Forms of Drama

Edited by

JAMES L. CALDERWOOD

and

HAROLD E. TOLIVER

University of California, Irvine

PRENTICE-HALL, INC., *Englewood Cliffs, New Jersey*

to Cleo and Mary

PRENTICE-HALL INTERNATIONAL, INC., *London*
PRENTICE-HALL OF AUSTRALIA, PTY. LTD., *Sydney*
PRENTICE-HALL OF CANADA, LTD., *Toronto*
PRENTICE-HALL OF INDIA PRIVATE LTD., *New Delhi*
PRENTICE-HALL OF JAPAN, INC., *Tokyo*

Prentice-Hall English Literature Series

MAYNARD MACK,   *Editor*

Library of Congress Catalog Card Number: 69–10491

Printed in the United States of America

Current Printing (last digit):

10 9 8 7 6 5 4 3 2 1

Preface

Our understanding of forms of drama, especially in their polychromed modern species, is not helped by the wavy and often riddled line between the art of illusion onstage and the art of role playing offstage. Performed drama is inherently lifelike (that is, it makes use of real people pretending to be other real people), and life in turn is nothing if not theatrical. It puzzles Hamlet that a man like himself, who dislikes the "windy suspiration of forced breath," is unable to enact his heart's promptings while a mere player, "in a fiction, in a dream of passion," can "force his soul so to his own conceit" that his eyes pour tears. Since Hamlet, Bottom, Jacques, and other Shakespearean characters threatened to step across the line between us and the play some 350 years ago, others have actually done so, entering the play from the audience or telling the audience that basically it is no different from the actors, the creatures of illusion. (Skill in histrionics begins with the infant's first strategically excessive wail for attention.)

Yet despite the apparent disregard for distinctions between art and life that many modern and a few older plays display, all plays impose some elements of coherent art on the chance, haphazard sequences and confusions of nature. It is true that modern plays tend to stress the tangled present of immediate scenes, amplified and reinforced in other scenes, rather than well-structured movement from definite beginnings to plotted conclusions. But no play surrenders completely to formlessness; and precisely because forms of drama are now so varied and complex the problem of form is more unavoidable than ever. A list of dramatic elements, old and new, that cannot be understood apart from a general considera-tion of form would be nearly exhaustive: recurrent imagery, stagecraft, style, lighting and scenery, character, prose and verse media, dialogue, editorial direc-tions, choral and lyric retardation, plot and subplot, rising and falling actions, circular and linear movement, tempo, acting technique, the limits of illusion (spatial dimensions of the stage, temporal dimensions of the performance), modes from realism to impressionism to ritual formality, dramatic schools and movements

(Restoration drama, theater of the absurd, classical tragedy, dark comedy), and so on. We have no sooner isolated such elements than we discover how dependent our view of them is upon our understanding of both the unique form of the individual play and the traditions out of which the play developed or against which it reacts.

Unfortunately, most general and introductory collections of plays either rest content with conventional headings and chronological order or merely set one play, uncomfortably, beside another. Even those that arrange plays by families frequently do not raise the problem of form seriously enough or pursue it far enough. In *Forms of Drama*, as in its companion volume, *Forms of Poetry*, we have emphasized genres, or kinds, on the assumption that most students need a substantial framework within which to consider literary works. To repeat what *Forms of Poetry* suggests with respect to the value of the forms approach: because everything a student reads influences, for better or worse, his subsequent reading, he should be asked to encounter not merely *a* work among an undifferentiated cluster of works but a particular kind of work whose structure, themes, conventions, etc. have immediate relevance to his study of the next work of that kind. The object is not, of course, to qualify the student in the craft of literary pigeon-holing or to teach him in reading drama to hold individual plays up against generic paradigms and to check off a list of criteria before admitting one to the inner sanctum of tragedy while banishing others to less hallowed precincts. Generic study is concerned with forms, not formulas, with dramatic categories sufficiently complex, capacious, and meaningful to do at least partial justice to the rich and elusive variety of individual plays. Though the student will rightly discover that each play possesses its own distinctive integrity, he should also discover that its individuality is most readily apparent if it is first placed in the company of others of its kind and then distinguished from them.

That uniqueness can only be determined by differentiation is still further reason that the study of genres is not irrelevant to modern innovations in drama. The search for new forms by writers like Beckett, Brecht, and Ionesco is clearly a response to earlier forms and fully definable only in terms of them, as an unplotted play is definable only in terms of its plotted predecessors. Tragicomedies presuppose tragedies and comedies, antiplays presuppose plays, and even so apparently novel a movement as the theater of the absurd, as Martin Esslin reminds us, is "a return to old, even archaic traditions." The interaction of old and new, then, demands that the study of drama have depth as well as variety.

We have represented each form by plays sufficiently spread out in time that the student may gain a sense of their historical conditioning. The general introduction attempts to define the rather protean anatomy of drama and to suggest some patterns that all drama illustrates. The introductions to different genres are designed to be broad and flexible enough to encompass the field and yet precise enough to be pertinent to individual plays. The headnotes make at least some preliminary connections between generic and individual form, and biographical notes add brief comments on the historical place of the authors and their works. In all this critical material, we have tried to maintain a distinction between guidance and coercion. In quantity the text offers enough material for quarter or semester courses in drama; supplemented by paperback editions, it could conceivably contribute to more ambitious undertakings.

Contents

Introduction

If we disregard the differences between farcical interludes, minstrelsy, mummery, opera, masques, puppet shows, charms, rain dances, and the like, the main distinction between drama (from *dran*, to do, act) and other forms of literature is relatively clear. Drama, though not always performed, is always performable: it can be "done." It is true that poetry and passages from novels are sometimes recited in public, but an authentic performance of either turns it into drama, and narrative forms presuppose a different audience "address." Plays also consist of talk *about* the action they imitate, of course, but unlike the talk of novels, dramatic dialogue is neither merely verbal nor ordinarily screened through a narrator; rather, it is an immediate, normally present-tense impersonation, a form of action and reaction before a group that is both engaged in it and detached from it. In contrast to real-life performances (as in the courtroom, for instance), plays are coherent "play," or pretence; the theater, as Thornton Wilder writes, "partakes of the nature of festival": "The excitement induced by pretending a fragment of life is such that it...requires a throng" (an audience). The actors do not intend to be mistaken for the characters they represent: murderers remove their makeup and go unpunished, and their victims rise from the rug to be murdered another day. The playwright reserves the right to conceal himself behind the masks of his characters and to complicate the dramatic illusion as he sees fit.

The distinction between art for its own sake and unrehearsed, pragmatic mimicry has not always been clear, however. In primitive cultures, the two overlap, drama doubling as religious ritual to promote collective well-being—for instance, the tribe's control of nature as invested in various gods. By imitating an action, the ritual participants hope to free themselves of "winter" and bring about a vernal rebirth. Such rites sometimes include impersonations demonstrating to the gods precisely what they are to do; the participants may actually imagine themselves becoming gods: they are "beside" or "outside" themselves in ecstasy (derived ultimately from *ek-histanai,* to cause to stand out, to derange). Or, to put it another way, they are "enthusiastic" (from *entheos,* the god within). Primitive tribal exercises of this kind are thus both frenetic ritual and programmed art.

In sophisticated drama as distinguished from rituals the purposive function is limited to instructing and pleasing the audience. It is also more verbal than dancelike. As the Greek theater gradually grew away from Dionysiac and other religious rites, for instance, it gave increasing emphasis to speech and characterization, adding speaking parts to dancing and singing choruses, then answering parts, and finally full-fledged actors. The players now spoke outward toward the spectators rather than upward toward the gods. (Shakespeare resurrects the notion of communal prayer in *The Tempest* in appealing, in the epilogue, for mercy and the "choral" participation of the audience:

> release me from my bands
> With the help of your good hands:
> Gentle breath of yours my sails
> Must fill, or else my project fails,
> Which was to please. Now I want
> Spirits to enforce, Art to enchant;
> And my ending is despair,
> Unless I be reliev'd by prayer,
> Which pierces so, that it assaults
> Mercy itself, and frees all faults.
> > As you from crimes would pardon'd be,
> > Let your indulgence set me free.)

In sum, what in primitive societies had been imprecation, by Aristotle's time had become a basic instinct for, and pleasure in, the "imitation of an action" before an audience. What was once literal "relief" sought for the community—say by summer's victory over winter—became "catharsis," the purgation of emotion, signaled by the applause of the audience.

The organization of a sophisticated play may, however, borrow more from ritual than we realize. Rather than the physical movement of a chorus, it has more intangible rhythms achieved through speech and plot and the arrangement of characters and situations. Even in "naturalistic" plays, which are less obviously dependent on balanced sets of characters, poetic speech, and ritual repetition, there are likely to be implicit ritual elements. Consider, for instance, the opening speeches of Chekhov's *The Cherry Orchard,* which may appear at first to have as little in common with the repeated gestures and formal movements of ritual as a tape-recorded talk from daily life.

Lopakhin. The train's arrived, thank God. What's the time?

Dunyasha. It will soon be two. (*Blows out candle.*) It is light already.

Lopakhin. How much was the train late? Two hours at least. (*Yawns and stretches himself.*) I have made a rotten mess of it! I came here on purpose to meet them at the station, and then overslept myself... In my chair. It's a pity. I wish you'd wakened me.

Despite its apparent casualness, the beginning contains the germ of what follows, especially in its tilting of the ceremonies of greeting to make them awkward. (The ending of the play is a purposely awkward departure.) In the light of later developments, this disturbance of repeated social formulas foreshadows a conflict between the old aristocratic manner and a new order beginning to displace it— more specifically, between the businessman Lopakhin and Mme. Ranevsky and her brother Gaev. Lopakhin does in fact make "a rotten mess" of the old family graces again and again. As he awakes, the time is coming to end the cherry orchard (and to "blow out the candle"). In his first appearance to those who have arrived, he looks in at a door and "moos," obviously impatient with the discussion going on and uncertain as to how to approach with his plans for saving the estate. The others insist on ignoring him until it is too late. The chance for a marriage between him and Mme. Ranevsky's daughter Varya (which would graft the new and the old) is lost as he bungles the ceremonies of courtship. While the clock of the seasons continues its ordinary pace, he quickens the human tempo and upsets the equilibrium of the natural order and a decaying society, both symbolized by the flowering orchard.

Lopakhin's initial impatience and maladroitness, then, are typical of his relationship with the society of the play and therefore *predictive*. They set a pattern that recurs several times in the play and is eventually completed with the chopping down of the trees, itself a rhythmic, destructive act—in a sense a ritual of the builder of villas destroying the ritual of the old order.

The pattern of even sophisticated drama, then, is in some way predictive and repetitive. Plays do not merely imitate an action; they structure their imitations in both the small patterns of rhythmic, poetic speech and pageantry and the larger pattern of the plot, with its anticipation, climax, and resolution. A play has tempo, symmetry, and an internal logic by which it unfolds, and the pattern that binds the members of its society together in a single or compound action is a central control equivalent to the program of primitive rituals, though different in aim and method. Characters are not allowed to walk on and off stage without relation to the governing design; they are made to appear at moments at which they can further its unfolding and combine in effective groupings. Once on stage they move, talk, and gesture not as in life but in accordance with the kind of organized impersonation of life that the playwright envisions. Whereas a man in isolation may provide material for fiction, a play usually meshes the lives of two or more people. Dramatic pattern is therefore *synchronized* unfolding.

It is also a *dialectical* unfolding, made dramatic by counteractions. (Greek choruses were divided into strophe and antistrophe, movement in one direction then the other.) In terms of character and motive, dramatic pattern usually calls for opposition by an antagonist to a protagonist's goals, brings their relationship to a climax, and resolves their conflict in a rhythmic design of complication, crisis, and catharsis. To put it another way, a dramatic plot unfolds in the form of intersecting intrigues by two or more people (it may be difficult to tell "protagonists" from "antagonists"), whose conflict produces passion and the statement and counterstatement of dramatic dialogue, which Bernard Shaw calls "retortive backchat." Not until a final clarification are all the differences between the intriguers resolved, because only when all masks are off is the interrelatedness of the parts manifest to everyone, and drama preeminently concerns the *connectives* of a society. Ignorance or failure to recognize the truth about someone or oneself (which seems to be what Aristotle meant by *hamartia,* tragic flaw) usually causes the antagonism of the characters, whereas *anagnorisis,* disclosure or recognition, clarifies what was mistaken and produces *catharsis,* or the feeling of peace after harrowing pathos and suffering. Each of these stages is essentially a step in the disclosure of true lines of communication in the society or in the clash of two or more competing modes of social order.

The resolving of dramatic tensions among characters on stage often coincides with a release of tension in the audience, which participates in the dramatic action indirectly, following its own structured program of reactions: it arrives with some ceremony at the theater, identifies with certain of the characters, and shares in the processes of ignorance and knowledge. Thus unlike most novels and poems, plays implicate an exterior group in their unfolding and force the writer to take into account the psychology of the audience as well as the psychology of the characters. The action may be punctuated by choral responses and by lyric pauses and soliloquies, as characters stop to analyze the ordeal posed by the obstacles they confront; but even these seemingly nondramatic elements are directed implicitly to the audience. They serve the double function of advancing the speaker's articulation of his state of mind and of keeping the knowledge of the audience abreast of the action.

The presence of the audience is important in another way as well. A play is tragic or comic only as it is received so by an audience. (Evidence as to how an informed audience understands a passage is legitimate critical evidence as to what it means and how it should be performed.) A play can be radically transformed—even distorted from its author's intent—either by the performers or by the audience that sees it, as excessive sympathy for Shylock makes *The Merchant of Venice* something other than romantic comedy and excessive dislike for Macbeth makes *Macbeth* something other than tragedy. (Russian audiences are said to laugh at *Hamlet* as an exposure of the carryings on of kings and nobles.) Hence the dialectic of protagonists and antagonists on stage is complemented by a dialectic between the play and its audience. A play has a manner toward the audience, and drama is both (1) a tension on stage among characters and (2) an author's playing to an audience through and above his characters. It is the latter sense that we mean when we call a lyric dramatic and label Browning's "Andrea del Sarto" a dramatic monologue. The writer intends us to understand more than his *personae* and to comprehend things immediately that the characters must realize gradually. This is the source of dramatic irony, a doubleness of perspective by which we both sympathize with a character and transcend his errors. Because of the play-audience dialectic, the time of disclosures and the resolution of the play are also double: they work dramatically in one sense on the characters and dramatically in the other sense on the audience, who knows what Oedipus and Macbeth do not.

Let us turn now to specific dramatic elements and conventions to examine their functions in this synchronized enactment that unfolds toward clarification.

Scenic Aspects: Stage Properties and Settings　In realistic novels, a given character's assets are likely to comprise a considerable list. The novelist may place him among scores of named objects, continents of geography, pantries of food, houses full of personal items, and innumerable things of the street and countryside that constitute his material environment, and unless the novelist uses a first-person narrator, he is privileged to tell us directly or by implication about his character's relation to these properties. Note Faulkner's typically novelistic handling of scenic influence on Talliaferro in *Mosquitoes*:

> Clasping his accursed bottle, feeling like a criminal, Mr. Talliaferro hurried on.
> He walked swiftly beside a dark wall, passing small indiscriminate shops dimly

lighted with gas and smelling of food of all kinds, fulsome, slightly overripe. The proprietors and their families sat before the doors in tilted chairs, women nursing babies into slumber spoke in soft South European syllables one to another. Children scurried before him and about him, ignoring him or becoming aware of him and crouching in shadows like animals, defensive, passive and motionless.

Although the shops could be represented on stage, they would dominate the limited space and lose the indiscriminate appearance Faulkner gives them among two pages' worth of petit bourgeois property through which Talliaferro passes. Furthermore, though sounds can be approximated on stage, smells can only be talked about. The novel does not actually present these things either, of course; it merely names them. But it does manage to give us a sense of Talliaferro's awkward movement through the bric-a-brac of his life, Faulkner's point being that he does not stand out against the series of belittling situations he confronts. Even his guilt is timid.

In contrast, if a play is to remain performable, it can introduce only a limited number of physical objects and must use them in a certain way. The outdoor life of Indians on the plains, for instance, would be impossible to dramatize, herds of buffalo and the theater being incompatible. A list of things that cannot be staged would include perhaps 75 per cent of the gross national product. Since emphasis falls on action and stage props are inactive, a dramatist finds it difficult to represent the *submergence* of character in environment. Hence stage properties limit the range of possible dramatic forms and even the kinds of characterization that can be introduced on stage. They are normally handled symbolically; an actor smuggles into his relationship with them as much of the character as he can. Each item singled out for use must count for something, as an emblem or a visual identity marker—like the skull that Hamlet holds up in the grave-digger scene as something roughly equivalent to the "quintessence of dust" to which Hamlet reduces all men.

Or consider the initial set of Chekhov's *Uncle Vanya,* which consists of a country house and terrace, an avenue of trees painted on a background design, an old poplar, a table set for tea, some benches and chairs, a samovar, and a guitar. Marina, an old woman, sits knitting a stocking while Astroff, an idealistic, overworked country doctor, paces up and down close by her:

MARINA. (*Pouring some tea into a glass.*) Take a little tea, my son.
ASTROFF. (*Takes the glass from her unwillingly.*) Somehow, I don't seem to want any.
MARINA. Then will you have a little vodka instead?
ASTROFF. No, I don't drink vodka every day, and besides, it is too hot now....

The properties include the weather, which both fosters and symbolizes the fatigue and discomfort of the characters, and a hint beyond the stage of an extensive middle-class estate that forms the outer circumference of the assembled cast. The immediate instrument of the enactment is the tea service. The actress playing Marina uses it and the knitting of the stocking as a sign of her grandmotherliness and maternal feeling for Astroff. The actor performing Astroff employs the refusal of tea as a sign of boredom: It is obvious that small daily events have lost their flavor, even when tempered by Marina's motherly concern. In refusing he is turning away from the "tea" of his life, which is made to stand for perhaps ten pages of description of things that a similar country doctor might find oppressive in a Zola novel. The guitar remains an enigma through most of the first scene and as such contributes implicitly to the forward thrust of the plot. By its suggestion of gaiety and song, it may seem to offer some counterpoint to Astroff's comment that "existence is tedious...it is a senseless, dirty business, this life, and goes heavily"; but we discover later that it belongs to "Waffles" Telegin, an impoverished, stupid, and extremely ugly landowner. (The song that Astroff commands him to play in the middle of the night turns into a parody of drunken revelry.)

With very few props, then, Chekhov creates not only a background setting consistent with the foreground action but also an interaction of character and scene in which the properties are made to "come forward" one by one and offer their comment on the lives of the characters. Whereas Talliaferro becomes an extension of the city itself, Astroff in the tea ceremony makes his boredom personal; he *enacts* it, even though he is not totally responsible for it. The thingness of poetry and fiction is thus replaced, here and in most plays, by a fundamentally social medium in which both the outside world and the internal condition of the characters are made visible in social action.

The interaction of scene and character may be complemented by that of audience and play if the scene is used to tell the audience what the players do not know. Managed well, a setting is the playwright's direct bridge to the audience over the players' heads. An astute observer of the setting of Ibsen's *Ghosts,* for instance, notices several indications of the meaning of the action in the mountains, the rain, and the sun that sometimes complement and sometimes contrast to the enclosed Oswald living room. When the characters come to read their environment with comparable awareness, the play's dramatic irony is resolved. Because they are set and inert, stage properties maintain their stance before us as the play unfolds: while the sequential action passes through one aspect of the plot and then another, they summarize in visual form a significant part of the whole pattern.

Mimetic Aspects: Symbol, Pageantry, Gesture, Stage Movement   Gesture and group movement are usually more prominent in verse drama than in prose or naturalistic drama since formality of verse speech is likely to be matched by formality of movement. Final elegiac pronouncements over the body of the tragic hero in Shakespeare, for instance, are often accompanied by off-stage drums and cortegelike movement:

AUFIDIUS. My rage is gone,
  And I am struck with sorrow. Take him up.
  Help, three o' th' chiefest soldiers; I'll be one.
  Beat thou the drum, that it speak mournfully.
  Trail your steel pikes. Though in this city he
  Hath widow'd and unchilded many a one,
  Which to this hour bewail the injury,
  Yet he shall have a noble memory....
(*Exeunt, bearing the body of* CORIOLANUS. *A dead march sounded.*)

Though the fullest use of such elements of pageantry and spectacle is illustrated by opera rather than tragedy, the slow, formal movement both of the players and of the rhythmic speech can be part of the cathartic effect of a play. Similarly, *King Lear* and *Hamlet* end with dead marches, and *Macbeth* concludes with a flourish of trumpets that proclaims the time free of its curse.

Though dialectical exchange stands still during such visual demonstrations, pageantry may be more than atmosphere—just as lyric odes and forms of choral commentary may be more than ornament. Pageantry used effectively is a compressed enactment of *public* relationships and institutions. The groupings around the king, alive or dead, in Shakespeare's king plays, for instance, represent visually the politics of the group. Even in plays without choruses or mass pageantry such as this, group movements are useful to demonstrate both the common society and the position of those outside it.

Ever since the invention of actors distinct from the chorus in Greek drama, central characters are more likely to be played off against than integrated with the spiritual currents of the main social body. In modern plays, particularly, the play's sympathy is likely to be with outcasts. (A martyr play such as Eliot's *Murder in the Cathedral* gives the protagonist his inner group distinct from the society at large that martyrs him.) Communal pageantry obviously breaks down if characters discover that they have no basis for unity. In Inge's *Bus Stop* people have come together by accident and end either isolated or paired off biologically. People in Chekhov's plays intersect occasionally, but no two lives coincide very closely, and the end of the play is generally a dispersal. Whereas in romantic comedy the playwright usually contrives to make a central "pairing off" symbolic of a healthy society (as in the happy choruses of musical comedy), in Chekhov's ironic drama both the love affairs and the friendships are broken. In O'Neill's *The Iceman Cometh,* which illustrates another variation of a crowd with no way to become a society, the people are drawn together in a barroom by common weaknesses, and as these are exposed they drift apart. Themes of social disaffection, absurdity, and estrangement, then, result in a pageantry of gathering and dispersal, arrivals, momentary associations, and departures. But even such loose arrangements, movement, and group gestures as these indicate the kind of spiritual and psychological engagement the characters make with each other.

Story Aspects: Plot and Sequence   With respect to plot, drama normally begins, as we have seen, in a state of uncertainty and imbalance and ends, again normally, in clarification. It is a variation of hide-and-seek whose goal is normally the definition of character and situation—whether a given character is innocent or guilty, for instance, or blessed or cursed, or merely has or has not done something. To be fully dramatic, a performance must have some variation of expectation, ordeal, and disclosure. Expectation is heightened by certain conventions that receive special emphasis in drama, such as oracles (predictive riddles that cause us to guess ahead), challenges and responses, anticipatory beseeching (which asks for something good to happen or something bad not to happen), threatening, masking and unmasking, strongly willed courses of action, and the like.

But dramatic plots are not often single movements toward a single clarification; more often they contain several related intrigues and discoveries, perhaps false clues, a subplot, and always some resistance or retardation. Shakespeare, for instance, often juxtaposes two or more societies—like forest and court groups in *As You Like It*—and then advances them with numerous cross references toward some common meeting ground. Each represents different values but shares in a central plot and unmasking. Ben Jonson's *The Alchemist* combines a central group of manipulators with a varied collection of gulls whom they fleece. The plot is multiple in one sense, single in another in that several parties take different paths to one end: loss of cash in hand. Just as the play has one main plot and several subplots, so its language includes separate kinds of jargon from several trades and professions but relates them to the central terms of alchemy and the common denominator of human greed. The gulls have in common the desire to change their "low" substance magically into something "high" (lead into gold) and discover instead that what they had thought magic is merely hocus-pocus pronounced over the base, untransformable stuff of their own humanity. In Shakespeare's *1 Henry IV* the low-life elements of the Falstaff group reflect ironically the chivalric order of Hotspur and the kingship, thus putting the central society of the play and its values in a different perspective from the perspective that those in power take toward themselves. But the detractors are eventually forced aside or reform: the main plot subordinates them.

Plot, then, is a progressive relation of various clusters of people whose relationships change under the influence of the information made available to them. Interim or apparent truths are likely to alter as the bedrock relationship is discovered—as appearance gives way to reality, concealment to disclosure.

The unity of multiple plots derives from thematic concerns that extend to all levels and from their ultimate intersection. Thus theme and plot are inseparable, and their combination amounts to something like a "master plot," or that which the various intrigues have in common. Like the tempo of the plot's progression, such a common pattern need not be readily visible; but if a play is an organic whole and not a collection of fragments, it will have a meaningful pattern of relationships. As a civil constitution arranges all its constituent branches and a primitive ritual arranges its intricate dances according to a single goal, such a pattern composes the elements of the play according to the ultimate pronouncement the play makes about the characters' identities. The master plot of *1 Henry IV,* for instance, is the gradual realization of the Prince's dedication to true kingship, the final demonstration of which comes on the battlefield. Other actions— the mock interview of the prince and Falstaff playing the king, the father-son relations of Hotspur and his elders, the plots of night robbers as opposed to noble rebels against the kingdom—are analogous to that plot. The master plot of *The Cherry Orchard* is the exchange of one social order for another and hence the realignment of each character with respect to the others. (The construction of both plays is discussed further in their respective headnotes.) So conceived, plot is perhaps the most basic of dramatic elements, encompassing the arrangement of properties and characters, the tempo of the unfolding, the visual symbols, and the recurrent themes.

It is possible, of course, for a play to imitate a group action or approach a riddle that it cannot fully illuminate, and still more likely that even in a fully coherent play readers and spectators may not understand what happens. But the inadequacy of audiences and the difficulty of works are not problems of drama alone, and, despite such difficulties, we can make tentative descriptions of dramatic form on the basis of its governing plots, moods, tempo, and conventions, and on the kind of disclosure it offers.

We have not tried to impose a rigid classification of types on the following plays according to the kind of social contract they embody—such as farce for plays whose people are related by pie-in-the-face incongruity, satire for the more bitter incongruities that a towel will not wipe off, or antiplays in which no communication takes place and no community is formed (as in Ionesco's *The Chairs*, in which a mock theater on stage is filled with empty chairs for most of the play; a climactic speech delivered to them proves to be complete nonsense). Instead, we have called the selections tragedy, comedy, and indeterminate forms in the hope that refinements of analysis and sensitivity to dramatic form can be managed with individual plays as well under these as under more inventive headings.

Tragedy

Introduction

Unlike the names for some literary forms such as satire and novel, tragedy has both literary and popular meanings; and in the normal way of the world the popular meanings, primarily because acquiring them takes a smaller expenditure of intellectual capital, tend to drive the literary ones out of the marketplace. In newspapers and magazines the words "Tragedy Strikes" can caption stories about falling airplanes and rising taxes, disease, unease, death, divorce, tidal waves, broken bones or hopes, and lost kittens. Blessed with this sort of unlimited, two-way semantic stretch, "tragedy" is also cursed with attenuated significance: meaning everything, it means nothing, or at best it merges into the indistinct conceptual haze of misfortune, adversity, and mischance. Though the word itself enjoys great currency, for too many people the concept has, in effect, ceased to exist.

Tragedy and Ritual   To set about restoring tragedy to meaning, we need to return to early concepts of tragic form and its ritual origins. In his *Poetics* Aristotle says that tragedy arose not as a deliberate literary invention but as a gradually sophisticated development of the "dithyramb"—a passionate choric hymn honoring the god Dionysus (sometimes called *dithyrambos,* or, figuratively, twice-born). Scholars differ about the precise connection between Dionysiac ritual and Greek tragedy, but one view suggests that the significance of the Greek *tragoidia* (from *tragon oide,* song of goats) lies in the fact that the goat, traditionally associated with virility, was sacred to Dionysus, and that Dionysiac ritual involved a symbolic *sparagmos* (dismemberment) of the god in which the goat as god-surrogate was torn apart and eaten raw. The purpose of the *sparagmos* may have been to foster communion with Dionysus, to enable the worshipers to absorb into themselves and hence to become one with the god (*entheos*), as in the Christian Eucharist.

Like the Babylonian Tammuz, the Phrygian Attis, and the Egyptian Osiris (with whom the Greeks specifically identified him), Dionysus was a vegetation deity or life-spirit, a dying and reviving god whose cyclic rhythm paralleled the seasonal dying and reviving of life in nature; and since time was based on the seasons, he was also a year-daemon who enacted the annual death and rebirth of time. The sprouting of plants in the spring, especially the vine sacred to him, marked the god's birth or rebirth—the bursting forth of impulse and desire, the procreative marriage of god and earth mother—and was celebrated at the vernal equinox in Athens by a festival called the City Dionysia. After the harvest in the fall, vegetation faded and the god died. Perhaps he died *because* of the harvest, like the Phrygian vegetation god Lityerses, who was slain by the sickles of the reapers. At any rate, his death was somehow the fault of the community and had to be atoned for. A *pharmakos* or scapegoat sacrifice, either human or animal, was chosen to serve as the community's "container" of sin and guilt, and in his death or banishment the community was purged of wrongdoing, the god propitiated, the slate of time wiped clean in preparation for the new year, the reborn god. It is believed by many scholars today that the structure of tragedy began in the cyclic rhythm of the dying-reviving god, and that the tragic protagonist may be likened to both the god himself and the *pharmakos*.

Of specific features of the seasonal ritual little is known for certain, and its drunken, orgiastic character bears small resemblance to Greek tragedy. Gilbert Murray hypothesizes a ritual including an *agon,* or contest, between the god and his enemies (Life against Death, Light against Darkness, Summer against Winter); a narration of a *pathos,* or scene-of-suffering, in which the god is slain, the *pharmakos* driven out, the king dismembered; a *threnos,* or lamentation; an *anagnorisis,* or discovery and recognition of the dead god by his followers; and a *theophany,* or rebirth-resurrection of the god. Whether correct in every detail or not, this would appear to be the general form of the rites, Dionysiac or other, lying behind Greek drama. The Greek historian Herodotus tells us that Dionysiac rites resembled those honoring Isis and Osiris, which he observed at Sais in Egypt, and central to these was a sacred drama in which worshipers re-enacted in a kind of lakeside theater the story of Osiris' sufferings, death, and rebirth. Osiris, the son of sky and earth gods, was attacked and dismembered by his brother Set (so, under the name of Dionysus Zagreus, Dionysus was caught and dismembered by the Titans, subsequently to be revivified by his grandmother Rhea) and his body scattered over the land like seed. His grieving sister-wife Isis, after a long search, found his fragmented body and with the help of the god Anubis and others sewed it together, whereupon Osiris acquired eternal life as king of the underworld.

This myth is thought to have served as a kind of script for the sacred dramas dedicated to Osiris and Isis. We may note that an analogous death, search, discovery, and resurrection sequence is evident in the *Quem Quaeritis* trope of the medieval Church liturgy. An interpolation into the Introit or first phase of the Easter Mass, the *Quem Quaeritis* trope takes the form of a very brief ritual drama in which three women (actually priests) carrying spices with which to aniont the body of Jesus and "stepping delicately as though seeking something" approach the altar-sepulchre. There a priest-actor in the role of an angel asks, "Whom do you seek in the sepulchre, followers of Christ?" They reply that they seek the body of the crucified Christ; the angel informs them that "He is risen," and everyone rejoices. From such a liturgical matrix as this, English drama arose, passed through the stages of miracle and morality play, assimilated elements from native folk drama and in the Renaissance from classical drama, and finally flowered in Elizabethan tragedy and comedy. Similarly, between Dionysiac ritual and Attic drama there were no doubt other transitional forms, perhaps one of which was a rural folk drama on the order of the English Mummers' Play featuring the death by combat and subsequent resurrection of a god-hero. Somewhere along the line the ritual of death-and-rebirth suffered a *sparagmos* of its own, the phase of the god's suffering and dying going to tragedy, that of his resurrection and sacred marriage to the earth mother going to comedy. (For Aristotle says that comedy derived from the phallic songs, which presumably celebrated the restoration of the god's sexual potency.)

Tragic Inevitability From the seasonal ritual, then, tragedy would appear to inherit a pattern of action originally based on the waxing and waning of the sun daily and of vegetation annually, a pattern traditionally associated with the rise and fall of the turning wheel. Like the myth-ritual of Dionysus-Attis-Osiris-Adonis, which dramatizes the quickening and weakening pulse of life in all things, the tragic pattern of rise-and-fall (maturing-and-wasting, flowering-and-withering, etc.) is an abstraction from the life process of man and organic nature generally, a foreshortening and intensifying of that process in the interests of significant form. In dramatic tragedy this rise-and-fall becomes what Aristotle called the "metabasis," the change of fortune from prosperity to adversity, which, as Chaucer's Monk reminds us, dominated the medieval view of tragedy:

> I wol biwaille in manere of tragedye
> The harm of hem that stoode in heigh degree,
> And fillen so that ther nas no remedye
> To bringe hem out of hir adversitee.

As an abstraction from the life process, the rise-and-fall pattern is significant, not as an illustration of life or an assertion about reality but as a structural principle shaping the tragic form, like the quest that shapes the form of most romances. Thus whereas the quest has a natural affinity to the erratic, episodic plots normally found in romance, the rise-and-fall pattern lends itself to plots following a strict sequence of action and reaction and hence exhibiting the sort of inevitability suggested by the phrase "what goes up must come down." Aristotle may have had this in mind in his seemingly over-obvious insistence on the tragic plot's having a beginning, middle, and end. That is, if tragedy as distinguished from epic were to be a representation of a single, unified action, then each phase of that action must grow logically and causally out of its predecessor.

What this amounts to in actual practice is an evolution of action in which possibilities become narrowed into probabilities and finally into inevitabilities, like parallel lines converging gradually in the distance into one. Accident, coincidence, and sheer whimsy are the specialties of comedy because the comic form is not grounded in causality. For the sake of the comic ending we will suffer gladly the miraculous reformations of an Oliver or a Duke Frederick in *As You Like It* or the *deus ex machina* of a King's Officer in *Tartuffe*. We are more resistant to gratuitous string-pulling in serious plays. A plot dealing in unmotivated suffering and undeserved death would result not in tragedy but in a kind of inverted melodrama. Even in so authentic a tragedy as *King Lear* the sense of action being manipulated in the death of Cordelia left eighteenth-century audiences feeling that the inevitable had been sacrificed to the perverse and afflicted a number of would-be tragic playwrights with an irresistible itch to correct Shakespeare.

If the tragic plot makes the action of rise-and-fall seem inevitable, something in the hero's situation even at the zenith of his fortunes must necessitate his fall. The seasonal god of myth and ritual was, of course, destined to fall simply because it is a condition of nature that the sun waxes and then wanes, that all life flowers and then fades. One view of tragedy holds that an equally impersonal and usually external law must govern the tragic hero. Critics of this persuasion may point to the gods and fates of Greek tragedy, to prophecies, wheels of fortune, family curses, astrological omens, and other indices of what Pope calls "supernatural machinery" shaping the destinies of tragic heroes. In modern works this machinery may be naturalized. If malevolent gods *above* nature seem outmoded, then nature itself may be malevolent toward man: in Hemingway's *A Farewell to Arms* Lieutenant Henry likens mankind to a colony of ants caught on a burning log. Or the outside cause of tragedy may seem to lie in the hero's society, which is in some way or another corrupt (like Hamlet's Denmark or the Norway of Ibsen's plays). Obviously, the more the stress falls on causes outside the hero working on or through him, the further he descends from hero toward victim, from active agent toward passive prey.

Many plays, however, do not exhibit this sort of determinism. King Lear is not impelled by any external agency to divide his kingdom, put his evil daughters in power, and banish Cordelia. Lear *acts,* and the world *reacts.* In a nontragic play like *Riders to the Sea* it is just the reverse, the heroine Maurya reacting to (by suffering) the world's infliction of death on her family. In *King Lear* the trigger of evil is in man himself, in *Riders to the Sea* it is entirely outside man—in nature or in an abstract fatality somewhere behind the scenes that makes the sea its instrument. In *Lear* man is an active agent shaping his destiny; in *Riders* he is a passive victim suffering his destiny. In the one his character participates in his fate, in the other it has no meaningful bearing on his fate. Thus in *Riders to the Sea* we have not tragedy but a drama of pathos.

That does not mean that we can have tragedy only when a hero acts in perfect freedom of will. The cause of tragic action normally falls somewhere in between the extremes of arbitrary fate and unqualified free will, in the indefinable territory where consciousness and compulsion collaborate. If the hero seems fated to act, his will ratifies his fate; if he seems to act in perfect freedom, his act fashions a subsequent fate.

Tragic Guilt and Praxis   The co-presence of fate, free will, and suffering in tragedy makes justice a perennial issue for the tragic dramatist, who generally stays within the extremes of totally deserved and totally undeserved punishment. The most influential formulation of the problem of justice in tragedy appears in Aristotle's *Poetics*. In genuine tragedy, he argues, the hero who suffers misfortune cannot be either good or bad separately but instead a mixture of both, the good man who falls by virtue of an *hamartia*—an error or ignorance or (as some would have it) a flaw in his character. To the extent that the hero is flawed, he merits his suffering, and hence tragedy becomes morally explicable. Here, too, a certain inevitability is guaranteed the tragic action, the hero's error or flaw in character preceding and in a sense forecasting his fall. In fact, the error normally attributed wholesale to Greek heroes—*hubris,* the kind of excessive pride that goes before a fall—seems to have been regarded by the Greeks themselves as a nearly inevitable consequence of a man's rise to high station in life, as though in reaping prosperity he also gathered the seeds of misfortune.

A major drawback of the concept of *hamartia* is that it implies perfection of character apart from a single isolable act of ignorance, error, or weakness, on the analogy of a perfect vase with a single chip or crack. Tragic heroes, however, do not ordinarily fit this prescription. The assorted faults and frailties of a Raskolnikov (*Crime and Punishment*), a Miss Julie (Strindberg's play of that name), or a Willie Loman (*Death of a Salesman*) could be inventoried at impressive length; and even with characters of a more heroic cut—Oedipus, Coriolanus, Samson—the notion of "a" flaw is optimistic. Though normally higher in the chain of being than the rest of us, the tragic hero is still tethered to the human condition where vices and virtues are given rather equal distribution.

Still, if most tragic heroes have their full quota of failings, some do not. The danger is that we shall set out on flaw-hunting expeditions through flawless territory, stalking about with high-powered Aristotelean weapons and bagging only a few undersized virtues. Given a critical permit, almost anyone will discover in himself a talent for detecting tragic flaws that borders on genius. Not, of course, that there is any argument about Tamburlaine's compulsion to depopulate heaven and earth or Macbeth's treasonous ambition or Medea's vindictiveness. But it is not very persuasive to regard Prometheus' pity for mankind as a flaw of character or to extract some species of moral frailty from Antigone's decision to bury Polyneices. These are by no means unflawed—which would be to say, morally perfect—characters, but the flaws they have do not cause or significantly contribute to the act from which their sufferings ultimately issue. And if we move still further along the moral spectrum, we come to characters like Eliot's Thomas Becket, Robert Bolt's Thomas More, and Christ in the *Passion,* at which point the search for operative moral flaws becomes an exercise in divination.

Unless we are to deny the high title of "goat-song" to all works whose heroes are morally innocent sufferers, it would seem necessary to modify the notion of *hamartia* as an ethical defect. *Hamartia* engenders actions that involve moral guilt, but moral guilt is possible only when there are innocent alternatives to a given action. Macbeth, for instance, is morally guilty in murdering Duncan because an innocent alternative—not murdering Duncan—was available to him. For Orestes, however, the alternative to murdering Clytemnestra is available only at the cost of disobeying Apollo and abandoning his duty to his father and king; and for Antigone, the alternative to burying Polyneices is available only at the cost of betraying family honor and divine law. So too with Prometheus, Agamemnon in sacrificing Iphigenia, Socrates in Plato's *Apology,* Christ before Pilate, Cordelia in *King Lear,* Becket in *Murder in the Cathedral,* More in *A Man for All Seasons:* each is caught between mutually exclusive imperatives. The laws of God and Caesar cannot both be honored, kings demand what conscience forbids, duty insists but love prohibits. In such situations any action, whether for good or ill, carries with it a measure of guilt in that it necessarily violates some imperative, and this guilt condemns the hero to subsequent suffering.

At the opposite extreme from moral guilt, then, is what can be called "situational guilt." Characters whose actions fall into this category are normally "good" men with whom we sympathize and whose suffering we deplore while acknowledging its inevitability. Between the extremes of moral guilt and situational guilt lies a continuum in which situation conspires with ethical failure in varying proportions to generate the tragic sequence.

What is common to tragic characters is not that they act in either guilt or innocence, nor that they act either with or without free will, but that they *act*—and suffer the consequences of their action. *Praxis,* Aristotle's term for the action of tragedy, seems an essential feature not only of the plot but of the tragic hero. Passive, uncommitted heroes inexplicably victimized by the world—like the trapped characters in Maeterlinck's *The Intruder*—are not agents of tragedy. "Tragic guilt" thus includes but transcends both moral and situational guilt, the hero being indicated for the "crime" of action itself. Any significant act—an act of commitment or assertion—is burdened by the guilt of its own preclusive identity, and this guilt is absorbed by the actor, who in choosing it performs *this* and not another act and hence becomes *this* and not another sort of character. Tragic guilt centers on the inevitable reduction of freedom involved in any commitment to action, the diminution of human potential, the straitening of the self as it goes through the needle's eye of choice. That one commitment precludes others is of course a commonplace of human experience, giving rise to a great many proverbs warning us about the dangers of putting all our eggs in one basket or reminding us that we cannot have our cake and eat it too. But tragedy is especially devoted to exploring the ways in which men suffer the consequences of preclusive acts.

In tragedy, as A. C. Bradley says, action issues from character, and hence the tragic hero will have a certain preclusiveness of character corresponding to the nature of his act. Like Lear or Oedipus, he may be subject to an imperious whimsy leading to irrevocable acts and unexamined decisions. Often he has a form of intellectual tunnel-vision, like Camus' Caligula, who "sees nothing but his own idea," or Euripides' Pentheus, who cannot see the god in Dionysus. Clytemnestra, Faustus, Coriolanus, Ahab, Willie Loman: the obsessed hero runs the length and breadth of tragedy. Even when the hero acts deliberately, in full consciousness of conflicting values and imperatives, he is not the sort to seek compromises that will do justice to both sides of an issue. It is in choruses, like the one in *Agamemnon,* that we find worldly wisdom and a search for negotiable positions: "For Ruin is revealed the child / Of not to be attempted actions... Measure is best." The tragic hero does not look for an Aristotelean mean but sets the issues in an *either/or* frame and commits himself irreversibly to one or the other. As Othello puts it:

> Like to the Pontic Sea,
> Whose icy current and compulsive course
> Ne'er feels retiring ebb, but keeps due on
> To the Propontic and the Hellespont,
> Even so my bloody thoughts, with violent pace,
> Shall ne'er look back, ne'er ebb to humble love,
> Till that a capable and wide revenge
> Swallow them up.

So Oedipus keeps a "compulsive course" in his search for Laius' killer, Racine's Phaedra in her love for Hippolytus, Ephraim Cabot (*Desire Under the Elms*) in his devotion to the rocky land. At one extreme, where the hero is in danger of not measuring up to tragic status, we have the insentient character who acts readily because he cannot perceive alternatives or consequences: Goethe's Egmont, for instance, whose blind naïveté hurries him to entrapment, or Marlowe's Tamburlaine and Jonson's Sejanus, whose egoism and brutality simply override all moral issues. At the other extreme, where the hero is in danger of not "measuring down" to tragic stature, we find the profoundly sentient character whose awareness of the complexities of his situation requires a prolonged preparation for action, as in the cases of Hamlet and Eliot's Thomas Becket.

Thus the gradually constricting scope of the tragic plot as it moves from the possible, to the probable, to the inevitable has its "interior" counterpart in the character of the tragic hero, and both plot and character emphasize the preclusiveness and the irreversibility of tragic action. In addition to the unyielding character of the hero, the irreversibility of his commitment is usually reinforced by some kind of outside constraint. This may take the form of the curse that cannot be revoked (for instance, Theseus' invocation to Poseidon to destroy Hippolytus), the legal sentence (Oedipus' pronouncement of death or banishment for Laius' killer), the pact or vow (Faustus' pact with the devils, Othello's "sacred vow" of vengeance), or the authoritarian decree (Lear's decision to divide his kingdom, Bernarda Alba's establishment of the eight-year mourning period). But whatever the reason, whether from sense of duty, allegiance to principle, rigidity of will, or sheer intransigence, the hero sticks to his commitment. "Break what break will," Oedipus cries as the truth becomes imminent, "My will is to see my origin, however mean!" "I have sworn," Lear says of Cordelia's banishment, "I am firm!" Macbeth speaks more wearily but no less resolutely: "I am in blood / Stepp'd in so far that, should I wade no more, / Returning were as tedious as go o'er." And Caligula says, "No, there's no return. I must go on and on, until the consummation." The hero's initial act sets him "on rails," and in suffering the world's reaction he "bears it out, even to the edge of doom." That does not mean that the tragic hero remains oblivious to the claims of the world or his own failures (a matter we shall take up a bit further on); but it does mean that he must retain the dignity of his position under attack, that he must make some assertion of self, register some impulse of resistance as the world closes in on him. Were he merely to collapse, like Shakespeare's King John, or to recant completely, like the heroes of morality plays, he would be something other than a tragic hero.

Pathos and Praxis   This brings us to the second phase of tragedy, the Aristotelean *pathos,* or suffering. By pathos Aristotle apparently means any kind of suffering; but we need to distinguish between pathetic and tragic suffering, both of which may occur in a single play. As we have suggested, for suffering to be tragic it must not simply descend on the hero out of nowhere, like the safe that falls on a pedestrian, but develop as a consequence of his acts. Desdemona suffers and dies not because of her actions but because of Othello's, and Duncan is destroyed by Macbeth, not himself. Cassandra in *Agamemnon,* Oedipus' children in *Oedipus Rex,* Job (unless we construe his devotion to virtue as an act of commitment that causes his subsequent ordeal), Ophelia in *Hamlet,* the paretic Oswald in Ibsen's *Ghosts,* Laura Wingfield in Williams' *The Glass Menagerie,* and the citizens of Oran in Camus' *The Plague* are all characters primarily acted upon rather than acting, recipients of unexpected and inexplicable suffering. If we call their suffering pathetic instead of tragic, we are not saying that it is somehow inferior to tragic suffering but only that it is different in terms of its cause, nature, and meaning. Tragic heroes are essentially self-made. They may be born as victims of pathetic suffering but graduate to tragic status by acting.

Racine's Phaedra, for instance, is initially pictured as the victim of a family curse, literally dying of the disease of love inflicted on her by Venus. But she does not let the disease remain an "outside" affliction; she accepts it, converting it into an instrument of her own will by declaring herself to Hippolytus and later accusing him to Theseus. Similarly, Hamlet at first is the victim of an outside situation not of his making, Othello the victim of Iago's malignity, and Macbeth the victim of both the witches' riddling prophecies and his wife's instigations. But for them suffering is not final; they transform it into a matrix of subsequent action. Refusing to remain victims, they make victims of others.

Since it is unusual to find an entirely passive character in drama, it is normally not so much *whether* he acts as how *significantly* he acts that is at issue in determining the tragic or nontragic nature of his suffering. What constitutes an act of tragic significance is not easily answered in a way that will apply to all tragic characters; but we would suggest that it is an act of engagement, commitment, or assertion in which the character of the hero is concentrated or summed up, his self defined, his values, aspirations, impulses for good or evil condensed and clarified. On this view the child who chases a ball into the street and is struck by a car acts, but not with tragic significance. The airplane pilot who misreads his altimeter or misjudges the height of a peak suffers from errors of eyesight, not, like tragic heroes, from failures of vision. We spoke earlier of Maurya, the heroine of Synge's *Riders to the Sea,* who in suffering the deaths of others never acts, only reacts. Her last son, however, does act; he sets out for Galway across the water to sell some horses at the fair, disregarding Maurya's pleas that he remain. Thus he comes nearer than she to being a tragic character. But as his sister says, "It's the life of a young man to be going on the sea." What we witness is not an act of tragic significance in which the self is summoned into realization but an act of routine courage, of a man going stolidly about his daily and dangerous business.

So far, for the most part, we have been stressing the hero's role as the radical individual who becomes increasingly isolated from his society through an uncompromising commitment to a course of action. Most tragic heroes do move toward isolation, usually in the form of death or banishment, and even before they reach this point they have become alienated from their normal world. Thus Christ, abandoned by his disciples and denied three times by Peter, cries out on the cross, "My God, my God, why hast Thou forsaken me?" Prometheus staked to his rock, Oedipus blinded, Faustus awaiting the devils, Lear on the stormy heath, Samson eyeless in Gaza, Halvard Solness-on his scaffolding (*The Master Builder*), Lavinia Mannon in her shuttered house (*Mourning Becomes Electra*): all present images of the isolated individual suffering the crime of individuality—of having asserted *his* will and values in the teeth of accepted norms, of having aspired like Icarus beyond the range of ordinary men. The mythic analogues to this aspect of the tragic hero are various self-assertive but suffering gods, like Prometheus, Dionysus, and Lucifer. Like such gods, the hero is a paradoxical figure. He is greater than us in his power for good and evil, goes beyond us in his drive for fulfillment, in the magnitude of the claims he makes for self or principle; but what is greater in him makes him more liable than we to loss, to suffering, and to death.

The self-deifying impulse in the tragic hero is usually crystalized in his social or political station; he is a king, general, nobleman, in some way or another a leader or focal point of his society. This initial connection with society becomes attenuated as the hero's fortunes alter for the worse; but it is rarely broken because as he loses political or social power the hero often gains a form of medicinal power, becoming a *pharmakos* or scapegoat figure in whom, logically (Richard III) or magically (Christ), society's guilts and ills are concentrated. Power passes into pollution, which becomes another form of power, the power to purge, cleanse, or free society. As Murray says, the Year-Daemon (Attis, Osiris, Dionysus) begins his annual life in purity, grows old and bloated with the sins of the community, and is slain as a pollution, thus cleansing the slate of the past in preparation for the new year. The limited political power that Christ might have exercised over the Jews is sacrificed to his spiritual power as *pharmakos,* the divine scapegoat carrying off man's sins. Thus behind a number of tragic heroes we can see, in varying degrees of clarity, the paradoxical figure of the god-scapegoat. Oedipus is both the godlike deliverer of Thebes from the curse of the Sphinx and the incestuous murderer whose banishment will release the city from the plague. Macbeth begins in glory, buying "golden opinions" from everyone as a queller of rebellion, and becomes the source of Scotland's contamination, the tyrant grown old in sin whose head must be carried in on the point of Macduff's pike before "the time is free." It is a comment on modern domestic tragedy that Willie Loman, whose name implies his unheroic stature, can aspire not to godlike status but only to the level of *pharmakos* when he seeks through one last sale, of his insured life, to carry off the economic and social ills that have burdened his family.

The paradox of the *pharmakos* is that he is valuable to society precisely to the extent that he is contaminated; as a version of Philoctetes (the Greek hero whose suppurating wound kept him out of the battle against Troy but whose bow had been declared essential to victory), he does not have a wound *and* a bow—his wound *is* his bow. When Oedipus stands revealed as the murderer, he becomes laden with sin but, because of that, with virtue too, since he now has the power to carry off the plague. Here we regard the hero as the sewer of society's guilt, sin, corruption; but it is not impossible to regard him as the chalice that contains society's most sacred virtues. The saint, no less than the great sinner, may have overtones of the *pharmakos*. Like Christ, he may miraculously take upon himself the sins of society; or from a more worldly standpoint, he may, by suffering or death, relieve others from the burden of self-reproach, the oppressive consciousness of not measuring up to the unattainable ideal that he embodies. Merely by existing, the saint demands too much and hence becomes, like Joan of Arc in Shaw's play, "insufferable" to ordinary men. So Job's friends take a certain consolation in regarding his suffering as punishment for sin. Lowering Job does not raise them, but it normalizes their shortcomings and thus purges them by redefinition. Nobody kills saints without first killing off their claims to saintliness and redefining them as sinners, heretics, imposters. And as with other *pharmakos* figures, in Heraclitus' phrase, "the way down is the way up": pollution is transformed into spiritual power, debasement into sanctity. So it is with some tragic heroes. "They told me I was everything," Lear says, " 'tis a lie, I am not ague-proof." In the storm Lear must cast off, with his clothes, his claims to majesty, reaching a rock bottom of the human condition before finding an order of recovery. Samson must play the role of muscular clown before the Philistines to earn the strength that topples the pillars. Oedipus must become a wandering pariah before, in *Oedipus at Colonus,* he is spiritually transfigured.

Anagnorisis This raises the question of what emerges from tragic suffering; the hero acts, he suffers, and then what? The earliest relevant answer is Aeschylus' "Through suffering—wisdom." Aristotle says nothing about the nature of tragic wisdom; but according to Hegel it consists in a recognition of cosmic justice. In his view the tragic hero is always a victim of what we called earlier situational guilt: he has chosen one kind of right at the expense of others that have equal claims on him. The result is an imbalance in the "Ethical Substance," which is the sum and source of all specific rights, but with the suffering and death of the offending agent this imbalance is stabilized. Out of the hero's suffering, then, comes his awareness of the role he has played in the grand scheme of things, his acknowledgement of the justice of a death that heals the breach he created in the Ethical Substance. Everything is ultimately for the best in this best of all possible tragic worlds. Not, however, for Schopenhauer, who feels that what we really see at the end of a tragedy is not the triumph of justice but of evil, of a malign cosmic will that frustrates and inexorably destroys even the well-endowed and apparently powerful. Amid defeat and general chaos, all we and the hero can achieve is a sense of tragic resignation of the sort coached by medieval *de casibus* tragedy and stoicism. These two positions—the one involving a sense of reconciliation verging on optimism, the other a sense of resignation verging on despair—are useful not because they represent the tragic vision but because they represent the limits of it, the points at which tragedy begins to turn into something else, into the melodrama of triumph, where at the end the hero's gains cancel out all losses, or the melodrama of disaster, where his losses cancel out all gains. At the upper limit, close to the drama of triumph, we find works like the *Eumenides,* Sophocles' *Electra, Samson Agonistes,* and *Murder in the Cathedral.* Near the lower limit, where we approach (and probably reach) the literature of disaster and despair, we find works like Hardy's *Tess of the D'Urbervilles* and *Jude the Obscure,* Hemingway's *A Farewell to Arms,* Gorki's *The Lower Depths,* O'Neill's *The Iceman Cometh,* and Ionesco's *The Chairs.*

The melodrama of triumph sees man only winning, that of disaster man only losing, but in the divided focus of the tragic vision victory and defeat become interinvolved. The hero's loss of material prosperity, power, or status in the eyes of others is figured in his suffering and rendered final by his death. But out of suffering and despite death something is gained—perception, insight, understanding, perhaps even wisdom—for which we can use Aristotle's term *anagnorisis* (strictly, recognition). To the victim of disaster in real life—the man stricken with a fatal disease, the mother whose child drowns, all those who die by accident and suffer by chance—suffering is a *post quam non.* Questions like "Where did I go wrong—or right?" and "What did I prove and was it worth it?" are meaningless; all that remains is the blank inscrutable fact that what has happened has happened, which is why we are so tongue-tied in the presence of disaster. If form consists in a meaningful relation between parts, disaster, which exhibits no relation between self and suffering, is at bottom formless, chaotic, disordered. The tragic *anagnorisis,* on the other hand, is essentially a recognition of form, a consciousness of how self, action, and suffering have cooperated to shape the hero's experience. Thus we normally find the hero near the end of the play looking back on a point of change, a crucial decision, a fatal act that led through a series of consequences to the present moment and seeing how the present, carried by the momentum of time and action, drives on to a determined future—how, as Faustus says, "The stars move still, time runs, the clock will strike." According to Thomas Hobbes,

"Hell is truth seen too late," and the sight of it causes Oedipus to blind himself, Lady Macbeth to lapse into an endless ritual of purification, and Joan of Arc to cry, "My voices have deceived me. I have been mocked by devils."

Despite the appalling nature of what is normally seen, the act of perception is an achievement of mind and spirit in which the hero transcends both self and suffering. In a sense, he breaks out of the limited role of a character *in* a drama and achieves a vision *of* the drama and his own part in it that is analogous to that of the playwright. From this new perspective the identity he felt he possessed is seen as an illusion, and he now recognizes his fallen self, as in Macbeth's—

> My way of life
> Is fallen into the sear, the yellow leaf;
> And that which should accompany old age,
> As honour, love, obedience, troops of friends,
> I must not look to have; but, in their stead,
> Curses, not loud but deep, mouth-honour, breath
> Which the poor heart would fain deny, and dare not.

Macbeth's world-weary realization of how what he might have been has dwindled into what he is underscores the preclusiveness of the tragic act as it bears on the self. The hero's decision to act, to go a certain route, not only precludes other acts but contributes to the formation of a self that precludes others: he *is* what he has done. Thus to some extent the hero, as he realizes the form his life has taken, mourns the potential selves that have been lost to him. At the end of the play, Caligula addresses his mirror-image, saying, "I've stretched out my hands... but it's always you I find, you only, confronting me, and I've come to hate you. I have chosen a wrong path, a path that leads to nothing." Even the search for unlimited freedom has created an entirely limited and now, he realizes, repellent identity—"you only." So Faustus laments the values he might have enjoyed: "for vain pleasure of twenty-four years hath Faustus lost eternal joy and felicity." And even Coriolanus, one of the least sentient of Shakespearean tragic heroes, seeks in dying to transcend the self he has become by recapturing his lost identity as Rome's soldier, dying not as "Marcius" but "Coriolanus."

Suffering for the tragic hero, then, however painful, destructive, and seemingly final, is not merely a crushing defeat but an incitement to knowledge, understanding, vision. Even Prometheus, the "Fore-thinker" who knew in advance all that was to follow, continues nevertheless to reassess and explore the issues involved in his tragedy, dominating his suffering not only through sustained defiance and courage but through repeated acts of understanding. Job, too, though an innocent victim, acts like a tragic hero in making suffering an avenue to self-knowledge. He does not simply cave in, on the one hand, nor automatically trumpet his innocence, on the other, but strives to master his experience through a re-examination of self, faith, the mystery of justice.

The range and profundity of *anagnorisis* will of course vary from hero to hero, but for *anagnorisis* to occur at all the hero must be endowed with a certain degree of vision and understanding. In this regard, Willie Loman's status as a tragic hero is seriously jeopardized. He goes to his death with all his illusions about winning friends and influencing people still intact, unable really to see his sons Biff and Happy or, more important, himself. As Biff says after his death, "He never knew who he was." At a slightly higher level, Anton Schill, the *pharmakos* hero of Duerrenmatt's *The Visit*, comes to see the death he will suffer in the light of his own conduct—"I made Clara what she is, and I made myself what I am...It's all my own work"—but his *anagnorisis*, like his life, is severely limited: "I only know that my meaningless life will end." Lear, on the other hand, undergoes a sustained *anagnorisis* in which he graduates from a foolish, egoistic, willful old man who "hath ever but slenderly known himself" to one shot through with humility, compassion, and self-knowledge. Macbeth does not undergo a transformation of character like Lear's, but as he perceives the inevitability of what lies before him, he refuses to exchange the role of tragic hero for that of victim. Unlike a lesser man, he accepts responsibility for his fate, facing the withering knowledge of what he has become without shifting guilt to fortune, the witches, or his wife. "The unexamined life," Socrates said, "is not worth living." For some tragic heroes, even the examined life may not seem worth living, but examine it they nevertheless do. As *anagnorisis* implies, tragic heroes, though they usually die, do not die blindly.

Oedipus Rex

Oedipus Rex is the most frequently mentioned play in the *Poetics* of Aristotle, where it is regarded as a model of tragic composition; but its date is unknown (scholars guess it to have appeared around 429 B.C.), and all we know of its theatrical life is that it was awarded, remarkably enough, only the second prize when first presented in competition. The Oedipus story had existed in myth long before Sophocles (496?–406 B.C.) chose to dramatize it; in literature it shows up as early as Homer, undergoing various alterations before appearing in dramatic form. Aeschylus wrote a Theban trilogy in which the second play, since lost, was entitled *Oedipus,* and Sophocles had himself written, about ten or twelve years earlier, *Antigone,* which treats the last phase of the Oedipus myth. In the form in which Sophocles used it, the entire myth runs as follows:

According to a prophecy, the son to be born of Laius and Jocasta, the King and Queen of Thebes, would kill his father and marry his mother. To prevent this, they "exposed" the child, that is, had him abandoned on Mount Cithairon, feet pinned together, to die. A compassionate shepherd, however, took the infant to Corinth, where he was adopted by the childless rulers, Polybus and Merope, who gave him the name "Oedipus" (swollen foot). Much later, as a young man, Oedipus learned of the prophecy concerning him and fled immediately from Corinth and his supposed parents. At a crossroads near Thebes he quarreled with an old man—actually his father Laius—over the right of way and in the ensuing fight killed him. Continuing on, he found Thebes suffering under the tyranny of the Sphinx, a creature part woman, part animal, who destroyed all who could not answer her riddle: "What is it that walks on four legs in the morning, two in the afternoon, and three in the evening?" Oedipus gave the right answer, "Man," who crawls on all fours in infancy, walks upright in his maturity, and employs a cane or other support in old age. The Sphinx destroyed herself, the city was released from its bondage, and, the news of Laius' death having arrived, Oedipus was awarded Jocasta and the rule of Thebes for his victory. He had four children by Jocasta, two girls, Antigone and Ismene, and two boys, Polynices and Eteocles; and all was well until a mysterious plague settled over Thebes that, according to an oracle, could be lifted only by the death or banishment of Laius' killer. At this point *Oedipus Rex* begins, continuing on to the banishment of Oedipus. After leaving Thebes Oedipus wanders for some time, a pariah, until he is given sanctuary in Athens by King Theseus, at which point in the story Sophocles' play *Oedipus at Colonus* begins, moving on to the death of Oedipus. After his death, the struggle for power in Thebes leads to a civil war in which Oedipus' two sons kill each other in single combat outside the gates. Creon then becomes king and decrees that the body of Polynices, who had opposed him and Eteocles, is to be left unburied and unhallowed. Antigone, Oedipus' elder daughter, defies this edict, and the remainder of the play *Antigone* explores the tragic consequences of her defiance and Creon's insistence.

From one standpoint, then, what Sophocles has dramatized in *Oedipus Rex* is a purgation ritual in which the hero, having freed the city from the dragon of death, becomes himself the center of pollution, radiating a plague of sterility and sickness that only his scapegoat sacrifice can cure. The play thus has a rich vein of religious and anthropological significance. But seeing the primary meaning of the play only in an underlying ritual structure is as reductive in its own way as trying to make the Freudian Oedipus-complex account for the complex Oedipus. Though tragedy and other kinds of drama draw on the reservoirs of human feeling tapped by ritual, the greater sophistication and artistry of drama and the linguistic and scenic power articulating these feelings and generating others count for more. Thus while we should by no means ignore the ritual dimension of drama, we should no more substitute ritual for drama than a moan of grief for an elegy.

For one thing, ritual is not especially noted for its irony, but Sophocles' play is freighted with it, the title itself, as Bernard Knox has pointed out, being a network of ironies. The Greek work *tyrannos,* usually translated as either king or tyrant, actually means neither. King implies the orderly succession of rule, primarily through lineal descent, and tyrant implies despotic rule; but *tyrannos* refers to the ruler who has acquired power on his own hook through force, intrigue, or, in Oedipus' case, cleverness—a self-made ruler who may or may not be despotic. The irony lies in the fact that while Oedipus is a *tyrannos* by virtue of his own riddle-answering talents the action of the play leads to his discovery that, as the son of Laius, he is also king. This same sort of irony invades Oedipus' own name, which means swollen foot, in reference, of course, to the injuries caused by the pinning of his feet in infancy. *Oidi* meaning "swell," however, is nearly identical to the Greek *oida,* which means "I know," and knowing is the means by which Oedipus became *tyrannos.* His intellectual victory over the Sphinx dominates the consciousness both of Oedipus himself and the citizens of Thebes throughout the play. (The student should glance through the play noting the extraordinary number of times the words "I know" get into Oedipus' language.) But if we accept the punning identity of *oida-oidi,* the result is a fusion of *oida* and *pous,* or "I know-foot," and yet it is precisely his mangled foot and the circumstances that caused it that Oedipus does not know.

So too with the celebrated imagery of sight. A play that presents so horrible an image as that of Oedipus emerging from his palace, eyes streaming blood, raises the critical question of whether this is horror for its own spectacular sake or horror somehow assimilated into dramatic form. Answering that question requires an examination of the imagery of seeing and of light and dark, which of course involves comparing Oedipus with Teiresias. Oedipus as the man of "seeing" and "knowing" ("I see" in the sense of "I understand") reflects the Greek spirit of self-sufficient rationalism, which Protagoras so confidently expressed by saying "Man is the measure of all things." From this perspective, the play is a critique of rationalism, in twentieth-century America as well as in fifth-century B.C. Greece; a critique designed not to reject but to set the limits of rationalism by distinguishing between knowledge, which may provide answers to the Sphinx, and wisdom, which may include an awareness that knowledge is not necessarily beneficial, that the truth may enslave as well as set free.

Reason and logic, the developing inevitability of action, are congenial to the tragic plot, but the tragic mode, as Oedipus discovers, also deals in the illogic of paradox. The man who finds himself to be the husband of his mother and the brother of his children, who is both judge and criminal, physician and disease, world-renowned and world-abhorred, has experienced the dissolution of the rational surfaces of reality and encountered a chaos within. Harrowing as it is, however, that encounter is paradoxically an achievement also, and the suffering that Oedipus undergoes upon seeing the truth is not more pitiable than his insistence on seeing it is ennobling. In a world shaped at least in part by the mysterious forces of the oracle, Oedipus transcends the role of blind victim by shaping his own form of awareness. Though fated to perform certain acts, he is not, as Sophocles has dramatized the myth, fated to discover what he has done. His tragedy lies less in killing his father and marrying his mother than in his courageous search for a knowledge that can only bring him suffering. Thus though Yeats' remark about heroism applies to most tragic heroes, it has special significance for Oedipus: "Why should we honor those who die on the field of battle? A man may show as reckless a courage in entering into the abyss of himself."

Oedipus Rex

OEDIPUS
A PRIEST
CREON
TEIRESIAS
IOCASTE

MESSENGER
SHEPHERD OF LAIOS
SECOND MESSENGER
CHORUS OF THEBAN ELDERS

THE SCENE. *Before the palace of Oedipus, King of Thebes. A central door and two lateral doors open onto a platform which runs the length of the façade. On the platform, right and left, are altars; and three steps lead down into the* orchestra, *or chorus-ground.*
The steps are crowded by suppliants who have brought branches and chaplets of olive leaves and who lie in various attitudes of despair. OEDIPUS *enters.*

OEDIPUS. My children, generations of the living
In the line of Kadmos, nursed at his ancient hearth:
Why have you strewn yourselves before these altars
In supplication, with your boughs and garlands?
The breath of incense rises from the city
With a sound of prayer and lamentation.
                    Children,
I would not have you speak through messengers,
And therefore I have come myself to

hear you—
I, Oedipus, who bear the famous name. [*To a* PRIEST.] You, there, since you are eldest in the company,
Speak for them all, tell me what preys upon you,
Whether you come in dread, or crave some blessing:
Tell me, and never doubt that I will help you
In every way I can; I should be heartless
Were I not moved to find you suppliant here.

PRIEST. Great Oedipus, O powerful King of Thebes!
You see how all the ages of our people
Cling to your altar steps: here are boys
Who can barely stand alone, and here are priests
By weight of age, as I am a priest of God,
And young men chosen from those yet unmarried;
As for the others, all that multitude,
They wait with olive chaplets in the squares,
At the two shrines of Pallas, and where Apollo
Speaks in the glowing embers.
                Your own eyes
Must tell you: Thebes is in her extremity

Translated by Dudley Fitts and Robert Fitzgerald.
The Oedipus Rex of Sophocles: *An English Version by Dudley Fitts and Robert Fitzgerald, copyright, 1949, by Harcourt, Brace & World, Inc. and reprinted with their permission.*

And cannot lift her head from the surge of death.
A rust consumes the buds and fruits of the earth;
The herds are sick; children die unborn,
And labor is vain. The god of plague and pyre
Raids like detestable lightning through the city,
And all the house of Kadmos is laid waste,
All emptied, and all darkened: Death alone
Battens upon the misery of Thebes.
You are not one of the immortal gods, we know;
Yet we have come to you to make our prayer
As to the man of all men best in adversity
And wisest in the ways of God. You saved us
From the Sphinx, that flinty singer, and the tribute
We paid to her so long; yet you were never
Better informed than we, nor could we teach you:
It was some god breathed in you to set us free.
Therefore, O mighty King, we turn to you:
Find us our safety, find us a remedy,
Whether by counsel of the gods or men.
A king of wisdom tested in the past
Can act in a time of troubles, and act well.
Noblest of men, restore
Life to your city! Think how all men call you
Liberator for your triumph long ago;
Ah, when your years of kingship are remembered,
Let them not say *We rose, but later fell*—
Keep the State from going down in the storm!
Once, years ago, with happy augury,

You brought us fortune; be the same again!
No man questions your power to rule the land:
But rule over men, not over a dead city!
Ships are only hulls, citadels are nothing,
When no life moves in the empty passageways.

OEDIPUS. Poor children! You may be sure I know
All that you longed for in your coming here.
I know that you are deathly sick; and yet,
Sick as you are, not one is as sick as I.
Each of you suffers in himself alone
His anguish, not another's; but my spirit
Groans for the city, for myself, for you.
I was not sleeping, you are not waking me.
No, I have been in tears for a long while
And in my restless thought walked many ways.
In all my search, I found one helpful course,
And that I have taken: I have sent Creon,
Son of Menoikeus, brother of the Queen,
To Delphi, Apollo's place of revelation,
To learn there, if he can,
What act or pledge of mine may save the city.
I have counted the days, and now, this very day,
I am troubled, for he has overstayed his time.
What is he doing? He has been gone too long.
Yet whenever he comes back, I should do ill
To scant whatever hint the god may give.

PRIEST. It is a timely promise. At this instant
They tell me Creon is here.

OEDIPUS.   O Lord Apollo!
May his news be fair as his face is radiant!

PRIEST. It could not be otherwise: he is crowned with bay,
The chaplet is thick with berries.

OEDIPUS.   We shall soon know;
He is near enough to hear us now.

[*Enter* CREON.]

                    O Prince:
Brother: son of Menoikeus:
What answer do you bring us from the god?

CREON. It is favorable. I can tell you, great afflictions
Will turn out well, if they are taken well.

OEDIPUS. What was the oracle? These vague words
Leave me still hanging between hope and fear.

CREON. Is it your pleasure to hear me with all these
Gathered around us? I am prepared to speak,
But should we not go in?

OEDIPUS.   Let them all hear it.
It is for them I suffer, more than for myself.

CREON. Then I will tell you what I heard at Delphi.
In plain words
The god commands us to expel from the land of Thebes
An old defilement that it seems we shelter.
It is a deathly thing, beyond expiation.
We must not let it feed upon us longer.

OEDIPUS. What defilement? How shall we rid ourselves of it?

CREON. By exile or death, blood for blood. It was
Murder that brought the plague-wind on the city.

OEDIPUS. Murder of whom? Surely the god has named him?

CREON. My lord: long ago Laïos was our king,
Before you came to govern us.

OEDIPUS.   I know;
I learned of him from others; I never saw him.

CREON. He was murdered; and Apollo commands us now
To take revenge upon whoever killed him.

OEDIPUS. Upon whom? Where are they? Where shall we find a clue
To solve that crime, after so many years?

CREON. Here in this land, he said. If we make enquiry,
We may touch things that otherwise escape us.

OEDIPUS. Tell me: Was Laïos murdered in his house,
Or in the fields, or in some foreign country?

CREON. He said he planned to make a pilgrimage.
He did not come home again.

OEDIPUS.   And was there no one,
No witness, no companion, to tell what happened?

CREON. They were all killed but one, and he got away
So frightened that he could remember one thing only.

OEDIPUS. What was that one thing? One may be the key
To everything, if we resolve to use it.

CREON. He said that a band of highwaymen attacked them,
Outnumbered them, and overwhelmed the King.

OEDIPUS. Strange, that a highwayman should be so daring—
Unless some faction here bribed him to do it.

CREON. We thought of that. But after Laïos' death
New troubles arose and we had no avenger.

OEDIPUS. What troubles could prevent

your hunting down the killers?

CREON. The riddling Sphinx's song
   Made us deaf to all mysteries but her
      own.

OEDIPUS. Then once more I must bring
      what is dark to light.
   It is most fitting that Apollo shows,
   As you do, this compunction for the
      dead.
   You shall see how I stand by you,
      as I should,
   To avenge the city and the city's god,
   And not as though it were for some
      distant friend,
   But for my own sake, to be rid of
      evil.
   Whoever killed King Laïos might—
      who knows?—
   Decide at any moment to kill me as
      well.
   By avenging the murdered king I
      protect myself.
   Come, then, my children: leave the
      altar steps,
   Lift up your olive boughs!
                         One of you go
   And summon the people of Kadmos
      to gather here.
   I will do all that I can; you may tell
      them that.   [*Exit a* PAGE.]
   So, with the help of God,
   We shall be saved—or else indeed we
      are lost.

PRIEST. Let us rise, children. It was
      for this we came,
   And now the King has promised it
      himself.
   Phoibos has sent us an oracle; may
      he descend
   Himself to save us and drive out the
      plague.

[*Exeunt* OEDIPUS *and* CREON *into the
palace by the central door. The* PRIEST
and the SUPPLIANTS *disperse R and L.
After a short pause the* CHORUS *enters
the* orchestra.]

CHORUS. What is the god singing in his
      profound
   Delphi of gold and shadow?

What oracle for Thebes, the sun-
   whipped city?
Fear unjoints me, the roots of my
   heart tremble.
Now I remember, O Healer, your
   power, and wonder:
Will you send doom like a sudden
   cloud, or weave it
Like nightfall of the past?
Ah no: be merciful, issue of holy
   sound:
Dearest to our expectancy: be ten-
   der!
Let me pray to Athenê, the immortal
   daughter of Zeus,
And to Artemis her sister
Who keeps her famous throne in the
   market ring,
And to Apollo, bowman at the far
   butts of heaven—
O gods, descend! Like three streams
   leap against
The fires of our grief, the fires of
   darkness;
Be swift to bring us rest!
   As in the old time from the bril-
   liant house
Of air you stepped to save us, come
   again!
Now our afflictions have no end,
Now all our stricken host lies down
And no man fights off death with his
   mind;
   The noble plowland bears no grain,
And groaning mothers cannot bear—
   See, how our lives like birds take
   wing,
Like sparks that fly when a fire soars,
To the shore of the god of evening.
   The plague burns on, it is pitiless,
Though pallid children laden with
   death
Lie unwept in the stony ways,
   And old gray women by every path
Flock to the strand about the altars
There to strike their breasts and cry
Worship of Zeus in wailing prayers:
Be kind, God's golden child!
There are no swords in this attack by
   fire,

No shields, but we are ringed with
cries.
   Send the besieger plunging from
our homes
Into the vast sea-room of the Atlantic
Or into the waves that foam eastward
of Thrace—
For the day ravages what the night
spares—
Destroy our enemy, lord of the
thunder!
Let him be riven by lightning from
heaven!
Phoibos Apollo, stretch the sun's
bowstring,
That golden cord, until it sing for us,
Flashing arrows in heaven!
                Artemis, Huntress,
Race with flaring lights upon our
mountains!
O scarlet god, O golden-banded
brow,
O Theban Bacchos in a storm of
Maenads,

[*Enter* OEDIPUS, *from the palace.*]

Whirl upon Death, that all the Undying hate!
Come with blinding cressets, come in
joy!

OEDIPUS. Is this your prayer? It may
be answered. Come,
Listen to me, act as the crisis
demands,
And you shall have relief from all
these evils.
Until now I was a stranger to this
tale,
As I had been a stranger to the crime.
Could I track down the murderer
without a clue?
But now, friends,
As one who became a citizen after
the murder,
I make this proclamation to all
Thebans:
If any man knows by whose hand
Laïos, son of Labdakos,
Met his death, I direct that man to
tell me everything,

No matter what he fears for having
so long withheld it.
Let it stand as promised that no
further trouble
Will come to him, but he may leave
the land in safety.
Moreover: If anyone knows the murderer to be foreign,
Let him not keep silent: he shall
have his reward from me.
However, if he does conceal it; if any
man
Fearing for his friend or for himself
disobeys this edict,
Hear what I propose to do:
I solemnly forbid the people of this
country,
Where power and throne are mine,
ever to receive that man
Or speak to him, no matter who he is,
or let him
Join in sacrifice, lustration, or in
prayer.
I decree that he be driven from every
house,
Being, as he is, corruption itself to
us: the Delphic
Voice of Zeus has pronounced this
revelation.
Thus I associate myself with the
oracle
And take the side of the murdered
king.
As for the criminal, I pray to
God—
Whether it be a lurking thief, or one
of a number—
I pray that that man's life be con-
sumed in evil and wretchedness.
And as for me, this curse applies no
less
If it should turn out that the culprit
is my guest here,
Sharing my hearth.
          You have heard the penalty.
I lay it on you now to attend to this
For my sake, for Apollo's, for the
sick
Sterile city that heaven has aban-
doned.

Suppose the oracle had given you no command:
Should this defilement go uncleansed for ever?
You should have found the murderer: your king,
A noble king, had been destroyed!
                                      Now I,
Having the power that he held before me,
Having his bed, begetting children there
Upon his wife, as he would have, had he lived—
Their son would have been my children's brother
If Laïos had had luck in fatherhood!
(But surely ill luck rushed upon his reign)—
I say I take the son's part, just as though
I were his son, to press the fight for him
And see it won! I'll find the hand that brought
Death to Labdakos' and Polydoros' child,
Heir of Kadmos' and Agenor's line.
And as for those who fail me,
May the gods deny them the fruit of the earth,
Fruit of the womb, and may they rot utterly!
Let them be wretched as we are wretched, and worse!
For you, for loyal Thebans, and for all
Who find my actions right, I pray the favor
Of justice, and of all the immortal gods.
CHORAGOS. Since I am under oath, my lord, I swear
I did not do the murder, I cannot name
The murderer. Might not the oracle
That has ordained the search tell where to find him?
OEDIPUS. An honest question. But no man in the world
Can make the gods do more than the gods will.
CHORAGOS. There is one last expedient—
OEDIPUS.   Tell me what it is.
Though it seem slight, you must not hold it back.
CHORAGOS. A lord clairvoyant to the lord Apollo,
As we all know, is the skilled Teiresias.
One might learn much about this from him, Oedipus.
OEDIPUS.   I am not wasting time:
Creon spoke of this, and I have sent for him—
Twice, in fact; it is strange that he is not here.
CHORAGOS. The other matter—that old report—seems useless.
OEDIPUS. Tell me. I am interested in all reports.
CHORAGOS. The King was said to have been killed by highwaymen.
OEDIPUS. I know. But we have no witnesses to that.
CHORAGOS. If the killer can feel a particle of dread,
Your curse will bring him out of hiding!
OEDIPUS.   No.
The man who dared that act will fear no curse.

[*Enter the blind seer* TEIRESIAS, *led by a* PAGE.]

CHORAGOS. But there is one man who may detect the criminal.
This is Teiresias, this is the holy prophet
In whom, alone of all men, truth was born.
OEDIPUS. Teiresias: seer: student of mysteries,
Of all that's taught and all that no man tells,
Secrets of Heaven and secrets of the earth:
Blind though you are, you know the city lies

Sick with plague; and from this plague, my lord,

We find that you alone can guard or save us.

Possibly you did not hear the messengers?

Apollo, when we sent to him,

Sent us back word that this great pestilence

Would lift, but only if we established clearly

The identity of those who murdered Laïos.

They must be killed or exiled.

                          Can you use

Bird flight or any art of divination

To purify yourself, and Thebes, and me

From this contagion? We are in your hands.

There is no fairer duty

Than that of helping others in distress.

TEIRESIAS. How dreadful knowledge of the truth can be

When there's no help in truth! I knew this well,

But did not act on it: else I should not have come.

OEDIPUS. What is troubling you? Why are your eyes so cold?

TEIRESIAS. Let me go home. Bear your own fate, and I'll

Bear mine. It is better so: trust what I say.

OEDIPUS. What you say is ungracious and unhelpful

To your native country. Do not refuse to speak.

TEIRESIAS. When it comes to speech, your own is neither temperate

Nor opportune. I wish to be more prudent.

OEDIPUS. In God's name, we all beg you—

TEIRESIAS.   You are all ignorant.

No; I will never tell you what I know.

Now it is my misery; then, it would be yours.

OEDIPUS. What! You do know something, and will not tell us?

You would betray us all and wreck the State?

TEIRESIAS. I do not intend to torture myself, or you.

Why persist in asking? You will not persuade me.

OEDIPUS. What a wicked old man you are! You'd try a stone's

Patience! Out with it! Have you no feeling at all?

TEIRESIAS. You call me unfeeling. If you could only see

The nature of your own feelings . . .

OEDIPUS.   Why,

Who would not feel as I do? Who could endure

Your arrogance toward the city?

TEIRESIAS.   What does it matter!

Whether I speak or not, it is bound to come.

OEDIPUS. Then, if "it" is bound to come, you are bound to tell me.

TEIRESIAS. No, I will not go on. Rage as you please.

OEDIPUS. Rage? Why, not!

    And I'll tell you what I think:

You planned it, you had it done, you all but

Killed him with your own hands: if you had eyes,

I'd say the crime was yours, and yours alone.

TEIRESIAS. So? I charge you, then,

Abide by the proclamation you have made:

From this day forth

Never speak again to these men or to me;

You yourself are the pollution of this country.

OEDIPUS. You dare say that! Can you possibly think you have

Some way of going free, after such insolence?

TEIRESIAS. I have gone free. It is the truth sustains me.

OEDIPUS. Who taught you shamelessness? It was not your craft.

TEIRESIAS. You did. You made me speak. I did not want to.

OEDIPUS. Speak what? Let me hear it again more clearly.

TEIRESIAS. Was it not clear before? Are you tempting me?

OEDIPUS. I did not understand it. Say it again.

TEIRESIAS. I say that you are the murderer whom you seek.

OEDIPUS. Now twice you have spat out infamy. You'll pay for it!

TEIRESIAS. Would you care for more? Do you wish to be really angry?

OEDIPUS. Say what you will. Whatever you say is worthless.

TEIRESIAS. I say that you live in hideous love with her
Who is nearest you in blood. You are blind to the evil.

OEDIPUS. It seems you can go on mouthing like this for ever.

TEIRESIAS. I can, if there is power in truth.

OEDIPUS.   There is:
But not for you, not for you,
You sightless, witless, senseless, mad old man!

TEIRESIAS. You are the madman. There is no one here
Who will not curse you soon, as you curse me.

OEDIPUS. You child of endless night! You cannot hurt me
Or any other man who sees the sun.

TEIRESIAS. True: it is not from me your fate will come.
That lies within Apollo's competence, As it is his concern.

OEDIPUS.   Tell me:
Are you speaking for Creon, or for yourself?

TEIRESIAS. Creon is no threat. You weave your own doom.

OEDIPUS. Wealth, power, craft of statesmanship!
Kingly position, everywhere admired!
What savage envy is stored up against these,

If Creon, whom I trusted, Creon my friend,
For this great office which the city once
Put in my hands unsought—if for this power
Creon desires in secret to destroy me!
He has bought this decrepit fortune-teller, this
Collector of dirty pennies, this prophet fraud—
Why, he is no more clairvoyant than I am!

                              Tell us:
Has your mystic mummery ever approached the truth?
When that hellcat the Sphinx was performing here,
What help were you to these people?
Her magic was not for the first man who came along:
It demanded a real exorcist. Your birds—
What good were they? or the gods, for the matter of that?
But I came by,
Oedipus, the simple man, who knows nothing—
I thought it out for myself, no birds helped me!
And this is the man you think you can destroy,
That you may be close to Creon when he's king!
Well, you and your friend Creon, it seems to me,
Will suffer most. If you were not an old man,
You would have paid already for your plot.

CHORAGOS. We cannot see that his words or yours
Have been spoken except in anger, Oedipus,
And of anger we have no need. How can God's will
Be accomplished best? That is what most concerns us.

TEIRESIAS. You are a king. But where argument's concerned

I am your man, as much a king as you.
I am not your servant, but Apollo's.
I have no need of Creon to speak for me.

Listen to me. You mock my blindness, do you?
But I say that you, with both your eyes, are blind:
You cannot see the wretchedness of your life,
Nor in whose house you live, no, nor with whom.
Who are your father and mother? Can you tell me?
You do not even know the blind wrongs
That you have done them, on earth and in the world below.
But the double lash of your parents' curse will whip you
Out of this land some day, with only night
Upon your precious eyes.
Your cries then—where will they not be heard?
What fastness of Kithairon will not echo them?
And that bridal-descant of yours—you'll know it then,
The song they sang when you came here to Thebes
And found your misguided berthing.
All this, and more, that you cannot guess at now,
Will bring you to yourself among your children.

Be angry, then. Curse Creon. Curse my words.
I tell you, no man that walks upon the earth
Shall be rooted out more horribly than you.

OEDIPUS. Am I to bear this from him?—Damnation
Take you! Out of this place! Out of my sight!

TEIRESIAS. I would not have come at all if you had not asked me.

OEDIPUS. Could I have told that you'd talk nonsense, that
You'd come here to make a fool of yourself, and of me?

TEIRESIAS. A fool? Your parents thought me sane enough.

OEDIPUS. My parents again!—Wait: who were my parents?

TEIRESIAS. This day will give you a father, and break your heart.

OEDIPUS. Your infantile riddles! Your damned abracadabra!

TEIRESIAS. You were a great man once at solving riddles.

OEDIPUS. Mock me with that if you like; you will find it true.

TEIRESIAS. It was true enough. It brought about your ruin.

OEDIPUS. But if it saved this town?

TEIRESIAS [*to the* PAGE]. Boy, give me your hand.

OEDIPUS. Yes, boy; lead him away.
                    —While you are here
We can do nothing. Go; leave us in peace.

TEIRESIAS. I will go when I have said what I have to say.
How can you hurt me? And I tell you again:
The man you have been looking for all this time,
The damned man, the murderer of Laïos,
That man is in Thebes. To your mind he is foreign-born,
But it will soon be shown that he is a Theban,
A revelation that will fail to please.
                    A blind man,
Who has his eyes now; a penniless man, who is rich now;
And he will go tapping the strange earth with his staff.
To the children with whom he lives now he will be
Brother and father—the very same; to her
Who bore him, son and husband—the very same
Who came to his father's bed, wet with his father's blood.

Enough. Go think that over.
If later you find error in what I have said,
You may say that I have no skill in prophecy.

[*Exit* TEIRESIAS, *led by his* PAGE. OEDIPUS *goes into the palace.*]

CHORUS. The Delphic stone of prophecies
Remembers ancient regicide
And a still bloody hand.
That killer's hour of flight has come.
He must be stronger than riderless
Coursers of untiring wind,
For the son of Zeus armed with his father's thunder
Leaps in lightning after him;
And the Furies follow him, the sad Furies.
Holy Parnassos' peak of snow
Flashes and blinds that secret man,
That all shall hunt him down:
Though he may roam the forest shade
Like a bull gone wild from pasture
To rage through glooms of stone.
Doom comes down on him; flight will not avail him;
For the world's heart calls him desolate,
And the immortal Furies follow, forever follow.

But now a wilder thing is heard
From the old man skilled at hearing
Fate in the wing beat of a bird.
Bewildered as a blown bird, my soul
hovers and cannot find
Foothold in this debate, or any reason or rest of mind.
But no man ever brought—none can bring
Proof of strife between Thebes' royal house,
Labdakos' line, and the son of Polybos;
And never until now has any man brought word
Of Laïos' dark death staining Oedipus the King.
Divine Zeus and Apollo hold
Perfect intelligence alone of all tales ever told;
And well though this diviner works, he works in his own night;
No man can judge that rough unknown or trust in second sight,
For wisdom changes hands among the wise.
Shall I believe my great lord criminal
At a raging word that a blind old man let fall?
I saw him, when the carrion woman faced him of old,
Prove his heroic mind! These evil words are lies.

CREON. Men of Thebes:
I am told that heavy accusations
Have been brought against me by King Oedipus.
I am not the kind of man to bear this tamely.
If in these present difficulties
He holds me accountable for any harm to him
Through anything I have said or done—why, then,
I do not value life in this dishonor.
It is not as though this rumor touched upon
Some private indiscretion. The matter is grave.
The fact is that I am being called disloyal
To the State, to my fellow citizens, to my friends.

CHORAGOS. He may have spoken in anger, not from his mind.

CREON. But did you not hear him say
I was the one
Who seduced the old prophet into lying?

CHORAGOS. The thing was said; I do not know how seriously.

CREON. But you were watching him! Were his eyes steady?
Did he look like a man in his right mind?

CHORAGOS.   I do not know.
I cannot judge the behavior of great men.

But here is the King himself.

[*Enter* OEDIPUS.]

OEDIPUS.   So you dared come back.
Why? How brazen of you to come to
my house,
You murderer!
            Do you think I do not know
That you plotted to kill me, plotted
to steal my throne?
Tell me, in God's name: am I coward,
a fool,
That you should dream you could
accomplish this?
A fool who could not see your slip-
pery game?
A coward, not to fight back when I
saw it?
You are the fool, Creon, are you not?
hoping
Without support or friends to get a
throne?
Thrones may be won or bought: you
could do neither.

CREON. Now listen to me. You have
talked; let me talk, too.
You cannot judge unless you know
the facts.

OEDIPUS. You speak well: there is one
fact; but I find it hard
To learn from the deadliest enemy I
have.

CREON. That above all I must dispute
with you.

OEDIPUS. That above all I will not hear
you deny.

CREON. If you think there is anything
good in being stubborn
Against all reason, then I say you
are wrong.

OEDIPUS. If you think a man can sin
against his own kind
And not be punished for it, I say you
are mad.

CREON. I agree. But tell me: what have
I done to you?

OEDIPUS. You advised me to send for
that wizard, did you not?

CREON. I did. I should do it again.

OEDIPUS.   Very well. Now tell me:

How long has it been since Laïos—

CREON.   What of Laïos?

OEDIPUS. Since he vanished in that
onset by the road?

CREON. It was long ago, a long time.

OEDIPUS.   And this prophet,
Was he practicing here then?

CREON. He was; and with honor, as
now.

OEDIPUS. Did he speak of me at that
time?

CREON.   He never did;
At least, not when I was present.

OEDIPUS.   But...the enquiry?
I suppose you held one?

CREON. We did, but we learned nothing.

OEDIPUS. Why did the prophet not
speak against me then?

CREON. I do not know; and I am the
kind of man
Who holds his tongue when he has no
facts to go on.

OEDIPUS. There's one fact that you
know, and you could tell it.

CREON. What fact is that? If I know it,
you shall have it.

OEDIPUS. If he were not involved with
you, he could not say
That it was I who murdered Laïos.

CREON. If he says that, you are the one
that knows it!—
But now it is my turn to question
you.

OEDIPUS. Put your questions. I am no
murderer.

CREON. First, then: You married my
sister?

OEDIPUS.   I married your sister.

CREON. And you rule the kingdom
equally with her?

OEDIPUS. Everything that she wants
she has from me.

CREON. And I am the third, equal to
both of you?

OEDIPUS. That is why I call you a bad
friend.

CREON. No. Reason it out, as I have
done.
Think of this first: Would any sane
man prefer

Power, with all a king's anxieties,
To that same power and the grace of
    sleep?
Certainly not I.
I have never longed for the king's
    power—only his rights.
Would any wise man differ from me
    in this?
As matters stand, I have my way in
    everything
With your consent, and no respon-
    sibilities.
If I were king, I should be a slave to
    policy.
    How could I desire a scepter more
Than what is now mine—untroubled
    influence?
No, I have not gone mad; I need no
    honors,
Except those with the perquisites I
    have now.
I am welcome everywhere; every man
    salutes me,
And those who want your favor seek
    my ear,
Since I know how to manage what
    they ask.
Should I exchange this ease for that
    anxiety?
Besides, no sober mind is treasonable.
I hate anarchy
And never would deal with any man
    who likes it.
    Test what I have said. Go to the
    priestess
At Delphi, ask if I quoted her cor-
    rectly.
And as for this other thing: if I am
    found
Guilty of treason with Teiresias,
Then sentence me to death! You
    have my word
It is a sentence I should cast my vote
    for—
But not without evidence!
                    You do wrong
When you take good men for bad,
    bad men for good.
A true friend thrown aside—why, life
    itself

Is not more precious!
    In time you will know this well:
For time, and time alone, will show
    the just man,
Though scoundrels are discovered in
    a day.
CHORAGOS. This is well said, and a
    prudent man would ponder it.
Judgments too quickly formed are
    dangerous.
OEDIPUS. But is he not quick in his
    duplicity?
And shall I not be quick to parry
    him?
Would you have me stand still, hold
    my peace, and let
This man win everything, through
    my inaction?
CREON. And you want—what is it,
    then? To banish me?
OEDIPUS. No, not exile. It is your death
    I want,
So that all the world may see what
    treason means.
CREON. You will persist, then? You will
    not believe me?
OEDIPUS. How can I believe you?
CREON.   Then you are a fool.
OEDIPUS. To save myself?
CREON.   In justice, think of me.
OEDIPUS. You are evil incarnate.
CREON. But suppose that you are wrong?
OEDIPUS. Still I must rule.
CREON.   But not if you rule badly.
OEDIPUS. O city, city!
CREON.   It is my city, too!
CHORAGOS. Now, my lords, be still. I see
    the Queen,
    Iocastê, coming from her palace
    chambers;
And it is time she came, for the sake
    of you both.
This dreadful quarrel can be resolved
    through her.

[*Enter* IOCASTE.]

IOCASTE. Poor foolish men, what wicked
    din is this?
With Thebes sick to death, is it not
    shameful

That you should rake some private
quarrel up?
[*To* OEDIPUS.] Come into the house.
        —And you, Creon, go now:
Let us have no more of this tumult
over nothing.
CREON. Nothing? No, sister: what your
husband plans for me
Is one of two great evils: exile or
death.
OEDIPUS. He is right.
Why, woman I have caught him
squarely
Plotting against my life.
CREON.   No! Let me die
Accurst if ever I have wished you
harm!
IOCASTE. Ah, believe it, Oedipus!
In the name of the gods, respect this
oath of his
For my sake, for the sake of these
people here!
CHORAGOS. Open your mind to her, my
lord. Be ruled by her, I beg you!
OEDIPUS. What would you have me do?
CHORAGOS. Respect Creon's word. He
has never spoken like a fool,
And now he has sworn an oath.
OEDIPUS.   You know what you ask?
CHORAGOS.   I do.
OEDIPUS.   Speak on, then.
CHORAGOS. A friend so sworn should not
be baited so,
In blind malice, and without final
proof.
OEDIPUS. You are aware, I hope, that
what you say
Means death for me, or exile at the
least.
CHORAGOS. No, I swear by Helios, first
in Heaven!
May I die friendless and accurst,
The worst of deaths, if ever I meant
that!
It is the withering fields
    That hurt my sick heart:
Must we bear all these ills,
    And now your bad blood as
well?
OEDIPUS. Then let him go. And let me

die, if I must,
Or be driven by him in shame from
the land of Thebes.
It is your unhappiness, and not his
talk,
That touches me.
    As for him—
Wherever he is, I will hate him as
long as I live.
CREON. Ugly in yielding, as you were
ugly in rage!
Natures like yours chiefly torment
themselves.
OEDIPUS. Can you not go? Can you not
leave me?
CREON.   I can.
You do not know me; but the city
knows me,
And in its eyes I am just, if not in
yours.   [*Exit* CREON.]
CHORAGOS. Lady Iocastê, did you not
ask the King to go to his cham-
bers?
IOCASTE. First tell me what has hap-
pened.
CHORAGOS. There was suspicion without
evidence; yet it rankled
As even false charges will.
IOCASTE.   On both sides?
CHORAGOS.   On both.
IOCASTE.   But what was said?
CHORAGOS. Oh let it rest, let it be done
with!
Have we not suffered enough?
OEDIPUS. You see to what your decency
has brought you:
You have made difficulties where my
heart saw none.
CHORAGOS. Oedipus, it is not once only
I have told you—
You must know I should count my-
self unwise
To the point of madness, should I
now forsake you—
You, under whose hand,
    In the storm of another time,
Our dear land sailed out free.
    But now stand fast at the helm!
IOCASTE. In God's name, Oedipus, in-
form your wife as well:

Why are you so set in this hard anger?

OEDIPUS. I will tell you, for none of these men deserves

My confidence as you do. It is Creon's work,

His treachery, his plotting against me.

IOCASTE. Go on, if you can make this clear to me.

OEDIPUS. He charges me with the murder of Laïos.

IOCASTE. Has he some knowledge? Or does he speak from hearsay?

OEDIPUS. He would not commit himself to such a charge,

But he has brought in that damnable soothsayer

To tell his story.

IOCASTE.   Set your mind at rest.

If it is a question of soothsayers, I tell you

That you will find no man whose craft gives knowledge

Of the unknowable.

                    Here is my proof:

An oracle was reported to Laïos once

(I will not say from Phoibos himself but from

His appointed ministers, at any rate)

That his doom would be death at the hands of his own son—

His son, born of his flesh and of mine!

Now, you remember the story: Laïos was killed

By marauding strangers where three highways meet;

But his child had not been three days in this world

Before the King had pierced the baby's ankles

And had him left to die on a lonely mountain.

Thus, Apollo never caused that child

To kill his father, and it was not Laïos' fate

To die at the hands of his son, as

he had feared.

This is what prophets and prophecies are worth!

Have no dread of them.

                    It is God himself

Who can show us what he wills, in his own way.

OEDIPUS. How strange a shadowy memory crossed my mind,

Just now while you were speaking; it chilled my heart.

IOCASTE. What do you mean? What memory do you speak of?

OEDIPUS. If I understand you, Laïos was killed

At a place where three roads meet.

IOCASTE.   So it was said;

We have no later story.

OEDIPUS.   Where did it happen?

IOCASTE. Phokis, it is called: at a place where the Theban Way

Divides into the roads toward Delphi and Daulia.

OEDIPUS. When?

IOCASTE. We had the news not long before you came

And proved the right to your succession here.

OEDIPUS. Ah, what net has God been weaving for me?

IOCASTE. Oedipus! Why does this trouble you?

OEDIPUS.   Do not ask me yet.

First, tell me how Laïos looked, and tell me

How old he was.

IOCASTE. He was tall, his hair just touched

With white; his form was not unlike your own.

OEDIPUS. I think that I myself may be accurst

By my own ignorant edict.

IOCASTE.   You speak strangely.

It makes me tremble to look at you, my King.

OEDIPUS. I am not sure that the blind man cannot see.

But I should know better if you were to tell me—

IOCASTE. Anything—though I dread to
hear you ask it.

OEDIPUS. Was the King lightly escorted,
or did he ride

With a large company, as a ruler
should?

IOCASTE. There were five men with him
in all: one was a herald;

And a single chariot, which he was
driving.

OEDIPUS. Alas, that makes it plain
enough!

But who—
Who told you how it happened?

IOCASTE.   A household servant,
The only one to escape.

OEDIPUS.   And is he still
A servant of ours?

IOCASTE. No; for when he came back at
last

And found you enthroned in the place
of the dead king,

He came to me, touched my hand
with his, and begged

That I would send him away to the
frontier district

Where only the shepherds go—

As far away from the city as I could
send him.

I granted his prayer; for although the
man was a slave,

He had earned more than this favor
at my hands.

OEDIPUS. Can he be called back
quickly?

IOCASTE.   Easily.
But why?

OEDIPUS. I have taken too much upon
myself

Without enquiry; therefore I wish to
consult him.

IOCASTE. Then he shall come.

But am I not one also
To whom you might confide these
fears of yours?

OEDIPUS. That is your right; it will not
be denied you,

Now least of all; for I have reached
a pitch

Of wild foreboding. Is there anyone

To whom I should sooner speak?
Polybos of Corinth is my father.
My mother is a Dorian: Meropê.
I grew up chief among the men of
Corinth
Until a strange thing happened—
Not worth my passion, it may be,
but strange.
At a feast, a drunken man maunder-
ing in his cups
Cries out that I am not my father's
son!
I contained myself that night, though
I felt anger
And a sinking heart. The next day I
visited
My father and mother, and ques-
tioned them. They stormed,
Calling it all the slanderous rant of
a fool;
And this relieved me. Yet the suspi-
cion
Remained always aching in my mind;
I knew there was talk; I could not
rest;
And finally, saying nothing to my
parents,
I went to the shrine at Delphi.
The god dismissed my question with-
out reply;
He spoke of other things.
Some were clear,
Full of wretchedness, dreadful, un-
bearable:
As, that I should lie with my own
mother, breed
Children from whom all men would
turn their eyes;
And that I should be my father's
murderer.
I heard all this, and fled. And from
that day
Corinth to me was only in the stars
Descending in that quarter of the sky,
As I wandered farther and farther
on my way
To a land where I should never see
the evil
Sung by the oracle. And I came to
this country

Where, so you say, King Laïos was
killed.
I will tell you all that happened
there, my lady.
There were three highways
Coming together at a place I passed;
And there a herald came towards me,
and a chariot
Drawn by horses, with a man such
as you describe
Seated in it. The groom leading the
horses
Forced me off the road at his lord's
command;
But as this charioteer lurched over
towards me
I struck him in my rage. The old
man saw me
And brought his double goad down
upon my head
As I came abreast.
   He was paid back, and more!
Swinging my club in this right hand
I knocked him
Out of his car, and he rolled on the
ground.
      I killed him.
I killed them all.
Now if that stranger and Laïos were
—kin,
Where is a man more miserable than
I?
More hated by the gods? Citizen and
alien alike
Must never shelter me or speak to
me—
I must be shunned by all.
     And I myself
Pronounced this malediction upon
myself!
Think of it: I have touched you with
these hands,
These hands that killed your hus-
band. What defilement!
Am I all evil, then? It must be
so,
Since I must flee from Thebes, yet
never again
See my own countrymen, my own
country,

For fear of joining my mother in
marriage
And killing Polybos, my father.
         Ah,
If I was created so, born to this fate,
Who could deny the savagery of
God?
O holy majesty of heavenly powers!
May I never see that day! Never!
Rather let me vanish from the race
of men
Than know the abomination destined
me!
CHORAGOS. We too, my lord, have felt
dismay at this.
But there is hope: you have yet to
hear the shepherd.
OEDIPUS. Indeed, I fear no other hope
is left me.
IOCASTE. What do you hope from him
when he comes?
OEDIPUS.   This much:
If his account of the murder tallies
with yours,
Then I am cleared.
IOCASTE.   What was it that I said
Of such importance?
OEDIPUS. Why, "marauders," you said,
Killed the King, according to this
man's story.
If he maintains that still, if there
were several,
Clearly the guilt is not mine: I was
alone.
But if he says one man, singlehanded,
did it,
Then the evidence all points to me.
IOCASTE. You may be sure that he said
there were several;
And can he call back that story now?
He cannot.
The whole city heard it as plainly
as I.
But suppose he alters some detail
of it:
He cannot ever show that Laïos'
death
Fulfilled the oracle: for Apollo said
My child was doomed to kill him;
and my child—

Poor baby!—it was my child that
died first.
No. From now on, where oracles are
concerned,
I would not waste a second thought
on any.
OEDIPUS. You may be right.
                    But come: let someone go
For the shepherd at once. This mat-
ter must be settled.
IOCASTE. I will send for him.
I would not wish to cross you in
anything,
And surely not in this.—Let us go in.

[*Exeunt into the palace, the* CHORUS
remaining.]

CHORUS. Let me be reverent in the
ways of right,
Lowly the paths I journey on;
Let all my words and actions keep
The laws of the pure universe
From highest Heaven handed down.
For Heaven is their bright nurse,
Those generations of the realms of
light;
Ah, never of mortal kind were they
begot,
Nor are they slaves of memory, lost
in sleep:
Their Father is greater than Time
and ages not.
The tyrant is a child of Pride
Who drinks from his great sickening
cup
Recklessness and vanity,
Until from his high crest headlong
He plummets to the dust of hope.
That strong man is not strong.
But let no fair ambition be denied;
May God protect the wrestler for the
State
In government, in comely policy,
Who will fear God, and on His ordi-
nance wait.
Haughtiness and the high hand of
disdain
Tempt and outrage God's holy law;
And any mortal who dares hold
No immortal Power in awe
Will be caught up in a net of pain:

The price for which his levity is sold.
Let each man take due earnings,
then,
And keep his hands from holy things,
And from blasphemy stand apart—
Else the crackling blast of heaven
Blows on his head, and on his desper-
ate heart;
Though fools will honor impious men,
In their cities no tragic poet sings.
Shall we lose faith in Delphi's
obscurities,
We who have heard the word's core
Discredited, and the sacred wood
Of Zeus at Elis praised no more?
The deeds and the strange prophecies
Must make a pattern yet to be under-
stood.
Zeus, if indeed you are lord of all,
Throned in light over night and day,
Mirror this in your endless mind:
Our masters call the oracle
Words on the wind, and the Delphic
vision blind!
Their hearts no longer know Apollo,
And reverence for the gods has died
away.

[*Enter* IOCASTE.]

IOCASTE. Princes of Thebes, it has oc-
curred to me
To visit the altars of the gods, bearing
These branches as a suppliant, and
this incense.
Our King is not himself: his noble
soul
Is overwrought with fantasies of
dread,
Else he would consider
The new prophecies in the light of
the old.
He will listen to any voice that
speaks disaster,
And my advice goes for nothing.

[*She approaches the altar.*]

                    To you, then, Apollo,
Lycean lord, since you are nearest,
I turn in prayer.
Receive these offerings, and grant us
deliverance

From defilement. Our hearts are
heavy with fear
When we see our leader distracted, as
helpless sailors
Are terrified by the confusion of their
helmsman.

[*Enter* MESSENGER.]

MESSENGER. Friends, no doubt you can
direct me:
Where shall I find the house of Oedipus,
Or, better still, where is the King
himself?
CHORAGOS. It is this very place,
stranger; he is inside.
This is his wife and mother of his
children.
MESSENGER. I wish her happiness in a
happy house,
Blest in all the fulfillment of her mar-
riage.
IOCASTE. I wish as much for you: your
courtesy
Deserves a like good fortune. But
now, tell me:
Why have you come? What have you
to say to us?
MESSENGER. Good news, my lady, for
your house and your husband.
IOCASTE. What news? Who sent you
here?
MESSENGER.   I am from Corinth.
The news I bring ought to mean joy
for you.
Though it may be you will find some
grief in it.
IOCASTE. What is it? How can it touch
us in both ways?
MESSENGER. The people of Corinth,
they say,
Intend to call Oedipus to be their
king.
IOCASTE. But old Polybos—is he not
reigning still?
MESSENGER. No. Death holds him in
his sepulchre.
IOCASTE. What are you saying? Polybos is dead?
MESSENGER. If I am not telling the
truth, may I die myself.

IOCASTE [*to a* MAIDSERVANT]. Go in,
go quickly; tell this to your
master.
O riddlers of God's will, where are
you now!
This was the man whom Oedipus,
long ago,
Feared so, fled so, in dread of
destroying him—
But it was another fate by which he
died.

[*Enter* OEDIPUS, *from palace.*]

OEDIPUS. Dearest Iocastê, why have
you sent for me?
IOCASTE. Listen to what this man says,
and then tell me
What has become of the solemn pro-
phecies.
OEDIPUS. Who is this man? What is his
news for me?
IOCASTE. He has come from Corinth to
announce your father's death!
OEDIPUS. Is it true, stranger? Tell me
in your own words.
MESSENGER. I cannot say it more
clearly: the King is dead.
OEDIPUS. Was it by treason? Or by an
attack of illness?
MESSENGER. A little thing brings old
men to their rest.
OEDIPUS. It was sickness, then?
MESSENGER. Yes, and his many years.
OEDIPUS. Ah!
Why should a man respect the
Pythian hearth, or
Give heed to the birds that jangle
above his head?
They prophesied that I should kill
Polybos,
Kill my own father; but he is dead
and buried,
And I am here—I never touched him,
never,
Unless he died of grief for my depar-
ture,
And thus, in a sense, through me.
No. Polybos
Has packed the oracles off with him
underground.
They are empty words.

IOCASTE.   Had I not told you so?

OEDIPUS. You had; it was my faint heart that betrayed me.

IOCASTE. From now on never think of those things again.

OEDIPUS. And yet—must I not fear my mother's bed?

IOCASTE. Why should anyone in this world be afraid,

Since Fate rules us and nothing can be foreseen?

A man should live only for the present day.

Have no more fear of sleeping with your mother:

How many men, in dreams, have lain with their mothers!

No reasonable man is troubled by such things.

OEDIPUS. That is true; only—

If only my mother were not still alive!

But she is alive. I cannot help my dread.

IOCASTE. Yet this news of your father's death is wonderful.

OEDIPUS. Wonderful. But I fear the living woman.

MESSENGER. Tell me, who is this woman that you fear?

OEDIPUS. It is Meropê, man; the wife of King Polybos.

MESSENGER. Meropê? Why should you be afraid of her?

OEDIPUS. An oracle of the gods, a dreadful saying.

MESSENGER. Can you tell me about it or are you sworn to silence?

OEDIPUS. I can tell you, and I will.

Apollo said through his prophet that I was the man

Who should marry his own mother, shed his father's blood

With his own hands. And so, for all these years

I have kept clear of Corinth, and no harm has come—

Though it would have been sweet to see my parents again.

MESSENGER. And is this the fear that drove you out of Corinth?

OEDIPUS. Would you have me kill my father?

MESSENGER.   As for that

You must be reassured by the news I gave you.

OEDIPUS. If you could reassure me, I would reward you.

MESSENGER. I had that in mind, I will confess: I thought

I could count on you when you returned to Corinth.

OEDIPUS. No: I will never go near my parents again.

MESSENGER. Ah, son, you still do not know what you are doing—

OEDIPUS. What do you mean? In the name of God tell me!

MESSENGER.—If these are your reasons for not going home.

OEDIPUS. I tell you, I fear the oracle may come true.

MESSENGER. And guilt may come upon you through your parents?

OEDIPUS. That is the dread that is always in my heart.

MESSENGER. Can you not see that all your fears are groundless?

OEDIPUS. How can you say that? They are my parents, surely?

MESSENGER. Polybos was not your father.

OEDIPUS.   Not my father?

MESSENGER. No more your father than the man speaking to you.

OEDIPUS. But you are nothing to me!

MESSENGER.   Neither was he.

OEDIPUS. Then why did he call me son?

MESSENGER.   I will tell you:

Long ago he had you from my hands, as a gift.

OEDIPUS. Then how could he love me so, if I was not his?

MESSENGER. He had no children, and his heart turned to you.

OEDIPUS. What of you? Did you buy me? Did you find me by chance?

MESSENGER. I came upon you in the crooked pass of Kithairon.

OEDIPUS. And what were you doing there?

MESSENGER.   Tending my flocks.

OEDIPUS. A wandering shepherd?

MESSENGER. But your savior, son, that day.

OEDIPUS. From what did you save me?

MESSENGER. Your ankles should tell you that.

OEDIPUS. Ah, stranger, why do you speak of that childhood pain?

MESSENGER. I cut the bonds that tied your ankles together.

OEDIPUS. I have had the mark as long as I can remember.

MESSENGER. That was why you were given the name you bear.

OEDIPUS. God! Was it my father or my mother who did it?
Tell me!

MESSENGER. I do not know. The man who gave you to me
Can tell you better than I.

OEDIPUS. It was not you that found me, but another?

MESSENGER. It was another shepherd gave you to me.

OEDIPUS. Who was he? Can you tell me who he was?

MESSENGER. I think he was said to be one of Laïos' people.

OEDIPUS. You mean the Laïos who was king here years ago?

MESSENGER. Yes; King Laïos; and the man was one of his herdsmen.

OEDIPUS. Is he still alive? Can I see him?

MESSENGER.   These men here
Know best about such things.

OEDIPUS.   Does anyone here
Know this shepherd that he is talking about?
Have you seen him in the fields, or in the town?
If you have, tell me. It is time things were made plain.

CHORAGOS. I think the man he means is that same shepherd
You have already asked to see. Iocastê perhaps

Could tell you something.

OEDIPUS.   Do you know anything
About him, Lady? Is he the man we have summoned?
Is that the man this shepherd means?

IOCASTE.   Why think of him?
Forget this herdsman. Forget it all.
This talk is a waste of time.

OEDIPUS.   How can you say that,
When the clues to my true birth are in my hands?

IOCASTE. For God's love, let us have no more questioning!
Is your life nothing to you?
My own is pain enough for me to bear.

OEDIPUS. You need not worry. Suppose my mother a slave,
And born of slaves: no baseness can touch you.

IOCASTE. Listen to me, I beg you: do not do this thing!

OEDIPUS. I will not listen; the truth must be made known.

IOCASTE. Everything that I say is for your own good!

OEDIPUS.   My own good
Snaps my patience, then; I want none of it.

IOCASTE. You are fatally wrong! May you never learn who you are!

OEDIPUS. Go, one of you, and bring the shepherd here.
Let us leave this woman to brag of her royal name.

IOCASTE. Ah, miserable!
That is the only word I have for you now.
That is the only word I can ever have.   [*Exit into the palace.*]

CHORAGOS. Why has she left us, Oedipus? Why has she gone
In such a passion of sorrow? I fear this silence:
Something dreadful may come of it.

OEDIPUS.   Let it come!
However base my birth, I must know about it.
The Queen, like a woman, is perhaps ashamed

To think of my low origin. But I
Am a child of Luck; I cannot be
dishonored.
Luck is my mother; the passing
months, my brothers,
Have seen me rich and poor.
                        If this is so,
How could I wish that I were some-
one else?
How could I not be glad to know my
birth?

CHORUS. If ever the coming time were
known
To my heart's pondering,
Kithairon, now by Heaven I see the
torches
At the festival of the next full moon,
And see the dance, and hear the
choir sing
A grace to your gentle shade:
Mountain where Oedipus was found,
O mountain guard of a noble race!
May the god who heals us lend his
aid,
And let that glory come to pass
For our king's cradling-ground.
Of the nymphs that flower beyond
the years,
Who bore you, royal child,
To Pan of the hills or the timberline
Apollo,
Cold in delight where the upland
clears,
Or Hermês for whom Kyllenê's
heights are piled?
Or flushed as evening cloud,
Great Dionysos, roamer of moun-
tains,
He—was it he who found you there,
And caught you up in his own proud
Arms from the sweet god-ravisher
Who laughed by the Muses' foun-
tains?

OEDIPUS. Sirs: though I do not know
the man,
I think I see him coming, this
shepherd we want:
He is old, like our friend here, and
the men
Bringing him seem to be servants of
my house.

But you can tell, if you have ever
seen him.

[*Enter* SHEPHERD *escorted by servants.*]

CHORAGOS. I know him, he was Laïos'
man. You can trust him.

OEDIPUS. Tell me first, you from
Corinth: is this the shepherd
We were discussing?

MESSENGER.   This is the very man.

OEDIPUS [*to* SHEPHERD]. Come here.
No, look at me. You must answer
Everything I ask.—You belonged to
Laïos?

SHEPHERD. Yes: born his slave, brought
up in his house.

OEDIPUS. Tell me: what kind of work
did you do for him?

SHEPHERD. I was a shepherd of his,
most of my life.

OEDIPUS. Where mainly did you go for
pasturage?

SHEPHERD. Sometimes Kithairon, sometimes the hills nearby.

OEDIPUS. Do you remember ever seeing
this man out there?

SHEPHERD. What would he be doing
there? This man?

OEDIPUS. This man standing here. Have
you ever seen him before?

SHEPHERD. No. At least, not to my
recollection.

MESSENGER. And that is not strange,
my lord. But I'll refresh
His memory: he must remember
when we two
Spent three whole seasons together,
March to September,
On Kithairon or thereabouts. He had
two flocks;
I had one. Each autumn I'd drive
mine home
And he would go back with his to
Laïos' sheepfold.—
Is this not true, just as I have
described it?

SHEPHERD. True, yes; but it was all
so long ago.

MESSENGER. Well, then: do you remember, back in those days,

That you gave me a baby boy to bring up as my own?

SHEPHERD. What if I did? What are you trying to say?

MESSENGER. King Oedipus was once that little child.

SHEPHERD. Damn you, hold your tongue!

OEDIPUS.   No more of that!
It is your tongue needs watching, not this man's.

SHEPHERD. My King, my Master, what is it I have done wrong?

OEDIPUS. You have not answered his question about the boy.

SHEPHERD. He does not know...He is only making trouble...

OEDIPUS. Come, speak plainly, or it will go hard with you.

SHEPHERD. In God's name, do not torture an old man!

OEDIPUS. Come here, one of you; bind his arms behind him.

SHEPHERD. Unhappy king! What more do you wish to learn?

OEDIPUS. Did you give this man the child he speaks of?

SHEPHERD.   I did.
And I would to God I had died that very day.

OEDIPUS. You will die now unless you speak the truth.

SHEPHERD. Yet if I speak the truth, I am worse than dead.

OEDIPUS. Very well; since you insist upon delaying—

SHEPHERD. No! I have told you already that I gave him the boy.

OEDIPUS. Where did you get him? From your house? From somewhere else?

SHEPHERD. Not from mine, no. A man gave him to me.

OEDIPUS. Is that man here? Do you know whose slave he was?

SHEPHERD. For God's love, my King, do not ask me any more!

OEDIPUS. You are a dead man if I have to ask you again.

SHEPHERD. Then...Then the child was from the palace of Laïos.

OEDIPUS. A slave child? or a child of his own line?

SHEPHERD. Ah, I am on the brink of dreadful speech!

OEDIPUS. And I of dreadful hearing. Yet I must hear.

SHEPHERD. If you must be told, then
...They said it was Laïos' child;
But it is your wife who can tell you about that.

OEDIPUS. My wife!—Did she give it to you?

SHEPHERD.   My lord, she did.

OEDIPUS. Do you know why?

SHEPHERD.   I was told to get rid of it.

OEDIPUS. An unspeakable mother!

SHEPHERD. There had been prophecies...

OEDIPUS.   Tell me.

SHEPHERD. It was said that the boy would kill his own father.

OEDIPUS. Then why did you give him over to this old man?

SHEPHERD. I pitied the baby, my King,
And I thought that this man would take him far away
To his own country.
He saved him—but for what a fate!
For if you are what this man says you are,
No man living is more wretched than Oedipus.

OEDIPUS.   Ah God!
It was true!
          All the prophecies!
                    —Now,
O Light, may I look on you for the last time!
I, Oedipus,
Oedipus, damned in his birth, in his marriage damned,
Damned in the blood he shed with his own hand!

[*He rushes into the palace.*]

CHORUS. Alas for the seed of men.
What measure shall I give these generations
That breathe on the void and are void
And exist and do not exist?
Who bears more weight of joy

Than mass of sunlight shifting in
images,
Or who shall make his thoughts stay
on
That down time drifts away?
Your splendor is all fallen.
O naked brow of wrath and tears,
O change of Oedipus!
I who saw your days call no man
blest—
Your great days like ghósts góne.
That mind was a strong bow.
Deep, how deep you drew it then,
hard archer,
At a dim fearful range,
And brought dear glory down!
You overcame the stranger—
The virgin with her hooking lion
claws—
And though death sang, stood like a
tower
To make pale Thebes take heart.
Fortress against our sorrow!
Divine king, giver of laws,
Majestic Oedipus!
No prince in Thebes had ever such
renown,
No prince won such grace of power.
And now of all men ever known
Most pitiful is this man's story:
His fortunes are most changed, his
state
Fallen to a low slave's
Ground under bitter fate.
O Oedipus, most royal one!
The great door that expelled you to
the light
Gave at night—ah, gave night to
your glory:
As to the father, to the fathering son.
All understood too late.
How could that queen whom Laïos
won,
The garden that he harrowed at his
height,
Be silent when that act was done?
But all eyes fail before time's eye,
All actions come to justice there.
Though never willed, though far
down the deep past,

Your bed, your dread sirings,
Are brought to book at last.
Child by Laïos doomed to die,
Then doomed to lose that fortunate
little death,
Would God you never took breath in
this air
That with my wailing lips I take to
cry:
For I weep the world's outcast.
Blind I was, and cannot tell why;
Asleep, for you had given ease of
breath;
A fool, while the false years went by.

[*Enter, from the palace,* SECOND MES-
SENGER.]

SECOND MESSENGER. Elders of Thebes,
most honored in this land,
What horrors are yours to see and
hear, what weight
Of sorrow to be endured, if, true to
your birth,
You venerate the line of Labdakos!
I think neither Istros nor Phasis,
those great rivers,
Could purify this place of the corrup-
tion
It shelters now, or soon must bring
to light—
Evil not done unconsciously, but
willed.
The greatest griefs are those we cause
ourselves.
CHORAGOS. Surely, friend, we have grief
enough already;
What new sorrow do you mean?
SECOND MESSENGER. The Queen is dead.
CHORAGOS. Iocastê? Dead? But at
whose hand?
SECOND MESSENGER.   Her own.
The full horror of what happened you
cannot know,
For you did not see it; but I, who
did, will tell you
As clearly as I can how she met her
death.
When she had left us,
In passionate silence, passing through
the court,

She ran to her apartment in the house,
Her hair clutched by the fingers of both hands.
She closed the doors behind her; then, by that bed
Where long ago the fatal son was conceived—
That son who should bring about his father's death—
We heard her call upon Laïos, dead so many years,
And heard her wail for the double fruit of her marriage,
A husband by her husband, children by her child.
Exactly how she died I do not know:
For Oedipus burst in moaning and would not let us
Keep vigil to the end: it was by him
As he stormed about the room that our eyes were caught.
From one to another of us he went, begging a sword,
Cursing the wife who was not his wife, the mother
Whose womb had carried his own children and himself.
I do not know: it was none of us aided him,
But surely one of the gods was in control!
For with a dreadful cry
He hurled his weight, as though wrenched out of himself,
At the twin doors: the bolts gave, and he rushed in.
And there we saw her hanging, her body swaying
From the cruel cord she had noosed about her neck.
A great sob broke from him, heartbreaking to hear,
As he loosed the rope and lowered her to the ground.
I would blot out from my mind what happened next!
For the King ripped from her gown the golden brooches
That were her ornament, and raised them, and plunged them down
Straight into his own eyeballs, crying, "No more,
No more shall you look on the misery about me,
The horrors of my own doing! Too long you have known
The faces of those whom I should never have seen,
Too long been blind to those for whom I was searching!
From this hour, go in darkness!" And as he spoke,
He struck at his eyes—not once, but many times;
And the blood spattered his beard,
Bursting from his ruined sockets like red hail.
So from the unhappiness of two this evil has sprung,
A curse on the man and woman alike. The old
Happiness of the house of Labdakos
Was happiness enough: where is it today?
It is all wailing and ruin, disgrace, death—all
The misery of mankind that has a name—
And it is wholly and forever theirs.

CHORAGOS. Is he in agony still? Is there no rest for him?

SECOND MESSENGER. He is calling for someone to lead him to the gates
So that all the children of Kadmos may look upon
His father's murderer, his mother's— no,
I cannot say it!
    And then he will leave Thebes,
Self-exiled, in order that the curse
Which he himself pronounced may depart from the house.
He is weak, and there is none to lead him,
So terrible is his suffering.
            But you will see:
Look, the doors are opening; in a moment

You will see a thing that would crush a heart of stone.

[*The central door is opened;* OEDIPUS, *blinded, is led in.*]

CHORAGOS. Dreadful indeed for men to see.
Never have my own eyes
Looked on a sight so full of fear.
Oedipus!
What madness came upon you, what daemon
Leaped on your life with heavier
Punishment than a mortal man can bear?
No: I cannot even
Look at you, poor ruined one.
And I would speak, question, ponder,
If I were able. No.
You make me shudder.

OEDIPUS. God.   God.
Is there a sorrow greater?
Where shall I find harbor in this world?
My voice is hurled far on a dark wind.
What has God done to me?

CHORAGOS. Too terrible to think of, or to see.

OEDIPUS. O cloud of night,
Never to be turned away: night coming on,
I cannot tell how: night like a shroud!
My fair winds brought me here.
                    O God. Again
The pain of the spikes where I had sight,
The flooding pain
Of memory, never to be gouged out.

CHORAGOS. This is not strange.
You suffer it all twice over, remorse in pain,
Pain in remorse.

OEDIPUS. Ah dear friend
Are you faithful even yet, you alone?
Are you still standing near me, will you stay here,
Patient, to care for the blind?

            The blind man!
Yet even blind I know who it is attends me,
By the voice's tone—
Though my new darkness hide the comforter.

CHORAGOS. Oh fearful act!
What god was it drove you to rake black
Night across your eyes?

OEDIPUS. Apollo. Apollo. Dear
Children, the god was Apollo.
He brought my sick, sick fate upon me.
But the blinding hand was my own!
How could I bear to see
When all my sight was horror everywhere?

CHORAGOS. Everywhere; that is true.

OEDIPUS. And now what is left?
Images? Love? A greeting even,
Sweet to the senses? Is there anything?
Ah, no, friends: lead me away.
Lead me away from Thebes.
                    Lead the great wreck
And hell of Oedipus, whom the gods hate.

CHORAGOS. Your fate is clear, you are not blind to that.
Would God you had never found it out!

OEDIPUS. Death take the man who unbound
My feet on that hillside
And delivered me from death to life!
What life?
If only I had died,
This weight of monstrous doom
Could not have dragged me and my darlings down.

CHORAGOS. I would have wished the same.

OEDIPUS. Oh never to have come here
With my father's blood upon me! Never
To have been the man they call his mother's husband!
Oh accurst! Oh child of evil,

To have entered that wretched bed—
> the selfsame one!
More primal than sin itself, this fell
to me.
CHORAGOS. I do not know how I can
answer you.
You were better dead than alive and
blind.
OEDIPUS. Do not counsel me any more.
This punishment
That I have laid upon myself is just.
If I had eyes,
I do not know how I could bear the
sight
Of my father, when I came to the
house of Death,
Or my mother: for I have sinned
against them both
So vilely that I could not make my
peace
By strangling my own life.
> Or do you think my children,
Born as they were born, would be
sweet to my eyes?
Ah never, never! Nor this town with
its high walls,
Nor the holy images of the gods.
> For I,
Thrice miserable!—Oedipus, noblest
of all the line
Of Kadmos, have condemned myself
to enjoy
These things no more, by my own
malediction
Expelling that man whom the gods
declared
To be a defilement in the house of
Laïos.
After exposing the rankness of my
own guilt,
How could I look men frankly in the
eyes?
No, I swear it,
If I could have stifled my hearing at
its source,
I would have done it and made all
this body
A tight cell of misery, blank to light
and sound:

So I should have been safe in a dark
agony
Beyond all recollection.
> Ah Kithairon!
Why did you shelter me? When I
was cast upon you,
Why did I not die? Then I should
never
Have shown the world my execrable
birth.
Ah Polybos! Corinth, city that I
believed
The ancient seat of my ancestors:
how fair
I seemed, your child! And all the
while this evil
Was cancerous within me!
> For I am sick
In my daily life, sick in my origin.
O three roads, dark ravine, woodland
and way
Where three roads met: you, drinking
my father's blood,
My own blood, spilled by my own
hand: can you remember
The unspeakable things I did there,
and the things
I went on from there to do?
> O marriage, marriage!
The act that engendered me, and
again the act
Performed by the son in the same
bed—
> Ah, the net
Of incest, mingling fathers, brothers,
sons,
With brides, wives, mothers: the last
evil
That can be known by men: no
tongue can say
How evil!
> No. For the love of God,
conceal me
Somewhere far from Thebes; or kill
me; or hurl me
Into the sea, away from men's eyes
forever.
Come, lead me. You need not fear
to touch me.

Of all men, I alone can bear this guilt.

[*Enter* CREON.]

CHORAGOS. We are not the ones to decide; but Creon here
May fitly judge of what you ask. He only
Is left to protect the city in your place.

OEDIPUS. Alas, how can I speak to him? What right have I
To beg his courtesy whom I have deeply wronged?

CREON. I have not come to mock you, Oedipus.
Or to reproach you, either.
[*To* ATTENDANTS.]—You, standing there:
If you have lost all respect for man's dignity,
At least respect the flame of Lord Helios:
Do not allow this pollution to show itself
Openly here, an affront to the earth
And Heaven's rain and the light of day. No, take him
Into the house as quickly as you can.
For it is proper
That only the close kindred see his grief.

OEDIPUS. I pray you in God's name, since your courtesy
Ignores my dark expectation, visiting
With mercy this man of all men most execrable:
Give me what I ask—for your good, not for mine.

CREON. And what is it that you would have me do?

OEDIPUS. Drive me out of this country as quickly as may be
To a place where no human voice can ever greet me.

CREON. I should have done that before now—only,
God's will had not been wholly revealed to me.

OEDIPUS. But his command is plain: the parricide
Must be destroyed. I am that evil man.

CREON. That is the sense of it, yes; but as things are,
We had best discover clearly what is to be done.

OEDIPUS. You would learn more about a man like me?

CREON. You are ready now to listen to the god.

OEDIPUS. I will listen. But it is to you
That I must turn for help. I beg you, hear me.
The woman in there—
Give her whatever funeral you think proper:
She is your sister.
            —But let me go, Creon!
Let me purge my father's Thebes of the pollution
Of my living here, and go out to the wild hills,
To Kithairon, that has won such fame with me,
The tomb my mother and father appointed for me,
And let me die there, as they willed I should.
And yet I know
Death will not ever come to me through sickness
Or in any natural way: I have been preserved
For some unthinkable fate. But let that be.
As for my sons, you need not care for them.
They are men, they will find some way to live.
But my poor daughters, who have shared my table,
Who never before have been parted from their father—
Take care of them, Creon; do this for me.
And will you let me touch them with my hands

A last time, and let us weep together?
Be kind, my lord,
Great prince, be kind!
        Could I but touch them,
They would be mine again, as when
    I had my eyes.

[*Enter* ANTIGONE *and* ISMENE, *attended.*]

Ah, God!
Is it my dearest children I hear weeping?
Has Creon pitied me and sent my
    daughters?
CREON. Yes, Oedipus: I knew that they
    were dear to you
In the old days, and know you must
    love them still.
OEDIPUS. May God bless you for this—
    and be a friendlier
Guardian to you than he has been to
    me!
Children, where are you?
Come quickly to my hands: they are
    your brother's—
Hands that have brought your
    father's once clear eyes
To this way of seeing —
        Ah dearest ones,
I had neither sight nor knowledge
    then, your father
By the woman who was the source of
    his own life!
And I weep for you—having no
    strength to see you—,
I weep for you when I think of the
    bitterness
That men will visit upon you all your
    lives.
What homes, what festivals can you
    attend
Without being forced to depart again
    in tears?
And when you come to marriageable
    age,
Where is the man, my daughters, who
    would dare
Risk the bane that lies on all my
    children?

Is there any evil wanting? Your
    father killed
His father; sowed the womb of her
    who bore him;
Engendered you at the fount of his
    own existence!
That is what they will say of you.
        Then, whom
Can you ever marry? There are no
    bridegrooms for you,
And your lives must wither away in
    sterile dreaming.
O Creon, son of Menoikeus!
You are the only father my daughters
    have,
Since we, their parents, are both of
    us gone for ever.
They are your own blood: you will
    not let them
Fall into beggary and loneliness;
You will keep them from the miseries
    that are mine!
Take pity on them; see, they are
    only children,
Friendless except for you. Promise
    me this,
Great Prince, and give me your hand
    in token of it. [CREON *clasps his
    right hand.*]
Children:
I could say much, if you could understand me,
But as it is, I have only this prayer
    for you:
Live where you can, be as happy as
    you can—
Happier, please God, than God has
    made your father!
CREON. Enough. You have wept enough.
    Now go within.
OEDIPUS. I must; but it is hard.
CREON.   Time eases all things.
OEDIPUS. But you must promise—
CREON.   Say what you desire.
OEDIPUS. Send me from Thebes!
CREON.   God grant that I may!
OEDIPUS. But since God hates me...
CREON.   No, he will grant your wish.
OEDIPUS. You promise?

CREON. I cannot speak beyond my knowledge.

OEDIPUS. Then lead me in.

CREON. Come now, and leave your children.

OEDIPUS. No! Do not take them from me!

CREON. Think no longer
That you are in command here, but rather think
How, when you were, you served your own destruction.

[*Exeunt into the house all but the* CHORUS; *the* CHORAGOS *chants directly to the audience.*]

CHORAGOS. Men of Thebes: look upon Oedipus.
This is the king who solved the famous riddle
And towered up, most powerful of men.
No mortal eyes but looked on him with envy,
Yet in the end ruin swept over him.
Let every man in mankind's frailty
Consider his last day; and let none
Presume on his good fortune until he find
Life, at his death, a memory without pain.

The Tragedy of Macbeth

Apart from *The Comedy of Errors, Macbeth* is William Shakespeare's shortest play. That is appropriate because a major concern of this tragedy is to explore the lock-step inevitability with which consequences follow from a fatal act, and by compressing his dramatic structure Shakespeare (1564–1616) intensifies this sense of inevitability. But if the play has linear compression, it also has a kind of vertical expansiveness. In the first brief scene we are introduced to the witches. Chanting prophetic verse on a heath tormented by thunder and lightning, they "look not like th' inhabitants o' th' earth," Banquo says, "And yet are on't" (I.iii.41–2). Though much has been written to "explain" the witches, explanations are rather beside the point. Whatever our beliefs or those (if we knew them) of Shakespeare and his Jacobean audiences, the *dramatic* function of the witches is to establish the range of the play's fictional universe, which extends literally from hell to heaven. The witches put us on notice that reality has been released from its usual confines in this play and that a certain imaginative free play on our parts is necessary. Norms of cause and effect, fact, credibility, must be suspended. No instruments of measurement will register Banquo's presence at the banquet, tell us what happened to Lady Macbeth's children, or account for the presence of the third murderer (III.iii). In short, Shakespeare has woven into the fabric of *Macbeth* patterns of mystery and surreality that will not abide our analysis.

The supernatural not only adds imaginative range to *Macbeth* but provides points of reference that help us evaluate characters and actions. After the witches have delivered their first prophecy, for instance, Banquo reminds Macbeth that sometimes

> The instruments of darkness tell us truths,
> Win us with honest trifles, to betray's
> In deepest consequence.
>
> (I.iii.124–26)

Banquo's remarks accurately forecast Macbeth's experience when, aligning himself with the "instruments of darkness" ("Let not light see my black and deep desires" —I.iv.51), he murders Duncan, only to discover ultimately that his own death is an unavoidable consequence of that act. If Macbeth's values are clarified by his association with the "instruments of darkness," those of the Scots exiles are, too, when they gather under the aegis of England's saintly king and become "instruments" of divine force:

> Macbeth
> Is ripe for shaking, and the powers above
> Put on their instruments.
>
> (IV.iii.237–39)

With powers both above and below involved, it is evident that human action in Macbeth occurs within a universe of exceeding sensitivity and responsiveness. Nothing takes place quite in isolation. The morning after Duncan's murder, Ross glances at the murky sky and says,

> Thou seest the heavens, as troubled with man's act,
> Threatens his bloody stage.
>
> (II.iv.5–6)

This basic moral division in the play between the divine and the demonic is reinforced at every turn by symbols and images; the student would do well to identify and analyze as many of these as he can isolate, beginning perhaps with such examples as light and dark, water and blood, fertility and sterility, growth and decay, natural and unnatural.

This moral division does not mean that *Macbeth* is reducible to a melodramatic confrontation of good and evil in the form of heroes and villains. Macbeth himself is far more deeply dyed in evil than Shakespeare's other tragic heroes. But in a world founded on paradox—"Fair is foul, and foul is fair," the witches claim (I.i)—we would not expect the hero to be exempt from complexity. In fact, like most tragic heroes, Macbeth combines good and evil, guilt and innocence so thoroughly that a keen sense of moral discrimination is required if we are to assess him justly. By the same token, a Lady Macbeth who can callously dismiss the murder of Duncan by saying "what's done is done" (III.ii.12) but whose dreams later on are racked by the thought that "what's done cannot be undone" (V.i.90–91) is hardly a stereotype of evil inviting us to respond with snap moral judgments.

Lady Macbeth's lines just cited illustrate the prominence in this play of the concept of act, deed, thing done. As we pointed out in the generic introduction, tragedy normally proceeds from act to suffering to understanding. *Macbeth* obviously traces this sequence: the act of murdering Duncan produces the profound anxiety that Macbeth seeks to still with subsequent murders that lead him ultimately to realize the full and damning implications of what he has done. In a sense, however, Macbeth is never more deeply sensitive to moral issues than prior to the murder when he weighs his ambition against the prohibitions of conscience, duty, justice (I.vii.1–28). He is fascinated at this point with the nature of action itself, its timing, its consequences, its irreversibility—

> If it were done when 'tis done, then 'twere well
> It were done quickly.

The sound "done" reverberates through these lines with a kind of ceaselessness, as though giving the lie to his hopes even while he voices them: the deed, generating as it does a sequence of reactions, will never be quite done. The inconclusiveness of action is further underscored by Macbeth's inability to say "Amen" immediately after the murder. Macbeth is responsible for three main acts in the play: the murder of Duncan, of Banquo, and of Lady Macduff and her son. Does the fact that Malcolm and Donalbain, Fleance, and Macduff escape on these three occasions reinforce the idea of the inconclusiveness of action?

An act is performed in time and in space. Consider the theme of time in *Macbeth*. At one point prior to the murder, Macbeth can think of time as reassuringly transitory: "Come what come may, / Time and the hour runs through the roughest day" (I.iii.146–47). When he responds to his wife's death with the famous "Tomorrow and tomorrow and tomorrow" soliloquy (V.v.), however, his conception of time has altered considerably. The student should analyze the many references to time in the play, with special attention to differences between Lady Macbeth and Macbeth, and between Banquo and Macbeth. Consider also the act of murder in relation to its spatial scene. Before the murder Macbeth's castle is associated with "heaven's breath" (I.vi.5); as he girds himself to perform the murder, Macbeth verbally transforms the castle, perhaps the world, into a place of horror (II.i.49–60); and after the murder, the Porter associates the castle with Hell (II.iii.1–28). The scene of the murder, though, is not merely Macbeth's castle; it is also Scotland and, ultimately, the many-dimensioned universe of which we spoke earlier. Is there, as with the castle, a coalescence of scene and act at these further ranges? Does the murderous act transform Scotland and the universe, too?

But perhaps of greatest interest is the way in which the act and its agent interact. Macbeth is the agent who brings an act into being; but the act also brings Macbeth into being, in that it imparts an identity or character to Macbeth. When the murder is "done" (though far from finished, as we know), Macbeth says, "To know my deed, 'twere best not know myself" (II.ii.72). What he has done has created an identity that he cannot bear to acknowledge. Thus the immediate effect of the murder is to stifle self-awareness, to make life endurable only at the cost of moral and spiritual oblivion. His subsequent murders are accompanied by an increasing numbness of thought and feeling, a willful dehumanization, as Macbeth thrusts into deeper and deeper regions of consciousness his awareness of what he is. Action becomes possible only by bypassing the mind and conscience: "The very firstlings of my heart shall be / The firstlings of my hand" (IV.i.147–48). But it is typical of tragic heroes that ultimately the courage to see—even though what is seen is appalling—triumphs over self-protective desires. That this is true of Macbeth helps rescue him from the nontragic category of the hero who, because he is incapable of recognizing values beyond the borders of self, merely dwindles into demonism or becomes fortified in evil.

The Tragedy of Macbeth

DUNCAN *King of Scotland*

MALCOLM } *his sons*
DONALBAIN

MACBETH
BANQUO
MACDUFF
LENNOX
ROSS } *noblemen of Scotland*
MENTEITH
ANGUS
CAITHNESS

FLEANCE *son to* BANQUO
SIWARD *Earl of Northumberland*
YOUNG SIWARD *his son*
SEYTON *an officer attending on* MACBETH
BOY *son to* MACBETH
A CAPTAIN
AN ENGLISH DOCTOR

A SCOTTISH DOCTOR
A PORTER
AN OLD MAN
THREE MURDERERS
LADY MACBETH
LADY MACDUFF
A GENTLEWOMAN *attending on* LADY MACBETH
THE WEIRD SISTERS
HECATE
THE GHOST OF BANQUO
APPARITIONS
LORDS
OFFICERS
SOLDIERS
MESSENGERS
ATTENDANTS

SCENE: *Scotland and England.*

ACT I

SCENE i. *Thunder and lightning. Enter three* WITCHES.

1. WITCH. When shall we three meet again?
   In thunder, lightning, or in rain?
2. WITCH. When the hurlyburly's done,
   When the battle's lost and won.
3. WITCH. That will be ere the set of sun. 5
1. WITCH. Where the place?
2. WITCH.   Upon the heath.
3. WITCH. There to meet with Macbeth.
1. WITCH. I come, Graymalkin!
2. WITCH. Paddock calls.

3. WITCH.   Anon!
ALL. Fair is foul, and foul is fair. 10
   Hover through the fog and filthy
      air.   *Exeunt.*

SCENE ii. *Alarum within. Enter* KING [DUNCAN], MALCOLM, DONALBAIN, LENNOX, *with* ATTENDANTS, *meeting a bleeding* CAPTAIN.

KING. What bloody man is that? He can report,
   As seemeth by his plight, of the revolt
   The newest state.
MALCOLM.   This is the sergeant
   Who like a good and hardy soldier fought

I.i.8–9 *Graymalkin, Paddock:* little gray cat and toad (spirits serving the witches).

'Gainst my captivity. Hail, brave
  friend!   5
Say to the King the knowledge of
  the broil
As thou didst leave it.

CAPTAIN.   Doubtful it stood,
As two spent swimmers that do cling
  together
And choke their art. The merciless
  Macdonwald
(Worthy to be a rebel, for to that 10
The multiplying villainies of nature
Do swarm upon him) from the West-
  ern Isles
Of kerns and gallowglasses is sup-
  plied;
And Fortune, on his damned quarrel
  smiling,
Showed like a rebel's whore. But all's
  too weak: 15`
For brave Macbeth (well he deserves
  that name),
Disdaining Fortune, with his bran-
  dished steel,
Which smoked with bloody execu-
  tion,
Like valor's minion carved out his
  passage
Till he faced the slave;   20
Which ne'er shook hands nor bade
  farewell to him
Till he unseamed him from the nave
  to the chops
And fixed his head upon our battlements.

KING. O valiant cousin! worthy gentleman!

CAPTAIN. As whence the sun 'gins his
  reflection   25
Shipwracking storms and direful
  thunders break,
So from that spring whence comfort
  seemed to come
Discomfort swells. Mark, King of
  Scotland, mark.
No sooner justice had, with valor
  armed,

Compelled these skipping kerns to
  trust their heels   30
But the Norweyan lord, surveying
  vantage,
With furbished arms and new supplies of men,
Began a fresh assault.

KING.   Dismayed not this
Our captains, Macbeth and Banquo?

CAPTAIN.   Yes,
As sparrows eagles, or the hare the
  lion.   35
If I say sooth, I must report they
  were
As cannons overcharged with double
  cracks,
So they doubly redoubled strokes
  upon the foe.
Except they meant to bathe in reek-
  ing wounds,
Or memorize another Golgotha, 40
I cannot tell—
But I am faint; my gashes cry for
  help.

KING. So well thy words become thee
  as thy wounds,
They smack of honor both. Go get
  him surgeons.

            [Exit CAPTAIN, *attended.]*

Enter ROSS *and* ANGUS.

Who comes here?

MALCOLM.   The worthy Thane
  of Ross.   45

LENNOX. What a haste looks through
  his eyes! So should he look
That seems to speak things strange.

ROSS.   God save the King!

KING. Whence cam'st thou, worthy
  Thane?

ROSS.   From Fife, great King,
Where the Norweyan banners flout
  the sky
And fan our people cold.   50
Norway himself, with terrible num-
  bers,

I.ii.13 *kerns and gallowglasses:* two kinds of
Irish soldiers. *22 nave:* navel.

31 *surveying vantage:* perceiving an opportunity. 37 *cracks:* explosive charges. 39 *Except:*
unless.

Assisted by that most disloyal traitor
The Thane of Cawdor, began a dis-
  mal conflict,
Till that Bellona's bridegroom, lap-
  ped in proof,
Confronted him with self-compari-
  sons,   55
Point against point, rebellious arm
  'gainst arm,
Curbing his lavish spirit: and to
  conclude,
The victory fell on us.
KING.   Great happiness!
Ross.   That now
Sweno, the Norways' king, craves
  composition;
Nor would we deign him burial of
  his men   60
Till he disbursed, at Saint Colme's
  Inch,
Ten thousand dollars to our general
  use.
KING. No more that Thane of Cawdor
  shall deceive
Our bosom interest. Go pronounce
  his present death
And with his former title greet
  Macbeth.   65
Ross. I'll see it done.
KING. What he hath lost, noble Macbeth
  hath won.   *Exeunt.*

SCENE iii. *Thunder. Enter the three*
WITCHES.

1. WITCH. Where hast thou been, sister?
2. WITCH. Killing swine.
3. WITCH. Sister, where thou?
1. WITCH. A sailor's wife had chest-
  nuts in her lap
And mounched and mounched and
  mounched. "Give me," quoth I. 5
"Aroint thee, witch!" the rump-
  fed ronyon cries.
Her husband's to Aleppo gone, master
  o' the Tiger:

But in a sieve I'll thither sail
And, like a rat without a tail,
I'll do, I'll do, and I'll do.   10
2. WITCH. I'll give thee a wind.
1. WITCH. Th' art kind.
3. WITCH. And I another.
1. WITCH. I myself have all the other,
And the very ports they blow,   15
All the quarters that they know
I' th' shipman's card.
I'll drain him dry as hay.
Sleep shall neither night nor day
Hang upon his penthouse lid.   20
He shall live a man forbid.
Weary sev'nights, nine times nine,
Shall he dwindle, peak, and pine.
Though his bark cannot be lost,
Yet it shall be tempest-tost.   25
Look what I have.
2. WITCH. Show me, show me.
1. WITCH. Here I have a pilot's thumb,
Wracked as homeward he did come.
Drum within.
3. WITCH. A drum, a drum!   30
Macbeth doth come.
ALL. The weird sisters, hand in hand,
Posters of the sea and land,
Thus do go about, about,   34
Thrice to thine, and thrice to mine,
And thrice again, to make up nine.
Peace! The charm's wound up.

Enter MACBETH *and* BANQUO.

MACBETH. So foul and fair a day I have
  not seen.
BANQUO. How far is't called to Forres?
  What are these,
So withered and so wild in their
  attire   40
That look not like the inhabitants o'
  the earth
And yet are on't? Live you, or are
  you aught
That man may question? You seem
  to understand me,
By each at once her choppy finger
  laying

---

54 *Bellona's bridegroom:* i.e., Macbeth, as
bridegroom of the goddess of war; *proof:*
armor. I.iii.6 *Aroint:* be gone.

17 *card:* compass. 20 *penthouse lid:* eyelid.
33 *Posters:* swift riders. 39 *Forres:* town
near Inverness.

Upon her skinny lips. You should be women,   45
And yet your beards forbid me to interpret
That you are so.
MACBETH.   Speak, if you can. What are you?
1. WITCH. All hail, Macbeth! Hail to thee, Thane of Glamis!
2. WITCH. All hail, Macbeth! Hail to thee, Thane of Cawdor!
3. WITCH. All hail, Macbeth, that shalt be King hereafter!   50
BANQUO. Good sir, why do you start and seem to fear
Things that do sound so fair? I' the name of truth,
Are ye fantastical, or that indeed
Which outwardly ye show? My noble partner
You greet with present grace and great prediction   55
Of noble having and of royal hope,
That he seems rapt withal. To me you speak not.
If you can look into the seeds of time
And say which grain will grow and which will not,
Speak then to me, who neither beg nor fear   60
Your favors nor your hate.
1. WITCH. Hail!
2. WITCH. Hail!
3. WITCH. Hail!
1. WITCH. Lesser than Macbeth, and greater.   65
2. WITCH. Not so happy, yet much happier.
3. WITCH. Thou shalt get kings, though thou be none.
So all hail, Macbeth and Banquo!
1. WITCH. Banquo and Macbeth, all hail!
MACBETH. Stay, you imperfect speakers, tell me more: 70
By Sinel's death I know I am Thane of Glamis,

But how of Cawdor? The Thane of Cawdor lives,
A prosperous gentleman; and to be King
Stands not within the prospect of belief,
No more than to be Cawdor. Say from whence   75
You owe this strange intelligence, or why
Upon this blasted heath you stop our way
With such prophetic greeting. Speak, I charge you.   WITCHES *vanish*.
BANQUO. The earth hath bubbles as the water has,
And these are of them. Whither are they vanished?   80
MACBETH. Into the air, and what seemed corporal melted
As breath into the wind. Would they had stayed.
BANQUO. Were such things here as we do speak about?
Or have we eaten on the insane root
That takes the reason prisoner?   85
MACBETH. Your children shall be kings.
BANQUO.   You shall be King.
MACBETH. And Thane of Cawdor too. Went it not so?
BANQUO. To the selfsame tune and words. Who's here?

Enter Ross *and* ANGUS.

ROSS. The King hath happily received, Macbeth,
The news of thy success; and when he reads   90
Thy personal venture in the rebels' fight,
His wonders and his praises do contend
Which should be thine or his. Silenced with that,
In viewing o'er the rest o' the selfsame day,

---

53 *fantastical:* imaginary.   71 *Sinel:* Macbeth's father.

84 *insane:* causing insanity.   90 *reads:* thinks about.

He finds thee in the stout Norweyan
 ranks,   95
Nothing afeard of what thyself didst
 make—
Strange images of death. As thick as
 hail
Came post with post, and everyone
 did bear
Thy praises in his kingdom's great
 defense
And poured them down before him.
ANGUS.   We are sent 100
 To give thee from our royal master
 thanks;
Only to herald thee into his sight,
Not pay thee.
ROSS. And for an earnest of a greater
 honor,
He bade me, from him, call thee
 Thane of Cawdor;   105
In which addition, hail, most worthy
 Thane,
For it is thine.
BANQUO.   What, can the devil
 speak true?
MACBETH. The Thane of Cawdor lives.
 Why do you dress me
In borrowed robes?
ANGUS.   Who was the
 Thane lives yet,
But under heavy judgment bears that
 life   110
Which he deserves to lose. Whether
 he was combined
With those of Norway, or did line
 the rebel
With hidden help and vantage, or
 that with both
He labored in his country's wrack, I
 know not;
But treasons capital, confessed and
 proved,   115
Have overthrown him.
MACBETH.   [*aside*] Glamis, and
 Thane of Cawdor—
The greatest is behind! [*to* Ross *and*

ANGUS] Thanks for your pains.
[*aside to* BANQUO] Do you not hope
 your children shall be kings,
When those that gave the Thane of
 Cawdor to me
Promised no less to them?
BANQUO. [*to* MACBETH] That, trust-
 ed home,   120
Might yet enkindle you unto the
 crown,
Besides the Thane of Cawdor. But
 'tis strange:
And oftentimes, to win us to our
 harm,
The instruments of darkness tell us
 truths,   124
Win us with honest trifles, to betray's
In deepest consequence.—
Cousins, a word, I pray you.
MACBETH.   [*aside*] Two
 truths are told,
As happy prologues to the swelling
 act
Of the imperial theme.—I thank you,
 gentlemen.—   129
[*aside*] This supernatural soliciting
Cannot be ill, cannot be good. If ill,
Why hath it given me earnest of
 success,
Commencing in a truth? I am Thane
 of Cawdor.
If good, why do I yield to that
 suggestion
Whose horrid image doth unfix my
 hair   135
And make my seated heart knock at
 my ribs
Against the use of nature? Present
 fears
Are less than horrible imaginings.
My thought, whose murder yet is but
 fantastical,
Shakes so my single state of man
 that function   140
Is smothered in surmise and nothing
 is
But what is not.

---

106 *addition:* honor. 109 *Who:* he who. 112
line: aid (literally, stuff). 117 *behind:* beyond,
in the distance or future.

120 *home:* completely. 137 *use:* normal func-
tioning. 140 *function:* normal activity.

BANQUO.   Look how our
partner's rapt.
MACBETH. [*aside*] If chance will have
me King, why chance may crown
me
Without my stir.
BANQUO.   New honors come
upon him
Like our strange garments, cleave not
to their mould   145
But with the aid of use.
MACBETH.   [*aside*] Come what
come may,
Time and the hour runs through the
roughest day.
BANQUO. Worthy Macbeth, we stay
upon your leisure.
MACBETH. Give me your favor. My
dull brain was wrought
With things forgotten. Kind gentle-
men, your pains   150
Are regist'red where every day I turn
The leaf to read them. Let us toward
the King.
[*aside to* BANQUO] Think upon what
hath chanced, and at more time,
The interim having weighed it, let
us speak
Our free hearts each to other.
BANQUO.   Very gladly. 155
MACBETH. Till then, enough.—Come,
friends.   *Exeunt*.

SCENE iv. *Flourish. Enter* KING [DUN-
CAN], LENNOX, MALCOLM, DONAL-
BAIN, *and* ATTENDANTS.

KING. Is execution done on Cawdor?
Are not
Those in commission yet returned?
MALCOLM.   My liege,
They are not yet come back. But I
have spoke
With one that saw him die; who did
report

That very frankly he confessed his
treasons,   5
Implored your Highness' pardon, and
set forth
A deep repentance. Nothing in his
life
Became him like the leaving it. He
died
As one that had been studied in his
death
To throw away the dearest thing he
owed   10
As 'twere a careless trifle.
KING.   There's no art
To find the mind's construction in
the face.
He was a gentleman on whom I built
An absolute trust.

Enter MACBETH, BANQUO, ROSS, *and*
ANGUS.

                    O worthiest cousin, 14
The sin of my ingratitude even now
Was heavy on me. Thou art so far
before
That swiftest wing of recompense is
slow
To overtake thee. Would thou hadst
less deserved,
That the proportion both of thanks
and payment
Might have been mine! Only I have
left to say,   20
More is thy due than more than all
can pay.
MACBETH. The service and the loyalty
I owe,
In doing it pays itself. Your High-
ness' part
Is to receive our duties, and our
duties
Are to your throne and state children
and servants,   25
Which do but what they should by
doing everything
Safe toward your love and honor.
KING.   Welcome hither.

---

154 *free:* open, honest. I.iv. 2 *Those in commission:* those assigned to execute Cawdor.

9 *studied:* schooled. 10 *owed:* owned. 16
before: ahead.

I have begun to plant thee and will
   labor
To make thee full of growing. Noble
   Banquo,
That hast no less deserved nor must
   be known   30
No less to have done so, let me enfold
   thee
And hold thee to my heart.
BANQUO.   There if I grow,
The harvest is your own.
KING.   My plenteous joys,
Wanton in fullness, seek to hide
   themselves
In drops of sorrow. Sons, kinsmen,
   thanes,   35
And you whose places are the near-
   est, know
We will establish our estate upon
Our eldest, Malcolm, whom we name
   hereafter
The Prince of Cumberland; which
   honor must   39
Not unaccompanied invest him only,
But signs of nobleness, like stars,
   shall shine
On all deservers. From hence to
   Inverness,
And bind us further to you.
MACBETH. The rest is labor which is
   not used for you.
I'll be myself the harbinger, and
   make joyful   45
The hearing of my wife with your
   approach;
So, humbly take my leave.
KING.   My worthy Cawdor!
MACBETH. [*aside*] The Prince of Cum-
   berland—that is a step
On which I must fall down or else
   o'erleap,
For in my way it lies. Stars, hide
   your fires;   50
Let no light see my black and deep
   desires.
The eye wink at the hand; yet let
   that be
Which the eye fears, when it is done,
   to see.   *Exit.*

KING. True, worthy Banquo: he is full
   so valiant,
And in his commendations I am
   fed;   55
It is a banquet to me. Let's after him,
Whose care is gone before to bid us
   welcome.
It is a peerless kinsman.

               Flourish. Exeunt.

SCENE v. *Enter* MACBETH'S WIFE,
alone, with a letter.

LADY. [*reads*] "They met me in the day
of success; and I have learned by the
perfect'st report they have more in
them than mortal knowledge. When
I burned in desire to question 5
them further, they made themselves
air, into which they vanished. Whiles
I stood rapt in the wonder of it,
came missives from the King, who
all-hailed me Thane of Cawdor, 10
by which title, before, these weird
sisters saluted me, and referred me
to the coming on of time with 'Hail,
King that shalt be!' This have I
thought good to deliver thee, my 15
dearest partner of greatness, that
thou mightst not lose the dues of
rejoicing by being ignorant of what
greatness is promised thee. Lay it
to thy heart, and farewell."   20
Glamis thou art, and Cawdor, and
   shalt be
What thou art promised. Yet do I
   fear thy nature.
It is too full o' th' milk of human
   kindness
To catch the nearest way. Thou
   wouldst be great
Art not without ambition, but without   25
The illness should attend it. What
   thou wouldst highly,
That wouldst thou holily; wouldst
   not play false,
And yet wouldst wrongly win.

Thou'dst have, great Glamis,
That which cries "Thus thou must
do" if thou have it;
And that which rather thou dost fear
to do   30
Than wishest should be undone. Hie
thee hither,
That I may pour my spirits in thine
ear
And chastise with the valor of my
tongue
All that impedes thee from the golden
round
Which fate and metaphysical aid
doth seem   35
To have thee crowned withal.

Enter MESSENGER.

                    What is your tidings?
MESSENGER. The King comes here to-
night.
LADY.   Thou'rt mad to say it!
Is not thy master with him? who,
were't so,
Would have informed for prepara-
tion.
MESSENGER. So please you, it is true.
Our Thane is coming.   40
One of my fellows had the speed of
him,
Who, almost dead for breath, had
scarcely more
Than would make up his message.
LADY.   Give him tending;
He brings great news.

                    Exit MESSENGER.

          The raven himself is hoarse
That croaks the fatal entrance of
Duncan   45
Under my battlements. Come, you
spirits
That tend on mortal thoughts, unsex
me here,

And fill me from the crown to the
toe top-full
Of direst cruelty. Make thick my
blood;
Stop up th' access and passage to
remorse,   50
That no compunctious visitings of
nature
Shake my fell purpose nor keep peace
between
Th' effect and it. Come to my woman's
breasts
And take my milk for gall, you
murd'ring ministers,   54
Wherever in your sightless substances
You wait on nature's mischief. Come,
thick night,
And pall thee in the dunnest smoke
of hell,
That my keen knife see not the
wound it makes,
Nor heaven peep through the blanket
of the dark
To cry "Hold, hold!"

Enter MACBETH.

Great Glamis! worthy Cawdor! 60
Greater than both, by the all-hail
hereafter!
Thy letters have transported me
beyond
This ignorant present, and I feel now
The future in the instant.
MACBETH.   My dearest love,
Duncan comes here tonight.
LADY.   And when goes hence? 65
MACBETH. Tomorrow, as he purposes.
LADY.   O, never
Shall sun that morrow see!
Your face, my Thane, is as a book
where men
May read strange matters. To beguile
the time,
Look like the time; bear welcome in
your eye,   70
Your hand, your tongue; look like
th' innocent flower,

I.v.28–31 *Thou'dst...undone:* You desire the crown, which can be gotten only by murder; and, moreover, you desire the murder of Duncan, too, your hesitance in the matter arising not from moral scruples but only from cowardice. 34 *round:* crown.

55 *sightless:* invisible. 56 *wait on:* assist.

But be the serpent under't. He that's coming
Must be provided for; and you shall put
This night's great business into my dispatch,
Which shall to all our nights and days to come   75
Give solely sovereign sway and masterdom.
MACBETH. We will speak further.
LADY.   Only look up clear.
To alter favor ever is to fear.
Leave all the rest to me.   *Exeunt.*

SCENE vi. *Hautboys and torches. Enter* KING [DUNCAN], MALCOLM, DONAL-BAIN, BANQUO, LENNOX, MACDUFF, ROSS, ANGUS, *and* ATTENDANTS.

KING. This castle hath a pleasant seat. The air
Nimbly and sweetly recommends itself
Unto our gentle senses.
BANQUO.   This guest of summer,
The temple-haunting martlet, does approve
By his loved mansionry that the heaven's breath   5
Smells wooingly here. No jutty, frieze,
Buttress, nor coign of vantage, but this bird
Hath made his pendent bed and procreant cradle.
Where they most breed and haunt, I have observed
The air is delicate.

Enter LADY [MACBETH].

KING.   See, see, our honored hostess!   10
The love that follows us sometime is our trouble,
Which still we thank as love. Herein I teach you
How you shall bid God 'ield us for your pains
And thank us for your trouble.
LADY.   All our service
In every point twice done, and then done double,   15
Were poor and single business to contend
Against those honors deep and broad wherewith
Your Majesty loads our house. For those of old,
And the late dignities heaped up to them,
We rest your hermits.
KING.   Where's the Thane of Cawdor?   20
We coursed him at the heels and had a purpose
To be his purveyor; but he rides well,
And his great love, sharp as his spur, hath holp him
To his home before us. Fair and noble hostess,
We are your guest tonight.
LADY.   Your servants ever   25
Have theirs, themselves, and what is theirs, in compt,
To make their audit at your Highness' pleasure,
Still to return your own.
KING.   Give me your hand.
Conduct me to mine host: we love him highly
And shall continue our graces towards him.   30
By your leave, hostess.   *Exeunt.*

SCENE vii. *Hautboys. Torches. Enter a* SEWER, *and divers* SERVANTS *with dishes and service over the stage. Then enter* MACBETH.

---

77 *look up clear:* appear undisturbed. 78 *favor:* color, i.e., to blanch. I.vi *Hautboys:* oboes. 11 *our trouble:* troublesome.

12 *which:* though. 13 *bid:* pray; *'ield us:* reward me. I. vii *Sewer:* chief servant.

MACBETH. If it were done when 'tis done, then 'twere well
It were done quickly. If the assassination
Could trammel up the consequence, and catch
With his surcease success, that but this blow
Might be the be-all and the end-all here, 5
But here, upon this bank and shoal of time,
We'ld jump the life to come. But in these cases
We still have judgment here, that we but teach
Bloody instructions, which, being taught, return
To plague the inventor. This even-handed justice 10
Commends the ingredients of our poisoned chalice
To our own lips. He's here in double trust:
First, as I am his kinsman and his subject,
Strong both against the deed; then, as his host,
Who should against his murderer shut the door, 15
Not bear the knife myself. Besides, this Duncan
Hath borne his faculties so meek, hath been
So clear in his great office, that his virtues
Will plead like angels, trumpet-tongued, against
The deep damnation of his taking-off; 20
And pity, like a naked newborn babe
Striding the blast, or heaven's cherubin horsed
Upon the sightless couriers of the air,
Shall blow the horrid deed in every eye
That tears shall drown the wind. I have no spur 25
To prick the sides of my intent, but only
Vaulting ambition, which o'erleaps itself
And falls on the other—

Enter LADY [MACBETH].

　　　　　　　　How now? What news?
LADY. He has almost supped. Why have you left the chamber?
MACBETH. Hath he asked for me?
LADY.　　Know you not he has? 30
MACBETH. We will proceed no further in this business.
He hath honored me of late, and I have bought
Golden opinions from all sorts of people,
Which would be worn now in their newest gloss,
Not cast aside so soon.
LADY.　　Was the hope drunk 35
Wherein you dressed yourself? Hath it slept since?
And wakes it now to look so green and pale
At what it did so freely? From this time
Such I account thy love. Art thou afeard
To be the same in thine own act and valor 40
As thou art in desire? Wouldst thou have that
Which thou esteem'st the ornament of life,
And live a coward in thine own esteem?
Letting "I dare not" wait upon "I would,"
Like the poor cat i' the adage.
MACBETH.　　Prithee, peace! 45

---

1 *done:* over, finished.　7 *jump:* risk.　17 *faculties:* prerogatives as king.　18 *clear:* guiltless, unstained.　23 *sightless couriers:* i.e., the winds.

---

45 *the adage:* "The cat would eat fish, but would not wet her feet."

I dare do all that may become a man;
Who dares do more is none.
LADY.   What beast was't then
That made you break this enterprise
  to me?
When you durst do it, then you were
  a man;
And to be more than what you were,
  you would   50
Be so much more the man. Nor time,
  nor place,
Did then adhere, and yet you would
  make both.
They have made themselves, and
  that their fitness now
Does unmake you. I have given suck,
  and know
How tender 'tis to love the babe that
  milks me: 55
I would, while it was smiling in my
  face,
Have plucked my nipple from his
  boneless gums
And dashed the brains out, had I so
  sworn as you
Have done to this.
MACBETH.   If we should fail?
LADY.   We fail?
But screw your courage to the stick-
  ing place   60
And we'll not fail. When Duncan is
  asleep
(Whereto the rather shall his day's
  hard journey
Soundly invite him), his two cham-
  berlains
Will I with wine and wassail so

convince
That memory, the warder of the
  brain,   65
Shall be a fume, and the receipt of
  reason
A limbeck only. When in swinish sleep
Their drenched natures lie as in a
  death,
What cannot you and I perform upon
The unguarded Duncan? what not
  put upon   70
His spongy officers, who shall bear
  the guilt
Of our great quell?
MACBETH.   Bring forth men-
  children only;
For thy undaunted mettle should
  compose
Nothing but males. Will it not be
  received,
When we have marked with blood
  those sleepy two   75
Of his own chamber and used their
  very daggers,
That they have done't?
LADY.   Who dares receive it other,
As we shall make our griefs and
  clamor roar
Upon his death?
MACBETH.   I am settled and bend up
Each corporal agent to this terrible
  feat.   80
Away, and mock the time with fairest
  show;
False face must hide what the false
  heart doth know.   *Exeunt.*

ACT II

SCENE i. *Enter* BANQUO, *and* FLEANCE
with a torch before him.

BANQUO. How goes the night, boy?
FLEANCE. The moon is down; I have
  not heard the clock.

BANQUO. And she goes down at twelve.
FLEANCE.   I take't, 'tis later, sir.
BANQUO. Hold, take my sword. There's
  husbandry in heaven;

---

52 *adhere:* seem suitable. 53 *that their:* that
very. 60 *But:* only.

67 *limbeck:* alembic, the cap of a still. 74
received: accepted as true. II.i.4 *husbandry:*
thrift.

Their candles are all out. Take thee
  that too.   5
A heavy summons lies like lead upon
  me,
And yet I would not sleep. Merciful
  powers,
Restrain in me the cursed thoughts
  that nature
Gives way to in repose.

Enter MACBETH, *and a* SERVANT *with
a torch.*

                         Give me my sword!
Who's there?   10
MACBETH. A friend.
BANQUO. What, sir, not yet at rest?
  The King's abed.
He hath been in unusual pleasure and
Sent forth great largess to your
  offices.
This diamond he greets your wife
  withal   15
By the name of most kind hostess,
  and shut up
In measureless content.
MACBETH.   Being unprepared,
  Our will became the servant to
  defect,
Which else should free have wrought.
BANQUO.   All's well.
  I dreamt last night of the three weird
  sisters.   20
To you they have showed some truth.
MACBETH.   I think not of them.
  Yet when we can entreat an hour to
  serve,
We would spend it in some words
  upon that business,
If you would grant the time.
BANQUO.   At your kind'st leisure.
MACBETH. If you shall cleave to my
  consent, when 'tis,   25
It shall make honor for you.

---

5 *that:* probably his dagger. 6 *summons:*
i.e., to sleep. 14 *offices:* servants' quarters.
17–19 *Being...wrought:* Being unprepared,
our will to receive the king generously could
not be carried out. 25 *cleave...when 'tis:*
side with me at the right time.

BANQUO.   So I lose none
  In seeking to augment it, but still
  keep
My bosom franchised and allegiance
  clear,
I shall be counseled.
MACBETH. Good repose the while.   29
BANQUO. Thanks, sir. The like to you.

        Exeunt BANQUO [*and* FLEANCE].

MACBETH. Go bid thy mistress, when
  my drink is ready,
She strike upon the bell. Get thee
  to bed.   *Exit* [SERVANT].
Is this a dagger which I see before
  me,
The handle toward my hand? Come,
  let me clutch thee!
I have thee not, and yet I see thee
  still.   35
Art thou not, fatal vision, sensible
To feeling as to sight? or art thou
  but
A dagger of the mind, a false creation
Proceeding from the heat-oppressed
  brain?
I see thee yet, in form as palpable 40
As this which now I draw.
Thou marshall'st me the way that
  I was going,
And such an instrument I was to use.
Mine eyes are made the fools o' the
  other senses,
Or else worth all the rest. I see thee
  still,   45
And on thy blade and dudgeon gouts
  of blood,
Which was not so before. There's no
  such thing.
It is the bloody business which
  informs
Thus to mine eyes. Now o'er the
  one half-world
Nature seems dead, and wicked
  dreams abuse   50
The curtained sleep. Witchcraft
  celebrates

---

46 *dudgeon:* handle. 48–49 *informs Thus:*
falsely communicates.

Pale Hecate's offerings; and withered
 murder,
Alarumed by his sentinel, the wolf,
Whose howl's his watch, thus with
 his stealthy pace,
With Tarquin's ravishing strides,
 towards his design   55
Moves like a ghost. Thou sure and
 firm-set earth,
Hear not my steps which way they
 walk, for fear
Thy very stones prate of my where-
 about
And take the present horror from
 the time,
Which now suits with it. Whiles I
 threat, he lives;   60
Words to the heat of deeds too cold
 breath gives. *A bell rings.*
I go, and it is done: the bell invites
 me.
Hear it not, Duncan, for it is a knell
That summons thee to heaven, or
 to hell.   *Exit.*

SCENE ii. *Enter* LADY [MACBETH].

LADY. That which hath made them
 drunk hath made me bold;
What hath quenched them hath given
 me fire. Hark! Peace!
It was the owl that shrieked, the
 fatal bellman
Which gives the stern'st good night.
 He is about it.
The doors are open, and the surfeited
 grooms   5
Do mock their charge with snores.
 I have drugged their possets,
That death and nature do contend
 about them
Whether they live or die.

---

52 *Hecate's offerings:* rituals of Hecate, goddess of witchcraft. 55 *Tarquin:* Roman
tyrant who raped Lucrece. II.ii.3 *fatal bellman:* who rang outside the cells of condemned
men the night before execution to remind
them of their crimes. 6 *possets:* nightcaps of
ale and warm milk.

MACBETH.   [*within*] Who's there?
 What, ho?
LADY. Alack, I am afraid they have
 awaked,
And 'tis not done! The attempt, and
 not the deed,   10
Confounds us. Hark! I laid their
 daggers ready—
He could not miss 'em. Had he not
 resembled
My father as he slept, I had done't.

Enter MACBETH.

        My husband!
MACBETH. I have done the deed. Didst
 thou not hear a noise?
LADY. I heard the owl scream and the
 crickets cry.   15
Did not you speak?
MACBETH.   When?
LADY.   Now.
MACBETH.   As I descended?
LADY. Ay.
MACBETH. Hark!
 Who lies i' the second chamber?
LADY.   Donalbain.
MACBETH. This is a sorry sight. 20
LADY. A foolish thought, to say a sorry
 sight.
MACBETH. There's one did laugh in's
 sleep, and one cried "Murder!"
That they did wake each other. I
 stood and heard them.
But they did say their prayers and
 addressed them
Again to sleep.
LADY.   There are two lodged
 together.   25
MACBETH. One cried "God bless us!"
 and "Amen!" the other,
As they had seen me with these
 hangman's hands,
List'ning their fear. I could not say
 "Amen!"
When they did say "God bless us!"
LADY.   Consider it not so deeply.
MACBETH. But wherefore could not I
 pronounce "Amen"?   30
I had most need of blessing, and
 "Amen"

Stuck in my throat.

LADY.   These deeds must not be thought
After these ways; so, it will make us mad.

MACBETH. Methought I heard a voice cry "Sleep no more!
Macbeth does murder sleep"—the innocent sleep,   35
Sleep that knits up the raveled sleave of care,
The death of each day's life, sore labor's bath,
Balm of hurt minds, great nature's second course,
Chief nourisher in life's feast.

LADY.   What do you mean?

MACBETH. Still it cried "Sleep no more!" to all the house;   40
"Glamis hath murdered Sleep, and therefore Cawdor
Shall sleep no more, Macbeth shall sleep no more."

LADY. Who was it that thus cried? Why, worthy Thane,
You do unbend your noble strength to think
So brainsickly of things. Go, get some water   45
And wash this filthy witness from your hand.
Why did you bring these daggers from the place?
They must lie there: go, carry them, and smear
The sleepy grooms with blood.

MACBETH.   I'll go no more.
I am afraid to think what I have done;   50
Look on't again I dare not.

LADY.   Infirm of purpose!
Give me the daggers. The sleeping, and the dead,
Are but as pictures. 'Tis the eye of childhood
That fears a painted devil. If he do bleed,
I'll gild the faces of the grooms withal,   55
For it must seem their guilt.

Exit. Knocking within.

MACBETH.   Whence is that knocking?
How is't with me when every noise appalls me?
What hands are here? Ha! they pluck out mine eyes.
Will all great Neptune's ocean wash this blood
Clean from my hand? No, this my hand will rather   60
The multitudinous seas incarnadine,
Making the green one red.

Enter LADY [MACBETH].

LADY. My hands are of your color, but I shame
To wear a heart so white. (*Knock.*) I hear a knocking
At the south entry. Retire we to our chamber.   65
A little water clears us of this deed.
How easy is it then! Your constancy
Hath left you unattended. (*Knock.*) Hark! more knocking.
Get on your nightgown, lest occasion call us
And show us to be watchers. Be not lost   70
So poorly in your thoughts.

MACBETH. To know my deed, 'twere best not know myself. (*Knock.*)
Wake Duncan with thy knocking! I would thou couldst.   *Exeunt.*

SCENE iii. *Enter a* PORTER. *Knocking within.*

PORTER. Here's a knocking indeed! If a man were porter of hell gate, he should have old turning the key. (*Knock.*) Knock, knock, knock. Who's there, i' the name of Beelze-   5

---

36 *raveled sleave:* tangled skein. 38 *second course:* sleep as an after-dinner nap.

67–68 *Your constancy...unattended:* Your resolution has abandoned you. II.iii.3 *old:* frequent.

bub? Here's a farmer that hanged himself on the expectation of plenty. Come in time! Have napkins enow about you; here you'll sweat for't. (*Knock.*) Knock, knock. Who's 10 there, in the other devil's name? Faith, here's an equivocator, that could swear in both the scales against either scale; who committed treason enough for God's sake, yet could 15 not equivocate to heaven. O come in, equivocator. (*Knock.*) Knock, knock, knock. Who's there? Faith, here's an English tailor come hither for stealing out of a French hose. Come 20 in, tailor. Here you may roast your goose. (*Knock.*) Knock, knock. Never at quiet! What are you?— But this place is too cold for hell. I'll devil-porter it no further. I 25 had thought to have let in some of all professions that go the primrose way to the everlasting bonfire. (*Knock.*) Anon, anon! [*Opens the gate.*] I pray you remember the 30 porter.

Enter MACDUFF *and* LENNOX.

MACDUFF. Was it so late, friend, ere you went to bed,
That you do lie so late?
PORTER. Faith, sir, we were carousing till the second cock; and drink, 35 sir, is a great provoker of three things.
MACDUFF. What three things does drink especially provoke?
PORTER. Marry, sir, nose-painting, 40 sleep, and urine. Lechery, sir, it provokes, and unprovokes: it provokes the desire, but it takes away the performance. Therefore much drink may be said to be an 45 equivocator with lechery: it makes

him, and it mars him; it sets him on, and it takes him off; it persuades him, and disheartens him; makes him stand to, and not stand to; 50 in conclusion, equivocates him in a sleep, and, giving him the lie, leaves him.
MACDUFF. I believe drink gave thee the lie last night. 55
PORTER. That it did, sir, i' the very throat on me; but I requited him for his lie; and, I think, being too strong for him, though he took up my legs sometime, yet I made a 60 shift to cast him.
MACDUFF. Is thy master stirring?

Enter MACBETH.

Our knocking has awaked him: here he comes.
LENNOX. Good morrow, noble sir.
MACBETH.   Good morrow, both. 65
MACDUFF. Is the King stirring, worthy Thane?
MACBETH.   Not yet.
MACDUFF. He did command me to call timely on him;
I have almost slipped the hour.
MACBETH.   I'll bring you to him.
MACDUFF. I know this is a joyful trouble to you;
But yet 'tis one. 70
MACBETH. The labor we delight in physics pain.
This is the door.
MACDUFF.   I'll make so bold to call,
For 'tis my limited service. [*Exit.*]
LENNOX. Goes the King hence today?
MACBETH.   He does; he did appoint so.
LENNOX. The night has been unruly. Where we lay, 75
Our chimneys were blown down; and, as they say,
Lamentings heard i' the air, strange screams of· death,

6–7 *a farmer...plenty:* who, having hoarded crops, killed himself when it became apparent that a plentiful harvest, which would lower prices, was forthcoming. 22 *goose:* pressing iron; also venereal disorder; also whore. 35 *second cock:* 3 A.M.

---

60 *made a shift:* managed; *cast:* throw (as a wrestler), throw up (as a drinker), urinate. 71 *physics:* eliminates. 73 *limited:* appointed.

And prophesying, with accents ter-
    rible,
Of dire combustion and confused
    events
New hatched to the woeful time. The
    obscure bird   80
Clamored the livelong night. Some
    say the earth
Was feverous and did shake.
MACBETH.   'Twas a rough night.
LENNOX. My young remembrance can-
    not parallel
A fellow to it.

Enter MACDUFF.

MACDUFF. O horror, horror, horror!
    Tongue nor heart   85
Cannot conceive nor name thee!
MACBETH and LENNOX.   What's
    the matter?
MACDUFF. Confusion now hath made
    his masterpiece:
Most sacrilegious murder hath broke
    ope
The Lord's anointed temple and stole
    thence
The life o' the building!
MACBETH.   What is't
    you say—the life?   90
LENNOX. Mean you his Majesty?
MACDUFF. Approach the chamber and
    destroy your sight
With a new Gorgon. Do not bid me
    speak—
See, and then speak yourselves.

    Exeunt MACBETH *and* LENNOX.

                        Awake, awake!
Ring the alarum bell! Murder and
    treason!   95
Banquo and Donalbain! Malcolm,
    awake!
Shake off this downy sleep, death's
    counterfeit,
And look on death itself. Up, up,
    and see
The great doom's image. Malcolm!

Banquo!
As from your graves rise up and
    walk like sprites   100
To countenance this horror. Ring the
    bell! *Bell rings.*

Enter LADY [MACBETH].

LADY. What's the business,
    That such a hideous trumpet calls to
        parley
    The sleepers of the house? Speak,
        speak!
MACDUFF. O gentle lady,
    'Tis not for you to hear what I can
        speak: 105
    The repetition in a woman's ear
    Would murder as it fell.

Enter BANQUO.

                    O Banquo, Banquo!
    Our royal master's murdered!
LADY.   Woe, alas!
    What, in our house?
BANQUO.   Too cruel anywhere.
    Dear Duff, I prithee contradict
        thyself   110
    And say it is not so.

Enter MACBETH, LENNOX, *and* ROSS.

MACBETH. Had I but died an hour
    before this chance,
    I had lived a blessed time; for from
        this instant
    There's nothing serious in mortality:
    All is but toys. Renown and grace is
        dead,   115
    The wine of life is drawn, and the
        mere lees
    Is left this vault to brag of.

Enter MALCOLM *and* DONALBAIN.

DONALBAIN. What is amiss?
MACBETH.   You are,
    and do not know't.
    The spring, the head, the fountain
        of your blood

80 *bird:* owl. 99 *great doom's image:* likeness of the day of judgment.

101 *countenance:* look upon and look like.
114 *serious in mortality:* worth taking
seriously in life. 115 *toys:* trifles.

Is stopped, the very source of it is
stopped.   120
MACDUFF. Your royal father's mur-
dered.
MALCOLM. O, by whom?
LENNOX. Those of his chamber, as it
seemed, had done't.
Their hands and faces were all badged
with blood;
So were their daggers, which unwiped
we found
Upon their pillows. They stared and
were distracted.   125
No man's life was to be trusted with
them.
MACBETH. O, yet I do repent me of
my fury
That I did kill them.
MACDUFF.   Wherefore did you so?
MACBETH. Who can be wise, amazed,
temp'rate and furious,
Loyal and neutral, in a moment? No
man.   130
The expedition of my violent love
Outrun the pauser, reason. Here lay
Duncan,
His silver skin laced with his golden
blood;
And his gashed stabs looked like a
breach in nature
For ruin's wasteful entrance: there,
the murderers,   135
Steeped in the colors of their trade,
their daggers
Unmannerly breeched with gore.
Who could refrain
That had a heart to love, and in that
heart
Courage to make's love known?
LADY.   Help me hence, ho!
MACDUFF. Look to the lady.
MALCOLM. [*aside to* DONALBAIN] Why
do we hold our tongues,   140
That most may claim this argument
for ours?
DONALBAIN. [*to* MALCOLM] What
should be spoken here,

Where our fate, hid in an auger hole,
May rush and seize us? Let's away:
Our tears are not yet brewed.
MALCOLM. [*to* DONALBAIN] Nor our
strong sorrow   145
Upon the foot of motion.
BANQUO.   Look to the lady.
[LADY MACBETH *is carried out.*]
And when we have our naked frailties
hid,
That suffer in exposure, let us meet
And question this most bloody piece
of work,
To know it further. Fears and scru-
ples shake us.   150
In the great hand of God I stand,
and thence
Against the undivulged pretense I
fight
Of treasonous malice.
MACDUFF.   And so do I.
ALL.   So all.
MACBETH. Let's briefly put on manly
readiness
And meet i' the hall together.
ALL.   Well contented.   155
Exeunt [*all but* MALCOLM *and* DONAL-
BAIN].

MALCOLM. What will you do? Let's not
consort with them.
To show an unfelt sorrow is an office
Which the false man does easy. I'll
to England.
DONALBAIN. To Ireland I. Our sepa-
rated fortune
Shall keep us both the safer. Where
we are,   160
There's daggers in men's smiles; the
near in blood,
The nearer bloody.
MALCOLM.   This murderous
shaft that's shot
Hath not yet lighted, and our safest
way
Is to avoid the aim. Therefore to
horse,

---

131 *expedition:* speed.   132 *pauser:* retarder.
140 *Look:* tend.

143 *auger:* i.e., a small (hole).   146 *Upon the
foot of motion:* begun.   149 *question:* discuss.   152 *undivulged pretense:* secret designs.

And let us not be dainty of leave-
taking   165
But shift away. There's warrant in
that theft
Which steals itself when there's no
mercy left.   *Exeunt.*

SCENE iv. *Enter* ROSS *with an* OLD
MAN.

OLD MAN. Threescore and ten I can
remember well;
Within the volume of which time I
have seen
Hours dreadful and things strange,
but this sore night
Hath trifled former knowings.
ROSS.   Ha, good father,
Thou seest the heavens, as troubled
with man's act,   5
Threatens his bloody stage. By the
clock 'tis day,
And yet dark night strangles the
traveling lamp.
Is't night's predominance, or the
day's shame,
That darkness does the face of earth
entomb
When living light should kiss it?
OLD MAN.   'Tis unnatural, 10
Even like the deed that's done. On
Tuesday last
A falcon, towering in her pride of
place,
Was by a mousing owl hawked at
and killed.
ROSS. And Duncan's horses (a thing
most strange and certain),
Beauteous and swift, the minions of
their race,   15
Turned wild in nature, broke their
stalls, flung out,
Contending 'gainst obedience, as they
would make
War with mankind.
OLD MAN.   'Tis said they eat
each other.

ROSS. They did so, to the amazement
of mine eyes
That looked upon't.

Enter MACDUFF.

                  Here comes the good Macduff. 20
How goes the world, sir, now?
MACDUFF.   Why, see you not?
ROSS. Is't known who did this more
than bloody deed?
MACDUFF. Those that Macbeth hath
slain.
ROSS.   Alas the day,
What good could they pretend?
MACDUFF.   They were suborned.
Malcolm and Donalbain, the King's
two sons,   25
Are stol'n away and fled, which puts
upon them
Suspicion of the deed.
ROSS.   'Gainst nature still.
Thriftless ambition, that will raven
up
Thine own live's means! Then 'tis
most like
The sovereignty will fall upon
Macbeth.   30
MACDUFF. He is already named, and
gone to Scone
To be invested.
ROSS.   Where is Duncan's body?
MACDUFF. Carried to Colmekill,
The sacred storehouse of his prede-
cessors
And guardian of their bones.
ROSS.   Will you to Scone? 35
MACDUFF. No, cousin, I'll to Fife.
ROSS.   Well, I will thither
MACDUFF. Well, may you see things
well done there—Adieu—
Lest our old robes sit easier than
our new!
ROSS. Farewell, father.
OLD MAN. God's benison go with you,
and with those   40
That would make good of bad, and
friends of foes.   *Exeunt omnes.*

II.iv.7 *traveling lamp:* the sun.

24 *pretend:* expect. 28 *raven up:* eat up. 40
benison: blessing.

ACT III

SCENE i. *Enter* BANQUO.

BANQUO. Thou hast it now—King, Cawdor, Glamis, all,
As the weird women promised; and I fear
Thou play'dst most foully for't. Yet it was said
It should not stand in thy posterity.
But that myself should be the root and father   5
Of many kings. If there come truth from them.
(As upon thee, Macbeth, their speeches shine),
Why, by the verities on thee made good,
May they not be my oracles as well
And set me up in hope? But hush, no more!   10

Sennet sounded. Enter MACBETH *as King,* LADY [MACBETH], LENNOX, ROSS, LORDS, *and* ATTENDANTS.

MACBETH. Here's our chief guest.
LADY.   If he had been forgotten,
It had been as a gap in our great feast,
And all-thing unbecoming.
MACBETH. Tonight we hold a solemn supper, sir,
And I'll request your presence.
BANQUO.   Let your Highness   15
Command upon me, to the which my duties
Are with a most indissoluble tie
Forever knit.
MACBETH.   Ride you this afternoon?
BANQUO. Ay, my good lord.
MACBETH. We should have else desired your good advice   20
(Which still hath been both grave and prosperous)

In this day's council; but we'll take tomorrow.
Is't far you ride?
BANQUO. As far, my lord, as will fill up the time
'Twixt this and supper. Go not my horse the better,   25
I must become a borrower of the night
For a dark hour or twain.
MACBETH.   Fail not our feast.
BANQUO. My lord, I will not.
MACBETH. We hear our bloody cousins are bestowed
In England and in Ireland, not confessing   30
Their cruel parricide, filling their hearers
With strange invention. But of that tomorrow,
When therewithal we shall have cause of state
Craving us jointly. Hie you to horse. Adieu,
Till you return at night. Goes Fleance with you?   35
BANQUO. Ay, my good lord. Our time does call upon's.
MACBETH. I wish your horses swift and sure of foot,
And so I do commend you to their backs.
Farewell.   *Exit* BANQUO.
Let every man be master of his time   40
Till seven at night. To make society
The sweeter welcome, we will keep ourself
Till supper time alone. While then, God be with you!

          Exeunt LORDS [*and others*].

Sirrah, a word with you. Attend those men
Our pleasure?   45

III.i.13 *all-thing:* entirely. 14 *solemn:* formal.

44 *Sirrah:* term used to address inferiors.

SERVANT. They are, my lord, without the palace gate.

MACBETH. Bring them before us.

Exit SERVANT.

To be thus is nothing, but to be safely thus—
Our fears in Banquo stick deep,
And in his royalty of nature reigns that   50
Which would be feared. 'Tis much he dares;
And to that dauntless temper of his mind
He hath a wisdom that doth guide his valor
To act in safety. There is none but he
Whose being I do fear; and under him   55
My genius is rebuked, as it is said
Mark Antony's was by Caesar. He chid the sisters
When first they put the name of King upon me,
And bade them speak to him. Then, prophetlike,
They hailed him father to a line of kings.   60
Upon my head they placed a fruitless crown
And put a barren sceptre in my gripe,
Thence to be wrenched with an unlineal hand,
No son of mine succeeding. If't be so,
For Banquo's issue have I filed my mind;   65
For them the gracious Duncan have I murdered;
Put rancors in the vessel of my peace,
Only for them, and mine eternal jewel
Given to the common enemy of man
To make them kings—the seed of Banquo kings!   70

Rather than so, come, Fate, into the list,
And champion me to th' utterance! Who's there?

Enter SERVANT *and two* MURDERERS.

Now go to the door and stay there till we call.   *Exit* SERVANT.
Was it not yesterday we spoke together?

MURDERERS. It was, so please your Highness.

MACBETH.   Well then, now   75
Have you considered of my speeches? Know
That it was he, in the times past, which held you
So under fortune, which you thought had been
Our innocent self. This I made good to you
In our last conference, passed in probation with you   80
How you were borne in hand, how crossed, the instruments,
Who wrought with them; and all things else that might
To half a soul and to a notion crazed
Say "Thus did Banquo."

1. MURDERER.   You made it known to us.

MACBETH. I did so; and went further, which is now   85
Our point of second meeting. Do you find
Your patience so predominant in your nature
That you can let this go? Are you so gospeled
To pray for this good man and for his issue,
Whose heavy hand hath bowed you to the grave   90
And beggared yours forever?

---

49 *in:* concerning. 56 *genius is rebuked:* spirit is put down. 65 *issue:* offspring; *filed:* defiled probably, but perhaps also sharpened and exacerbated. 68 *eternal jewel:* immortal soul.

72 *champion:* combat; *utterance:* uttermost point (death). 80 *passed in probation with:* proved to. 81 *borne in hand:* duped along; *crossed:* frustrated. 88 *gospeled:* subdued by gospel teachings such as "Love thy enemies."

1. MURDERER.   We are
men, my liege.
MACBETH. Ay, in the catalogue ye go
for men,
As hounds and greyhounds, mongrels,
spaniels, curs,
Shoughs, water-rugs, and demiwolves
are clept
All by the name of dogs. The valued
file   95
Distinguishes the swift, the slow, the
subtle,
The housekeeper, the hunter, every
one
According to the gift which bounteous
nature
Hath in him closed, whereby he does
receive
Particular addition, from the bill   100
That writes them all alike; and so
of men.
Now, if you have a station in the file,
Not i' the worst rank of manhood,
say't;
And I will put that business in your
bosoms
Whose execution takes your enemy
off,   105
Grapples you to the heart and love
of us,
Who wear our health but sickly in
his life,
Which in his death were perfect.
2. MURDERER.   I am one, my liege,
Whom the vile blows and buffets of
the world
Have so incensed that I am reckless
what   110
I do to spite the world.
1. MURDERER.   And I another,
So weary with disasters, tugged with
fortune,
That I would set my life on any
chance
To mend it or be rid on't.

MACBETH.   Both of you
Know Banquo was your enemy.
MURDERERS.   True, my lord.   115
MACBETH. So is he mine, and in such
bloody distance
That every minute of his being
thrusts
Against my near'st of life; and
though I could
With barefaced power sweep him
from my sight
And bid my will avouch it, yet I
must not,   120
For certain friends that are both his
and mine,
Whose loves I may not drop, but wail
his fall
Who I myself struck down. And
thence it is
That I to your assistance do make
love,
Masking the business from the com-
mon eye   125
For sundry weighty reasons.
2. MURDERER.   We shall, my lord,
Perform what you command us.
1. MURDERER.   Though our lives—
MACBETH. Your spirits shine through
you. Within this hour at most
I will advise you where to plant
yourselves,
Acquaint you with the perfect spy o'
the time,   130
The moment on't, for't must be done
tonight
And something from the palace (always thought
That I require a clearness); and with
him,
To leave no rubs nor botches in the
work,
Fleance his son, that keeps him com-
pany,   135
Whose absence is no less material to
me

---

94 *shoughs:* shaggy-haired lapdogs. 95 *valued
file:* list of ratings. 100 *Particular addition:*
special distinction; *from:* contrary to. 113
set: risk.

---

116 *distance:* disagreement. 120 *avouch:*
justify. 132 *always thought:* constantly keeping in mind. 134 *rubs:* imperfections.

Than is his father's, must embrace
the fate
Of that dark hour. Resolve yourselves
apart;
I'll come to you anon.
MURDERERS.   We are re-
solved, my lord.
MACBETH. I'll call upon you straight.
Abide within.   140

[*Exeunt* MURDERERS.]

It is concluded. Banquo, thy soul's
flight,
If it find heaven, must find it out
tonight.   *Exeunt.*

SCENE ii. *Enter* MACBETH's LADY *and
a* SERVANT.

LADY. Is Banquo gone from court?
SERVANT. Ay, madam, but returns again
tonight.
LADY. Say to the King I would attend
his leisure
For a few words.
SERVANT.   Madam, I will. [*Exit.*]
LADY.   Naught's had, all's
spent,
Where our desire is got without con-
tent.   5
'Tis safer to be that which we destroy
Than by destruction dwell in doubt-
ful joy.

Enter MACBETH.

How now, my lord? Why do you keep
alone,
Of sorriest fancies your companions
making,
Using those thoughts which should
indeed have died   10
With them they think on? Things
without all remedy
Should be without regard. What's
done is done.
MACBETH. We have scorched the snake,
not killed it.
She'll close and be herself, whilst our
poor malice

Remains in danger of her former
tooth.   15
But let the frame of things disjoint,
both the worlds suffer,
Ere we will eat our meal in fear,
and sleep
In the affliction of these terrible
dreams
That shake us nightly. Better be with
the dead,
Whom we, to gain our peace, have
sent to peace,   20
Than on the torture of the mind to lie
In restless ecstasy. Duncan is in his
grave;
After life's fitful fever he sleeps well.
Treason has done his worst: nor steel
nor poison,
Malice domestic, foreign levy, noth-
ing,   25
Can touch him further.
LADY.   .   Come on,
Gentle my lord, sleek o'er your rug-
ged looks;
Be bright and jovial among your
guests tonight.
MACBETH. So shall I, love; and so, I
pray, be you.
Let your remembrance apply to
Banquo;   30
Present him eminence both with eye
and tongue:
Unsafe the while, that we must lave
Our honors in these flattering streams
And make our faces vizards to our
hearts,
Disguising what they are.
LADY.   You must leave this.   35
MACBETH. O, full of scorpions is my
mind, dear wife!
Thou know'st that Banquo, and his
Fleance, lives.
LADY. But in them Nature's copy's not
eterne.

III.ii.16 *disjoint:* break apart; *both the
worlds:* heaven and earth. 21 *torture:* torturing rack. 22 *ecstasy:* fever, madness. 31
Present him eminence: treat him deferentially.
34 *vizards:* masks. 38 *copy:* copyhold, lease.

MACBETH. There's comfort yet; they
  are assailable.
  Then be thou jocund. Ere the bat
  hath flown   40
  His cloistered flight, ere to black
  Hecate's summons
  The shard-born beetle with his drowsy
  hums
  Hath rung night's yawning peal, there
  shall be done
  A deed of dreadful note.
LADY.   What's to be done?
MACBETH. Be innocent of the knowl-
  edge, dearest chuck,   45
  Till thou applaud the deed. Come,
  seeling night,
  Scarf up the tender eye of pitiful
  day,
  And with thy bloody and invisible
  hand
  Cancel and tear to pieces that great
  bond
  Which keeps me pale. Light thickens,
  and the crow   50
  Makes wing to the rooky wood.
  Good things of day begin to droop
  and drowse,
  Whiles night's black agents to their
  preys do rouse.
  Thou marvell'st at my words, but
  hold thee still;
  Things bad begun make strong them-
  selves by ill.   55
  So prithee go with me.   *Exeunt.*

SCENE iii. *Enter three* MURDERERS.

1. MURDERER. But who did bid thee
  join with us?
3. MURDERER.   Macbeth.

---

42 *shard-born:* dung-engendered. 46 *seeling:*
stitching together (as a hawk's eyelids were
stitched to make him tractable). 49 *bond:*
Banquo's lease on life. III.iii.2–4 *He...just:*
We need not mistrust this man since he
repeats our instructions from Macbeth exactly.

2. MURDERER. He needs not our mistrust, since he delivers
  Our offices and what we have to do
  To the direction just.
1. MURDERER.   Then stand with us.
  The west yet glimmers with some
  streaks of day.   5
  Now spurs the lated traveler apace
  To gain the timely inn, and near
  approaches
  The subject of our watch.
3. MURDERER.   Hark, I hear horses.
BANQUO. (*within*) Give us a light there,
  ho!
2. MURDERER.   Then 'tis he: the rest
  That are within the note of expectation   10
  Already are i' the court.
1. MURDERER.   His horses go about.
3. MURDERER. Almost a mile; but he
  does usually,
  So all men do, from hence to the
  palace gate
  Make it their walk.

Enter BANQUO, *and* FLEANCE, *with a
torch.*

2. MURDERER. A light, a light!
3. MURDERER.   'Tis he.
1. MURDERER.   Stand to't. 15
BANQUO. It will be rain tonight.
1. MURDERER.   Let it come down!
BANQUO. O,   treachery!   Fly,   good
  Fleance, fly, fly, fly!
  Thou mayst revenge—O slave!

[*Dies.* FLEANCE *escapes.*]

3. MURDERER. Who did strike out the
  light?
1. MURDERER.   Was't not the way?
3. MURDERER. There's but one down:
  the son is fled.   20
2. MURDERER. We have lost best half
  of our affair.
1. MURDERER. Well, let's away, and say
  how much is done.   *Exeunt.*

---

10 *within the note of expectation:* i.e., on the
guest list.

SCENE iv. *A Banquet prepared. Enter*
MACBETH, LADY [MACBETH], ROSS,
LENNOX, LORDS, *and* ATTENDANTS.

MACBETH. You know your own degrees
  —sit down:
  At first and last, the hearty welcome.
LORDS. Thanks to your Majesty.
MACBETH. Ourself will mingle with
  society
  And play the humble host.   5
  Our hostess keeps her state, but in
  best time
  We will require her welcome.
LADY. Pronounce it for me, sir, to all
  our friends,
  For my heart speaks they are wel-
  come.

Enter FIRST MURDERER, *to the door.*

MACBETH. See, they encounter thee
  with their hearts' thanks.   10
  Both sides are even. Here I'll sit i'
  the midst.
  Be large in mirth; anon we'll drink
  a measure
  The table round. [*Goes to door.*]
  There's blood upon thy face.
MURDERER.   'Tis Banquo's then.
MACBETH. 'Tis better thee without than
  he within.   15
  Is he dispatched?
MURDERER.   My lord, his throat
  is cut:
  That I did for him.
MACBETH.   Thou art the best o'
  th' cutthroats.
  Yet he's good that did the like for
  Fleance:
  If thou didst it, thou art the non-
  pareil.
MURDERER. Most royal sir, Fleance is
  scaped.   20
MACBETH. [*aside*] Then comes my fit
  again. I had else been perfect;
  Whole as the marble, founded as the
  rock,
  As broad and general as the casing air.

But now I am cabined, cribbed, con-
  fined, bound in
  To saucy doubts and fears.—But
  Banquo's safe?   25
MURDERER. Ay, my good lord. Safe in
  a ditch he bides,
  With twenty trenched gashes on his
  head,
  The least a death to nature.
MACBETH.   Thanks for that.—
  [*aside*] There the grown serpent lies;
  the worm that's fled
  Hath nature that in time will venom
  breed,   30
  No teeth for the present.—Get thee
  gone. Tomorrow
  We'll hear ourselves again.

Exit MURDERER.

LADY.   My royal lord,
  You do not give the cheer. The feast
  is sold
  That is not often vouched, while 'tis
  a-making,
  'Tis given with welcome. To feed
  were best at home;   35
  From thence, the sauce to meat is
  ceremony:
  Meeting were bare without it.

Enter the GHOST OF BANQUO *and sits
in* MACBETH'S *place.*

MACBETH.   Sweet remembrancer!
  Now good digestion wait on appetite,
  And health on both!
LENNOX.   May't please your
  Highness sit.
MACBETH. Here had we now our coun-
  try's honor roofed   40
  Were the graced person of our
  Banquo present—

III.iv.23 *casing:* encasing, enclosing.

29 *worm:* serpent. 33 *sold:* not given freely.
34 *vouched:* authenticated by cordial speech.
35 *To feed:* merely to eat. 36 *From thence:*
away from home. 40 *our country's honor
roofed:* all Scotland's honored men under one
roof.

Who may I rather challenge for un-
kindness
Than pity for mischance!
Ross.   His absence, sir,
Lays blame upon his promise. Please't
your Highness
To grace us with your royal com-
pany?   45
Macbeth. The table's full.
Lennox.   Here is a
place reserved, sir.
Macbeth. Where?
Lennox. Here, my good lord. What
is't that moves your Highness?
Macbeth. Which of you have done
this?
Lords.   What, my good lord?
Macbeth. Thou canst not say I did it;
never shake   50
Thy gory locks at me.
Ross. Gentlemen, rise. His Highness is
not well.
Lady. Sit, worthy friends. My lord is
often thus,
And hath been from his youth. Pray
you keep seat.
The fit is momentary; upon a
thought   55
He will again be well. If much you
note him,
You shall offend him and extend his
passion.
Feed, and regard him not.—Are you
a man?
Macbeth. Ay, and a bold one, that
dare look on that
Which might appall the devil.
Lady.   O proper stuff!   60
This is the very painting of your
fear.
This is the air-drawn dagger which
you said
Led you to Duncan. O, these flaws
and starts,
Impostors to true fear, would well
become
A woman's story at a winter's fire, 65
Authorized by her grandam. Shame
itself!

Why do you make such faces? When
all's done,
You look but on a stool.
Macbeth.   Prithee see there!
Behold! Look! Lo!—How say you?
Why, what care I? If thou canst
nod, speak too.   70
If charnel houses and our graves
must send
Those that we bury back, our
monuments
Shall be the maws of kites.

[*Exit* Ghost.]

Lady.   What,
quite unmanned in folly?
Macbeth. If I stand here, I saw him.
Lady.   Fie, for shame!
Macbeth. Blood hath been shed ere
now, i' the olden time,   75
Ere humane statute purged the gentle
weal;
Ay, and since too, murders have been
performed
Too terrible for the ear. The time
has been
That, when the brains were out, the
man would die,
And there an end. But now they rise
again,   80
With twenty mortal murders on their
crowns,
And push us from our stools. This is
more strange
Than such a murder is.
Lady.   My worthy lord,
Your noble friends do lack you.
Macbeth.   I do forget.
Do not muse at me, my most worthy
friends;   85
I have a strange infirmity, which is
nothing
To those that know me. Come, love
and health to all!
Then I'll sit down. Give me some
wine, fill full.

Enter Ghost.

---

62 *air-drawn:* carried on the air.

72 *our monuments:* our only graves.   73
maws of kites: bellies of birds of prey.   76
purged the gentle weal: civilized society.

I drink to the general joy o' the whole table,
And to our dear friend Banquo, whom we miss. 90
Would he were here! To all, and him, we thirst,
And all to all.
LORDS.   Our duties, and the pledge..
MACBETH. Avaunt, and quit my sight!
Let the earth hide thee!
Thy bones are marrowless, thy blood is cold;
Thou hast no speculation in those eyes 95
Which thou dost glare with!
LADY.   Think of this, good peers,
But as a thing of custom. 'Tis no other.
Only it spoils the pleasure of the time.
MACBETH. What man dare, I dare.
Approach thou like the rugged Russian bear, 100
The armed rhinoceros, or the Hyrcan tiger;
Take any shape but that, and my firm nerves
Shall never tremble. Or be alive again
And dare me to the desert with thy sword.
If trembling I inhabit then, protest me 105
The baby of a girl. Hence, horrible shadow!
Unreal mock'ry, hence!

[*Exit* GHOST.]

Why, so—Being gone,
I am a man again. Pray you sit still.
LADY. You have displaced the mirth, broke the good meeting,
With most admired disorder.
MACBETH.   Can such things be, 110
And overcome us like a summer's cloud
Without our special wonder? You make me strange

Even to the disposition that I owe,
When now I think you can behold such sights
And keep the natural ruby of your cheeks 115
When mine is blanched with fear.
ROSS.   What sights, my lord?
LADY. I pray you speak not; he grows worse and worse.
Question enrages him. At once, good night.
Stand not upon the order of your going,
But go at once.
LENNOX.   Good night and better health 120
Attend his Majesty.
LADY.   A kind good night to all.

Exeunt LORDS.

MACBETH. It will have blood, they say: blood will have blood.
Stones have been known to move and trees to speak;
Augures and understood relations have
By maggot-pies and choughs and rooks brought forth 125
The secret'st man of blood. What is the night?
LADY. Almost at odds with morning, which is which.
MACBETH. How say'st thou, that Macduff denies his person
At our great bidding?
LADY.   Did you send to him, sir?
MACBETH. I hear it by the way; but I will send. 130
There's not a one of them but in his house
I keep a servant fee'd. I will to-morrow
(And betimes I will) to the weird sisters.
More shall they speak, for now I am bent to know
By the worst means the worst. For mine own good 135

---

109 *admired:* dumbfounding. 111 *overcome:* happen to. 112–113 *make me...owe:* usurp my role as a brave man.

124 *Augures:* auguries; *understood relations:* omens (often contained in birds' cries) properly interpreted. 133 *betimes:* quickly.

All causes shall give way. I am in
blood
Stepped in so far that, should I wade
no more,
Returning were as tedious as go o'er.
Strange things I have in head, that
will to hand,
Which must be acted ere they may
be scanned.   140
LADY. You lack the season of all
natures, sleep.
MACBETH. Come, we'll to sleep. My
strange and self-abuse
Is the initiate fear that wants hard
use.
We are yet but young in deed.

Exeunt.

SCENE v. *Thunder. Enter the three*
WITCHES, *meeting* HECATE.

1. WITCH. Why, how now, Hecate!
You look angerly.
HECATE. Have I not reason, beldams
as you are,
Saucy and overbold? How did you
dare
To trade and traffic with Macbeth
In riddles and affairs of death;   5
And I, the mistress of your charms,
The close contriver of all harms,
Was never called to bear my part
Or show the glory of our art?
And, which is worse, all you have
done   10
Hath been but for a wayward son,
Spiteful and wrathful, who, as others
do,
Loves for his own ends, not for you.
But make amends now: get you gone
And at the pit of Acheron   15
Meet me i' the morning. Thither he

Will come to know his destiny.
Your vessels and your spells provide,
Your charms and everything beside.
I am for the air. This night I'll
spend   20
Unto a dismal and a fatal end.
Great business must be wrought ere
noon.
Upon the corner of the moon
There hangs a vap'rous drop pro-
found;
I'll catch it ere it come to ground;   25
And that, distilled by magic sleights,
Shall raise such artificial sprites
As by the strength of their illusion
Shall draw him on to his confusion.
He shall spurn fate, scorn death, and
bear   30
His hopes 'bove wisdom, grace, and
fear;
And you all know security
Is mortals' chiefest enemy. *Music
and a song.*
Hark! I am called. My little spirit,
see,
Sits in a foggy cloud and stays for
me.   [*Exit.*]   35
[*Sing within* "Come away, come away,"
etc.]
1. WITCH. Come, let's make haste:
she'll soon be back again. *Exeunt.*

SCENE vi. *Enter* LENNOX *and another*
LORD.

LENNOX. My former speeches have but
hit your thoughts,
Which can interpret farther. Only I
say
Things have been strangely borne.
The gracious Duncan
Was pitied of Macbeth. Marry, he
was dead!
And the right valiant Banquo walked
too late,   5

---

136 *All causes...way:* all else must take
second place.   142 *self-abuse:* self-imposed
delusion.   143 *initiate fear:* the fearfulness of
the inexperienced.   III.v.2 *beldams:* old hags.
7 *close:* secret.   15 *Acheron:* river in Hell
(here, Hell itself).

---

27 *artificial sprites:* spirits produced by magic.
III.vi.1 *hit:* matched.   3 *borne:* managed.

Whom you may say (if't please you)
Fleance killed,
For Fleance fled. Men must not walk
too late.
Who cannot want the thought how
monstrous
It was for Malcolm and for Donalbain
To kill their gracious father? Dam-
ned fact,   10
How it did grieve Macbeth! Did he
not straight,
In pious rage, the two delinquents
tear
That were the slaves of drink and
thralls of sleep?
Was not that nobly done? Ay, and
wisely too,
For 'twould have angered any heart
alive   15
To hear the men deny 't. So that I
say
He has borne all things well. And
I do think
That, had he Duncan's sons under
his key
(As, an't please heaven, he shall
not), they should find
What 'twere to kill a father. So should
Fleance.   20
But peace! for from broad words, and
'cause he failed
His presence at the tyrant's feast,
I hear
Macduff lives in disgrace. Sir, can
you tell
Where he bestows himself?
LORD.   The son of Duncan,
From whom this tyrant holds the due
of birth,   25
Lives in the English court and is
received
Of the most pious Edward with such
grace

That the malevolence of fortune
nothing
Takes from his high respect. Thither
Macduff
Is gone to pray the holy King upon
his aid   30
To wake Northumberland and war-
like Siward;
That by the help of these (with Him
above
To ratify the work) we may again
Give to our tables meat, sleep to our
nights,
Free from our feasts and banquets
bloody knives,   35
Do faithful homage and receive free
honors—
All which we pine for now. And this
report
Hath so exasperate the King that he
Prepares for some attempt of war.
LENNOX.   Sent he to Macduff?
LORD. He did; and with an absolute
"Sir, not I,"   40
The cloudy messenger turns me his
back
And hums, as who should say, "You'll
rue the time
That clogs me with this answer."
LENNOX.   And that well might
Advise him to a caution, t' hold what
distance
His wisdom can provide. Some holy
angel   45
Fly to the court of England and
unfold
His message ere he come, that a swift
blessing
May soon return to this our suffering
country
Under a hand accursed!
LORD.   I'll send my
prayers with him.   *Exeunt.*

---

8 *cannot want the thought:* can help thinking.
21 *broad:* plain, open.

30 *upon:* for.

ACT IV

SCENE i. *Thunder. Enter the three*
WITCHES.

1. WITCH. Thrice the brinded cat hath
   mewed.
2. WITCH. Thrice, and once the hedge-
   pig whined.
3. WITCH. Harpier cries.—'Tis time,
   'tis time!
1. WITCH. Round about the cauldron
   go;
   In the poisoned entrails throw.   5
   Toad, that under cold stone
   Days and nights has thirty-one
   Swelt'red venom, sleeping got,
   Boil thou first i' the charmed pot.
ALL. Double, double, toil and trou-
   ble,   10
   Fire burn, and cauldron bubble.
2. WITCH. Fillet of a fenny snake,
   In the cauldron boil and bake;
   Eye of newt, and toe of frog,
   Wool of bat, and tongue of dog,   15
   Adder's fork, and blindworm's sting,
   Lizard's leg, and howlet's wing—
   For a charm of pow'rful trouble
   Like a hell broth boil and bubble.
ALL. Double, double, toil and trou-
   ble,   20
   Fire burn, and cauldron bubble.
3. WITCH. Scale of dragon, tooth of
   wolf,
   Witch's mummy, maw and gulf
   Of the ravined salt-sea shark,
   Root of hemlock digged i' the dark, 25
   Liver of blaspheming Jew,
   Gall of goat, and slips of yew
   Slivered in the moon's eclipse,
   Nose of Turk, and Tartar's lips,
   Finger of birth-strangled babe   30
   Ditch-delivered by a drab
   Make the gruel thick and slab.

Add thereto a tiger's chaudron
For the ingredients of our cauldron.
ALL. Double, double, toil and trou-
   ble,   35
   Fire burn, and cauldron bubble.
2. WITCH. Cool it with a baboon's
   blood,
   Then the charm is firm and good.

Enter HECATE *and the other three*
WITCHES.

HECATE. O, well done! I commend
   your pains,
   And everyone shall share i' the
   gains.   40
   And now about the cauldron sing
   Like elves and fairies in a ring,
   Enchanting all that you put in.

Music and a song, "Black spirits," etc.
[*Exeunt* HECATE *and singers.*]

2. WITCH. By the pricking of my
   thumbs,
   Something wicked this way comes. 45
   Open locks,
   Whoever knocks!

Enter MACBETH.

MACBETH. How now, you secret, black,
   and midnight hags,
   What is't you do?
ALL.   A deed without a name.
MACBETH. I conjure you by that which
   you profess,   50
   Howe'er you come to know it, answer
   me.
   Though you untie the winds and let
   them fight
   Against the churches, though the
   yesty waves
   Confound and swallow navigation up,
   Though bladed corn be lodged and
   trees blown down,   55
   Though castles topple on their war-
   ders' heads,

IV.i.1 *brinded:* striped. 3 *Harpier:* the third
witch's spirit. 12 *fenny:* fen-like. 16 *blindworm:* slow-worm, mistakenly thought to be
poisonous. 23 *mummy:* medicine made from
a mummy, or flesh of a mummy. 31 *drab:*
whore.

33 *chaudron:* entrails. 50 *that...profess:*
i.e., black magic.

Though palaces and pyramids do slope
Their heads to their foundations, though the treasure
Of nature's germens tumble all together
Even till destruction sicken, answer me   60
To what I ask you.
1. WITCH.   Speak.
2. WITCH.   Demand.
3. WITCH.   We'll answer.
1. WITCH. Say if th' hadst rather hear it from our mouths
Or from our masters'.
MACBETH.   Call 'em. Let me see 'em.
1. WITCH. Pour in sow's blood that hath eaten
Her nine farrow; grease that's sweaten   65
From the murderer's gibbet throw
Into the flame.
ALL.   Come, high or low,
Thyself and office deftly show!

Thunder. FIRST APPARITION, *an armed Head.*

MACBETH. Tell me, thou unknown power—
1. WITCH.   He knows thy thought:
Hear his speech, but say thou naught.   70
1. APPARITION. Macbeth, Macbeth, Macbeth, beware Macduff!
Beware the Thane of Fife! Dismiss me.—Enough.   *He descends.*
MACBETH. Whate'er thou art, for thy good caution thanks:
Thou hast harped my fear aright.
But one word more—
1. WITCH. He will not be commanded. Here's another,   75
More potent than the first.

Thunder. SECOND APPARITION, *a bloody Child.*

2. APPARITION.   Macbeth, Macbeth, Macbeth—

MACBETH. Had I three ears, I'ld hear thee.
2. APPARITION. Be bloody, bold, and resolute! Laugh to scorn
The power of man, for none of woman born   80
Shall harm Macbeth.   *Descends.*
MACBETH. Then live, Macduff—what need I fear of thee?
But yet I'll make assurance double sure
And take a bond of fate. Thou shalt not live;
That I may tell pale-hearted fear it lies   85
And sleep in spite of thunder.

Thunder. THIRD APPARITION, *a Child crowned, with a tree in his hand.*

                    What is this
That rises like the issue of a king
And wears upon his baby brow the round
And top of sovereignty?
ALL.   Listen, but speak not to't.
3. APPARITION. Be lion-mettled, proud, and take no care   90
Who chafes, who frets, or where conspirers are!
Macbeth shall never vanquished be until
Great Birnam Wood to high Dunsinane Hill
Shall come against him.   *Descends.*
MACBETH.   That will never be.
Who can impress the forest, bid the tree   95
Unfix his earth-bound root? Sweet bodements, good!
Rebellious dead rise never till the Wood
Of Birnam rise, and our high-placed Macbeth
Shall live the lease of nature, pay his breath

---

59 *nature's germens:* seeds of life. 68 *office:* special powers.

88 *round:* crown. 95 *impress:* draft into military service. 99 *lease of nature:* natural lifespan.

To time and mortal custom. Yet my
   heart   100
Throbs to know one thing. Tell me,
   if your art
Can tell so much: Shall Banquo's
   issue ever
Reign in this kingdom?
ALL.   Seek to know no more.
MACBETH. I will be satisfied. Deny me
   this,
And an eternal curse fall on you!
   Let me know.   105
Why sinks that cauldron? and what
   noise is this? *Hautboys.*
1. WITCH. Show!
2. WITCH. Show!
3. WITCH. Show!
ALL. Show his eyes, and grieve his
   heart!   110
Come like shadows, so depart!

A show of eight KINGS *and* BANQUO'S
GHOST, [*the last* KING] *with a glass in
his hand.*

MACBETH. Thou art too like the spirit
   of Banquo. Down!
Thy crown does sear mine eyeballs.
   And thy hair,
Thou other gold-bound brow, is like
   the first.
A third is like the former. Filthy
   hags,   115
Why do you show me this? A fourth?
   Start, eyes!
What, will the line stretch out to the
   crack of doom?
Another yet? A seventh? I'll see no
   more.
And yet the eighth appears, who
   bears a glass
Which shows me many more; and
   some I see   120
That twofold balls and treble sceptres
   carry.

Horrible sight! Now I see 'tis true;
For the blood-boltered Banquo smiles
   upon me
And points at them for his. What?
   Is this so?
1. WITCH. Ay, sir, all this is so. But
   why   125
Stands Macbeth thus amazedly?
Come, sisters, cheer we up his sprites
And show the best of our delights.
I'll charm the air to give a sound
While   you   perform   your   antic
   round,   130
That this great king may kindly say
Our duties did his welcome pay.

Music. The WITCHES *dance and vanish.*

MACBETH. Where are they? Gone? Let
   this pernicious hour
Stand aye accursed in the calendar!
Come in, without there!

Enter LENNOX.

LENNOX.   What's your
   Grace's will?   135
MACBETH. Saw you the weird sisters?
LENNOX.   No, my lord.
MACBETH. Came they not by you?
LENNOX.   No indeed, my lord.
MACBETH. Infected be the air whereon
   they ride,
And dammed all those that trust
   them! I did hear
The galloping of horse. Who was't
   came by?   140
LENNOX. 'Tis two or three, my lord,
   that bring you word
Macduff is fled to England.
MACBETH.   Fled to England?
LENNOX. Ay, my good lord.
MACBETH. [*aside*] Time, thou antici-
   pat'st my dread exploits.
The flighty purpose never is o'er-
   took   145
Unless the deed go with it. From
   this moment

---

100 *mortal custom:* natural death.   121 *twofold...sceptres:* insignia of England and Scotland, united when King James V of Scotland
became, in 1603, King James I of England.
Banquo was supposed to be an ancestor of
James.

---

123 *blood-boltered:* blood-coated.   130 *antic
round:* fantastic circular dance.   144 *antici-
pat'st:* forestall'st.   145 *flighty:* hastening.

The very firstlings of my heart shall be
The firstlings of my hand. And even now,
To crown my thoughts with acts, be it thought and done:
The castle of Macduff I will surprise,   150
Seize upon Fife, give to the edge o' the sword
His wife, his babes, and all unfortunate souls
That trace him in his line. No boasting like a fool;
This deed I'll do before this purpose cool.
But no more sights!—Where are these gentlemen?   155
Come, bring me where they are.

Exeunt.

SCENE ii. *Enter* MACDUFF'S WIFE, *her* SON, *and* ROSS.

WIFE. What had he done to make him fly the land?
ROSS. You must have patience, madam.
WIFE.   He had none.
His flight was madness. When our actions do not,
Our fears do make us traitors.
ROSS.   You know not
Whether it was his wisdom or his fear.   5
WIFE. Wisdom? To leave his wife, to leave his babes,
His mansion and his titles in a place
From whence himself does fly? He loves us not,
He wants the natural touch. For the poor wren
(The most diminutive of birds) will fight,   10
Her young ones in her nest, against the owl.
All is the fear and nothing is the love;

As little is the wisdom, where the flight
So runs against all reason.
ROSS.   My dearest coz,
I pray you school yourself. But for your husband,   15
He is noble, wise, judicious, and best knows
The fits o' the season. I dare not speak much further,
But cruel are the times when we are traitors
And do not know ourselves; when we hold rumor
From what we fear, yet know not what we fear   20
But float upon a wild and violent sea
Each way and none. I take my leave of you.
Shall not be long but I'll be here again.
Things at the worst will cease, or else climb upward
To what they were before.—My pretty cousin,   25
Blessing upon you!
WIFE. Fathered he is, and yet he's fatherless.
ROSS. I am so much a fool, should I stay longer
It would be my disgrace and your discomfort.
I take my leave at once.   [*Exit.*]
WIFE.   Sirrah, your father's dead;   30
And what will you do now? How will you live?
SON. As birds do, mother.
WIFE.   What, with worms and flies?
SON. With what I get, I mean; and so do they.
WIFE. Poor bird! thou'dst never fear the net nor lime,
The pitfall nor the gin.   35

IV.ii.9 *wants...touch:* lacks natural protectiveness.

14 *coz:* cousin. 15 *school:* learn restraint.
19 *know ourselves:* know that we are traitors.
29 *It would...discomfort:* i.e., he would weep. 34 *lime:* birdlime. 35 *gin:* trap.

SON. Why should I, mother? Poor birds they are not set for.

My father is not dead for all your saying.

WIFE. Yes, he is dead. How wilt thou do for a father?

SON. Nay, how will you do for a husband?

WIFE. Why, I can buy me twenty at any market. 40

SON. Then you'll buy 'em to sell again.

WIFE. Thou speak'st with all thy wit; and yet, i' faith,

With wit enough for thee.

SON. Was my father a traitor, mother?

WIFE. Ay, that he was! 45

SON. What is a traitor?

WIFE. Why, one that swears and lies.

SON. And be all traitors that do so?

WIFE. Everyone that does so is a traitor and must be hanged. 50

SON. And must they all be hanged that swear and lie?

WIFE. Everyone.

SON. Who must hang them?

WIFE. Why, the honest men.

SON. Then the liars and swearers 55 are fools, for there are liars and swearers enow to beat the honest men and hang up them.

WIFE. Now God help thee, poor monkey! But how wilt thou do for 60 a father?

SON. If he were dead, you'ld weep for him. If you would not, it were a good sign that I should quickly have a new father. 65

WIFE. Poor prattler, how thou talk'st!

Enter a MESSENGER.

MESSENGER. Bless you, fair dame! I am not to you known,

Though in your state of honor I am perfect.

I doubt some danger does approach you nearly.

If you will take a homely man's advice, 70

Be not found here. Hence with your little ones!

To fright you thus methinks I am too savage;

To do worse to you were fell cruelty,

Which is too nigh your person. Heaven preserve you!

I dare abide no longer. *Exit.*

WIFE. Whither should I fly? 75

I have done no harm. But I remember now

I am in this earthly world, where to do harm

Is often laudable, to do good sometime

Accounted dangerous folly. Why then, alas,

Do I put up that womanly defense 80

To say I have done no harm?

Enter MURDERERS.

What are these faces?

MURDERER. Where is your husband?

WIFE. I hope in no place so unsanctified

Where such as thou mayst find him.

MURDERER. He's a traitor.

SON. Thou liest, thou shag-eared villain!

MURDERER. What, you egg! 85

[*Stabs him.*]

Young fry of treachery!

SON. He has killed me, mother.

Run away, I pray you! [*Dies.*]

Exit [LADY MACDUFF], *crying* "Murder!" [*pursued by* MURDERERS].

SCENE iii. *Enter* MALCOLM *and* MACDUFF.

MALCOLM. Let us seek out some desolate shade, and there

Weep our sad bosoms empty.

MACDUFF. Let us rather

Hold fast the mortal sword, and like good men,

---

41 *sell:* sell them out, betray. 68 *in your...
perfect:* I know your high rank. 69 *doubt:* fear.

Bestride our downfall'n birthdom.
  Each new morn
New widows howl, new orphans cry,
  new sorrows   5
Strike heaven on the face, that it
  resounds
As if it felt with Scotland and yelled
  out
Like syllable of dolor.
MALCOLM.   What I believe, I'll wail;
  What know, believe; and what I can
  redress,
As I shall find the time to friend, I
  will.   10
What you have spoke, it may be so
  perchance.
This tyrant, whose sole name blisters
  our tongues,
Was once thought honest; you have
  loved him well;
He hath not touched you yet. I am
  young; but something
You may deserve of him through me,
  and wisdom   15
To offer up a weak, poor, innocent
  lamb
T' appease an angry god.
MACDUFF. I am not treacherous.
MALCOLM.   But Macbeth is.
A good and virtuous nature may
  recoil
In an imperial charge. But I shall
  crave your pardon.   20
That which you are, my thoughts
  cannot transpose:
Angels are bright still though the
  brightest fell;
Though all things foul would wear
  the brows of grace,
Yet grace must still look so.
MACDUFF.   I have lost my hopes.
MALCOLM. Perchance even there where
  I did find my doubts.   25

Why in that rawness left you wife
  and child,
Those precious motives, those strong
  knots of love,
Without leave-taking? I pray you,
Let not my jealousies be your dis-
  honors,
But mine own safeties. You may be
  rightly just   30
Whatever I shall think.
MACDUFF.   Bleed, bleed,
  poor country!
Great tyranny, lay thou thy basis
  sure,
For goodness dare not check thee,
  wear thou thy wrongs,
The title is affeered! Fare thee well,
  lord.
I would not be the villain that thou
  think'st   35
For the whole space that's in the
  tyrant's grasp
And the rich East to boot.
MALCOLM.   Be not offended.
I speak not as in absolute fear of you.
I think our country sinks beneath the
  yoke.
It weeps, it bleeds, and each new day
  a gash   40
Is added to her wounds. I think
  withal
There would be hands uplifted in my
  right;
And here from gracious England have
  I offer
Of goodly thousands. But, for all
  this,
When I shall tread upon the tyrant's
  head   45
Or wear it on my sword, yet my poor
  country
Shall have more vices than it had
  before,
More suffer, and more sundry ways
  than ever,
By him that shall succeed.

IV.iii.8 *Like syllable:* with comparable sounds.
14–15 *but...me:* but you may be rewarded
by him for betraying me. 15 *wisdom:* it
would be smart. 19 *recoil:* give way. 20
In an imperial charge: before a king's command. 22 *the brightest:* Lucifer.

---

26 *rawness:* vulnerable state. 29 *jealousies:*
suspicions. 34 *affeered:* confirmed. 38 *absolute:* total.

MACDUFF.   What should he be?

MALCOLM. It is myself I mean, in
   whom I know   50
  All the particulars of vice so grafted
  That, when they shall be opened,
   black Macbeth
  Will seem as pure as snow, and the
   poor state
  Esteem him as a lamb, being com-
   pared
  With my confineless harms.

MACDUFF.   Not in the legions 55
  Of horrid hell can come a devil more
   damned
  In evils to top Macbeth.

MALCOLM.   I grant him bloody,
  Luxurious, avaricious, false, deceitful,
  Sudden, malicious, smacking of every
   sin
  That has a name. But there's no
   bottom, none,   60
  In my voluptuousness. Your wives,
   your daughters,
  Your matrons, and your maids could
   not fill up
  The cistern of my lust; and my
   desire
  All continent impediments would
   o'erbear
  That did oppose my will. Better
   Macbeth   65
  Than such an one to reign.

MACDUFF.   Boundless intemperance
  In nature is a tyranny. It hath been
  The untimely emptying of the happy
   throne
  And fall of many kings. But fear
   not yet
  To take upon you what is yours.
   You may   70
  Convey your pleasures in a spacious
   plenty
  And yet seem cold—the time you
   may so hoodwink.
  We have willing dames enough. There
   cannot be

  That vulture in you to devour so
   many
  As will to greatness dedicate themselves,   75
  Finding it so inclined.

MALCOLM.   With this there grows
  In my most ill-composed affection
   such
  A stanchless avarice that, were I
   King
  I should cut off the nobles for their
   lands,
  Desire his jewels, and this other's
   house,   80
  And my more-having would be as a
   sauce
  To make me hunger more, that I
   should forge
  Quarrels unjust against the good and
   loyal,
  Destroying them for wealth.

MACDUFF.   This avarice
  Sticks deeper, grows with more per-
   nicious root   85
  Than summer-seeming lust, and it
   hath been
  The sword of our slain kings. Yet do
   not fear.
  Scotland hath foisons to fill up your
   will
  Of your mere own. All these are
   portable,
  With other graces weighed.   90

MALCOLM. But I have none. The king-
   becoming graces,
  As justice, verity, temp'rance, stable-
   ness,
  Bounty, perseverance, mercy, lowli-
   ness,
  Devotion, patience, courage, fortitude,
  I have no relish of them, but
   abound   95
  In the division of each several crime,
  Acting it many ways. Nay, had I
   power, I should

---

51 *particulars:* various aspects. 58 *Luxurious:*
lecherous. 64 *continent:* chaste and restraining.

77 *ill-composed affection:* disordered will. 87
sword: killer. 88 *foisons:* plenty. 89 *mere
own:* own property; *portable:* bearable. 96
In the division of: in every part of.

They presently amend.

MALCOLM.   I thank you, doctor. 145

Exit [DOCTOR].

MACDUFF. What's the disease he means?

MALCOLM.   'Tis called the evil.
A most miraculous work in this good
King,
Which often since my here-remain in
England
I have seen him do: how he solicits
heaven
Himself best knows, but strangely
visited people,   150
All swol'n and ulcerous, pitiful to
the eye,
The mere despair of surgery, he
cures,
Hanging a golden stamp about their
necks,
Put on with holy prayers; and 'tis
spoken,   154
To the succeeding royalty he leaves
The healing benediction. With this
strange virtue,
He hath a heavenly gift of prophecy,
And sundry blessings hang about his
throne
That speak him full of grace.

Enter ROSS.

MACDUFF.   See who comes here.

MALCOLM. My countryman; but yet
I know him not.   160

MACDUFF. My ever gentle cousin, welcome hither.

MALCOLM. I know him now. Good God
betimes remove
The means that makes us strangers!

ROSS.   Sir, amen.

MACDUFF. Stands Scotland where it
did?

ROSS.   Alas, poor country,
Almost afraid to know itself. It
cannot   165
Be called our mother but our grave,
where nothing

But who knows nothing is once seen
to smile;
Where sighs and groans, and shrieks
that rent the air,
Are made, not marked; where violent
sorrow seems
A modern ecstasy. The dead man's
knell   170
Is there scarce asked for who, and
good men's lives
Expire before the flowers in their
caps,
Dying or ere they sicken.

MACDUFF.   O, relation
Too nice, and yet too true!

MALCOLM.   What's
the newest grief?

ROSS. That of an hour's age doth hiss
the speaker;   175
Each minute teems a new one.

MACDUFF.   How does my wife?

ROSS. Why, well.

MACDUFF. And all my children?

ROSS.   Well too.

MACDUFF. The tyrant has not battered
at their peace?

ROSS. No, they were well at peace
when I did leave 'em.

MACDUFF. Be not a niggard of your
speech. How goes't?   180

ROSS. When I came hither to transport
the tidings
Which I have heavily borne, there
ran a rumor
Of many worthy fellows that were
out,
Which was to my belief witnessed the
rather
For that I saw the tyrant's power
afoot.   185
Now is the time of help. Your eye
in Scotland
Would create soldiers, make our
women fight

---

167 *who:* the man who. 169 *marked:* noticed.
170 *modern ecstasy:* ordinary emotion. 173
or ere: before. 173–74 *relation Too nice:*
account too detailed and exact. 176 *teems:*
brings forth. 183 *out:* in arms. 184 *witnessed:* affirmed.

---

146 *evil:* king's evil (scrofula). 150 *visited:*
afflicted. 152 *mere:* total. 162 *betimes:*
hastily.

Pour the sweet milk of concord into
hell,
Uproar the universal peace, confound
All unity on earth.
MACDUFF. O Scotland, Scotland! 100
MALCOLM. If such a one be fit to
govern, speak.
I am as I have spoken.
MACDUFF.   Fit to govern?
No, not to live! O nation miserable,
With an untitled tyrant bloody-
sceptred,
When shalt thou see thy wholesome
days again,   105
Since that the truest issue of thy
throne
By his own interdiction stands
accursed
And does blaspheme his breed? Thy
royal father
Was a most sainted king; the queen
that bore thee,
Oft'ner upon her knees than on her
feet,   110
Died every day she lived. Fare thee
well.
These evils thou repeat'st upon thy-
self
Hath banished me from Scotland. O
my breast,
Thy hope ends here!
MALCOLM.   Macduff, this
noble passion,
Child of integrity, hath from my
soul   115
Wiped the black scruples, reconciled
my thoughts
To thy good truth and honor. Devilish
Macbeth
By many of these trains hath sought
to win me
Into his power; and modest wisdom
plucks me
From overcredulous haste; but God
above   120
Deal between thee and me, for even
now

I put myself to thy direction and
Unspeak mine own detraction, h(
abjure
The taints and blames I laid up
myself
For strangers to my nature. I
yet
Unknown to woman, never was f
sworn,
Scarcely have coveted what was m
own,
At no time broke my faith, wo
not betray
The devil to his fellow, and delight
No less in truth than life. My f
false speaking
Was this upon myself. What I
truly,
Is thine and my poor country'!
command;
Whither indeed, before thy h
approach,
Old Siward with ten thousand wai
men
Already at a point was setting f(
Now we'll together; and the ch;
of goodness
Be like our warranted quarrel! '
are you silent?
MACDUFF. Such welcome and un
come things at once
'Tis hard to reconcile.

Enter a DOCTOR.

MALCOLM. Well, more anon. Come!
King forth, I pray you?
DOCTOR. Ay, sir. There are a cre'
wretched souls
That stay his cure. Their ma
convinces
The great assay of art; but a'
touch,
Such sanctity hath heaven give!
hand,

---

107 *interdiction:* prohibition. 111 *Died:*
renounced worldly life. 118 *trains:* devices.

131 *upon:* against. 135 *at a point:* :
and ready. 136 *goodness:* success. 137
ranted: justified. 142 *convinces:* d(
143 *assay of art:* efforts of medical s(

To doff their dire distresses.

MALCOLM.   Be't their comfort
We are coming thither. Gracious
  England hath
Lent us good Siward and ten thousand
  men,   190
An older and a better soldier none
That Christendom gives out.

ROSS.   Would I could answer
This comfort with the like. But I
  have words
That would be howled out in the
  desert air,
Where hearing should not latch them.

MACDUFF.   What concern they, 195
The general cause or is it a fee-grief
Due to some single breast?

ROSS.   No mind that's honest
But in it shares some woe, though
  the main part
Pertains to you alone.

MACDUFF.   If it be mine,
Keep it not from me, quickly let
  me have it.   200

ROSS. Let not your ears despise my
  tongue forever,
Which shall possess them with the
  heaviest sound
That ever yet they heard.

MACDUFF.   Humh! I guess at it.

ROSS. Your castle is surprised, your
  wife and babes
Savagely slaughtered. To relate the
  manner   205
Were, on the quarry of these murdered deer,
To add the death of you.

MALCOLM.   Merciful heaven!
What, man! Ne'er pull your hat
  upon your brows.
Give sorrow words. The grief that
  does not speak
Whispers the o'erfraught heart and
  bids it break.   210

MACDUFF. My children too?

ROSS.   Wife, children, servants, all
That could be found.

MACDUFF.   And I must be
  from thence?
My wife killed too?

ROSS.   I have said.

MALCOLM.   Be comforted.
Let's make us med'cines of our great
  revenge
To cure this deadly grief.   215

MACDUFF. He has no children. All my
  pretty ones?
Did you say all? O hell-kite! All?
What, all my pretty chickens and
  their dam
At one fell swoop?

MALCOLM. Dispute it like a man.

MACDUFF.   I shall do so; 220
But I must also feel it as a man.
I cannot but remember such things
  were
That were most precious to me. Did
  heaven look on
And would not take their part? Sinful
  Macduff,
They were all struck for thee! Naught
  that I am,   225
Not for their own demerits but for
  mine
Fell slaughter on their souls. Heaven
  rest them now!

MALCOLM. Be this the whetstone of
  your sword. Let grief
Convert to anger; blunt not the
  heart, enrage it.

MACDUFF. O, I could play the woman
  with mine eyes   230
And braggart with my tongue. But,
  gentle heavens,
Cut short all intermission. Front to
  front
Bring thou this fiend of Scotland and
  myself.
Within my sword's length set him.
  If he scape,
Heaven forgive him too!

---

195 *latch:* catch. 196 *fee-grief:* private grief.
197 *honest:* honorable. 204 *surprised:* suddenly attacked. 206 *quarry:* heap of slaughtered animals.

220 *Dispute:* fight against. 225 *Naught:*
wicked. 232 *intermission:* postponement;
Front: face.

MALCOLM.   This time goes manly.
Come, go we to the King. Our power
  is ready;
Our lack is nothing but our leave.
  Macbeth
Is ripe for shaking, and the powers

above
Put on their instruments. Receive
  what cheer you may.
The night is long that never finds
  the day.   *Exeunt.* 240

ACT V

SCENE i. *Enter a* DOCTOR *of Physic and
a* WAITING GENTLEWOMAN.

DOCTOR. I have two nights watched
with you, but can perceive no truth
in your report. When was it she
last walked?

GENTLEWOMAN. Since his Majesty 5
went into the field I have seen her
rise from her bed, throw her nightgown upon her, unlock her closet,
take forth paper, fold it, write upon't,
read it, afterwards seal it, and 10
again return to bed; yet all this
while in a most fast sleep.

DOCTOR. A great perturbation in nature, to receive at once the benefit
of sleep and do the effects of 15
watching! In this slumb'ry agitation,
besides her walking and other actual
performances, what (at any time)
have you heard her say?

GENTLEWOMAN. That, sir, which I 20
will not report after her.

DOCTOR. You may to me, and 'tis most
meet you should.

GENTLEWOMAN. Neither to you nor
anyone, having no witness to 25
confirm my speech.

Enter LADY [MACBETH], *with a taper.*

Lo you, here she comes! This is her
very guise, and, upon my life, fast
asleep! Observe her; stand close.

DOCTOR. How came she by that 30
light?

GENTLEWOMAN. Why, it stood by her.
She has light by her continually.
'Tis her command.

DOCTOR. You see her eyes are open. 35

GENTLEWOMAN. Ay, but their sense are
shut.

DOCTOR. What is it she does now?
Look how she rubs her hands.

GENTLEWOMAN. It is an accustomed 40
action with her, to seem thus washing her hands. I have known her
continue in this a quarter of an hour.

LADY. Yet here's a spot.

DOCTOR. Hark, she speaks. I will 45
set down what comes from her, to
satisfy my remembrance the more
strongly.

LADY. Out, damned spot! Out, I say!
One—two—why then 'tis time to 50
do't. Hell is murky. Fie, my lord, fie!
a soldier and afeard? What need we
fear who knows it, when none can
call our power to accompt? Yet who
would have thought the old man 55
to have had so much blood in him?

DOCTOR. Do you mark that?

LADY. The Thane of Fife had a wife.
Where is she now? What, will these
hands ne'er be clean? No more 60
o' that, my lord, no more o' that!
You mar all with this starting.

DOCTOR. Go to, go to! You have known
what you should not.

GENTLEWOMAN. She has spoke what 65
she should not, I am sure of that.
Heaven knows what she has known.

LADY. Here's the smell of the blood
still. All the perfumes of Arabia will
not sweeten this little hand. Oh, 70
oh, oh!

DOCTOR. What a sigh is there! The
heart is sorely charged.

---

239 *Put on:* advance; *instruments:* agents.
V.i.62 *starting:* shying.

GENTLEWOMAN. I would not have such a heart in my bosom for the dig- 75 nity of the whole body.
DOCTOR. Well, well, well.
GENTLEWOMAN. Pray God it be, sir.
DOCTOR. This disease is beyond my practice. Yet I have known those 80 which have walked in their sleep who have died holily in their beds.
LADY. Wash your hands, put on your nightgown, look not so pale! I tell you yet again, Banquo's buried. 85 He cannot come out on's grave.
DOCTOR. Even so?
LADY. To bed, to bed! There's knocking at the gate. Come, come, come, come, give me your hand! What's 90 done cannot be undone. To bed, to bed, to bed! *Exit.*
DOCTOR. Will she go now to bed?
GENTLEWOMAN. Directly.
DOCTOR. Foul whisp'rings are abroad. Unnatural deeds 95
Do breed unnatural troubles. Infected minds
To their deaf pillows will discharge their secrets.
More needs she the divine than the physician.
God, God forgive us all! Look after her;
Remove from her the means of all annoyance, 100
And still keep eyes upon her. So good night.
My mind she has mated, and amazed my sight.
I think, but dare not speak.
GENTLEWOMAN. Good night, good doctor. *Exeunt.*

SCENE ii. *Drum and Colors. Enter* MENTEITH, CAITHNESS, ANGUS, LENNOX, *and* SOLDIERS.

MENTEITH. The English pow'r is near, led on by Malcolm,
His uncle Siward, and the good Macduff.
Revenges burn in them; for their dear causes
Would to the bleeding and the grim alarm
Excite the mortified man.
ANGUS. Near Birnam Wood 5
Shall we well meet them; that way are they coming.
CAITHNESS. Who knows if Donalbain be with his brother?
LENNOX. For certain, sir, he is not. I have a file
Of all the gentry. There is Siward's son
And many unrough youths that even now 10
Protest their first of manhood.
MENTEITH. What does the tyrant?
CAITHNESS. Great Dunsinane he strongly fortifies.
Some say he's mad; others, that lesser hate him,
Do call it valiant fury; but for certain
He cannot buckle his distempered cause 15
Within the belt of rule.
ANGUS. Now does he feel
His secret murders sticking on his hands.
Now minutely revolts upbraid his faith-breach.
Those he commands move only in command,
Nothing in love. Now does he feel his title 20
Hang loose about him, like a giant's robe
Upon a dwarfish thief.
MENTEITH. Who then shall blame
His pestered senses to recoil and start,
When all that is within him does condemn

---

100 *annoyance:* physical harm. 102 *mated:* bewildered.

V.ii.5 *mortified:* dead. 18 *minutely:* every minute; *revolts:* defectors.

Itself for being there?

CAITHNESS   Well, march we on   25
To give obedience where 'tis truly
    owed.
Meet we the med'cine of the sickly
    weal;
And with him pour we in our coun-
    try's purge
Each drop of us.

LENNOX.   Or so much as it needs
To dew the sovereign flower and
    drown the weeds.   30
Make we our march towards Birnam.

Exeunt, marching.

SCENE iii. *Enter* MACBETH, DOCTOR,
and ATTENDANTS.

MACBETH. Bring me no more reports.
    Let them fly all!
Till Birnam Wood remove to Dunsi-
    nane,
I cannot taint with fear. What's the
    boy Malcolm?
Was he not born of woman? The
    spirits that know
All mortal consequences have pro-
    nounced me thus: 5
"Fear not, Macbeth. No man that's
    born of woman
Shall e'er have power upon thee."
    Then fly, false thanes,
And mingle with the English epicures.
The mind I sway by and the heart
    I bear
Shall never sag with doubt nor shake
    with fear.   10

Enter SERVANT.

The devil damn thee black, thou
    cream-faced loon!
Where got'st thou that goose look?

SERVANT. There is ten thousand—

MACBETH.   Geese, villain?

SERVANT.   Soldiers, sir,

MACBETH. Go prick thy face and over-

---

27 *med'cine:* i.e., Malcolm; *weal:* country.
V.iii.14 *prick...fear:* draw blood and smear
it over your pallor.

---

red thy fear,
Thou lily-livered boy. What soldiers,
    patch?   15
Death of thy soul; those linen cheeks
    of thine
Are counsellors to fear. What sol-
    diers, whey-face?

SERVANT. The English force, so please
    you.

MACBETH. Take thy face hence.

[*Exit* SERVANT.]

    Seyton!—I am sick at heart,
When I behold—Seyton, I say—This
    push   20
Will cheer me ever, or disseat me
    now.
I have lived long enough. My way
    of life
Is fall'n into the sear, the yellow leaf,
And that which should accompany
    old age,
As honor, love, obedience, troops of
    friends,   25
I must not look to have; but, in their
    stead,
Curses not loud but deep, mouth-
    honor, breath,
Which the poor heart would fain
    deny, and dare not.
Seyton!

Enter SEYTON.

SEYTON. What's your gracious pleasure?

MACBETH.   What news more?   30

SEYTON. All is confirmed, my lord,
    which was reported.

MACBETH. I'll fight till from my bones
    my flesh be hacked.
Give me my armor.

SEYTON.   'Tis not needed yet.

MACBETH. I'll put it on.
Send out moe horses, skirr the coun-
    try round,   35
Hang those that talk of fear. Give
    me mine armor.
How does your patient, doctor?

DOCTOR.   Not so sick, my lord,
As she is troubled with thick-coming

---

15 *patch:* dolt. 35 *skirr:* scour.

fancies
That keep her from her rest.
MACBETH.　　　　　Cure her of that!
Canst thou not minister to a mind
　diseased,　　　　　　　　　40
Pluck from the memory a rooted
　sorrow,
Raze out the written troubles of the
　brain,
And with some sweet oblivious anti-
　dote
Cleanse the stuffed bosom of that
　perilous stuff
Which weighs upon the heart?
DOCTOR.　　　Therein the patient　45
Must minister to himself.
MACBETH. Throw physic to the dogs,
　I'll none of it!
Come, put mine armor on. Give me
　my staff.
Seyton, send out.—Doctor, the thanes
　fly from me.—
Come, sir, dispatch.—If thou couldst,
　doctor, cast　　　　　　　50
The water of my land, find her
　disease,
And purge it to a sound and pristine
　health,
I would applaud thee to the very
　echo,
That should applaud again.—Pull't
　off, I say.—
What rhubarb, senna, or what purga-
　tive drug　　　　　　　55
Would scour these English hence?
　Hear'st thou of them?
DOCTOR. Ay, my good lord. Your royal
　preparation
Makes us hear something.
MACBETH.　　　　Bring it after me!
I will not be afraid of death and
　bane
Till Birnam Forest come to Dunsi-
　nane.　　　　　　　　　60
　　　[*Exeunt all but the* DOCTOR.]
DOCTOR. Were I from Dunsinane away
　and clear,

Profit again should hardly draw me
　here.　　　　　　　　*Exit.*

SCENE iv. *Drum and colors. Enter*
MALCOLM, SIWARD, MACDUFF, SIWARD'S
SON, MENTEITH, CAITHNESS, ANGUS,
[LENNOX, ROSS,] *and* SOLDIERS, *march-
ing.*

MALCOLM. Cousins, I hope the days
　are near at hand
That chambers will be safe.
MENTEITH.　　　We doubt it nothing.
SIWARD. What wood is this before us?
MENTEITH.　　　The Wood of Birnam.
MALCOLM. Let every soldier hew him
　down a bough
And bear't before him. Thereby shall
　we shadow　　　　　　　5
The numbers of our host and make
　discovery
Err in report of us.
SOLDIERS.　　　　　It shall be done.
SIWARD. We learn no other but the
　confident tyrant
Keeps still in Dunsinane and will
　endure
Our setting down before't.
MALCOLM.　　　'Tis his main hope,　10
For where there is advantage to be
　given
Both more and less have given him
　the revolt,
And none serve with him but con-
　strained things
Whose hearts are absent too.
MACDUFF.　　　Let our just censures
Attend the true event, and put we
　on　　　　　　　　　15
Industrious soldiership.
SIWARD.　　　　The time approaches
That will with due decision make
　us know
What we shall say we have and what
　we owe.

---

47 *physic:* medicine. 50 *dispatch:* hurry.
50–51 *cast...water:* analyze the urine.

V.iv.2 *chambers:* sleeping rooms. 12 *more
and less:* nobles and commoners. 15 *Attend
...event:* await the outcome.

Thoughts speculative their unsure hopes relate,
But certain issue strokes must arbitrate—   20
Towards which advance the war.

Exeunt, marching.

SCENE V. *Enter* MACBETH, SEYTON, *and* SOLDIERS, *with drum and colors.*

MACBETH. Hang out our banners on the outward walls.
The cry is still, "They come!" Our castle's strength
Will laugh a siege to scorn. Here let them lie
Till famine and ague eat them up.
Were they not forced with those that should be ours,   5
We might have met them dareful, beard to beard,
And beat them backward home.

A cry within of women.

What is that noise?
SEYTON. It is the cry of women, my good lord.   [*Exit.*]
MACBETH. I have almost forgot the taste of fears.
The time has been my senses would have cooled   10
To hear a night-shriek, and my fell of hair
Would at a dismal treatise rouse and stir
As life were in't. I have supped full with horrors.
Direness, familiar to my slaughterous thoughts,
Cannot once start me.

[*Enter* SEYTON.]

Wherefore was that cry?   15
SEYTON. The Queen, my lord, is dead.
MACBETH. She should have died hereafter;

There would have been a time for such a word.
Tomorrow, and tomorrow, and tomorrow
Creeps in this petty pace from day to day,   20
To the last syllable of recorded time;
And all our yesterdays have lighted fools
The way to dusty death. Out, out, brief candle!
Life's but a walking shadow, a poor player
That struts and frets his hour upon the stage   25
And then is heard no more. It is a tale
Told by an idiot, full of sound and fury,
Signifying nothing.

Enter a MESSENGER.

Thou com'st to use thy tongue: thy story quickly!
MESSENGER. Gracious my lord,   30
I should report that which I say I saw,
But know not how to do't.
MACBETH.   Well, say, sir.
MESSENGER. As I did stand my watch upon the hill,
I looked toward Birnam, and anon methought
The wood began to move.
MACBETH.   Liar and slave!   35
MESSENGER. Let me endure your wrath if't be not so.
Within this three mile may you see it coming.
I say, a moving grove.
MACBETH.   If thou speak'st false,
Upon the next tree shall thou hang alive
Till famine cling thee. If thy speech be sooth,   40
I care not if thou dost for me as much.
I pull in resolution, and begin

---

19 *Thoughts...relate:* guesses as to the future merely reflect our hopes. V.v.5 *forced:* reinforced. 11 *fell:* pelt.

40 *cling:* shrivel; *sooth:* true. 42 *pull in:* rein in.

To doubt the equivocation of the fiend,
That lies like truth. "Fear not, till Birnam Wood
Do come to Dunsinane!" and now a wood   45
Comes toward Dunsinane. Arm, arm, and out!
If this which he avouches does appear,
There is nor flying hence nor tarrying here.
I 'gin to be aweary of the sun,
And wish the estate o' the world were now undone.   50
Ring the alarum bell! Blow wind, come wrack,
At least we'll die with harness on our back.   *Exeunt.*

SCENE vi. *Drum and colors. Enter* MALCOLM, SIWARD, MACDUFF, *and their* ARMY, *with boughs.*

MALCOLM. Now near enough. Your leavy screens throw down
And show like those you are. You, worthy uncle,
Shall with my cousin, your right noble son,
Lead our first battle. Worthy Macduff and we
Shall take upon's what else remains to do,   5
According to our order.
SIWARD.   Fare you well.
Do we but find the tyrant's power tonight,
Let us be beaten if we cannot fight.
MACDUFF. Make all our trumpets speak, give them all breath,
Those clamorous harbingers of blood and death.   10

          Exeunt. Alarums continued.

SCENE vii. *Enter* MACBETH.

MACBETH. They have tied me to a stake. I cannot fly,
But bearlike I must fight the course. What's he
That was not born of woman? Such a one
Am I to fear, or none.

Enter YOUNG SIWARD.

YOUNG SIWARD. What is thy name?
MACBETH.   Thou'lt be afraid to hear it.   5
YOUNG SIWARD. No, though thou call'st thyself a hotter name
Than any is in hell.
MACBETH.   My name's Macbeth.
YOUNG SIWARD. The devil himself could not pronounce a title
More hateful to mine ear.
MACBETH.   No, nor more fearful.
YOUNG SIWARD. Thou liest, abhorred tyrant! With my sword   10
I'll prove the lie thou speak'st.

Fight, and YOUNG SIWARD *slain.*

MACBETH.   Thou wast born of woman.
But swords I smile at, weapons laugh to scorn,
Brandished by man that's of a woman born.   *Exit.*

Alarums. Enter MACDUFF.

MACDUFF. That way the noise is. Tyrant, show thy face!
If thou beest slain and with no stroke of mine,   15
My wife and children's ghosts will haunt me still.
I cannot strike at wretched kerns, whose arms
Are hired to bear their staves. Either thou, Macbeth,
Or else my sword with an unbattered edge
I sheathe again undeeded. There thou shouldst be: 20

V.vii.1 *stake:* to which bears were chained to be baited by dogs. 17 *kerns:* ordinary foot soldiers. 18 *staves:* spears.

V.vi.4 *battle:* battalion. 6 *order:* plans.

By this great clatter one of greatest
note
Seems bruited. Let me find him,
Fortune,
And more I beg not! *Exit. Alarums.*

Enter MALCOLM *and* SIWARD.

SIWARD. This way, my lord. The castle's
gently rend'red:
The tyrant's people on both sides do
fight,   25
The noble thanes do bravely in the
war,
The day almost itself professes yours
And little is to do.
MALCOLM.   We have met with foes
That strike beside us.
SIWARD.   Enter, sir, the castle.
                    Exeunt. Alarum.

SCENE viii. *Enter* MACBETH.

MACBETH. Why should I play the
Roman fool and die
On mine own sword? Whiles I see
lives, the gashes
Do better upon them.

Enter MACDUFF.

MACDUFF.   Turn, hellhound, turn!
MACBETH. Of all men else I have
avoided thee.
But get thee back! My soul is too
much charged   5
With blood of thine already.
MACDUFF.   I have no words;
My voice is in my sword, thou
bloodier villain
Than terms can give thee out!

Fight. Alarum.

MACBETH.   Thou losest labor.
As easy mayst thou the intrenchant
air
With thy keen sword impress as make
me bleed.   10

---

22 *bruited:* announced.   24 *rend'red:* sur-
rendered.

Let fall thy blade on vulnerable
crests.
I bear a charmed life, which must
not yield
To one of woman born.
MACDUFF.   Despair thy charm,
And let the angel whom thou still
hast served
Tell thee, Macduff was from his
mother's womb   15
Untimely ripped.
MACBETH. Accursed be that tongue
that tells me so,
For it hath cowed my better part of
man!
And be these juggling fiends no more
believed,
That palter with us in a double
sense,   20
That keep the word of promise to
our ear
And break it to our hope. I'll not fight
with thee.
MACDUFF. Then yield thee, coward,
And live to be the show and gaze o'
the time.
We'll have thee, as our rarer mon-
sters are,   25
Painted upon a pole, and underwrit
"Here may you see the tyrant."
MACBETH.   I will not yield,
To kiss the ground before young
Malcolm's feet
And to be baited with the rabble's
curse.
Though Birnam Wood be come to
Dunsinane,   30
And thou opposed, being of no woman
born,
Yet I will try the last. Before my
body
I throw my warlike shield. Lay on,
Macduff,
And damned be him that first cries
"Hold, enough!"

*Exeunt fighting. Alarums. [Re-enter
fighting, and* MACBETH *slain. Exit*

V.viii.20 *palter:* quibble.

MACDUFF.] *Retreat and flourish. Enter, with drum and colors,* MALCOLM, SIWARD, ROSS, THANES, *and* SOLDIERS.

MALCOLM. I would the friends we miss were safe arrived.   35
SIWARD. Some must go off; and yet, by these I see,
 So great a day as this is cheaply bought.
MALCOLM. Macduff is missing, and your noble son.
ROSS. Your son, my lord, has paid a soldier's debt.
 He only lived but till he was a man,   40
 The which no sooner had his prowess confirmed
 In the unshrinking station where he fought
 But like a man he died.
SIWARD.   Then he is dead?
ROSS. Ay, and brought off the field. Your cause of sorrow
 Must not be measured by his worth, for then   45
 It hath no end.
SIWARD.   Had he his hurts before?
ROSS. Ay, on the front.
SIWARD.   Why then, God's soldier be he.
 Had I as many sons as I have hairs,
 I would not wish them to a fairer death.
 And so his knell is knolled.
MALCOLM.   He's worth more sorrow,   50
 And that I'll spend for him.
SIWARD.   He's worth no more.
 They say he parted well and paid his score,
 And so, God be with him. Here comes newer comfort.

Enter MACDUFF, *with* MACBETH'S *head.*

MACDUFF. Hail, King, for so thou art. Behold where stands
 The usurper's cursed head. The time is free.   55
 I see thee compassed with thy kingdom's pearl,
 That speak my salutation in their minds,
 Whose voices I desire aloud with mine—
 Hail, King of Scotland!
ALL.   Hail, King of Scotland!

Flourish.

MALCOLM. We shall not spend a large expense of time   60
 Before we reckon with your several loves
 And make us even with you. My Thanes and kinsmen,
 Henceforth be Earls, the first that ever Scotland
 In such an honor named. What's more to do
 Which would be planted newly with the time—   65
 As calling home our exiled friends abroad
 That fled the snares of watchful tyranny,
 Producing forth the cruel ministers
 Of this dead butcher and his fiend-like queen,
 Who (as 'tis thought) by self and violent hands   70
 Took off her life—this, and what needful else
 That calls upon us, by the grace of Grace
 We will perform in measure, time, and place.
 So thanks to all at once and to each one,
 Whom we invite to see us crowned at Scone.   75

Flourish. Exeunt omnes.

---

36 *go off:* die.

56 *compassed:* surrounded.   73 *in measure:* in the proper manner.

Phaedra

Like most of Jean Racine's tragedies, *Phaedra* derives from classical sources, its main events and characters coming from Euripides' play *Hippolytus*. But as he explains in his preface to *Phaedra*, Racine has by no means taken his duty to be that of mere imitator. Thus, as the altered title would suggest, Phaedra is given a prominence in Racine's play that she did not have in that of Euripides, where she appears in only two scenes before dying in mid-play. Racine (1639–1699) also notes that to bring the play in line with propriety he has lessened the purity of Euripides' Hippolytus by having him betray a weakness in falling in love with Aricia (who did not appear in *Hippolytus*), and he has ennobled Phaedra somewhat by having the idea of accusing Hippolytus come from Oenone, not herself. He has also eliminated the goddesses Aphrodite and Artemis, whose appearances at the beginning and the end of Euripides' play provide a structural frame, and the chorus of Troezenian ladies.

Despite the disappearance of the chorus, *Phaedra* is a neoclassic work consciously modeled on the form of Greek tragedy; hence its employment of the dramatic unities of time, place, and action so often ridiculed by critics as arbitrary and unnatural. It is true that many neoclassic dramatists with little talent and much respect for rules turned out absurdly contrived plays, such as Joseph Addison's *Cato*. But Racine manages to conform to the unities with such ease and naturalness that they pass almost unnoticed. Not merely that; so managed, the unities and the neoclassic form in general impart a distinctive character to Racinian tragedy. Perhaps this is best described in contrast to Shakespeare.

Turning from Shakespearean to Racinian tragedy is a bit like turning from epic to lyric. In the Shakespearean form action shifts back and forth from main plot to subplot, scenes change from one country to another, time-gaps are frequent, the number of characters is large, and the tone is not exclusively tragic but also comic or satiric on occasion. Tragedy of this sort embraces a great range of human experience; but what it gains in scope, it tends to lose in concentration. Just the reverse is true in Racine's tragedies. The manifold levels and variety of action in Shakespeare give way in Racine to a simple, highly compressed structure of events, a scaffolding of bare incidents designed to exhibit an inner psychological and emotional intensity. Whereas the whole course of Macbeth's tragic career is presented from the beginning, the action of *Phaedra* commences *in medias res*— at a well advanced point in the plot—in the approved Aristotelean fashion. Reading *Phaedra* is thus like reading an expanded last act of a Shakespearean tragedy.

The neoclassic form of *Phaedra* gives the play an air of order and balance. From this perspective, it acts as a rational envelope or boundary restraining the play of emotional energy in the characters. But the dramatic form of *Phaedra* is not merely an artificial outside container; it is an informing element that coalesces with and helps shape Racine's tragic vision. His beginning *in medias res,* for example, quite apart from merely curtailing the scope of presentation, contributes certain meanings to Phaedra's experience. By giving the action a momentum it would otherwise have to generate on its own, it augments the sense of inevitability with which the tragedy evolves. Corollary to this, beginning at an advanced point in the action also suggests the inescapable constraints narrowing down the range of human freedom. Contrast *Phaedra* and *Macbeth* in this regard. Because Racine begins his play with Phaedra's fatal love for Hippolytus already an accomplished fact, whereas Shakespeare begins his play well before the murder of Duncan, dramatic form itself appears to withhold from Phaedra the freedom of choice that it grants Macbeth.

In this respect, dramatic form reinforces thematic import, for Racine's play repeatedly thrusts before us a view of man as victimized by forces from within and without. When Freud said that the poets discovered the unconscious long before he did, he might have been thinking of Racine, who reveals the futility of reason, will, and conscience in competing with passion in shaping human fate. Phaedra is suffering from a love that is less desire than disease: "She dies in my arms," Oenone says, "of an ill that she conceals" (I.147). And of Hippolytus' love for Aricia, so contrary to filial duty and political wisdom, Theramenes says: "You are dying from an ill which you would hide" (I.137). Even Theseus' six-month imprisonment in the earth, which plays a crucial role in the evolving tragedy, results directly from the "unwise passion" of his friend Pirithous (III.230–51).

It would seem, then, that the motive force in the play is an irrepressible passion that in expressing itself creates a web of incrimination from which no one escapes. If so, as Meredith's sonnet has it, "We are betrayed by what is false within." But Racine's characters, especially Phaedra, are doubly betrayed, from without as well as within. Though there are no gods directly exhibited, their shadow falls over the action. The hereditary curse upon the women of Minos—Pasiphae, Ariadne, and Phaedra—goes back in Cretan myth to Minos' flouting of the will of Neptune, which should remind us that the sea-monster that destroys Hippolytus is also directed by Neptune. Phaedra's passion, as she well knows, is generated as much by Venus as by herself; and her pathological sense of contamination is partly guilt coming from within and partly shame coming from her awareness of outside ancestral disapproval (the fiery passion within, as the imagery puts it, subjects her to the flames of Minos' judgment and to the exposing light of Jupiter the sun).

In addition to being dominated by passion and the gods, Phaedra is prey to accident, coincidence, mistakes. She is twice thrown into the company of Hippolytus by the oblivious Theseus, being brought to Troezen in the first place and then being left there in her husband's absence. The ill-timed report of Theseus' death prompts her to reveal her love, and his equally ill-timed return transforms that indiscretion into catastrophe. Able for awhile to resist Oenone's urgings to accuse Hippolytus, she then misinterprets his expression when he enters with Theseus (III.180 ff.), assuming from his grave looks that he intends to expose her, and authorizes Oenone to proceed. And finally, when she is prepared to exonerate Hippolytus, her good intentions are perversely intercepted by Theseus' revelation that Hippolytus loves Aricia.

With this stress on internal passions and external gods, family curses, mistakes, and adverse coincidences, the student may well feel that Racine has loaded the dramatic dice against Phaedra from the start. If so, is she really a tragic heroine or merely a victim of cosmic persecution? Victimization is incompatible with tragedy emotionally, since it draws only on pity; morally, since it oversimplifies in its stress on the evil outside man; and intellectually, since it specializes in blind suffering. *Phaedra* is more complex than this. Racine's heroine does not merely suffer a passion inflicted on her by Venus; she commits herself to it and acts on it, thus transcending the role of pathetic victim. Nor is evil represented as outside the pale of human responsibility; Phaedra is not just the innocent pawn of evil gods and circumstances but the guilty agent of Hippolytus' destruction, "neither completely guilty nor completely innocent," as Racine says in his preface. If we feel that at the end of the play she fails fully to declare her independence in guilt from Oenone, still in committing suicide she is executing justice on herself.

Phaedra confronts a world in which the range of human freedom is severely limited. Caught between contraries that are mutually exclusive, she can choose and act only with reluctance and a sense of loss. This curtailment of action, however, does not entail a reduction of vision. Her mind is as restive as her passions, constantly exploring, testing, sharpening the issues that engage her. *Anagnorisis* is not limited to any one phase of her experience but is distributed throughout. Action becomes transformed into thought and feeling. Unable to do, she suffers. But her suffering is far from the unexpressive helplessness of the persecuted; it is an active encounter, a debate of the spirit in crisis, rendered with the eloquence of an inflamed and brilliant imagination.

Phaedra

THESEUS   *king of Athens, son of Aegeus*
PHAEDRA   *wife of* THESEUS, *daughter of Minos and of Pasiphae*
HIPPOLYTUS   *son of* THESEUS *and of Antiope, queen of the Amazons*
ARICIA   *a princess of the royal house of Athens*

OENONE   *nurse and confidant of* PHAEDRA
THERAMENES   *tutor and friend of* THESEUS
ISMENE   *confidant of* ARICIA
PANOPE   *a lady in the court of* PHAEDRA
GUARDS

ACT I

THE SCENE *is at Troezen, a city in the Peloponnesus.*

[HIPPOLYTUS *and* THERAMENES *enter.*]

HIPPOLYTUS. My mind is made up. I am leaving, Theramenes,
And ending my stay in gracious Troezen,
For, shaken as I am by dreadful doubts,
I begin to feel shame at my idleness.
Six months and more my father has been away,   5
And yet I do not know the fate of one so dear to me;
I do not even know what regions may be hiding him.
THERAMENES. And in what regions, my lord, would you then search?
Already, in answer to your just fears,
I have sailed the two seas that surround Corinth;   10
I have asked for Theseus of the people on those shores
Where one sees Acheron lose itself among the dead;
I have visited Elis and, leaving Taenarus,
Have gone on to the sea where Icarus fell.
With what new hope, in what happy place,   15
Do you expect to find the trace of his steps?
Who knows, indeed, if the King your father
Wants the secret of his absence learned?
While we, along with you, fear for his life,
He may be quietly hiding his newest loves,   20

I.10 *the two seas:* the Ionian and the Aegean seas.

12 *Acheron:* a river flowing from Epirus, a country of northwestern Greece, into Hades. 13 *Elis:* a country of ancient Greece, on the western shore of the Peloponnesus; *Taenarus:* southernmost tip of the Peloponnesus. 14 *Icarus:* the son of Daedalus; he fell in the Aegean, having escaped from the labyrinth of Crete by the use of wings insecurely fastened on with wax, which melted in the sun. 20 *his newest loves:* Theseus had already seduced Antiope, Ariadne, Phaedra, Helen, and Peribea.

From Phaedra *by Jean Racine, translated by Wesley Goddard, published by Chandler Publishing Company, San Francisco. Copyright © 1961 by Chandler Publishing Company. Reprinted by permission.*

Waiting, that some deluded loving
  girl...
HIPPOLYTUS. Theramenes, stop, and
  show respect for Theseus.
Long since recovered from his youth-
  ful ways,
He is now held back by no unworthy
  obstacle;
And with his inconstancy ended by
  his own vows,   25
Phaedra for long has feared no rivals.
    In short, by searching for him,
    I will follow duty,
And I will flee this place which I
  dare see no more.
THERAMENES. Since when, my lord, do
  you fear the sight
Of this peaceful place, so dear to
  your childhood,   30
And which I have seen that you
  prefer
To the pompous tumult of Athens
  and the court?
What danger, or rather what pain,
  sends you away?
HIPPOLYTUS. Those happy times are
  gone. All has changed
Since the gods have sent here to these
  shores   35
The daughter of Minos and Pasiphae.
THERAMENES. I understand. I know the
  cause of your suffering.
Phaedra here distresses you and hurts
  your sight:
A dangerous stepmother, who showed
  her true self
By sending you to exile when first
  she saw you.   40
But her hate, which once enveloped
  you,
Either has vanished or is now much
  weakened.
    Besides, what risks can you be
      made to face
By a dying woman, by one who wants

to die?
Phaedra, struck by an ill of which
  she will not speak,   45
Weary of herself and of the very day,
Can she form plots against you?
HIPPOLYTUS. Her empty hate is not
  what I fear.
Hippolytus, in leaving, flees another
  enemy.
I flee, I will admit it, that young
  Aricia,   50
Descendant of a fatal line conspir-
  ing against us.
THERAMENES. What! Do you yourself,
  my lord, persecute her?
Did ever this sweet sister of the cruel
  Pallantides
Have a hand in the schemes of her
  treacherous brothers?
Must you now hate her innocent
  charms?   55
HIPPOLYTUS. If I hated her, I would
  not flee.
THERAMENES [*after a pause*]. My lord,
  may I be allowed to interpret your
  flight?
Could it be you are no more that
  proud Hippolytus,
Implacable enemy of the laws of love
And of the yoke that Theseus has so
  often worn?   60
Is Venus, so long disdained by your
  pride,
Trying in this to justify Theseus,
And by putting you on a level with
  other men
Has she forced you to burn incense
  on her altars?
    Would you be in love, my
      lord?   65
HIPPOLYTUS. Friend, what are you say-
  ing?
You who have known my thoughts
  since I first took breath,
Can you ask me to disavow in shame

---

36 *daughter of Minos and Pasiphae:* this early
mention of Pasiphae, famous because of her
unnatural love for a bull, establishes the
hereditary taint in Phaedra's character.

53 *Pallantides:* the fifty brothers of Aricia
(reduced to six by Racine) who were killed
by their cousin Theseus, with whom they
were rivals for the throne of Athens.

The feelings of a heart so proud, so disdainful?
Small wonder that an Amazon mother should give   70
With her milk this pride which seems to astound you.
Indeed, with years and growing knowledge of myself,
I came to approve of what I saw in me.
    Attached to me by a sincere devotion,
You would tell me then the story of my father.   75
You know how my heart, attentive to your voice,
Warmed to hear the tale of his noble exploits,
When you painted for me this fearless hero
Consoling the mortals upon the absence of Alcides—
The monsters destroyed and the brigands punished,   80
Procrustes, Cercyon, and Sciron, and Sinis,
And the scattered bones of the giant of Epidaurus,
And Crete smoking with the blood of the Minotaur.
    But then you told of less glorious deeds:
His faith offered everywhere and everywhere received,   85
Helen stolen from her parents in Sparta,
Salamis a witness to the tears of Peribea;
So many more, whose names have escaped him,
Too credulous hearts that his love has deceived:
Ariadne telling the rocks of her abandonment,   90
Phaedra, too, abducted, but to a happier end.
    You know how, regretting to hear this talk,
I often pressed you to shorten your account;
Happy, had I been able to erase from memory   94
This shameful half of so fine a tale!
    Would I, in my turn, see myself bound by love?
And would the gods have so degraded me?
Unmanly sighs are all the more contemptible
Without the great deeds which can excuse the King;
For no monsters subdued by me as yet   100
Have given me the right to be as frail as he.
    Yet even had my resistance been softened,
Would I have chosen Aricia to be my conqueror?
Would not my wandering senses remember
The eternal obstacle which lies between us?   105
My father rejects her, and by severest laws
He forbids any heirs be given to her brothers,
For he fears an offspring of this guilty stock.

---

70 *Amazon mother:* Antiope, Hippolytus' mother by an earlier marriage of Theseus, had been queen of the Amazons, a warlike nation of women. 79 *Alcides:* another name for Hercules. 81 *Procrustes, etc.:* all Greek brigands, famous for their methods of torture, who were killed by Theseus. 82 *Epidaurus:* a town on the Aegean coast, the home of another of Theseus' victims. 83 *Minotaur:* a monster—half man, half bull—shut up in the labyrinth of Crete, living off human sacrifices until killed by Theseus. The Minotaur was born of the union between Pasiphae and a bull and was thus the half-brother of Phaedra. 86 *Helen:* abducted by Theseus, later the wife of Menelaus, and eventually the cause of the Trojan War.

87 *Peribea:* abandoned by Theseus and later married to the king of Salamis. 90 *Ariadne:* Phaedra's sister, abandoned by Theseus on the Island of Naxos. 91 *happier end:* because Phaedra, at least, was legitimately married to Theseus.

With their sister he wants to bury
their name,
And never for her will wedding fires
be lit   110
While yet she lives and still is in his
care.
Should I espouse her rights against
an angry father?
Shall I make a show of such temerity
And like a fool embark upon an
insane love...

THERAMENES. My lord, though one's
final hour be known above,   115
Still heaven ignores the reasons that
guide our acts.
Theseus opens your eyes while wishing to close them,
And his hate, fanning in you a rebellious love,
Lends to his enemy one grace she did
not have.
    So why be afraid of a love that
    is pure?   120
If its promise is sweet, do you not
dare to taste it,
Or will you always maintain such a
timorous scruple?
Do you fear being lost in the path
of Hercules?
What hearts has Venus not been
known to master?
And where would you be, you who
are fighting the goddess,   125
If Antiope, like you, opposed to her
laws,
Had not burned with a chaste love
for Theseus?
    But what do you gain by affect-
    ing this proud talk?
Admit it; you are changed. And for
some days
One sees you less often, arrogant and
alone,   130
Now making a chariot fly along the
shore,
Now, wise in the art invented by

Neptune,
Making docile a courser till then un-
broken.
Today the forests echo less often to
our cries.
Charged with an inner fire, your eyes
are heavy.   135
There can be no doubt: you are in
love, you burn;
You are dying from an ill which you
would hide.
Has Aricia cast a spell and been able
to please you?

HIPPOLYTUS. Theramenes, I am leaving and will search for my father.

THERAMENES. Will you see Phaedra
before you go, my lord?   140

HIPPOLYTUS. Such is my plan. You may
tell her of it.

[*Exit* THERAMENES.]

Let us see her, since thus my duty
orders.

[*He sees* OENONE *entering.*]

    But what new distress troubles
    her dear Oenone?

OENONE. Alas, my lord, what trouble
can equal mine?
The Queen has nearly reached her
fated end,   145
And though I watch both night and
day,
She dies in my arms of an ill that
she conceals.
Some eternal disorder reigns within
her soul.
Her uneasy grief takes her from her
bed;
She wants to see the day; yet her
deep sadness   150
Commands me ever to let her be
alone...
    She comes

HIPPOLYTUS. It is enough. I will leave
her here

---

123 *Hercules:* Hercules was also noted as a
woman-chaser.   126 *Antiope:* the mother of
Hippolytus.

132 *Neptune:* though god of the sea, he also
was responsible for introducing the horse and
horsemanship to the Greeks.

And will not show to her a hateful face.

[*Exit* HIPPOLYTUS *as* PHAEDRA *enters.*]

PHAEDRA. Let us go no farther. Let us stop, dear Oenone.   155
I can hold up no more. My strength abandons me.
My eyes are blinded by the light I see again,
And my trembling knees give way beneath me. [*She sits.*]
Alas!
OENONE. Almighty gods, may our tears appease you!   160
PHAEDRA. How these vain jewels, how these veils weigh upon me!
What meddling hand, in making all these knots,
Has thus arranged my hair upon my brow?
Everything overwhelms me and hurts me and conspires to hurt me.
OENONE. Thus one sees how her wishes overrule one another!   165
You yourself, condemning your unjust resolve,
Urged on our hands to adorn you;
You yourself, remembering your earlier strength,
Wanted to show yourself and to see again the light.
You see it, Madam; and, ready now to hide,   170
You hate the day that you came out to find.
PHAEDRA [*looking toward the sun*].
Noble and brilliant father of a woeful family,
You whose daughter my mother was proud to be,
Who blush in shame at the trouble you see me in,
Sun, I come to look on you for one last time.   175

OENONE. What! You will not give up this cruel desire?
Shall I always see you, renouncing life,
Make dismal preparations for your death?
PHAEDRA. Oh, gods! That I might be seated in the forest shade,
That I might, through a cloud of noble dust,   180
Follow with my eye a chariot coursing down the field!
OENONE. What, Madam?
PHAEDRA. I am mad. Where am I, and what have I said?
Where have I let wander my wishes —and my mind?
I have lost it; the gods have robbed me of its use.   185
Oenone, the blush of shame covers my face;
I let you see too well my miseries,
And my eyes, despite me, fill with tears.
OENONE. Ah, if you must blush, blush for the silence
Which but aggravates the violence of your hurt.   190
Refusing all our aid, deaf to all our words,
Do you, without pity, want to end your days?
What madness cuts them short in the middle of their run?
What spell or what poison has dried up their source?
Three times have the shadows darkened the heavens   195
Since sleep last entered upon your eyes;
And three times the day has chased away dark night
Since your body has languished without food.
By what frightful purpose are you tempted?
By what right do you lay hands upon yourself?   200
You offend the gods, the authors of your life;

158 [*She sits*]: the only stage direction given by Racine in the entire play. 175 *Sun:* Phaedra's mother, Pasiphae, was the daughter of Apollo, the sun god.

You betray the husband to whom
your promise binds you;
You betray, in the end, your own
unhappy children,
Whom you thrust beneath a yoke of
iron.
Consider that the same day will rob
them of their mother   205
And give hope to the foreign woman's
son,
To that implacable enemy of you and
of your blood,
The son whom an Amazon has borne,
That Hippolytus...
PHAEDRA. Oh, gods!   210
OENONE. This reproach touches you.
PHAEDRA. Wretch, what name did your
mouth utter?
OENONE. Well, your anger burst forth
with good reason.
I like to see you tremble at this
baleful name.
Live then. May love and duty bring
you back to life.   215
Live. Do not let the son of a
Scythian,
Crushing your children beneath a
hateful power,
Command the finest blood of Greece
and of the gods.
But do not delay. Each moment
brings you nearer death.
Build up at once your weakened
strength,   220
While still the torch of life endures
And, though nearly out, can yet be
lit again.
PHAEDRA. I have made it burn too long,
in guilt.
OENONE. What, do you feel torn by
some remorse?
What crime has brought about such
torment?   225
Can your hands be stained by inno-
cent blood?

PHAEDRA. Thanks be to heaven, my
hands bear no guilt.
If only my heart were as innocent
as they!
OENONE. What awful project, then,
have you begotten
That your heart should still be struck
with terror?   230
PHAEDRA. I have said enough. Spare me
the rest.
I die, to save myself so painful a
confession.
OENONE. Die, then, and keep your
inhuman silence;
But seek another hand to close your
eyes.
Though you have but a spark of life
within you,   235
My soul will be the first to go among
the dead.
A thousand open roads lead always
down,
And my just bitterness will find the
shortest way.
Cruel one, when has my devotion
proved untrue?
Do you recall that my arms held you
at your birth?   240
For you I left all—my native land,
my children.
Is this the way to repay my loyalty?
PHAEDRA. What fruit do you want from
so much argument?
You would tremble with horror
should I break my silence.
OENONE. And what could you tell me
that would equal   245
The horror of seeing you expire be-
fore my eyes?
PHAEDRA. When you know my crime
and the fate which crushes me,
I shall die nonetheless, but I shall
die more guilty yet.
OENONE [*kneeling*]. Madam, in the
name of the tears I have shed for
you,
By your knees which I clasp to my
heart,   250
Free my mind of this dreadful doubt.
PHAEDRA. You wish it. Rise.

---

216 *Scythian:* i.e., an Amazon, Scythia being
an area north of the Caspian Sea inhabited by
the Amazons. 218 *of Greece and of the gods:*
Phaedra's sons have Theseus as a father and
both Apollo and Jupiter as ultimate ancestors.

OENONE. Speak. I listen to your words.

PHAEDRA. Heaven, what shall I say, and where do I begin?

OENONE. Offend me no more with these vain fears.   255

PHAEDRA. This is the fatal anger of Venus, and her hate!

To what madness my mother was driven by love!

OENONE. Forget the past, Madam, and may to all posterity

An eternal silence hide this memory.

PHAEDRA. Ariadne, my sister, wounded too by such love,   260

You died on the shores where you were abandoned.

OENONE. What are you doing, Madam? And what torment

Stirs you against all your family today?

PHAEDRA. Since Venus wishes it, of this piteous line

I perish the last, the most wretched of all.   265

OENONE. Are you in love?

PHAEDRA. I know love in all its fury.

OENONE. For whom?

PHAEDRA. You are about to hear the ultimate horror.

I love...At this fatal name I tremble, I quake.   270

I love...

OENONE. Whom?

PHAEDRA. You know the son of the Amazon,

That prince whom so long I myself have oppressed?

OENONE. Hippolytus! Great gods!   275

PHAEDRA. It is you who have named him.

OENONE. Merciful heaven! My blood freezes in my veins.

The despair and crime that befall a cursed race!

That fated voyage that led to this unhappy strand!

Did you need to come here to this dangerous shore?   280

PHAEDRA. My ill comes from further back. No sooner

Was I engaged by law to the son of Aegeus,

Than my repose, my happiness, seemed assured.

Then Athens showed me my proud enemy;

I saw him, I blushed, I paled at his sight.   285

A new emotion troubled my lost soul.

My eyes no longer saw; I could not speak;

I felt my whole body both burning and benumbed.

In all this I saw Venus and her fearful fires,

Inevitable torments of the family she pursues—   290

Torments I thought I could avoid by vows:

I built a temple to her and adorned it with care;

I surrounded myself with victims of sacrifice

And sought in their entrails my wandering mind.

Powerless remedies for an incurable love!   295

In vain on the altars my hand burned the incense.

While to the name of the goddess my lips formed prayers,

I adored Hippolytus. And seeing him always,

Even at the foot of the altars that I caused to smoke,

I offered all to this god I dared not name.   300

I avoided him everywhere; then, height of misery!

I found him again in the face of his father.

Against myself at last I dared revolt:

---

257 *driven by love:* Venus was responsible for Pasiphae's love of the bull. 279 *fated voyage:* the trip of Phaedra and Oenone to Troezen.

290 *the family she pursues:* Venus continues to punish Phaedra's family because it was Apollo who had revealed the secret of the love between the goddess and Mars.

I inflamed my heart that I might
persecute him.

To banish the enemy whom I wor-
shiped   305

I assumed the ill-will of an unjust
stepmother;

I urged his exile, and by my constant
cries

Tore him from his father's arms and
heart.

  I breathed at last, Oenone, and
  since his going,

My calmer days have flowed in inno-
cence.   310

Submissive to my husband, and hiding my torment,

I nursed the fruit of this ill-fated
marriage.

  Vain precautions against a cruel
  destiny!

Brought to Troezen by my husband
himself,

I saw again the enemy I had
banished.   315

My wound, still too fresh, bled again.

It is no longer an ardor hidden in
my veins;

It is Venus clutching tight her prey.

  I have conceived a just terror of
  my crime

And held my life in hate, my love in
horror.   320

I wanted in death to preserve my
honor

And to rob the day of so criminal a
love.

  I could not withstand your tears
  and your arguments;

I have confessed all to you, nor do
I repent it,

If only, respecting the nearness of
my death,   325

You no longer afflict me with unjust
reproaches

And if you cease to preserve to no
avail

The last bit of warmth on the point
of vanishing.

---

312 *fruit of this ill-fated marriage:* i.e., her
two sons by Theseus.

[*Enter* PANOPE.]

PANOPE. I wish that I could hide this
tragic news,

  Madam, but to you I must reveal
  it.   330

  Death has robbed you of your in-
  vincible husband,

  And this calamity is known to all
  but you.

OENONE. Panope, what did you say?

PANOPE. That the Queen, deluded,

  In vain prays heaven for Theseus'
  return,   335

  And that from the ships just arrived
  in port

  Hippolytus, his son, has learned of
  his death.

PHAEDRA. Heaven!

PANOPE. For the choice of a master,
Athens is divided.

  Some give their vote to your son,
  Madam;   340

  Others, forgetting the law of the
  state,

  Dare give their voice to the son of
  the foreigner.

  It is even said that one insolent group

  Wants to put Aricia on the throne.

    I felt that I should warn you of
    this peril.   345

  Hippolytus is about to leave, and it
  is feared

  That if he should go to Athens in
  this unforeseen storm

  He might carry with him a whole
  inconstant people.

OENONE. Panope, that is enough. The
Queen, who hears you,

  Will not neglect this important
  news.   [*Exit* PANOPE.]   350

    Madam, I had ceased urging you
    to live;

  Already I expected to follow you to
  the tomb

  And had no voice left to change
  your mind,

  But this new misfortune prescribes
  new obligations.

  Your situation changes and takes another face.   355

The King is no more, Madam. You
must take his place.
His death leaves you a son to whom
you owe yourself:
A slave if he loses you, a king if you
live.
On whom, in his grief, do you want
him to lean?
His tears will have no hand to wipe
them away;   360
And his innocent cries, rising to the
gods,
Will turn his ancestors against his
mother.
          Live. You need reproach your-
self no more.
Your love has become an ordinary
love.
Theseus in dying has just undone the
knots   365
Which made all the crime and horror
of your passion.
Hippolytus becomes for you less dangerous,
And you can see him now with no
trace of guilt.
          Perhaps, convinced of your aver-
sion,
He plans to serve as leader to sedi-
tion.   370
Correct his error. Change his heart
and mind.
As king of these happy shores, Troe-
zen is his portion,
But he knows that the laws give to
your son
The proud ramparts which Minerva
built.
You have, both of you, a legitimate
enemy: 375
Unite, both of you, to fight Aricia.
PHAEDRA. Very well, by your counsel
I will let myself be led.
Let us live, if I can be brought to
life,
And if the love of a son at this dismal
time
Can awaken my feeble spirits once
again.   380

ACT II

[*Enter* ARICIA *and* ISMENE.]

ARICIA. Hippolytus asks to see me in
this place?
Hippolytus seeks me and wants to
say farewell?
Ismene, is this true? You are not
mistaken?
ISMENE. This is the first effect of
Theseus' death.
Prepare yourself, Madam, to see on
every side   5
Men turn to you who were held off
by Theseus.
Aricia at last is mistress of her days.
And soon at her feet she will see all
Greece.
ARICIA. This is not, Ismene, an un-
founded tale?
I am no more a slave and have no
enemies?   10
ISMENE. No, Madam, the gods no
longer are opposed to you,
And Theseus has joined the ghosts of
your brothers.
ARICIA. Do they say what accident has
ended his days?
ISMENE. Unbelievable stories are told of
his death.
They say that as the ravisher of his
newest love,   15
This faithless husband was swallowed
by the seas.
They say too—and this account is
widely spread—
That with Pirithous he descended
into hell,
Where he saw the Cocytus and its
shadowy banks

---

374 *ramparts which Minerva built:* i.e.,
Athens. II.18 *Pirithous:* king of the Lapithae,
who was thought to have gone to Hades with
his friend Theseus to abduct Persephone. 19
Cocytus: a river of Hades.

And showed himself alive among the
infernal shades,   20
But that he could not return from
those gloomy parts
And recross the border that can be
crossed but once.
ARICIA. Shall I believe that a mortal,
before his final hour,
Can descend early to the abode of
the dead?
What spell drew him to those fearful
shores?   25
ISMENE. Theseus is dead, Madam, and
you alone still doubt.
Athens already mourns, Troezen has
heard the news
And recognizes Hippolytus for king.
Phaedra in this palace, fearful for
her son,
Asks counsel of her troubled
friends.   30
ARICIA. And you think that Hippolytus,
more human than his father,
Will lighten the burden of my chains,
That he will have pity on my misfor-
tune?
ISMENE. Madam, I do believe it.
ARICIA. Do you really know the insen-
sitive Hippolytus?   35
By what foolish hope do you believe
he pities me
And respects in me alone a sex which
he disdains?
You can see for how long he has
avoided our path
And has sought only those places
where we cannot be found.
ISMENE. I know all that has been said
of his coldness.   40
But I have seen this proud Hippoly-
tus beside you,
And even as I looked, the fame of
his aloofness
Redoubled my curiosity. And yet his
aspect
Agreed in no way with the stories
that they tell.
At your first glance upon him, I saw
he was troubled.   45
His eyes, already languishing, tried

to avoid you,
But in vain; they could not turn
away.
The name of lover perhaps wounds
his pride;
But he has a lover's eyes, though he
lack the words.
ARICIA. How my heart, dear Ismene,
listens eagerly   50
To a tale that may have little base!
You who know me, can you believe
That this sad plaything of a pitiless
fate,
This heart ever nourished on bitter-
ness and tears,
Should know love and all its foolish
pain?   55
    Descendant of a king, noble son
    of the Earth,
I alone escaped from the fury of war.
I lost, in the flower of their youth, six
brothers—
They were the hope of an illustrious
house.
The sword reaped all, and the
dampened ground   60
Drank with regret the blood of
Erechtheus' heirs.
    You know, since their death, by
    what stern laws
All Greeks are forbidden to show
pity for me.
It is feared that the sister's rash
flame of love
May bring to life the ashes of her
brothers.   65
But you know too with what disdain-
ful eye
I looked on the concern of the dis-
trustful King.
You know that, always contemptuous
of love,
I often forgave the unjust Theseus,

---

56 *son of the Earth:* Aricia is a descendant
in a direct line from the Earth, through his
son Erechtheus. 61 *Drank with regret:* because the Pallantides were descended from the
Earth.

Whose harshness seconded my scorn. 70
At that time my eyes had not yet seen his son.
Not that by my eyes alone, shamefully bewitched,
Do I love his beauty and his much-praised grace,
Gifts that nature has freely accorded him,
Which he scorns and of which he seems unaware. 75
I love, I prize in him, more noble wealth:
The virtues of his father, but not the weaknesses.
I love, I will confess, that splendid pride
Which never has submitted to the yoke of love.
Phaedra thinks herself honored by the sighs of Theseus. 80
As for me, I am more proud and flee the easy glory
Of winning an homage offered to a thousand more
And of entering a heart open on every side.
But to sway a will till then inflexible,
To bring pain to an insensitive soul, 85
To enchain a captive, amazed to be in irons,
Revolting in vain against a pleasing yoke:
That is what I want; that is what excites me.
Hercules was easier to disarm than Hippolytus
And, vanquished more often and sooner overcome, 90
Brought less renown to those who subdued him.
But, dear Ismene, alas, what rash hope is mine!
I can meet with nothing but his too great resistance.
You may someday hear me, humble in my pain,
Bemoaning the same pride which I admire today. 95
Can Hippolytus love? By what good fortune
Could I have swayed...
ISMENE. You will hear him speak himself.
He comes to you.

[*Enter* HIPPOLYTUS.]

HIPPOLYTUS. Madam, before I leave, 100
I felt that I should speak of what awaits you.
My father no longer lives. My well-founded fears
Foretold the reason for his too-long absence:
Death alone, putting an end to his brilliant deeds,
Could hide him from the universe so long. 105
At last the gods surrender to the deadly Fates
The friend, the companion, the successor to Alcides.
(Surely even your hate, admitting his virtues,
Listens without distaste to these names that are his due.)
One hope lightens my deathly grief: 110
I can free you from a strict surveillance;
I revoke the laws whose harshness I deplored;
You are mistress of yourself and of your heart.
And in this Troezen, which now belongs to me,
Once the heritage of my forefather Pittheus, 115
And which, without debate, has named me king,
I leave you free, and more free than I.

---

90 *vanquished more often:* i.e., by love.

106 *Fates:* the three goddesses of destiny and death. 115 *Pittheus:* the maternal grandfather of Theseus, founder of Troezen.

ARICIA. Restrain your goodness, whose excess confounds me.

To honor my misfortune with such generous care

Is to place me, my lord, more than you think,   120

Under as severe laws as those from which you free me.

HIPPOLYTUS. In the choice of a successor, uncertain Athens

Speaks of you, of me, of the son of the Queen.

ARICIA. Of me, my lord?

HIPPOLYTUS. I know, without wishing to deceive myself,   125

That an insolent law appears to reject me:

Greece reproaches me my foreign mother.

But if as a rival I had only my brother,

I could well save from capricious laws

Certain genuine rights that I have over him.   130

A more legitimate brake puts a stop to my daring:

I cede to you, or rather I return, a place

And sceptre received of old by your forebears

From that famous mortal conceived by the Earth.

Adoption put them in Aegeus' hands.   135

Later Athens, enhanced and protected by my father,

Recognized with joy so noble a king

And left your unhappy brothers to forgetfulness.

Now Athens calls you back within her walls.

She has suffered enough from a lengthy quarrel,   140

And long enough has the blood of your family

Made the fields smoke from which they came.

Troezen obeys me. The countryside of Crete

Offers a rich retreat to the son of Phaedra.

Attica is yours. I go and will unite for you   145

All the voices now divided between us.

ARICIA. Of all that I hear, astonished and confused,

I almost fear, I do fear a dream deceives me.

Am I awake? Can I believe that such a plan is true?

What god, my lord, has put it in your heart?   150

How right that your fame is spread afar,

And yet the truth surpasses reputation!

In my favor do you really give over your claim?

Was it not enough that you should not hate me

And that for so long you could preserve your soul   155

From that enmity...

HIPPOLYTUS. I hate you, Madam?

In whatever light my pride may have been painted,

Can one believe a monster gave me birth?

What savage ways, what hardened hate   160

Could not be softened merely by seeing you?

Could I resist the delusive charm...

ARICIA. What, my lord?

HIPPOLYTUS. I have gone too far.

I see that reason yields to the violence of love.   165

But since I have now begun to break my silence,

Madam, I must go on. I must inform you

---

134 *famous mortal:* Erechtheus.   135 *Adoption put them in Aegeus' hands:* Aegeus, the father of Theseus, and Pallas, the father of Aricia, were both sons of Pandion, king of Athens. But Aegeus was only an adopted son, whereas Pallas was legitimate. Thus Aricia's claim to the throne of Athens is valid.

Of a secret my heart no longer can
contain.
    You see before you a pitiful
prince,
An enduring example of a presumptuous pride. 170
I have been haughtily rebellious
against love,
Have long jeered at the irons of her
captives,
And, deploring the shipwreck of
weaker men,
Hoped always to watch the storms
from shore.
    But now, enslaved by the com-
mon law, 175
By what passion I see myself carried
away!
One moment has vanquished my rash
audacity;
My arrogant soul is at last depen-
dent.
For nearly six months, ashamed and
in despair,
Bearing everywhere the arrow by which
I am torn, 180
I have contended in vain against you,
against myself.
With you present, I flee; absent, I
find you.
In the depths of the forest your
image follows me.
The light of the day, the shades of
the night,
Everything retraces for my eyes the
charms that I avoid. 185
Everything vies to deliver the rebel
Hippolytus to you.
And as the only fruit of all my use-
less efforts,
I search now for myself but can no
longer find me.
My bow, my javelins, my chariot, all
annoy me;
I no longer remember the lessons of
Neptune; 190
Only my groans re-echo in the
woods,

And my idle coursers have forgotten
my voice.
    Perhaps the tale of a love so
unrestrained
Makes you blush in shame at the
work you have done.
And what uncouth speech to offer
you a heart! 195
What a strange captive for so fair a
bond!
Yet the offer, to your eyes, should be
the more precious.
Remember that I speak a language
strange to me;
So do not reject these vows, badly
expressed,
Which Hippolytus without you would
never have made. 200

[*Enter* THERAMENES.]

THERAMENES. My lord, the Queen
comes, and I have come ahead.
She seeks you.
HIPPOLYTUS. Me?
THERAMENES. I do not know her
thought,
But you are being asked for in her
behalf. 205
Phaedra wants to speak to you before
your leaving.
HIPPOLYTUS. Phaedra? What can I say
to her? And what can she expect?
ARICIA. My lord, you cannot refuse to
hear her.
Though you are too convinced of her
ill feeling,
You owe to her tears some shadow
of pity. 210
HIPPOLYTUS [*to* ARICIA]. Meanwhile
you go. And I am leaving. And I
do not know
If I offend the charms which I adore!
I do not know if the heart I leave in
your hands...
ARICIA. Go, Prince, and follow your
generous designs. 215
Make Athens submissive to my
power.
I accept all the gifts that you offer
me.

190 *lessons of Neptune:* i.e., horsemanship.

But this empire, after all so great,
so glorious,
Is not of your gifts the dearest to my
eyes.
[*Exeunt* ARICIA *and* ISMENE.]
HIPPOLYTUS. Friend, are you ready?
But the Queen comes near.   220
Go, that all for our departure be
prepared in haste.
Have the signal given, run, order,
and return
To deliver me soon from this un-
welcome talk.

[*Exit* THERAMENES *as* PHAEDRA *and*
OENONE *enter.*]

PHAEDRA. Here he is. All my blood
flows back to my heart.
I forget, in seeing him, what I came
to say.   225
OENONE. Remember a son who has
hope but in you.
PHAEDRA [*to* HIPPOLYTUS]. They say
a quick departure takes you from
us,
My lord. To your grief I come to
join my tears.
And I come to expose my fears
for a son.
My son has now no father, and the
day is not far   230
That will make him witness to my
death besides.
Already a thousand enemies attack
him in his youth.
You alone can take up his defense
against them.
But a secret remorse troubles my
spirit.
I fear I have closed your ear to his
cries.   235
I tremble lest your rightful anger
Against his hateful mother should fall
on him.
HIPPOLYTUS. Madam, I have no
thoughts so base as that.
PHAEDRA. If you should hate me, I
would not complain,
My lord. You have seen me striving
to hurt you,   240

And could not read in the depths of
my heart.
I have taken pains to expose myself
to your enmity.
I could not permit you on the shores
where I lived.
Declaring myself against you in pub-
lic and alone,   244
I tried to put the seas between us.
I even forbade, by a special law,
That anyone utter your name before
me.
If, however, the pain be mea-
sured by the offense,
If only hate can bring about your
hate,
Then never was woman more deserv-
ing of pity,   250
And less deserving, my lord, of your
enmity.
HIPPOLYTUS. For the rights of her chil-
dren a jealous mother
Rarely forgives the son of another
wife.
Madam, I know this. Harassing sus-
picions
Are the most common fruits of a
second marriage.   255
Anyone else would have taken the
same offense.
And I might have suffered more out-
rages yet.
PHAEDRA. Ah, my lord, here I dare
attest that heaven
Has excepted me from that common
law,
That a very different care troubles
and consumes me!   260
HIPPOLYTUS. Madam, this is not the
time still to torment yourself.
Perhaps your husband yet sees the
light of day.
Heaven may answer our tears and
accord his return.
Neptune protects him, and this
guardian god
Will not be implored in vain by my
father.   265
PHAEDRA. No one sees twice the shores
of the dead,

My lord. Since Theseus has seen
that somber place,
You hope in vain a god will send him
back to you.
And the miserly Acheron does not
loose its prey.   269
  What am I saying? He is not
  dead, for he breathes in you.
Still before my eyes I think I see my
husband.
I see him, I speak to him, and my
heart...I wander.
My lord, my insane passion declares
itself despite me.
HIPPOLYTUS. I see the marvelous effect
of your love.
Dead though he is, Theseus is present
to your eyes;   275
Your soul is still afire with love of
him.
PHAEDRA. Yes, Prince, I languish, I
burn for Theseus.
I love him, but not as he is seen in
hell—
Inconstant lover of a thousand
women,
Gone to dishonor the couch of the
god of the dead—   280
But faithful, but proud, and even a
little shy,
Charming, young, trailing all hearts
behind him,
Such as our gods are painted—or
such as I see you.
He had your bearing, your eyes, your
speech;
The same noble modesty colored his
face   285
When he crossed the waters of our
Crete,
Well deserving the love of the
daughters of Minos.
  What were you doing then?
  Why, without Hippolytus,
Did he assemble the elite of the

heroes of Greece?
Why could you not then, though still
too young,   290
Board the ship which put him on
our shores?
Through you, the monster of Crete
would have perished,
Despite all the turnings of his endless
lair.
To lead you in safety through the
bewildering maze
My sister would have armed you with
the fateful thread.   295
  But no, I would have acted before her in this plan;
Love would first have given the
thought to me.
It is I, Prince, it is I whose useful
aid
Would have taught you the turnings
of the Labyrinth.
What care that charming head would
then have cost me!   300
A thread would not have made your
lover sure enough.
Companion in the peril which you
had to seek,
I myself before you would have
wished to walk;
And Phaedra, gone down with you
into the Labyrinth,
With you would have been saved or
lost.   305
HIPPOLYTUS. Gods! What do I hear?
Madam, do you forget
That Theseus is my father, and that
he is your husband?
PHAEDRA. And what makes you think
that I have lost this memory,
Prince? Have I abandoned all con-
cern for my name?
HIPPOLYTUS. Madam, pardon me. I
admit, blushing,   310
That I misunderstood an innocent
speech.

---

280 *god of the dead:* Theseus was said to
have gone to Hades with Pirithous to abduct
Persephone, wife of Pluto. 287 *daughters of
Minos:* Ariadne and Phaedra.

292 *monster of Crete:* the Minotaur. 295
fateful thread: Ariadne had given Theseus a
thread to enable him to find his way out of
the labyrinth after killing the Minotaur.

My shame forbids me to look upon
you;
And I go...
PHAEDRA. Oh, cruel one, you under-
stood me too well.
I have told you enough for you to
see the truth.   315
So now you know Phaedra and all of
her passion.
I love. Think not that at the moment
when I love you,
I approve of myself, innocent in my
own eyes,
Nor that an easy complaisance has
strengthened the poison
Of the mad love that troubles my
reason.   320
The ill-fated object of a heavenly
vengeance,
I abhor myself more even than you
detest me.
The gods are my witness, those gods
who in my breast
Kindled the fatal fire of all my line,
Those gods who have taken a cruel
pride   325
In leading astray the heart of a fee-
ble woman.
     You, in your own mind, recall
          the past.
To shun you was not enough; I drove
you away.
I wanted to seem odious to you,
inhuman;
The better to resist you, I sought
your hate.   330
But how did my vain efforts bring
me any gain?
You hated me more; I loved you no
less.
Your misfortunes but lent you more
and newer charms.
I languished and was consumed, by
flames and by tears.
You need only your eyes to be convinced,   335
If for a moment your eyes could look
at me.
     What am I saying? This avowal
          I have made,
This so shameful avowal, do you

think that I willed it?
Trembling for a son whom I dared
not fail,
I came to beg you not to hate
him.   340
Futile hope of a heart too full of
what it loves!
Alas, I could speak to you only of
yourself.
     Avenge yourself, punish me for
          an odious love.
Worthy son of the hero who gave
you life,
Deliver the universe from a monster
that offends you.   345
The widow of Theseus dares to love
his son!
     Believe me, this awful monster
          must not escape you.
Here is my heart. Here your hand
must strike.
Impatient already to expiate its
offense,
I feel it advance as if to meet your
arm.   350
Strike! Or if you think it unworthy
of your blows,
If your hate refuse me so mild a
punishment,
Or if your hand would be dipped in
blood too vile,
Stay your arm, but lend me your
sword.
Give me it! [*She pulls his sword
from its scabbard.*]   355
OENONE [*rushing to* PHAEDRA *and
seizing the sword*]. What are you
doing, Madam? Merciful gods!
But someone comes. Avoid a hateful
witness.
Come, go in, flee certain shame.

[*Exeunt* PHAEDRA *and* OENONE *as*
THERAMENES *enters.*]

THERAMENES. Is that Phaedra who
flees, or rather is dragged away?
Why, my lord, why these marks of
grief?   360
I see you without your sword,
abashed and pale.
HIPPOLYTUS. Theramenes, let us escape.

My surprise has overwhelmed me.
I cannot without horror look upon
myself.
Phaedra...But no, may this horrible
secret
Lie buried forever in deep forgetful-
ness.   365
THERAMENES. If you wish to leave, the
ship is set to sail.
But Athens, my lord, has already
declared itself.
Its chiefs have heard the votes of
all its tribes.
Your brother has won, and Phaedra
has the upper hand.
HIPPOLYTUS. Phaedra?   370
THERAMENES. A herald, charged with
the will of Athens,
Has just put in her hands the reins
of the State.

Her son is king, my lord.
HIPPOLYTUS. Gods, you who know her,
Is it then her virtue you are reward-
ing?   375
THERAMENES. However, a secret rumor
says the King still lives.
They claim that Theseus has ap-
peared in Epirus.
But I, who searched for him, my
lord, I know too well...
HIPPOLYTUS. No matter, let us hear all
and neglect nothing.
Let us examine this rumor; let us go
to the source.   380
If it does not deserve to delay my
going,
Then let us leave and at whatever
price
Place the scepter in hands that are
worthy of holding it.

ACT III

[*Enter* PHAEDRA *and* OENONE.]

PHAEDRA. Oh, take away these honors
that are sent me!
How can you hope that I should
show myself?
Why do you try to calm my tormented mind?
Hide me well, instead, for I have
spoken but too much.
The transports of my madness have
been spread abroad;   5
I have said what one should never
hear.
Heaven, how he listened to me! And
by what detours
He tried, unfeeling, to elude my
words!
How he hoped for nothing but a
quick escape,
And how his shame did but increase
my own!   10
    Why did you turn me from my
    fatal plan?
Alas, when I held his sword against

my breast,
Did he pale for me? Did he snatch it
away?
It was enough that I should touch
it once
To make it horrible to his inhuman
eyes;   15
That steel thereafter would profane
his hands.
OENONE. Thus in your misery, thinking
only of your woes,
You nourish a flame that you had
best put out.
Is it not better, worthy daughter of
Minos,
To seek your repose in more noble
concerns   20
And, in place of the ingrate who
resorts to flight,
To reign and to direct the affairs of
state?
PHAEDRA. I, reign! I, bring a state
under my law,
When my feeble reason rules me no
more!

III.1 *take away these honors:* sent by Athens
to the mother of the new king.

383 *hands that are worthy of holding it:* i.e.,
in the hands of Aricia.

When I have abandoned control of
my senses! 25
When under a yoke of shame I barely
breathe!
When I am dying!

OENONE. Then flee!

PHAEDRA. I cannot leave him.

OENONE. You dared to banish him, yet
dare not go away! 30

PHAEDRA. It is too late. He knows of
my mad love.
The limits of strict modesty are
passed;
I have revealed my shame to the eyes
of my conqueror,
And hope, despite me, has crept into
my heart.
You yourself, calling back my waning
strength 35
And my breath, already hovering on
my lips,
By your deceiving counsel made me
live again.
You made me glimpse the truth that
I could love him.

OENONE. Alas, whether innocent or
guilty of your misfortune,
What would I not have done to save
you? 40
But if ever an offense angered your
spirit,
Can you forget the scorn of an arrogant man?
With what cruel eyes his stubborn
indifference
Left you nearly prostrate at his feet.
How odious he was in his savage
pride! 45
Why, at that moment, could Phaedra
not have my eyes?

PHAEDRA. Oenone, he may abandon this
pride that hurts you.
He was reared in the forests, and so
he is uncouth,
And, hardened by savage ways, Hip-
polytus 49
Hears talk of love for the first time.
Perhaps his silence was due to his
surprise,
And perhaps our complaints have

been too severe.

OENONE. Remember that a barbarian
formed him in her womb.

PHAEDRA. Though a barbarian and a
Scythian, still she loved.

OENONE. He has for all the sex a hate
that is his destiny. 55

PHAEDRA. I shall then see no rival
preferred to me.
So all of your counsels are now out
of place.
Serve my madness, Oenone, and not
my reason.
Since to love he shows an inac-
cessible heart,
Let us hunt a more sensitive spot to
attack. 60
The charms of an empire seemed to
affect him.
Athens attracted him; he could not
hide the fact.
Already his ships had turned their
prows that way,
And the sails floated free in the wind.
Go find for me this young ambi-
tious man, 65
Oenone; make the crown shine before
his eyes.
On his brow must be placed the
sacred diadem;
I want only the honor of fixing it
there myself.
Let us give him this power that I can
hold no more.
He will instruct my son in the art of
command 70
And may perhaps be willing to play
a father's role.
In his power I place both son and
mother.
Try any means, indeed, to sway
him.
Your words will be received more
readily than mine.
Press him, weep, wail; bemoan a
dying Phaedra. 75
Do not be ashamed to take a pleading voice.
I will approve all you do; in you lies
my only hope.

Go. I await your return, that I may
live or die.   [*Exit* OENONE.]
   Oh you, who see the shame to
      which I have come,
Implacable Venus, am I humbled
   enough?   80
You cannot further push your
   cruelty.
Your triumph is complete; your every
   shaft has carried.
      Cruel goddess, if you wish more
         glory yet,
Attack an enemy who is more rebel-
   lious to you.
Hippolytus flees from you, and, brav-
   ing your wrath,   85
Never has bent his knee before your
   altars.
Your name seems to offend his proud
   ears.
Goddess, avenge yourself. Our cause
   is the same.
May he love...

[*Enter* OENONE.]

   But already you return,
      Oenone?   90
He hates me; he will not listen.
OENONE. You must give up all thought
   of this fruitless love,
Madam. Remember your past virtue.
The King, thought dead, will appear
   before your eyes.
Theseus has arrived. Theseus is in
   this place.   95
To see him, the people rush headlong.
I was going, at your command, to
   seek Hippolytus,
When a thousand cries burst forth
   toward heaven...
PHAEDRA. My husband lives, Oenone;
   that is enough.
I have confessed in shame a love that
   wrongs him.   100
He lives. I want to know no more.
OENONE. What?
PHAEDRA. I had foretold it; but you
   would not believe.
Your tears prevailed over my rightful
   remorse.

I might have died this morning,
   worthy to be mourned.   105
I followed your counsel; and I die
   dishonored.
OENONE. You die?
PHAEDRA. Just heaven! What have I
   done today?
My husband will appear, and with
   him his son.
I will see the witness of my adulter-
   ous love   110
Watch in what fashion I dare ap-
   proach his father,
My heart full of sighs which he
   would not hear,
My eyes wet with tears which he
   cruelly rebuffed.
Do you think, sensitive as he is to
   the honor of Theseus,
That he will hide from him the love
   which enflames me?   115
Will he let his father be betrayed,
   and his king?
Can he restrain the horror he feels
   for me?
      Even his silence would be in
         vain. I know my guilt,
Oenone, and am not of those brazen
   women
Who, enjoying calm peace even in
   their crime,   120
Can prepare a brow which never
   shows a blush.
I know my passions; I recall them,
   every one.
Even now I feel these walls and these
   arches
Are about to speak and, ready to
   accuse me,
Wait only for my husband, that they
   may tell him all.   125
      Let me die, that death deliver
         me from so much horror.
Is the end of life so great a calamity?
Death holds no terror for those who
   are wretched.
I fear only the name that I shall
   leave behind—
What a frightful heritage for my unhappy sons!   130

The blood of Jupiter must strengthen
their hearts;
But whatever just pride this lineage
inspires,
The crime of a mother is a heavy
load.
I tremble lest talk, alas too true,
May someday reproach them for a
guilty mother.   135
I tremble lest, weighted down by this
hateful burden,
Neither will dare to raise his eyes
again.
OENONE. You must not doubt that I
pity them both;
And never was fear better founded
than yours.
But why must you expose them to
such affronts?   140
Why must you stand as witness
against yourself?
If you do this, they will say that the
guilty Phaedra
Flees the fearful sight of a husband
she has wronged.
Hippolytus is happy that, at the cost
of your life,
You support, by dying, the charges
that he makes.   145
    What then could I answer to him
    who accuses you?
Too easily before him would I be
rendered silent.
In his awful triumph I can see him
rejoice
And tell of your shame to whomever
wants to hear.
Ah, may rather the fire of heaven
consume me!   150
    But do not deceive me. Is he still
    dear to you?
With what eye do you look upon that
audacious prince?
PHAEDRA. I see him as a monster,
frightful to my eyes.
OENONE. Why then concede to him a

---

131 *Jupiter:* through Minos, her two sons are
descended from Jupiter.

full victory?
You fear him. Dare to accuse him
first   155
Of the crime with which he may
charge you today.
What will belie you? Everything
speaks against him:
His sword, happily left in your own
hands,
Your present agitation, your anger in
the past,
His father warned against him by
your cries,   160
And his exile, which you yourself
obtained.
PHAEDRA. Am I then to crush and
blacken innocence?
OENONE. My zeal needs nothing but
your silence,
Though, trembling like you, I too
feel some remorse.
You would see me meet more readily
a thousand deaths.   165
But since I would lose you, without
this painful cure,
Everything yields before the value of
your life.
I will speak.
    Theseus, embittered by what I
    tell him,
Will limit his vengeance to the exile
of his son.   170
A punishing father, Madam, is still a
father;
A light penalty is all his wrath
demands.
But even should innocent blood be
spilled,
What is too much when your honor
is at stake?
It is too dear a treasure to risk a
compromise.   175
Whatever law it imposes, you must
submit,
Madam, and to save your embattled
honor,
You must sacrifice all, even virtue
itself.
    Someone comes. I see Theseus.

PHAEDRA. Ah, I see Hippolytus. 180
  In his insolent eyes, I can see my
    ruin written.
  [*To* OENONE] Do what you wish; I
    surrender to your will.
  In my present turmoil, I can do
    nothing for myself.

[*Enter* THESEUS *and* HIPPOLYTUS,
separately.]

THESEUS. Fortune no longer runs coun-
    ter to my hopes,
  Madam, and puts within your
    arms... 185
PHAEDRA. Stop, Theseus,
  And do not profane such pleasing
    raptures,
  For I deserve no more this tender
    show of feeling.
  You have been wronged. In your
    absence
  Jealous fortune has not spared your
    wife. 190
  Unworthy to please you or even to
    come near,
  I must henceforth think only of hid-
    ing myself. [*Exit* PHAEDRA.]
THESEUS. What is this strange welcome
    given to your father,
  My son?
HIPPOLYTUS. Phaedra alone can explain
    this mystery.
  But if my earnest wishes can move
    you, 195
  Allow me, my lord, to see her no
    more.
  Permit this shaken Hippolytus for-
    ever
  To quit those regions where Phaedra
    lives.
THESEUS. You will leave me, my son?
HIPPOLYTUS. I did not seek her
    out; 200
  It is you who led her to these shores.
  It was your wish, my lord, in the
    land of Troezen
  To leave in trust Aricia and the
    Queen,
  And I was given the duty of guard-

ing them.
  But what duty now can hold me
    here? 205
    Long enough in the forests has
      my idle youth
  Shown its skill against lowly enemies.
  May I not flee this unworthy repose
  And color my lance in more noble
    blood?
    You had not yet reached my
      present age 210
  When your arm had already felt the
    weight
  Of more than one tyrant, one fero-
    cious beast.
  Already the favored persecutor of
    oppression,
  You had made safe the shores of the
    two seas;
  The free voyager feared no further
    outrage. 215
  Already Hercules, hearing the fame
    of your blows,
  Could rest from his labors and put
    his faith in you.
    And I, the unknown son of a
      glorious father,
  I am still far from even my mother's
    steps.
  Allow my courage at last to find a
    goal, 220
  And if ever some monster was able to
    escape you,
  Let me lay at your feet his worthy
    hide.
  Or let the lasting memory of a beau-
    tiful death,
  Immortalizing my days so nobly
    ended,
  Prove to the universe that I was your
    son. 225
THESEUS. What do I see? What horror,
    spread about this place,
  Makes my distracted family flee
    before my eyes?
  If I return so feared, so little wanted,

---

214 *two seas:* the Ionian and the Aegean
seas.

Why, heaven, did you free me from
my prison?
 I had but one friend. His unwise
  passion   230
Ravished the wife of the tyrant of
Epirus.
To my sorrow I served his amorous
designs;
But angered fate blinded the two of
us.
The tyrant surprised me without
defense, without arms;
I saw Pirithous, unhappy object of
my tears,   235
Thrown by the barbarian to cruel
monsters
Which feed on the blood of unlucky
mortals.
As for me, he shut me in somber
caves,
Deep regions near the kingdom of
the dead.
The gods, six months after, at last
remembered me,   240
And I deceived the eyes by which I
was guarded.
I purged nature of a perfidious
enemy;
To his own monsters he served as
fodder.
 And when with joy I think I
  am returning
To what the gods have left that was
dearest to me—   245
When my soul, delivered to itself
again,
Comes to feast upon so dear a sight,
I meet only trembling by way of
welcome.
All flee; all refuse my embrace.
And I myself, feeling the terror I
inspire,   250
Could wish to be again in the prisons
of Epirus.

Speak. Phaedra complains that
I am wronged.
Who has betrayed me? Why am I
not avenged?
Has Greece, to whom my arm has so
often been of aid,
Accorded some asylum to the crimi-
nal?   255
You do not answer me. My son, my
own son,
Is he in collusion with my enemies?
 I will go in. It is clinging to a
  doubt that crushes me.
I will learn at one time both the
crime and the guilty one;
Let Phaedra explain at last the dis-
tress I see in her.   260

 [*Exit* THESEUS.]

HIPPOLYTUS. What did those words
mean, which chilled me with fear?
Does Phaedra, still a prey to her wild
madness,
Want to accuse herself and bring her-
self to ruin?
Gods, what will the King say? What
mortal poison
Love has spread throughout his
house!   265
 Myself, full of a fire which he
  condemns—
How he looked upon me once, and
how he finds me now!
 Black forebodings come to
  frighten me.
But innocence, after all, has nothing
to fear.
Come, let us seek elsewhere by what
happy means   270
I can move my father to tenderness
And tell him of a love he may wish
to change
But which he, with all his power, can
never shake.

---

230 *I had but one friend:* Pirithous. 231
tyrant of Epirus: As Racine points out in
his preface, Theseus accompanied Pirithous to
Epirus, not to Hades.

---

261 *What did those words mean:* i.e., Phaedra's last speech.

ACT IV

[*Enter* THESEUS *and* OENONE.]

THESEUS. Ah, what is this I hear? A
  brazen traitor
  Planned this outrage against the
  honor of his father?
  With what harshness you pursue me,
  destiny!
  I know not where I am going, I know
  not where I am.
  Oh, tenderness and goodness too ill
  rewarded!   5
  Audacious scheme! Detestable
  thought!
    To achieve the goal of his black
    love
  The shameless wretch made use of
  force.
  I recognized the sword, the weapon of
  his fury,
  That steel with which I armed him
  for a nobler cause.   10
  Could no ties of blood hold him in
  check?
  And did Phaedra defer his punishment?
  Did Phaedra's silence spare the guilty
  one?
OENONE. Phaedra spared instead a piti-
  ful father.
  Shamed by the scheme of a lover lost
  to passion   15
  And by the criminal fire that burned
  within him,
  Phaedra was about to die, and her
  murderous hand
  Would have extinguished the innocent light in her eyes.
  I saw her lifted arm. I ran to save
  her.
  I alone preserved her for your
  love,   20
  And bemoaning at once her trouble
  and your alarm,
  I came, despite me, to interpret her
  tears.
THESEUS. False-hearted son! He could
  not keep from paling.

I saw him shudder from fear at meet-
  ing me
And was amazed to see his lack of
  joy;   25
His cold embrace froze my tender-
  ness.
    But this guilty love by which he
    is devoured,
  Had it already been declared in
  Athens?
OENONE. My lord, remember the com-
  plaint of the Queen.
  A criminal love was cause of all her
  hate.   30
THESEUS. And this passion then began
  anew in Troezen?
OENONE. I have told you, my lord, all
  that has occurred.
  But the Queen is left too long in her
  mortal grief;
  Allow me to leave you, to be nearer
  to her.   [*Exit* OENONE.]
THESEUS [*alone, seeing* HIPPOLYTUS
  approach]. Ah, here he is. Great
  gods, at this noble bearing,   35
What eye would not have been
  deceived like mine?
Must it be that the sacred mark of
  virtue
Can shine on the brow of a profane
  adulterer?
Should one not be able, by positive
  signs,
To recognize the heart of perfidious
  mortals?   40

[*Enter* HIPPOLYTUS.]

HIPPOLYTUS. May I ask what gloomy
  cloud, my lord,
  Has come to trouble your august
  brow?
  Dare you not confide in me the
  secret?
THESEUS. Traitor! Can you really show
  yourself before me?
  Monster, whom the thunderbolts too
  long have spared,   45

Foul remnant of the brigands of
whom I purged the earth!

After the transports of horror-tainted
love

Have brought their madness to your
father's bed,

You dare to show your hateful self
to me;

You appear in a place you have filled
with infamy,   50

And you do not seek, under an unknown sky,

Some land where my name has not
yet reached!

Fly, traitor. Do not come here
to defy my hate

And tempt a wrath that I can
scarcely hold.

It is enough for me to earn the
eternal disgrace   55

Of having given life to so treacherous
a son,

Without having your death, shameful
blot on my name,

Defile the glory of my noble deeds.

Fly; and if you do not wish a
sudden punishment

To add your name to those my hand
has scourged,   60

Take care that the sun which gives
us light

May never see you set your rash foot
here.

Fly, I say, with speed and no return.

Let none of my States see your
countenance again.

And Neptune, remember—when
through my courage   65

Your shores were cleansed of foul
assassins—

Remember that to reward my successful efforts

You promised to grant the first of my
wishes.

Through all the long hardship of a
cruel prison

I did not ask aid of your immortal
power.   70

Miserly of the help that I await from
you,

I have saved my wishes for some
greater need.

I implore you today. Avenge an unhappy father.

Now I abandon this traitor to your
wrath.

Smother in his blood his shameless
desires.   75

By your fury will Theseus know
your goodness.

HIPPOLYTUS. Phaedra accuses me of a
criminal love!

Such an excess of horror strikes my
soul dumb;

So many unforeseen blows crush me
at one time

That they steal my speech and choke
my voice.   80

THESEUS. Traitor, you assumed that in
cowardly silence

Phaedra would bury your brutal insolence,

But in fleeing, you should not have
abandoned

The sword that in her hands helps
to condemn you.

Or rather, at one blow, adding to
your treachery,   85

You should have robbed her of both
speech and life.

HIPPOLYTUS. Justly angered by so black
a lie,

I should here let truth speak out, my
lord,

But I suppress a secret touching
you.

Be pleased with the respect which
seals my lips,   90

And without seeking to add to your
own grief,

Examine my life, and think of what
I am.

Crimes must always come before
great crimes.

Whoever has crossed the borders fixed
by law

May in the end violate the most
sacred rights.   95

But like virtue itself, crime has its
degrees,

And never has timid innocence been
    seen
To pass abruptly to the extremes of
    license.
A single day does not turn a virtuous
    mortal
Into a false-hearted murderer, an in-
    cestuous coward.   100
        Reared at the bosom of a vir-
            tuous woman,
I have not been untrue to her divine
    origin;
And Pittheus, considered a sage
    among all men,
Deigned to instruct me when I left
    her care.
        I do not wish to paint myself
            with vanity;   105
But if some virtue has fallen to my
    share,
I believe I have above all displayed
The hate of those crimes imputed to
    me.
It is thus that I am known in Greece.
I have pushed virtue to the point of
    bluntness.   110
You know the inflexible rigor of my
    mind,
Nor is the day more pure than the
    depths of my heart.
And yet they claim Hippolytus, lost
    in a profane love...
THESEUS. Yes, it is this same pride,
    wretch, that condemns you.
I see the hateful nature of your cold-
    ness: 115
Phaedra alone has charmed your
    shameless eyes,
And for all other women your indif-
    ferent soul
Has disdained to burn with an inno-
    cent flame.
HIPPOLYTUS. No, I cannot hide from
    you that my heart
Has not disdained to burn with a
    chaste love.   120

At your feet I confess my true
    offense:
I love. I love, it is true, despite your
    prohibition,
For Aricia holds my hopes in slavery
    to her law.
The daughter of Pallas has conquered
    your son.
I adore her, and my soul, rebellious
    to your command,   125
Can neither sigh nor burn but for
    her alone.
THESEUS. You love her? Heaven! But
    no, the stratagem is gross.
You pretend to be a criminal, to
    justify yourself.
HIPPOLYTUS. My lord, six months I
    have shunned her, and I love.
Tremblingly I came to tell you this
    yourself.   130
And now, can nothing show you your
    mistake?
By what awful oath can you be reas-
    sured?
May the earth, may heaven, may all
    nature...
THESEUS. Villains must always have
    recourse to perjury.
Cease, cease, and spare me an un-
    welcome speech,   135
If your false virtue can do nothing
    else.
HIPPOLYTUS. To you it seems false and
    full of artifice.
Phaedra, in her heart, does me
    greater justice.
THESEUS. Oh, how your impudence
    arouses my wrath!
HIPPOLYTUS [*after a pause*]. What
    time do you prescribe for my exile,
    and what place?   140
THESEUS. If you were beyond the
    columns of Alcides,
I would still think myself too near
    a traitor.
HIPPOLYTUS. What friends will pity
    when you abandon me

---

102 *her divine origin:* his mother Antiope was
the daughter of Mars.   103 *Pittheus:* king of
Troezen, who brought up both his grandson
Theseus and his great-grandson Hippolytus.

141 *columns of Alcides:* the Straits of Gibral-
tar, the farthest limit of Hercules' voyages.

And charge me with this awful crime
which you suspect?

THESEUS. Go seek some friends whose
perverse esteem   145
Honors adultery and applauds
incest—
Traitors, wretches without honor and
without law,
Worthy of protecting an evil one like
you.

HIPPOLYTUS. You speak to me still of
adultery and incest?
I say no more. Yet Phaedra had a
mother,   150
Phaedra is of a blood, as you well
know,
More tainted with these horrors than
is mine.

THESEUS. What! Your madness now
loses all restraint.
For the last time, take yourself from
my sight.
Leave, traitor. Do not wait for a
furious father   155
To have you dragged from here in
disgrace.   [*Exit* HIPPOLYTUS.]
Wretch, you go to your certain
death.
Neptune, by the river terrible to the
gods themselves,
Gave me his word and now will
execute it.
A vengeful god follows you; you
cannot avoid him.   160
I loved you; and I feel, despite
your offense,
My heart already troubled at your
fate.
But you have obliged me to condemn you.
Has ever a father, indeed, been more
wronged?
Just gods, who see the grief that
overwhelms me,   165
How could I have bred so guilty a
son?

---

158 *river terrible to the gods themselves:* the
Styx, by which the gods swore irrevocable
oaths.

[*Enter* PHAEDRA.]

PHAEDRA. My lord, I come to you, filled
with a just fear,
For your redoubtable voice reached
to where I stood.
I am afraid a prompt result may
have followed your threat,
But if there still is time, then spare
your son.   170
Respect your own blood, I come to
beg of you.
Save me from the horror of hearing
it cry out;
Do not prepare for me the eternal
grief
Of letting it be shed by a father's
hand.

THESEUS. No, Madam, my hand has
not dipped into my blood,   175
But nonetheless, the wretch has not
escaped me.
An immortal hand is charged with
his destruction;
Neptune owes me this, and you will
be avenged.

PHAEDRA. Neptune owes it to you! So
then your angry prayers...

THESEUS. What! Do you already fear
they may be heard?   180
Rather, join me in my lawful prayers.
Retrace his crimes for me in all their
blackness;
Arouse my anger, still too slow, too
restrained.
All of his crimes are still un-
known to you.
His fury against you pours out in
abuse: 185
Your mouth, he says, is full of decep-
tion.
He claims that Aricia has his heart
and pledge,
That he loves her.

PHAEDRA. What, my lord?

THESEUS. He said it before me.   190
But I know how to pass off an empty
artifice.
Let us hope for prompt justice from
Neptune;

I myself go again to the foot of his altars

To press him to fulfill his immortal oath. [*Exit* THESEUS.]

PHAEDRA. He leaves. What is this news that has struck my ear?   195

What fire, scarcely out, awakens in my heart?

What bolt of thunder, oh heaven, what fatal tidings!

I flew with all speed to the aid of his son,

And, tearing myself from the arms of Oenone,

I gave in to the remorse which tortured me.   200

Who knows where this repentance might have led?

Perhaps I would have ended by accusing myself.

Perhaps, if my voice had not been stopped,

The awful truth would have escaped me.

Hippolytus feels, yet feels nothing for me!   205

Aricia has his heart! Aricia has his pledge!

Oh gods! When at my pleas the unrelenting ingrate

Showed so proud an eye, so austere a brow,

I thought his heart, still shut against love,

Was armed against all my sex alike.   210

Another, however, has broken his indifference;

Before his cruel eyes, another has found compassion.

Perhaps he has a heart easy to be moved,

And I am the only one he cannot endure.

Should I then undertake to defend him?   215

[*Enter* OENONE.]

Dear Oenone, do you know what I have learned?

OENONE. No, but in truth I come to you in trembling,

Pale at the intention which made you leave;

I feared a frenzy that might be fatal to you.

PHAEDRA. Oenone, who would believe it? I had a rival.   220

OENONE. What?

PHAEDRA. Hippolytus loves, and I cannot doubt it.

This proud enemy whom none could subdue,

Whom respect offended, whom pleas importuned,

This tiger, whom I could never meet without fear,   225

Submissive, tamed, admits a conqueror:

Aricia has found the way into his heart.

OENONE. Aricia?

PHAEDRA. Oh, pain never before felt!

For what new torment have I saved myself?   230

All that I have suffered—my fears, my transports,

The fury of my fires, the horror of my remorse,

And the unbearable hurt of a cruel refusal—

Was but a pale foretaste of my torment now.

They love. By what spell did they deceive my eyes?   235

How have they seen each other? Since when? And where?

[*To* OENONE] You knew. Why did you leave me in ignorance?

Could you not tell me of their furtive love?

Have they been often seen speaking, searching for one another?

In the depths of the forest did they go to hide?   240

Alas, they saw each other with full liberty.

As heaven approved the innocence of their sighs,

They followed without remorse their
  lovers' inclination.
For them the days dawned serene and
  clear,
And I, sad reject of all nature, 245
I hid from the day; I fled the light.
  Death was the only god I dared
    to implore,
And I awaited the moment when I
  should expire.
Nourished with gall and with my
  tears,
Still too closely observed in my mis-
  fortune, 250
I dared not drown myself in weeping.
Trembling, I tasted this deathly
  pleasure,
And, disguising my sorrow behind a
  serene brow,
I had often to deny myself my tears.
OENONE. What fruit will they receive
  from their vain love? 255
They will not meet again.
PHAEDRA. They will always love.
  At the moment that I speak—oh,
    awful thought—
They defy the fury of my insane
  passion.
Despite the very exile which is to
  separate them, 260
They take a thousand oaths never to
  be parted.
No, I cannot bear a happiness that
  so offends me,
Oenone. Have pity of my jealous
  rage.
    Aricia must die. Against a hate-
      ful line
I must arouse the anger of my hus-
  band. 265
Let him not be content to punish
  lightly,
For the crime of the sister surpasses
  that of her brothers.
In my jealous transport, I want to
  beg this of him.
    What am I doing? Where does
      my reason wander?

I, jealous? And is Theseus the one
  whom I implore? 270
My husband lives, and I still burn
  with love.
For whom? To whose heart does my
  love aspire?
    Each word I utter stands my
      hair upright.
My crimes now have overflowed the
  measure;
I exhale a scent of incest and decep-
  tion; 275
My murderous hands, ready for
  revenge,
Burn to plunge themselves in innocent blood.
    And yet I live, and I can stand
      the sight
Of that sacred sun from whom I am
  descended?
My ancestor is the father and master
  of the gods; 280
The heavens, the whole universe, are
  full of my forebears.
Where can I hide? Let me fly into
  the infernal night.
But what do I say? My father Minos
  holds the fatal urn;
Destiny, they say, placed it in his
  stern hands,
And there in hell he judges all the
  palid mortals. 285
Ah, how his shade, appalled, will
  tremble
When he sees his daughter before his
  eyes,
Obliged to admit so many varied
  crimes,
And crimes perhaps as yet unknown
  in hell!
    What will you say, my father,
      at this fearful sight? 290
I think I see the urn fall from your
  hand;

---

280 *My ancestor is the father and master of
the gods:* on her father's side, Phaedra is
descended from Jupiter.

I think I see you, seeking some new torture,
Become the tormentor of your own blood.
Pardon! A cruel goddess has destroyed your family;
See her vengeance in the madness of your daughter. 295
Alas, of the awful crime whose shame follows me,
My unhappy heart has never reaped the fruit.
Pursued by misfortune unto my last breath,
I end in torment a life of pain.

OENONE. Thrust aside, Madam, a terror that has no base, 300
And look with another eye upon an excusable mistake.
You love. One cannot vanquish his destiny;
You were carried along by a spell of fate.
Is this, then, an unheard-of marvel among us?
Has love triumphed over none but you? 305
Weakness is but too natural to human beings;
Mortal, you must suffer the fate of a mortal.
You complain of a yoke imposed long ago.
The very gods, the gods who live on Olympus,
Those who strike terror into criminals, 310
Have themselves sometimes burned with illicit fire.

PHAEDRA. What do I hear? What counsel dare you give?

So till the end you wish to poison me,
Wretch? That is how you have ruined me.
You gave me back the light that I tried to flee; 315
Your prayers made me forget my duty;
I was avoiding Hippolytus, and you made me see him.
How was this your affair? Why has your blasphemous mouth,
By accusing him, dared to blacken his life?
He now may die, and the sacrilegious prayer 320
Of a maddened father will be fulfilled.

I listen to you no more. Go, hateful beast!
Go. Leave to me the care of my pitiful fate.
May a just heaven repay you worthily,
And may your punishment forever frighten 325
All those who, like you, by cowardly guile,
Nourish the weakness of the unhappy great,
Push them to the brink toward which their heart inclines,
And smooth for them the road to crime—
Detestable flatterers, the most deadly gift 330
That heavenly anger can make to those who rule! [*Exit* PHAEDRA.]

OENONE [*alone*]. Oh, gods! To serve her I have done all, left all;
And I am thus repaid. [*Long pause.*]
I have well deserved it.

---

294 *A cruel goddess:* Venus.

ACT V

[*Enter* ARICIA *and* HIPPOLYTUS.]

ARICIA. What, you can keep silent in
　this extreme peril
And leave in error a father who loves
　you?
Cruel one, if, disdaining the power of
　my tears,
You consent so easily to see me no
　more,
Then go. Leave behind a sad
　Aricia.   5
But at least in leaving, safeguard
　your life,
Defend your honor from a shameful
　reproach,
And force your father to revoke his
　prayers.
There still is time. Why, by what
　caprice,
Do you leave the field free to your
　accuser?   10
Enlighten Theseus.
HIPPOLYTUS. Ah, what have I not said?
Should I have brought to light his
　bed's disgrace?
Should I, in telling too truthful a
　story,
Have made my father blush with
　unworthy shame?   15
You alone have pierced this hateful
　mystery;
To pour out my heart, I have but
　you and the gods.
I could not hide from you—judge
　whether I love—
All that I wanted to hide from my-
　self.
　　But remember that I revealed
　　it under seal of secrecy.   20
Forget, if you can, that I have
　spoken to you,
Madam, and never may so pure a
　mouth
Open to tell of this horrible adven-
　ture.
Let us place our trust in the fairness
　of the gods,

For they have every reason to vindi-
　cate me,   25
And Phaedra, soon or late punished
　for her crime,
Will not avoid her merited disgrace.
This is as much as I require of you;
All the rest I leave to my free wrath.
　　Quit the slavery to which you
　　are reduced;   30
Dare to follow me; dare to join me
　in flight;
Tear yourself from a baleful and
　ungodly place,
Where virtue breathes a poisoned
　air.
To hide your quick departure, take
　advantage
Of the confusion that my disgrace
　creates.   35
I can assure you of the means of
　flight,
For as yet you have no guards but
　mine.
Powerful defenders will take up our
　quarrel;
Argos extends its arms, and Sparta
　calls to us.
To our common friends let us carry
　our just complaints.   40
Let us not allow Phaedra, profiting
　by our disgrace,
To drive the two of us from my
　father's throne
And promise to her son both my her-
　itage and yours.
　　The opportunity is good; we
　　must embrace it.
What fear withholds you? You bal-
　ance undecided?   45
It is your interest alone that inspires
　my daring.
When I am all fire, whence comes
　your ice?
Are you afraid to follow in the steps
　of an exile?
ARICIA. Alas, how such banishment
　would be dear to me!

In what joyful transports, tied to
your fate,   50
Would I live forgotten by all other
mortals,
But not being united by so sweet a
bond,
Can I with honor flee with you?
I know, without wounding the most
exacting honor,
I can deliver myself from the hands
of your father;   55
I am not tearing myself from my
parents' bosom,
And flight is allowed him who flees
his tyrants.
But you love me, my lord, and my
threatened name...

HIPPOLYTUS. No, no, I have too much
regard for your reputation.
A nobler plan brings me before
you: 60
Flee from your enemies, and follow
your husband.
Free in our misfortune, since so
heaven decrees,
The pledging of our faith depends on
no one else.
Not always must a wedding be lit by
torches.
At the gates of Troezen, and among
the tombs,   65
Ancient sepulchre of the princes of
my people,
Is a sacred temple, fearful to per-
jurers.
It is there that mortals dare not
swear in vain.
The perfidious receive a sudden
punishment,
And no greater barrier to a lie
exists   70
Than fear of finding inevitable death.
There, if you believe me, with an
eternal love,
We will go to confirm our solemn
troth.
We will take as witness the god we
worship there,
And we both will pray him to serve
as father to us.   75

I will call upon the most sacred of
our gods.
Both chaste Diana and august Juno
And all gods, indeed, in witness to
my love,
Will guarantee the worth of my holy
promises.
ARICIA. The King comes. Flee, Prince,
and leave at once.   80
To hide my departure, I will stay a
while.
Go. And leave me some faithful guide
To lead my timid steps toward you.

[*Exit* HIPPOLYTUS *as* THESEUS *enters.*]

THESEUS. Gods, shed light on my trouble, and deign
To show me the truth I come here to
seek.   85
ARICIA [*to* ISMENE]. Think of everything, dear Ismene, and be ready
for flight.   [*Exit* ISMENE.]
THESEUS. You change color and seen
abashed, Madam.
What was Hippolytus doing in this
place?
ARICIA. My lord, he was bidding me an
eternal farewell.
THESEUS. Your eyes were able to sub-
due that rebellious heart,   90
And his first sighs are your trium-
phant work.
ARICIA. My lord, I cannot deny the
truth to you.
He has not inherited your unjust
hate;
He did not treat me as a criminal.
THESEUS. I understand. He swore eter-
nal love to you.   95
But do not feel assured of that incon-
stant heart,
For he has sworn as much to others.
ARICIA. He, my lord?
THESEUS. You should have rendered
him less flighty.
How could you bear this horrible
sharing?   100
ARICIA. And how can you bear that this
horrible slander

Should blacken the course of so fine
a life?
Have you so little knowledge of his
heart?
Do you so ill distinguish crime from
innocence?
Must it be that to your eyes alone
a hateful cloud   105
Conceals his virtue that shines to
other eyes?
Oh, this is giving him up to perfidious
tongues.
Stop. Repent of your murderous
prayers.
Fear, my lord, fear lest a stern
heaven
Should hate you enough to fulfill
your wish.   110
Often in its anger it accepts our
sacrifice;
Its gifts are often the punishment of
our crimes.
THESEUS. No, you wish in vain to excuse his outrage;
Your love blinds you in favor of the
wretch.
But I believe positive, irreproachable
witnesses.   115
I have seen tears, I have seen true
tears flow.
ARICIA. Take care, my lord. Your in-
vincible hands
Have freed men from monsters with-
out number,
But all are not destroyed, and you
let one
Still live... Your son, my lord, for-
bids me to go on.   120
Aware of the respect for you he
wishes to preserve,
I would afflict him too much if I
dared to finish.
I imitate his reserve and flee from
your presence
That I may not be forced to break
my silence.   [*Exit* ARICIA.]
THESEUS [*alone*]. What is her thought?
What do her words hide,   125
Begun so many times, and always
interrupted?

Do they seek to disturb me through
a vain pretense?
Are the two of them agreed to put
me to the torture?
    And as for me, despite my harsh
    severity,
What plaintive voice cries in the
depths of my heart?   130
A secret pity afflicts and moves me.
A second time I will question Oenone.
I wish to be better informed of all
the crime.
Guards, have Oenone come out and
approach alone.

[*Enter* PANOPE.]

PANOPE. I do not know the project that
the Queen debates,   135
My lord, but from the emotion that
stirs her I fear the worst.
A mortal despair is painted on her
face.
And the pallor of death already is
upon her.
    Already, sent away in shame
    from her presence,
Oenone has thrown herself into the
sea.   140
No one knows from whence came this
mad intent,
And the waves evermore will hide her
from our view.
THESEUS. What do I hear?
PANOPE. Her death has not relieved
the Queen;
The trouble seems to grow in her
uncertain soul.   145
Sometimes, to soften her secret pain,
She takes her children and bathes
them in tears,
And suddenly, renouncing maternal
love,
Her hand with horror pushes them
away.
Her irresolute steps lead her at ran-
dom;   150
Her distracted eye no longer recog-
nizes us.
Three times she has written, and,
changing her mind,

Three times she has torn the letter
she had begun.
Deign to see her, my lord; deign to
give her aid.
THESEUS. Oh, heaven, Oenone is dead,
and Phaedra wants to die?　155
Have my son recalled; let him come
to his defense!
Let him come to speak to me. I am
ready to listen.
　　Do not hasten, Neptune, your
　　deadly godsend,
For I prefer my wishes never to be
granted.
I perhaps believed too soon unfaithful witnesses,　160
And too soon I lifted my cruel hands
to you.
　　Ah, what anguish may follow
　　that prayer!

[*Enter* THERAMENES.]

　　Theramenes, is that you? What
　　have you done with my son?
I entrusted him to you from the
tenderest age.
But whence come these tears I see
you shed?　165
What is my son doing?
THERAMENES. Oh, tardy and super-
fluous care!
Futile tenderness! Hippolytus is no
more.
THESEUS. Gods!
THERAMENES. I have seen perish the
most gracious of mortals,　170
And, I dare to say again, my lord, the
least guilty.
THESEUS. My son is no more? When I
hold out to him my arms
The impatient gods have hastened
his end?
What blow stole him from me? What
sudden thunderbolt?
THERAMENES. Scarcely had we left the
gates of Troezen,　175
Than he was in his chariot. His griev-
ing guards,
Ranged all about him, were silent
as he.

Pensively he followed the road to
Mycena,
Letting the reins float free above his
horses.
His proud coursers, which one used
to see　180
Full of noble zeal, obedient to his
voice,
Now with saddened eye and lowered
head
Seemed to conform to his sad
thoughts.
　　A terrible cry, come from the
　　depths of the sea,
At that moment troubled the quiet of
the air;　185
And from the bosom of the earth a
formidable voice
Answered with a moan this dreadful
sound.
In our very hearts our blood was
frozen,
And on the alerted horses the mane
stood up.
　　Meanwhile on the face of the
　　liquid plain　190
There rises, boiling, a watery moun-
tain.
The wave comes near, breaks, and
vomits before our eyes,
Amid a flood of foam, a furious
monster.
His wide brow is armed with menac-
ing horns,
His whole body covered with yellow-
ing scales;　195
Untamable bull, hot-headed dragon—
His crupper curls in tortuous folds.
His long bellowing makes the shore
tremble.
With horror heaven looks on this
savage shape.
The earth is aroused, the air in-
fected;　200
The sea, which brought him, with-
draws in terror.
All flee. Without making show of
fruitless courage,
In the nearby temple they seek
safety.

Hippolytus alone, worthy son of
a hero,
Stops his coursers, seizes his jave-
lins,   205
Rushes upon the beast, and with
well-thrown spear
Makes a great wound in his side.
In rage and in pain the leaping mon-
ster
Falls moaning at the feet of the
horses,
Rolls and turns on them a flaming
mouth,   210
Which covers them with smoke, with
blood and fire.
Fear carries them off, and deaf this
one time,
They no longer know either rein or
voice.
In useless effort their master exhausts
himself.
They redden the bit with a bloody
foam.   215
It is said that in this awful confusion
there was even seen
A god who pressed their dusty flanks
with goads.
Across the rocks, fright rushes them.
The axle cries and breaks. The
intrepid Hippolytus
Sees his shattered chariot fly in
splinters;   220
He himself falls, entangled in the
reins.
        Excuse my grief. This cruel scene
Will be for me an eternal source of
tears.
I saw, my lord, I saw your unhappy
son
Dragged by the horses whom his
hand had fed.   225
He wants to call them back, and his
voice frightens them.
They run. His whole body is soon but
one wound.
The plain re-echoes to our grievous
cries.
        At last their impetuous dash is
slowed;

They stop, not far from those ancient
tombs   230
Where lie the cold remains of the
kings his ancestors.
I run, panting, and his guard follows
me.
The trail of his noble blood shows
us the way;
The rocks are stained; the dripping
brambles
Carry the bloody strands of his
hair.   235
I arrive; I call him. Then, giving me
his hand,
He opens his dying eyes, and closes
them at once.
"Heaven," he says, "takes an inno-
cent life.
After my death, care well for sad
Aricia.
Dear friend, if my father, one day
disabused,   240
Regrets the misfortune of a son
falsely blamed,
To appease my blood and my plain-
tive shade,
Tell him to treat his captive with
gentleness,
To give her back . . ." At this word,
the hero, dead,
Left in my arms but his disfigured
body,   245
A sad thing, in which triumphed the
anger of the gods,
And which the eye of his very father
would not know.
THESEUS. Oh, my son! Dear hope of
which I have robbed myself!
Inexorable gods who have served me
too well!
To what mortal regrets my life is now
given over!   250
THERAMENES. Timid Aricia then
arrived.
She was coming, my lord, flying from
your wrath,

---

230 *those ancient tombs:* where Aricia was to
meet Hippolytus.

To take him as husband before the
gods.

She approaches. She sees the grass,
red and smoking;

She sees (what a sight for the eyes
of a lover!)   255

Hippolytus outstretched, without
form, without color.

She tries for a time to doubt her
misfortune,

And, no longer knowing this hero
she adores,

She sees Hippolytus and yet asks for
him.

But too sure at last that he is before
her eyes,   260

By a sorrowing look she accuses the
gods;

And cold, moaning, and almost inani-
mate,

She falls in a swoon at the feet of
her lover.

Ismene is beside her; Ismene, all in
tears,

Calls her back to life, or rather back
to grief.   265

    And as for me, I have come,
cursing life,

To tell you the last wish of a hero

And to fulfill, my lord, the unhappy
duty

Which his dying heart placed upon
me.

But I see his mortal enemy ap-
proach.   270

[*Enter* PHAEDRA.]

THESEUS [*to* PHAEDRA]. Well, you
triumph, and my son is without
life.

Ah, what I have cause to fear, and
what cruel suspicion,

Excusing him in my heart, alarms
me with reason!

But, Madam, he is dead. Take your
victim.

Enjoy his death, unjust or legitimate.   275

I consent that my eyes may always

be deluded.

I believe him a criminal, since you
accuse him.

His death offers reason enough for
my tears

Without my going to seek hateful
enlightenment,

Which, unable to return him to my
just grief,   280

Might only serve to increase my
misery.

    Let me, far from you and far
from these shores,

Flee the bloody image of my torn
son.

Bewildered, pursued by this memory
of death,

I would banish myself from the entire universe.   285

    Everything seems to rise against
my injustice.

The glory of my name even increases
my torture.

Less known to mortals, I could hide
myself the better.

I hate the very care with which the
gods honor me,

And I leave to bewail their murdering
favors,   290

Without bothering them more with
futile prayers.

Whatever they do for me, their
deadly goodness

Can never repay me for what they
have taken.

PHAEDRA. No, Theseus, I must break
an unjust silence.

I must give back his innocence to
your son.   295

He was not guilty.

THESEUS. Ah, unhappy father!

And it was on your word that I
condemned him!

Cruel one, do you believe yourself
sufficiently excused...

PHAEDRA. Moments are dear to me.
Listen to me, Theseus.   300

It is I who on this chaste and respectful son

Dared to cast an impure and incestuous eye.
Heaven placed in my breast a deadly
flame;
The detestable Oenone did all the
rest.
She feared that Hippolytus, learning
of my madness,   305
Might reveal the love that horrified
him;
So the treacherous woman, imposing
on my weakness,
Hastened to accuse him first before
you.
She has punished herself and, fleeing
my wrath,
Has sought in the waves too easy a
penalty.   310
The sword would already have cut
short my destiny,
But I allowed Virtue, compromised,
to moan.
Exposing my remorse before you, I
wanted
To go down among the dead by a
slower route.
I have poured into my burning
veins   315
A poison which Medea brought to
Athens.
Already the venom, having reached

my dying heart,
Casts upon it a cold it has never
known.
Already I see but through a cloud
Both the sky and the husband that
my presence offends;   320
And death, hiding from my eyes the
light,
Gives back to the day, which they
defiled, all its purity.

PANOPE. She dies, my lord!

THESEUS. Of so black an act
Would that the memory might die
with her.   325
Let us go, too well aware, alas, of
my error,
To mix our tears with the blood of
my unhappy son.
Let us go to embrace what remains
of him,
To expiate the madness of a prayer
I curse.
Let us render him the honors he has
deserved,   330
And the better to appease his angered
shade,
Despite the plotting of an unjust
family,
Let his loved one be for me a
daughter, from today.

---

303 *Heaven:* more specifically, Venus.   316
Medea: wife of Jason, famous for her magic
philters.

---

332 *an unjust family:* the Pallantides.

The Master Builder

The central conflict of *The Master Builder* is revealed both in Solness' relationships with the three women, Mrs. Solness, Kaia Fosli, and Hilda Wangel, and
in three kinds of buildings that correspond roughly to them: the old-fashioned
houses of a previous generation (Mrs. Solness' lifeless dolls burn in one, her two
babies dying subsequently from her shock and the poisoning of her milk); Solness'
special kind of houses for people to be happy in (for assistance in building these
he has taken Kaia as scribe and drained the resources of Ragnar and the elder
Brovik); and buildings of high aspiration (houses with towers, churches, and
castles in the air). Since the creation of one kind destroys another, Solness is
caught in a dilemma: he cannot live on all these levels at the same time. As the
exposition of the first act carries him back to an earlier, crucial decision concerning
what woman to follow (or use) and what to build, the immediate action of the play
carries him forward to a reversal of that decision. Recapturing a moment of past
exaltation in which he "climbed high," he rejects his ten years of moderate success
and dies trying to "do the impossible" once again.

Whatever course Solness chooses, however, will destroy him, because if he does
not transcend his "domestic" work the new generation will ruin him as he has
ruined those before him; yet his own fatal weakness will also destroy him if he
tries to reach new heights. The fatal discontinuity between the generations is
clear both in his own empty dwelling and in old Brovik's decline. In the first
act he is merely trying to postpone the inevitable by repressing Ragnar, his most
imminent challenger, and transferring Mrs. Solness into a house comfortable on
the ground floor but possessing a high tower. When Hilda comes knocking as the
spirit of the new generation (escaping the old), she cannot reverse the inevitable;
she can only make Solness perish heroically rather than pathetically. As the conflict
between romantic aspiration (Viking freedom) and safe, conventional building
sharpens, it appears momentarily as though she might enable him not only to
dispense with his other youthful help but also to use youth against youth to
triumph over his rivals; and certainly she works a spiritual cleansing of his
morbidity, guilt, arrogance, pettiness, and underhanded use of others, scraping
enough deposits from his ego to free what is left of his brilliance. (As the name
Wangel suggests, she is his good angel, though perhaps more Valkyrie—and less
either than an energetic, dreaming, erotic woman.)

Yet in a sense it is Solness' own ambiguous spirit that summons her (as though
by occult means); and in any case he cannot translate himself entirely into her
image of him. She is not so much an exterior cause of the change in him as a
correlative to inner causes, and these are too complex to allow a simple return
to youth. Both Hilda and his own conscience are instruments of tragic *retribution*
as well as *aspiration*. The new tower proves as unsuitable for him as the ground
floor is for his wife: he cannot escape the part of him that is represented by
the older woman: "I am chained alive to a dead woman," he says, "I who cannot

live without joy in life." Hilda herself comes to understand that after talking with Mrs. Solness and realizes that she ought to leave.

Solness, then, cannot be renewed in Hilda (though she sleeps in the nursery as though his child), any more than Mrs. Solness was able to renew herself in her twin children. He is surrounded by bitter envy, partly veiled behind and partly transformed into the slavishness of Brovik, Ragnar, and Kaia. That he clears away some of the emotional and social tangle that weighs him down is evident in the soaring mood of the final act in which the fearful doubts of Mrs. Solness, Ragnar, and Solness himself are counterbalanced by his courage and Hilda's rejuvenated spirit. But Mrs. Solness' and Ragnar's view of him is as valid as Hilda's: he both climbs *and* falls.

In this twofold movement of Solness toward catastrophe and rejuvenation, the play's symbolic means reinforce its realistic surface and give compressed expression to his destructive alternatives. But in other respects, critics have found the play's symbolism incompatible with its realism. If Solness and Hilda are interpreted as strictly an admiring young lady and a builder, the play's claim to tragic status becomes very tenuous. Considered this way, as one reader points out, the play presents us with an aging architect who falls from a scaffold while trying to show off for a young lady. What are we to make of a builder who puts high towers on houses? Or who believes in occult powers and the influence of trolls and apparently in all seriousness decides to build henceforth castles in the air (on firm foundation!)? Or what are we to make of a starry-eyed girl who hears voices and harps in the air and demands a queendom from an aging designer of housing projects? If we limit ourselves to strict realism, as Ibsen suggested, we are apparently obliged to consider both Hilda and Solness candidates for an asylum. (Mrs. Solness, still recuperating from the shock of her burned dolls, already visits one.) The play then becomes a study in near-pathological psychology. Certainly psychoanalysis can tell us much of phallic spires, *anima* figures like Hilda, and perhaps even of trolls, as it has told us of Oedipus complexes. On this level, the castles are sublimated passion, airy eroticism; and Solness' desire to build them on firm foundation suggests something like an intent to set up an apartment for Hilda where a tired architect can escape his wife. Human love replaces devotion to art, and Hilda brings not blueprints for houses but unqualified devotion and an obvious physical liveliness.

One way of avoiding the shrinkage of the play in this reading is very inviting to biographers of Henrik Ibsen (1828–1906), who recognize a number of striking parallels between Solness and Ibsen, the master builder of plays. Solness' early high-rise construction they take to be roughly equivalent to Ibsen's early plays with romantic superhuman heroes (though that equation ignores Ibsen's ironic treatment of his own heroes); modest homes become the predominantly realistic plays of Ibsen's middle period; and plays subsequent to *The Master Builder* are found again to aspire, conveniently, beyond realism. It is also true that Ibsen received both adoration and hostile attacks from younger writers during the year he began work on the play. In Vienna he said in response to a toast to him, "This is a beautiful hour," and promised that "the beautiful, the clear, the free" that he then saw would become "part of a work of art." (He was accustomed to allow a year for germination after finishing one work before starting another, during which time just such personal experience as this was transformed into dramatic material.) Attacked during the same period by the young writer Knut Hamsun, he may well have felt threatened by new modes of drama that would discredit his own. More important, he may have felt the truth of Georg Brandes' charge that his idealism as a poet was impractical, that his high aspirations failed to change society. (He could not climb as high as he built.) The younger social revolutionary suggested that Ibsen expressed ideals only through dramatic characters, thus freeing himself of responsibility for them, and that such practice separated "the theoretical from the practical" and created a dualism that only a poet living in exile (as Ibsen did) could indulge in.

These parallels have a legitimate claim on our attention, especially since it is obviously impossible to make literal castles in the air, with a hammer and saw, though Solness insists twice that he *will* build them and says that they are the "only possible dwelling-place for human happiness." Despite disclaimers to the contrary, Ibsen appears at these points to demand that we abandon either surface realism or belief in Solness' sanity. But a translation of Solness into Ibsen and airy castles into idealistic dreams, to be instrumented in future plays (despite the author's own dizziness at high altitudes), raises the question, what kind of dramatic mode or variety of tragedy do we then have? Actually, at some point much earlier than the emergence of Solness' unexpected powers of imagination we realize that he is more than a carpenter; he is a forceful creator, or would be if he could free himself from his own limitations. The play clearly concerns the tension between creation and social entanglement. That Ibsen felt that tension personally and was vulnerable to Brandes' charge is perhaps less relevant to an interpretation of the play, however, than that such a disjunction between *means of action* and *idealistic masterplans* threatens all builders. Solness may be a carpenter and still represent universal problems, including some that troubled Ibsen.

The critical as opposed to the biographical point, then, is that the play contains an ironic comment on its own construction and that a sophisticated reaction to it must negotiate between symbolism and realism. We can perhaps put the formal repercussions of theme in this way: idea and form, imagination and architectural structure (including the conventions of theatrical realism) are so distinct as to require that the creator defy his own tangible means (defy the building code) by trying the impossible. In Solness' case this means crowning his work with a wreath; in Ibsen's case chancing romantic elements in realistic plays. Such a crowning does not change the basic nature of the building, but it does require a revaluation that emphasizes the tower and the romantic gesture toward transcendence as opposed to things that make better sense. Descriptively, we can say that Solness, the literal builder surrounded with the documentary stuff of realism—chained to a dead woman and a disbelieving society—seeks for a means to liberate himself from the limitations of his vocation. Biographically, some aspects of the old Ibsen must be sacrificed to the Viking creator who wrote predictively as a young man:

> I will build me a cloud castle. Two wings shall shape it forth;
> A great one and a small one. I shall shine across the North.
> The greater shall shelter a singer immortal;
> The smaller to a maiden shall open its portal.

With respect to the tragic necessity involved in either position, we can say that it is metaphysically impossible to incarnate romantic ideals in structures, whether conventional, social, and marital institutions, houses, churches, or plays. To be reborn, a tragic hero must die to his less heroic self; and to transcend nature romantically and live in castles in the air, a writer must destroy nature as daily reality.

Full awareness of this law of spiritual dynamics may belong to Ibsen and to the audience rather than to Solness, but we should remember Solness' recognition that he has built "nothing" and made no sacrifices "for the chance of building. Nothing, nothing! The whole is nothing." And he clearly realizes that dreams transcend such realities as he has negotiated with. We need only add to this that as allegorical meaning is both realized in and destroys the literal "letter" at some point, or as talk in "high" romantic terms necessitates abandoning "low" realism (one cannot wear priestly robes and work clothes at the same time), so the soaring language of Solness must put aside his frail, mortal self; and if he rises high enough, the fall will be fatal. Solness, then, could well be Ibsen's dramatic answer both to quick-acting revolutionaries, like Brandes, and romantics who suppose that instituting ideals is a matter of female suffrage and a change in government.

In this dimension of the play, Ibsen works a new variation of a typical tragic paradox in which the sublimity or nobility of the hero emerges as his accustomed status is reversed. For tragic peripety is often ennobling as well as destructive: Lear must be broken as king to become a greater man; Oedipus must be cast down as a rational man to prove the higher truths of oracles and prove himself worthy of enlightenment. In most tragedies the new figure that emerges from the reversal is expended in a few lines without displacing the pity and fear of his destruction. In *The Master Builder* the harps that Hilda hears counterbalance but do not cancel the horror of the fall. Nor does her love, though important to Solness (on any level) in ridding himself of inner weaknesses, offer a new vocation that allows him to escape the ambiguity of realistic-romantic creation. (We note that the young Ibsen placed the "singer immortal" in the major wing of his castle, leaving the smaller wing for the maiden who comes to join him. Indications are that Ibsen's young women either joined him on his terms or not at all.) Hilda, then, provides a choral commentary on the defiant act and bears witness to it as its perfect audience—as one among the new generations who knows how to read the master. But unlike her and like Mrs. Solness, we, the "outside" audience, remember that Solness is also a dizzy mortal who on two special occasions proved that he could climb as high as he built but in neither case managed to sustain himself in the air: at the peak of his performance, the realities of gravity and aging bodies crash through the triumphs of creative imagination. Shakespeare might well have followed with an epilogue by a character coming forth from the theatrical illusion (to give us transition back to the real world) who puts aside his mask to tell us:

> Now my charms are all o'erthrown,
> And what strength I have's mine own,
> Which is most faint.
>
> *(The Tempest)*

The Master Builder

HALVARD SOLNESS   *Master Builder*
ALINE SOLNESS   *his wife*
DOCTOR HERDAL   *physician*
KNUT BROVIK   *formerly an architect, now in* SOLNESS' *employment*

RAGNAR BROVIK   *his son, draftsman*
KAIA FOSLI   *his niece, bookkeeper*
MISS HILDA WANGEL
SOME LADIES

ACT I

SCENE. *A crowd in the street. The action passes in and about* SOLNESS' *house.*

A plainly furnished workroom in the house of HALVARD SOLNESS. *Folding doors on the left lead out to the hall. On the right is the door leading to the inner rooms of the house. At the back is an open door into the draftsmen's office. In front, on the left, a desk with books, papers, and writing materials. Farther back than the folding door, a stove. In the right-hand corner, a sofa, a table, and one or two chairs. On the table a water bottle and glass. A smaller table, with a rocking chair and armchair, in front on the right. Lighted lamps, with shades, on the table in the draftsmen's office, on the table in the corner, and on the desk.*
In the draftsmen's office sit KNUT BROVIK *and his son* RAGNAR, *occupied with plans and calculations. At the desk in the outer office stands* KAIA FOSLI, *writing in the ledger.* KNUT BROVIK *is a spare old man with white hair and beard. He wears a rather threadbare*

but well-brushed black coat, spectacles and a somewhat discoloured white neckcloth. RAGNAR BROVIK *is a well-dressed, light-haired man in his thirties, with a slight stoop.* KAIA FOSLI *is a slightly built girl, a little over twenty, carefully dressed and delicate looking. She has a green shade over her eyes. All three go on working for some time in silence.*

KNUT BROVIK [*rises suddenly, as if in distress, from the table; breathes heavily and laboriously as he comes forward into the doorway*]. No, I can't bear it much longer!

KAIA [*going up to him*]. You are feeling ill this evening, are you not, uncle?

BROVIK. Oh, I seem to get worse every day.

RAGNAR [*has risen and advances*]. You ought to go home, father. Try to get a little sleep——

BROVIK [*impatiently*]. Go to bed, I suppose? Would you have me stifled outright?

KAIA. Then take a little walk.

RAGNAR. Yes, do. I will come with you.

BROVIK [*with warmth*]. I will not go till he comes! I am determined to have it out this evening with—[*in a tone of suppressed bitterness*]—with him—with the chief.

Reprinted from Six Great Modern Plays *edited by Edward Parone and published by Dell Publishing Co., Inc.*

KAIA [*anxiously*]. Oh no, uncle—do wait awhile before doing that.

RAGNAR. Yes, better wait, father!

BROVIK [*draws his breath laboriously*]. Ha—ha——! I haven't much time for waiting.

KAIA [*listening*]. Hush! I hear him on the stairs.

[*All three go back to their work. A short silence.* HALVARD SOLNESS *comes in through the hall door. He is a man no longer young, but healthy and vigorous, with close-cut curly hair, dark moustache, and dark thick eyebrows. He wears a grayish-green buttoned jacket with an upstanding collar and broad lapels. On his head he wears a soft gray felt hat, and he has one or two light portfolios under his arm.*]

SOLNESS [*near the door, points toward the draftsmen's office and asks in a whisper*]. Are they gone?

KAIA [*softly, shaking her head*]. No.

[*She takes the shade off her eyes.* SOLNESS *crosses the room, throws his hat on a chair, places the portfolios on the table by the sofa, and approaches the desk again.* KAIA *goes on writing without intermission but seems nervous and uneasy.*]

SOLNESS [*aloud*]. What is that you are entering, Miss Fosli?

KAIA [*starts*]. Oh, it is only something that——

SOLNESS. Let me look at it, Miss Fosli. [*Bends over her, pretends to be looking into the ledger, and whispers:*] Kaia!

KAIA [*softly, still writing*]. Well?

SOLNESS. Why do you always take that shade off when I come?

KAIA [*as before*]. I look so ugly with it on.

SOLNESS [*smiling*]. Then you don't like to look ugly, Kaia?

KAIA [*half glancing up at him*]. Not for all the world. Not in your eyes.

SOLNESS [*stroking her hair gently*]. Poor, poor little Kaia—

KAIA [*bending her head*]. Hush—they can hear you.

[SOLNESS *strolls across the room to the right, turns, and pauses at the door of the draftsmen's office.*]

SOLNESS. Has anyone been here for me?

RAGNAR [*rising*]. Yes, the young couple who want a villa built, out at Löv-strand.

SOLNESS [*growling*]. Oh, those two! They must wait. I am not quite clear about the plans yet.

RAGNAR [*advancing, with some hesitation*]. They were very anxious to have the drawings at once.

SOLNESS [*as before*]. Yes, of course—so they all are.

BROVIK [*looks up*]. They say they are longing so to get into a house of their own.

SOLNESS. Yes, yes—we know all that! And so they are content to take whatever is offered them. They get a—a roof over their heads—an address—but nothing to call a home. No thank you! In that case, let them apply to somebody else. Tell them that, the next time they call.

BROVIK [*pushes his glasses up on to his forehead and looks in astonishment at him*]. To somebody else? Are you prepared to give up the commission?

SOLNESS [*impatiently*]. Yes, yes, yes, devil take it! If that is to be the way of it——. Rather that than build away at random. [*vehemently*] Besides, I know very little about these people as yet.

BROVIK. The people are safe enough. Ragnar knows them. He is a friend of the family. Perfectly safe people.

SOLNESS. Oh, safe—safe enough! That is not at all what I mean. Good Lord—don't you understand me either? [*angrily*] I won't have anything to do with these strangers. They may apply to whom they please, so far as I am concerned.

BROVIK [*rising*]. Do you really mean that?

SOLNESS [*sulkily*]. Yes, I do,—for once in a way.

[*He comes forward.* BROVIK *exchanges a glance with* RAGNAR, *who makes a warning gesture. Then* BROVIK *comes into the front room.*]

BROVIK. May I have a few words with you?

SOLNESS. Certainly.

BROVIK [*to* KAIA]. Just go in there for a moment, Kaia.

KAIA [*uneasily*]. Oh, but uncle—

BROVIK. Do as I say, child. And shut the door after you.

[KAIA *goes reluctantly into the draftsmen's office, glances anxiously and imploringly at* SOLNESS, *and shuts the door.*]

BROVIK [*lowering his voice a little*]. I don't want the poor children to know how ill I am.

SOLNESS. Yes, you have been looking very poorly of late.

BROVIK. It will soon be all over with me. My strength is ebbing—from day to day.

SOLNESS. Won't you sit down?

BROVIK. Thanks—may I?

SOLNESS [*placing the armchair more conveniently*]. Here—take this chair. —And now?

BROVIK [*has seated himself with difficulty*]. Well, you see, it's about Ragnar. That is what weighs most upon me. What is to become of him?

SOLNESS. Of course your son will stay with me as long as ever he likes.

BROVIK. But that is just what he does not like. He feels that he cannot stay here any longer.

SOLNESS. Why, I should say he was very well off here. But if he wants more money, I should not mind—

BROVIK. No, no! It is not that. [*impatiently*] But sooner or later he, too, must have a chance of doing something on his own account.

SOLNESS [*without looking at him*]. Do you think that Ragnar has quite talent enough to stand alone?

BROVIK. No, that is just the heartbreaking part of it—I have begun to have my doubts about the boy. For you have never said so much as—as one encouraging word about him. And yet I cannot but think there must be something in him—he can't be without talent.

SOLNESS. Well, but he has learnt nothing—nothing thoroughly, I mean. Except, of course, to draw.

BROVIK [*looks at him with covert hatred and says hoarsely*]. You had learned little enough of the business when you were in my employment. But that did not prevent you from setting to work—[*breathing with difficulty*]—and pushing your way up and taking the wind out of my sails —mine, and so many other people's.

SOLNESS. Yes, you see—circumstances favored me.

BROVIK. You are right there. Everything favored you. But then how can you have the heart to let me go to my grave—without having seen what Ragnar is fit for? And of course I am anxious to see them married, too—before I go.

SOLNESS [*sharply*]. Is it she who wishes it?

BROVIK. Not Kaia so much as Ragnar —he talks about it every day. [*appealingly*] You must—you must help him to get some independent work now! I must see something that the lad has done. Do you hear?

SOLNESS [*peevishly*]. Hang it, man, you can't expect me to drag commissions down from the moon for him!

BROVIK. He has the chance of a capital commission at this very moment. A big bit of work.

SOLNESS [*uneasily, startled*]. Has he?

BROVIK. If you would give your consent.

SOLNESS. What sort of work do you mean?

BROVIK [*with some hesitation*]. He can have the building of that villa out at Lövstrand.

SOLNESS. That! Why, I am going to build that myself.

BROVIK. Oh, you don't much care about doing it.

SOLNESS [*flaring up*]. Don't care! I? Who dares to say that?

BROVIK. You said so yourself just now.

SOLNESS. Oh, never mind what I say. —Would they give Ragnar the building of that villa?

BROVIK. Yes. You see, he knows the family. And then—just for the fun of the thing—he has made drawings and estimates and so forth——

SOLNESS. Are they pleased with the drawings? The people who will have to live in the house?

BROVIK. Yes. If you would only look through them and approve of them.

SOLNESS. Then they would let Ragnar build their home for them?

BROVIK. They were immensely pleased with his idea. They thought it exceedingly original, they said.

SOLNESS. Oho! Original! Not the old-fashioned stuff that *I* am in the habit of turning out!

BROVIK. It seemed to them different.

SOLNESS [*with suppressed irritation*]. So it was to see Ragnar that they came here—whilst I was out!

BROVIK. They came to call upon you —and at the same time to ask whether you would mind retiring——

SOLNESS [*angrily*]. Retire? I?

BROVIK. In case you thought that Ragnar's drawings——

SOLNESS. I? Retire in favor of your son!

BROVIK. Retire from the agreement, they meant.

SOLNESS. Oh, it comes to the same thing. [*Laughs angrily.*] So that is it, is it? Halvard Solness is to see about retiring now! To make room for younger men! For the very youngest, perhaps! He must make room! Room! Room!

BROVIK. Why, good heavens! there is surely room for more than one single man——

SOLNESS. Oh, there's not so very much room to spare either. But, be that as it may—I will never retire! I will never give way to anybody! Never of my own free will. Never in this world will I do that!

BROVIK [*rises with difficulty*]. Then I am to pass out of life without any certainty? Without a gleam of happiness? Without any faith or trust in Ragnar? Without having seen a single piece of work of his doing? Is that to be the way of it?

SOLNESS [*turns half aside and mutters*]. H'm—don't ask more just now.

BROVIK. I must have an answer to this one question. Am I to pass out of life in such utter poverty?

SOLNESS [*seems to struggle with himself; finally he says, in a low but firm voice:*] You must pass out of life as best you can.

BROVIK. Then be it so.

[*He goes up the room.*]

SOLNESS [*following him, half in desperation*]. Don't you understand that I cannot help it? I am what I am, and I cannot change my nature!

BROVIK. No, no; I suppose you can't. [*Reels and supports himself against the sofa table.*] May I have a glass of water?

SOLNESS. By all means.

[*Fills a glass and hands it to him.*]

BROVIK. Thanks.

[*Drinks and puts the glass down again. SOLNESS goes up and opens the door of the draftsmen's office.*]

SOLNESS. Ragnar—you must come and take your father home.

[RAGNAR *rises quickly. He and* KAIA *come into the workroom.*]

RAGNAR. What is the matter, father?

BROVIK. Give me your arm. Now let us go.

RAGNAR. Very well. You had better put your things on, too, Kaia.

SOLNESS. Miss Fosli must stay—just for a moment. There is a letter I want written.

BROVIK [*looks at* SOLNESS]. Good night. Sleep well—if you can.

SOLNESS. Good night.

[BROVIK *and* RAGNAR *go out by the hall door.* KAIA *goes to the desk.* SOLNESS *stands with bent head, to the right, by the armchair.*]

KAIA [*dubiously*]. Is there any letter ——?

SOLNESS [*curtly*]. No, of course not. [*Looks sternly at her.*] Kaia!

KAIA [*anxiously, in a low voice*]. Yes!

SOLNESS [*points imperatively to a spot on the floor*]. Come here! At once!

KAIA [*hesitatingly*]. Yes.

SOLNESS [*as before*]. Nearer!

KAIA [*obeying*]. What do you want with me?

SOLNESS [*looks at her for a while*]. Is it you I have to thank for all this?

KAIA. No, no, don't think that!

SOLNESS. But confess now—you want to get married!

KAIA [*softly*]. Ragnar and I have been engaged for four or five years, and so——

SOLNESS. And so you think it time there were an end to it. Is not that so?

KAIA. Ragnar and Uncle say I must. So I suppose I shall have to give in.

SOLNESS [*more gently*]. Kaia, don't you really care a little bit for Ragnar, too?

KAIA. I cared very much for Ragnar once—before I came here to you.

SOLNESS. But you don't now? Not in the least?

KAIA [*passionately, clasping her hands and holding them out toward him*]. Oh, you know very well there is only one person I care for now! One, and one only, in all the world! I shall never care for anyone else.

SOLNESS. Yes, you say that. And yet you go away from me—leave me alone here with everything on my hands.

KAIA. But could I not stay with you, even if Ragnar——?

SOLNESS [*repudiating the idea*]. No, no, that is quite impossible. If Ragnar leaves me and starts work on his own account, then of course he will need you himself.

KAIA [*wringing her hands*]. Oh, I feel as if I could not be separated from you! It's quite, quite impossible!

SOLNESS. Then be sure you get those foolish notions out of Ragnar's head. Marry him as much as you please— [*Alters his tone.*] I mean—don't let him throw up his good situation with me. For then I can keep you, too, my dear Kaia.

KAIA. Oh yes, how lovely that would be, if it could only be managed!

SOLNESS [*clasps her head with his two hands and whispers*]. For I cannot get on without you, you see. I must have you with me every single day.

KAIA [*in nervous exaltation*]. My God! My God!

SOLNESS [*kisses her hair*]. Kaia—Kaia!

KAIA [*sinks down before him*]. Oh, how good you are to me! How unspeakably good you are!

SOLNESS [*vehemently*]. Get up! For goodness' sake get up! I think I hear someone!

[*He helps her to rise. She staggers over to the desk.*]

[MRS. SOLNESS *enters by the door on the right. She looks thin and wasted with grief but shows traces of bygone beauty. Blonde ringlets. Dressed with good taste, wholly in black. Speaks somewhat slowly and in a plaintive voice.*]

MRS. SOLNESS [*in the doorway*]. Halvard!

SOLNESS [*turns*]. Oh, are you there, my dear——?

MRS. SOLNESS [*with a glance at* KAIA]. I am afraid I am disturbing you.

SOLNESS. Not in the least. Miss Fosli has only a short letter to write.

MRS. SOLNESS. Yes, so I see.

SOLNESS. What do you want with me, Aline?

MRS. SOLNESS. I merely wanted to tell you that Dr. Herdal is in the drawing room. Won't you come and see him, Halvard?

SOLNESS [*looks suspiciously at her*]. H'm—is the doctor so very anxious to talk to me?

MRS. SOLNESS. Well, not exactly anxious. He really came to see me; but he would like to say how-do-you-do to you at the same time.

SOLNESS [*laughs to himself*]. Yes, I daresay. Well, you must ask him to wait a little.

MRS. SOLNESS. Then you will come in presently?

SOLNESS. Perhaps I will. Presently, presently, dear. In a little while.

MRS. SOLNESS [*glancing again at* KAIA]. Well, now, don't forget Halvard.

[*Withdraws and closes the door behind her.*]

KAIA [*softly*]. Oh dear, oh dear—I am sure Mrs. Solness thinks ill of me in some way!

SOLNESS. Oh, not in the least. Not more than usual, at any rate. But all the same, you had better go now, Kaia.

KAIA. Yes, yes, now I must go.

SOLNESS [*severely*]. And mind you get that matter settled for me. Do you hear?

KAIA. Oh, if it only depended on me——

SOLNESS. I will have it settled, I say!

And tomorrow too—not a day later!

KAIA [*terrified*]. If there's nothing else for it, I am quite willing to break off the engagement.

SOLNESS [*angrily*]. Break it off? Are you mad? Would you think of breaking it off?

KAIA [*distracted*]. Yes, if necessary. For I must—I must stay here with you! I can't leave you! That is utterly—utterly impossible!

SOLNESS [*with a sudden outburst*]. But deuce take it—how about Ragnar then! It's Ragnar that I——

KAIA [*looks at him with terrified eyes*]. It is chiefly on Ragnar's account, that—that you——

SOLNESS [*collecting himself*]. No, no, of course not! You don't understand me either. [*gently and softly*] Of course it is you I want to keep—you above everything, Kaia. But for that very reason, you must prevent Ragnar, too, from throwing up his situation. There, there,—now go home.

KAIA. Yes, yes—good night, then.

SOLNESS. Good night. [*as she is going*] Oh, stop a moment! Are Ragnar's drawings in there?

KAIA. I did not see him take them with him.

SOLNESS. Then just go and find them for me. I might perhaps glance over them, after all.

KAIA [*happy*]. Oh yes, please do!

SOLNESS. For your sake, Kaia dear. Now, let me have them at once, please.

[KAIA *hurries into the draftsmen's office, searches anxiously in the table drawer, finds a portfolio, and brings it with her.*]

KAIA. Here are all the drawings.

SOLNESS. Good. Put them down there on the table.

KAIA [*putting down the portfolio*]. Good night, then. [*beseechingly*] And please, please think kindly of me.

SOLNESS. Oh, that I always do. Good night, my dear little Kaia. [*Glances to the right.*] Go, go now!

[MRS. SOLNESS *and* DR. HERDAL *enter by the door on the right. He is a stoutish, elderly man, with a round, good-humored face, clean shaven, with thin, light hair, and gold spectacles.*]

MRS. SOLNESS [*still in the doorway*]. Halvard, I cannot keep the doctor any longer.

SOLNESS. Well then, come in here.

MRS. SOLNESS [*to* KAIA *who is turning down the desk lamp*]. Have you finished the letter already, Miss Fosli?

KAIA [*in confusion*]. The letter———?

SOLNESS. Yes, it was quite a short one.

MRS. SOLNESS. It must have been very short.

SOLNESS. You may go now, Miss Fosli. And please come in good time tomorrow morning.

KAIA. I will be sure to. Good night, Mrs. Solness.

[*She goes out by the hall door.*]

MRS. SOLNESS. She must be quite an acquisition to you, Halvard, this Miss Fosli.

SOLNESS. Yes, indeed. She is useful in all sorts of ways.

MRS. SOLNESS. So it seems.

DR. HERDAL. Is she good at book-keeping too?

SOLNESS. Well———of course she has had a good deal of practice during these two years. And then she is so nice and willing to do whatever one asks of her.

MRS. SOLNESS. Yes, that must be very delightful———

SOLNESS. It is. Especially when one is not too much accustomed to that sort of thing.

MRS. SOLNESS [*in a tone of gentle remonstrance*]. Can you say that, Halvard?

SOLNESS. Oh, no, no, my dear Aline; I beg your pardon.

MRS. SOLNESS. There's no occasion. ———Well then, doctor, you will come back later on and have a cup of tea with us?

DR. HERDAL. I have only that one patient to see and then I'll come back.

MRS. SOLNESS. Thank you.

[*She goes out by the door on the right.*]

SOLNESS. Are you in a hurry, doctor?

DR. HERDAL. No, not at all.

SOLNESS. May I have a little chat with you?

DR. HERDAL. With the greatest of pleasure.

SOLNESS. Then let us sit down. [*He motions the doctor to take the rocking chair and sits down himself in the armchair. Looks searchingly at him.*] Tell me—did you notice anything odd about Aline?

DR. HERDAL. Do you mean just now, when she was here?

SOLNESS. Yes, in her manner to me. Did you notice anything?

DR. HERDAL [*smiling*]. Well, I admit —one couldn't well avoid noticing that your wife—h'm———

SOLNESS. Well?

DR. HERDAL. ———that your wife is not particularly fond of this Miss Fosli.

SOLNESS. Is that all? I have noticed that myself.

DR. HERDAL. And I must say I am scarcely surprised at it.

SOLNESS. At what?

DR. HERDAL. That she should not exactly approve of your seeing so much of another woman, all day and every day.

SOLNESS. No, no, I suppose you are right there—and Aline too. But it's impossible to make any change.

DR. HERDAL. Could you not engage a clerk?

SOLNESS. The first man that came to

hand? No, thank you—that would never do for me.

DR. HERDAL. But now, if your wife ———? Suppose, with her delicate health, all this tries her too much?

SOLNESS. Even then—I might almost say—it can make no difference. I must keep Kaia Fosli. No one else could fill her place.

DR. HERDAL. No one else?

SOLNESS [*curtly*]. No, no one.

DR. HERDAL [*drawing his chair closer*]. Now listen to me, my dear Mr. Solness. May I ask you a question, quite between ourselves?

SOLNESS. By all means.

DR. HERDAL. Women, you see—in certain matters, they have a deucedly keen intuition———

SOLNESS. They have, indeed. There·is not the least doubt of that. But—?

DR. HERDAL. Well, tell me now——— if your wife can't endure this Kaia Fosli———?

SOLNESS. Well, what then?

DR. HERDAL. ———may she not have just—just the least little bit of reason for this instinctive dislike?

SOLNESS [*looks at him and rises*]. Oho!

DR. HERDAL. Now don't be offended— but hasn't she?

SOLNESS [*with curt decision*]. No.

DR. HERDAL. No reason of any sort?

SOLNESS. No other reason than her own suspicious nature.

DR. HERDAL. I know you have known a good many women in your time.

SOLNESS. Yes, I have.

DR. HERDAL. And have been a good deal taken with some of them, too.

SOLNESS. Oh, yes, I don't deny it.

DR. HERDAL. But as regards Miss Fosli, then? There is nothing of that sort in the case?

SOLNESS. No, nothing at all—on my side.

DR. HERDAL. But on her side.

SOLNESS. I don't think you have any right to ask that question, doctor.

DR. HERDAL. Well, you know, we were discussing your wife's intuition.

SOLNESS. So we were. And for that matter—[*Lowers his voice.*]—Aline's intuition, as you call it—in a certain sense, it has not been so far astray.

DR. HERDAL. Aha! there we have it!

SOLNESS [*sits down*]. Doctor Herdal —I am going to tell you a strange story—if you care to listen to it.

DR. HERDAL. I like listening to strange stories.

SOLNESS. Very well then. I daresay you recollect that I took Knut Brovik and his son into my employment— after the old man's business had gone to the dogs.

DR. HERDAL. Yes, so I have understood.

SOLNESS. You see, they really are clever fellows, these two. Each of them has talent in his own way. But then the son took it into his head to get engaged; and the next thing, of course, was that he wanted to get married—and begin to build on his own account. That is the way with all these young people.

DR. HERDAL [*laughing*]. Yes, they have a bad habit of wanting to marry.

SOLNESS. Just so. But of course that did not suit my plans; for I needed Ragnar myself—and the old man, too. He is exceedingly good at calculating bearing strains and cubic contents— and all that sort of devilry, you know.

DR. HERDAL. Oh, yes, no doubt that's indispensable.

SOLNESS. Yes, it is. But Ragnar was absolutely bent on setting to work for himself. He would hear of nothing else.

DR. HERDAL. But he has stayed with you all the same.

SOLNESS. Yes, I'll tell you how that came about. One day this girl, Kaia Fosli, came to see them on some errand or other. She had never been here before. And when I saw how utterly infatuated they were with each other, the thought occurred to me: If I could only get her into the office here, then perhaps Ragnar, too, would stay where he is.

DR. HERDAL. That was not at all a bad idea.

SOLNESS. Yes, but at the time I did not breathe a word of what was in my mind. I merely stood and looked at her—and kept on wishing intently that I could have her here. Then I talked to her a little, in a friendly way—about one thing and another. And then she went away.

DR. HERDAL. Well?

SOLNESS. Well, then, next day, pretty late in the evening, when old Brovik and Ragnar had gone home, she came here again and behaved as if I had made an arrangement with her.

DR. HERDAL. An arrangement? What about?

SOLNESS. About the very thing my mind had been fixed on. But I hadn't said one single word about it.

DR. HERDAL. That was most extraordinary.

SOLNESS. Yes, was it not? And now she wanted to know what she was to do here—whether she could begin the very next morning, and so forth.

DR. HERDAL. Don't you think she did it in order to be with her sweetheart?

SOLNESS. That was what occurred to me at first. But no, that was not it. She seemed to drift quite away from him—when once she had come here to me.

DR. HERDAL. She drifted over to you, then?

SOLNESS. Yes, entirely. If I happen to look at her when her back is turned, I can tell that she feels it. She quivers and trembles the moment I come near her. What do you think of that?

DR. HERDAL. H'm—that's not very hard to explain.

SOLNESS. Well, but what about the other thing? That she believed I had said to her what I had only wished and willed—silently—inwardly—to

myself? What do you say to that? Can you explain that, Dr. Herdal?

DR. HERDAL. No, I won't undertake to do that.

SOLNESS. I felt sure you would not; and so I have never cared to talk about it till now. But it's a cursed nuisance to me in the long run, you understand. Here I have to go on day after day pretending———. And it's a shame to treat her so, too, poor girl. [*vehemently*] But I cannot do anything else. For if she runs away from me—then Ragnar will be off too.

DR. HERDAL. And you have not told your wife the rights of the story?

SOLNESS. No.

DR. HERDAL. Then why on earth don't you?

SOLNESS [*looks fixedly at him and says in a low voice:*] Because I seem to find a sort of—of salutary self-torture in allowing Aline to do me an injustice.

DR. HERDAL [*shakes his head*]. I don't in the least understand what you mean.

SOLNESS. Well, you see—it is like paying off a little bit of a huge, immeasurable debt———

DR. HERDAL. To your wife?

SOLNESS. Yes; and that always helps to relieve one's mind a little. One can breathe more freely for a while, you understand.

DR. HERDAL. No, goodness knows, I don't understand at all———

SOLNESS [*breaking off, rises again*]. Well, well, well—then we won't talk any more about it. [*He saunters across the room, returns, and stops beside the table. Looks at the doctor with a sly smile.*] I suppose you think you have drawn me out nicely now, doctor?

DR. HERDAL [*with some irritation*]. Drawn you out? Again I have not the faintest notion what you mean, Mr. Solness.

SOLNESS. Oh come, out with it; I have seen it quite clearly, you know.

DR. HERDAL. What have you seen?

SOLNESS [*in a low voice, slowly*]. That you have been quietly keeping an eye upon me.

DR. HERDAL. That *I* have! And why in all the world should I do that?

SOLNESS. Because you think that I ———[*passionately*] Well, devil take it—you think the same of me as Aline does.

DR. HERDAL. And what does she think of you?

SOLNESS [*having recovered his self-control*]. She has begun to think that I am—that I am—ill.

DR. HERDAL. Ill! You! She has never hinted such a thing to me. Why, what can she think is the matter with you?

SOLNESS [*leans over the back of the chair and whispers*]. Aline has made up her mind that I am mad. That is what she thinks.

DR. HERDAL [*rising*]. Why, my dear good fellow———!

SOLNESS. Yes, on my soul she does! I tell you it is so. And she has got you to think the same! Oh, I can assure you, doctor, I see it in your face as clearly as possible. You don't take me in so easily, I can tell you.

DR. HERDAL [*looks at him in amazement*]. Never, Mr. Solness—never has such a thought entered my mind.

SOLNESS [*with an incredulous smile*]: Really? Has it not?

DR. HERDAL. No, never! Nor your wife's mind either, I am convinced. I could almost swear to that.

SOLNESS. Well, I wouldn't advise you to. For, in a certain sense, you see, perhaps—perhaps she is not so far wrong in thinking something of the kind.

DR. HERDAL. Come now, I really must say———

SOLNESS [*interrupting with a sweep of his hand*]. Well, well, my dear doctor —don't let us discuss this any further. We had better agree to differ.

[*Changes to a tone of quiet amusement.*] But look here now, doctor— h'm———

DR. HERDAL. Well?

SOLNESS. Since you don't believe that I am—ill—and crazy, and mad, and so forth———

DR. HERDAL. What then?

SOLNESS. Then I daresay you fancy that I am an extremely happy man.

DR. HERDAL. Is that mere fancy?

SOLNESS [*laughs*]. No, no—of course not! Heaven forbid! Only think—to be Solness the master builder! Halvard Solness! What could be more delightful?

DR. HERDAL. Yes, I must say it seems to me you have had the luck on your side to an astounding degree.

SOLNESS [*suppresses a gloomy smile*]. So I have, I can't complain on that score.

DR. HERDAL. First of all that grim old robbers' castle was burnt down for you. And that was certainly a great piece of luck.

SOLNESS [*seriously*]. It was the home of Aline's family. Remember that.

DR. HERDAL. Yes, it must have been a great grief to her.

SOLNESS. She has not got over it to this day—not in all these twelve or thirteen years.

DR. HERDAL. Ah, but what followed must have been the worst blow for her.

SOLNESS. The one thing with the other.

DR. HERDAL. But you—yourself—you rose upon the ruins. You began as a poor boy from a country village— and now you are at the head of your profession. Ah, yes, Mr. Solness, you have undoubtedly had the luck on your side.

SOLNESS [*looking at him with embarrassment*]. Yes, but that is just what makes me so horribly afraid.

DR. HERDAL. Afraid? Because you have the luck on your side!

SOLNESS. It terrifies me—terrifies me every hour of the day. For sooner or

later the luck must turn, you see.

DR. HERDAL. Oh nonsense! What should make the luck turn?

SOLNESS [*with firm assurance*]. The younger generation.

DR. HERDAL. Pooh! The younger generation! You are not laid on the shelf yet, I should hope. Oh no—your position here is probably firmer now than it has ever been.

SOLNESS. The luck will turn. I know it —I feel the day approaching. Someone or other will take it into his head to say: Give me a chance! And then all the rest will come clamoring after him and shake their fists at me and shout: Make room—make room—make room! Yes, just you see, doctor—presently the younger generation will come knock at my door——

DR. HERDAL [*laughing*]. Well, and what if they do?

SOLNESS. What if they do? Then there's an end of Halvard Solness.

[*There is a knock at the door on the left.*]

SOLNESS [*starts*]. What's that? Did you not hear something?

DR. HERDAL. Someone is knocking at the door.

SOLNESS [*loudly*]. Come in.

[HILDA WANGEL *enters by the hall door. She is of middle height, supple, and delicately built. Somewhat sunburned. Dressed in a tourist costume, with skirt caught up for walking, a sailor's collar open at the throat and a small sailor hat on her head. Knapsack on back, plaid in strap, and alpenstock.*]

HILDA [*goes straight up to* SOLNESS, *her eyes sparkling with happiness*]. Good evening!

SOLNESS [*looks doubtfully at her*]. Good evening——

HILDA [*laughs*]. I almost believe you don't recognise me!

SOLNESS. No—I must admit that—just for the moment——

DR. HERDAL [*approaching*]. But I recognize you, my dear young lady ——

HILDA [*pleased*]. Oh, is it you that—

DR. HERDAL. Of course it is. [*to* SOLNESS] We met at one of the mountain stations this summer. [*to* HILDA] What became of the other ladies?

HILDA. Oh, they went westward.

DR. HERDAL. They didn't much like all the fun we used to have in the evenings.

HILDA. No, I believe they didn't.

DR. HERDAL [*holds up his finger at her*]. And I am afraid it can't be denied that you flirted a little with us.

HILDA. Well that was better fun than to sit there knitting stockings with all those old women.

DR. HERDAL [*laughs*]. There I entirely agree with you.

SOLNESS. Have you come to town this evening?

HILDA. Yes, I have just arrived.

DR. HERDAL. Quite alone, Miss Wangel?

HILDA. Oh, yes!

SOLNESS. Wangel? Is your name Wangel?

HILDA [*looks in amused surprise at him*]. Yes, of course it is.

SOLNESS. Then you must be a daughter of the district doctor up at Lysanger?

HILDA [*as before*]. Yes, who else's daughter should I be?

SOLNESS. Oh, then I suppose we met up there, that summer when I was building a tower on the old church.

HILDA [*more seriously*]. Yes, of course it was then we met.

SOLNESS. Well, that is a long time ago.

HILDA [*looks hard at him*]. It is exactly ten years.

SOLNESS. You must have been a mere child then, I should think.

HILDA [*carelessly*]. Well, I was twelve or thirteen.

DR. HERDAL. Is this the first time you have ever been up to town, Miss Wangel?

HILDA. Yes, it is indeed,

SOLNESS. And don't you know anyone here?

HILDA. Nobody but you. And of course, your wife.

SOLNESS. So you know her, too?

HILDA. Only a little. We spent a few days together at the sanitorium.

SOLNESS. Ah, up there?

HILDA. She said I might come and pay her a visit if ever I came up to town. [*Smiles.*] Not that that was necessary.

SOLNESS. Odd that she should never have mentioned it.

[HILDA *puts her stick down by the stove, takes off the knapsack and lays it and the plaid on the sofa.* DR. HERDAL *offers to help her.* SOLNESS *stands and gazes at her.*]

HILDA [*going toward him*]. Well, now I must ask you to let me stay the night here.

SOLNESS. I am sure there will be no difficulty about that.

HILDA. For I have no other clothes than those I stand in, except a change of linen in my knapsack. And that has to go to the wash, for it's very dirty.

SOLNESS. Oh, yes, that can be managed. Now I'll just let my wife know——

DR. HERDAL. Meanwhile I will go and see my patient.

SOLNESS. Yes, do; and come again later on.

DR. HERDAL [*playfully, with a glance at* HILDA]. Oh, that I will, you may be very certain! [*Laughs.*] So your prediction has come true, Mr. Solness!

SOLNESS. How so?

DR. HERDAL. The younger generation did come knocking at your door.

SOLNESS [*cheerfully*]. Yes, but in a very different way from what I meant.

DR. HERDAL. Very different, yes. That's undeniable.

[*He goes out by the hall door.* SOLNESS *opens the door on the right and speaks into the side room.*]

SOLNESS. Aline! Will you come in here, please. Here is a friend of yours— Miss Wangel.

MRS. SOLNESS [*appears in the doorway*]. Who did you say it is? [*Sees* HILDA.] Oh, is it you, Miss Wangel? [*Goes up to her and offers her hand.*] So you have come to town after all.

SOLNESS. Miss Wangel has this moment arrived and she would like to stay the night here.

MRS. SOLNESS. Here with us? Oh yes, certainly.

SOLNESS. Till she can get her things a little in order, you know.

MRS. SOLNESS. I will do the best I can for you. It's no more than my duty. I suppose your trunk is coming on later?

HILDA. I have no trunk.

MRS. SOLNESS. Well, it will be all right, I daresay. In the meantime, you must excuse my leaving you here with my husband, until I can get a room made a little comfortable for you.

SOLNESS. Can we not give her one of the nurseries? They are all ready as it is.

MRS. SOLNESS. Oh, yes. There we have room and to spare. [*to* HILDA] Sit down now and rest a little.

[*She goes out to the right.*]

[HILDA, *with her hands behind her back, strolls about the room and looks at various objects.* SOLNESS *stands in front, beside the table, also with his hands behind his back, and follows her with his eyes.*]

HILDA [*stops and looks at him*]. Have you several nurseries?

SOLNESS. There are three nurseries in the house.

HILDA. That's a lot. Then I suppose you have a great many children?

SOLNESS. No. We have no child. But now you can be the child here, for the time being.

HILDA. For tonight, yes. I shall not cry. I mean to sleep as sound as a stone.

SOLNESS. Yes, you must be very tired, I should think.

HILDA. Oh, no! But all the same——— It's so delicious to lie and dream.

SOLNESS. Do you dream much of nights?

HILDA. Oh, yes! Almost always.

SOLNESS. What do you dream about most?

HILDA. I shan't tell you tonight. Another time, perhaps.

[*She again strolls about the room, stops at the desk, and turns over the books and papers a little.*]

SOLNESS [*approaching*]. Are you searching for anything?

HILDA. No, I am merely looking at all these things. [*Turns.*] Perhaps I mustn't?

SOLNESS. Oh, by all means.

HILDA. Is it you that writes in this great ledger?

SOLNESS. No, it's my bookkeeper.

HILDA. Is it a woman?

SOLNESS [*smiles*]. Yes.

HILDA. One you employ here, in your office?

SOLNESS. Yes.

HILDA. Is she married?

SOLNESS. No, she is single.

HILDA. Oh, indeed!

SOLNESS. But I believe she is soon going to be married.

HILDA. That's good thing for her.

SOLNESS. But not such a good thing for me. For then I shall have nobody to help me.

HILDA. Can't you get hold of someone else who will do just as well?

SOLNESS. Perhaps you would stay here and write in the ledger?

HILDA [*measures him with a glance*]. Yes, I daresay! No, thank you— nothing of that sort for me.

[*She again strolls across the room and sits down in the rocking chair.* SOLNESS, *too, goes to the table.*]

HILDA [*continuing*]. For there must surely be plenty of other things to be done here. [*Looks smiling at him.*] Don't you think so, too?

SOLNESS. Of course. First of all, I suppose, you want to make a round of the shops and get yourself up in the height of fashion.

HILDA [*amused*]. No, I think I shall let that alone!

SOLNESS. Indeed.

HILDA. For you must know I have run through all my money.

SOLNESS [*laughs*]. Neither trunk nor money, then.

HILDA. Neither one nor the other. But never mind—it doesn't matter now.

SOLNESS. Come now, I like you for that.

HILDA. Only for that?

SOLNESS. For that among other things. [*Sits in the armchair.*] Is your father alive still?

HILDA. Yes, father's alive.

SOLNESS. Perhaps you are thinking of studying here?

HILDA. No, that hadn't occurred to me.

SOLNESS. But I suppose you will be staying for some time?

HILDA. That must depend upon circumstances.

[*She sits awhile rocking herself and looking at him, half seriously, half with a suppressed smile. Then she takes off her hat and puts it on the table in front of her.*]

HILDA. Mr. Solness!

SOLNESS. Well?

HILDA. Have you a very bad memory?

SOLNESS. A bad memory? No, not that I am aware of.

HILDA. Then have you nothing to say to me about what happened up there?

SOLNESS [*in momentary surprise*]. Up at Lysanger? [*indifferently*] Why, it was nothing much to talk about, it seems to me.

HILDA [*looks reproachfully at him*]. How can you sit there and say such things?

SOLNESS Well, then, you talk to me about it.

HILDA. When the tower was finished,

we had grand doings in the town.

SOLNESS. Yes, I shall not easily forget that day.

HILDA [*smiles*]. Will you not? That comes well from you.

SOLNESS. Comes well?

HILDA. There was music in the church-yard—and many, many hundreds of people. We schoolgirls were dressed in white; and we all carried flags.

SOLNESS. Ah yes, those flags—I can tell you I remember them!

HILDA. Then you climbed right up the scaffolding, straight to the very top; and you had a great wreath with you; and you hung that wreath right away up on the weather vane.

SOLNESS [*curtly interrupting*]. I always did that in those days. It was an old custom.

HILDA. It was so wonderfully thrilling to stand below and look up at you. Fancy, if he should fall over! He—the master builder himself!

SOLNESS [*as if to divert her from the subject*]. Yes, yes, yes that might very well have happened, too. For one of those white-frocked little devils,—she went on in such a way and screamed up at me so——

HILDA [*sparkling with pleasure*]. "Hurrah for Master Builder Solness!" Yes!

SOLNESS. ——and waved and flour-ished with her flag, so that I—so that it almost made me giddy to look at it.

HILDA [*in a lower voice, seriously*]. That little devil—that was *I*.

SOLNESS [*fixes his eyes steadily upon her*]. I am sure of that now. It must have been you.

HILDA [*lively again*]. Oh, it was so gloriously thrilling! I could not have believed there was a builder in the whole world that could build such a tremendously high tower. And then, that you yourself should stand at the very top of it, as large as life! And that you should not be the least bit

dizzy! It was that above everything that made one—made one dizzy to think of.

SOLNESS. How could you be so certain that I was not——?

HILDA [*scouting the idea*]. No indeed! Oh, no! I knew that instinctively. For if you had been, you could never have stood up there and sung.

SOLNESS [*looks at her in astonishment*]. Sung? Did I sing?

HILDA. Yes, I should think you did.

SOLNESS [*shakes his head*]. I have never sung a note in my life.

HILDA. Yes indeed, you sang then. It sounded like harps in the air.

SOLNESS [*thoughtfully*]. This is very strange—all this.

HILDA [*is silent awhile, looks at him and says in a low voice:*] But then, —it was after that—and the real thing happened.

SOLNESS. The real thing?

HILDA [*sparkling with vivacity*]. Yes, I surely don't need to remind you of that?

SOLNESS. Oh, yes, do remind me a little of that, too.

HILDA. Don't you remember that a great dinner was given in your honor at the Club?

SOLNESS. Yes, to be sure. It must have been the same afternoon, for I left the place next morning.

HILDA. And from the Club you were invited to come round to our house to supper.

SOLNESS. Quite right, Miss Wangel. It is wonderful how all these trifles have impressed themselves on your mind.

HILDA. Trifles! I like that! Perhaps it was a trifle, too, that I was alone in the room when you came in?

SOLNESS. Were you alone?

HILDA [*without answering him*]. You didn't call me a little devil then!

SOLNESS. No, I suppose I did not.

HILDA. You said I was lovely in my white dress and that I looked like a little princess.

SOLNESS. I have no doubt you did, Miss Wangel.—And besides—I was feeling so buoyant and free that day————

HILDA. And then you said that when I grew up I should be your princess.

SOLNESS [*laughing a little*]. Dear, dear —did I say that, too?

HILDA. Yes, you did. And when I asked how long I should have to wait, you said that you would come again in ten years—like a troll and carry me off—to Spain or some such place. And you promised you would buy me a kingdom there.

SOLNESS [*as before*]. Yes, after a good dinner one doesn't haggle about the halfpence. But did I really say all that?

HILDA [*laughs to herself*]. Yes. And you told me, too, what the kingdom was to be called.

SOLNESS. Well, what was it?

HILDA. It was to be called the kingdom of Orangia,* you said.

SOLNESS. Well, that was an appetizing name.

HILDA. No, I didn't like it a bit; for it seemed as though you wanted to make a game of me.

SOLNESS. I am sure that cannot have been my intention.

HILDA. No, I should hope not—considering what you did next————

SOLNESS. What in the world did I do next?

HILDA. Well, that's the finishing touch, if you have forgotten that, too. I should have thought no one could help remembering such a thing as that.

SOLNESS. Yes, yes, just give me a hint, and then perhaps———— Well————

HILDA [*looks fixedly at him*]. You came and kissed me, Mr. Solness.

SOLNESS [*open mouthed, rising from his chair*]. *I* did!

HILDA. Yes, indeed you did. You took

---

* In the original *Appelsina, appelsin* meaning orange.

me in both your arms and bent my head back and kissed me—many times.

SOLNESS. Now really, my dear Miss Wangel————!

HILDA [*rises*]. You surely cannot mean to deny it?

SOLNESS. Yes, I do. I deny it altogether!

HILDA [*looks scornfully at him*]. Oh, indeed!

[*She turns and goes slowly close up to the stove, where she remains standing motionless, her face averted from him, her hands behind her back. Short pause.*]

SOLNESS [*goes cautiously up behind her*]. Miss Wangel————!

[HILDA *is silent and does not move.*]

SOLNESS. Don't stand there like a statue. You must have dreamt all this. [*Lays his hand on her arm.*] Now just listen————

[HILDA *makes an impatient movement with her arm.*]

SOLNESS [*as a thought flashes upon him*]. Or————! Wait a moment! There is something under all this, you may depend!

[HILDA *does not move.*]

SOLNESS [*in a low voice, but with emphasis*]. I must have thought all that. I must have wished it—have willed it—have longed to do it. And then————. May not that be the explanation?

[HILDA *is still silent.*]

SOLNESS [*impatiently*]. Oh very well, deuce take it all—then I did it, I suppose.

HILDA [*turns her head a little but without looking at him*]. Then you admit it now?

SOLNESS. Yes—whatever you like.

HILDA. You came and put your arms around me?

SOLNESS. Oh, yes!

HILDA. And bent my head back?

SOLNESS. Very far back.

HILDA. And kissed me?

SOLNESS. Yes, I did.

HILDA. Many times?

SOLNESS. As many as ever you like.

HILDA [*turns quickly toward him and has once more the sparkling expression of gladness in her eyes*]. Well, you see, I got it out of you at last!

SOLNESS [*with a slight smile*]. Yes— just think of my forgetting such a thing as that.

HILDA [*again a little sulky, retreats from him*]. Oh, you have kissed so many people in your time, I suppose.

SOLNESS. No, you mustn't think that of me. [HILDA *seats herself in the armchair.* SOLNESS *stands and leans against the rocking chair. Looks observantly at her.*] Miss Wangel!

HILDA. Yes!

SOLNESS. How was it now? What came of all this—between us two?

HILDA. Why, nothing more came of it. You know that quite well. For then the other guests came in, and then— bah!

SOLNESS. Quite so! The others came in. To think of my forgetting that, too!

HILDA. Oh, you haven't really forgotten anything: You are only a little ashamed of it all. I am sure one doesn't forget things of that kind.

SOLNESS. No, one would suppose not.

HILDA [*lively again, looks at him*]. Perhaps you have even forgotten what day it was?

SOLNESS. What day———?

HILDA. Yes, on what day did you hang the wreath on the tower? Well? Tell me at once!

SOLNESS. H'm—I confess I have forgotten the particular day. I only knew it was ten years ago. Sometime in the autumn.

HILDA [*nods her head slowly several times*]. It was ten years ago—on the 19th of September.

SOLNESS. Yes, it must have been about that time. Fancy your remembering that, too! [*Stops.*] But wait a moment———! Yes—it's the 19th of September today.

HILDA. Yes, it is; and the ten years are gone. And you didn't come—as you promised me.

SOLNESS. Promised you? Threatened, I suppose you mean?

HILDA. I don't think there was any sort of threat in that.

SOLNESS. Well then, a little bit of fun.

HILDA. Was that all you wanted? To make fun of me?

SOLNESS. Well, or to have a little joke with you. Upon my soul, I don't recollect. But it must have been something of that kind for you were a mere child then.

HILDA. Oh, perhaps I wasn't quite such a child either. Not such a mere chit as you imagine.

SOLNESS [*looks searchingly at her*]. Did you really and seriously expect me to come again?

HILDA [*conceals a half-teasing smile*]. Yes, indeed; I did expect that of you.

SOLNESS. That I should come back to your home and take you away with me?

HILDA. Just like a troll—yes.

SOLNESS. And make a princess of you?

HILDA. That's what you promised.

SOLNESS. And give you a kingdom as well?

HILDA [*looks up at the ceiling*]. Why not? Of course it need not have been an actual, everyday sort of kingdom.

SOLNESS. But something else just as good?

HILDA. Yes, at least as good. [*Looks at him a moment.*] I thought, if you could build the highest church towers in the world, you could surely manage to raise a kingdom of one sort or another as well.

SOLNESS [*shakes his head*]. I can't quite make you out, Miss Wangel.

HILDA. Can you not? To me it seems all so simple.

SOLNESS. No, I can't make up my mind whether you mean all you say or are simply having a joke with me.

HILDA [*smiles*]. Making fun of you, perhaps? I, too?

SOLNESS. Yes, exactly. Making fun— of both of us. [*Looks at her.*] Is it long since you found out that I was married?

HILDA. I have known it all along. Why do you ask me that?

SOLNESS [*lightly*]. Oh, well, it just occurred to me. [*Looks earnestly at her and says in a low voice.*] What have you come for?

HILDA. I want my kingdom. The time is up.

SOLNESS [*laughs involuntarily*]. What a girl you are!

HILDA [*gaily*]. Out with my kingdom, Mr. Solness! [*Raps with her fingers.*] The kingdom on the table!

SOLNESS [*pushing the rocking chair nearer and sitting down*]. Now, seriously speaking—what have you come for? What do you really want to do here?

HILDA. Oh, first of all, I want to go around and look at all the things that you have built.

SOLNESS. That will give you plenty of exercise.

HILDA. Yes, I know you have built a tremendous lot.

SOLNESS. I have indeed—especially of late years.

HILDA. Many church towers among the rest? Immensely high ones?

SOLNESS. No. I build no more church towers now. Nor churches either.

HILDA. What do you build, then?

SOLNESS. Homes for human beings.

HILDA [*reflectively*]. Couldn't you build a little—a little bit of a church tower over these homes as well?

SOLNESS [*starting*]. What do you mean by that?

HILDA. I mean—something that points —points up into the free air. With the vane at a dizzy height.

SOLNESS [*pondering a little*]. Strange that you should say that—for that is just what I am most anxious to do.

HILDA [*impatiently*]. Why don't you do it, then?

SOLNESS [*shakes his head*]. No, the people will not have it.

HILDA. Fancy their not wanting it!

SOLNESS [*more lightly*]. But now I am building a new home for myself— just opposite here.

HILDA. For yourself?

SOLNESS. Yes. It is almost finished. And on that there is a tower.

HILDA. A high tower?

SOLNESS. Yes.

HILDA. Very high?

SOLNESS. No doubt people will say it is too high—too high for a dwelling-house.

HILDA. I'll go out and look at that tower the first thing tomorrow morning.

SOLNESS [*sits resting his cheek on his hand and gazes at her*]. Tell me, Miss Wangel—what is your name? Your Christian name, I mean?

HILDA. Why, Hilda, of course.

SOLNESS [*as before*]. Hilda? Indeed?

HILDA. Don't you remember that? You called me Hilda yourself—that day when you misbehaved.

SOLNESS. Did I really?

HILDA. But then you said "little Hilda"; and I didn't like that.

SOLNESS. Oh, you didn't like that, Miss Hilda?

HILDA. No, not at such a time as that. But—"Princess Hilda"—that will sound very well, I think.

SOLNESS. Very well indeed. Princess Hilda of—of—what was to be the name of the kingdom?

HILDA. Pooh! I won't have anything to do with that stupid kingdom. I have set my heart upon quite a different one!

SOLNESS [*has leaned back in the chair, still gazing at her*]. Isn't it strange ———? The more I think of it now, the more it seems to me as though I had gone about all these years torturing myself with—h'm————

HILDA. With what?

SOLNESS. With the effort to recover something—some experience, which I seemed to have forgotten. But I never had the least inkling of what it could be.

HILDA. You should have tied a knot in your pocket handkerchief, Mr. Solness.

SOLNESS. In that case, I should simply have had to go racking my brains to discover what the knot could mean.

HILDA. Oh, yet, I suppose there are trolls of that kind in the world, too.

SOLNESS [*rises slowly*]. What a good thing it is that you have come to me now.

HILDA [*looks deeply into his eyes*]. Is it a good thing?

SOLNESS. For I have been so lonely here. I have been gazing so helplessly at it all. [*in a lower voice*] I must tell you—I have begun to be so afraid —so terribly afraid of the younger generation.

HILDA [*with a little snort of contempt*]. Pooh—is the younger generation a thing to be afraid of?

SOLNESS. It is indeed. And that is why I have locked and barred myself in. [*mysteriously*] I tell you the younger generation will one day come and thunder at my door! They will break in upon me!

HILDA. Then I should say you ought to go out and open the door to the younger generation.

SOLNESS. Open the door?

HILDA. Yes. Let them come in to you on friendly terms, as it were.

SOLNESS. No, no, no! The younger generation—it means retribution, you see. It comes, as if under a new banner, heralding the turn of fortune.

HILDA [*rises, looks at him, and says with a quivering twitch of her lips*]. Can I be of any use to you, Mr. Solness?

SOLNESS. Yes, you can indeed! For you, too, come—under a new banner, it seems to me. Youth marshaled against youth————!

[DR. HERDAL *comes in by the hall door.*]

DR. HERDAL. What—you and Miss Wangel here still?

SOLNESS. Yes. We have had no end of things to talk about.

HILDA. Both old and new.

DR. HERDAL. Have you really?

HILDA. Oh, it has been the greatest fun. For Mr. Solness—he has such a miraculous memory. All the least little details he remembers instantly.

[MRS. SOLNESS *enters by the door on the right.*]

MRS. SOLNESS. Well, Miss Wangel, your room is quite ready for you now.

HILDA. Oh, how kind you are to me!

SOLNESS [*to* MRS. SOLNESS]. The nursery?

MRS. SOLNESS. Yes, the middle one. But first let us go in to supper.

SOLNESS [*nods to* HILDA]. Hilda shall sleep in the nursery, she shall.

MRS. SOLNESS [*looks at him*]. Hilda?

SOLNESS. Yes, Miss Wangel's name is Hilda. I knew her when she was a child.

MRS. SOLNESS. Did you really, Halvard? Well, shall we go? Supper is on the table.

[*She takes* DR. HERDAL'S *arm and goes out with him to the right.* HILDA *has meanwhile been collecting her traveling things.*]

HILDA [*softly and rapidly to* SOLNESS]. Is it true, what you said? Can I be of use to you?

SOLNESS [*takes the things from her*]. You are the very being I have needed most.

HILDA [*looks at him with happy, wondering eyes and clasps her* hands]. But then, great heavens—!

SOLNESS [*eagerly*]. What———?

HILDA. Then I have my kingdom!

SOLNESS [*involuntarily*]. Hilda———!

HILDA [*again with the quivering twitch of her lips*]. Almost—I was going to say.

[*She goes out to the right,* SOLNESS *follows her.*]

ACT II

A prettily furnished small drawing room in SOLNESS' *house. In the back, a glass door leading out to the verandah and garden. The right-hand corner is cut off transversely by a large bay window, in which are flower stands. The left-hand corner is similarly cut off by a transverse wall, in which is a small door papered like the wall. On each side, an ordinary door. In front, on the right, a console table with a large mirror over it. Well-filled stands of plants and flowers. In front, on the left, a sofa with a table and chairs. Farther back, a bookcase. Well forward in the room, before the bay window, a small table and some chairs. It is early in the day.*

SOLNESS *sits by the little table with* RAGNAR BROVIK'S *portfolio open in front of him. He is turning the drawings over and closely examining some of them.* MRS. SOLNESS *moves about noiselessly with a small watering pot, attending to her flowers. She is dressed in black as before. Her hat, cloak, and parasol lie on a chair near the mirror. Unobserved by her,* SOLNESS *now and again follows her with his eyes. Neither of them speaks.*

KAIA FOSLI *enters quietly by the door on the left.*

SOLNESS [*turns his head and says in an off-hand tone of indifference*]. Well, is that you?

KAIA. I merely wished to let you know that I have come.

SOLNESS. Yes, yes, that's all right. Hasn't Ragnar come, too?

KAIA. No, not yet. He had to wait a little while to see the doctor. But he is coming presently to hear———

SOLNESS. How is the old man today?

KAIA. Not well. He begs you to excuse him; he is obliged to keep his bed today.

SOLNESS. Why, of course; by all means let him rest. But now, get to work.

KAIA. Yes. [*Pauses at the door.*] Do you wish to speak to Ragnar when he comes?

SOLNESS. No—I don't know that I have anything particular to say to him.

[KAIA *goes out again to the left.* SOLNESS *remains seated, turning over the drawings.*]

MRS. SOLNESS [*over beside the plants*]. I wonder if he isn't going to die now, as well?

SOLNESS [*looks up to her*]. As well as who?

MRS. SOLNESS [*without answering*]. Yes, yes—depend upon it, Halvard, old Brovik is going to die, too. You'll see that he will.

SOLNESS. My dear Aline, ought you not to go out for a little walk?

MRS. SOLNESS. Yes, I suppose I ought to.

[*She continues to attend to the flowers.*]

SOLNESS [*bending over the drawings*]. Is she still asleep?

MRS. SOLNESS [*looking at him*]. Is it Miss Wangel you are sitting there thinking about?

SOLNESS [*indifferently*]. I just happened to recollect her.

MRS. SOLNESS. Miss Wangel was up long ago.

SOLNESS. Oh, was she?

MRS. SOLNESS. When I went in to see her, she was busy putting her things in order.

[*She goes in front of the mirror and slowly begins to put on her hat.*]

SOLNESS [*after a short pause*]. So we have found a use for one of our nurseries after all, Aline.

MRS. SOLNESS. Yes, we have.

SOLNESS. That seems to me better than to have them all standing empty.

MRS. SOLNESS. That emptiness is dreadful; you are right there.

SOLNESS [*closes the portfolio, rises, and approaches her*]. You will find that we shall get on far better after this, Aline. Things will be more comfortable. Life will be easier—especially for you.

MRS. SOLNESS [*looks at him*]. After this?

SOLNESS. Yes, believe me, Aline———

MRS. SOLNESS. Do you mean—because she has come here?

SOLNESS [*checking himself*]. I mean, of course—when once we have moved into the new house.

MRS. SOLNESS [*takes her cloak*]. Ah, do you think so, Halvard? Will it be better then?

SOLNESS. I can't think otherwise. And surely you think so, too?

MRS. SOLNESS. I think nothing at all about the new house.

SOLNESS [*cast down*]. It's hard for me to hear you say that; for you know it is mainly for your sake that I have built it.

[*He offers to help her on with her cloak.*]

MRS. SOLNESS [*evades him*]. The fact is, you do far too much for my sake.

SOLNESS [*with certain vehemence*]. No, no, you really mustn't say that, Aline! I cannot bear to hear you say such things!

MRS. SOLNESS. Very well, then I won't say it, Halvard.

SOLNESS. But I stick to what *I* said. You'll see that things will be easier for you in the new place.

MRS. SOLNESS. O heavens—easier for me———!

SOLNESS [*eagerly*]. Yes, indeed they will! You may be quite sure of that! For you see—there will be so very, very much there that will remind you of your own home———

MRS. SOLNESS. The home that used to be father's and mother's—and that was burned to the ground———

SOLNESS [*in a low voice*]. Yes, yes, my poor Aline. That was a terrible blow for you.

MRS. SOLNESS [*breaking out in lamentation*]. You may build as much as ever you like, Halvard—you can never build up again a real home for me!

SOLNESS [*crosses the room*]. Well, in heaven's name, let us talk no more about it, then.

MRS. SOLNESS. Oh, yes, Halvard, I understand you very well. You are so anxious to spare me—and to find excuses for me, too—as much as ever you can.

SOLNESS [*with astonishment in his eyes*]. *You!* Is it you—yourself, that you are talking about, Aline?

MRS. SOLNESS. Yes, who else should it be but myself?

SOLNESS [*involuntarily to himself*]. That, too!

MRS. SOLNESS. As for the old house, I wouldn't mind so much about that. When once misfortune was in the air—why———

SOLNESS. Ah, you are right there. Misfortune will have its way—as the saying goes.

MRS. SOLNESS. But it's what came of the fire—the dreadful thing that followed———! That is the thing! That, that, that!

SOLNESS [*vehemently*]. Don't think about that, Aline!

MRS. SOLNESS. Ah, that is exactly what I cannot help thinking about. And now, at last, I must speak about it, too; for I don't seem able to bear it any longer. And then never to be able to forgive myself——

SOLNESS [*exclaiming*]. Yourself——!

MRS. SOLNESS. Yes, for I had duties on both sides—both towards you and towards the little ones. I ought to have hardened myself—not to have let the horror take such hold upon me—nor the grief for the burning of my old home. [*Wrings her hands.*] Oh, Halvard, if I had only had the strength!

SOLNESS [*softly, much moved, comes closer*]. Aline—you must promise me never to think these thoughts any more.—Promise me that, dear!

MRS. SOLNESS. Oh, promise, promise! One can promise anything.

SOLNESS [*clenches his hands and crosses the room*]. Oh, but this is hopeless, hopeless! Never a ray of sunlight! Not so much as a gleam of brightness to light up our home!

MRS. SOLNESS. This is no home, Halvard.

SOLNESS. Oh no, you may well say that. [*gloomily*] And God knows whether you are not right in saying that it will be no better for us in the new house, either.

MRS. SOLNESS. It will never be any better. Just as empty—just as desolate—there as here.

SOLNESS [*vehemently*]. Why in all the world have we built it then? Can you tell me that?

MRS. SOLNESS. No; you must answer that question for yourself.

SOLNESS [*glances suspiciously at her*]. What do you mean by that, Aline?

MRS. SOLNESS. What do I mean?

SOLNESS. Yes, in the devil's name! You said it so strangely—as if you had hidden some meaning in it.

MRS. SOLNESS. No, indeed, I assure you——

SOLNESS [*comes closer*]. Oh, come now

—I know what I know. I have both my eyes and my ears about me, Aline—you may depend upon that!

MRS. SOLNESS. Why, what are you talking about? What is it?

SOLNESS [*places himself in front of her*]. Do you mean to say you don't find a kind of lurking, hidden meaning in the most innocent word I happen to say?

MRS. SOLNESS. *I*, do you say? *I* do that?

SOLNESS [*laughs*]. Ho-ho-ho! It's natural enough, Aline! When you have a sick man on your hands——

MRS. SOLNESS [*anxiously*]. Sick? Are you ill, Halvard?

SOLNESS [*violently*]. A half-mad man then! A crazy man! Call me what you will.

MRS. SOLNESS [*feels blindly for a chair and sits down*]. Halvard—for God's sake——

SOLNESS. But you are wrong, both you and the doctor. I am not in the state you imagine.

[*He walks up and down the room.* MRS. SOLNESS *follows him anxiously with her eyes. Finally he goes up to her.*]

SOLNESS [*calmly*]. In reality there is nothing whatever the matter with me.

MRS. SOLNESS. No, there isn't, is there? But then what is it that troubles you so?

SOLNESS. Why this, that I often feel ready to sink under this terrible burden of debt——

MRS. SOLNESS. Debt, do you say? But you owe no one anything, Halvard!

SOLNESS [*softly, with emotion*]. I owe a boundless debt to you—to you—to you, Aline.

MRS. SOLNESS [*rises slowly*]. What is behind all this? You may just as well tell me at once.

SOLNESS. But there is nothing behind it; I have never done you any wrong —not wittingly and willfuly, at any rate. And yet—and yet it seems as though a crushing debt rested upon me and weighed me down.

MRS. SOLNESS. A debt to me?

SOLNESS. Chiefly to you.

MRS. SOLNESS. Then you are—ill after all, Halvard.

SOLNESS [*gloomily*]. I suppose I must be—or not far from it. [*Looks toward the door to the right, which is opened at this moment.*] Ah! now it grows lighter.

[HILDA WANGEL *comes in. She has made some alteration in her dress and let down her skirt.*]

HILDA. Good morning, Mr. Solness!

SOLNESS [*nods*]. Slept well?

HILDA. Quite deliciously! Like a child in a cradle. Oh—I lay and stretched myself like—like a princess!!

SOLNESS [*smiles a little*]. You were thoroughly comfortable then?

HILDA. I should think so.

SOLNESS. And no doubt you dreamed, too.

HILDA. Yes, I did. But that was horrid.

SOLNESS. Was it?

HILDA. Yes, for I dreamed I was falling over a frightfully high, sheer precipice. Do you never have that kind of dream?

SOLNESS. Oh yes—now and then———

HILDA. It is tremendously thrilling—when you fall and fall———

SOLNESS. It seems to make one's blood run cold.

HILDA. Do you draw your legs up under you while you are falling?

SOLNESS. Yes, as high as ever I can.

HILDA. So do I.

MRS. SOLNESS [*takes her parasol*]. I must go into town now, Halvard. [*to* HILDA] And I'll try to get one or two things that you may require.

HILDA [*making a motion to throw her arms round her neck*]. Oh, you dear, sweet Mrs. Solness! You are really much too kind to me! Frightfully kind———

MRS. SOLNESS [*deprecatingly, freeing herself*]. Oh, not at all. It's only my duty, so I am very glad to do it.

HILDA [*offended, pouts*]. But really, I think I am quite fit to be seen in the streets—now that I've put my dress to rights. Or do you think I am not?

MRS. SOLNESS. To tell the truth, I think people would stare at you a little.

HILDA [*contemptuously*]. Pooh! Is that all? That only amuses me.

SOLNESS [*with suppressed ill-humor*]. Yes, but people might take it into their heads that you were mad, too, you see.

HILDA. Mad? Are there so many mad people here in town, then?

SOLNESS [*points to his own forehead*]. Here you see one, at all events.

HILDA. You—Mr. Solness!

MRS. SOLNESS. Oh, don't talk like that, my dear Halvard!

SOLNESS. Have you not noticed that yet?

HILDA. No, I certainly have not. [*Reflects and laughs a little.*] And yet—perhaps in one single thing.

SOLNESS. Ah, do you hear that, Aline?

MRS. SOLNESS. What is that one single thing, Miss Wangel?

HILDA. No, I won't say.

SOLNESS. Oh, yes, do!

HILDA. No, thank you—I am not so mad as that.

MRS. SOLNESS. When you and Miss Wangel are alone, I daresay she will tell you, Halvard.

SOLNESS. Ah—you think she will?

MRS. SOLNESS. Oh, yes, certainly. For you have known her so well in the past. Ever since she was a child—you tell me.

[*She goes out by the door on the left.*]

HILDA [*after a little while*]. Does your wife dislike me very much?

SOLNESS. Did you think you noticed anything of the kind?

HILDA. Did you not notice it yourself?

SOLNESS [*evasively*]. Aline has become exceedingly shy with strangers of late years.

HILDA. Has she really?

SOLNESS. But if only you could get to know her thoroughly————! Ah! she is so good—so kind—so excellent a creature————

HILDA [*impatiently*]. But if she is all that—what made her say that about her duty?

SOLNESS. Her duty?

HILDA. She said that she would go out and buy something for me because it was her duty. Oh, I can't bear that ugly, horrid word!

SOLNESS. Why not?

HILDA. It sounds so cold and sharp and stinging. Duty—duty—duty. Don't you think so, too? Doesn't it seem to sting you?

SOLNESS. H'm—haven't thought much about it.

HILDA. Yes, it does. And if she is so good—as you say she is—why should she talk in that way?

SOLNESS. But, good Lord, what would you have had her say, then?

HILDA. She might have said she would do it because she had taken a tremendous fancy to me. She might have said something like that—something really warm and cordial, you understand.

SOLNESS [*looks at her*]. Is that how you would like to have it?

HILDA. Yes, precisely. [*She wanders about the room, stops at the bookcase, and looks at the books.*] What a lot of books you have.

SOLNESS. Yes, I have got together a good many.

HILDA. Do you read them all, too?

SOLNESS. I used to try to. Do you read much?

HILDA. No, never! I have given it up. For it all seems so irrelevant.

SOLNESS. That is just my feeling.

[HILDA *wanders about a little, stops at the small table, opens the portfolio, and turns over the contents.*]

HILDA. Are all these drawings yours?

SOLNESS. No, they are drawn by a young man whom I employ to help me.

HILDA. Someone you have taught?

SOLNESS. Oh, yes, no doubt he has learned something from one, too.

HILDA [*sits down*]. Then I suppose he is very clever. [*Looks at a drawing.*] Isn't he?

SOLNESS. Oh, he might be worse. For my purpose————

HILDA. Oh, yes—I'm sure he is frightfully clever.

SOLNESS. Do you think you can see that in the drawings?

HILDA. Pooh—these scrawlings! But if he has been learning from you————

SOLNESS. Oh, so far as that goes—there are plenty of people that have learned from me and have come to little enough for all that.

HILDA [*looks at him and shakes her head*]. No, I can't for the life of me understand how you can be so stupid.

SOLNESS. Stupid? Do you think I am so very stupid?

HILDA. Yes, I do indeed. If you are content to go about here teaching all these people————

SOLNESS [*with a slight start*]. Well, and why not?

HILDA [*rises, half serious, half laughing*]. No indeed, Mr. Solness! What can be the good of that? No one but you should be allowed to build. You should stand quite alone—do it all yourself. Now you know it.

SOLNESS [*involuntarily*]. Hilda————!

HILDA. Well!

SOLNESS. How in the world did that come into your head?

HILDA. Do you think I am so very far wrong, then?

SOLNESS. No, that's not what I mean. But now I'll tell you something.

HILDA. Well?

SOLNESS. I keep on—incessantly—in

silence and alone—brooding on that very thought.

HILDA. Yes, that seems to me perfectly natural.

SOLNESS [*looks somewhat searchingly at her*]. Perhaps you have noticed it already?

HILDA. No, indeed I haven't.

SOLNESS. But just now—when you said you thought I was—off my balance? In one thing, you said———

HILDA. Oh, I was thinking of something quite different.

SOLNESS. What was is?

HILDA. I am not going to tell you.

SOLNESS [*crosses the room*]. Well, well —as you please. [*Stops at the bow window.*] Come here, and I will show you something.

HILDA [*approaching*]. What is it?

SOLNESS. Do you see—over there in the garden———?

HILDA. Yes.

SOLNESS [*points*]. Right above the great quarry———?

HILDA That new house, you mean?

SOLNESS. The one that is being built, yes. Almost finished.

HILDA. It seems to have a very high tower.

SOLNESS. The scaffolding is still up.

HILDA. Is that your new house?

SOLNESS. Yes.

HILDA. The house you are soon going to move into?

SOLNESS. Yes.

HILDA [*looks at him*]. Are there nurseries in that house, too?

SOLNESS. Three, as there are here.

HILDA. And no child.

SOLNESS. And there never will be one.

HILDA [*with a half smile*]. Well, isn't it just as I said———?

SOLNESS. That———?

HILDA. That you are a little—a little mad after all.

SOLNESS. Was that what you were thinking of?

HILDA. Yes, of all the empty nurseries I slept in.

SOLNESS [*lowers his voice*]. We have had children—Aline and I.

HILDA [*looks eagerly at him*]. Have you———?

SOLNESS. Two little boys. They were of the same age.

HILDA. Twins, then.

SOLNESS. Yes, twins. It's eleven or twelve years ago now.

HILDA [*cautiously*]. And so both of them———? You have lost both the twins, then?

SOLNESS [*with quiet emotion*]. We kept them only about three weeks. Or scarcely so much. [*Bursts forth.*] Oh, Hilda, I can't tell you what a good thing it is for me that you have come! For now at last I have someone I can talk to!

HILDA. Can you not talk to—her, too?

SOLNESS. Not about this. Not as I want to talk and must talk. [*gloomily*] And not about so many other things, either.

HILDA [*in a subdued voice*]. Was that all you meant when you said you needed me?

SOLNESS. That was mainly what I meant—at all events, yesterday. For today I am not so sure———[*breaking off*] Come here and let us sit down, Hilda. Sit there on the sofa— so that you can look into the garden. [HILDA *seats herself in the corner of the sofa.* SOLNESS *brings a chair closer.*] Should you like to hear about it?

HILDA. Yes, I shall love to sit and listen to you.

SOLNESS [*sits down*]. Then I will tell you all about it.

HILDA. Now I can see both the garden and you, Mr. Solness. So now, tell away! Begin!

SOLNESS [*points toward the bow window*]. Out there on the rising ground—where you see the new house———

HILDA. Yes?

SOLNESS. Aline and I lived there in the first years of our married life. There was an old house up there that had belonged to her mother; and we inherited it, and the whole of the great garden with it.

HILDA. Was there a tower on that house, too?

SOLNESS. No, nothing of the kind. From the outside it looked like a great, dark, ugly wooden box; but all the same, it was snug and comfortable enough inside.

HILDA. Then did you pull down the ramshackle old place?

SOLNESS. No, it burned down.

HILDA. The whole of it?

SOLNESS. Yes.

HILDA. Was that a great misfortune for you?

SOLNESS. That depends on how you look at it. As a builder, the fire was the making of me——

HILDA. Well, but——?

SOLNESS. It was just after the birth of the two little boys——

HILDA. The poor little twins, yes.

SOLNESS. They came healthy and bonny into the world. And they were growing too—you could see the difference from day to day.

HILDA. Little children do grow quickly at first.

SOLNESS. It was the prettiest sight in the world to see Aline lying with the two of them in her arms.—But then came the night of the fire——

HILDA [*excitedly*]. What happened? Do tell me! Was anyone burned?

SOLNESS. No, not that. Everyone got safe and sound out of the house

——

HILDA. Well, and what then——?

SOLNESS. The fright had shaken Aline terribly. The alarm—the escape—the break-neck hurry—and then the ice-cold night air—for they had to be carried out just as they lay—both she and the little ones.

HILDA. Was it too much for them?

SOLNESS. Oh no, they stood it well enough. But Aline fell into a fever, and it affected her milk. She would insist on nursing them herself because it was her duty, she said. And both our little boys, they—[*clenching his hands*]—they—oh!

HILDA. They did not get over that?

SOLNESS. No, that they did not get over. That was how we lost them.

HILDA. It must have been terribly hard for you.

SOLNESS. Hard enough for me; but ten times harder for Aline. [*clenching his hands in suppressed fury*] Oh, that such things should be allowed to happen here in the world! [*shortly and firmly*] From the day I lost them, I had no heart for building churches.

HILDA. Did you not like the church tower in our town?

SOLNESS. I didn't like it. I know how free and happy I felt when the tower was finished.

HILDA. *I* know that, too.

SOLNESS. And now I shall never—never build anything of that sort again! Neither churches nor church towers.

HILDA [*nods slowly*]. Nothing but houses for people to live in.

SOLNESS. Homes for human beings, Hilda.

HILDA. But homes with high towers and pinnacles upon them.

SOLNESS. If possible. [*Adopts a lighter tone.*] But, as I said before, that fire was the making of me—as a builder, I mean.

HILDA. Why don't you call yourself an architect, like the others?

SOLNESS. I have not been systematically enough taught for that. Most of what I know, I have found out for myself.

HILDA. But you succeeded all the same.

SOLNESS. Yes, thanks to the fire. I laid out almost the whole of the garden in villa lots; and there I was able to build after my own heart.

So I came to the front with a rush.

HILDA [*looks keenly at him*]. You must surely be a very happy man, as matters stand with you.

SOLNESS [*gloomily*]. Happy? Do you say that, too—like all the rest of them?

HILDA. Yes, I should say you must be. If you could only cease thinking about the two little children——

SOLNESS [*slowly*]. The two little children—they are not so easy to forget, Hilda.

HILDA [*somewhat uncertainly*]. Do you still feel their loss so much—after all these years?

SOLNESS [*looks fixedly at her, without replying*]. A happy man you said

——

HILDA. Well, now, are you not happy—in other respects?

SOLNESS [*continues to look at her*]. When I told you all this about the fire—h'm——

HILDA. Well?

SOLNESS. Was there not one special thought that you—that you seized upon?

HILDA [*reflects in vain*]. No. What thought should that be?

SOLNESS [*with subdued emphasis*]. It was simply and solely by that fire that I was enabled to build homes for human beings. Cozy, comfortable, bright homes, where father and mother and the whole troop of children can live in safety and gladness, feeling what a happy thing it is to be alive in the world—and most of all to belong to each other—in great things and in small.

HILDA [*ardently*]. Well, and is it not a great happiness for you to be able to build such beautiful homes?

SOLNESS. The price, Hilda! The terrible price I had to pay for the opportunity!

HILDA. But can you never get over that?

SOLNESS. No. That I might build homes for others I had to forgo—to forgo for all time—the home that might have been my own. I mean a home for a troop of children—and for father and mother, too.

HILDA [*cautiously*]. But need you have done that? For all time, you say?

SOLNESS [*nods slowly*]. That was the price of this happiness that people talk about. [*Breathes heavily.*] This happiness—h'm—this happiness was not to be bought any cheaper, Hilda.

HILDA [*as before*]. But may it not come right even yet?

SOLNESS. Never in this world—never. That is another consequence of the fire—and of Aline's illness afterwards.

HILDA [*looks at him with an indefinable expression*]. And yet you build all these nurseries?

SOLNESS [*seriously*]. Have you never noticed, Hilda, how the impossible—how it seems to beckon and cry aloud to one?

HILDA [*reflecting*]. The impossible? [*with animation*] Yes, indeed! Is that how you feel too?

SOLNESS. Yes, I do.

HILDA. There must be—a little of the troll in you, too.

SOLNESS. Why of the troll?

HILDA. What would you call it, then?

SOLNESS [*rises*]. Well, well, perhaps you are right. [*vehemently*] But how can I help turning into a troll, when this is how it always goes with me in everything—in everything!

HILDA. How do you mean?

SOLNESS [*speaking low, with inward emotion*]. Mark what I say to you, Hilda. All that I have succeeded in doing, building, creating—all the beauty, security, cheerful comfort—ay, and magnificence, too—[*Clenches his hands.*] Oh, is it not terrible even to think of——!

HILDA. What is so terrible?

SOLNESS. That all this I have to make up for, to pay for—not in money, but in human happiness. And not with my own happiness only, but with other people's, too. Yes, yes, do you see that, Hilda? That is the price which my position as an artist has cost me—and others. And every single day I have to look on while the price is paid for me anew. Over again, and over again—and over again for ever!

HILDA [*rises and looks steadily at him*]. Now I can see that you are thinking of—of her.

SOLNESS. Yes, mainly of Aline. For Aline—she, too, had her vocation in life, just as much as I had mine. [*His voice quivers.*] But her vocation has had to be stunted and crushed and shattered—in order that mine might force its way to—to a sort of great victory. For you must know that Aline—she, too, had a talent for building.

HILDA. She! For building?

SOLNESS [*shakes his head*]. Not houses and towers, and spires—not such things as I work away at——

HILDA. Well, but what then?

SOLNESS [*softly, with emotion*]. For building up the souls of little children, Hilda. For building up children's souls in perfect balance and in noble and beautiful forms. For enabling them to soar up into erect and full-grown human souls. That was Aline's talent. And there it all lies now———unused and unusable forever—of no earthly service to anyone—just like the ruins left by a fire.

HILDA. Yes, but even if this were so ———?

SOLNESS. It is so! It is so! I know it!

HILDA. Well, but in any case it is not your fault.

SOLNESS [*fixes his eyes on her and nods slowly*]. Ah, that is the great, terrible question. That is the doubt that is gnawing me—night and day.

HILDA. That?

SOLNESS. Yes. Suppose the fault was mine—in a certain sense.

HILDA. Your fault! The fire!

SOLNESS. All of it; the whole thing. And yet, perhaps—I may not have had anything to do with it.

HILDA [*looks at him with a troubled expression*]. Oh, Mr. Solness—if you can talk like that, I am afraid you must be—ill, after all.

SOLNESS. H'm—I don't think I shall ever be of quite sound mind on that point.

[RAGNAR BROVIK *cautiously opens the little door in the left-hand corner.* HILDA *comes forward.*]

RAGNAR [*when he sees* HILDA]. Oh, I beg pardon, Mr. Solness—

[*He makes a movement to withdraw.*]

SOLNESS. No, no, don't go. Let us get it over.

RAGNAR. Oh, yes—if only we could.

SOLNESS. I hear your father is no better?

RAGNAR. Father is fast growing weaker —and therefore I beg and implore you to write a few kind words for me on one of the plans! Something for father to read before he——

SOLNESS [*vehemently*]. I won't hear anything more about those drawings of yours!

RAGNAR. Have you looked at them?

SOLNESS. Yes—I have.

RAGNAR. And they are good for nothing? And *I* am good for nothing, too?

SOLNESS [*evasively*]. Stay here with me, Ragnar. You shall have everything your own way. And then you can marry Kaia and live at your ease—and happily, too, who knows? Only don't think of building on your own account.

RAGNAR. Well, well, then I must go home and tell father what you say —I promised I would.—Is this what I am to tell father—before he dies?

SOLNESS [*with a groan*]. Oh tell him

—tell him what you will, for me. Best to say nothing at all to him! [*with a sudden outburst*] I cannot do anything else, Ragnar!

RAGNAR. May I have the drawings to take with me?

SOLNESS. Yes, take them—take them by all means. They are lying there on the table.

RAGNAR [*goes to the table*]. Thanks.

HILDA [*puts her hand on the portfolio*]. No, no; leave them here.

SOLNESS. Why?

HILDA. Because I want to look at them, too.

SOLNESS. But you have been——— [*to* RAGNAR] Well, leave them here, then.

RAGNAR. Very well.

SOLNESS. And go home at once to your father.

RAGNAR. Yes. I suppose I must.

SOLNESS [*as if in desperation*]. Ragnar —you must not ask me to do what is beyond my power! Do you hear, Ragnar? You must not!

RAGNAR. No, no. I beg your pardon
———

[*He bows and goes out by the corner door.* HILDA *goes over and sits down on a chair near the mirror.*]

HILDA [*looks angrily at* SOLNESS]. That was a very ugly thing to do.

SOLNESS. Do you think so, too?

HILDA. Yes, it was horribly ugly—and hard and bad and cruel as well.

SOLNESS. Oh, you don't understand my position.

HILDA. No matter———. I say you ought not to be like that.

SOLNESS. You said yourself, only just now, that no one but *I* ought to be allowed to build.

HILDA. *I* may say such things—but you must not.

SOLNESS. I most of all, surely, who have paid so dear for my position.

HILDA. Oh yes—with what you call domestic comfort—and that sort of thing.

SOLNESS. And with my peace of soul into the bargain.

HILDA [*rising*]. Peace of soul! [*with feeling*] Yes, yes, you are right in that! Poor Mr. Solness—you fancy that———

SOLNESS [*with a quiet, chuckling laugh*]. Just sit down again, Hilda, and I'll tell you something funny.

HILDA [*sits down; with intent interest*]. Well?

SOLNESS. It sounds such a ludicrous thing for, you see, the whole story turns upon nothing but a crack in a chimney.

HILDA. No more than that?

SOLNESS. No, not to begin with.

[*He moves a chair nearer to* HILDA *and sits down.*]

HILDA [*impatiently, taps on her knee*]. Well, now for the crack in the chimney!

SOLNESS. I had noticed the split in the flue long, long before the fire. Every time I went up into the attic, I looked to see if it was still here.

HILDA. And it was?

SOLNESS. Yes; for no one else knew about it.

HILDA. And you said nothing?

SOLNESS. Nothing.

HILDA. And did not think of repairing the flue either?

SOLNESS. Oh, yes, I thought about it —but never got any further. Every time I intended to set to work, it seemed just as if a band held me back. Not today, I thought—tomorrow; and nothing ever came of it.

HILDA. But why did you keep putting it off like that?

SOLNESS. Because I was revolving something in my mind. [*slowly, and in a low voice*] Through that little black crack in the chimney, I might, perhaps, force my way upwards— as a builder.

HILDA [*looking straight in front of her*]. That must have been thrilling.

SOLNESS. Almost irresistible—quite ir-resistible. For at that time it appeared to me a perfectly simple and straightforward matter. I would have had it happen in the wintertime —a little before midday. I was to be out driving Aline in the sleigh. The servants at home would have made huge fires in the stoves.

HILDA. For, of course, it was to be bitterly cold that day?

SOLNESS. Rather biting, yes—and they would want Aline to find it thorough-ly snug and warm when she came home.

HILDA. I suppose she is very chilly by nature?

SOLNESS. She is. And as we drove home, we were to see the smoke.

HILDA. Only the smoke?

SOLNESS. The smoke first. But when we came up to the garden gate, the whole of the old timber box was to be a rolling mass of flames.—That is how I wanted it to be, you see.

HILDA. Oh why, why could it not have happened so!

SOLNESS. You may well say that, Hilda.

HILDA. Well, but now listen, Mr. Sol-ness. Are you perfectly certain that the fire was caused by that little crack in the chimney?

SOLNESS. No, on the contrary—I am perfectly certain that the crack in the chimney had nothing whatever to do with the fire.

HILDA. What?

SOLNESS. It has been clearly ascertained that the fire broke out in a clothes cupboard—in a totally different part of the house.

HILDA. Then what is all this nonsense you are talking about the crack in the chimney?

SOLNESS. May I go on talking to you a little, Hilda?

HILDA. Yes, if you'll only talk sensibly

SOLNESS. I will try. [*He moves his chair nearer.*]

HILDA. Out with it, then, Mr. Solness.

SOLNESS [*confidentially*]. Don't you agree with me, Hilda, that there exist special, chosen people who have been endowed with the power and faculty of desiring a thing, craving for a thing, willing a thing—so persistently and so—so inexorably—that at last it has to happen? Don't you believe that?

HILDA [*with an indefinable expression in her eyes*]. If that is so, we shall see, one of these days, whether *I* am one of the chosen.

SOLNESS. It is not one's self that can do such great things. Oh, no,—the helpers and the servers—they must do their part, too, if it is to be of any good. But they never come of themselves. One has to call upon them very persistently—inwardly, you understand.

HILDA. What are these helpers and servers?

SOLNESS. Oh, we can talk about that some other time. For the present, let us keep to this business of the fire.

HILDA. Don't you think that fire would have happened all the same—even without your wishing for it?

SOLNESS. If the house had been old Knut Brovik's, it would never have burned down so conveniently for him. I am sure of that for he does not know how to call for the helpers— no, nor for the servers, either. [*Rises in unrest.*] So you see, Hilda—it is my fault, after all, that the lives of the two little boys had to be sacri-ficed. And do you think it is not my fault, too, that Aline has never been the woman she should and might have been—and that she most longed to be?

HILDA. Yes, but if it is all the work of those helpers and servers———?

SOLNESS. Who called for the helpers and servers? It was I! And they came and obeyed my will. [*in in-creasing excitement*] That is what people call having the luck on your side; but I must tell you what this sort of luck feels like! It feels like a great raw place here on my breast. And the helpers and servers keep on flaying pieces of skin off other people in order to close my sore!—But still the sore is not healed—never, never! Oh, if you knew how it can sometimes gnaw and burn.

HILDA [*looks attentively at him*]. You are ill, Mr. Solness. Very ill, I almost think.

SOLNESS. Say mad for that is what you mean.

HILDA. No, I don't think there is much amiss with your intellect.

SOLNESS. With what then? Out with it!

HILDA. I wonder whether you were not sent into the world with a sickly conscience.

SOLNESS. A sickly conscience? What devilry is that?

HILDA. I mean that your conscience is feeble—too delicately built, as it were—hasn't strength to take a grip of things—to lift and bear what is heavy.

SOLNESS [*growls*]. H'm! May I ask, then, what sort of conscience one ought to have?

HILDA. I should like your conscience to be—to be thoroughly robust.

SOLNESS. Indeed? Robust, eh? Is your own conscience robust, may I ask?

HILDA. Yes, I think it is. I have never noticed that it wasn't.

SOLNESS. It has not been put very severely to the test, I should think.

HILDA [*with a quivering of the lips*]. Oh, it was no such simple matter to leave father—I am so awfully fond of him.

SOLNESS. Dear me! for a month or two——

HILDA. I think I shall never go home again.

SOLNESS. Never? Then why did you leave him?

HILDA [*half-seriously, half-banteringly*]. Have you forgotten that the ten years are up?

SOLNESS. Oh nonsense. Was anything wrong at home? Eh?

HILDA [*quite seriously*]. It was this impulse within me that urged and goaded me to come—and lured and drew me on, as well.

SOLNESS [*eagerly*]. There we have it! There we have it, Hilda! There is a troll in you, too, as in me. For it's the troll in one, you see—it is that that calls to the powers outside us. And then you must give in—whether you will or no.

HILDA. I almost think you are right, Mr. Solness.

SOLNESS [*walks about the room*]. Oh, there are devils innumerable abroad in the world, Hilda, that one never sees!

HILDA. Devils, too?

SOLNESS [*stops*]. Good devils and bad devils; light-haired devils and black-haired devils. If only you could always tell whether it is the light or dark ones that have got hold of you! [*Paces about.*] Ho-ho! Then it would be simple enough.

HILDA [*follows him with her eyes*]. Or if one had a really vigorous, radiantly healthy conscience—so that one dared to do what one would.

SOLNESS [*stops beside the console table*]. I believe, now, that most people are just as puny creatures as I am in that respect.

HILDA. I shouldn't wonder.

SOLNESS [*leaning against the table*]. In the sagas————Have you read any of the old sagas?

HILDA. Oh, yes! When I used to read books, I————

SOLNESS. In the sagas you read about vikings, who sailed to foreign lands, and plundered and burned and killed men————

HILDA. And carried off women————

SOLNESS. ————and kept them in captivity————

HILDA. ————took them home in their ships————

SOLNESS. ————and behaved to them like—like the very worst of trolls.

HILDA [*looks straight before her, with a half-veiled look*]. I think that must have been thrilling.

SOLNESS [*with a short, deep laugh*]. To carry off women.

HILDA. To be carried off.

SOLNESS [*looks at her a moment*]. Oh, indeed.

HILDA [*as if breaking the thread of the conversation*]. But what made you speak of these vikings, Mr. Solness?

SOLNESS. Why, those fellows must have had robust consciences, if you like! When they got home again, they could eat and drink and be as happy as children. And the women, too! They often would not leave them on any account. Can you understand that, Hilda?

HILDA. Those women I can understand exceedingly well.

SOLNESS. Oho! Perhaps you could do the same yourself?

HILDA. Why not?

SOLNESS. Live—of your own free will —with a ruffian like that?

HILDA. If it was a ruffian I had come to love————

SOLNESS. Could you come to love a man like that?

HILDA. Good heavens, you know very well one can't choose whom one is going to love.

SOLNESS [*looks meditatively at her*]. Oh, no, I suppose it is the troll within one that's responsible for that.

HILDA [*half laughing*]. And all those blessed devils, that you know so well —both the light-haired and the dark-haired ones.

SOLNESS [*quietly and warmly*]. Then I hope with all my heart that the devils will choose carefully for you, Hilda.

HILDA. For me they have chosen already—once and for all.

SOLNESS [*looks earnestly at her*]. Hilda —you are like a wild bird of the woods.

HILDA. Far from it. I don't hide myself away under the bushes.

SOLNESS. No, no. There is rather something of the bird of prey in you.

HILDA. That is nearer it—perhaps. [*very earnestly*] And why not a bird of prey? Why should not *I* go a-bunting—I, as well as the rest. Carry off the prey I want—if only I can get my claws into it and do with it as I will.

SOLNESS. Hilda—do you know what you are?

HILDA. Yes, I suppose I am a strange sort of bird.

SOLNESS. No. You are like a dawning day. When I look at you—I seem to be looking towards the sunrise.

HILDA. Tell me, Mr. Solness—are you certain that you have never called me to you? Inwardly, you know?

SOLNESS [*softly and slowly*]. I almost think I must have.

HILDA. What did you want with me?

SOLNESS. You are the younger generation, Hilda.

HILDA [*smiles*]. That younger generation that you are so afraid of?

SOLNESS [*nods slowly*]. And which, in my heart, I yearn towards so deeply.

[HILDA *rises, goes to the little table, and fetches* RAGNAR BROVIK'S *portfolio.*]

HILDA [*holds out the portfolio to him*]. We were talking of these drawings————

————

SOLNESS [*shortly, waving them away*]. Put those things away! I have seen enough of them.

HILDA. Yes, but you have to write your approval on them.

SOLNESS. Write my approval on them? Never!

HILDA. But the poor old man is lying at death's door! Can't you give him and his son this pleasure before they are parted? And perhaps he might get the commission to carry them out, too.

SOLNESS. Yes, that is just what he would get. He has made sure of that —has my fine gentleman!

HILDA. Then, good heavens—if that is so—can't you tell the least little bit of a lie for once in a way?

SOLNESS. A lie? [*raging*] Hilda—take those devil's drawings out of my sight!

HILDA [*draws the portfolio a little nearer to herself*]. Well, well, well—don't bite me.—You talk of trolls—but I think you go on like a troll yourself. [*Looks around.*] Where do you keep your pen and ink?

SOLNESS. There is nothing of the sort in here.

HILDA [*goes toward the door*]. But in the office where that young lady is

———

SOLNESS. Stay where you are, Hilda!— I ought to tell a lie, you say. Oh, yes, for the sake of his old father I might well do that—for in my time I have crushed him, trodden him under foot———

HILDA. Him, too?

SOLNESS. I needed room for myself. But this Ragnar—he must on no account be allowed to come to the front.

HILDA. Poor fellow, there is surely no fear of that. If he has nothing in him———

SOLNESS [*comes closer, looks at her and whispers*]. If Ragnar Brovik gets his chance, he will strike me to the earth. Crush me—as I crushed his father.

HILDA. Crush you? Has he the ability for that?

SOLNESS. Yes, you may depend upon it; he has the ability! He is the younger generation that stands ready to knock at my door—to make an end of Halvard Solness.

HILDA [*looks at him with quiet reproach*]. And yet you would bar him out. Fie, Mr. Solness!

SOLNESS. The fight I have been fighting has cost heart's blood enough.—And I am afraid, too, that the helpers and servers will not obey me any longer.

HILDA. Then you must go ahead without them. There is nothing else for it.

SOLNESS. It is hopeless, Hilda. The luck is bound to turn. A little sooner or a little later. Retribution is inexorable.

HILDA [*in distress, putting her hands over her ears*]. Don't talk like that! Do you want to kill me? To take from me what is more than my life?

SOLNESS. And what is that?

HILDA. The longing to see you great. To see you, with a wreath in your hand, high, high up upon a church tower. [*Calm again.*] Come, out with your pencil now. You must have a pencil about you?

SOLNESS [*takes out his pocketbook*]. I have one here.

HILDA [*lays the portfolio on the sofa table*]. Very well. Now let us two sit down here, Mr. Solness. [SOLNESS *seats himself at the table.* HILDA *stands behind him, leaning over the back of the chair.*] And now we will write on the drawings. We must write very, very nicely and cordially—for this horrid Ruar—or whatever his name is.

SOLNESS [*writes a few words, turns his head, and looks at her*]. Tell me one thing, Hilda.

HILDA. Yes!

SOLNESS. If you have been waiting for me all these ten years———

HILDA. What then?

SOLNESS. Why have you never written to me? Then I could have answered you.

HILDA [*hastily*]. No, no, no! That was just what I did not want.

SOLNESS. Why not?

HILDA. I was afraid the whole thing might fall to pieces.—But we were going to write on the drawings, Mr. Solness.

SOLNESS. So we were.

HILDA [*bends forward and looks over his shoulder while he writes*]. Mind now, kindly and cordially! Oh how I hate—how I hate this Ruald——

SOLNESS [*writing*]. Have you never really cared for anyone, Hilda?

HILDA [*harshly*]. What do you say?

SOLNESS. Have you never cared for anyone?

HILDA. For anyone else, I suppose you mean?

SOLNESS [*looks up at her*]. For anyone else, yes. Have you never? In all these ten years? Never?

HILDA. Oh, yes, now and then. When I was perfectly furious with you for not coming.

SOLNESS. Then you did take an interest in other people, too?

HILDA. A little bit—for a week or so. Good heavens, Mr. Solness, you surely know how such things come about.

SOLNESS. Hilda—what is it you have come for?

HILDA. Don't waste time talking. The poor old man might go and die in the meantime.

SOLNESS. Answer me, Hilda. What do you want of me?

HILDA. I want my kingdom.

SOLNESS. H'm——

[*He gives a rapid glance toward the door on the left and then goes on writing on the drawings. At the same moment* MRS. SOLNESS *enters; she has some packages in her hand.*]

MRS. SOLNESS. Here are a few things I have got for you, Miss Wangel. The large parcels will be sent later on.

HILDA. Oh, how very, very kind of you!

MRS. SOLNESS. Only my simple duty. Nothing more than that.

SOLNESS [*reading over what he has written*]. Aline!

MRS. SOLNESS. Yes?

SOLNESS. Did you notice whether the —the bookkeeper was out there?

MRS. SOLNESS. Yes, of course, she was out there.

SOLNESS [*puts the drawings in the portfolio*]. H'm——

MRS. SOLNESS. She was standing at the desk, as she always is—when *I* go through the room.

SOLNESS [*rises*]. Then I'll give this to her and tell her that——

HILDA [*takes the portfolio from him*]. Oh, no, let me have the pleasure of doing that! [*Goes to the door, but turns.*] What is her name?

SOLNESS. Her name is Miss Fosli.

HILDA. Pooh, that sounds too cold! Her Christian name, I mean?

SOLNESS. Kaia—I believe.

HILDA [*opens the door and calls out*]. Kaia, come in here! Make haste! Mr. Solness wants to speak to you.

[KAIA FOSLI *appears at the door.*]

KAIA [*looking at him in alarm*]. Here I am——?

HILDA [*handing her the portfolio*]. See here, Kaia! You can take this home; Mr. Solness has written on them now.

KAIA. Oh, at last!

SOLNESS. Give them to the old man as soon as you can.

KAIA. I will go straight home with them.

SOLNESS. Yes, do. Now Ragnar will have a chance of building for himself.

KAIA. Oh, may he come and thank you for all——?

SOLNESS [*harshly*]. I won't have any thanks! Tell him that from me.

KAIA. Yes, I will——

SOLNESS. And tell him at the same time that henceforward I do not require his services—nor yours either.

KAIA [*softly and quiveringly*]. Not mine either?

SOLNESS. You will have other things to think of now and to attend to; and that is a very good thing for you. Well, go home with the drawings now, Miss Fosli. At once! Do you hear?

KAIA [*as before*]. Yes, Mr. Solness.

[*She goes out.*]

MRS. SOLNESS. Heavens! what deceitful eyes she has.

SOLNESS. She? That poor little creature?

MRS. SOLNESS. Oh—I can see what I can see, Halvard.————Are you really dismissing them?

SOLNESS. Yes.

MRS. SOLNESS. Her as well?

SOLNESS. Was not that what you wished?

MRS. SOLNESS. But how can you get on without her————? Oh, well, no doubt you have someone else in reserve, Halvard.

HILDA [*playfully*]. Well, I for one am not the person to stand at that desk.

SOLNESS. Never mind, never mind—it will be all right, Aline. Now all you have to do is to think about moving into our new home—as quickly as you can. This evening we will hang up the wreath—[*Turns to Hilda.*] —right on the very pinnacle of the tower. What do you say to that, Miss Hilda?

HILDA [*looks at him with sparkling eyes*]. It will be splendid to see you so high up once more.

SOLNESS. Me!

MRS. SOLNESS. For heaven's sake, Miss Wangel, don't imagine such a thing! My husband!—when he always gets so dizzy!

HILDA. He get dizzy! No, I know quite well he does not!

MRS. SOLNESS. Oh, yes, indeed he does.

HILDA. But I have seen him with my own eyes right up at the top of a high church tower!

MRS. SOLNESS. Yes, I hear people talk of that; but it is utterly impossible ————

SOLNESS [*vehemently*]. Impossible— impossible, yes! But there I stood all the same!

MRS. SOLNESS. Oh, how can you say so, Halvard? Why, you can't even bear to go out on the second-story balcony here. You have always been like that.

SOLNESS. You may perhaps see something different this evening.

MRS. SOLNESS [*in alarm*]. No, no, no! Please God I shall never see that. I will write at once to the doctor—and I am sure he won't let you do it.

SOLNESS. Why, Aline————!

MRS. SOLNESS. Oh, you know you're ill, Halvard. This proves it! Oh God— Oh God!

[*She goes hastily out to the right.*]

HILDA [*looks intently at him*]. Is it so, or is it not?

SOLNESS. That I turn dizzy?

HILDA. That my master builder dares not—cannot—climb as high as he builds?

SOLNESS. Is that the way you look at it?

HILDA. Yes.

SOLNESS. I believe there is scarcely a corner in me that is safe from you.

HILDA [*looks toward the bow window*]. Up there, then. Right up there————

SOLNESS [*approaches her*]. You might have the topmost room in the tower, Hilda—there you might live like a princess.

HILDA [*indefinably, between earnest and jest*]. Yes, that is what you promised me.

SOLNESS. Did I really?

HILDA. Fie, Mr. Solness! You said I should be a princess and that you would give me a kingdom. And then you went and————Well!

SOLNESS [*cautiously*]. Are you quite certain that this is not a dream— a fancy, that has fixed itself in your mind?

HILDA [*sharply*]. Do you mean that you did not do it?

SOLNESS. I scarcely know myself. [*more softly*] But now I know so much for certain, that I————

HILDA. That you————? Say it at once!

SOLNESS. —that I ought to have done it.

HILDA [*exclaims with animation*]. Don't tell me you can ever be dizzy!

SOLNESS. This evening, then, we will hang up the wreath—Princess Hilda.

HILDA [*with a bitter curve of the lips*]. Over your new home, yes.

SOLNESS. Over the new house, which will never be a home for me.

[*He goes out through the garden door.*]

HILDA [*looks straight in front of her with a far-away expression and whispers to herself. The only words audible are*]. —frightfully thrilling

———

ACT III

The large, broad verandah of SOLNESS' *dwelling house. Part of the house, with outer door leading to the verandah, is seen to the left. A railing along the verandah to the right. At the back, from the end of the verandah, a flight of steps leads down to the garden below. Tall old trees in the garden spread their branches over the verandah and toward the house. Far to the right, in among the trees, a glimpse is caught of the lower part of the new villa, with scaffolding round so much as is seen of the tower. In the background the garden is bounded by an old wooden fence. Outside the fence, a street with low, tumble-down cottages.*

Evening sky with sun-lit clouds.

On the verandah, a garden bench stands along the wall of the house, and in front of the bench a long table. On the other side of the table, an armchair and some stools. All the furniture is of wickerwork.

MRS. SOLNESS, *wrapped in a large white crepe shawl, sits resting in the armchair and gazes over to the right. Shortly after,* HILDA WANGEL *comes up the flight of steps from the garden. She is dressed as in the last act and wears her hat. She has in her bodice a little nosegay of small common flowers.*

MRS. SOLNESS [*turning her head a little*]. Have you been round the garden, Miss Wangel?

HILDA. Yes, I have been taking a look at it.

MRS. SOLNESS. And found some flowers, too, I see.

HILDA. Yes, indeed! There are such heaps of them in among the bushes.

MRS. SOLNESS. Are there really? Still? You see I scarcely ever go there.

HILDA [*closer*]. What! Don't you take a run down into the garden every day, then?

MRS. SOLNESS [*with a faint smile*]. I don't "run" anywhere, nowadays.

HILDA. Well, but do you not go down now and then to look at all the lovely things there?

MRS. SOLNESS. It has all become so strange to me. I am almost afraid to see it again.

HILDA. Your own garden!

MRS. SOLNESS. I don't feel that it is mine any longer.

HILDA. What do you mean———?

MRS. SOLNESS. No, no, it is not—not —not as it was in my mother's and father's time. They have taken away so much—so much of the garden, Miss Wangel. Fancy—they have parceled it out—and built houses for strangers—people that I don't know. And they can sit and look in upon me from their windows.

HILDA [*with a bright expression*]. Mrs. Solness!

MRS. SOLNESS. Yes!

HILDA. May I stay here with you a little?

MRS. SOLNESS. Yes, by all means, if you care to.

[HILDA *moves a stool close to the armchair and sits down.*]

HILDA. Ah—here one can sit and sun oneself like a cat.

MRS. SOLNESS [*lays her hand softly on* HILDA's *neck*]. It is nice of you to be willing to sit with me. I thought you wanted to go in to my husband.

HILDA. What should I want with him?

MRS. SOLNESS. To help him, I thought.

HILDA. No, thank you. And besides, he is not in. He is over there with the workmen. But he looked so fierce that I did not care to talk to him.

MRS. SOLNESS. He is so kind and gentle in reality.

HILDA. He!

MRS. SOLNESS. You do not really know him yet, Miss Wangel.

HILDA [*looks affectionately at her*]. Are you pleased at the thought of moving over to the new house?

MRS. SOLNESS. I ought to be pleased; for it is what Halvard wants——

HILDA. Oh, not just on that account, surely.

MRS. SOLNESS. Yes, yes, Miss Wangel; for it is only my duty to submit myself to him. But very often it is dreadfully difficult to force one's mind to obedience.

HILDA. Yes, that must be difficult indeed.

MRS. SOLNESS. I can tell you it is— when one has so many faults as I have——

HILDA. When one has gone through so much trouble as you have——

MRS. SOLNESS. How do you know about that?

HILDA. Your husband told me.

MRS. SOLNESS. To me he very seldom mentions these things. ——Yes, I can tell you I have gone through more than enough trouble in my life, Miss Wangel.

HILDA [*looks sympathetically at her and nods slowly*]. Poor Mrs. Solness. First of all there was the fire——

MRS. SOLNESS [*with a sigh*]. Yes, everything that was mine was burned.

HILDA. And then came what was worse.

MRS. SOLNESS [*looking inquiringly at her*]. Worse?

HILDA. The worst of all.

MRS. SOLNESS. What do you mean?

HILDA [*softly*]. You lost the two little boys.

MRS. SOLNESS. Oh, yes, the boys. But, you see, that was a thing apart. That was a dispensation of Providence; and in such things one can only bow in submission—yes, and be thankful, too.

HILDA. Then you are so?

MRS. SOLNESS. Not always, I am sorry to say. I know well enough that it is my duty—but all the same I cannot.

HILDA. No, no, I think that is only natural.

MRS. SOLNESS. And often and often I have to remind myself that it was a righteous punishment for me——

HILDA. Why?

MRS. SOLNESS. Because I had not fortitude enough in misfortune.

HILDA. But I don't see that ——

MRS. SOLNESS. Oh, no, no, Miss Wangel—do not talk to me any more about the two little boys. We ought to feel nothing but joy in thinking of them; for they are so happy—so happy now. No, it is the small losses in life that cut one to the heart—the loss of all that other people look upon as almost nothing.

HILDA [*lays her arms on* MRS. SOLNESS' *knees and looks up at her affectionately*]. Dear Mrs. Solness— tell me what things you mean!

MRS. SOLNESS. As I say, only little things. All the old portraits were burned on the walls. And all the old silk dresses were burned, that had belonged to the family for generations and generations. And all mother's and grandmother's lace—that was burned, too. And only think—the jewels, too! [*sadly*] And then all the dolls.

HILDA. The dolls?

MRS. SOLNESS [*choking with tears*]. I had nine lovely dolls.

HILDA. And they were burned, too?

MRS. SOLNESS. All of them. Oh, it was hard—so hard for me.

HILDA. Had you put by all these dolls, then? Ever since you were little?

MRS. SOLNESS. I had not put them by. The dolls and I had gone on living together.

HILDA. After you were grown up?

MRS. SOLNESS. Yes, long after that.

HILDA. After you were married, too?

MRS. SOLNESS. Oh, yes, indeed. So long as he did not see it———. But they were all burned up, poor things. No one thought of saving them. Oh, it is so miserable to think of. You mustn't laugh at me, Miss Wangel.

HILDA. I am not laughing in the least.

MRS. SOLNESS. For you see, in a certain sense, there was life in them, too. I carried them under my heart —like little unborn children.

[DR. HERDAL, *with his hat in his hand, comes out through the door and observes* MRS. SOLNESS *and* HILDA.]

DR. HERDAL. Well, Mrs. Solness, so you are sitting out here catching cold?

MRS. SOLNESS. I find it so pleasant and warm here today.

DR. HERDAL. Yes, yes. But is there anything going on here? I got a note from you.

MRS. SOLNESS [*rises*]. Yes, there is something I must talk to you about.

DR. HERDAL. Very well; then perhaps we had better go in. [*to* HILDA] Still in your mountaineering dress, Miss Wangel?

HILDA [*gaily, rising*]. Yes—in full uniform! But today I am not going climbing and breaking my neck. We two will stop quietly below and look on, doctor.

DR. HERDAL. What are we to look on at?

MRS. SOLNESS [*softly, in alarm, to* HILDA]. Hush, hush—for God's sake! He is coming. Try to get that idea out of his head. And let us be friends, Miss Wangel. Don't you think we can?

HILDA [*throws her arms impetuously round* MRS. SOLNESS' *neck*]. Oh, if we only could!

MRS. SOLNESS [*gently disengages herself*]. There, there, there! There he comes, doctor. Let me have a word with you.

DR. HERDAL. Is it about him?

MRS. SOLNESS. Yes, to be sure it's about him. Do come in.

[*She and the doctor enter the house. Next moment* SOLNESS *comes up from the garden by the flight of steps. A serious look comes over* HILDA's *face.*]

SOLNESS [*glances at the house door, which is closed cautiously from within*]. Have you noticed, Hilda, that as soon as I come she goes?

HILDA. I have noticed that as soon as you come, you make her go.

SOLNESS. Perhaps so. But I cannot help it. [*Looks observantly at her.*] Are you cold, Hilda? I think you look cold.

HILDA. I have just come up out of a tomb.

SOLNESS. What do you mean by that?

HILDA. That I have got chilled through and through, Mr. Solness.

SOLNESS [*slowly*]. I believe I understand———

HILDA. What brings you up here just now?

SOLNESS. I caught sight of you from over there.

HILDA. But then you must have seen her too?

SOLNESS. I knew she would go at once I came.

HILDA. Is it very painful for you that

she should avoid you in this way?

SOLNESS. In one sense, it's a relief as well.

HILDA. Not to have her before your eyes?

SOLNESS. Yes.

HILDA. Not to be always seeing how heavily the loss of the little boys weighs upon her?

SOLNESS. Yes. Chiefly that.

[HILDA *drifts across the verandah with her hands behind her back, stops at the railing and looks out over the garden.*]

SOLNESS [*after a short pause*]. Did you have a long talk with her?

[HILDA *stands motionless and does not answer.*]

SOLNESS. Had you a long talk, I asked?

[HILDA *is silent as before.*]

SOLNESS. What was she talking about, Hilda?

[HILDA *continues silent.*]

SOLNESS. Poor Aline! I suppose it was about the little boys.

[*A nervous shudder runs through* HILDA; *then she nods hurriedly once or twice.*]

SOLNESS. She will never get over it—never in this world. [*Approaches her.*] Now you are standing there again like a statue; just as you stood last night.

HILDA [*turns and looks at him, with great serious eyes*]. I am going away.

SOLNESS [*sharply*]. Going away!

HILDA. Yes.

SOLNESS. But I won't allow you to!

HILDA. What am I to do here now?

SOLNESS. Simply to be here, Hilda!

HILDA [*measures him with a look*]. Oh, thank you. You know it wouldn't end there.

SOLNESS [*heedlessly*]. So much the better!

HILDA [*vehemently*]. I cannot do any

harm to one whom I know! I can't take away anything that belongs to her.

SOLNESS. Who wants you to do that?

HILDA [*continuing*]. A stranger, yes! for that is quite a different thing! A person I have never set eyes on. But one that I have come into close contact with————! Oh, no! Oh, no! Ugh!

SOLNESS. Yes, but I never proposed you should.

HILDA. Oh, Mr. Solness, you know quite well what the end of it would be. And that is why I am going away.

SOLNESS. And what is to become of me when you are gone? What shall I have to live for then?—After that?

HILDA [*with the indefinable look in her eyes*]. It is surely not so hard for you. You have your duties to her. Live for those duties.

SOLNESS. Too late. These powers—these—these————

HILDA. —devils————

SOLNESS. Yes, these devils! And the troll within me as well—they have drawn all the life blood out of her. [*Laughs in desperation.*] They did it for my happiness! Yes, yes! [*sadly*] And now she is dead—for my sake. And I am chained alive to a dead woman. [*in wild anguish*] I—I who cannot live without joy in life!

[HILDA *moves round the table and seats herself on the bench, with her elbows on the table and her head supported by her hands.*]

HILDA [*sits and looks at him awhile*]. What will you build next?

SOLNESS [*shakes his head*]. I don't believe I shall build much more.

HILDA. Not those cozy, happy homes for mother and father, and for the troop of children?

SOLNESS. I wonder whether there will be any use for such homes in the coming time.

HILDA. Poor Mr. Solness! And you have gone all these ten years—and staked your whole life—on that alone.

SOLNESS. Yes, you may well say so, Hilda.

HILDA [*with an outburst*]. Oh, it all seems to me so foolish—so foolish!

SOLNESS. All what?

HILDA. Not to be able to grasp at your own happiness—at your own life! Merely because someone you know happens to stand in the way!

SOLNESS. One whom you have no right to set aside.

HILDA. I wonder whether one really has not the right! And yet, and yet ————. Oh, if one could only sleep the whole thing away!

[*She lays her arms flat on the table, rests the left side of her head on her hands, and shuts her eyes.*]

SOLNESS [*turns the armchair and sits down at the table*]. Had you a cozy, happy home—up there with your father, Hilda?

HILDA [*without stirring, answers as if half asleep*]. I had only a cage.

SOLNESS. And you are determined not to go back to it?

HILDA [*as before*]. The wild bird never wants to go into the cage.

SOLNESS. Rather range through the free air————

HILDA [*still as before*]. The bird of prey loves to range————

SOLNESS [*lets his eyes rest on her*]. If only one had the viking spirit in life ————

HILDA [*in her usual voice; opens her eyes but does not move*]. And the other thing? Say what that was!

SOLNESS. A robust conscience.

[HILDA *sits erect on the bench, with animation. Her eyes have once more the sparkling expression of gladness.*]

HILDA [*nods to him*]. I know what you are going to build next!

SOLNESS. Then you know more than I do, Hilda.

HILDA. Yes, builders are such stupid people.

SOLNESS. What is it to be then?

HILDA [*nods again*]. The castle.

SOLNESS. What castle?

HILDA. My castle, of course.

SOLNESS. Do you want a castle now?

HILDA. Don't you owe me a kingdom, I should like to know?

SOLNESS. You say I do.

HILDA. Well—you admit you owe me this kingdom. And you can't have a kingdom without a royal castle, I should think!

SOLNESS [*more and more animated*]. Yes, they usually go together.

HILDA. Good! Then build it for me! This moment!

SOLNESS [*laughing*]. Must you have that on the instant, too?

HILDA. Yes, to be sure! For the ten years are up now, and I am not going to wait any longer. So—out with the castle, Mr. Solness!

SOLNESS. It's no light matter to owe you anything, Hilda.

HILDA. You should have thought of that before. It is too late now. So— [*tapping the table*]—the castle on the table! It is my castle! I will have it at once!

SOLNESS [*more seriously, leans over toward her, with his arms on the table*]. What sort of castle have you imagined, Hilda?

[*Her expression becomes more and more veiled. She seems gazing inward at herself.*]

HILDA [*slowly*]. My castle shall stand on a height—on a very great height —with a clear outlook on all sides, so that I can see far—far around.

SOLNESS. And no doubt it is to have a high tower!

HILDA. A tremendously high tower. And at the very top of the tower there shall be a balcony. And I will stand out upon it————

SOLNESS [*involuntarily clutches at his forehead*]. How can you like to stand at such a dizzy height————?

HILDA. Yes, I will, right up there will I stand and look down on the other people—on those that are building churches, and homes for mother and father and the troop of children. And you may come up and look on at it, too.

SOLNESS [*in a low tone*]. Is the builder to be allowed to come up beside the princess?

HILDA. If the builder will.

SOLNESS [*more softly*]. Then I think the builder will come.

HILDA [*nods*]. The builder—he will come.

SOLNESS. But he will never be able to build any more. Poor builder!

HILDA [*animated*]. Oh yes, he will! We two will set to work together. And then we will build the loveliest —the very loveliest—thing in all the world.

SOLNESS [*intently*]. Hilda—tell me what that is!

HILDA [*looks smilingly at him, shakes her head a little, pouts, and speaks as if to a child*]. Builders—they are such very—very stupid people.

SOLNESS. Yes, no doubt they are stupid. But now tell me what it is—the loveliest thing in the world—that we two are to build together?

HILDA [*is silent a little while, then says with an indefinable expression in her eyes*]. Castles in the air.

SOLNESS. Castles in the air?

HILDA [*nods*]. Castles in the air, yes! Do you know what sort of thing a castle in the air is?

SOLNESS. It is the loveliest thing in the world, you say.

HILDA [*rises with vehemence and makes a gesture of repulsion with her hand*]. Yes, to be sure it is! Castles in the air—they are so easy to take refuge in. And so easy to build, too—[*Looks scornfully at*

him.]—especially for the builders who have a—a dizzy conscience.

SOLNESS [*rises*]. After this day we two will build together, Hilda.

HILDA [*with a half-dubious smile*]. A real castle in the air?

SOLNESS. Yes. One with a firm foundation under it.

[RAGNAR BROVIK *comes out from the house. He is carrying a large, green wreath with flowers and silk ribbons.*]

HILDA [*with an outburst of pleasure*]. The wreath! Oh, that will be glorious!

SOLNESS [*in surprise*]. Have you brought the wreath, Ragnar?

RAGNAR. I promised the foreman I would.

SOLNESS [*relieved*]. Ah, then I suppose your father is better?

RAGNAR. No.

SOLNESS. Was he not cheered by what I wrote?

RAGNAR. It came too late.

SOLNESS. Too late!

RAGNAR. When she came with it he was unconscious. He had had a stroke.

SOLNESS. Why, then, you must go home to him! You must attend to your father!

RAGNAR. He does not need me any more.

SOLNESS. But surely you ought to be with him.

RAGNAR. She is sitting by his bed.

SOLNESS [*rather uncertainly*]. Kaia?

RAGNAR [*looking darkly at him*].—Yes —Kaia.

SOLNESS. Go home, Ragnar—both to him and to her. Give me the wreath.

RAGNAR [*suppresses a mocking smile*]. You don't mean that you yourself ————?

SOLNESS. I will take it down to them myself: [*Takes the wreath from him.*] And now you go home; we don't require you today.

RAGNAR. I know you do not require

me any more; but today I shall remain.

SOLNESS. Well, remain then, since you are bent upon it.

HILDA [*at the railing*]. Mr. Solness, I will stand here and look on at you.

SOLNESS. At me!

HILDA. It will be fearfully thrilling.

SOLNESS [*in a low tone*]. We will talk about that presently, Hilda.

[*He goes down the flight of steps with the wreath and away through the garden.*]

HILDA [*looks after him, then turns to RAGNAR*]. I think you might at least have thanked him.

RAGNAR. Thanked him? Ought I to have thanked him?

HILDA. Yes, of course you ought!

RAGNAR. I think it is rather you I ought to thank.

HILDA. How can you say such a thing?

RAGNAR [*without answering her*]. But I advise you to take care, Miss Wangel! For you don't know him rightly yet.

HILDA [*ardently*]. Oh, no one knows him as I do!

RAGNAR [*laughs in exasperation*]. Thank him, when he has held me down year after year! When he made father disbelieve in me—made me disbelieve in myself! And all merely that he might————!

HILDA [*as if divining something*]. That he might————? Tell me at once!

RAGNAR. That he might keep her with him.

HILDA [*with a start toward him*]. The girl at the desk.

RAGNAR. Yes.

HILDA [*threateningly, clenching her hands*]. That is not true! You are telling falsehoods about him!

RAGNAR. I would not believe it either until today—when she said so herself.

HILDA [*as if beside herself*]. What did she say? I will know! At once! at once!

RAGNAR. She said that he had taken possession of her mind—her whole mind—centered all her thoughts upon himself alone. She says that she can never leave him—that she will remain here, where he is————

HILDA [*with flashing eyes*]. She will not be allowed to!

RAGNAR [*as if feeling his way*]. Who will not allow her?

HILDA [*rapidly*]. He will not either!

RAGNAR. Oh no—I understand the whole thing now. After this, she would merely be—in the way.

HILDA. You understand nothing—since you can talk like that! No, *I* will tell you why he kept hold of her.

RAGNAR. Well then, why?

HILDA. In order to keep hold of you.

RAGNAR. Has he told you so?

HILDA. No, but it is so. It must be so. [*wildly*] I will—I will have it so!

RAGNAR. And at the very moment when you came—he let her go.

HILDA. It was you—you that he let go. What do you suppose he cares about strange women like her?

RAGNAR [*reflects*]. Is it possible that all this time he has been afraid of me?

HILDA. He afraid! I would not be so conceited if I were you.

RAGNAR. Oh, he must have seen long ago that I had something in me, too. Besides—cowardly—that is just what he is, you see.

HILDA. He! Oh, yes. I am likely to believe that!

RAGNAR. In a certain sense he is cowardly—he, the great master builder. He is not afraid of robbing others of their life's happiness—as he has done both for my father and for me. But when it comes to climbing up a paltry bit of scaffolding—he will do anything rather than that.

HILDA. Oh, you should just have seen him high, high up—at the dizzy height where I once saw him.

RAGNAR. Did you see that?

HILDA. Yes, indeed I did. How free and great he looked as he stood and fastened the wreath to the church vane!

RAGNAR. I know that he ventured that, once in his life—one solitary time. It is legend among us younger men. But no power on earth would induce him to do it again.

HILDA. Today he will do it again!

RAGNAR [*scornfully*]. Yes, I daresay!

HILDA. We shall see it!

RAGNAR. That neither you nor I will see.

HILDA [*with uncontrollable vehemence*]. I will see it! I will and must see it!

RAGNAR. But he will not do it. He simply dare not do it. For you see he cannot get over this infirmity—master builder though he be.

[MRS. SOLNESS *comes from the house on to the verandah.*]

MRS. SOLNESS [*looks around*]. Is he not here? Where has he gone to?

RAGNAR. Mr. Solness is down with the men.

HILDA. He took the wreath with him.

MRS. SOLNESS [*terrified*]. Took the wreath with him! Oh, God! oh, God! Brovik—you must go down to him! Get him to come back here!

RAGNAR. Shall I say you want to speak to him, Mrs. Solness?

MRS. SOLNESS. Oh, yes, do!—No, no—don't say that *I* want anything! You can say that somebody is here, and that he must come at once.

RAGNAR. Good. I will do so, Mrs. Solness.

[*He goes down the flight of steps and away through the garden.*]

MRS. SOLNESS. Oh, Miss Wangel, you can't think how anxious I feel about him.

HILDA. Is there anything in this to be so terribly frightened about?

MRS. SOLNESS. Oh, yes; surely you can understand. Just think, if he were really to do it! If he should take it into his head to climb up the scaffolding!

HILDA [*eagerly*]. Do you think he will?

MRS. SOLNESS. Oh, one can never tell what he might take into his head. I am afraid there is nothing he mightn't think of doing.

HILDA. Aha! Perhaps you too think that he is—well———?

MRS. SOLNESS. Oh, I don't know what to think about him now. The doctor has been telling me all sorts of things; and putting it all together with several things I have heard him say———

[DR. HERDAL *looks out, at the door.*]

DR. HERDAL. Is he not coming soon?

MRS. SOLNESS. Yes, I think so. I have sent for him at any rate.

DR. HERDAL [*advancing*]. I am afraid you will have to go in, my dear lady———

MRS. SOLNESS. Oh, no! Oh, no! I shall stay out here and wait for Halvard.

DR. HERDAL. But some ladies have just come to call on you———

MRS. SOLNESS. Good heavens, that too! And just at this moment!

DR. HERDAL. They say they positively must see the ceremony.

MRS. SOLNESS. Well, well, I suppose I must go to them after all. It is my duty.

HILDA. Can't you ask the ladies to go away?

MRS. SOLNESS. No, that would never do. Now that they are here, it is my duty to see them. But do you stay out here in the meantime—and receive him when he comes.

DR. HERDAL. And try to occupy his attention as long as possible———

MRS. SOLNESS. Yes, do, dear Miss Wangel. Keep a firm hold of him as ever you can.

HILDA. Would it not be best for you to do that?

MRS. SOLNESS. Yes! God knows that is my duty. But when one has duties in so many directions———

DR. HERDAL [*looks toward the garden*]. There he is coming.

MRS. SOLNESS. And I have to go in!

DR. HERDAL [*to* HILDA]. Don't say anything about my being here.

HILDA. Oh, no! I daresay I shall find something else to talk to Mr. Solness about.

MRS. SOLNESS. And be sure you keep firm hold of him. I believe you can do it best.

[MRS. SOLNESS *and* DR. HERDAL *go into the house.* HILDA *remains standing on the verandah.* SOLNESS *comes from the garden, up the flight of steps.*]

SOLNESS. Somebody wants me, I hear.

HILDA. Yes; it is I, Mr. Solness.

SOLNESS. Oh, is it you, Hilda? I was afraid it might be Aline or the doctor.

HILDA. You are very easily frightened, it seems!

SOLNESS. Do you think so?

HILDA. Yes; people say that you are afraid to climb about—on the scaffoldings, you know.

SOLNESS. Well, that is quite a special thing.

HILDA. Then it is true that you are afraid to do it?

SOLNESS. Yes, I am.

HILDA. Afraid of falling down and killing yourself?

SOLNESS. No, not of that.

HILDA. Of what, then?

SOLNESS. I am afraid of retribution, Hilda.

HILDA. Of retribution? [*Shakes her head.*] I don't understand that.

SOLNESS. Sit down and I will tell you something.

HILDA. Yes, do! At once!

[*She sits on a stool by the railing and looks expectantly at him.*]

SOLNESS [*throws his hat on the table*].

You know that I began by building churches.

HILDA [*nods*]. I know that well.

SOLNESS. For, you see, I came as a boy from a pious home in the country; and so it seemed to me that this church-building was the noblest task I could set myself.

HILDA. Yes, yes.

SOLNESS. And I venture to say that I built those poor little churches with such honest and warm and heartfelt devotion that—that———

HILDA. That———? Well?

SOLNESS. Well, that I think that he ought to have been pleased with me.

HILDA. He? What he?

SOLNESS. He who was to have the churches, of course! He to whose honor and glory they were dedicated.

HILDA. Oh, indeed! But are you certain, then, that—that he was not—pleased with you?

SOLNESS [*scornfully*]. He pleased with me! How can you talk so, Hilda? He who gave the troll in me leave to lord it just as it pleased. He who bade them be at hand to serve me, both day and night—all these—all these———

HILDA. Devils———

SOLNESS. Yes, of both kinds. Oh, no, he made me feel clearly enough that he was not pleased with me. [*mysteriously*] You see, that was really the reason why he made the old house burn down.

HILDA. Was that why?

SOLNESS. Yes, don't you understand? He wanted to give me the chance of becoming an accomplished master in my own sphere—so that I might build all the more glorious churches for him. At first I did not understand what he was driving at; but all of a sudden it flashed upon me.

HILDA. When was that?

SOLNESS. It was when I was building the church tower up at Lysanger.

HILDA. I thought so.

SOLNESS. For you see, Hilda—up there, amidst those new surroundings, I used to go about musing and pondering within myself. Then I saw plainly why he had taken my little children from me. It was that I should have nothing else to attach myself to. No such thing as love and happiness, you understand. I was to be only a master builder—nothing else. And all my life long I was to go on building for him. [*Laughs.*] But I can tell you nothing came of that.

HILDA. What did you do, then?

SOLNESS. First of all, I searched and tried my own heart——

HILDA. And then?

SOLNESS. Then I did the impossible—I no less than he.

HILDA. The impossible?

SOLNESS. I had never before been able to climb up to a great, free height. But that day I did it.

HILDA [*leaping up*]. Yes, yes, you did!

SOLNESS. And when I stood there, high over everything, and was hanging the wreath over the vane, I said to him: Hear me now, thou Mighty One! From this day forward I will be a free builder—I, too, in my sphere—just as thou in thine. I will never more build churches for thee—only homes for human beings.

HILDA [*with great sparkling eyes*]. That was the song that I heard through the air!

SOLNESS. But afterwards his turn came.

HILDA. What do you mean by that?

SOLNESS [*looks despondently at her*]. Building homes for human beings—is not worth a rap, Hilda.

HILDA. Do you say that now?

SOLNESS. Yes, for now I see it. Men have no use for these homes of theirs—to be happy in. And I should not have had any use for such a home, if I had had one. [*with a quiet, bitter laugh*] See, that is the upshot of the whole affair, however far back I look. Nothing really built; nor anything sacrificed for the chance of building. Nothing, nothing! the whole is nothing.

HILDA. Then you will never build anything more?

SOLNESS [*with animation*]. On the contrary, I am just going to begin!

HILDA. What, then? What will you build? Tell me at once!

SOLNESS. I believe there is only one possible dwelling-place for human happiness—and that is what I am going to build now.

HILDA [*looks fixedly at him*]. Mr. Solness—you mean our castle?

SOLNESS. The castles in the air—yes.

HILDA. I am afraid you would turn dizzy before we got halfway up.

SOLNESS. Not if I can mount hand in hand with you, Hilda.

HILDA [*with an expression of suppressed resentment*]. Only with me? Will there be no others of the party?

SOLNESS. Who else should there be?

HILDA. Oh—that girl—that Kaia at the desk. Poor thing—don't you want to take her with you, too?

SOLNESS. Oho! Was it about her that Aline was talking to you?

HILDA. Is it so—or is it not?

SOLNESS [*vehemently*]. I will not answer such a question. You must believe in me, wholly and entirely!

HILDA. All these ten years I have believed in you so utterly—so utterly.

SOLNESS. You must go on believing in me!

HILDA. Then let me see you stand free and high up!

SOLNESS [*sadly*]. Oh Hilda—it is not every day that I can do that.

HILDA [*passionately*]. I will have you do it! I will have it! [*imploringly*] Just once more Solness! Do the impossible once again!

SOLNESS [*stands and looks deep into her eyes*]. If I try it, Hilda, I will stand up there and talk to him as I did that time before.

HILDA [*in rising excitement*]. What will you say to him?

SOLNESS. I will say to him: Hear me, Mighty Lord—thou may'st judge me as seems best to thee. But hereafter I will build nothing but the loveliest thing in the world————

HILDA [*carried away*]. Yes—yes—yes!

SOLNESS. —build it together with a princess, whom I love————

HILDA. Yes, tell him that! Tell him that!

SOLNESS. Yes. And then I will say to him: Now I shall go down and throw my arms round her and kiss her ————

HILDA. —many times! Say that!

SOLNESS. —many, many times, I will say.

HILDA. And then————?

SOLNESS. Then I will wave my hat—and come down to the earth—and do as I said to him.

HILDA [*with outstretched arms*]. Now I see you again as I did when there was song in the air.

SOLNESS [*looks at her with his head bowed*]. How have you become what you are, Hilda?

HILDA. How have you made me what I am?

SOLNESS [*shortly and firmly*]. The princess shall have her castle.

HILDA [*jubilant, clapping her hands*]. Oh, Mr. Solness————! My lovely, lovely castle. Our castle in the air!

SOLNESS. On a firm foundation.

[*In the street a crowd of people has assembled, vaguely seen through the trees. Music of wind instruments is heard far away behind the new house. MRS. SOLNESS, with a fur collar round her neck, DOCTOR HERDAL with her white shawl on his arm, and some ladies come out on the verandah. RAGNAR BROVIK comes at the same time up from the garden.*]

MRS. SOLNESS [*to RAGNAR*]. Are we to have music, too?

RAGNAR. Yes. It's the band of the Mason's Union. [*to SOLNESS*] The foreman asked me to tell you that he is ready now to go up with the wreath.

SOLNESS [*takes his hat*]. Good. I will go down to him myself.

MRS. SOLNESS [*anxiously*]. What have you to do down there, Halvard?

SOLNESS [*curtly*]. I must be down below with the men.

MRS. SOLNESS. Yes, down below—only down below.

SOLNESS. That is where I always stand —on everyday occasions.

[*He goes down the flight of steps and away through the garden.*]

MRS. SOLNESS [*calls after him over the railing*]. But do beg the man to be careful when he goes up? Promise me that, Halvard!

DR. HERDAL [*to MRS. SOLNESS*]. Don't you see that I was right? He has given up all thought of that folly.

MRS. SOLNESS. Oh, what a relief! Twice workmen have fallen, and each time they were killed on the spot. [*Turns to HILDA.*] Thank you, Miss Wangel, for having kept such a firm hold upon him. I should never have been able to manage him.

DR. HERDAL [*playfully*]. Yes, yes, Miss Wangel, you know how to keep firm hold on a man, when you give your mind to it.

[MRS. SOLNESS *and* DR. HERDAL *go up to the ladies, who are standing nearer to the steps and looking over the garden.* HILDA *remains standing beside the railing in the foreground.* RAGNAR *goes up to her.*]

RAGNAR [*with suppressed laughter, half whispering*]. Miss Wangel—do you see all those young fellows down in the street?

HILDA. Yes.

RAGNAR. They are my fellow students, come to look at the master.

HILDA. What do they want to look at him for?

RAGNAR. They want to see how he

daren't climb to the top of his own house.

HILDA. Oh, that is what those boys want, is it?

RAGNAR [*spitefully and scornfully*]. He has kept us down so long—now we are going to see him keep quietly down below himself.

HILDA. You will not see that—not this time.

RAGNAR [*smiles*]. Indeed! Then where shall we see him?

HILDA. High—high up by the vane! That is where you will see him!

RAGNAR [*laughs*]. Him! Oh, yes, I daresay!

HILDA. His will is to reach the top—so at the top you shall see him.

RAGNAR. His will, yes; that I can easily believe. But he simply cannot do it. His head would swim round, long, long before he got half way. He would have to crawl down again on his hands and knees.

DR. HERDAL [*points across*]. Look! There goes the foreman up the ladders.

MRS. SOLNESS. And of course he has the wreath to carry, too. Oh, I do hope he will be careful!

RAGNAR [*stares incredulously and shouts*]. Why, but it's———

HILDA [*breaking out in jubilation*]. It is the master builder himself!

MRS. SOLNESS [*screams with terror*]. Yes, it is Halvard! Oh, my great God———! Halvard! Halvard!

DR. HERDAL. Hush! Don't shout to him!

MRS. SOLNESS [*half beside herself*]. I must go to him! I must get him to come down again!

DR. HERDAL [*holds her*]. Don't move, any of you! Not a sound!

HILDA [*immovable, follows* SOLNESS *with her eyes*]. He climbs and climbs. Higher and higher! Higher and higher! Look! Just look!

RAGNAR [*breathless*]. He must turn now. He can't possibly help it.

HILDA. He climbs and climbs. He will soon be at the top now.

MRS. SOLNESS. Oh, I shall die of terror. I cannot bear to see it.

DR. HERDAL. Then don't look up at him.

HILDA. There he is standing on the topmost planks. Right at the top!

DR. HERDAL. Nobody must move! Do you hear?

HILDA [*exulting, with quiet intensity*]. At last! At last! Now I see him great and free again!

RAGNAR [*almost voiceless*]. But this is im———

HILDA. So I have seen him all through these ten years. How secure he stands! Frightfully thrilling all the same. Look at him! Now he is hanging the wreath round the vane.

RAGNAR. I feel as if I were looking at something utterly impossible.

HILDA. Yes, it is the impossible that he is doing now! [*with the indefinable expression in her eyes*] Can you see anyone else up there with him?

RAGNAR. There is no one else.

HILDA. Yes, there is one he is striving with.

RAGNAR. You are mistaken.

HILDA. Then do you hear no song in the air, either?

RAGNAR. It must be the wind in the treetops.

HILDA. *I* hear a song—a mighty song! [*Shouts in wild jubilation and glee.*] Look, look! Now he is waving his hat! He is waving it to us down here! Oh, wave, wave back to him. For now it is finished! [*Snatches the white shawl from the doctor, waves it, and shouts up to* SOLNESS.] Hurrah for Master Builder Solness!

DR. HERDAL. Stop! Stop! For God's sake———!

[*The ladies on the verandah wave their pocket handkerchiefs, and the shouts of "Hurrah" are taken up in the street below. Then they are suddenly silenced,* and the crowd bursts out into a shriek of horror. A human body, with planks and fragments of wood, is vaguely perceived crashing down behind the trees.]

MRS. SOLNESS AND THE LADIES [*at the same time*]. He is falling! He is falling!

[MRS. SOLNESS *totters, falls backward, swooning, and is caught, amid cries and confusion, by the ladies. The crowd in the street breaks down the fence and storms into the garden. At the same time* DR. HERDAL, *too, rushes down thither. A short pause.*]

HILDA [*stares fixedly upward and says, as if petrified*]. My Master Builder.

RAGNAR [*supports himself, trembling, against the railing*]. He must be dashed to pieces—killed on the spot.

ONE OF THE LADIES [*whilst* MRS. SOL-NESS *is carried into the house*]. Run down for the doctor——

RAGNAR. I can't stir a foot——

ANOTHER LADY. Then call to someone!

RAGNAR [*tries to call out*]. How is it? Is he alive?

A VOICE [*below in the garden*]. Mr. Solness is dead!

OTHER VOICES [*nearer*]. The head is all crushed.—— He fell right into the quarry.

HILDA [*turns to* RAGNAR *and says quietly*]. I can't see him up there now.

RAGNAR. This is terrible. So, after all, he could not do it.

HILDA [*as if in quiet spellbound triumph*]. But he mounted right to the top. And I heard harps in the air. [*Waves her shawl in the air and shrieks with wild intensity.*] My— my Master Builder!

Purgatory

As a great lyric poet, William Butler Yeats (1865–1939) would not seem at first glance to have been well equipped for dramatic art. The great lyric poets of the nineteenth century—Blake, Coleridge, Wordsworth, Byron, Shelley, Keats, Tennyson, Browning, etc.—were undistinguished playwrights, and the major dramatists—Ibsen, Strindberg, Chekhov, etc.—wrote nothing in the way of lyric poetry. Their drama, the tradition most immediately available to Yeats, was naturalistic, with stress on realism of situation, character, and dialogue. For Yeats such drama fell into the category of "unimaginative art," which was "content to set a piece of the world as we know it in a place by itself." The lyric imagination is normally not anxious to restrict anything to "a place by itself" and usually prefers to transcend rather than imitate "the world as we know it." For drama to become an "imaginative art," then, it must purify reality in the interests of artifice, creating a theater in which verse, ritual, music, and dance keep the ordinary world at a distance, giving the undistracted mind access to its own "inner deeps."

In the Nō theater of Japan Yeats found a dramatic form wonderfully suited to his aims. Designed for an aristocratic audience of initiates, the Nō is a highly ritualized dramatic form in which all the elements of enactment—scenery, stage properties, number of actors—are reduced to a bare minimum. The actors wear masks (they are often gods, ghosts, or demons), speak in formal prose and verse, and perform in a ceremonial style. As in neoclassic tragedy, concentration of means and elevation of style are the governing laws. Everything irrelevant having been burned away, what remains is a purified form in which each word and gesture is full of symbolic intensity.

With its two actors starkly outlined between a ruined house and a bare tree, *Purgatory* obviously reflects the Nō theater. But it also reflects the lyric predispositions of its author. Its charged emotional atmosphere, dreamlike movement, brevity, and associative verse style make it a kind of dramatic analogue to the lyric. The plot of the play is spare, less a structure of specific incidents and actions than a frame in which phases of imaginative apprehension may be exhibited. As the play opens, an old man tells a boy to "study that house," a ruined house once owned, he says, by his aristocratic mother but burned down years ago by her drunken husband, "a groom in a training stable," who wasted her fortune and degraded her family name. During the fire, the old man confesses, he stabbed and killed his father, ran away, and became a pedlar, fathering his bastard son upon a "tinker's daughter in a ditch." Now, on the anniversary of his mother's wedding, the pedlar hears the hoofbeats of the past, his father riding drunkenly home once more, and as a light goes on in the house, he sees images of his parents re-enacting his own conception. His son, seeing nothing and thinking him mad, attempts to make off with their bag of money, but the old man stops him. As they struggle for the bag of money, the boy suddenly sees the same images in the house and covers his eyes in horror. The old man takes this opportunity to stab his son with the same knife he used to kill his father. Immediately afterward, the lighted window darkens—in acknowledgement, the old man feels, of the fact that he has prevented the guilt and degradation of his mother's marriage from being perpetuated through the boy, who would have "begot, and passed pollution on." But as he cleans his knife and picks up the money, the hoofbeats commence again. Despite his actions, he realizes, his mother remains in her purgatory of guilt, condemned endlessly to repeat her sin.

Yeats conceived of *Purgatory* as, in his phrase, "a scene of tragic intensity," which is perhaps not quite the same thing as a tragedy. Structurally, however, the play traces out the tragic sequence of action-suffering-understanding, the old man murdering both his father and his son and suffering the realization of futility: "Twice a murderer and all for nothing." On the other hand, the old man would seem to lack the tragic stature of such heroes as Oedipus, Macbeth, Phaedra, and Solness, all of whom dominate their dramatic worlds in a way that he does not. From kings to pedlars is quite a falling off. Yet this is no ordinary pedlar. In some regards, he seems less than ordinary. He has none of the social and psychological reality of salesmen like Willie Loman in *Death of a Salesman*. He lacks even that most basic of individualizing features, a name, and instead of being defined by his practical relations to such things as the house and the tree, he is metaphorically identified with them: a gutted mansion, all inner values burned out; a thunderbolt-riven tree once full of "fat, greasy life," now "stripped bare." Ironically, in depriving the old man of ordinary life as a dramatic character, Yeats invests him with something more, an archetypal intensity of being that stations him out of time on the fringes of reality, in at least tenuous contact with the supernatural, as Oedipus and Hamlet and Macbeth were. Like Hamlet, he inherits a polluted world and seeks the purgation of past and present through a murderous act. Like most tragic heroes, too, he is a divided personality, shaped both by the patrician influences of his mother's family and by the vulgarity of his father. Thus he can, in the final stage direction, both clean his knife, in an act symbolic of his impulse to purify corruption, and pick up the scattered money, in an act that associates him with both his grasping father and his son, in whom the groom's materialistic grossness has recurred in intensified form. As that recurrence would suggest, the old man and the boy are both victims of the pollution passed on through his mother's marriage, a kind of genetic deterioration analogous to the role of the family curse in Greek tragic cycles like the *Oresteia* and the Theban plays. Short of killing himself, the old man has done what he can to purge the consequences in others of his mother's transgression (see lines 38–39); but the cycle of remorse and sin in his mother's dream continues. Like most tragic heroes, he comes to acknowledge the limits of human aspiration— "Mankind can do no more"—and in the process to discover his own identity, newly defined in guilt, misery, and remorse.

Purgatory

A BOY   AN OLD MAN

SCENE: *A ruined house and a bare tree in the background.*

BOY. Half door, hall door,
　Hither and thither day and night,
　Hill or hollow, shouldering this pack,
　Hearing you talk.
OLD MAN.　　　Study that house.
　I think about its jokes and stories;　5
　I try to remember what the butler
　Said to a drunken gamekeeper
　In mid-October, but I cannot.
　If I cannot, none living can.
　Where are the jokes and stories of a
　　house,　10
　Its threshold gone to patch a pigsty?
BOY. So you have come this path be-
　　fore?
OLD MAN. The moonlight falls upon the
　　path,
　The shadow of a cloud upon the
　　house,
　And that's symbolical; study that
　　tree,　15
　What is it like?
BOY.　　　　A silly old man.
OLD MAN. It's like—no matter what
　　it's like.
　I saw it a year ago stripped bare as
　　now,
　So I chose a better trade.
　I saw it fifty years ago　20
　Before the thunderbolt had riven it,

Green leaves, ripe leaves, leaves thick
　as butter,
Fat, greasy life. Stand there and look,
Because there is somebody in that
　house.

[*The* BOY *puts down pack and stands in the doorway.*]

BOY. There's nobody here.　25
OLD MAN. There's somebody there.
BOY. The floor is gone, the windows
　gone,
　And where there should be roof
　　there's sky,
　And here's a bit of an egg shell
　　thrown
　Out of a jackdaw's nest.
OLD MAN.　　　But there are some　30
　That do not care what's gone, what's
　　left:
　The souls in Purgatory that come
　　back
　To habitations and familiar spots.
BOY. Your wits are out again.
OLD MAN.　　　　　　Relive
　Their transgressions, and that not
　　once　35
　But many times; they know at last
　The consequence of those transgres-
　　sions
　Whether upon others or upon them-
　　selves;
　Upon others, others may bring help,
　For when the consequence is at an
　　end　40
　The dream must end; if upon them-
　　selves,
　There is no help but in themselves
　And in the mercy of God.

BOY.   I have had enough!
  Talk to the jackdaws, if talk you
    must.
OLD MAN. Stop! Sit there upon that
    stone.   45
  That is the house where I was born.
BOY. The big old house that was burnt
    down?
OLD MAN. My mother that was your
    grand-dam owned it,
  This scenery and this countryside,
  Kennel   and   stable,   horse   and
    hound—   50
  She had a horse at the Curragh, and
    there met
  My father, a groom in a training
    stable,
  Looked at him and married him.
  Her mother never spoke to her again,
  And she did right.
BOY.   What's right and wrong? 55
  My granddad got the girl and the
    money.
OLD MAN. Looked at him and married
    him,
  And he squandered everything she
    had.
  She never knew the worst, because
  She died in giving birth to me,   60
  But now she knows it all, being dead.
  Great people lived and died in this
    house;
  Magistrates, colonels, members of
    Parliament,
  Captains and Governors, and long
    ago
  Men that had fought at Aughrim and
    the Boyne.   65
  Some that had gone on Government
    work
  To London or to India came home to
    die,
  Or came from London every spring
  To look at the may-blossom in the
    park.
  They had loved the trees that he cut
    down   70
  To pay what he had lost at cards
  Or   spent   on   horses,   drink   and
    women;

Had loved the house, had loved all
  The intricate passages of the house,
  But he killed the house; to kill a
    house   75
  Where great men grew up, married,
    died,
  I here declare a capital offence.
BOY. My God, but you had luck!
    Grand clothes,
  And maybe a grand horse to ride.
OLD MAN. That he might keep me upon
    his level   80
  He never sent me to school, but some
  Half-loved me for my half of her:
  A gamekeeper's wife taught me to
    read,
  A Catholic curate taught me Latin.
  There were old books and books
    made fine   85
  By eighteenth-century French bind-
    ing, books
  Modern and ancient, books by the
    ton.
BOY. What education have you given
    me?
OLD MAN. I gave the education that
    befits
  A bastard that a pedlar got   90
  Upon a tinker's daughter in a ditch.
  When I had come to sixteen years old
  My father burned down the house
    when drunk.
BOY. But that is my age, sixteen years
    old,
  At the Puck Fair.
OLD MAN.   And   everything   was
    burnt;   95
  Books, library, all were burnt.
BOY. Is what I have heard upon the
    road the truth,
  That you killed him in the burning
    house?
OLD MAN. There's nobody here but
    our two selves?
BOY. Nobody, Father.
OLD MAN.   I stuck him with
    a knife,   100
  That knife that cuts my dinner now,
  And after that I left him in the fire.
  They dragged him out, somebody saw

The knife-wound but could not be
certain
Because the body was all black and
charred.   105
Then some that were his drunken
friends
Swore they would put me upon trial,
Spoke of quarrels, a threat I had
made.
The gamekeeper gave me some old
clothes,
I ran away, worked here and
there   110
Till I became a pedlar on the roads,
No good trade, but good enough
Because I am my father's son,
Because of what I did or may do.
Listen to the hoof beats; Listen,
listen!   115

BOY. I cannot hear a sound.

OLD MAN.   Beat! Beat!
This night is the anniversary
Of my mother's wedding night,
Or of the night wherein I was be-
gotten.
My father is riding from the public
house,   120
A whiskey-bottle under his arm.

[*A window is lit showing a young girl.*]

Look at the window; she stands there
Listening, the servants are all in bed,
She is alone, he has stayed late
Bragging and drinking in the public
house   125

BOY. There's nothing but an empty
gap in the wall.
You have made it up. No, you are
mad!
You are getting madder every day.

OLD MAN. It's louder now because he
rides
Upon a gravelled avenue   130
All grass to-day. The hoof-beat stops,
He has gone to the other side of the
house,
Gone to the stable, put the horse up.
She has gone down to open the door.
This night she is no better than her
man   135

And does not mind that he is half
drunk,
She is mad about him. They mount
the stairs,
She brings him into her own cham-
ber.
And that is the marriage-chamber
now.
The window is dimly lit again.   140
Do not let him touch you! It is not
true
That drunken men cannot beget,
And if he touch he must beget
And you must bear his murderer.
Deaf! Both deaf! If I should
throw   145
A stick or a stone they would not
hear;
And that's a proof my wits are out.
But there's a problem: she must live
Through everything in exact detail,
Driven to it by remorse, and yet   150
Can she renew the sexual act
And find no pleasure in it, and if
not,
If pleasure and remorse must both be
there,
Which is the greater?
                    I lack schooling.
Go fetch Tertullian; he and I   155
Will ravel all that problem out
Whilst those two lie upon the mat-
tress
Begetting me.
            Come back! Come back!
And so you thought to slip away,
My bag of money between your
fingers,   160
And that I could not talk and see!
You have been rummaging in the
pack.

[*The light in the window has faded
out.*]

BOY. You never gave me my right share.

OLD MAN. And had I given it, young
as you are,
You would have spent it upon
drink.   165

BOY. What if I did? I had a right

To get it and spend it as I chose.
OLD MAN. Give me that bag and no
more words.
BOY. I will not.
OLD MAN.   I will break your fingers.

[*They struggle for the bag. In the
struggle it drops, scattering the money.
The* OLD MAN *staggers but does not
fall. They stand looking at each other.
The window is lit up. A man is seen
pouring whiskey into a glass.*]

BOY. What if I killed you? You killed
my grand-dad,   170
Because you were young and he was
old.
Now I am young and you are old.
OLD MAN [*staring at window*]. Better
looking, those sixteen years—
BOY. What are you muttering?
OLD MAN.   Younger—and yet
She should have known he was not
her kind.   175
BOY. What are you saying? Out with
it! [OLD MAN *points to window.*]
My God! The window is lit up
And somebody stands there, although
The floorboards are all burnt away.
OLD MAN. The window is lit up because
my father   180
Has come to find a glass for his whis-
key.
He leans there like some tired beast.
BOY. A dead, living, murdered man!
OLD MAN. "Then the bride-sleep fell
upon Adam":
Where did I read those words?
                        And yet   185
There's nothing leaning in the win-
dow
But the impression upon my mother's
mind;
Being dead she is alone in her
remorse.
BOY. A body that was a bundle of old
bones
Before I was born. Horrible! Horri-
ble! [*He covers his eyes.*]   190
OLD MAN. That beast there would know
nothing, being nothing,

If I should kill a man under the
window
He would not even turn his head.

[*He stabs the* BOY.]

My father and my son on the same
jack-knife!
That finishes—there—there—there—

[*He stabs again and again. The window
grows dark.*]

"Hush-a-bye baby, thy father's a
knight,   196
Thy mother a lady, lovely and
bright."
No, that is something that I read in
a book,
And if I sing it must be to my
mother,
And I lack rhyme.

[*The stage has grown dark except
where the tree stands in white light.*]

                Study that tree. 200
It stands there like a purified soul,
All cold, sweet, glistening light.
Dear mother, the window is dark
again,
But you are in the light because
I finished all that consequence.   205
I killed that lad because had he
grown up
He would have struck a woman's
fancy,
Begot, and passed pollution on.
I am a wretched foul old man
And therefore harmless. When I have
stuck   210
This old jack-knife into a sod
And pulled it out all bright again,
And picked up all the money that he
dropped,
I'll to a distant place, and there
Tell my old jokes among new
men.   215

[*He cleans the knife and begins to pick
up money.*]

Hoof beats! Dear God,
How quickly it returns—beat—

beat—!
Her mind cannot hold up that dream.
Twice a murderer and all for nothing,
And she must animate that dead
  night   220
Not once but many times!

O God,
Release my mother's soul from its
  dream!
Mankind can do no more. Appease
The misery of the living and the
  remorse of the dead.

Comedy

Introduction

Like tragedy, comedy has suffered from the infiltration of popular meanings into a literary context. Since the comic in ordinary experience is roughly synonymous with funny and laughable, it is only natural to think of laughter as the distinctive feature of dramatic comedy. But defining any genre by its effects upon us—laughter, tears, spiritual uplift, etc.—is risky. What a work does and what it is are different things, and we do not establish the latter by exploring the former. Nevertheless, comic theory from Plato to Arthur Koestler has been regularly seduced away from the objective properties of comedy—structure, theme, style, characterization—to pursue the elusive nature of laughter. More recent criticism has come to recognize that not every funny play is a comedy (for instance, Harold Pinter's *The Dumbwaiter*) nor every comedy a funny play (Shakespeare's *Measure for Measure*). Still, the persistence of affective theories reminds us that comedy does have an enduring affiliation to laughter that we need to take account of, however glancingly.

What laughter actually is, whether a "sudden glory," a "surge of vital feeling," a catharsis of psychic tension, or something else, is less to the point here than its pattern of development. One generally acknowledged cause of laughter is the incongruous, which implies a forced linkage of disparate categories. The clown's distended nose, the motley fool in court, the pompous strut leading to a pratfall,

---

"Introduction to Comedy" reprinted from Perspectives on Drama, *New York, Oxford University Press, 1968, by permission of the Oxford University Press.*

verbal devices like hyperbole, understatement, and pun: all accord in being some-how discordant. The incongruous in space is the disproportionate or asymmetrical; the incongruous in time is the unexpected. Thus Kant says that humor consists of a "strained expectation being suddenly reduced to nothing." Anticipation set up and then reversed, or fulfilled explosively, characterizes physical slapstick no less than the witty joke. Even disastrous reversals can sometimes seem funny after the initial dismay has worn off. (At the end of the movie *The Treasure of Sierra Madre* when the gold dust for which three men have suffered and nearly died is blown away by the wind, their "expectations being suddenly reduced to nothing," they slump to the ground and then gradually commence laughing.) In humor, as in magic, the false lead prepares the way for the irrational effect; hence our bafflement at the magical act can easily pass on into bemused laughter. As the analogy to magic suggests, there is a certain freedom to the comic; it is an open society where any association (or dissociation) is permissible, and everything is more or less than it seems. The banana peel and the punchline both disclose to us that a prior situation contained undreamed of potentials, that our bondage to the appearances of things was itself only apparent.

If we take a kind of "a, b, c, X!" sequence as typical of humor, then in structure at least, much comedy is a joke writ large. For the comic plot normally puts its major characters, usually young lovers, on a path toward frustration but then intercepts this development with a "punchline" reversal in which victory and a happy ending are wrested out of apparent defeat. Tragic plots unfold the probabilities of a given situation, showing us a world harnessed to the irrevers-ibility of cause and effect, action and reaction. Comedy, on the other hand, like humor, specializes in the improbable, the reversible, the redemption that comes from nowhere. Nothing in *Tartuffe* prepares us for the officer of a suddenly omniscient king, or in *Arms and the Man* for Bluntschli's inheriting, just in time to qualify him as a suitor to Raina, two hundred horses, seventy carriages, four thousand tablecloths, nine thousand six hundred sheets and blankets, and so on. In looking back over them, tragic plots, like some dice, seem "loaded" in that given *that* starting point *this* ending seems unavoidable. Comic plots are also loaded but rather in the sense of being fertile, capable of multiplying in all direc-tions. They do not exhaust possibilities but escape them, liberating their characters from the laws of action and reaction. That does not mean, however, that comedy is less realistic than tragedy, since reality does not noticeably prefer logic to illogic or causality to coincidence; it means merely that each genre sets its own ground rules in the process of transforming reality.

Comedy and Ritual   Like tragedy, comedy may have had its origins in ritual—the same fertility rituals in which the dying and reviving god of nature (Dionysus, Attis, Osiris, etc.) was imitatively worshiped. Tragedy is believed to reflect the phase of the ritual in which the god-king-scapegoat suffers and dies; comedy, it is held, passes beyond this to a final phase in which the god's rebirth and sacred marriage to the earth goddess are celebrated, in part by a festive procession called the *komos* (hence, *komedia*). Comedy thus completes a pattern begun by tragedy, moving around or beyond death to events suggestive of ongoing life. Not that specific comedies in moving around death to life are slavishly adhering to ancient ritual formuli. A potential death phase may appear in comedies by authors totally unaware of such rituals merely because the traditional happy ending of comedy becomes happy by evading potential unhappiness, and unhappiness in the intensified realm of dramatic action normally figures as death: the ending of Christopher Fry's *The Lady's Not for Burning,* for instance, is happy at least partly in virtue of the fact that the lady might have been *for* burning.

Though a melodramatic Renaissance comedy like Peele's *Mucedorus* may kill off half the cast enroute to a happy ending, for survivors death is encountered only symbolically. The ritual combat between a young man and an old man (summer against winter, life against death, fertility against sterility) is sometimes suggested in comedy by the conflict between a son and his father over the issue of marriage. If life is to continue, youth must be served, which means that old age must not be literally killed but transformed somehow. If the *senex,* or old man, is cast as the hero, as in the early Greek comedies of Aristophanes, we may encounter a miraculous regeneration. In *The Knights,* for instance, the old man Demos grows young again through the ministrations of a sausage-selling magician-cook, perhaps thus reflecting, as F. M. Cornford argues, the resurrection of the slain god-king in fertility rituals. In Shakespeare a pseudo-death and subsequent revival is frequently accorded the heroine—for example, Hero in *Much Ado About Nothing,* Helena in *All's Well That Ends Well,* Imogen in *Cymbeline,* Hermione and Perdita in *The Winter's Tale.* Nearly everyone qualifies for the role in *The Tempest,* where a *senex* figure, Prospero, manipulates the action in the interests of youth, to which he graciously gives way at the end. Normally, however, young lovers are at the center of the comic action, and repressive father figures must be converted to paternal permissiveness, often by harrassments and humiliations of a nearly fatal sort. Thus the misanthropic father in Menander's *The Grouch (ca.* 317 B.C.) is obliged by comic necessity to fall into a well so that a young man can earn both his gratitude and his daughter by fetching him out again. In Synge's *The Playboy of the Western World* (1907) the young hero becomes a center of sexual attraction because he is thought to have killed his father (for trying to marry him off to an elderly widow). When the father reappears, alive and crusty as ever, the son flattens him once again with a spade, and though he rises yet again, he is now willing to pass the mantle of family authority to the son. The convention of symbolically killing off the *senex* is evidently as indestructible as most of the *senex* figures themselves. A recent British play by Joe Orton, *Entertaining Mr. Sloane* (1964), blandly exploits the implication of the convention by having the young Mr. Sloane actually murder the old and moralistic Kemp so that he is free to be "entertained," in the cyclic fashion of fertility gods like Adonis, half a year by one lover and half a year by another. Even in extreme cases when death does occur in comedy, it is by no means the all-absorbing, conclusive death of tragedy but merely one phase of an over-all comic movement.

The ritual origins of comedy appear to have left an imprint on its endings also. Most fertility rituals begin on a note of inhibition as the worshipers abstain from sex and food—thus imitating the suspension of life and time during the transition period between the god's death and his rebirth, between winter and spring, between the old and the new year—and then work towards a final release of such inhibitions in sexual promiscuity and feasting suggestive of the rejuvenation of life. The feast, probably once the eating of an animal symbolizing the god (the Dionysiac bull or goat, for instance), brought the worshipers into a state of communion both with the god and with one another. Comedy too, whether directly indebted to ritual in given cases or not, fosters a sense of the continuity and community of life. Whereas tragedy, with the death of a hero who has been the focal point of his society, ends with an old order breaking up or greatly devitalized, comedy goes on to form a new society around the young couple whose wedding usually marks the play's conclusion. In less decorous comedies like Machiavelli's *Mandragola* and Wycherley's *The Country Wife,* the wedding is supplanted by a youth's success in seducing an old man's wife or daughter. The idea of social communion behind the ritual feast also helps account for the large number of comedies that end with some suggestion of eating, whether it be formal feasting as in Aristophanes' *The Wasps,* a simple invitation to dinner as in Plautus' *The Rope,* or merely routine preparations for breakfast as in Peele's *The Old Wives' Tale.* In any event, comedy is traditionally dedicated to bringing together at its close a happy society liberated from such restraints on human impulse as age, law, sterility, and guilt and surrounded by images of abundant and continuing life.

Kinds of Comedy: Romance and Satire   Judging from the descriptive terms that have been applied to it, nothing multiplies and mutates so rapidly as comedy. Critics have identified such classes as Old and New Comedy, classical and medieval comedy, high and low comedy, sweet and bitter, dark, farcical, pastoral, sentimental, laughing, comedy of manners, of humours, of ideas, of intrigue, and so on. Almost, it would seem, a genre for every play—which suggests that shaping such a clutter into a reasonably coherent or manageable form is difficult. Nevertheless, some guidelines are necessary, if only as general boundaries within which individual plays can exhibit their individuality.

Northrop Frye's argument that comedy lies between satire and romance may be helpful here. Such a positioning means not that comedy *is* satire or romance—each a legitimate genre in its own right—but that it is influenced by them. The earliest surviving Greek comedy, the Old Comedy of Aristophanes, is indeed satiric: a tightly structured but loosely plotted sort of musical revue drama that gives the dramatist maximum freedom to attack either individuals, like Socrates in *The Clouds,* or social, political, and moral abuses in general. In the line of satiric descent from Old Comedy would appear the plays of Machiavelli, Ben Jonson, Molière, Congreve, Sheridan, and Shaw, to mention merely a few. New Comedy, on the other hand, as represented by Menander of Athens and the Roman dramatists Plautus and Terence, though not exclusively romantic, contains enough in the way of shipwrecks, separated lovers, lost children, concealed identities, and other such improbabilities, all leading to a final recognition and reconciliation scene, to suggest its affinities to romance. Romantic comedy, it should be stressed, does not mean merely plays concerned with love or courtship, which while normally present in romantic comedy may also be the concern of essentially satiric comedies like Congreve's *The Way of the World.* What is meant, rather, is a kind of comedy that reflects the literary genre of romance in a light but on the whole sympathetic manner, as, for instance, in Plautus' *The Rope* or in the comedies of Lyly, Peele, Greene, and for the most part Shakespeare.

Satire usually represents human experience as degraded, romance as elevated. Comedies animated by a satiric spirit may present us with characters like Jonson's Volpone or Molière's Tartuffe, whose greed, cunning, and hypocrisy enable them to dominate societies composed of the hopelessly foolish and the helplessly virtuous. Romantic comedy, on the other hand, may give us a world in which both nature and society accede to the benevolent magic of a Prospero, and viciousness is rendered either harmless or humorous. Romance normally affirms the saving graces of life, depicting the human condition from a perspective of charity. Thus *The Tempest* concludes upon images of a redeemed world, even potentially dangerous characters being absorbed into an atmosphere of forgiveness. But in *Volpone* and *Tartuffe,* though certain characters are redeemed, it is at the expense of other characters, and the stress is not on charity but punishment. All ends well, perhaps, but not convincingly so: Tartuffe is restrained less by moral than by theatrical means, and as the major characters in *Volpone* line up for sentencing we do not feel that the organized processes of social order have succeeded but that depravity has failed—just barely.

The structure of comedy no less than its view of human experience is varyingly affected by romance and satire. Satiric comedy naturally centers in characters who are somehow ridiculous—misers, misanthropes, hypocrites, braggarts, who in one way or another violate the canons of common sense or deviate from conventional standards. The normal way of structuring such a play is to make the traditional happy ending contingent upon the defeat of the ridiculous characters. Defeat means primarily exposure, the stripping away of delusions and pretense. This sort of exposure is most effective, of course, after the success of the ridiculous seems assured. Absurdities are given free rein and then at some crowning moment brought up short—while Tartuffe stands greedily surveying his spoils or when Mosca in *Volpone* thinks he has maneuvered Volpone into a corner and himself into a fortune. The movement here, then, is through freedom (or license) to frustration and restraint. In romantic comedy, on the other hand, since the focus is on sympathetic characters like Rosalind and Orlando in *As You Like It,* the happy ending arises not from restraining the ridiculous characters but from liberating the hero and heroine. The movement here tends to be through frustration to freedom; hence the standard plot in which boy and girl, after meeting, are kept apart by various restraints from which they finally disengage themselves.

One way of viewing this structural distinction is in terms of movements to or away from law. Continuing with the examples of *Volpone* and *Tartuffe,* for instance, we note that both plays end on climactic scenes in which the law suddenly clamps down on transgressors, whereas romantic comedies tend to begin with stress on a rule of law that is subsequently circumvented or relaxed. *A Midsummer Night's Dream* begins with an entire society in bondage to the Athenian law requiring a daughter to marry a husband of her father's choosing; at the end of the play Duke Theseus simply sets the law aside. In *The Merchant of Venice* Portia reveals that if it is subjected to closer scrutiny, the law apparently guaranteeing Shylock his pound of Antonio's flesh can become in itself an avenue to freedom. Thus romantic and satiric comedy define law in different ways. In the latter it stands for norms of good sense and general experience that have been violated and need to be reinstated if life is to be conducted on a fairly reasonable basis. The violators, of course, need not be persons; they may as easily be ideas, such as the idea of war as a glorious enterprise, which it is the aim of Shaw's *Arms and the Man* to deflate. Nor need law be taken literally: in Shaw's play the law that reasserts itself at the end is simply the standard of practical reason and straightforward fact. In romantic comedy however, law, if it is of the statutory sort, it less a curb on excesses than excessive itself, like the law of slavery in Roman comedies or the repressive rule of Duke Frederick in *As You Like It.* Here again we need to consider law figuratively as a symbol of blighting influences in general: the economic injustices harped on at the opening of *The Second Shepherds' Pageant,* the puritanism of Malvolio in *Twelfth Night,* the rigid sense of honor that causes Bertram to reject Helena in *All's Well That Ends Well.* So inherent in the structure of comedy is this movement through restraint to release that even a benign parent like Prospero is obliged to sentence Ferdinand to a period of "wooden slavery," his log-carrying chores, if only, as he explains, to make his subsequent release the more attractive. In either event, however, whether society is freed of tyranny through imposing the law or freed from the tyranny of law itself, the result is an elimination of extremes and a return to a sane and liberal normality.

Tragedy and Comedy   Speaking of an elimination of extremes may well remind us of tragedy and its tendency to expel by banishment or death the exceptional individual. No doubt there are points at which comedy and tragedy touch, however tentatively. The tragic hero is often an extremist, an overreacher like Faustus or Macbeth, and yet it is in a comedy by Massinger that we find a dominating figure called Sir Giles Overreach, whose comic fate is to suffer madness upon discovering that his grasp has exceeded the length of his arm. Characters like Sir Giles, Shylock, Volpone, Tartuffe, and Alceste (in Molière's *The Misanthrope*) have their scapegoat functions no less than tragic heroes like Oedipus or Samson; and in their uncompromising commitment to particular vices they may even achieve a kind of largeness in folly that is comically analogous to tragic grandeur. The analogy, however, is more a matter of burlesque or parody than of equation; hence criticism since Aristotle has been busier contrasting than comparing the two genres.

By way of contrast, then, we might remind ourselves that although both forms originated in fertility rituals, they reflect different phases of those rituals. Tragedy, centering in the suffering and death of the god-hero, partially develops a ritual whose full cycle is completed by comedy. Thus Northrop Frye speaks of tragedy as "uncompleted comedy" and of comedy as containing tragedy implicitly within itself. At first glance the death with which tragedy normally ends would certainly seem complete, but death is complete only when it terminates a cycle of youth, maturity, and age: the premature deaths of tragic heroes are curtailments, not completions. The tragic hero moves down a linear path that breaks off in a chasm —he "falls." But the pattern of ritual is cyclical rather than linear, tracing as it does the cycle of the seasons. The rebirth and marriage of the god that conclude fertility rituals do not represent progress, which is a linear conception; they represent a *return*—of the god to life, of nature from the sterile winter to the fertile spring, of society to the state it occupied before. Everything returns to its beginnings, and this cyclical pattern of ritual is carried over into comedy, the "return to before" being a temporal expression of what we referred to in spatial terms as comedy's re-establishment of a balance or norm at its conclusion.

As this cyclical return-to-before suggests, comedy is a more conservative genre than tragedy, more self-protective. It does not venture everything at the risk of great losses or in the expectation of large gains but conserves what it has in the interests of continuity. Tragedy presents us with heroes who take up extreme positions on the ledges and limbs of human experience and risk everything in remaining there. Its most recurrent feature is thus a sense of loss, most commonly the loss of life. And yet in the process of losing, tragic heroes also gain a great deal in the qualitative refinement of consciousness we have called *anagnorisis*. Comedy, too, deals in losses, but unlike those of tragedy they are temporary, for the full comic sequence is actually loss-and-recovery. Prospero's dukedom and Alonzo's son, Orgon's peace of mind and possessions, Millamant's fortune, hosts of heroines: all are lost only as a preliminary to being triumphantly found again.

The stress here is not on achievement, an improving movement beyond the present, but on a recapturing of the past. And from this vantage point we can see that the theme of loss-and-recovery subsumes the motif of death and rebirth discussed earlier. In dying, Mr. Roberts is not really lost; the play finds him again in the form of Ensign Pulver, who will hurl the Captain's palm tree overboard and restore the ship to its earlier norm of quasi-mutiny.

Thus, though comedy is more complete than tragedy, it is less final. As Lear says of Cordelia after her death, "Thou'lt come no more, / Never, never, never, never, never!" Nor will any of the tragic heroes; the Lear or Oedipus or Phaedra experience at its end is over, a unique and final action. But comedy is recurrent, always coming around, like ritual, to where it was and ought to be, where we want it to be. Its endings are always beginnings or rebeginnings. The Callimachos, Ferdinands, Mirabels, and Bluntschlis are sufficiently non-unique to be always with us, and there is no guarantee that even prison can permanently contain the Tartuffian spirit.

The tragic sequence is from *praxis* (action) through *pathos* (suffering) to *anagnorisis* (recognition). Comedy also concludes with recognition scenes but of a different sort from those in tragedy. For one thing, in tragedy the *anagnorisis* is usually experienced by the hero alone, while in comedy it is generalized, in the proper spirit of comic community, to include as many characters as possible. What Samson thinks and feels during the moment of inwardness before he turns his strength upon the pillars, only he knows; and though Hamlet tries to convey to Horatio his sense of expanded awareness after his ocean voyage, his words fly out, but his thoughts—if we are to judge from Horatio's monosyllabic replies—apparently remain behind. Shakespearean comedy, on the other hand—and comedy in general—typically concludes with scenes in which most of the characters troop forward in a state of headshaking mystification to be enlightened by a Portia or a Rosalind or a Prospero. Thus the comic *anagnorisis* is often a kind of unearned dividend of information—such as the fact that Cesario is really Viola in *Twelfth Night* or that Mirabel in *The Way of the World* has all along held a secret deed of conveyance—that is gratuitously distributed by a character who throughout the play has gratuitously withheld it from circulation. This revealing of something that has been present but concealed all along is in marked contrast to the tragic *anagnorisis* as something not present to begin with but created by the action of the play and the ordeal of the hero.

The *anagnorisis* in either comedy or tragedy may be a discovery of identity, as it is for Oedipus in *Oedipus Tyrannos* and for Jack Worthing in *The Importance of Being Earnest*. The tragic hero, however, discovers not merely his real identity but the quality and substance of it—what he has been and done, and what, therefore, he now is. The stress is on the constricting effects of time as the hero's past catches up with his present, subjecting him to a moral redefinition, the innocent Oedipus becoming the polluted Oedipus. But Jack Worthing's discovery that he is actually Ernest Moncrieff is a liberation of the present by the past, an opening up of certain future opportunities, such as marriage to Gwendolyn. Oedipus is compelled to revise his view of himself in radical fashion, recognizing that he has changed not merely in surface identity or in his external relations to others, but in essence. Thus the action of Sophocles' play *redefines* Oedipus while that of Wilde's play simply *renames* Jack Worthing.

This renaming as distinguished from redefining is typical of comedy in that comic identities are often shifted about like counters over a surface of unvarying essences. This is true not only in cases of misplaced identity, such as Jack Worthing's, but in cases of disguised identity as well, Viola-as-Cesario being no different in essence from Viola-as-Viola in *Twelfth Night*. Nor on the whole do comic characters develop. By the end of her play Viola is neither better nor worse than she was at the beginning, despite the fact that a good deal has happened to her. By the same token Volpone is Volpone is Volpone; he is led off finally, not chastened, merely foiled, his unregeneracy and incapacity for change appropriately figured in his being confined to a hospital for "incurables." So, too, at the end of Menander's *The Grouch*, where the confirmed misanthrope Cnemon, like his descendants Jaques in *As You Like It* and Alceste in Molière's *The Misanthrope*, sets out to achieve permanent petrifaction of character as a hermit.

It is true that remarkable character changes sometimes occur in comedy. At the end of Plautus' *The Rope*, for instance, a villainous slave-trader whose evil schemes are disastrously undermined suddenly turns all smiles and graciousness as he goes jovially off to dine with a man he has good cause to hate. But such changes are usually unconvincing. They nearly always occur at the end of a comedy where the demands of plot and the convention of the happy ending provoke an arbitrary substitution of one mask for another instead of an authentic evolution of inner impulses and convictions.

Unlike tragedy, then, comedy tends to register the impact of experience on character quantitatively rather than qualitatively. Experience and character do not, as they do in tragedy, interpenetrate. Happenings multiply in the life of the comic character but do not modify him.

Thus comedy specializes in two-dimensional, flat, or surface characterization. The profound individuality of tragic heroes is embodied even in the titles of their plays: *Prometheus, Agamemnon, Antigone, Oedipus Tyrannos, Medea, Doctor Faustus, Hamlet, Othello, Phaedra*, etc. If, as a sort of index of the difference in focus, we compare these with the titles of comedies, the individual coloring of tragic titles bleaches out into a generic blankness in comedy—e.g., Menander's *Double Deceiver, Hero, Hated Man, Selfish Person*, etc.; Molière's *The Miser, The Intellectual Ladies*, or *The Misanthrope;* Wycherley's *The Country Wife;* Goldsmith's *The Good Natured Man;* Somerset Maugham's *The Constant Wife;* and so on. It is equally suggestive that there has occurred in each period of great comedy an efflorescence of the "character" as a minor literary genre (New Comedy and the characters of Theophrastus; Elizabethan-Jacobean comedy and the characters of Joseph Hall and Sir Thomas Overbury; neoclassic French comedy and the characters of La Bruyère; and early eighteenth century English comedy and the characters of Addison and Steele). We need to add, of course, that tragedy too has its full quota of stock characters; but the function of such characters in tragedy is to provide an environment in which the tragic hero's individuality is fortified by contrast. The individuality of Hamlet, for instance, is framed by such stock types as the sentential Polonius, the innocent maiden Ophelia, the soldier Fortinbras, the fop Osric, and the faithful friend Horatio.

There are various reasons for the presence of stock characters in comedy. For one thing, repetition is a great source of humor, the clown who gets flattened by a swinging door becoming funnier each time it happens; and repetition is the essence of the stock character. The reason, in fact, that we can type such a character in the first place is that from situation to situation he keeps repeating himself, just as from play to play he is repeated by dramatists. The complex character is unique because he registers the differences between situations and hence responds to each with stylistic appropriateness, or at least discloses a potential for varying responses. In contrast, the stock character suffers from situation-deafness: all occasions register alike to him, their differences lying outside the restricted tonal range of his mind and conduct. In Thomas Love Peacock's *Nightmare Abbey,* a character called Mr. Toobad channels every situation through a filter of religious paranoia and responds on all occasions, whatever the context, by crying in alarm, "The devil is come among us, having great wrath!" To the fop both dining rooms and desert islands are appropriate scenes for a flourishing of fashions; and to the *miles gloriosus,* or braggart warrior, all places are substitute battlefields calling as insistently as Pavlov's bells for verbal foamings at the mouth.

By virtue of his constricted, repetitive style of mind and action, the stock character carries his own "alienation effect" (to use the phrase of the modern German playwright Bertolt Brecht), which serves the comic cause. A certain emotional distance on the part of the audience seems a prerequisite for laughter, familiarity in this respect breeding not contempt but concern, as when our amusement at the stumbling drunk turns to something else when we learn that he drinks, say, out of grief for a child's death. The perpetual smile on the clown's painted face serves this distancing requirement of humor by keeping us from perceiving any real winces of pain when he takes a header. So with the stock character, whose unalterable oversimplicity, *idée fixe* mentality, and repetitious style of conduct constitute a kind of character-mask preventing us from seeing anything beneath that could lay claim to our feelings. Even a character like Falstaff, who is infinitely variable in his responses to the world and hence by no means two-dimensional in either character or physique, is given a painted smile of witty invulnerability to wear on all occasions. It is at the end of *2 Henry IV,* when Shakespeare momentarily erases that smile and discloses the face beneath, that Falstaff becomes other than funny.

Invulnerability and Comic Detachment The mask of invulnerability covers not merely comic characters but comedy itself, which specializes in the art of remaining unmarked by experience. If we consider the prevalence of funny stories about "The Time the Drains Plugged Up" or "Our Trip Through Paris During the Rush Hour," it is evident that humor capitalizes on trouble. Or perhaps we should say on troubles survived, for surviving trouble or escaping potential injury seems to provide the sort of relief that in itself borders on humor. The humor of the drains or the drive through Paris, however, is not in the experience itself, when our feelings of frustration, annoyance, dismay are too immediately involved, but after the fact, in the retelling of the experience. Temporal distance in this case supplies the invulnerability that enables us, having survived, to laugh with a sense of detachment. But temporal distance is not available in drama, where the action is primarily in the present tense; so detachment, and the invulnerability of characters that helps produce it, must be bought in other ways. In the ramshackle world of farce, where everything from suspenders to suspension bridges collapses, where mountains disintegrate, trains collide, and human bodies reverberate like kettledrums under a constant rain of blows, characters like Laurel and Hardy or the Three Stooges are invulnerable by convention. After the first brain-addling, spine-curling, head-on smashup has produced no more than a ripple of annoyance among the victims, we can sit back and watch them fall out second-story windows, off speeding cars, and down precipices, assured that they will have only our laughter to show for it. In sophisticated comedies like *The Tempest,* the same convention is in effect, though handled differently. We quickly gather that compassionate feelings are unnecessary when Prospero's magic arches its protective rainbow over the tempests of human affairs.

In *The Tempest* we view the action over Prospero's shoulder. He is a kind of "interior dramatist," stationing the players, ordering the plot, creating with his magical art the comic spectacle; and through him we become conscious of Shakespeare, the controlling dramatist outside the play, who, in fidelity to the comic form, is maneuvering everything toward desired ends. Shakespeare used many such interior dramatists—Oberon, Rosalind, Viola, the Duke in *Measure for Measure.* They know something the other characters are unaware of, and when they produce their knowledge everything resolves into harmony. In this, Shakespeare is only personifying within his comedies a fact of comedy in general: that the maneuvering hand of the playwright is more obvious here than in other genres. Compare, for instance, two crucial bits of action, the murder of Duncan in *Macbeth* and the assumption of a disguise by Viola in *Twelfth Night.* Shakespeare wants both actions to occur; his plots demand that they occur. But in the tragedy he lets the action issue from the character of Macbeth. Macbeth is ambitious, therefore he kills Duncan. Viola's action, however, does not arise from her character. She does not assume a boy's disguise because, say, she is guileful, cowardly, latently homosexual, or something else. Virtually no reason is given, nor are any inferences about her character appropriate. She assumes the disguise because Shakespeare's comic plot hinges upon her doing so. In tragedy the plot dances to the tune of the characters, in comedy the characters dance to the tune of the plot. The effect of this arbitrariness of action is to keep the audience emotionally removed from the dramatic experience, wary of investing affective capital in events that may turn inside out in an instant.

From another angle, comedy's maneuvering us into a state of emotional detachment can be seen as an enabling of intellectual engagement. Horace Walpole said that life is a tragedy to the man who feels, a comedy to the man who thinks. That is oversimple, but it is true that as spectators of tragedy we tend to register experience through the consciousness of the tragic hero, inevitably absorbing some of the emotional impact of his ordeal, whereas in comedy we are spared the pain of vicarious injuries and forgo the comforts of uncritical involvement because we have been led away from individual perspectives to an intellectual overview analogous to that of the playwright. From that altitude we look down on a world of mortal foolishness and redeeming vitality from which our own world, we begin uneasily to realize, is separated only by the thin line of artistic illusion.

The Second Shepherds' Pageant

The Second Shepherds' Pageant, by common consent the best of the early English comedies, comes from a manuscript that dates from the second half of the fifteenth century. It was one of a group of Towneley plays performed by the medieval crafts of Wakefield and ranging in type from simple amplifications of liturgical ceremony to dramatized biblical episodes of broad comedy and tragedy. The method of the play's apparent madness is indicated by the parallels among its sections. Though through some 637 lines the setting is medieval England, in the last few lines the shepherds are transported backward in time to Bethlehem, the anachronism of the first scenes proving to be part of a general contrast between low humor and high veneration, local farce and ceremonial praise. Such a change of scenes and moods may appear to be illogical, but it is no more so than Milton's imaginative journey from 1629 to the day of Christ's birth in "On the Morning of Christ's Nativity": the implication of both texts is that the divine birth supersedes time and requires a translation of the terms of local daily life into those of timeless Christian miracle. Mak, the thief, serves as a kind of devil outcast, and the misogyny of the shepherds (obviously justified if Gill is an example of womanhood) clears the way for a simple, unironic respect for the Virgin mother.

The numerous parallels between the two main parts reinforce the translation from one scene to the other. Actually, the first movement is itself divided into two sections (the initial complaints of the three shepherds and the results of Mak's theft), each related in slightly different ways to the conclusion. The first shepherd complains of a class system that makes them all "hand-tamed" and crushes them in poverty, the second of bad wives, and the third of cold weather and nature's general inhospitality. The three of them then pool their discontent, mixing with it a certain amount of personal friction that betrays a class conflict even among themselves. This combined lament is a form of antipastoral that sets the problem and predicts the pastoral terms of its solution: they live not in a golden age of pleasant nymphs, democratic equality, and eternal spring but in great marital, social, and natural distress. The first melioration of their "jangling" is a song of mirth that prefigures a greater harmony to come but is obviously only a temporary expedient.

At this point Mak enters and lodges complaints of his own, and the shepherds sleep, marking the first division of the play. Mak then escapes with the lamb, and a "sacred parody" follows: the three shepherds awake as though resurrected from death, but instead of discovering a Virgin and child who bring unlooked for blessings to poor shepherds (including a proper resurrection) they encounter Mak's wife Gill, whose frequent (and not immaculate) conceptions bring only increased poverty. The farce of the lamb-in-the-cradle prepares *incongruously* for the child in the manger, the finding of which constitutes the recognition of the shepherds and the end of their search. It results not in comic retribution as the discovery of the other "lamb" does, but in the serious resolution of their problems. Thus after their second sleep, they awaken to the entirely revised condition of the Christian Shepherd who shares their poverty and cold with them. After ritualized speeches of some dignity and a sign—an unseasonal bob of cherries—that vernal rebirth is coming, they exit singing in contented harmony, their mood as close to religious joy as we could expect from them.

The Second Shepherds' Pageant

COLL   *the First Shepherd*
GIB   *the Second Shepherd*
DAW   *the Third Shepherd*
MAK   *the Sheep Stealer*

GILL   MAK'S *Wife*
ANGEL
MARY   *with the Christ-child*

SCENE i. *The open fields.*

1 SHEPHERD. Lord, what these weathers
    are cold! And I am ill happed.
I am near-hand dold,   *nearly numb*
    so long have I napped;
My legs they fold,   *give way*
    my fingers are chapped.
It is not as I would, for I am all
    lapped   *wrapped*
In sorrow.   5
In storms and tempest,
Now in the east, now in the west,
Woe is him has never rest
Mid-day nor morrow!
But we sely husbands that walk on
    the moor,   10
In faith, we are near-hands out of
    the door.
No wonder, as it stands if we be
    poor,
For the tilth of our lands lies fallow
    as the floor,
As ye ken.   14
We are so hammed,   *crippled*

---

1 How cold this weather is! And I am poorly clad. 10 But we poor husbandmen. 11
We are nearly homeless. 13 *tilth:* arable
part.

From the book Everyman and Medieval
Miracle Plays *edited by A. C. Cawley.
Dutton Paperback Edition (1959). Re-
printed by permission of E. P. Dutton &
Co., Inc. Also from Everyman's Library
Text, reprinted by permission of J. M.
Dent & Sons Ltd.: Publishers.*

Fortaxed and   *overtaxed*
    rammed,   *crushed*
We are made hand-tamed
With these gentlery-men.
Thus they reave us our rest, our
    Lady them wary!
These men that are lord-fast, they
    cause the plough tarry.   20
That, men say, is for the best; we
    find it contrary.
Thus are husbands oppressed, in
    point to miscarry
On live.
Thus hold they us under,   24
Thus they bring us in
    blunder;   *trouble*
It were great wonder
And ever should we thrive.   *if*
For may he get a paint sleeve or a
    brooch, nowadays,
Woe is him that him grieve, or
    once again-says!   *gainsays*
Dare no man him repreve, what
    mastery he mays;   30
And yet may no man lieve   *believe*
    one word that he says—
No letter.
He can make purveyance
With boast and bragance,   *bragging*

17–18 We are reduced to submission by these
gentry. 19 They rob us of our rest, our Lady
curse them! 20 *lord-fast:* bound to a lord.
22–23 In danger of coming to mortal harm.
28 If he is able to get an embroidered sleeve,
i.e., a lord's livery. 30 No man dare repreve
him, no matter what force he uses. 33 He can
requisition [our belongings].

And all is through
    maintenance   *support*
Of men that are greater.   36
There shall come a swain as proud
    as a po;   *peacock*
He must borrow my wain, my plough
    also;
Then I am full fain to grant ere he
    go.
Thus live we in pain, anger, and
    woe   40
By night and day.
He must have, if he langed,
If I should forgang it;
I were better be hanged
Than once say him nay.   45
It does me good, as I walk thus by
    mine own,   *myself*
Of this world for to
    talk in manner of moan.   *grumble*
To my sheep will I stalk and harken
    anon,
There abide on a balk, or sit on a
    stone
Full soon;   50
For I trow, pardie,   *by God*
True men if they be,
We get more company
Ere it be noon.   54

[*Enter* SECOND SHEPHERD.]

2 SHEPHERD. Benste and Dominus,
    what may this bemean?   *mean*
Why fares this world thus? Oft have
    we not seen.
Lord, these weathers are
    spitous, and the winds   *cruel*
    full keen,
And the frosts so hideous they water
    mine een—   *eyes*
No lie.
Now in dry, now in wet,   60
Now in snow, now in sleet,

When my shoon freeze to my feet
It is not all easy.
But as far as I ken, or yet as I go,
We   sely   wedmen   dree   mickle
    woe: 65
We have sorrow then and then; it
    falls oft so.
Silly Copple, our hen, both to and
    fro
She cackles;
But begin she to croak,
To groan or to cluck,   70
Woe is him our cock,
For he is in the shackles.
These men that are wed have not all
    their will;
When they are full hard sted, they
    sigh full still.
God wot they are led full hard and
    full ill;   75
In bower nor in bed they say nought
    theretill.
This tide
My part have I fun,
I know my lesson: 79
Woe is him that is
    bun,   *bound (in marriage)*
For he must abide.   *remain so*
But now late in our lives—a marvel
    to me,
That I think my heart rives   *breaks*
    such wonders to see;
What that destiny drives it should
    so be—
Some men will have two wives, and
    some men three   85
In store;
Some are woe that   *miserable*
    have any.
But so far can I: *know*
Woe is him that has many,   89
For he feels sore.   *pain*

42–43 He must have what he wants, even if I have to go without it. 49 *balk:* a strip of rough grassland dividing two ploughed portions of a common field. 55 *Benste: benedicite* (bless us). 56 We have not often seen the like.

64–66 But as far as I know or as my experience goes, we poor married men suffer much woe: we have sorrow time and again. 71 Unhappy is our cock. 74 When they are hard put to it they sigh unceasingly. 76–78 They never answer back. Now I've found out what I have to do. 84 Whatever destiny compels must come to pass.

[Turns to the audience.]

But, young men, of wooing, for God
that you bought,
Be well ware of   *very wary*
wedding, and think in your thought:
"Had I wist" is a thing that serveth
of nought.
Mickle still mourning has   *constant*
wedding home brought,
And griefs,   95
With many a sharp shower; *pang*
For thou mayst catch in an hour
That shall sow thee full sour
As long as thou lives.
For, as ever read I epistle, I have
one to my fere   100
As sharp as thistle, as rough as a
briar.
She is browed like a bristle, with a
sour-loten cheer;
Had she once wet her whistle, she
could sing full clear
Her paternoster.
She is as great as a whale,   105
She has a gallon of gall;
By him that died for us all,
I would I had run to   *till*
I had lost her!
1 SHEPHERD. God look over the raw!
Full deafly ye stand.
2 SHEPHERD. Yea, the devil in thy
maw, so tariand!   110
Saw'st thou awre of Daw?
1 SHEPHERD.   Yea, on a lea-land
Heard I him blow. He comes here at
hand,
Not far.

Stand still.
2 SHEPHERD. Why?   114
1 SHEPHERD. For he comes,
hope I.   *think*
2 SHEPHERD. He will make us both a
lie,   *tell*
But if we beware.   *unless*

[Enter THIRD SHEPHERD.]

3 SHEPHERD. Christ's cross me speed,
and Saint Nicholas!
Thereof had I need; it is worse than
it was.
Whoso could take heed and let the
world pass,   120
It is ever in dread and brickle as
glass,
And slithes.
This world fared never so,
With marvels mo and mo— *more*
Now in weal, now in woe,   125
And all thing writhes. *changes*
Was never since Noah's flood such
floods seen,
Winds and rains so rude, and storms
so keen:
Some stammered, some stood in
doubt, as I ween.   *fear*
Now God turn all to good! I say as
I mean,   130
For ponder: *consider*
These floods so they drown,
Both in fields and in town,
And bear all down;
And that is a wonder.   135
We that walk on the nights our cat-
tle to keep,
We see sudden sights when other men
sleep.
Yet methink my heart
lights; I see   *grows light*
shrews peep.   *rogues*
Ye are two all-wights— *monsters*

---

91 But, young men, as for wooing, by God who redeemed you. 93 "If only I had known" is something that does not help you. 98 What shall grieve you most bitterly. 100 I have one for my mate. 102 She has bristly brows and a sour-looking face. 109 God save the audience! You stand there as deaf as a post. (The First Shepherd has evidently been trying to attract the other's attention.) 110–12 The devil in your belly for tarrying so long! Have you seen Daw anywhere?...Yea, in a fallow field I heard him blow [his horn].

---

119 *it:* i.e., the world. 120–23 Anyone who could look on and let the world go by [would see that] it is always fearful and as brittle as glass, and slides away (i.e., is transitory). But the world never behaved in this way before.

I will give my sheep
A turn.   140
But full ill have I meant;
As I walk on this bent,
I may lightly repent,
My toes if I spurn.
Ah, sir, God you save, and master
mine!   145
A drink fain would I have, and some-
what to dine.
1 SHEPHERD. Christ's curse, my knave,
thou art a lither hine!   *lazy hind*
2 SHEPHERD. What, the boy list rave!
Abide unto syne;
We have made it.   149
Ill thrift on thy pate!   *luck*
Though the shrew came late,
Yet is he in state   *ready*
To dine—if he had it.
3 SHEPHERD. Such servants as I, that
sweat and swinks,   *toil*
Eat our bread full dry, and that me
forthinks.   *displeases*
We are oft wet and weary when
master-men winks;   *sleep*
Yet come full lately both   *tardily*
dinners and drinks.   157
But nately   *thoroughly*
Both our dame and our sire,
When we have run in the mire,   160
They can nip at our hire,
And pay us full lately.
But hear my truth, master: for the
fare that ye make,
I shall do thereafter—work as I take.
I shall do a little, sir, and among
ever lake,   165
For yet lay my supper never on my
stomach
In fields.

Whereto should I threap?   *haggle*
With my staff can I leap;
And men say "Light cheap   170
Litherly foryields."
1 SHEPHERD. Thou wert an ill lad to
ride on wooing
With a man that had but little of
spending.
2 SHEPHERD. Peace, boy, I bade. No
more jangling,
Or I shall make thee full rad, by the
heaven's king!   175
With thy guads—
Where are our sheep, boy?—we
scorn.
3 SHEPHERD. Sir, this same day at
morn
I them left in the corn,
When they rang Lauds.   180
They have pasture good, they cannot
go wrong.
1 SHEPHERD. That is right. By the
rood, these nights are long! *cross*
Yet I would, ere we yode,   *went*
one gave us a song.
2 SHEPHERD. So I thought as I stood, to
mirth us among.
3 SHEPHERD. I grant.   185
1 SHEPHERD. Let me sing the
tenory.   *tenor*
2 SHEPHERD. And I the treble so high.
3 SHEPHERD. Then the mean falls to
me.
Let see how ye chant. [*They sing.*]

[*Then* MAK *enters with a cloak covering his tunic.*]

MAK. Now, Lord, for thy names seven,

139–44 I will turn my sheep away. But I
have been ill disposed [to the shepherds]; as
I walk on this field, I may stub my toes in
easy penance. 148–49 What, the boy is pleased
to rave! Wait till later; we have finished it
(i.e., our meal). 161 They can stint our
wages. 163–65 But hear my promise, master:
In return for the food you provide, I shall do
accordingly—work as I'm paid. I shall do but
little, sir, and between whiles play all the
time.

170–73 "A cheap bargain repays badly.". . .
You'd be the wrong lad for anyone that's
hard up to take a-wooing with him (cf.
Othello III.iii.71). 174–77 Stop your wran-
gling, or I'll quickly make you, by the king of
heaven! We scorn your pranks—where are
our sheep, boy? 180 *Lauds:* the first of the
seven canonical offices, usually sung at day-
break. 184 To gladden us meanwhile. 190–
92 Now, Lord, by thy seven names, who made
both moon and stars far more than I can
name, thy will concerning me, Lord, is lacking. I am all at sixes and sevens; that often
unsettles my brain.

that made both moon and
starns   190
Well more than I can neven, thy will,
Lord, of me tharns.
I am all uneven; that moves oft my
harns.
Now would God I were in heaven, for
there weep no bairns
So still.   *incessantly*
1 SHEPHERD. Who is that pipes so
poor?   195
MAK. Would God ye wist   *knew*
how I foor!   *fared*
Lo, a man that walks on the moor,
And has not all his will.
2 SHEPHERD. Mak, where hast thou
gone? Tell us tiding.   *news*
3 SHEPHERD. Is he come? Then
ilkone take heed   *everyone*
to his thing. [*He takes* MAK's
cloak from him.]   200
MAK. What! I be a yeoman, I tell you,
of the king,
The self and the same,
sond from a great   *messenger*
lording,
And sich.   *such like*
Fie on you! Go hence
Out of my presence!   205
I must have reverence.
Why, who be ich?
1 SHEPHERD. Why make ye it so
quaint? Mak, ye do wrong.
2 SHEPHERD. But, Mak, list ye saint?
I trow that ye long.
3 SHEPHERD. I trow the shrew can
paint, the devil might   *deceive*
him hang!   210
MAK. I shall make complaint, and make
you all to thwang
At a word,
And tell even how ye doth.   *do*
1 SHEPHERD. But, Mak, is that sooth?
Now take out that Southern

tooth,   215
And set in a turd!   *put*
2 SHEPHERD. Mak, the devil in your
eye! A stroke would I lene   *give*
you.
3 SHEPHERD. Mak, know ye not me?
By God, I could teen you.   *hurt*
MAK. God look you all three!   *save*
Methought I had seen you.
Ye are a fair company.
1 SHEPHERD.   Can ye now
mean you?   220
2 SHEPHERD. Shrew, peep!   *pry about*
Thus late as thou goes,
What will men suppose?   *suspect*
And thou hast an ill
noise   *reputation*
Of stealing of sheep.   *for*
MAK. And I am true as steel, all men
wot;   226
But a sickness I feel that holds me
full hot: *severely*
My belly fares not well, it is out of
estate.   *condition*
3 SHEPHERD. Seldom lies the devil dead
by the gate.
MAK. Therefore   230
Full sore am I and ill;
If I stand stone-still,
I eat not a needle   *morsel*
This month and more.
1 SHEPHERD. How fares thy wife? By
my hood, how fares she?   235
MAK. Lies waltering—   *sprawling*
by the rood—by the fire, lo!
And a house full of brood.   *children*
She drinks well, too;
Ill speed other good that she will do!
But she
Eats as fast as she can,   240
And ilk year that comes   *every*
to man
She brings forth a lakan—   *baby*
And, some years, two.
But were I now more

---

195 Who is it that cries so piteously? 208
Why are you so uppish? 209 But, Mak, do
you want to play the saint? I believe you do.
211 And have you all flogged. 215 Southern
speech. (Mak has been trying to talk Southern English.)

220 Can you remember now? 229 Seldom
lies the devil dead by the roadside, i.e., appearances may be deceptive. 232–33 May I be
turned to stone if I have eaten a morsel. 238
I.e., there is no hope of her doing much else.

gracious, and richer   *prosperous*
by far,   244
I were eaten out of house and of
harbor.   *home*
Yet is she a foul dowse,   *wench*
if ye come near;
There is none that trows nor knows
a war
Than ken I.
Now will ye see what I proffer?
To give all in my coffer   250
To-morn at next to offer
Her head-masspenny.
2 SHEPHERD. I wot so forwaked is none
in this shire;
I would sleep if I taked less to my
hire.
3 SHEPHERD. I am cold and naked, and
would have a fire.   255
1 SHEPHERD. I am weary, forraked, and
run in the mire—
Wake thou!
2 SHEPHERD. Nay, I will lie down
by.   *nearby*
For I must sleep, truly.
3 SHEPHERD. As good a man's son was
I   260
As any of you.
But, Mak, come hither!
· Between shalt thou   *between us*
lie down.
MAK. Then might I let you bedene of
that ye would rown,
No dread.
From my top to my toe,   265

[*He recites a night-spell.*]

Manus tuas commendo,
Pontio Pilato.
Christ's cross me speed!
Now were time for a man that lacks
what he would

To stalk privily then unto a fold,   270
And nimbly to work then, and be not
too bold,
For he might abuy the bargain, if it
were told
At the ending.
Now were time for to
reel;   *move quickly*
But he needs good counsel   275
That fain would fare well,
And has but little
spending.   *money*
But about you a
circle, as round   *(magic) circle*
as a moon,
To I have done what I will,   *till*
till that it be noon,
That ye lie stone-still to that I have
done;   280
And I shall say theretill of good
words a fone:
"On height,   *high*
Over your heads, my hand I lift.
Out go your eyes! Fordo your sight!"
But yet I must make better
shift,   285
And it be right.
Lord, what they sleep hard!—that
may ye all hear.
Was I never a shepherd, but now
will I lere.   *learn*
If the flock be scared, yet shall I nip
near.
How! draw hitherward! Now mends
our cheer   290
From sorrow
A fat sheep, I dare say,
A good fleece, dare I lay.
Eft-quit when I may,   *repay*
But this will I borrow.   295

[*He goes home with the sheep.*]

---

247 There is none who believes [he knows]
or [really] knows a worse one. 251–52 Tomorrow at the latest to give all in my coffer
as an offering for her soul. 253 *forwaked:*
wearied with waking. 254 Even if I should
get less wages. 256 *forraked:* worn out with
walking. 263–64 Then I might keep you from
whispering what you want, no doubt.

272–73 For he might pay dearly for it, if it
came to a final reckoning. 281 And I shall
also say a few good words. 284–87 "Lose your
power of sight." But yet I must make better
efforts, if things are to come right. Lord, how
soundly they sleep! 289 Yet I shall grab [a
sheep] tightly. 290–92 Now a fat sheep shall
comfort us.

SCENE ii. MAK's *cottage.*

MAK. How, Gill, art thou in? Get us
some light.

WIFE. Who makes such din this time of
the night?
I am set for to spin; I hope not I
might
Rise a penny to win, I shrew them
on height!
So fares   300
A housewife that has been,
To be raised thus between.
Here may no note be seen
For such small chares.

MAK. Good wife, open the
heck! See'st thou not   *inner door*
what I bring?   305

WIFE. I may thole thee draw the sneck.
Ah, come in, my sweeting!

MAK. Yea, thou thar not reck of my
long standing.

WIFE. By the naked neck art thou like
for to hang.   308

MAK. Do way!   *enough!*
I am worthy my meat,   *food*
For in a strait can I get   *fix*
More than they that swink   *toil*
and sweat
All the long day.
Thus it fell to my lot, Gill; I had
such grace.

WIFE. It were a foul blot   *deed*
to be hanged for the case.   315

MAK. I have scaped, Jelott, oft as
hard a glase.   *blow*

WIFE. "But so long goes the pot to the
water," men says,
"At last
Comes it home broken."   319

MAK. Well know I the token,   *portent*
But let it never be spoken!
But come and help fast.

I would he were flain; I list well eat.
This twelvemonth was I not so fain
of one sheepmeat.

WIFE. Come they ere he be slain, and
hear the sheep bleat—   325

MAK. Then might I be ta'en: that were
a cold sweat!
Go spar   *fasten*
The gate-door.   *outer door*

WIFE.   Yes, Mak,
For and they come at thy back— *if*

MAK. Then might I buy, for all the
pack,   330
The devil of the war.

WIFE. A good bourd have   *jest*
I spied, since thou
canst none: *knowest*
Here shall we him hide, till they be
gone,
In my cradle. Abide! Let me alone,
And I shall lie beside in childbed and
groan.   335

MAK. Thou red,   *get ready*
And I shall say thou
wast light   *delivered*
Of a knave-child this night.   *boy*

WIFE. Now well is me day bright
That ever was I bred!   340
This is a good guise and a far cast;
Yet a woman's advice helps at the
last.
I wot never who spies; again go thou
fast.

MAK. But I come ere they rise,
else blows a cold blast!   *unless*
I will go sleep.   345

[MAK *prepares to return to the shepherds.*]

Yet sleep all this meny;   *company*
And I shall go stalk privily,
As it had never been I
That carried their sheep.

298–304 I don't think I can earn a penny by
getting up [from my spinning], curse them!
Any woman who has been a housewife knows
what it means to be got up from her work
continually. I have no work to show because
of such small chores.   306 I will let you draw
the latch.   307 You needn't mind about my
standing [outside] so long.

323–24 I wish he were skinned; I am eager to
eat. At no time this year have I been so glad
of a meal of mutton.   330–31 Then I may
get the devil of a bad time from the whole
pack of them.   339–41 I'm happy when I
think of the bright day I was born! This is
a good method and a cunning trick.   343
Return again quickly [to the others].

SCENE iii. *The open fields.*

1 SHEPHERD. *Resurrex a mortruis!*
    have hold my hand!   350
Judas carnas dominus! I may not
    well stand:
My foot sleeps, by Jesus, and I
    walter fastand.
I thought that we laid us full near
    England.
2 SHEPHERD. Ah, yea?   *oh, really*
Lord, what I have slept well!   355
As fresh as an eel,
As light I me feel
As leaf on a tree.
3 SHEPHERD. Benste be   *blessing*
    herein! So me quakes,
My heart is out of skin, what-so it
    makes.   360
Who makes all this din? So my brow
    blakes,   *darkens*
To the door will I win.   *go*
    Hark, fellows, wakes!   *wake up*
We were four:
See ye awre of Mak now?
1 SHEPHERD. We were up ere thou.   365
2 SHEPHERD. Man, I give God avow
Yet yede he nawre.
3 SHEPHERD. Methought he was lapped
    in a wolf-skin.
1 SHEPHERD. So are many happed now
    —namely within.   369
3 SHEPHERD. When we had long napped,
    methought with a gin   *snare*
A fat sheep he trapped; but he made
    no din.
2 SHEPHERD. Be still!
Thy dream makes thee
    wood;   *mad*
It is but phantom, by the rood.
1 SHEPHERD. Now God turn all to
    good,   375
If it be his will.

2 SHEPHERD. Rise, Mak, for shame!
    Thou liest right long.
MAK. Now Christ's holy name be us
    among!
What is this? For Saint Jame, I may
    not well gang!   *walk*
I trow I be the same. Ah, my neck
    has lain wrong   380
Enough. [*They help him to get up.*]
Mickle thank! Since yester-even,
Now by Saint Stephen,
I was flayed with a sweven—
My heart out of slough.   385
I thought Gill began to croak and
    travail full sad,   *hard*
Well-nigh at the first cock, of a
    young lad
For to mend our flock.   *increase*
Then be I never glad;
I have tow on my rock more than
    ever I had.
Ah, my head!   390
A house full of young
    tharms,   *bellies*
The devil knock out their
    harns!   *brains*
Woe is him has many bairns,
And thereto little bread.   394
I must go home, by your leave, to
    Gill, as I thought.   *intended*
I pray you look my   *examine*
    sleeve, that I steal nought;
I am loath you to grieve or from you
    take aught.
3 SHEPHERD. Go forth, ill might thou
    chieve! Now would I we   *prosper*
    sought,
This morn,
That we had all our store.   400
1 SHEPHERD. But I will go before.
Let us meet.
2 SHEPHERD. Where?
3 SHEPHERD. At the crooked thorn.

352 I'm tottering with hunger. 355 How well I have slept! 359–60 I tremble so much, my heart is in my mouth, whatever the reason for it. 364 Have you seen Mak anywhere? 366–67 I vow to God he's gone nowhere yet. 369 Many are covered like that nowadays—especially underneath.

379 By Saint James. 380–81 My neck has been lying very crookedly. 384–85 I was terrified by a dream—I nearly jumped out of my skin. 389 I have more tow on my distaff (i.e., more trouble in store) than ever I had. 398–400 Now I want us this morning to see that we have all our stock.

Scene iv. Mak's *cottage.*

Mak. Undo this door! Who is here?
How long shall I stand?

Wife. Who makes such a bere?   *din*
Now walk in the wenyand!   405

Mak. Ah, Gill, what cheer? It is I,
Mak, your husband.

Wife. Then may we see here the devil
in a band,   *noose*
Sir Guile!

Lo, he comes with a lote,   *noise*
As he were holden in the   *held by*
throat.   410

I may not sit at my note   *work*
A hand-long while.   *brief*

Mak. Will ye hear what fare she makes
to get her a glose?

And does naught but lakes,   *play*
and claws her toes.

Wife. Why, who wanders, who wakes?
Who comes, who goes?   415

Who brews, who bakes? What makes
me thus hoarse?

And then

It is ruth to behold—   *a pity*
Now in hot, now in cold,

Full woeful is the household   420
That wants a woman.   *lacks*

But what end hast thou made with
the herds, Mak?   *shepherds*

Mak. The last word that they said
when I turned my back,

They would look that they had their
sheep, all the pack.

I hope they will not be   *think*
well paid when they   *pleased*
their sheep lack,   425
Pardie!

But how-so the game goes,   *however*
To me they will suppose,

And make a foul noise,

And cry out upon me.   430

But thou must do as thou
hight.   *promised*

Wife.   I accord me theretill;
I shall swaddle him right in my
cradle.

If it were a greater
sleight, yet could I help   *trick*
till.

I will lie down straight.   *straightway*
Come hap me.   *cover*

Mak.   I will.

Wife. Behind!   435
Come Coll and his narrow,   *mate*
They will nip us full narrow.   *hard*

Mak. But I may cry "Out, harrow!"
The sheep if they find.

Wife. Harken ay when they call; they
will come anon.   440

Come and make ready all, and sing
by thine own;

Sing lullay thou shall,   *lullaby*
for I must groan,

And cry out by the wall on Mary
and John,

For sore.   *pain*
Sing lullay on fast,   *quickly*
When thou hearest at the last;   446
And but I play a false cast,

Trust me no more.

Scene v. *The crooked thorn.*

3 Shepherd. Ah, Coll, good morn!
Why sleepest thou not?

1 Shepherd. Alas, that ever was I
born! We have a foul blot—   450
A fat wether have we lorn.   *lost*

3 Shepherd.   Marry,
God's forbot!   *God forbid*

2 Shepherd. Who should do us that
scorn? That were   *insult*
a foul spot.   *disgrace*

1 Shepherd. Some shrew.
I have sought with my dogs
All Horbury shrogs,   *thickets*
And, of fifteen hogs,   456

---

405 Walk in the waning moon, i.e., at an unlucky time. 413 Will you listen to the fuss she makes in the hope of excusing herself? 419 I.e., at all times. 428 They will suspect me. 431 I agree to that.

433 I could still help with it. 438 A cry for help. 447 And if I don't play a false trick. 455 Horbury, near Wakefield.

Found I but one ewe.

3 SHEPHERD. Now trow me, if ye will
   —by Saint Thomas of Kent,
Either Mak or Gill was at that
   assent.

1 SHEPHERD. Peace, man, be still! I saw
   when he went.   460
Thou slander'st him ill; thou ought
   to repent
Good speed.   *quickly*

2 SHEPHERD. Now as ever might I thee,
If I should even here die,
I would say it were he   465
That did that same deed.

3 SHEPHERD. Go we thither,
   I rede, and run on our   *advise*
   feet.
Shall I never eat bread, the sooth
   to I wit.

1 SHEPHERD. Nor drink in my head,
   with him till I meet.

2 SHEPHERD. I will rest in no
   stead till that I him greet,   *place*
My brother.   471
One I will hight:
Till I see him in sight,
Shall I never sleep one night
There I do another.   *where*

SCENE vi. MAK's *cottage.*

3 SHEPHERD. Will ye hear how they
   hack? Our sire list croon.   476

1 SHEPHERD. Heard I never none
   crack so clear out of   *bawl*
   tone.   *tune*
Call on him.

2 SHEPHERD. Mak, undo your door
   soon!   *immediately*

MAK. Who is it that spake, as it were
   noon,
On loft?   480
Who is that, I say?

3 SHEPHERD. Good fellows,
   were it day.   *if only it were*

MAK. As far as ye may,
Good, speak soft,   *good sirs*
Over a sick woman's head, that is at
   malease;   485
I had liefer be dead ere she had any
   disease.

WIFE. Go to another stead! I may not
   well quease;   *breathe*
Each foot that ye tread goes thorough
   my nose
So high.   489

1 SHEPHERD. Tell us, Mak, if ye may,
How fare ye, I say?

MAK. But are ye in this town today?
Now how fare ye?
Ye have run in the mire, and are wet
   yet;
I shall make you a fire, if ye will
   sit.   495
A nurse would I hire. Think ye on
   yet?
Well quit is my hire—my dream, this
   is it—
A season.
I have bairns, if ye knew,
Well more than enew;   *enough*
But we must drink as we brew,   501
And that is but reason.
I would ye dined ere ye yode.   *went*
Methink that ye sweat.

2 SHEPHERD. Nay, neither mends our
   mood drink nor meat.

456–57 Among fifteen hogs (or young sheep) I found only a ewe, i.e., the wether was missing. 458 St. Thomas of Canterbury. 459 Either Mak or Gill was a party to it. 463 As I hope to prosper. 468 Till I know the truth. 471 *My brother:* a friendly form of address. 472 One thing I will promise. 476 Do you hear them trilling? Our gentleman is pleased to croon.

479–80 Who is it that spoke aloud, as though it were noon? 485–86 Because of a sick woman who is in distress; I had rather die than she should suffer any discomfort. 488–89 Every step you tread goes through my nose so strongly, i.e., goes right through my head. 496–98 I would like to hire a nurse. Do you still remember [my dream about a new addition to the family]? I've been paid my wages in full for a while—this is my dream come true.

MAK. Why, sir, ails you aught but
   good? 505
3 SHEPHERD.   Yea, our sheep that
   we gete   *tend*
   Are stolen as they yode. Our loss is
   great.
MAK. Sirs, drink!
   Had I been there,
   Some should have bought   *paid for*
   it full sore.
1 SHEPHERD. Marry, some men trow
   that ye were, 510
   And that us forthinks.   *displeases*
2 SHEPHERD. Mak, some men
   trow that it should   *believe*
   be ye.
3 SHEPHERD. Either ye or your spouse,
   so say we.
MAK. Now if ye have
   suspouse to Gill   *suspicion*
   or to me,
   Come and rip our house,   *ransack*
   and then may ye see 515
   Who had her.
   If I any sheep fot,   *fetched*
   Either cow or stot—   *heifer*
   And Gill, my wife, rose not
   Here since she laid her— 520
   As I am true and leal,   *honest*
   to God here I pray
   That this be the first meal that I
   shall eat this day.
1 SHEPHERD. Mak, as have I sele,
   advise thee, I say:
   He learned timely to steal that could
   not say nay. 524
WIFE. I swelt!   *feel faint*
   Out, thieves, from my wones! *house*
   Ye come to rob us for the nonce.
MAK. Hear ye not how she groans?
   Your hearts should melt.
WIFE. Out, thieves, from my bairn!
   Nigh him not there. 530

MAK. Wist ye how she had farn, your
   hearts would be sore.
   Ye do wrong, I you warn, that thus
   come before
   To a woman that has farn; but I
   say no more.
WIFE. Ah, my middle!
   I pray to God so mild, 535
   If ever I you beguiled,
   That I eat this child   *may eat*
   That lies in this cradle.
MAK. Peace, woman, for God's pain,
   and cry not so!
   Thou spillest thy brain,   *injurest*
   and makest me full woe. 540
2 SHEPHERD. I trow our sheep be slain.
   What find ye two?
3 SHEPHERD. All work we in vain; as
   well may we go.
   But hatters!   *confound it*
   I can find no flesh,
   Hard nor nesh,   *soft*
   Salt nor fresh, 546
   But two tome platters. *only; empty*
   Quick cattle but this, tame nor wild,
   None, as have I bliss, as loud as he
   smelled.
WIFE. No, so God me bless, and give
   me joy of my child! 550
1 SHEPHERD. We have marked amiss;
   I hold us beguiled.
2 SHEPHERD. Sir, don.   *completely*
   Sir—our Lady him save!—
   Is your child a knave?   *boy*
MAK. Any lord might him have, 555
   This child, to his son.
   When he wakens he kips,   *snatches*
   that joy is to see.
3 SHEPHERD. In good time to his hips,
   and in sely.
   But who were his

---

505 Why, sir, is anything wrong with you?
523–24 Mak, as I hope for happiness, take
thought I say: He learned early to steal who
could not say no [to another's property].
527 You come on purpose to rob us. 530 Do
not go near him there.

531 If you knew what she had been through.
533 To a woman who has been in labor.
548–49 Live stock but this (i.e., the "baby"
in the cradle), tame or wild, none [have I
found], as I hope to be happy, that smelled
as loud as he (i.e., the missing sheep). 551
Aimed wrongly, i.e., made a mistake. 558 A
good and happy future to him.

gossips so soon   *godparents*
ready?
MAK. So fair fall their lips!
1 SHEPHERD [*aside*].   Hark now,
  a lie!   560
MAK. So God them thank,
Parkin, and Gibbon Waller, I say,
And gentle John Horne, in good
  fay—   *faith*
He made all the
  garray—   *commotion*
With the great shank.   *long legs*
2 SHEPHERD. Mak, friends will we be,
  for we are all one.   *agreed*
MAK. We? Now I hold for me, for
  mends get I none.
Farewell all three!—all glad were ye
  gone.
3 SHEPHERD. Fair words may there be,
  but love is there none   569
This year.
[*They leave the cottage.*]
1 SHEPHERD. Gave ye the child anything?
2 SHEPHERD. I trow not one farthing.
3 SHEPHERD. Fast again will I fling;
Abide ye me there.

[*He returns to the cottage.*]

Mak, take it to no grief, if I come to
  thy bairn.   575
MAK. Nay, thou dost me great reprief,
  and foul hast thou farn.
3 SHEPHERD. The child will it not
  grieve, that little day-starn.   *star*
Mak, with your leave, let me give
  your bairn
But sixpence.
MAK. Nay, do way! He sleeps.   580
3 SHEPHERD. Methink he peeps.
MAK. When he wakens he weeps.

I pray you go hence.
3 SHEPHERD. Give me leave him to kiss,
  and lift up the clout.   *cloth*

[*He glimpses the sheep.*]

What the devil is this? He has a long
  snout!   585
1 SHEPHERD. He is marked amiss. We
  wait ill about.
2 SHEPHERD. Ill-spun weft, iwis, ay
  comes foul out.
Aye, so! [*He recognizes the sheep.*]
He is like to our sheep!
3 SHEPHERD.   How, Gib, may I
  peep?   590
1 SHEPHERD. I trow kind will creep
Where it may not go.
2 SHEPHERD. This was a quaint gaud
  and a far cast;
It was a high fraud.
3 SHEPHERD.   Yea, sirs, was't.
Let burn this bawd and bind her
  fast.   595
A false scold hangs at the last;
So shalt thou.
Will ye see how they swaddle
His four feet in the middle?
Saw I never in a cradle   600
A horned lad ere now.
MAK. Peace, bid I. What, let be your
  fare!   *uproar*
I am he that him begat, and yond
  woman him bare.
1 SHEPHERD. What devil shall he
  hat, Mak? Lo, God,   *be called*
Mak's heir!
2 SHEPHERD. Let be all that. Now God
  give him care,   *sorrow*
I sagh.   606
WIFE. A pretty child is he
As sits on a woman's knee;
A dillydown, pardie,   *darling*

---

560 Good luck to them. 563 John Horne is the shepherd in the *First Shepherds' Pageant* who quarrels with Gyb about the pasturing of an imaginary flock of sheep. 567 For my own part, I'm holding back, for I get no amends. 568 [I should be] very glad if you were gone. (Probably an aside.) 573 I will dash back. 575 Don't take offence. 576 Nay, you do me great shame, and you have behaved badly.

586–87 He is misshapen. We do wrong to pry about.... Ill-spun weft, indeed, always comes out badly, i.e., what is bred in the bone will come out in the flesh. 591–93 Nature will creep where it cannot walk, i.e., assert itself in one way or another.... This was a clever dodge and a cunning trick. 606 I saw [the sheep myself].

To gar a man laugh.   *make*
3 SHEPHERD. I know him by the ear-
mark; that is a good token.   611
MAK. I tell you, sirs, hark! his nose
was broken.
Since told me a clerk that he was
forspoken.   *bewitched*
1 SHEPHERD. This is a false work; I
would fain be wroken.   *avenged*
Get weapon!   615
WIFE. He was taken with an elf,   *by*
I saw it myself;
When the clock struck twelve,
Was he forshapen.   *transformed*
2 SHEPHERD. Ye two are well feft sam
in a stead.   620
1 SHEPHERD. Since they maintain their
theft, let do them to dead.   *death*
MAK. If I trespass eft,   *again*
gird off my head.   *strike*
With you will I be left.
3 SHEPHERD.   Sirs, do my rede:
For this trespass
We will neither
ban ne flite,   *curse; quarrel*
Fight nor chide,   626
But have done as tite,   *at once*
And cast him in canvas.

[*They toss* MAK *in a blanket.*]

SCENE vii. *The open fields.*

1 SHEPHERD. Lord, what I am sore, in
point for to burst!
In faith, I may no more; therefore
will I rest.   630
2 SHEPHERD. As a sheep of seven score
he weighed in my fist.
For to sleep aywhere methink that
I list.
3 SHEPHERD. Now I pray you
Lie down on this green.   634

1 SHEPHERD. On these thieves yet
I mean.   *think*
3 SHEPHERD. Whereto should ye
teen?   *vex yourself*
Do as I say you.

[*An* ANGEL *sings "Gloria in excelsis,"
and then says:*]

ANGEL. Rise, herdmen hend,   *gentle*
for now is he born
That shall take from the fiend that
Adam had lorn;
That warlock to shend,   *destroy*
this night is he born.   640
God is made your friend now at this
morn,
He behests.   *promises*
At Bedlem go see   *Bethlehem*
There lies that   *where*
free   *noble one*
In a crib full poorly,   645
Betwixt two beasts.
1 SHEPHERD. This was a
quaint steven that   *elegant voice*
ever yet I heard.
It is a marvel to neven,   *tell of*
thus to be scared.
2 SHEPHERD. Of God's son of heaven
he spoke upward.   *on high*
All the wood on a leven methought
that he gard   650
Appear.
3 SHEPHERD. He spake of a bairn
In Bedlem, I you warn.
1 SHEPHERD.   That betokens yond
starn;
Let us seek him there.   655
2 SHEPHERD. Say, what was his song?
Heard ye not how he
cracked it,   *sang*
Three breves to a long?
3 SHEPHERD.   Yea, marry, he
hacked it: *trilled*
Was no crochet wrong, nor no thing
that lacked it.

---

620 You two are well endowed together in
one place, i.e., are as clever a pair of rascals
as ever lived under one roof. 623 I throw
myself on your mercy.... Take my advice.
632 I think I would be glad to sleep anywhere.

---

640 *warlock:* the devil. 650–51 I thought he
made the whole wood appear as if lit up by
lightning. 658 No crochet was wrong, and there
was nothing it lacked.

1 SHEPHERD. For to sing us among,
   right as he knacked it,   *sang*
I can.   660
2 SHEPHERD. Let see how ye croon.
Can ye bark at the moon?
3 SHEPHERD. Hold your tongues! Have
   done!
1 SHEPHERD. Hark after, then. [*Sings.*]
2 SHEPHERD. To Bedlem he bade that
   we should gang;   *go*
I am full adrad   *afraid*
   that we tarry too long.   666
3 SHEPHERD. Be merry and not sad—
   of mirth is our song!
Everlasting glad to meed may we
   fang
Without noise.   669
1 SHEPHERD. Hie we thither
   forthy,   *therefore*
If we be wet and weary,   *even if*
To that child and that lady;
We have it not to lose.
2 SHEPHERD. We find by the prophecy
   —let be your din!—
Of David and Isay,   *Isaiah*
   and more than I min—   *remember*
They prophesied by   *learning*
   clergy—that in a virgin   676
Should he light and lie, to   *alight*
   sloken our sin,   *quench*
And slake it,   *relieve*
Our kind, from woe;   *race*
For Isay said so: 680
Ecce virgo
Concipiet a child that is naked.
3 SHEPHERD. Full glad may we be, and
   abide that day
That lovely to see, that all mights
   may.
Lord, well were me for once and for
   ay,   685
Might I kneel on my knee, some
   word for to say
To that child.

But the angel said
In a crib was he laid;
He was poorly arrayed,   690
Both meek and mild.
1 SHEPHERD. Patriarchs that have been,
   and prophets beforn,   *in the past*
They desired to have seen this child
   that is born.
They are gone full clean; that have
   they lorn.
We shall see him, I ween, ere it be
   morn,   695
To token.   *as a sign*
When I see him and feel,
Then wot I full well
It is true as steel
That prophets have spoken: 700
To so poor as we are that he would
   appear,
First find, and declare by his mes-
   senger.
2 SHEPHERD. Go we now, let us fare;
   the place is us near.
3 SHEPHERD. I am ready and
   yare; go we in   *eager*
   fere   *together*
To that bright.   *bright one*
Lord, if thy will be—   706
We are lewd all three—   *simple*
Thou grant us some kins glee
To comfort thy wight.

SCENE viii. *The stable in Bethlehem.*

1 SHEPHERD. Hail, comely and
   clean; hail, young child!   *pure*
Hail, maker, as I mean,   *born of*
   of a maiden so mild!   711
Thou hast waried,   *cursed*
   I ween, the warlock so wild:
The false guiler of teen, now goes
   he beguiled.
Lo, he merries,   *is merry*

668–69 We can get everlasting joy as our
reward without any fuss. 673 We must not
forget it. 681–82 Behold, a virgin conceive. 684–85 To see that lovely one who is
almighty. Lord, I would be happy for once
and all.

694 That chance have they lost. 702 Find
[us] first of all, and make known [his birth]
through his messenger. 708–9 Grant us some
joyful way of comforting thy child. 713
The false and malicious deceiver, i.e., the
devil.

Lo, he laughs, my sweeting! 715
A well fare meeting! *very fine*
I have holden my heting:
Have a bob of cherries. *bunch*
2 SHEPHERD. Hail, sovereign saviour,
for thou hast us sought!
Hail, freely food and *noble child*
flower, that all thing hast wrought!
Hail, full of favor, that made all of
nought! 721
Hail! I kneel and I cower. A bird
have I brought
To my bairn.
Hail, little tiny mop! *moppet*
Of our creed thou art crop; 725
I would drink on thy cop,
Little day-starn.
3 SHEPHERD. Hail, darling dear, full of
Godhead!
I pray thee be near when that I have
need.
Hail, sweet is thy cheer! My heart
would bleed 730
To see thee sit here in so poor
weed, *clothing*
With no pennies.
Hail! Put forth thy dall! *hand*
I bring thee but a ball:
Have and play thee withal, 735
And go to the tennis.

MARY. The Father of heaven, God
omnipotent,
That set all on seven, his Son has
he sent.
My name could he neven, and light
ere he went.
I conceived him full even through
might, as he meant; 740
And now is he born.
He keep you from woe!—
I shall pray him so.
Tell forth as ye go,
And min on this morn. *remember*
1 SHEPHERD. Farewell, lady, so fair to
behold, 746
With thy child on thy knee.
2 SHEPHERD. But he
lies full cold.
Lord, well is me! Now we go, thou
behold.
3 SHEPHERD. Forsooth, already it seems
to be told
Full oft. 750
1 SHEPHERD. What grace we have fun!
2 SHEPHERD. Come forth; now are we
won! *redeemed*
3 SHEPHERD. To sing are we
bun: *bound*
Let take on loft.

[*They exit singing.*]

---

717 I have kept my promise. 725–26 You are
the head of our faith; I would drink in your
cup (i.e., the cup of the Eucharist).

738 That made all the world in seven days.
739–40 He named my name and alighted in
me before He went. I conceived him indeed
through God's might, as His purpose was.
754 Let us begin loudly.

The Tempest

The Tempest is not William Shakespeare's last play—he wrote *Henry VIII* in collaboration with John Fletcher a year or two later—but it is his last solo performance as a dramatist. It was probably composed around 1611, since it is known to have been acted before King James on November 1 of that year; and it was first published in the 1623 Folio edition of Shakespeare's works.

The sources of the play are mostly conjectural. Shakespeare (1564–1616) may have gotten the idea from several pamphlets written around 1610 concerning shipwrecked sailors in the Bermudas; he may have been influenced by the Italian *commedia dell' arte,* by Longus' romance *Daphnis and Chloe,* and by various other works. But no specific source is recognized, and the general features of the play— the setting adrift, the desert island, the "wild man" of nature, the magician whose power is sought by others, the ethereal servant—are all stock material of romance. But this stock material has passed through the transforming sea of the Shakespearean imagination, suffering, as Ariel's song in Act I, scene ii has it,

a sea change
Into something rich and strange.

Phrases from Ariel's song are appropriate because the major mode of action in *The Tempest* is metamorphosis. If the sea in its slow and apparently destructive erosion of human eyes and bones ultimately produces pearl and coral, Prospero's magic (under the controlling influence of Shakespeare's magic) accelerates the process, transforming the sea itself into a tempest that seems to destroy but actually changes for the better. Changing for the better is not an easy job, however, and the tension of the play arises from the dialectical encounter of destructive and redemptive forces. The real world of Italy, like most fictional Italies in Renaissance works, is essentially Machiavellian, an arena of competing egos where, as Antonio observes (II.i.283), the shortest distance between two points is three inches of obedient steel. In Milan transformations are uprisings that tear down, revolutions intended to dispossess others and better oneself in power instead of moral character, as in Antonio's seizure of Prospero's dukedom. When the court party is shipwrecked on the island, they bring with them the disruptive impulses of Renaissance realpolitik to confront the stabilizing influences of Prospero's magic: hence, the plot by Antonio and Sebastian against the King of Naples (a repetition of the plot that dispossessed Prospero years earlier) and, at a lower social and stylistic level, the plot of the comic villains Stephano, Trinculo, and Caliban against Prospero, both of which are neutralized by Ariel.

What we have talked about so far suggests a standard kind of Renaissance pastoral romance in which corruption is associated with an urban or court society whose subdued longings for innocence are figured in the escape of certain characters into a pastoral retreat abounding in simplicity and natural goodness.

But it is too easy, Shakespeare knows, to distribute good and evil geographically. Therefore he represents Italy not merely by the evil Antonio and Sebastian but by the good Gonzalo, Ferdinand, and, for that matter, Prospero and Miranda as well. And he invests the pastoral world of the island not merely with the native goodness of Ariel but also with an indigenous and (before Prospero's arrival) dominating waywardness in Sycorax and her man-fish son Caliban. Good and evil are not simply environmental problems but mysteries rooted in the human condition, in man himself, so that coming to terms with them means coming to terms with man's own nature, which contains something of both Italy and the island within it.

If Shakespeare bypasses the easy solutions of naive pastoral to the enigmas of good and evil, it is because he realizes that moral and spiritual sea-changes in man are· harder to bring about than the physical transformations of flesh and bone into pearl and coral on the ocean floor. But good and evil are pretty high-powered terms to apply to what is, after all, a comedy; and we need to remind ourselves that, although the play does deal with fundamental issues of human nature, it does not engage in the sort of profound probing of moral reality that takes place in Shakespeare's tragedies. For one thing, the fictional deck is stacked against evil from the start by the very nature of the island and its society. Hamlet, Lear, Macbeth, Othello would all be out of place here, and even Iago would dwindle into an Antonio if he had to operate in a world peopled with Calibans and Ariels. Antonio is murderous enough, but he lacks an environment in which he can be genuinely threatening. "Be not afeard," Caliban tells Stephano and Trinculo, "The isle is full of noises, / Sounds and sweet airs, that give delight and hurt not." (III.ii.144–45). It is an island that has painful pinches as well as sweet airs, but they are corrective pinches, and the general impression is of a place where, as Prospero reassures Miranda after the storm (I.ii.15], "There's no harm done."

If evil is contained or protectively enveloped by the island environment, we need to remember how much that environment is controlled by Prospero. His magic provides additional insulation against the inroads of evil, enabling us to contemplate the dialectic of corruption and redemption from a vantage point of emotional detachment (which, of course, is precisely what the dramatic art that controls Prospero's magical art also enables us to do). It may seem, in fact, that by equipping Prospero with magical power Shakespeare has not given evil a fair chance. But Prospero's magic is cooperative, not coercive. He cannot compel Alonzo to experience a reformation of ˌcharacter. If he could, all his elaborate manipulations of nature and reality—the illusion of shipwreck and storm, of the death of Ferdinand, of the banquet, of the dancing shapes—would be unnecessary. But his magic can create a scene or context in which Alonzo's better impulses, his capacity for "heart's sorrow / And a clear life ensuing" (III.iii.81–2), may appropriately express themselves. Prospero's magical art (or Shakespeare's dramatic art) cannot make the spiritually blind see again, though it can cast the light that makes vision possible. Thus it is significant that whereas Alonzo and Gonzalo are transfigured by their island experiences, and even Caliban can say "I'll be wise hereafter / And seek for grace" (V.i.294–95), neither Antonio nor Sebastian makes any overt gesture of penitence at the end. For them, it seems, discipline must come always from the outside, not from within. Finally, it is more important to note that the dominion of Prospero's magic does not extend to his own soul. There, like less gifted men, he must work with the familiar, awkward tools—

conscience, intelligence, understanding, sense of justice. It is not magic but his own hard-earned moral awareness that enables him to say in defense of mercy that "the rarer action is / In virtue than in vengeance" (V.i.27–28).

In structural movement, also, Shakespeare's play is more complex than escapist pastoral, which is conditioned by the notion that bucolic retreats are unqualified ideals for which characters purchase one-way tickets. In comic structure generally, however, withdrawal or escape is merely one phase of a development that concludes with the reintegration of individuals into a social order from which they were temporarily excluded: they withdraw, undergo transformations, and return. Prospero's island, like the pastoral forests of *Two Gentlemen of Verona, A Midsummer Night's Dream*, and *As You Like It*, is thus a regenerative waystation, not a terminal. The implication is that one comes to terms with social and political injustice in the real world, not by flights into freedom but by disciplined acceptance of responsibility in private and public life. In fact, Shakespeare is wonderfully aware how easily irresponsible license can parade under the banner of freedom: "Freedom, high-day high-day, freedom!" Caliban chants gaily as he goes off to rape Miranda and knock a nail through Prospero's head (II.ii.190). It is ironic that Prospero, who had earlier withdrawn into his ivory study, freeing himself from his political obligations (cf. I.ii.66ff.), comes to understand his responsibilities as governor of both others and himself in so unlikely a spot as the island. What this suggests is that the island is not merely a desert island somewhere in the Mediterranean but a microcosm of civilization as well.

Freedom and restraint, as suggested above, are important concepts in *The Tempest*, and the student ought to explore the various forms in which they are dramatized. There is, for instance, the totally free commonwealth imagined by Gonzalo (II.i.147ff.), which assumes the instinctive goodness of things in a state of nature. In contrast to this are the authoritarian restraints of Prospero, who has learned from direct experience how humane and liberal treatment is responded to by ignoble savages like Caliban (cf. I.ii.344ff.); the slavery that Ariel suffered while penned in the pine tree by Sycorax and the "slavery" he now accepts (unlike the other slave, Caliban) under Prospero; the "wooden slavery" undergone by Ferdinand, designed not to punish but to confirm love; and the "slavery" of marriage, which Prospero repeatedly admonishes Ferdinand and Miranda to accept as appropriate to the free (but not licentious) exercise of sexual desire. The transformation of the Italians is a matter either of physical restraints (the spells) or of an education into an acceptance of moral restraints. And even Prospero, who is free to employ his magical power as he chooses, learns freely to renounce it and to accept the limiting conditions of normal humanity. Thus, though the comic spirit of release characterizes the conclusion of *The Tempest*, Shakespeare underscores the fact that genuine freedom is as far from license as it is from slavery.

The Tempest

ALONSO   *King of Naples*
SEBASTIAN   *his brother*
PROSPERO   *the right Duke of Milan*
ANTONIO   *his brother, the usurping Duke of Milan*
FERDINAND   *son to the King of Naples*
GONZALO   *an honest old councilor*
ADRIAN ⎱ *lords*
FRANCISCO ⎰
CALIBAN   *a savage and deformed slave*
TRINCULO   *a jester*
STEPHANO   *a drunken butler*

MASTER   *of a ship*
BOATSWAIN
MARINERS
MIRANDA   *daughter to Prospero*
ARIEL   *an airy spirit*
IRIS ⎫
CERES ⎪
JUNO ⎬ *presented by spirits*
NYMPHS ⎪
REAPERS ⎭
OTHER SPIRITS   *attending on Prospero*

SCENE: [*A ship at sea;*] *an uninhabited island.*

ACT I

SCENE i. [*On a ship at sea;*] *a tempestuous noise of thunder and lightning heard.*

Enter a SHIPMASTER *and a* BOATSWAIN.

MASTER. Boatswain!
BOATSWAIN. Here, master. What cheer?
MASTER. Good, speak to the mariners. Fall to't yarely, or we run ourselves aground. Bestir, bestir.   [*Exit.*]

Enter MARINERS.

BOATSWAIN. Heigh, my hearts!   5
Cheerly, cheerly, my hearts! Yare, yare! Take in the topsail. Tend to the master's whistle. Blow till thou burst thy wind, if room enough!

Enter ALONSO, SEBASTIAN, ANTONIO, FERDINAND, GONZALO, *and others.*

ALONSO. Good boatswain, have care.   10
Where's the master? Play the men.
BOATSWAIN. I pray now, keep below.
ANTONIO. Where is the master, boatswain?
BOATSWAIN. Do you not hear him?   15
You mar our labor. Keep your cabins. You do assist the storm.
GONZALO. Nay, good, be patient.
BOATSWAIN. When the sea is. Hence! What cares these roarers for the   20
name of King? To cabin. Silence! Trouble us not.
GONZALO. Good, yet remember whom thou hast aboard.
BOATSWAIN. None that I more love   25
than myself. You are a councilor. If you can command these elements to silence, and work the peace of

---

I.i.3 *Good:* my good man.   4 *yarely:* quickly.   7 *Tend:* attend.   9 *room:* sea room.

11 *Play...men:* act like men.   28–29 *work... present:* bring us peace at once.

the present, we will not hand a rope more. Use your authority. If you 30 cannot, give thanks you have lived so long, and make yourself ready in your cabin for the mischance of the hour, if it so hap. Cheerly, good hearts! Out of our way, I say. 35

[*Exit.*]

GONZALO. I have great comfort from this fellow. Methinks he hath no drowning mark upon him, his complexion is perfect gallows. Stand fast, good Fate, to his hanging. Make 40 the rope of his destiny our cable, for our own doth little advantage. If he be not born to be hanged, our case is miserable.   [*Exeunt.*]

Re-enter BOATSWAIN.

BOATSWAIN. Down with the top- 45 mast! Yare! Lower, lower! Bring her to try with main course. [*a cry within*] A plague upon this howling! They are louder than the weather or our office. 50

Re-enter SEBASTIAN, ANTONIO, *and* GONZALO.

Yet again! What do you here? Shall we give o'er and drown? Have you a mind to sink?

SEBASTIAN. A pox o' your throat, you bawling, blasphemous, inchari- 55 table dog!

BOATSWAIN. Work you then.

ANTONIO. Hang, cur! hang, you whore-son, insolent noisemaker! We are less afraid to be drowned than thou 60 art.

GONZALO. I'll warrant him for drowning, though the ship were no stronger than a nutshell and as leaky as an unstanched wench. 65

37–39 *hath...gallows:* refers to the proverb "He that is born to be hanged will never be drowned." 47 *try...course:* i.e., use only the mainsail to heave her to; *course:* sail. 50 *office:* business. 65 *unstanched:* wide open.

BOATSWAIN. Lay her a-hold, a-hold! Set her two courses off to sea again; lay her off.

Enter MARINERS *wet.*

MARINERS. All lost! To prayers, to prayers! All lost!

BOATSWAIN. What, must our mouths be cold? 70

GONZALO. The king and prince at prayers! Let's assist them, For our case is as theirs.

SEBASTIAN.   I'm out of patience.

ANTONIO. We are merely cheated of our lives by drunkards. This wide-chapped rascal—would thou mightst lie drowning 75 The washing of ten tides!

GONZALO.   He'll be hanged yet, Though every drop of water swear against it And gape at widest to glut him.

A confused noise within:

"Mercy on us!"— "We split, we split!"—"Farewell my wife and children!"— "Farewell, brother!"—"We split, we split, we split!" 80

ANTONIO. Let's all sink with the king.

SEBASTIAN. Let's take leave of him.

Exeunt [ANTONIO *and* SEBASTIAN].

GONZALO. Now would I give a thousand furlongs of sea for an acre of barren ground, long heath, brown furze, 85 anything. The wills above be done! But I would fain die a dry death.

[*Exeunt.*]

SCENE ii. [*The island. Before* PROSPERO's *cell.*]

Enter PROSPERO *and* MIRANDA.

MIRANDA. If by your art, my dearest father, you have Put the wild waters in this roar, allay them.

---

74 *merely:* totally.

The sky, it seems, would pour down stinking pitch,
But that the sea, mounting to the welkin's cheek,
Dashes the fire out. O, I have suffered 5
With those that I saw suffer. A brave vessel,
Who had, no doubt, some noble creature in her,
Dashed all to pieces. O, the cry did knock
Against my very heart. Poor souls, they perished.
Had I been any god of power, I would 10
Have sunk the sea within the earth or ere
It should the good ship so have swallowed and
The fraughting souls within her.
PROSPERO.   Be collected.
No more amazement. Tell your piteous heart
There's no harm done.
MIRANDA.   O, woe the day!
PROSPERO.   No harm. 15
I have done nothing but in care of thee,
Of thee, my dear one, thee, my daughter, who
Art ignorant of what thou art, nought knowing
Of whence I am, nor that I am more better
Than Prospero, master of a full poor cell, 20
And thy no greater father.
MIRANDA.   More to know
Did never meddle with my thoughts.
PROSPERO.   'Tis time
I should inform thee farther. Lend thy hand,
And pluck my magic garment from me. So— [*Lays down his mantle.*]
Lie there, my art. Wipe thou thine eyes; have comfort. 25

The direful spectacle of the wreck, which touched
The very virtue of compassion in thee,
I have with such provision in mine art
So safely ordered that there is no soul,
No, not so much perdition as an hair, 30
Betid to any creature in the vessel
Which thou heard'st cry, which thou saw'st sink. Sit down,
For thou must now know farther.
MIRANDA.   You have often
Begun to tell me what I am, but stopped
And left me to a bootless inquisition, 35
Concluding "Stay, not yet."
PROSPERO.   The hour's now come.
The very minute bids thee ope thine ear.
Obey and be attentive. Canst thou remember
A time before we came unto this cell?
I do not think thou canst, for then thou wast not 40
Out three years old.
MIRANDA.   Certainly, sir, I can.
PROSPERO. By what? By any other house or person?
Of anything the image tell me, that
Hath kept with thy remembrance.
MIRANDA.   'Tis far off
And rather like a dream than an assurance 45
That my remembrance warrants. Had I not
Four or five women once that tended me?
PROSPERO. Thou hadst, and more, Miranda. But how is it
That this lives in thy mind? What seest thou else
In the dark backward and abysm of time? 50

I.ii.13 *fraughting:* freighted.   20 *full:* quite.   41 *out:* quite.

If thou remember'st aught ere thou
    camest here,
How thou camest here thou mayst.
MIRANDA.   But that I do not.
PROSPERO. Twelve year since, Miranda,
    twelve year since,
Thy father was the Duke of Milan
    and
A prince of power.
MIRANDA.   Sir, are not you
    my father?   55
PROSPERO. Thy mother was a piece of
    virtue, and
She said thou wast my daughter. And
    thy father
Was Duke of Milan, and thou his
    only heir
And princess, no worse issued.
MIRANDA.   O the heavens!
What foul play had we, that we came
    from thence?   60
Or blessed was 't we did?
PROSPERO.   Both, both, my girl.
By foul play, as thou say'st, were
    we heaved thence,
But blessedly holp hither.
MIRANDA.   O, my heart bleeds
To think o' the teen that I have
    turned you to,
Which is from my remembrance!
    Please you, farther.   65
PROSPERO. My brother and thy uncle,
    called Antonio—
I pray thee, mark me—that a brother
    should
Be so perfidious!—he whom, next
    thyself,
Of all the world I loved, and to him
    put
The manage of my state; as at that
    time   70
Through all the signories it was the
    first
And Prospero the prime duke, being
    so reputed
In dignity, and for the liberal arts

Without a parallel. Those being all
    my study,
The government I cast upon my
    brother   75
And to my state grew stranger, being
    transported
And rapt in secret studies. Thy false
    uncle—
Dost thou attend me?
MIRANDA.   Sir, most heedfully.
PROSPERO. Being once perfected how to
    grant suits,
How to deny them, who to advance
    and who   80
To trash for over-topping, new
    created
The creatures that were mine, I say,
    or changed 'em,
Or else new formed 'em—having both
    the key
Of officer and office, set all hearts i'
    the state
To what tune pleased his ear, that
    now he was   85
The ivy which had hid my princely
    trunk,
And sucked my verdure out on 't.
    Thou attend'st not.
MIRANDA. O, good sir, I do.
PROSPERO.   I pray thee, mark me.
I, thus neglecting worldly ends, all
    dedicated
To closeness and the bettering of my
    mind,   90
With that which, but by being so
    retired,
O'er-prized all popular rate, in my
    false brother
Awaked an evil nature. And my trust,
Like a good parent, did beget of
    him
A falsehood in its contrary as great   95

---

79 *perfected:* well practiced in. 81 *trash for*
over-topping: restrain from exceeding their
authority. 83 *key:* by which a stringed instrument is tuned. 90 *closeness:* privacy. 91
but...retired: except that it (i.e., bettering of
the mind) kept him away from his public
duties. 92 *O'er-prized...rate:* exceeded its
usual valuation.

---

56 *piece:* masterpiece. 59 *no worse issued:*
no less well born. 64 *teen:* sorrow. 65 *from:*
beyond. 71 *signories:* dukedoms.

As my trust was—which had indeed no limit,
A confidence sans bound. He being thus lorded,
Not only with what my revenue yielded,
But what my power might else exact, like one
Who having into truth, by telling of it, 100
Made such a sinner of his memory,
To credit his own lie, he did believe
He was indeed the duke. Out o' the substitution,
And executing the outward face of royalty,
With all prerogative, hence his ambition growing— 105
Dost thou hear?

MIRANDA.   Your tale, sir, would cure deafness.

PROSPERO. To have no screen between this part he played
And him he played it for, he needs will be
Absolute Milan. Me, poor man, my library
Was dukedom large enough. Of temporal royalties 110
He thinks me now incapable; confederates—
So dry he was for sway—wi' the King of Naples
To give him annual tribute, do him homage,
Subject his coronet to his crown and bend
The dukedom yet unbowed—alas, poor Milan!— 115
To most ignoble stooping.

MIRANDA.   O the heavens!

PROSPERO. Mark his condition and the event, then tell me

99–102 *like one...own lie:* who has told a lie so often he believes it himself. 103–5 *Out o'...prerogative:* because he substituted for me, playing my role and publicly exercising my powers. 111 *confederates:* joins in conspiracy. 112 *dry:* thirsty; *sway:* power. 117 *event:* sequel.

If this might be a brother.

MIRANDA.   I should sin
To think but nobly of my grandmother.
Good wombs have borne bad sons.

PROSPERO.   Now the condition. 120
This King of Naples, being an enemy
To me inveterate, hearkens my brother's suit.
Which was that he, in lieu o' the premises,
Of homage, and I know not how much tribute,
Should presently extirpate me and mine 125
Out of the dukedom and confer fair Milan
With all the honours on my brother. Whereon,
A treacherous army levied, one midnight
Fated to the purpose did Antonio open
The gates of Milan, and, i' the dead of darkness, 130
The ministers for the purpose hurried thence
Me and thy crying self.

MIRANDA.   Alack, for pity!
I, not remembering how I cried out then,
Will cry it o'er again: it is a hint
That wrings mine eyes to 't.

PROSPERO.   Hear a little further 135
And then I'll bring thee to the present business
Which now's upon's; without the which this story
Were most impertinent.

MIRANDA.   Wherefore did they not
That hour destroy us?

PROSPERO.   Well demanded, wench:
My tale provokes that question. Dear, they durst not, 140
So dear the love my people bore me; nor set

---

123 *in lieu o':* in return for. 141 *nor set:* nor did they dare set.

A mark so bloody on the business, but
With colours fairer painted their foul ends.
In few, they hurried us aboard a bark,
Bore us some leagues to sea, where they prepared 145
A rotten carcass of a butt, not rigged,
Nor tackle, sail, nor mast. The very rats
Instinctively have quit it. There they hoist us,
To cry to the sea that roared to us, to sigh
To the winds whose pity, sighing back again, 150
Did us but loving wrong.
MIRANDA.   Alack, what trouble
Was I then to you!
PROSPERO.   O, a cherubin
Thou wast that did preserve me. Thou didst smile,
Infused with a fortitude from heaven,
When I have decked the sea with drops full salt, 155
Under my burthen groaned. Which raised in me
An undergoing stomach, to bear up
Against what should ensue.
MIRANDA.   How came we ashore?
PROSPERO. By Providence divine.
Some food we had and some fresh water that 160
A noble Neapolitan, Gonzalo,
Out of his charity, who being then appointed
Master of this design, did give us, with
Rich garments, linens, stuffs and necessaries,
Which since have steaded much. So, of his gentleness, 165
Knowing I loved my books, he furnished me
From mine own library with volumes that

I prize above my dukedom.
MIRANDA.   Would I might
But ever see that man!
PROSPERO.   Now I arise.

[Resumes his mantle.]

Sit still, and hear the last of our sea-sorrow. 170
Here in this island we arrived. And here
Have I, thy schoolmaster, made thee more profit
Than other princesses can that have more time
For vainer hours and tutors not so careful.
MIRANDA. Heavens thank you for 't!
And now, I pray you, sir, 175
For still 'tis beating in my mind, your reason
For raising this sea-storm?
PROSPERO.   Know thus far forth.
By accident most strange, bountiful Fortune,
Now my dear lady, hath mine enemies
Brought to this shore. And by my prescience 180
I find my zenith doth depend upon
A most auspicious star, whose influence
If now I court not but omit, my fortunes
Will ever after droop. Here cease more questions,
Thou art inclined to sleep. 'Tis a good dulness, 185
And give it way. I know thou canst not choose. [MIRANDA *sleeps.*]
Come away, servant, come. I am ready now.
Approach, my Ariel, come.

Enter ARIEL.

ARIEL. All hail, great master! Grave sir, hail! I come
To answer thy best pleasure. Be 't to fly, 190

---

146 *butt:* tub of a boat. 165 *steaded much:* served us well.

183 *omit:* fail to court, or woo.

To swim, to dive into the fire, to ride
On the curled clouds, to thy strong bidding task
Ariel and all his quality.
PROSPERO.   Hast thou, spirit,
Performed to point the tempest that I bade thee?
ARIEL. To every article.   195
I boarded the king's ship. Now on the beak,
Now in the waist, the deck, in every cabin,
I flamed amazement. Sometime I'd divide,
And burn in many places. On the topmast,
The yards and bowsprit, would I flame distinctly,   200
Then meet and join. Jove's lightnings, the precursors
O' the dreadful thunder-claps, more momentary
And sight-outrunning were not. The fire and cracks
Of sulphurous roaring the most mighty Neptune
Seem to besiege and make his bold waves tremble,   205
Yea, his dread trident shake.
PROSPERO.   My brave spirit!
Who was so firm, so constant, that this coil
Would not infect his reason?
ARIEL.   Not a soul
But felt a fever of the mad and played
Some tricks of desperation. All but mariners   210
Plunged in the foaming brine and quit the vessel,
Then all afire with me. The king's son, Ferdinand,
With hair upstaring—then like reeds, not hair—

Was the first man that leaped, cried, "Hell is empty,
And all the devils are here."
PROSPERO.   Why, that's my spirit!   215
But was not this nigh shore?
ARIEL.   Close by, my master.
PROSPERO. But are they, Ariel, safe?
ARIEL.   Not a hair perished,
On their sustaining garments not a blemish,
But fresher than before. And, as thou badest me,
In troops I have dispersed them 'bout the isle.   220
The king's son have I landed by himself,
Whom I left cooling of the air with sighs
In an odd angle of the isle and sitting,
His arms in this sad knot.
PROSPERO.   Of the king's ship
The mariners say how thou hast disposed,   225
And all the rest o' the fleet.
ARIEL.   Safely in harbour
Is the king's ship. In the deep nook, where once
Thou call'dst me up at midnight to fetch dew
From the still-vexed Bermoothes, there she's hid.
The mariners all under hatches stowed,   230
Who, with a charm joined to their suffered labour,
I have left asleep. And for the rest o' the fleet
Which I dispersed, they all have met again
And are upon the Mediterranean flote,
Bound sadly home for Naples,   235
Supposing that they saw the king's ship wrecked
And his great person perish.
PROSPERO.   Ariel, thy charge

---

192 *task:* assign a job to. 193 *quality:* talents. 194 *to point:* perfectly in all respects. 198 *flamed amazement:* spread confusion and fear by appearing as flame. 206 *brave:* excellent. 207 *coil:* confusion.

---

229 *still-vexed:* constantly stormy. 234 *flote:* sea.

Exactly is performed. But there's more work—
What is the time o' the day?
ARIEL.   Past the mid season.
PROSPERO. At least two glasses. The time 'twixt six and now   240
Must by us both be spent most preciously.
ARIEL. Is there more toil? Since thou dost give me pains,
Let me remember thee what thou hast promised,
Which is not yet performed me.
PROSPERO.   How now? Moody?
What is 't thou canst demand?
ARIEL.   My liberty. 245
PROSPERO. Before the time be out? No more!
ARIEL.   I prithee,
Remember I have done thee worthy service,
Told thee no lies, made thee no mistakings, served
Without or grudge or grumblings. Thou didst promise
To bate me a full year.
PROSPERO.   Dost thou forget 250
From what a torment I did free thee?
ARIEL. No.
PROSPERO. Thou dost, and think'st it much to tread the ooze
Of the salt deep,
To run upon the sharp wind of the north,
To do me business in the veins o' the earth   255
When it is baked with frost.
ARIEL.   I do not, sir.
PROSPERO. Thou liest, malignant thing! Hast thou forgot
The foul witch Sycorax, who with age and envy
Was grown into a hoop? Hast thou forgot her?
ARIEL. No, sir.
PROSPERO.   Thou hast. Where was she born? Speak, tell me.   260

ARIEL. Sir, in Argier.
PROSPERO.   O, was she so? I must
Once in a month recount what thou hast been,
Which thou forget'st. This damned witch Sycorax,
For mischiefs manifold and sorceries terrible
To enter human hearing, from Argier,   265
Thou know'st, was banished. For one thing she did
They would not take her life. Is not this true?
ARIEL. Ay, sir.
PROSPERO. This blue-eyed hag was hither brought with child
And here was left by the sailors. Thou, my slave,   270
As thou report'st thyself, wast then her servant.
And, for thou wast a spirit too delicate
To act her earthy and abhorred commands,
Refusing her grand hests, she did confine thee,
By help of her more potent ministers   275
And in her most unmitigable rage,
Into a cloven pine. Within which rift
Imprisoned thou didst painfully remain
A dozen years. Within which space she died
And left thee there, where thou did'st vent thy groans   280
As fast as mill-wheels strike. Then was this island—
Save for the son that she did litter here,
A freckled whelp hag-born—not honoured with
A human shape.

---

240 *glasses:* hourglasses. 250 *bate me:* lessen my period of service by.

261 *Argier:* Algiers. 266 *one thing:* i.e., sexual intercourse (which left her pregnant with Caliban and therefore not liable to capital punishment). 274 *hests:* commands.

ARIEL.   Yes, Caliban her son.
PROSPERO. Dull thing, I say so—he,
    that Caliban   285
    Whom now I keep in service. Thou
        best know'st
    What torment I did find thee in. Thy
        groans
    Did make wolves howl and penetrate
        the breasts
    Of ever angry bears. It was a torment
    To lay upon the damned, which
        Sycorax   290
    Could not again undo. It was mine
        art,
    When I arrived and heard thee, that
        made gape
    The pine and let thee out.
ARIEL.   I thank thee, master.
PROSPERO. If thou more murmur'st, I
    will rend an oak
    And peg thee in his knotty entrails
        till   295
    Thou hast howled away twelve
        winters.
ARIEL.   Pardon, master,
    I will be correspondent to command
    And do my spiriting gently.
PROSPERO.   Do so,
    and after two days
    I will discharge thee.
ARIEL.   That's my noble master!
    What shall I do? Say what. What
        shall I do?   300
PROSPERO. Go make thyself like a
    nymph o' the sea. Be subject
    To no sight but thine and mine,
        invisible
    To every eyeball else. Go take this
        shape
    And hither come in 't. Go, hence
        with diligence!   *Exit* [ARIEL].
    Awake, dear heart, awake! Thou hast
        slept well.   305
    Awake!
MIRANDA. The strangeness of your
    story put
    Heaviness in me.
PROSPERO.   Shake it off. Come on,

We'll visit Caliban my slave, who
    never
Yields us kind answer.
MIRANDA.   'Tis a villain, sir,
    I do not love to look on.
PROSPERO.   But, as 'tis,   310
    We cannot miss him. He does make
        our fire,
    Fetch in our wood and serves in
        offices
    That profit us. What, ho! slave!
        Caliban!
    Thou earth, thou! Speak.
CALIBAN.   *within.* There's wood
    enough within.
PROSPERO. Come forth, I say! There's
    other business for thee.   315
    Come, thou tortoise! When?

Re-enter ARIEL *like a water nymph.*

    Fine apparition! My quaint Ariel,
    Hark in thine ear.
ARIEL.   My lord, it shall be done.
                              [*Exit.*]
PROSPERO. Thou poisonous slave, got
    by the devil himself
    Upon thy wicked dam, come
        forth!   320

[*Enter* CALIBAN.]

CALIBAN. As wicked dew as e'er my
    mother brushed
    With raven's feather from unwhole-
        some fen
    Drop on you both! A southwest blow
        on ye
    And blister you all o'er!
PROSPERO. For this, be sure, tonight
    thou shalt have cramps,   325
    Side stitches that shall pen thy
        breath up. Urchins
    Shall, for that vast of night that they
        may work,
    All exercise on thee. Thou shalt be
        pinched
    As thick as honeycomb, each pinch
        more stinging

---

297 *correspondent:* obedient.

311 *miss:* do without.   327 *vast:* desolate
period.

Than bees that made 'em.

CALIBAN.   I must eat my dinner. 330
This island's mine, by Sycorax my
   mother,
Which thou takest from me. When
   thou camest first,
Thou strokedst me, and madest much
   of me, wouldst give me
Water with berries in't. And teach
   me how
To name the bigger light, and how
   the less, 335
That burn by day and night. And
   then I loved thee,
And showed thee all the qualities o'
   th' isle,
The fresh springs, brine pits, barren
   place and fertile.
Cursed be I that did so! All the
   charms
Of Sycorax, toads, beetles, bats, light
   on you! 340
For I am all the subjects that you
   have,
Which first was mine own king. And
   here you sty me
In this hard rock whiles you do keep
   from me
The rest o' the island.

PROSPERO.   Thou most lying slave,
Whom stripes may move, not kind-
   ness! I have used thee, 345
Filth as thou art, with human care,
   and lodged thee
In mine own cell till thou didst seek
   to violate
The honour of my child.

CALIBAN. Oh, ho, oh ho! Would 't had
   been done!
Thou didst prevent me. I had peopled else 350
This isle with Calibans.

[PROSPERO.]   Abhorred slave,
Which any print of goodness wilt
   not take,
Being capable of all ill! I pitied thee,
Took pains to make thee speak,
   taught thee each hour

One thing or other. When thou didst
   not, savage, 355
Know thine own meaning, but
   wouldst gabble like
A thing most brutish, I endowed thy
   purposes
With words that made them known.
   But thy vile race,
Though thou didst learn, had that
   in't which good natures
Could not abide to be with. Therefore
   wast thou 360
Deservedly confined into this rock,
Who hadst deserved more than a
   prison.

CALIBAN. You taught me language, and
   my profit on't
Is I know how to curse. The red
   plague rid you
For learning me your language!

PROSPERO.   Hagseed, hence! 365
Fetch us in fuel, and be quick, thou'rt
   best,
To answer other business. Shrug'st
   thou, malice?
If thou neglect'st, or dost unwillingly
What I command, I'll rack thee with
   old cramps,
Fill all thy bones with achés, make
   thee roar 370
That beasts shall tremble at thy din.

CALIBAN. No, pray thee.
   [*aside*] I must obey. His art is of
      such power
It would control my dam's god,
   Setebos,
And make a vassal of him.

PROSPERO.   So, slave. Hence!

[*Exit* CALIBAN.]

Re-enter ARIEL, *invisible, playing and
singing;* [FERDINAND *following*].

ARIEL'S SONG.

Come unto these yellow sands, 375
   And then take hands.
Curtsied when you have and kissed

---

352 *print:* impression.

364 *rid:* destroy.   370 *achés:* pronounced
"aitches."

The wild waves whist,
Foot it featly here and there,
And, sweet sprites, the burden
bear.   380
BURTHEN. *dispersedly.* Hark, hark!
                              Bow-wow.
ARIEL. The watch dogs bark:
[BURTHEN. *dispersedly*] Bow-wow.
ARIEL. Hark, hark! I hear
    The strain of strutting chanticleer
    Cry— [BURTHEN.] cock-a-diddle-
    dow.   385
FERDINAND. Where should this music
    be? I' the air or the earth?
    It sounds no more. And, sure, it waits
    upon
    Some god o' the island. Sitting on a
    bank,
    Weeping again the king my father's
    wreck,
    This music crept by me upon the
    waters,   390
    Allaying both their fury and my
    passion
    With its sweet air. Thence I have
    followed it,
    Or it hath drawn me rather. But 'tis
    gone.
    No, it begins again.

ARIEL'S SONG.

Full fathom five thy father lies, 395
    Of his bones are coral made,
Those are pearls that were his eyes.
    Nothing of him that doth fade
But doth suffer a sea-change
Into something rich and strange. 400
Sea nymphs hourly ring his knell.
BURDEN. Ding-dong.
ARIEL. Hark! now I hear them—ding-
    dong, bell.
FERDINAND. The ditty does remember
    my drowned father.
    This is no mortal business. Nor no
    sound   405
    That the earth owes—I hear it now
    above me.

PROSPERO. The fringed curtains of thine
    eye advance
    And say what thou seest yond.
MIRANDA.   What is 't—a spirit?
    Lord, how it looks about! Believe me,
    sir,
    It carries a brave form. But 'tis a
    spirit.   410
PROSPERO. No, wench, it eats and sleeps
    and hath such senses
    As we have, such. This gallant which
    thou seest
    Was in the wreck; and, but he's
    something stained
    With grief (that's beauty's canker)
    thou mightst call him
    A goodly person. He hath lost his
    fellows   415
    And strays about to find 'em.
MIRANDA.   I might call him
    A thing divine, for nothing natural
    I ever saw so noble.
PROSPERO.   [*aside*] It goes on, I see,
    As my soul prompts it. Spirit, fine
    spirit! I'll free thee
    Within two days for this.
FERDINAND.   Most sure,
    the goddess   420
    On whom these airs attend! Vouch-
    safe my prayer
    May know if you remain upon this
    island,
    And that you will some good instruc-
    tion give
    How I may bear me here. My prime
    request,
    Which I do last pronounce, is, O you
    wonder!   425
    If you be maid or no?
MIRANDA.   No wonder, sir,
    But certainly a maid.
FERDINAND.   My language!
    Heavens!
    I am the best of them that speak this
    speech,
    Were I but where 'tis spoken.

---

378 *whist:* silent. 379 *featly:* nimbly. 380
burden: refrain. 406 *owes:* owns, possesses.

410 *brave:* fine. 418 *It goes on:* i.e., Prospero's plan that they fall in love is working
out. 422 *May know:* may I know; *remain:*
dwell.

PROSPERO. How? The best?
What wert thou, if the King of
Naples heard thee? 430
FERDINAND. A single thing, as I am
now, that wonders
To hear thee speak of Naples. He
does hear me,
And that he does I weep. Myself am
Naples,
Who with mine eyes, never since at
ebb, beheld
The king my father wrecked.
MIRANDA. Alack, for mercy! 435
FERDINAND. Yes, faith, and all his
lords, the Duke of Milan
And his brave son being twain.
PROSPERO. [*aside*] The Duke of Milan
And his more braver daughter could
control thee,
If now 'twere fit to do 't. At the first
sight
They have changed eyes. Delicate
Ariel, 440
I'll set thee free for this. [*to* FERDI-
NAND] A word, good sir.
I fear you have done yourself some
wrong. A word.
MIRANDA. Why speaks my father so
ungently? This
Is the third man that e'er I saw, the
first
That e'er I sighed for. Pity move my
father 445
To be inclined my way!
FERDINAND. O, if a virgin,
And your affection not gone forth,
I'll make you
The queen of Naples.
PROSPERO. Soft, sir! one
word more.
[*aside*] They are both in either's
powers. But this swift business
I must uneasy make, lest too light
winning 450
Make the prize light. [*to* FERDI-

NAND] One word more. I charge
thee
That thou attend me. Thou dost here
usurp
The name thou owest not, and hast
put thyself
Upon this island as a spy, to win it
From me, the lord on 't.
FERDINAND. No, as I am a man. 455
MIRANDA. There's nothing ill can dwell
in such a temple.
If the ill spirit have so fair a house,
Good things will strive to dwell
with 't.
PROSPERO. Follow me.
Speak not you for him. He's a traitor.
Come,
I'll manacle thy neck and feet to-
gether. 460
Sea-water shalt thou drink; thy food
shall be
The fresh-brook muscles, withered
roots and husks
Wherein the acorn cradled. Follow.
FERDINAND. No.
I will resist such entertainment till
Mine enemy has more power.

Draws, and is charmed from moving.

MIRANDA. O dear father, 465
Make not too rash a trial of him, for
He's gentle and not fearful.
PROSPERO. What? I say,
My foot my tutor? Put thy sword
up, traitor,
Who makest a show but darest not
strike, thy conscience
Is so possessed with guilt. Come from
thy ward, 470
For I can here disarm thee with this
stick
And make thy weapon drop.
MIRANDA. Beseech you, father.
PROSPERO. Hence! Hang not on my
garments.
MIRANDA. Sir, have pity.
I'll be his surety.

---

431 *single:* solitary. 433 *that:* because. 437
being twain: being two of those who drowned.
447 *affection...forth:* love not already given
another.

---

467 *fearful:* to be feared, dangerous. 470
ward: fighting stance.

PROSPERO.　　　Silence! One word more
　Shall make me chide thee, if not hate
　　thee. What!　　　　　　　475
　An advocate for an imposter! Hush!
　Thou think'st there is no more such
　　shapes as he,
　Having seen but him and Caliban.
　　Foolish wench!
　To the most of men this is a Caliban
　And they to him are angels.
MIRANDA.　　　My affections　480
　Are then most humble; I have no
　　ambition
　To see a goodlier man.
PROSPERO.　　　Come on, obey.
　Thy nerves are in their infancy again
　And have no vigour in them.
FERDINAND.　　　So they are.
　My spirits, as in a dream, are all
　　bound up.　　　　　　485
　My father's loss, the weakness which
　　I feel,
　The wreck of all my friends, nor this
　　man's threats,
　To whom I am subdued, are but
　　light to me,

Might I but through my prison once
　a day
Behold this maid. All corners else o'
　the earth　　　　　　490
Let liberty make use of; space enough
Have I in such a prison.
PROSPERO.　　　[*aside*] It works.
　[*to* FERDINAND] Come on.
Thou hast done well, fine Ariel! [*to*
　FERDINAND] Follow me.
　[*To* ARIEL.] Hark what thou else
　shalt do me.
MIRANDA.　　　Be of comfort.
My father's of a better nature,
　sir,　　　　　　　495
Than he appears by speech. This is
　unwonted
Which now came from him.
PROSPERO.　　　Thou shalt be as free
As mountain winds. But then exactly
　do
All points of my command.
ARIEL.　　　　　To the syllable.
PROSPERO. Come, follow. Speak not for
　him.　　　　　[*Exeunt.*]　500

ACT II

SCENE i. [*Another part of the island.*]

Enter ALONSO, SEBASTIAN, ANTONIO,
GONZALO, ADRIAN, FRANCISCO, *and*
others.

GONZALO. Beseech you, sir, be merry.
　You have cause,
　So have we all, of joy, for our escape
　Is much beyond our loss. Our hint
　　of woe
　Is common. Every day some sailor's
　　wife,
　The masters of some merchant, and
　　the merchant　　　　5
　Have just our theme of woe. But for
　　the miracle—
　I mean our preservation—few in
　　millions

Can speak like us. Then wisely, good
　sir, weigh
Our sorrow with our comfort.
ALONSO.　　　　Prithee, peace.
SEBASTIAN. He receives comfort like
　cold porridge.　　　　　10
ANTONIO. The visitor will not give him
　o'er so.
SEBASTIAN. Look, he's winding up the
　watch of his wit. By and by it will
　strike.
GONZALO. Sir—
SEBASTIAN. One. Tell.　　　　15
GONZALO. When every grief is enter-
　tained that's offered,
　Comes to the entertainer—
SEBASTIAN. A dollar.
GONZALO. Dolour comes to him, indeed.

---

479 *To:* compared to.

II.i.15 *Tell:* count.

You have spoken truer than you purposed. 20

SEBASTIAN. You have taken it wiselier than I meant you should.

GONZALO. Therefore, my lord—

ANTONIO. Fie, what a spendthrift is he of his tongue!

ALONSO. I prithee, spare. 25

GONZALO. Well, I have done. But yet—

SEBASTIAN. He will be talking.

ANTONIO. Which, of he or Adrian, for a good wager, first begins to crow?

SEBASTIAN. The old cock. 30

ANTONIO. The cockerel.

SEBASTIAN. Done. The wager?

ANTONIO. A laughter.

SEBASTIAN. A match!

ADRIAN. Though this island seem to be desert— 35

SEBASTIAN. Ha, ha, ha!—So, you're paid.

ADRIAN. Uninhabitable and almost inaccessible—

SEBASTIAN. Yet—

ADRIAN. Yet—

ANTONIO. He could not miss 't. 40

ADRIAN. It must needs be of subtle, tender and delicate temperance.

ANTONIO. Temperance was a delicate wench.

SEBASTIAN. Ay, and a subtle, as he most learnedly delivered. 45

ADRIAN. The air breathes upon us here most sweetly.

SEBASTIAN. As if it had lungs and rotten ones.

ANTONIO. Or as 'twere perfumed by a fen.

GONZALO. Here is everything advantageous to life.

ANTONIO. True, save means to live. 50

SEBASTIAN. Of that there's none, or little.

GONZALO. How lush and lusty the grass looks! How green!

ANTONIO. The ground indeed is tawny.

SEBASTIAN. With an eye of green in 't. 55

ANTONIO. He misses not much.

SEBASTIAN. No, he doth but mistake the truth totally.

GONZALO. But the rarity of it is— which is indeed almost beyond credit—

SEBASTIAN. As many vouched rarities are. 60

GONZALO. That our garments, being, as they were, drenched in the sea, hold notwithstanding their freshness and glosses, being rather new-dyed than stained with salt water. 65

ANTONIO. If but one of his pockets could speak, would it not say he lies?

SEBASTIAN. Ay, or very falsely pocket up his report. 69

GONZALO. Methinks our garments are now as fresh as when we put them on first in Afric, at the marriage of the king's fair daughter Claribel to the King of Tunis.

SEBASTIAN. 'Twas a sweet marriage, and we prosper well in our return.

ADRIAN. Tunis was never graced before with such a paragon to their queen. 75

GONZALO. Not since widow Dido's time.

ANTONIO. Widow! A pox o' that! How came that widow in? Widow Dido!

SEBASTIAN. What if he had said "widower Æneas" too? Good Lord, how you take it! 80

ADRIAN. "Widow Dido" said you? You make me study of that. She was of Carthage, not of Tunis.

GONZALO. This Tunis, sir, was Carthage. 85

---

25 *spare:* save your words. 36 *So...paid:* i.e., I just laughed, thus paying the bet. 42 *temperance:* temperature.

55 *eye:* trace. 75 *to:* for. 76 *Dido:* Dido was Queen of Carthage. In Virgil's *Aeneid* she falls in love with Aeneas, who is enroute from the ruined Troy to Italy, and kills herself when he leaves. Antonio and Sebastian ridicule Gonzalo for calling her "widow" when she was not married to Aeneas; but Gonzalo is right since she was married and widowed before Aeneas arrived in Carthage, as he is also right about modern Tunis being ancient Carthage.

ADRIAN. Carthage?

GONZALO. I assure you, Carthage.

SEBASTIAN. His word is more than the miraculous harp: he hath raised the wall and houses too.   90

ANTONIO. What impossible matter will he make easy next?

SEBASTIAN. I think he will carry this island home in his pocket and give it his son for an apple.

ANTONIO. And, sowing the kernels of it in the sea, bring forth more islands.

GONZALO. Ay.

ANTONIO. Why, in good time.   95

GONZALO. Sir, we were talking that our garments seem now as fresh as when we were at Tunis at the marriage of your daughter, who is now queen.

ANTONIO. And the rarest that e'er   100 came there.

SEBASTIAN. Bate, I beseech you, widow Dido.

ANTONIO. O, widow Dido! Ay, widow Dido.

GONZALO. Is not, sir, my doublet as fresh as the first day I wore it? I mean, in a sort.

ANTONIO. That sort was well fished for.

GONZALO. When I wore it at your daughter's marriage?   105

ALONZO. You cram these words into mine ears against

The stomach of my sense. Would I had never

Married my daughter there! For, coming thence,

My son is lost and, in my rate, she too

Who is so far from Italy removed 110

I ne'er again shall see her. O thou mine heir

Of Naples and of Milan, what strange fish

Hath made his meal on thee?

FRANCISCO.   Sir, he may live.

I saw him beat the surges under him

And ride upon their backs. He trod the water,   115

Whose enmity he flung aside, and breasted

The surge most swoln that met him. His bold head

'Bove the contentious waves he kept, and oared

Himself with his good arms in lusty stroke

To the shore, that o'er his wave-worn basis bowed,   120

As stooping to relieve him. I not doubt

He came alive to land.

ALONSO.   No, no, he's gone.

SEBASTIAN. Sir, you may thank yourself for this great loss,

That would not bless our Europe with your daughter,

But rather lose her to an African,   125

Where she, at least, is banished from your eye,

Who hath cause to wet the grief on 't.

ALONSO. Prithee, peace.

SEBASTIAN. You were kneeled to and importuned otherwise

By all of us, and the fair soul herself

Weighed   between   loathness   and obedience, at   130

Which end o' the beam should bow. We have lost your son,

I fear, forever. Milan and Naples have

Moe widows in them of this business' making

Than we bring men to comfort them. The fault's your own.

ALONSO.   So is the dear'st o' the loss.   135

GONZALO. My lord Sebastian,

The truth you speak doth lack some
    gentleness
And time to speak it in. You rub the
    sore,
When you should bring the plaster.
SEBASTIAN. Very well.
ANTONIO. And most chirurgeonly.   140
GONZALO. It is foul weather in us all,
    good sir,
When you are cloudy.
SEBASTIAN.   Foul weather?
ANTONIO.   Very foul.
GONZALO. Had I plantation of this isle,
    my lord—
ANTONIO. He'd sow 't with nettle-seed.
SEBASTIAN. Or docks, or mallows.
GONZALO. And were the king on 't,
    what would I do?   145
SEBASTIAN. 'Scape being drunk for
    want of wine.
GONZALO. I' the commonwealth I would
    by contraries
Execute all things. For no kind of
    traffic
Would I admit, no name of magis-
    trate.
Letters should not be known. Riches,
    poverty,   150
And use of service, none. Contract,
    succession,
Bourn, bound of land, tilth, vineyard,
    none.
No use of metal, corn, or wine, or oil;
No occupation, all men idle, all;
And women too, but innocent and
    pure;   155
No sovereignty—
SEBASTIAN.   Yet he would be
    king on 't.
ANTONIO. The latter end of his com-
    monwealth forgets the beginning.
GONZALO. All things in common nature
    should produce
Without sweat or endeavour. Trea-
    son, felony,   160
Sword, pike, knife, gun, or need of
    any engine

Would I not have; but nature should
    bring forth
Of it own kind, all foison, all abun-
    dance,
To feed my innocent people.
SEBASTIAN. No marrying 'mong his sub-
    jects?   165
ANTONIO. None, man, all idle—whores
    and knaves.
GONZALO. I would with such perfection
    govern, sir,
To excel the golden age.
SEBASTIAN.   God save his majesty!
ANTONIO. Long live Gonzalo!
GONZALO.   And—do
    you mark me, sir?
ALONSO. Prithee, no more. Thou dost
    talk nothing to me.   170
GONZALO. I do well believe your high-
    ness, and did it to minister occasion
    to these gentlemen, who are of such
    sensible and nimble lungs that they
    always use to laugh at nothing.   175
ANTONIO. 'Twas you we laughed at.
GONZALO. Who in this kind of merry
    fooling am nothing to you—so you
    may continue and laugh at nothing
    still.
ANTONIO. What a blow was there
    given!   180
SEBASTIAN. An it had not fallen flat-
    long.
GONZALO. You are gentlemen of brave
    mettle. You would lift the moon out of
    her sphere, if she would contin-   185
    ue in it five weeks without changing.

Enter ARIEL *[invisible] playing solemn
music.*

SEBASTIAN. We would so, and then go
    a bat-fowling.
ANTONIO. Nay, good my lord, be not
    angry.
GONZALO. No, I warrant you, I will
    not adventure my discretion so weak-
    ly. Will you laugh me asleep, for
    I am very heavy?

---

140 *chirurgeonly:* surgeonlike.   143 *plantation:* colonization (though taken by Antonio
in the sense of "planting").

163 *it:* its; *foison:* plenty.   187 *bat-fowling:*
hunting birds at night with torches and bats
(sticks).

ANTONIO. Go sleep, and hear us. 190

[*All sleep except* ALONSO, SEBASTIAN, *and* ANTONIO.]

ALONSO. What, all so soon asleep! I wish mine eyes
Would, with themselves, shut up my thoughts. I find
They are inclined to do so.
SEBASTIAN.   Please you, sir,
Do not omit the heavy offer of it.
It seldom visits sorrow; when it doth, 195
It is a comforter.
ANTONIO.   We two, my lord,
Will guard your person while you take your rest,
And watch your safety.
ALONSO.   Thank you.
Wondrous heavy.

[ALONSO *sleeps. Exit* ARIEL.]

SEBASTIAN. What a strange drowsiness possesses them!
ANTONIO. It is the quality o' the climate.
SEBASTIAN. Why 200
Doth it not then our eyelids sink?
I find not
Myself disposed to sleep.
ANTONIO.   Nor I. My spirits are nimble.
They fell together all, as by consent;
They dropped as by a thunder-stroke. What might,
Worthy Sebastian—? O, what might —?—No more— 205
And yet methinks I see it in thy face.
What thou shouldst be. The occasion speaks thee, and
My strong imagination sees a crown
Dropping upon thy head.
SEBASTIAN.   What, art thou waking?
ANTONIO. Do you not hear me speak?
SEBASTIAN. I do, and surely 210
It is a sleepy language and thou speak'st
Out of thy sleep. What is it thou didst say?

This is a strange repose, to be asleep
With eyes wide open—standing, speaking, moving,
And yet so fast asleep.
ANTONIO.   Noble Sebastian, 215
Thou let'st thy fortune sleep—die, rather—wink'st
Whiles thou art waking.
SEBASTIAN.   Thou dost snore distinctly.
There's meaning in thy snores.
ANTONIO. I am more serious than my custom. You
Must be so too, if heed me; which to do 220
Trebles thee o'er.
SEBASTIAN.   Well, I am standing water.
ANTONIO. I'll teach you how to flow.
SEBASTIAN.   Do so. To ebb
Hereditary sloth instructs me.
ANTONIO.   O,
If you but knew how you the purpose cherish
Whiles thus you mock it! How in stripping it 225
You more invest it! Ebbing men, indeed,
Most often do so near the bottom run
By their own fear or sloth.
SEBASTIAN.   Prithee, say on.
The setting of thine eye and cheek proclaim
A matter from thee, and a birth indeed 230
Which throes thee much to yield.
ANTONIO.   Thus, sir:
Although this lord of weak remembrance, this,

---

220 *if heed me:* if you are to pay proper attention to me. 221 *Trebles thee o'er:* will triple your importance in the world; *standing water:* still water, i.e., inclined in no particular direction. 222–23 *To ebb...me:* I ebb (am retiring) because I am the younger son; the first-born son flows (advances). 223–26 *O...invest it:* In mocking the situation you suggest the solution to it, which is to eliminate the real hereditary obstacle, Alonzo. 232 *this lord:* Gonzalo.

Who shall be of as little memory
When he is earthed, hath here almost
persuaded—
For he's a spirit of persuasion,
only   235
Professes to persuade—the king his
son's alive,
'Tis as impossible that he's un-
drowned
As he that sleeps here swims.
SEBASTIAN.   I have no hope
That he's undrowned.
ANTONIO.   O, out of that
"no hope"
What great hope have you! No hope
that way is   240
Another way so high a hope that
even
Ambition cannot pierce a wink
beyond,
But doubt discovery there. Will you
grant with me
That Ferdinand is drowned?
SEBASTIAN.   He's gone.
ANTONIO.   Then, tell me,
Who's the next heir of Naples?
SEBASTIAN.   Claribel. 245
ANTONIO. She that is queen of Tunis,
she that dwells
Ten leagues beyond man's life, she
that from Naples
Can have no note, unless the sun
were post—
The man i' the moon's too slow—
till newborn chins
Be rough and razorable. She that
from whom   250
We all were sea-swallowed, though
some cast again,
And by that destiny to perform an
act
Whereof what's past is prologue, what
to come
In yours and my discharge.
SEBASTIAN.   What stuff
is this! How say you?

'Tis true, my brother's daughter's
queen of Tunis,   255
So is she heir of Naples, 'twixt which
regions
There is some space.
ANTONIO.   A space whose
every cubit
Seems to cry out, "How shall that
Claribel
Measure us back to Naples? Keep in
Tunis,
And let Sebastian wake." Say this
were death   260
That now hath seized them—why,
they were no worse
Than now they are. There be that
can rule Naples
As well as he that sleeps, lords that
can prate
As amply and unnecessarily
As this Gonzalo. I myself could
make   265
A chough of as deep chat. O, that
you bore
The mind that I do! What a sleep
were this
For your advancement! Do you
understand me?
SEBASTIAN. Methinks I do.
ANTONIO.   And how
does your content
Tender your own good fortune?
SEBASTIAN.   I remember 270
You did supplant your brother Pros-
pero.
ANTONIO. True.
And look how well my garments sit
upon me,
Much feater than before. My bro-
ther's servants
Were then my fellows; now they are
my men.
SEBASTIAN. But, for your con-
science?   275
ANTONIO. Ay, sir, where lies that? If
'twere a kibe,

---

234 *earthed:* buried. 248 *Can have no note:* cannot hear what has happened, so distant from Naples is Tunis. 250 *from whom:* coming from whom. 254 *discharge:* power to accomplish.

259 *Measure us back:* find (her) way. 266 *chough...chat:* I could make a crow talk as wisely. 269–70 *content...fortune:* How do you like your good fortune? 273 *feater:* more handsomely. 276 *kibe:* sore heel.

'Twould put me to my slipper; but
 I feel not
This deity in my bosom. Twenty
 consciences
That stand 'twixt me and Milan,
 candied be they
And melt ere they molest! Here lies
 your brother,   280
No better than the earth he lies
 upon,
If he were that which now he's like,
 that's dead.
Whom I, with this obedient steel,
 three inches of it,
Can lay to bed forever whiles you,
 doing thus,
To the perpetual wink for aye might
 put   285
This ancient morsel, this Sir Pru-
 dence, who
Should not upbraid our course. For
 all the rest,
They'll take suggestion as a cat laps
 milk.
They'll tell the clock to any business
 that
We say befits the hour.
SEBASTIAN.   Thy case, dear
 friend,   290
Shall be my precedent. As thou got'st
 Milan,
I'll come by Naples. Draw thy
 sword. One stroke
Shall free thee from the tribute which
 thou payest,
And I the king shall love thee.
ANTONIO.   Draw together,
And when I rear my hand, do you
 the like,   295
To fall it on Gonzalo.
SEBASTIAN.   O, but one
 word. [*They talk apart.*]

Re-enter [ARIEL *invisible*], *with music
and song.*

ARIEL. My master through his art
 foresees the danger

That you, his friend, are in, and sends
 me forth—
For else his project dies—to keep
 them living.

[*Sings in* GONZALO's *ear.*]

While you here do snoring lie,   300
Open-eyed conspiracy
  His time doth take.
If of life you keep a care,
  Shake off slumber, and beware.
  Awake, awake!   305
ANTONIO. Then let us both be sudden.
GONZALO. Now, good angels
 Preserve the king! [*They wake.*]
ALONSO. Why, how now? Ho, awake!
 Why are you drawn?
Wherefore this ghastly looking?
GONZALO.   What's the matter?
SEBASTIAN. Whiles we stood here secur-
 ing your repose,   310
Even now, we heard a hollow burst
 of bellowing
Like bulls, or rather lions. Did 't
 not wake you?
It struck mine ear most terribly.
ALONSO.   I heard nothing.
ANTONIO. O, 'twas a din to fright a
 monster's ear,
To make an earthquake! Sure, it
 was the roar   315
Of a whole herd of lions.
ALONSO.   Heard you
 this, Gonzalo?
GONZALO. Upon mine honour, sir, I
 heard a humming,
And that a strange one too, which
 did awake me.
I shaked you, sir, and cried. As mine
 eyes opened,
I saw their weapons drawn. There
 was a noise,   320
That's verily. 'Tis best we stand upon
 our weapons
Or that we quit this place. Let's draw
 our weapons.
ALONSO. Lead off this ground, and let's
 make further search
For my poor son.
GONZALO.   Heavens keep him
 from these beasts!

For he is, sure, i' the island.
ALONSO.   Lead away. 325
ARIEL. Prospero my lord shall know
    what I have done:
So, king, go safely on to seek thy son.

                              Exeunt.

SCENE ii. [*Another part of the island.*]

Enter CALIBAN *with a burden of wood.
A noise of thunder heard.*

CALIBAN. All the infections that the
    sun sucks up
    From bogs, fens, flats, on Prosper
        fall and make him
    By inchmeal a disease! His spirits
        hear me
    And yet I needs must curse. But
        they'll nor pinch,
    Fright me with urchin-shows, pitch
        me i' the mire,   5
    Nor lead me, like a firebrand, in the
        dark
    Out of my way, unless he bid 'em.
        But
    For every trifle are they set upon me.
    Sometime like apes that mow and
        chatter at me
    And after bite me, then like hedge-
        hogs which   10
    Lie tumbling in my barefoot way and
        mount
    Their pricks at my footfall. Some-
        time am I
    All wound with adders who with
        cloven tongues
    Do hiss me into madness.

Enter TRINCULO.

                         Lo, now, lo!
    Here comes a spirit of his, and to
        torment me   15
    For bringing wood in slowly. I'll fall
        flat—
    Perchance he will not mind me.
TRINCULO. Here's neither bush nor

shrub, to bear off any weather at
all, and another storm brewing.   20
I hear it sing i' the wind. Yond same
black cloud, yond huge one, looks
like a foul bombard that would shed
his liquor. If it should thunder as
it did before, I know not where   25
to hide my head. Yond same cloud
cannot choose but fall by pailfuls.
What have we here, a man or a fish?
Dead or alive? A fish. He smells like
a fish, a very ancient and fish-   30
like smell, a kind of not of the newest
Poor-John. A strange fish! Were
I in England now, as once I was,
and had but this fish painted, not a
holiday fool there but would give   35
a piece of silver. There would this
monster make a man. Any strange
beast there makes a man. When they
will not give a doit to relieve a lame
beggar, they will lay out ten to   40
see a dead Indian. Legged like a man
and his fins like arms! Warm o' my
troth! I do now let loose my opinion,
hold it no longer: this is no fish, but
an islander that hath lately suf-   45
fered by a thunderbolt. [*thunder*]
Alas, the storm is come again! My
best way is to creep under his gaberdine; there is no other shelter here-
about. Misery acquaints a man with   50
strange bed-fellows. I will here shroud
till the dregs of the storm be past.

Enter STEPHANO, *singing:* [*a bottle in
his hand.*]

STEPHANO. I shall no more to sea, to
    sea,
    Here shall I die ashore—
This is a very scurvy tune to   55
sing at a man's funeral. Well, here's
my comfort. *Drinks. Sings.*
    The master, the swabber, the boat-
        swain and I,
    The gunner and his mate

II.ii.3 *By inchmeal:* inch by inch. 5 *urchin-
shows:* apparitions. 9 *mow:* make faces.

19 *bear off:* fend off. 32 *Poor-John:* salted
hake (codfish). 39 *doit:* small coin. 48
gaberdine: cloak. 51 *shroud:* take shelter.

Loved Mall, Meg and Marian and
    Margery,   60
      But none of us cared for Kate.
      For she had a tongue with a
        tang,
      Would cry to a sailor, Go hang!
She loved not the savour of tar nor
    of pitch,
Yet a tailor might scratch her
    where'er she did itch.   65
      Then to sea, boys, and let her
      go hang!
This is a scurvy tune too, but here's
my comfort. *Drinks.*

CALIBAN. Do not torment me—Oh!

STEPHANO. What's the matter? Have we
devils here? Do you put tricks   70
upon 's with savages and men of Ind,
ha? I have not 'scaped drowning to
be afeard now of your four legs, for it
hath been said, As proper a man as
ever went on four legs cannot   75
make him give ground. And it shall be
said so again while Stephano breathes
at nostrils.

CALIBAN. The spirit torments me—Oh!

STEPHANO. This is some monster of   80
the isle with four legs, who hath got,
as I take it, an ague. Where the
devil should he learn our language?
I will give him some relief if it be
but for that. If I can recover him   85
and keep him tame and get to Naples
with him, he's a present for any
emperor that ever trod on neat's
leather.

CALIBAN. Do not torment me, pri-   90
thee. I'll bring my wood home faster.

STEPHANO. He's in his fit now and does
not talk after the wisest. He shall
taste of my bottle. If he have never
drunk wine afore, it will go near   95
to remove his fit. If I can recover him
and keep him tame, I will not take
too much for him. He shall pay for
him that hath him, and that soundly.

CALIBAN. Thou dost me yet but   100
little hurt; thou wilt anon, I know it
by thy trembling. Now Prosper works
upon thee.

STEPHANO. Come on your ways. Open
your mouth. Here is that which   105
will give language to you, cat. Open
your mouth. This will shake your
shaking, I can tell you, and that
soundly. You cannot tell who's your
friend: open your chaps again.   110

TRINCULO. I should know that voice.
It should be—but he is drowned.
And these are devils! O defend me!

STEPHANO. Four legs and two voices—
a most delicate monster! His   115
forward voice now is to speak well of
his friend, his backward voice is to
utter foul speeches and to detract. If
all the wine in my bottle will recover
him, I will help his ague. Come.   120
Amen! I will pour some in thy other
mouth.

TRINCULO. Stephano!

STEPHANO. Doth thy other mouth call
me? Mercy, mercy! This is a   125
devil, and no monster. I will leave
him, I have no long spoon.

TRINCULO. Stephano! If thou beest
Stephano, touch me and speak to
me, for I am Trinculo—be not   130
afeard—thy good friend Trinculo.

STEPHANO. If thou beest Trinculo, come
forth. I'll pull thee by the lesser
legs. If any be Trinculo's legs, these
are they. Thou art very Trinculo   135
indeed! How camest thou to be the
siege of this moon-calf? Can he vent
Trinculos?

TRINCULO. I took him to be killed with
a thunderstroke. But art thou   140
not drowned, Stephano? I hope now
thou art not drowned. Is the storm

---

103 *trembling:* symptom of demonic possession. 106 *cat:* refers to the proverb, "Good
liquor will make a cat speak." 127 *long
spoon:* refers to the proverb, "He that sups
with the devil has need of a long spoon."
137 *siege:* excrement; *moon-calf:* monstrosity,
abortion (supposedly caused by the moon).

---

71 *Ind:* India (vaguely, the East). 74 *proper:*
handsome. 85 *recover:* restore, heal. 88–89
neat's leather: cowhide.

overblown? I hid me under the dead moon-calf's gaberdine for fear of the storm. And art thou living, Ste- 145 phano? O Stephano, two Neapolitans 'scaped!

STEPHANO. Prithee, do not turn me about, my stomach is not constant.

CALIBAN. [*aside*] These be fine things, an if they be not sprites. 150 That's a brave god and bears celestial liquor. I will kneel to him.

STEPHANO. How didst thou 'scape? How camest thou hither? Swear by this bottle how thou camest 155 hither. I escaped upon a butt of sack which the sailors heaved o'erboard, by this bottle! which I made of the bark of a tree with mine own hands since I was cast ashore. 160

CALIBAN. I'll swear upon that bottle to be thy true subject, for the liquor is not earthly.

STEPHANO. Here, swear then how thou escapedst. 165

TRINCULO. Swum ashore, man, like a duck. I can swim like a duck, I'll be sworn.

STEPHANO. Here, kiss the book. Though thou canst swim like a duck, 170 thou art made like a goose.

TRINCULO. O Stephano, hast any more of this?

STEPHANO. The whole butt, man. My cellar is in a rock by the sea- 175 side where my wine is hid. How now, moon-calf! How does thine ague?

CALIBAN. Hast thou not dropped from heaven?

STEPHANO. Out o' the moon, I do 180 assure thee. I was the man i' the moon when time was.

CALIBAN. I have seen thee in her and I do adore thee. My mistress showed me thee and thy dog and thy bush. 185

STEPHANO. Come, swear to that. Kiss the book. I will furnish it anon with new contents. Swear.

TRINCULO. By this good light, this is a very shallow monster! I afeard 190 of him? A very weak monster! The man i' the moon! A most poor credulous monster! Well drawn, monster, in good sooth!

CALIBAN. I'll show thee every fertile inch o' the island; 195 And I will kiss thy foot. I prithee, be my god.

TRINCULO. By this light, a most perfidious and drunken monster! When 's god's asleep, he'll rob his bottle.

CALIBAN. I'll kiss thy foot, I'll 200 swear myself thy subject.

STEPHANO. Come on, then, down and swear.

TRINCULO. I shall laugh myself to death at this puppy-headed monster. A most scurvy monster! I could 205 find in my heart to beat him—

STEPHANO. Come, kiss.

TRINCULO. But that the poor monster's in drink. An abominable monster!

CALIBAN. I'll show thee the best springs, I'll pluck thee berries, 210 I'll fish for thee and get thee wood enough. A plague upon the tyrant that I serve! I'll bear him no more sticks, but follow thee, Thou wondrous man.

TRINCULO. A most ridiculous 215 monster, to make a wonder of a poor drunkard!

CALIBAN. I prithee, let me bring thee where crabs grow, And I with my long nails will dig thee pignuts, Show thee a jay's nest and instruct thee how 220 To snare the nimble marmoset. I'll bring thee

---

185 *dog...bush:* According to a folk tale, a peasant was transported to the moon for cutting bushes on Sunday; his dog and the last bush he cut accompanied him.

---

193 *Well drawn:* well drunk. 218 *crabs:* crab apples.

To clustering filberts and sometimes
I'll get thee
Young scamels from the rock. Wilt
thou go with me?
STEPHANO. I prithee now, lead the way
without any more talking. 225
Trinculo, the king and all our company else being drowned, we will
inherit here. Here, bear my bottle,
fellow Trinculo, we'll fill him by and
by again. 230
CALIBAN. *Sings drunkenly.* Farewell,
master, farewell, farewell!

TRINCULO. A howling monster, a drunk-
en monster!
CALIBAN. No more dams I'll make for
fish;
Nor fetch in firing
At requiring, 235
Nor scrape trencher, nor wash dish.
'Ban, 'Ban, Ca-Caliban
Has a new master. Get a new man.
Freedom, heyday! heyday, freedom!
freedom, heyday, freedom! 240
STEPHANO. O brave monster! Lead the
way. *Exeunt.*

ACT III

SCENE i. [*Before* PROSPERO'S *cell.*]

Enter FERDINAND, *bearing a log.*

FERDINAND. There be some sports are
painful, and their labour
Delight in them sets off. Some kinds
of baseness
Are nobly undergone and most poor
matters
Point to rich ends. This my mean
task
Would be as heavy to me as odious,
but 5
The mistress which I serve quickens
what's dead
And makes my labours pleasures. O,
she is
Ten times more gentle than her
father's crabbed,
And he's composed of harshness. I
must remove
Some thousands of these logs and
pile them up, 10
Upon a sore injunction. My sweet
mistress
Weeps when she sees me work, and
says such baseness
Had never like executor. I forget.
But these sweet thoughts do even

refresh my labours,
Most busy lest when I do it.

Enter MIRANDA; *and* PROSPERO [*at a
distance unseen*].

MIRANDA. Alas, now, pray you, 15
Work not so hard. I would the light-
ning had
Burnt up those logs that you are
enjoined to pile!
Pray, set it down and rest you. When
this burns,
'Twill weep for having wearied you.
My father
Is hard at study. Pray now, rest
yourself, 20
He's safe for these three hours.
FERDINAND. O most
dear mistress,
The sun will set before I shall dis-
charge
What I must strive to do.
MIRANDA. If you'll sit down,
I'll bear your logs the while. Pray,
give me that,
I'll carry it to the pile.
FERDINAND. No, precious
creature, 25

223 *scamels:* perhaps seagulls. 227 *inherit:* take possession. 236 *trencher:* wooden plate.

III.i.11 *sore:* grievous. 15 *Most...lest:* perhaps, most busily thinking when most apparently inactive. 19 *weep:* exude sap.

I had rather crack my sinews, break
  my back,
Than you should such dishonour
  undergo
While I sit lazy by.
MIRANDA.   It would become me.
  As well as it does you. And I should
  do it
With much more ease, for my good
  will is to it,   30
And yours it is against.
PROSPERO.   Poor worm,
  thou art infected!
This visitation shows it.
MIRANDA.   You look wearily.
FERDINAND. No, noble mistress, 'tis
  fresh morning with me
When you are by at night. I do
  beseech you—
Chiefly that I might set it in my
  prayers—   35
What is your name?
MIRANDA.   Miranda.—O my father,
I have broke your hest to say so!
FERDINAND.   Admired Miranda!
Indeed the top of admiration! Worth
What's dearest to the world! Full
  many a lady
I have eyed with best regard and
  many a time   40
The harmony of their tongues hath
  into bondage
Brought my too diligent ear. For
  several virtues
Have I liked several women. Never
  any
With so full soul, but some defect
  in her
Did quarrel with the noblest grace
  she owed   45
And put it to the foil. But you, O
  you,
So perfect and so peerless, are created
Of every creature's best!
MIRANDA.   I do not know

One of my sex—no woman's face
  remember,
Save, from my glass, mine own. Nor
  have I seen   50
More that I may call men than you,
  good friend,
And my dear father. How features
  are abroad,
I am skilless of. But, by my mo-
  desty—
The jewel in my dower—I would
  not wish
Any companion in the world but
  you.   55
Nor can imagination form a shape
Besides yourself to like of. But I
  prattle
Something too wildly and my father's
  precepts
I therein do forget.
FERDINAND.   I am in my con-
  dition
A prince, Miranda—I do think, a
  king—   60
I would, not so!—and would no more
  endure
This wooden slavery than to suffer
The flesh-fly blow my mouth. Hear
  my soul speak.
The very instant that I saw you, did
My heart fly to your service, there
  resides,   65
To make me slave to it, and for your
  sake
Am I this patient log-man.
MIRANDA.   Do you love me?
FERDINAND. O heaven, O earth, bear
  witness to this sound
And crown what I profess with kind
  event
If I speak true! If hollowly, invert 70
What best is boded me to mischief! I
Beyond all limit of what else i' the
  world
Do love, prize, honour you.

---

37 *hest:* command; *Admired Miranda:* a play
on Miranda—"to be wondered at, admired."
42 *several:* separate.

53 *skilless:* unaware. 59 *condition:* rank.
63 *blow:* lay its eggs on. 69 *event:* outcome.
71 *boded:* destined.

MIRANDA.   I am a fool
  To weep at what I am glad of.
PROSPERO.   Fair encounter
  Of two most rare affections! Heavens
    rain grace   75
  On that which breeds between 'em!
FERDINAND.   Wherefore weep you?
MIRANDA. At mine unworthiness that
  dare not offer
  What I desire to give, and much less
  take
  What I shall die to want. But this
  is trifling,
  And all the more it seeks to hide
  itself   80
  The bigger bulk it shows. Hence,
  bashful cunning!
  And prompt me, plain and holy
  innocence!
  I am your wife if you will marry me;
  If not, I'll die your maid. To be
  your fellow
  You may deny me, but I'll be your
  servant   85
  Whether you will or no.
FERDINAND.   My mistress, dearest,
  And I thus humble ever.
MIRANDA.   My husband, then?
FERDINAND. Ay, with a heart as willing
  As bondage e'er of freedom. Here's
  my hand.
MIRANDA. And mine, with my heart in
  't. And now farewell   90
  Till half an hour hence.
FERDINAND.   A thousand thousand!

Exeunt [FERDINAND *and* MIRANDA
severally].

PROSPERO. So glad of this as they I
  cannot be,
  Who are surprised withal; but my
  rejoicing
  At nothing can be more. I'll to my
  book,
  For yet ere supper-time must I
  perform   95
  Much business appertaining.   *Exit.*

---

79 *want:* lack. 84 *fellow:* wife. 86 *mistress:*
fair lady.

SCENE ii. [*Another part of the island.*]

Enter CALIBAN, STEPHANO, *and* TRIN-
CULO.

STEPHANO. Tell not me. When the butt
is out, we will drink water—not a
drop before. Therefore bear up and
board 'em. Servant-monster, drink to
me.   5
TRINCULO. Servant-monster! The folly
of this island! They say there's but
five upon this isle. We are three of
like. If the other two be brained
like us, the state totters.   10
STEPHANO.   Drink,   servant-monster,
when I bid thee. Thy eyes are almost
set in thy head.
TRINCULO. Where should they be set
else? He were a brave monster   15
indeed, if they were set in his tail.
STEPHANO.   My   man-monster   hath
drowned his tongue in sack. For my
part, the sea cannot drown me; I
swam, ere I could recover the   20
shore, five and thirty leagues off and
on. By this light, thou shalt be my
lieutenant, monster, or my standard.
TRINCULO. Your lieutenant, if you list;
he's no standard.   25
STEPHANO. We'll not run, Monsieur
Monster.
TRINCULO. Nor go neither, but you'll
lie like dogs and yet say nothing
neither.   30
STEPHANO. Moon-calf, speak once in
thy life, if thou beest a good moon-
calf.
CALIBAN. How does thy honour? Let
me lick thy shoe.   34
  I'll not serve him, he is not valiant.
TRINCULO. Thou liest, most ignorant
monster, I am in case to justle a

III.ii.1 *Tell not me:* don't tell me to drink
slower. 3 *bear up:* raise the helm so as to
bring the ship into the wind. 4 *board 'em:*
climb aboard ship. Both phrases mean, in
effect, "Drink up!" 13 *set:* fixed in a dim
stare. 23 *standard:* standard bearer. 28 *go:*
walk. 37 *in case:* in a condition; *justle:* push
around.

constable. Why, thou deboshed fish, thou, was there ever man a coward that hath drunk so much sack as 40 I today? Wilt thou tell a monstrous lie, being but half a fish and half a monster?

CALIBAN. Lo, how he mocks me! Wilt thou let him, my lord?   45

TRINCULO. "Lord," quoth he. That a monster should be such a natural!

CALIBAN. Lo, lo, again! Bite him to death, I prithee.

STEPHANO. Trinculo, keep a good 50 tongue in your head. If you prove a mutineer—the next tree! The poor monster's my subject and he shall not suffer indignity.

CALIBAN. I thank my noble lord. 55 Wilt thou be pleased to hearken once again to the suit I made to thee?

STEPHANO. Marry, will I. Kneel and repeat it. I will stand, and so shall Trinculo.   60

Enter ARIEL, *invisible.*

CALIBAN. As I told thee before, I am subject to a tyrant, a sorcerer, that by his cunning hath cheated me of the island.

ARIEL. Thou liest.   65

CALIBAN. Thou liest, thou jesting monkey, thou. I would my valiant master would destroy thee! I do not lie.

STEPHANO. Trinculo, if you trouble 70 him any more in 's tale, by this hand, I will supplant some of your teeth.

TRINCULO. Why, I said nothing.

STEPHANO. Mum, then, and no more. Proceed.   75

CALIBAN. I say, by sorcery he got this isle,
From me he got it. If thy greatness will
Revenge it on him—for I know thou darest,
But this thing dare not—

STEPHANO. That's most certain. 80

CALIBAN. Thou shalt be lord of it and I'll serve thee.

STEPHANO. How now shall this be compassed?
Canst thou bring me to the party?

CALIBAN. Yea, yea, my lord. I'll yield him thee asleep,
Where thou mayst knock a nail into his head.   85

ARIEL. Thou liest, thou canst not.

CALIBAN. What a pied ninny's this! Thou scurvy patch!
I do beseech thy greatness, give him blows
And take his bottle from him. When that's gone
He shall drink nought but brine, for I'll not show him   90
Where the quick freshes are.

STEPHANO. Trinculo, run into no further danger. Interrupt the monster one word further and, by this hand, I'll turn my mercy out o' doors 95 and make a stock-fish of thee.

TRINCULO. Why, what did I? I did nothing. I'll go farther off.

STEPHANO. Didst thou not say he lied?

ARIEL. Thou liest.   100

STEPHANO. Do I so? Take thou that.
[*Beats* TRINCULO.] As you like this, give me the lie another time.

TRINCULO. I did not give the lie. Out o' your wits and hearing too? A 105 pox o' your bottle! This can sack and drinking do. A murrain on your monster, and the devil take your fingers!

CALIBAN. Ha, ha, ha!   110

STEPHANO. How, forward with your tale. Prithee, stand farther off.

CALIBAN. Beat him enough. After a little time
I'll beat him too.

STEPHANO.   Stand farther. Come, proceed.   115

---

38 *deboshed:* debauched.   47 *natural:* idiot.

82 *compassed:* managed.   87 *pied:* vari-colored, as a fool's motley dress; *patch:* dolt. 96 *stock-fish:* dried cod pounded soft for boiling.   107 *murrain:* plague.

CALIBAN. Why, as I told thee, 'tis a custom with him
I' the afternoon to sleep. There thou mayst brain him,
Having first seized his books, or with a log
Batter his skull, or paunch him with a stake,
Or cut his wezand with thy knife. Remember   120
First to possess his books, for without them
He's but a sot, as I am, nor hath not
One spirit to command. They all do hate him
As rootedly as I. Burn but his books.
He has brave utensils—for so he calls them—   125
Which, when he has a house, he'll deck withal.
And that most deeply to consider is
The beauty of his daughter. He himself
Calls her a nonpareil. I never saw a woman,   129
But only Sycorax my dam and she,
But she as far surpasseth Sycorax
As great'st does least.
STEPHANO. Is it so brave a lass?
CALIBAN. Ay, lord, she will become thy bed, I warrant.   134
And bring thee forth brave brood.
STEPHANO. Monster, I will kill this man. His daughter and I will be king and queen—save our graces!—and Trinculo and thyself shall be viceroys. Dost thou like the plot,   140
Trinculo?
TRINCULO. Excellent.
STEPHANO. Give me thy hand. I am sorry I beat thee, but while thou livest, keep a good tongue in   145
thy head.
CALIBAN. Within this half hour will he be asleep.
Wilt thou destroy him then?

STEPHANO.   Ay, on mine honour.
ARIEL. This will I tell my master.
CALIBAN. Thou makest me merry; I am full of pleasure.   150
Let us be jocund! Will you troll the catch
You taught me but while-ere?
STEPHANO. At thy request, monster, I will do reason, any reason. Come on, Trinculo, let us sing. *Sings.*   155
Flout 'em and scout 'em
And scout 'em and flout 'em,
Thought is free.
CALIBAN. That's not the tune.

ARIEL *plays the tune on a tabor and pipe.*

STEPHANO. What is this same?   160
TRINCULO. This is the tune of our catch, played by the picture of Nobody.
STEPHANO. If thou beest a man, show thyself in thy likeness. If thou   165
beest a devil, take 't as thou list.
TRINCULO. O, forgive me my sins!
STEPHANO. He that dies pays all debts: I defy thee.
Mercy upon us!
CALIBAN. Art thou afeard?   170
STEPHANO. No, monster, not I.
CALIBAN. Be not afeard. The isle is full of noises,
Sounds and sweet airs, that give delight and hurt not.
Sometimes a thousand twangling instruments
Will hum about mine ears, and sometime voices   175
That, if I then had waked after long sleep,
Will make me sleep again. And then, in dreaming,

---

151 *troll the catch:* sing the round (song for three voices). 152 *while-ere:* a while since. 154 *any reason:* anything within reason. 156 *scout:* deride. 162–63 *picture of Nobody:* i.e., by an invisible actor. A drawing of Nobody looks like Humpty Dumpty, all head and no body. 168 *He...debts:* i.e., a dead man pays no debts, hence all debts (by cancellation).

---

119 *paunch:* stab in the belly. 120 *wezand:* windpipe. 125 *brave utensils:* fine furnishings.

The clouds methought would open and show riches
Ready to drop upon me, that when I waked
I cried to dream again.   180
STEPHANO. This will prove a brave kingdom to me, where I shall have my music for nothing.
CALIBAN. When Prospero is destroyed.   185
STEPHANO. That shall be by and by; I remember the story.
TRINCULO. The sound is going away; let's follow it, and after do our work.
STEPHANO. Lead, monster, we'll 190 follow. I would I could see this taborer, he lays it on.
TRINCULO. Wilt come? I'll follow, Stephano.   *Exeunt.*

SCENE iii. [*Another part of the island.*]

Enter ALONSO, SEBASTIAN, ANTONIO, GONZALO, ADRIAN, FRANCISCO, *etc.*

GONZALO. By 'r lakin, I can go no further, sir;
My old bones ache. Here's a maze trod indeed
Through forth-rights and meanders! By your patience,
I needs must rest me.
ALONSO.   Old lord, I cannot blame thee,
Who am myself attached with weariness,   5
To the dulling of my spirits. Sit down and rest.
Even here I will put off my hope and keep it
No longer for my flatterer. He is drowned
Whom thus we stray to find, and the sea mocks
Our frustrate search on land. Well, let him go.   10

ANTONIO. [*aside to* SEBASTIAN] I am right glad that he's so out of hope.
Do not, for one repulse, forego the purpose
That you resolved to effect.
SEBASTIAN. [*aside to* ANTONIO] The next advantage
Will we take throughly.
ANTONIO. [*aside to* SEBASTIAN] Let it be tonight,
For now they are oppressed with travel, they   15
Will not, nor cannot, use such vigilance
As when they are fresh.
SEBASTIAN. [*aside to* ANTONIO] I say, tonight. No more.

[*Solemn and strange music.*]

ALONSO. What harmony is this? My good friends, hark!
GONZALO. Marvellous sweet music!

Solemn and strange music; and PROS-PERO *on the top invisible. Enter several strange* SHAPES; *bringing in a banquet; and dance about it with gentle actions of salutation; and inviting the King, etc., to eat, they depart.*

ALONSO. Give us kind keepers, heavens! What were these?   20
SEBASTIAN. A living drollery. Now I will believe
That there are unicorns, that in Arabia
There is one tree, the phœnix' throne, one phœnix
At this hour reigning there.
ANTONIO.   I'll believe both,
And what does else want credit, come to me,   25
And I'll be sworn 'tis true. Travelers ne'er did lie,
Though fools at home condemn 'em.
GONZALO. If in Naples
I should report this now, would they believe me?

---

186 *by and by:* directly.   III.iii.1 *By 'r lakin:* by Our Lady.

20 *keepers:* guardians.   21 *drollery:* puppet show.   25 *want credit:* is not believed.

If I should say I saw such islanders—
For, certes, these are people of the
island—   30
Who, though they are of monstrous
shape, yet, note,
Their manners are more gentle-kind
than of
Our human generation you shall find
Many, nay, almost any.
PROSPERO.   [*aside*] Honest lord,
Thou hast said well, for some of you
there present   35
Are worse than devils.
ALONSO.   I cannot too much muse
Such shapes, such gesture and such
sound, expressing,
Although they want the use of
tongue, a kind
Of excellent dumb discourse.
PROSPERO.   [*aside*] Praise in
departing.
FRANCISCO. They vanished strangely.
SEBASTIAN.   No matter, since   40
They have left their viands behind;
for we have stomachs.
Will 't please you taste of what is
here?
ALONSO. Not I.
GONZALO. Faith, sir, you need not fear.
When we were boys,
Who would believe that there were
mountaineers
Dew-lapped like bulls, whose throats
had hanging at 'em   45
Wallets of flesh, or that there were
such men
Whose heads stood in their breasts?
Which now we find
Each putter-out of five for one will
bring us
Good warrant of.
ALONSO.   I will stand to and feed,
Although my last. No matter, since
I feel   50
The best is past. Brother, my lord
the duke,
Stand to and do as we.

Thunder and lightning. Enter ARIEL,
*like a harpy; claps his wings upon the
table; and, with a quaint device, the
banquet vanishes.*

ARIEL. You are three men of sin, whom
Destiny,
That hath to instrument this lower
world
And what is in 't, the never-surfeited
sea   55
Hath caused to belch up you. And on
this island
Where man doth not inhabit, you
'mongst men
Being most unfit to live. I have made
you mad,
And even with such-like valour men
hang and drown
Their proper selves.

[ALONSO, SEBASTIAN, *etc. draw their
swords.*]

You fools! I and my fellows 60
Are ministers of Fate. The elements,
Of whom your swords are tempered,
may as well
Wound the loud winds, or with
bemocked-at stabs
Kill the still-closing waters, as
diminish
One dowle that's in my plume. My
fellow ministers   65
Are like invulnerable. If you could
hurt,
Your swords are now too massy for
your strengths
And will not be uplifted. But remem-
ber—
For that's my business to you—that
you three
From Milan did supplant good Pros-
pero,   70
Exposed unto the sea, which hath
requit it,
Him and his innocent child. For
which foul deed

---

39 *Praise in departing:* a proverb meaning
"Don't praise your entertainment until you've
seen how it ends."

54 *to instrument:* for its instrument. 60
proper: own. 65 *dowle:* tiny feather. 66
like: similarly. 71 *hath requit it:* hath, by
storm-tossing you, revenged the crime you did.

The powers, delaying, not forgetting, have
Incensed the seas and shores, yea, all the creatures,
Against your peace. Thee of thy son, Alonso,   75
They have bereft, and do pronounce by me
Lingering perdition, worse than any death
Can be at once, shall step by step attend
You and your ways. Whose wraths to guard you from—
Which here, in this most desolate isle, else falls   80
Upon your heads—is nothing but heart-sorrow
And a clear life ensuing.

He vanishes in thunder; then, to soft music, enter the SHAPES *again, and dance, with mocks and mows, and carrying out the table.*

PROSPERO. Bravely the figure of this harpy hast thou
Performed, my Ariel—a grace it had devouring.
Of my instruction hast thou nothing bated   85
In what thou hadst to say. So, with good life
And observation strange, my meaner ministers
Their several kinds have done. My high charms work,
And these mine enemies are all knit up
In their distractions. They now are in my power,   90
And in these fits I leave them, while I visit
Young Ferdinand, whom they sup-

pose is drowned,
And his and mine loved darling.

                    [*Exit.*]

GONZALO. I' the name of something holy, sir, why stand you
In this strange stare?
ALONSO. O, it is monstrous, monstrous!   95
Methought the billows spoke and told me of it,
The winds did sing it to me, and the thunder,
That deep and dreadful organ-pipe, pronounced
The name of Prosper. It did bass my trespass.
Therefore my son i' the ooze is bedded, and   100
I'll seek him deeper than e'er plummet sounded
And with him there lie mudded.

                    Exit.

SEBASTIAN.   But one fiend at a time,
I'll fight their legions o'er.
ANTONIO.   I'll be thy second.

Exeunt [SEBASTIAN *and* ANTONIO].

GONZALO. All three of them are desperate. Their great guilt,
Like poison given to work a great time after,   105
Now 'gins to bite the spirits. I do beseech you
That are of suppler joints, follow them swiftly
And hinder them from what this ecstasy
May now provoke them to.
ADRIAN.   Follow, I pray you.

                    [*Exeunt omnes.*]

---

82 *clear:* reformed, guiltless. 84 *devouring:* a play, apparently, upon a "devouring grace" (a consuming or taking grace), the "devouring" of the banquet by magical disappearance, and perhaps the "wasting" of the saying of "grace" before eating.

99 *bass my trespass:* deeply proclaim my high crime—a matter of moral harmonics, with "undertones" of the depths in which Ferdinand presumably lies. 108 *ecstasy:* frenzy.

ACT IV

SCENE i. [*Before* PROSPERO's *cell.*]

Enter PROSPERO, FERDINAND, *and* MIRANDA.

PROSPERO. If I have too austerely
  punished you,
  Your compensation makes amends, for I
  Have given you here a third of mine own life,
  Or that for which I live, who once again
  I tender to thy hand. All thy vexations   5
  Were but my trials of thy love, and thou
  Hast strangely stood the test. Here, afore Heaven,
  I ratify this my rich gift. O Ferdinand,
  Do not smile at me that I boast her off,
  For thou shalt find she will outstrip all praise   10
  And make it halt behind her.
FERDINAND.   I do believe it
  Against an oracle.
PROSPERO. Then, as my gift and thine own acquisition
  Worthily purchased, take my daughter. But
  If thou dost break her virgin-knot before   15
  All sanctimonious ceremonies may
  With full and holy rite be ministered,
  No sweet aspersion shall the heavens let fall
  To make this contract grow; but barren hate,
  Sour-eyed disdain and discord shall bestrew   20

The union of your bed with weeds so loathly
  That you shall hate it both. Therefore take heed,
  As Hymen's lamps shall light you.
FERDINAND.   As I hope
  For quiet days, fair issue and long life,
  With such love as 'tis now, the murkiest den,   25
  The most opportune place, the strong'st suggestion
  Our worser genius can, shall never melt
  Mine honour into lust, to take away
  The edge of that day's celebration
  When I shall think, or Phœbus' steeds are foundered,   30
  Or Night kept chained below.
PROSPERO.   Fairly spoke.
  Sit then and talk with her, she is thine own.
  What, Ariel! My industrious servant, Ariel!

Enter ARIEL.

ARIEL. What would my potent master?
  Here I am.
PROSPERO. Thou and thy meaner fellows your last service   35
  Did worthily perform, and I must use you
  In such another trick. Go bring the rabble,
  O'er whom I give thee power, here to this place.
  Incite them to quick motion, for I must
  Bestow upon the eyes of this young couple   40
  Some vanity of mine art. It is my promise
  And they expect it from me.

IV.i.3 *a third...life:* Miranda as that third of Prospero's life (along with himself and his dead wife) associated especially with his future. 7 *strangely:* unusually well. 12 *Against an oracle:* even though an oracle should proclaim otherwise. 18 *aspersion:* shower (of grace; cf. III.i.75).

23 *Hymen's:* Greek and Roman god of marriage. 26 *suggestion:* temptation. 37 *rabble:* minor spirits.

ARIEL.   Presently?
PROSPERO. Ay, with a twink.
ARIEL. Before you can say "come" and
     "go,"
     And breathe twice and cry "so,
     so,"   45
     Each one, tripping on his toe,
     Will be here with mop and mow.
     Do you love me, master? No?
PROSPERO. Dearly, my delicate Ariel.
     Do not approach
     Till thou dost hear me call.
ARIEL.   Well, I conceive. 50

                              [*Exit.*]

PROSPERO. Look thou be true. Do not
     give dalliance
     Too much the rein. The strongest
     oaths are straw
     To the fire i' the blood. Be more
     abstemious
     Or else good night your vow!
FERDINAND.   I warrant you, sir,
     The white cold virgin snow upon my
     heart   55
     Abates the ardour of my liver.
PROSPERO.   Well.
     Now come, my Ariel! Bring a corol-
     lary
     Rather than want a spirit. Appear,
     and pertly!
     No tongue! All eyes! Be silent.

Soft music.

Enter IRIS.

IRIS. Ceres, most bounteous lady, thy
     rich leas   60
     Of wheat, rye, barley, vetches, oats
     and pease;
     Thy turfy mountains, where live
     nibbling sheep,
     And flat meads thatched with stover,
     them to keep;
     Thy banks with pioned and twilled
     brims,
     Which spongy April at thy hest
     betrims,   65

To make cold nymphs chaste crowns;
     and thy broom-groves,
Whose shadow the dismissed bachelor
     loves,
Being lass-lorn; thy pole-clipt vine-
     yard;
And thy sea-marge, sterile and rocky
     hard
Where thou thyself dost air—the
     queen o' the sky,   70
Whose watery arch and messenger
     am I,
Bids thee leave these, and with her
     sovereign grace,

JUNO *descends.*

Here on this grass-plot, in this very
     place,
To come and sport. Her peacocks
     fly amain.
Approach, rich Ceres, her to enter-
     tain.   75

Enter CERES.

CERES. Hail, many-coloured messenger,
     that ne'er
     Dost disobey the wife of Jupiter.
     Who with thy saffron wings upon my
     flowers
     Diffusest   honey-drops,   refreshing
     showers,
     And with each end of thy blue bow
     dost crown   80
     My bosky acres and my unshrubbed
     down,
     Rich scarf to my proud earth. Why
     hath thy queen
     Summoned me hither to this short-
     grassed green?
IRIS. A contract of true love to cele-
     brate,
     And some donation freely to estate 85
     On the blest lovers.
CERES.   Tell me, heavenly bow,
     If Venus or her son, as thou dost
     know,

---

56 *liver:* regarded as the center of passions.
65 *hest:* command.

67 *dismissed:* rejected. 68 *pole-clipt:* poles
entwined with vines. 70 *air:* take the air;
queen: Juno. 71 *watery arch:* rainbow. 81
bosky: full of foliage.

Do now attend the queen? Since they
  did plot
The means that dusky Dis my daugh-
  ter got,
Her and her blind boy's scandaled
  company   90
I have forsworn.
IRIS.   Of her society
  Be not afraid. I met her deity
  Cutting the clouds towards Paphos
    and her son
  Dove-drawn with her. Here thought
    they to have done
  Some wanton charm upon this man
    and maid—   95
  Whose vows are that no bed-right
    shall be paid
  Till Hymen's torch be lighted—but
    in vain.
  Mars' hot minion is returned again,
  Her waspish-headed son has broke
    his arrows,
  Swears he will shoot no more but
    play with sparrows   100
  And be a boy right out.
CERES.   High'st queen of state,
  Great Juno, comes; I know her by
    her gait.

[*Enter* JUNO.]

JUNO. How does my bounteous sister?
  Go with me
  To bless this twain, that they may
    prosperous be
  And honoured in their issue.   105

[*They sing:*]

JUNO. Honour, riches, marriage-
      blessing,
    Long continuance, and
      increasing,
    Hourly joys be still upon you!
    Juno sings her blessings on you.
CERES. Earth's increase, foison plenty,

Barns and garners never empty,
Vines with clustering bunches
  growing,   112
Plants with goodly burthen
  bowing;
Spring come to you at the
  farthest
In the very end of harvest!   115
Scarcity and want shall shun
  you,
Ceres' blessing so is on you.
FERDINAND. This is a most majestic
  vision, and
  Harmonious charmingly. May I be
    bold
  To think these spirits?
PROSPERO.   Spirits which
  by mine art   120
  I have from their confines called to
    enact
  My present fancies.
FERDINAND.   Let me live here
  ever.
  So rare a wondered father and a wife
  Makes this place Paradise.

JUNO *and* CERES *whisper, and send* IRIS
on employment.

PROSPERO.   Sweet, now, silence!
  Juno and Ceres whisper seriously.
  There's something else to do. Hush
    and be mute   126
  Or else our spell is marred.
IRIS. You nymphs, called Naiads, of
    the windring brooks,
  With your sedged crowns and ever-
    harmless looks,
  Leave your crisp channels and on
    this green land   130
  Answer your summons, Juno does
    command.
  Come, temperate nymphs, and help
    to celebrate
  A contract of true love, be not too
    late.

Enter certain NYMPHS.

---

89 *Dis:* Pluto, who abducted Ceres' daughter,
Proserpine, and made her his queen in the
underworld. 93 *Paphos:* town in Cyprus
sacred to Venus. 98 *hot minion:* hot-blooded
darling. 99 *son:* Cupid. 110 *foison plenty:*
bountiful harvest.

129 *sedged crowns:* garlands of sweet
flag.

You sunburnt sicklemen, of August
weary,
Come hither from the furrow and be
merry. 135
Make holiday, your rye-straw hats
put on
And these fresh nymphs encounter
everyone
In country footing.

Enter certain REAPERS, *properly
habited: they join with the* NYMPHS *in
a graceful dance; towards the end
whereof* PROSPERO *starts suddenly, and
speaks; after which, to a strange, hollow, and confused noise, they heavily
vanish.*

PROSPERO. [*aside*] I had forgot that
foul conspiracy.
Of the beast Caliban and his con-
federates 140
Against my life—the minute of their
plot
Is almost come. [*to the* SPIRITS]
Well done! Avoid! No more!
FERDINAND. This is strange. Your
father's in some passion
That works him strongly.
MIRANDA.　　　　Never till this day
Saw I him touched with anger so
distempered 145
PROSPERO. You do look, my son, in a
moved sort,
As if you were dismayed. Be cheerful,
sir.
Our revels now are ended. These our
actors,
As I foretold you, were all spirits and
Are melted into air, into thin air. 150
And like the baseless fabric of this
vision,
The cloud-capped towers, the gor-
geous palaces,
The solemn temples, the great globe
itself,
Yea, all which it inherit, shall dis-
solve

And like this insubstantial pageant
faded, 155
Leave not a rack behind. We are
such stuff
As dreams are made on, and our
little life
Is rounded with a sleep. Sir, I am
vexed.
Bear with my weakness, my old brain
is troubled.
Be not disturbed with my infirmity. 160
If you be pleased, retire into my
cell
And there repose. A turn or two I'll
walk,
To still my beating mind.
FERDINAND. MIRANDA.　　We wish
your peace.　　　　　　*Exeunt.*
PROSPERO. Come with a thought. I
thank thee, Ariel. Come.

Enter ARIEL.

ARIEL. Thy thoughts I cleave to. What's
thy pleasure?
PROSPERO.　　　Spirit, 165
We must prepare to meet with
Caliban.
ARIEL. Aye, my commander. When I
presented Ceres,
I thought to have told thee of it, but
I feared
Lest I might anger thee.
PROSPERO. Say again, where didst thou
leave these varlets? 170
ARIEL. I told you, sir, they were red-
hot with drinking,
So full of valour that they smote the
air
For breathing in their faces, beat the
ground
For kissing of their feet; yet always
bending
Towards their project. Then I beat
my tabor, 175
At which, like unbacked colts, they
pricked their ears,

---

137 *encounter:* pair off.　148 *revels:* performances.

156 *rack:* wisp.　158 *rounded:* both encircled
and rounded off.　175 *project:* i.e., to kill
Prospero.

Advanced their eyelids, lifted up their noses
As they smelt music. So I charmed their ears
That calf-like they my lowing followed through
Toothed briers, sharp furzes, pricking goss and thorns,   180
Which entered their frail shins. At last I left them
I' the filthy-mantled pool beyond your cell,
There dancing up to the chins, that the foul lake
O'erstunk their feet.
PROSPERO.   This was well done, my bird.
Thy shape invisible retain thou still.   185
The trumpery in my house, go bring it hither,
For stale to catch these thieves.
ARIEL.   I go, I go. [*Exit.*]
PROSPERO. A devil, a born devil, on whose nature
Nurture can never stick, on whom my pains,
Humanely taken, all, all lost, quite lost.   190
And as with age his body uglier grows,
So his mind cankers. I will plague them all,
Even to roaring.

Re-enter ARIEL, *loaden with glistering apparel, etc.*

Come, hang them on this line.

[PROSPERO *and* ARIEL *remain, invisible.*]
Enter CALIBAN, STEPHANO, *and* TRINCULO, *all wet.*

CALIBAN. Pray you, tread softly, that the blind mole may not
Hear a foot fall. We now are near his cell.   195

STEPHANO. Monster, your fairy, which you say is a harmless fairy, has done little better than played the Jack with us.
TRINCULO. Monster, I do smell   200 all horse-piss, at which my nose is in great indignation.
STEPHANO. So is mine. Do you hear, monster? If I should take a displeasure against you, look you—   205
TRINCULO. Thou wert but a lost monster.
CALIBAN. Good my lord, give me thy favour still.
Be patient, for the prize I'll bring thee to
Shall hoodwink this mischance. Therefore speak softly.   210
All's hushed as midnight yet.
TRINCULO. Ay, but to lose our bottles in the pool—
STEPHANO. There is not only disgrace and dishonour in that, monster,   215 but an infinite loss.
TRINCULO. That's more to me than my wetting. Yet this is your harmless fairy, monster.
STEPHANO. I will fetch off my   220 bottle, though I be o'er ears for my labour.
CALIBAN. Prithee, my king, be quiet. See'st thou here,
This is the mouth o' the cell. No noise, and enter.
Do that good mischief which may make this island
Thine own forever, and I, thy Caliban,   225
For aye thy foot-licker.
STEPHANO. Give me thy hand. I do begin to have bloody thoughts.
TRINCULO. O king Stephano! O peer! O worthy Stephano! Look what   230 a wardrobe here is for thee!
CALIBAN. Let it alone, thou fool, it is but trash.
TRINCULO. O, ho, monster! We know

---

182 *filthy-mantled:* scum-covered. 187 *stale:* decoy. 189 *Nurture:* education, training. 192 *cankers:* decays. 193 *line:* lime tree.

198 *Jack:* knave. 210 *hoodwink:* wipe out (be a blinder to).

what belongs to a frippery. O king
Stephano!   235
STEPHANO. Put off that gown, Trinculo.
By this hand, I'll have that gown.
TRINCULO. Thy grace shall have it.
CALIBAN. The dropsy drown this fool!
What do you mean
To dote thus on such luggage? Let's
alone   240
And do the murder first. If he
awake,
From toe to crown he'll fill our skins
with pinches,
Make us strange stuff.
STEPHANO. Be you quiet, monster.
Mistress line, is not this my   245
jerkin? Now is the jerkin under the
line. Now, jerkin, you are like to lose
your hair and prove a bald jerkin.
TRINCULO. Do, do. We steal by line
and level, an't like your grace.   250
STEPHANO. I thank thee for that jest,
here's a garment for 't. Wit shall
not go unrewarded while I am king
of this country. "Steal by line and
level" is an excellent pass of   255
pate. There's another garment for 't.
TRINCULO. Monster, come, put some
lime upon your fingers, and away
with the rest.
CALIBAN. I will have none on 't. We
shall lose our time   260
And all be turned to barnacles, or to
apes
With foreheads villainous low.

STEPHANO. Monster, lay to your
fingers. Help to bear this away where
my hogshead of wine is, or I'll   265
turn you out of my kingdom. Go to,
carry this!
TRINCULO. And this.
STEPHANO. Ay, and this.

A noise of hunters heard. Enter divers
SPIRITS, *in shape of dogs and hounds,*
hunting them about, PROSPERO *and*
ARIEL *setting them on.*

PROSPERO. Hey, Mountain, hey!   270
ARIEL. Silver! There it goes, Silver!
PROSPERO. Fury, Fury! There, Tyrant,
there! Hark! Hark!

[CALIBAN, STEPHANO, *and* TRINCULO
are driven out.]

Go charge my goblins that they grind
their joints
With dry convulsions, shorten up
their sinews
With aged cramps, and more pinch-
spotted make them   275
Than pard or cat o' mountain.
ARIEL.   Hark, they roar!
PROSPERO. Let them be hunted soundly.
At this hour
Lie at my mercy all mine enemies.
Shortly shall all my labours end, and
thou
Shalt have the air at freedom. For
a little   280
Follow, and do me service. *Exeunt.*

ACT V

SCENE i. [*Before* PROSPERO'S *cell.*]

Enter PROSPERO *in his magic robes,*

and ARIEL.

PROSPERO. Now does my project gather
to a head.
My charms crack not, my spirits
obey, and time
Goes upright with his carriage. How's
the day?

---

234 *frippery:* old-clothes shop.   238 *Thy*
grace: your Majesty. 240 *Let's alone:* let it
be. 246 *jerkin:* short jacket; *under the line:*
under the lime tree and under the equator.
247–48 *lose your hair:* i.e., because of equa-
torial fevers. 249 *Do, do:* keep it up; *line:*
plumb line. 250 *level:* carpenter's level. 255–
56 *pass of pate:* maneuver of wit. 258 *lime:*
birdlime; i.e., become sticky-fingered.

276 *pard:* leopard. V.i.2 *crack not:* remain
flawless. 3 *Goes upright:* i.e., moves swiftly,
unburdened.

ARIEL. On the sixth hour, at which time, my lord,
You said our work should cease.
PROSPERO.   I did say so, 5
When first I raised the tempest. Say, my spirit,
How fares the king and 's followers?
ARIEL. Confined together
In the same fashion as you gave in charge,
Just as you left them. All prisoners, sir,
In the line-grove which weather-fends your cell.   10
They cannot budge till your release. The king,
His brother and yours, abide all three distracted
And the remainder mourning over them,
Brimful of sorrow and dismay, but chiefly
Him that you termed, sir, "The good old lord, Gonzalo."   15
His tears run down his beard, like winter's drops
From eaves of reeds. Your charm so strongly works 'em
That if you now beheld them, your affections
Would become tender.
PROSPERO.   Dost thou think so, spirit?
ARIEL. Mine would, sir, were I human.
PROSPERO. And mine shall.   20
Hast thou, which art but air, a touch, a feeling
Of their afflictions, and shall not myself
One of their kind, that relish all as sharply
Passion as they, be kindlier moved than thou art?
Though with their high wrongs I am struck to the quick,   25
Yet with my nobler reason 'gainst my fury
Do I take part. The rarer action is

In virtue than in vengeance. They being penitent,
The sole drift of my purpose doth extend
Not a frown further. Go release them, Ariel.   30
My charms I'll break, their senses I'll restore,
And they shall be themselves.
ARIEL.   I'll fetch them, sir.

Exit.

PROSPERO. Ye elves of hills, brooks, standing lakes and groves,
And ye that on the sands with printless foot
Do chase the ebbing Neptune and do fly him   35
When he comes back; you demi-puppets that
By moonshine do the green sour ringlets make,
Whereof the ewe not bites, and you whose pastime
Is to make midnight mushrooms, that rejoice
To hear the solemn curfew, by whose aid,   40
Weak masters though ye be, I have bedimmed
The noontide sun, called forth the mutinous winds,
And 'twixt the green sea and the azured vault
Set roaring war. To the dread rattling thunder
Have I given fire and rifted Jove's stout oak   45
With his own bolt. The strong-based promontory
Have I made shake and by the spurs plucked up

10 *line-grove:* lime tree grove. 27 *rarer:* finer.

33 *standing:* currentless. 35 *ebbing Neptune:* ebbing tide. 36 *demi-puppets:* half-sized puppets. 37 *green sour ringlets:* fairy rings, supposedly caused by fairies dancing in a circle, actually by toadstools. 40 *curfew:* nine o'clock at night, after which time fairy creatures came forth. 42 *mutinous:* turbulent. 47 *spurs:* roots.

The pine and cedar. Graves at my command
Have waked their sleepers, oped, and let 'em forth
By my so potent art. But this rough magic   50
I here abjure, and when I have required
Some heavenly music, which even now I do,
To work mine end upon their senses that
This airy charm is for, I'll break my staff,
Bury it certain fathoms in the earth,   55
And deeper than did ever plummet sound
I'll drown my book. *Solemn music.*

Here enters ARIEL *before: then* ALONSO, *with a frantic gesture, attended by* GONZALO; SEBASTIAN *and* ANTONIO *in like manner, attended by* ADRIAN *and* FRANCISCO: *they all enter the circle which* PROSPERO *had made, and there stand charmed; which* PROSPERO *observing, speaks:*

A solemn air and the best comforter
To an unsettled fancy cure thy brains,
Now useless, boiled within thy skull! There stand,   60
For you are spell-stopped.
Holy Gonzalo, honourable man,
Mine eyes, even sociable to the show of thine,
Fall fellowly drops. The charm dissolves apace,
And as the morning steals upon the night,   65
Melting the darkness, so their rising senses
Begin to chase the ignorant fumes that mantle
Their clearer reason. O good Gonzalo,
My true preserver, and a loyal sir

To him thou follow'st! I will pay thy graces   70
Home both in word and deed. Most cruelly
Didst thou, Alonso, use me and my daughter.
Thy brother was a furtherer in the act.
Thou art pinched for 't now, Sebastian. Flesh and blood,
You, brother mine, that entertained ambition,   75
Expelled remorse and nature, who, with Sebastian—
Whose inward pinches therefore are most strong—
Would here have killed your king, I do forgive thee,
Unnatural though thou art. Their understanding
Begins to swell, and the approaching tide   80
Will shortly fill the reasonable shore
That now lies foul and muddy. Not one of them
That yet looks on me, or would know me. Ariel,
Fetch me the hat and rapier in my cell.
I will discase me, and myself present   85
As I was sometime Milan. Quickly, spirit!
Thou shalt ere long be free.

ARIEL *sings and helps to attire him.*

Where the bee sucks, there suck I.
In a cowslip's bell I lie.
There I couch when owls do cry.   90
On the bat's back I do fly
After summer merrily.
Merrily, merrily shall I live now
Under the blossom that hangs on the bough.
PROSPERO. Why, that's my dainty Ariel!
I shall miss thee,   95

---

54 *staff:* magic wand. 63 *sociable:* responsive.

70–71 *pay...Home:* repay your kindnesses in full. 81 *reasonable shore:* shore of reason.

But yet thou shalt have freedom. So,
so, so.
To the king's ship, invisible as thou
art.
There shalt thou find the mariners
asleep
Under the hatches. The master and
the boatswain
Being awake, enforce them to this
place.   100
And presently, I prithee.
ARIEL. I drink the air before me, and
return
Or ere your pulse twice beat. *Exit.*
GONZALO. All torment, trouble, wonder
and amazement
Inhabits here. Some heavenly power
guide us   105
Out of this fearful country!
PROSPERO.   Behold, sir king,
The wronged Duke of Milan, Pros-
pero.
For more assurance that a living
prince
Does now speak to thee, I embrace
thy body.
And to thee and thy company I
bid   110
A hearty welcome.
ALONSO.   Whether thou be'st
he or no,
Or some enchanted trifle to abuse me,
As late I have been, I not know.
Thy pulse
Beats as of flesh and blood, and since
I saw thee,
The affliction of my mind amends,
with which,   115
I fear, a madness held me. This must
crave,
An if this be at all, a most strange
story.
Thy dukedom I resign and do entreat
Thou pardon me my wrongs. But
how should Prospero
Be living and be here?
PROSPERO.   First, noble friend,   120

Let me embrace thine age, whose
honour cannot
Be measured or confined.
GONZALO.   Whether this be
Or be not, I'll not swear.
PROSPERO.   You do yet taste
Some subtleties o' the isle that will
not let you
Believe things certain. Welcome, my
friends all!   125

[*aside to* SEBASTIAN *and* ANTONIO]

But you, my brace of lords, were
I so minded,
I here could pluck his highness' frown
upon you
And justify you traitors. At this time
I will tell no tales.
SEBASTIAN. [*aside*] The devil speaks
in him.
PROSPERO. No.
For you, most wicked sir, whom to
call brother   130
Would even infect my mouth, I do
forgive
Thy rankest fault—all of them—and
require
My dukedom of thee, which perforce,
I know,
Thou must restore.
ALONSO.   If thou be'st Prospero,
Give us particulars of thy preserva-
tion,   135
How thou hast met us here, who
three hours since
Were wrecked upon this shore, where
I have lost—
How sharp the point of this remem-
brance is!—
My dear son Ferdinand.
PROSPERO.   I am woe for 't, sir.
ALONSO. Irreparable is the loss, and
patience   140
Says it is past her cure.
PROSPERO.   I rather think
You have not sought her help, of
whose soft grace

---

101 *presently:* immediately. 112 *trifle:* apparition generated by magic.

128 *justify:* prove.

For the like loss I have her sovereign
aid
And rest myself content.
ALONSO.　　　　　You the like loss!
PROSPERO. As great to me as late, and,
supportable　　　　　　　　　145
To make the dear loss, have I means
much weaker
Than you may call to comfort you,
for I
Have lost my daughter.
ALONSO.　　　　　A daughter?
O heavens, that they were living both
in Naples,
The king and queen there! That
they were, I wish　　　　　150
Myself were mudded in that oozy
bed
Where my son lies. When did you
lose your daughter?
PROSPERO. In this last tempest. I per-
ceive, these lords
At this encounter do so much admire
That they devour their reason and
scarce think　　　　　155
Their eyes do offices of truth, their
words
Are natural breath. But howsoe'er
you have
Been justled from your senses, know
for certain
That I am Prospero and that very
duke
Which was thrust forth of Milan,
who most strangely　　　　　160
Upon this shore, where you were
wrecked, was landed,
To be the lord on 't. No more yet
of this,
For 'tis a chronicle of day by day,
Not a relation for a breakfast nor
Befitting this first meeting. Welcome,
sir.　　　　　165
This cell's my court. Here have I
few attendants
And subjects none abroad. Pray you,

look in.
My dukedom since you have given
me again,
I will requite you with as good a
thing—
At least bring forth a wonder to
content ye　　　　　170
As much as me my dukedom.

Here PROSPERO *discovers* FERDINAND
and MIRANDA *playing at chess.*

MIRANDA. Sweet lord, you play me
false.
FERDINAND. No, my dear'st love,
I would not for the world.
MIRANDA. Yes, for a score of kingdoms
you should wrangle,
And I would call it fair play.
ALONSO.　　　　　If this prove　175
A vision of the island, one dear son
Shall I twice lose.
SEBASTIAN.　　　　A most high miracle!
FERDINAND. Though the seas threaten,
they are merciful.
I have cursed them without cause.

[*Kneels.*]

ALONSO.　　　　　Now all the blessings
Of a glad father compass thee
about!　　　　　180
Arise, and say how thou camest here.
MIRANDA. O, wonder!
How many goodly creatures are there
here!
How beauteous mankind is! O brave
new world,
That has such people in 't!
PROSPERO.　　　　　'Tis new to thee.
ALONSO. What is this maid with whom
thou wast at play?　　　　　185
Your eld'st acquaintance cannot be
three hours.
Is she the goddess that hath severed
us
And brought us thus together?

---

145 *as late:* as the recency of its occurrence.
146 *dear:* painful, costly. 154 *admire:* stand
astonished.

169 *requite:* repay. 170 *wonder:* marvel,
with a play on "Miranda" (—wonder). 183
brave: fine, splendid. 186 *eld'st:* longest possible.

FERDINAND.   Sir, she is mortal,
But by immortal Providence she's
mine.
I chose her when I could not ask my
father   190
For his advice, nor thought I had
one. She
Is daughter to this famous Duke of
Milan,
Of whom so often I have heard
renown
But never saw before, of whom I
have
Received a second life, and second
father   195
This lady makes him to me.
ALONSO.   I am hers.
But, O, how oddly will it sound
that I
Must ask my child forgiveness!
PROSPERO.   There, sir, stop.
Let us not burthen our remembrance
with
A heaviness that's gone.
GONZALO.   I have inly wept   200
Or should have spoke ere this. Look
down, you gods,
And on this couple drop a blessed
crown!
For it is you that have chalked forth
the way
Which brought us hither.
ALONSO.   I say Amen, Gonzalo!
GONZALO. Was Milan thrust from
Milan, that his issue   205
Should become kings of Naples? O,
rejoice
Beyond a common joy! And set it
down
With gold on lasting pillars: In one
voyage
Did Claribel her husband find at
Tunis
And Ferdinand, her brother, found a
wife   210
Where he himself was lost, Prospero
his dukedom

In a poor isle, and all of us ourselves
When no man was his own.
ALONSO.   [*to* FERDINAND *and*
MIRANDA]   Give me your hands.
Let grief and sorrow still embrace his
heart
That doth not wish you joy!
GONZALO.   Be it so! Amen!   215

Re-enter ARIEL, *with the* MASTER *and*
BOATSWAIN *amazedly following.*

O, look, sir, look, sir! here is more
of us.
I prophesied, if a gallows were on
land,
This fellow could not drown. Now,
blasphemy,
That swear'st grace o'erboard, not
an oath on shore?
Hast thou no mouth by land? What
is the news?   220
BOATSWAIN. The best news is that we
have safely found
Our king and company. The next,
our ship—
Which, but three glasses since, we
gave out split—
Is tight and yare and bravely rigged
as when
We first put out to sea.
ARIEL. [*aside to* PROSPERO] Sir, all
this service   225
Have I done since I went.
PROSPERO.   [*aside to* ARIEL]   My
tricksy spirit!
ALONSO. These are not natural events,
they strengthen
From strange to stranger. Say, how
came you hither?
BOATSWAIN. If I did think, sir, I were
well awake,
I'd strive to tell you. We were dead
of sleep   230
And—how we know not—all clapped
under hatches;
Where but even now with strange
and several noises

---

196 *hers:* her father, i.e., I accept her as a
daughter. 200 *heaviness:* sorrow.

219 *swear'st...o'erboard:* frighten God's grace
from the ship with swearing.   223 *glasses:*
hours.

Of roaring, shrieking, howling, jin-
gling chains,
And moe diversity of sounds, all
horrible,
We were awaked, straightway at
liberty.   235
Where we, in all her trim, freshly
beheld
Our royal, good and gallant ship, our
master
Capering to eye her. On a trice, so
please you,
Even in a dream, were we divided
from them
And were brought moping hither.
ARIEL.   [*aside to* PROSPERO] Was't
well done?   240
PROSPERO. [*aside to* ARIEL] Bravely,
my diligence. Thou shalt be free.
ALONSO. This is as strange a maze as
e'er men trod,
And there is in this business more
than nature
Was ever conduct of. Some oracle
Must rectify our knowledge.
PROSPERO.   Sir, my liege, 245
Do not infest your mind with beat-
ing on
The strangeness of this business. At
picked leisure
Which shall be shortly, single I'll
resolve you,
Which to you shall seem probable,
of every
These happened accidents. Till when,
be cheerful   250
And think of each thing well. [*aside
to* ARIEL] Come hither, spirit.
Set Caliban and his companions free,
Untie the spell.   [*Exit* ARIEL.]
How fares my gracious sir?
There are yet missing of your com-
pany
Some few odd lads that you remem-
ber not.   255

Re-enter ARIEL, *driving in* CALIBAN,
STEPHANO *and* TRINCULO, *in their
stolen apparel.*

STEPHANO. Every man shift for all the
rest, and let no man take care for
himself, for all is but fortune.
Coragio, bully-monster, coragio!
TRINCULO. If these be true spies 260
which I wear in my head, here's a
goodly sight.
CALIBAN. O Setebos, these be brave
spirits indeed!
How fine my master is! I am afraid
He will chastise me.
SEBASTIAN.   Ha, ha!   265
What things are these, my lord
Antonio?
Will money buy 'em?
ANTONIO.   Very like. One
of them
Is a plain fish, and no doubt market-
able.
PROSPERO. Mark but the badges of these
men, my lords,
Then say if they be true. This mis-
shapen knave,   270
His mother was a witch, and one so
strong
That could control the moon, make
flows and ebbs,
And deal in her command without
her power.
These three have robbed me. And
this demi-devil—
For he's a bastard one—had plotted
with them   275
To take my life. Two of these fellows
you
Must know and own. This thing of
darkness I
Acknowledge mine.
CALIBAN.   I shall be pinched
to death.
ALONSO. Is not this Stephano, my
drunken butler?

240 *moping:* dazedly. 244 *conduct of:* capable
of managing; *oracle:* divine enlightenment.
246 *infest:* molest. 247 *picked:* chosen. 248
single: privately, or perhaps simply. 253
gracious sir: Alonzo.

258 *bully:* fine. 269 *badges:* arm insignia
worn by servants; here, the stolen clothes.
273 *And deal...power:* wield the moon's
authority without the moon's permission. 277
own: admit to be yours.

SEBASTIAN. He is drunk now. Where had he wine? 280

ALONSO. And Trinculo is reeling ripe. Where should they
Find this grand liquor that hath gilded 'em?
How camest thou in this pickle?

TRINCULO. I have been in such a pickle since I saw you last that, I fear 285
me, will never out of my bones. I shall not fear fly-blowing.

SEBASTIAN. Why, how now, Stephano!

STEPHANO. O, touch me not, I am not Stephano but a cramp. 290

PROSPERO. You'll be king o' the isle, sirrah?

STEPHANO. I should have been a sore one then.

ALONSO. This is a strange thing as e'er I looked on. [*pointing to* CALIBAN]

PROSPERO. He is as disproportioned in his manners
As in his shape. Go, sirrah, to my cell. 295
Take with you your companions. As you look
To have my pardon, trim it handsomely.

CALIBAN. Ay, that I will. And I'll be wise hereafter
And seek for grace. What a thrice-double ass
Was I to take this drunkard for a god 300
And worship this dull fool!

PROSPERO.   Go to, away!

ALONSO. Hence, and bestow your luggage where you found it.

SEBASTIAN. Or stole it, rather.

[*Exeunt* CALIBAN, STEPHANO, *and* TRINCULO.]

PROSPERO. Sir, I invite your highness and your train
To my poor cell, where you shall take your rest 305
For this one night, which, part of it, I'll waste
With such discourse as, I not doubt, shall make it
Go quick away—the story of my life
And the particular accidents gone by
Since I came to this isle. And in the morn 310
I'll bring you to your ship and so to Naples,
Where I have hope to see the nuptial
Of these our dear-beloved solemnized,
And thence retire me to my Milan, where
Every third thought shall be my grave.

ALONSO. I long 315
To hear the story of your life, which must
Take the ear strangely.

PROSPERO.   I'll deliver all,
And promise you calm seas, auspicious gales
And sail so expeditious that shall catch
Your royal fleet far off. [*aside to* ARIEL] My Ariel, chick, 320
That is thy charge. Then to the elements
Be free, and fare thou well! Please you, draw near. *Exeunt omnes.*

---

282 *gilded:* flushed. 283 *in this pickle:* to be so pickled. 287 *fly-blowing:* i.e., pickled meat cannot get fly-blown.

309 *accidents:* incidents.

EPILOGUE

SPOKEN BY PROSPERO.

Now my charms are all o'erthrown,
And what strength I have's mine
  own,
Which is most faint. Now, 'tis true,
I must be here confined by you,
Or sent to Naples. Let me not,   5
Since I have my dukedom got
And pardoned the deceiver, dwell
In this bare island by your spell,
But release me from my bands
With the help of your good hands. 10

Gentle breath of yours my sails
Must fill, or else my project fails,
Which was to please. Now I want
Spirits to enforce, art to enchant,
And my ending is despair   15
Unless I be relieved by prayer,
Which pierces so that it assaults
Mercy itself and frees all faults.
As you from crimes would pardoned
  be,
Let your indulgence set me free. 20

Exit.

Epilogue.9 *bands:* bonds. 10 *hands:* i.e.,
clapping applause. 11 *Gentle breath:* ap-
preciative remarks.

13 *want:* lack. 16 *prayer:* i.e., the plea he is
now making.

Tartuffe

The text of *Tartuffe* is somewhat complicated by the circumstances of its early stagings and nonstagings. In 1664 Molière (1622–1673) presented before the court of Louis XIV at Versailles three acts of a play called *Le Tartuffe*. Though personally approving, Louis, apparently pressured by the archbishop of Paris and perhaps the queen mother, forbade further performances. Opposition to the play centered in the Compagnie du Saint-Sacrement, a secret society of moral vigilantes some of whose members were attached, like Tartuffe, to wealthy households as spiritual advisors (Directors of Conscience). This "cabal of the pious," as the society was called, along with other religious bodies like the Jesuits (whose treatises on "casuistry," or the art of adjusting morality to convenience, seemed also under attack by Molière: "There is a science / Of loosening the conscience so compliance is easy," Tartuffe says in IV, v) managed to keep *Tartuffe* off the stage for several years. In 1667, evidently with some prior encouragement by Louis, Molière brought forth a revised version called *The Impostor*, in which the *faux dévot* Tartuffe was now cast as Panulphe, a nonclerical dandy. Even these changes were not enough, however, and after one performance the play was suppressed by the president (the king was off with his armies in Flanders), backed by the archbishop of Paris' threat to excommunicate anyone in his diocese who attended it. Not until 1669, when various religious developments increased Louis' power, did *Tartuffe* appear in its present form.

The form is most obviously neoclassic, with implicit commitments to sanity, artifice, order. Thus, like *Phaedra*, *Tartuffe* is shaped to accord with the dramatic unities. The action is single (though there is a trace of a subplot in the Valère-Mariane situation), the time is held down to a day, and the scene is localized. The sense of formal containment brought about by Molière's adherence to the unities is reinforced by his poetic style. The French original is written throughout in rhyming Alexandrine couplets (in translation these have been cut back to pentameter couplets) that no amount of rhythmic variation can keep from sounding stiffly formal. Thought and feeling, however violent, rash, or uncontrolled, must pass through the regularizing mechanism of the verse to be expressed.

This normalizing process is at work in characterization as well. The characters and some of the action in *Tartuffe* are influenced by Italian drama, specifically the "professional drama" of Italy called *commedia dell'arte*, which specialized in vaguely outlined plots filled with improvisations by stock character types like Pantalone, an old Venetian merchant in loose pants and slippers, Dottore, a Bolognese pedant in black gown, and Capitano, a soldier in the *miles gloriosus* tradition. Dorine in *Tartuffe*, the quick-witted, commonsensical maid, is related to an Italian stock character of this type that goes back ultimately to the tricky slave of Roman comedy; Valère and Mariane are typical young lovers, nice, stubborn, anonymous; Orgon, the deceived, tyrannical parent, is a heavy father type popular from one end of comedy to the other; and Tartuffe comes under the label of *faux dévot,* or religious impostor. Even the action inherits from *commedia dell'arte* something of the stock comic routine *(lazzo),* as in II, ii when Orgon keeps urging the impertinent Dorine to say one more word as he stands with arm cocked; in III, iii when Elmire and Tartuffe reduce the maneuverings of desire to a chase of chairs; or in III, vi when Orgon and Tartuffe both plop to their knees.

These elements of regularity in the style and form of *Tartuffe* are conditioned by Molière's comic standard of values. Comedy normally endorses normality and order at the expense of the deviant and individualistic; but this is especially true in seventeenth-century France with its scrupulous attention to norms of dress, speech, and conduct and its reverence for reason and authority. Dorine's blunt honesty ("What stuff! Get out! You must be chaffing!"–II, ii), Elmire's level-headedness ("pray don't be scandalized if I seem to behave / Quite forwardly"— IV, iii), and Cléante's doctrine of rational moderation ("don't rush away/Too hastily, but keep to the middle way"—V, i) obviously offer perspectives from which we evaluate hypocrisy and irrationality. From this we might expect a plot based on a morality play triangle: Orgon as Everyman wooed by Tartuffe as Hypocrisy and the rest of his family as Right Reason. In such a scheme the climax would consist of the exposure of Hypocrisy and the enlightenment of Everyman. And that is precisely what Elmire plans with her pseudo-seduction scene. "Some men," she says to and of Orgon (IV, iii), "are easily fooled by infatuation; / Such blindness must be cured by illumination." But Molière has shaped his play in terms of a more complex awareness, for the illumination of Orgon, however personally redemptive it may be, does not save the family, which appears doomed to lose everything. A restoration of order can only come from a god-king in whom are focused all the normative values that Orgon and Tartuffe have abandoned during the play.

Molière has been frequently criticized for failing to prepare in any way for the sudden appearance of the King's officer. The very artlessness with which he employs this *rex ex machina,* however, calls attention to its artfulness and gives an ironic twist to the comic convention of the happy ending. Evil is controlled not by logic or virtue, not by any plausible development of the events of the play, but purely by theatrical artifice. The regal dramatist of France, Louis XIV, may have temporarily suppressed the pseudo-pious and redeemed Molière by allowing *Tartuffe* itself to be staged, but Molière seems to suggest that the material of actual life is normally more recalcitrant than that with which playwrights work.

Another way of viewing the appearance of the King's officer is as a logical conclusion to a play that specializes in the inconclusive. The student should note the number of scenes in which some form of interruption occurs. In I, i, for instance, we encounter a verbal world in which dialogue is impossible because Madame Pernelle will not permit anyone to complete a statement. By the same token, no one in Orgon's household can complete a normal relationship to anyone else because of the interruption of Tartuffe, who wedges his pious presence between Orgon and Elmire (whom he would seduce), between Orgon and Damis (whom he would disinherit), and between Valère and Mariane (whom he would marry). It is perfectly in keeping with the play's "interruptive mode," then, that the interrupter himself be interrupted just when he seems about to complete his triumph. Only the King, it seems, can genuinely conclude anything, though whether he has effectively concluded Tartuffe's career is questionable.

The family in this play is a disciplined social structure in which each person is allotted his role and function under the authoritarian rule of Orgon. In so patterned a group, Tartuffe is not only an interrupter but a sort of "wild card" who gets around normal requirements, who has no fixed identity of his own but is constantly absorbing the identities of others, especially Orgon. Perhaps this is what gives him, despite his broadly comic features, a certain ominousness. He is an unknown quantity, as hypocrites must always be, since we only see what they are not. But also, he acquires power by using others. The deluded Orgon is increasingly deprived of his own identity as he becomes the instrument of Tartuffe's will. In this sense Tartuffe is the parasite that feeds on and gradually envelops the host organism. Thus he becomes Orgon as head of household, Orgon as husband, Orgon as father, since Orgon's action in each of these roles is dictated by Tartuffe. Tartuffe steals Orgon's identity in another sense, too, by stealing his property. Orgon is what he owns, and he owns not merely land, house, chattel, and money but also people. Under Tartuffe's influence he becomes a domestic tyrant whose absolute authority is asserted by reducing his family to objects of his will, to mere property. He has learned not to "waste" his love on his wife (I, vi), he "disowns" his son Damis (III, vi), and he wants to "give" his daughter Mariane to Tartuffe:

> Give him your wealth [Mariane says], if that's what you want to do
> And, if that's not enough, why, take mine too.
> Give him all that I have; it cannot worsen
> My grief. But don't consign to him my person!
>
> (IV, iii)

When Orgon has given everything over to Tartuffe, there is a sense in which he has given himself as well, which perhaps accounts for the bleaching out of Orgon as a character near the end of the play. From this point of view, we see Tartuffe as a personality-vacuum seeking fulfillment through others. His ill-disguised lust for the women of the house is the physiological equivalent to this spiritual rapacity by which he attempts to renew himself. Thus it is not merely an accident that Tartuffe's presence causes Orgon to alter the provisions of his "will," for in his tyrannical assertions of his will over his family Orgon has become the agent of Tartuffe's will. The question is whose will shall dominate, whose absorptive powers are greater; the final answer is, the King's.

Tartuffe

MADAME PERNELLE *mother of* ORGON
ORGON
ELMIRE ORGON'S *wife*
DAMIS *son of* ORGON, *stepson of* ELMIRE
MARIANE *daughter of* ORGON *and step-daughter of* ELMIRE
VALÈRE

CLÉANTE *brother-in-law of* ORGON, *brother of* ELMIRE
TARTUFFE
DORINE *companion of* MARIANE
MONSIEUR LOYAL *bailiff*
A POLICE OFFICER
FLIPOTE MADAME PERNELLE'S *servant*

The setting throughout is the salon of ORGON'S *house in Paris. The furnishings are those of a well-to-do bourgeois.*

ACT I

SCENE i. MADAME PERNELLE, FLIPOTE, ELMIRE, MARIANE, DORINE, DAMIS, *and* CLÉANTE.

MME. PERNELLE. Come on, Flipote, away from their mad chatter.

ELMIRE. Heavens, Madame! Now what can be the matter?

MME. PERNELLE. Enough, enough; spare me their smiling faces.
I can well dispense with certain airs and graces.

ELMIRE. Madame, no one has given you cause to grieve;   5
Why, I pray, are you so resolved to leave?

MME. PERNELLE. I cannot stand this place a minute more;
My every wish is trampled and spurned to the floor.
I leave your house no wiser, but much sadder,
And now—heigh ho!—you ask me what's the matter.   10
None honors age, all speak with impudence,
This house has become like a Court of Insolence.

DORINE. If...

MME. PERNELLE. You are, my girl, a humble maid, a minion,
And yet you talk and give us your free opinion
Like the veriest, blabbiest, gabbling hobbledehoy!   15

DAMIS. But...

MME. PERNELLE. In words of single syllables, my boy,
You are a fool. And that's all there is to that.
You've no more common sense than my old cat.
I've warned your father, not once, but a hundred times
That in the end you'd not be worth a dime.   20

MARIANE. I think...

From Tartuffe *by* Molière, *translated by James L. Rosenberg, published by Chandler Publishing Company, San Francisco. Copyright* © *1962 by Chandler Publishing Company. Reprinted by permission.*

MME. PERNELLE. And you, his sister, so demure and shy!
But I suspect that sparkle in your eye;
I note the adage about waters running deep
When I hear you sweetly sigh and softly weep.
ELMIRE. But, mother...
MME. PERNELLE. And you who should above all play the role 25
Of modesty and grace; upon the whole
I find your conduct shocking. Is it your place
To squander your husband's money, paint your face,
And boldly parade your charms before the world
Like a golden galleon with all her sails unfurled? 30
A woman who only seeks to attract her spouse
Does not so gaily decorate the house!
CLÉANTE. But, madame, after all...
MME. PERNELLE. And you, my lad,
I honor, love and respect you, need I add?
But if I were in my son her husband's place 35
I'd earnestly ask you not to show your face
Ever again in my house. It seems you preach
Tireless moral maxims, but what you teach
And what you live do not precisely agree.
Forgive my bluntness; my manner of speech is free. 40
DAMIS. I'm sure, madame, your Tartuffe is fortunate...
MME. PERNELLE. He is a man you might well imitate,
And it makes me furious through and through
To hear him maligned by a fool and a dolt like you.
DAMIS. What the devil? (Pardon the expression!) 45
Am I to live at the bigoted discretion
Of a puritanical tyrant and beg his consent
To live or breathe in my father's establishment?
DORINE. According to him and his maxims, we can't begin
To wiggle a toe without committing a sin. 50
He's got his nose in everything, sniffing out wrongs.
MME. PERNELLE. Wherever his nose is, there, I'm sure, it belongs.
He seeks to lead you with him on Heaven's path,
And you, like silly geese, just sit and laugh.
DAMIS. Neither the due respect I owe to my father 55
Nor anything else could make me go to the bother
Of trying to like that unctuous hypocrite,
And I cannot live at ease with myself and sit
At the table with him, smiling and wishing him well,
Or wishing, in short, he were anywhere else but in Hell! 60
DORINE. Indeed, I say it's a monstrous and scandalous thing
To see a stranger come and put a ring
In the master's nose and lead him around like a bull—
A penniless tramp whose belly was seldom full,
Whose shoes and coat were as holy as now he allows 65
His precious soul is—having the run of the house!
MME. PERNELLE. Ah! mercy on us! how happy we would be
If we all obeyed his wise and pious decrees.
DORINE. He's a shining saint in your imagination
But a hypocrite in our frank estimation. 70

MME. PERNELLE. Hold your tongue!

DORINE.   I
  wouldn't trust him, by the book,
  As far as I could throw a ten-ton
  rock.

MME. PERNELLE. All your malicious lies
    leave me unmoved.
  In my opinion, Tartuffe stands
    approved
  In every way. You hate him, you
    foolish things,   75
  Because he tells you of your faults
    and brings
  A message calling your souls away
    from sin.
  Heaven's all he's interested in.

DORINE. Oh, yes, indeed! But tell me
    why, I pray,
  He wants to drive all visitors away.
  When someone calls, is Heaven so
    offended   81
  That he must rave as though the
    world had ended?
  Do you know what I think of the
    affair? [*pointing to* ELMIRE]
  I think he's jealous of Madame—so
    there!

MME. PERNELLE. Hold your tongue and
    mind what you are saying.   85
  He's not alone in finding your giddy
    playing
  And all your social life a bit too
    much:
  These carriages and servants, crowds
    and such,
  Disturb the neighborhood with an
    uproar
  The like of which has not been heard
    before   90
  By decent folk. No doubt there's no
    harm done,
  But gossip breeds like flies in the
    summer sun.

CLÉANTE. Ah, madame, would you cure
    the human race
  Of gossiping or showing the double
    face?
  And what a sorry world now this
    would be   95
  If every little lie that touched on me

Forced me to lose a friend. The fact
Is, no one's ever legislated tact.
No one's safe against the tongue of
  slander
Or those malicious souls who long to
  pander   100
To the mob's desire for scandal. No,
  each man
Must merely live as wisely as he
  can.

DORINE. Isn't it old Daphne and that
    shrimp
  Of a husband of hers—the little
    pimp!—
  Who've been busy spreading their
    gossip and lies   105
  About us? We're sinners in their
    eyes,
  Or so they say. But why, pray, is it
    those
  Whose own inane behavior, Heaven
    knows,
  Is always most ridiculous or suspect
  Who seem to feel it's their duty to
    inflict   110
  Their stupid opinions upon the rest
    of us?
  Can it be these peccadilloes they dis-
    cuss
  Are exactly the things they're up to
    on the sly
  And they think the insinuating lie
  Of who was seen ascending someone's
    stairs   115
  Will leave them free to conduct their
    own affairs?

MME. PERNELLE. All this chitchat's
    quite beside the point.
  You all, I'm sure, know my dear
    friend Orante,
  A good and saintly woman, full of
    grace;
  She's not pleased with what goes on
    in this place.   120

DORINE. A fine example, and a most
    chaste wife!
  It's true indeed she lives an austere
    life,
  But age has waked that cold reform-
    ing zeal;

The fire dies down when one runs
out of fuel.
Many a prude's born when youth's
beauty dies 125
And looks perforce on life with
saintly eyes.
Orante now hides beneath discretion's
veil
Those fading charms that from
henceforth must fail
To win esteem. These veteran
coquettes
Revenge themselves on a world that
soon forgets 130
Their fast-decaying beauty and retire
To rectitude, renouncing all desire;
Cheated of love, they turn to criti-
cism
And make Morality their catechism;
They censure all who taste the joy
of life 135
And concentrate on stirring endless
strife.
Not principle, but envy, activates
Their tireless tongues and bitterly
creates
That twisted malice which insanely
drives them
To hate those pleasures of which age
deprives them. 140
MME. PERNELLE [*to* ELMIRE]. These
are the things that you delight to
hear,
And it seems this gracious lady has
your ear
And is allowed to go on talking all
the day
While I must keep my peace and go
my way.
Alas, the sins of this world! Yet I'll
be heard 145
And give you, will-you nill-you, this
last word:
The wisest decision my son has ever
made
Was in taking this holy man to be
his guide;
God has sent him here to redeem
your sins
And show you where the road to

Heaven begins. 150
All those balls and dances, conversa-
tions,
Those goings to and fro, those visi-
tations
Are surely inspired by the Evil One's
decrees;
One never hears a pious word or sees
A modest action; all come in for their
share 155
In the tide of malicious gossip run-
ning there.
In short, all sensible people lose their
sense
In that sea of shallow frippery and
pretense.
A thousand silly stories spread in a
day,
And I heard a certain noted doctor
say 160
This house has become a virtual
Tower of Babel
Where everyone talks as fast and
loud as he's able.
And to explain how this comment
came to be...

[*Pointing to* CLÉANTE.]

But I see yon gentleman secretly
smiling at me.
Eh bien, go find the fools who make
you gay. [*to* ELMIRE] 165
To you, my daughter, I've nothing
more to say,
Except that I disapprove of your
home and friends;
Good-bye. Farewell. Here our
acquaintance ends.

[*Giving* FLIPOTE *a box on the ear.*]

Come on, wake up, you silly gaping
goose!
I'll fetch you a wallop will knock
your senses loose! 170
Come on, away, away!

SCENE ii. CLÉANTE *and* DORINE.

CLÉANTE. I'll not go rushing

After her, for fear of more tongue-
lashing.
That old battle-axe...
DORINE.   Ah, it's a pity
She can't hear you. What a lively
ditty
She would sing you now—she'd shout
and scold   175
To let you know she's not so awfully
old!
CLÉANTE. How angry she was with us,
and all for nothing!
Tartuffe has got her poor old brain
a-buzzing.
DORINE. All this is a minor situation
Compared to the master's infatuation.
If you could only see him, you'd say
he's turned   181
An utter fool. In recent years he'd
earned
The reputation of a man of sense,
But since Tartuffe's bewitched him,
all pretense
Of plain intelligence has left his head.
He calls him "brother" and has often
said   186
He loves him more than daughter,
son, or wife.
He makes him the director of his life
And his secret soul's true confidant;
A mistress or a sweetheart couldn't
want   190
More tender demonstrations of his
love;
At the dining table, Tartuffe sits
above
In the place of honor, like a greedy
glutton
Devouring vast slabs of beef and
mutton;
The choicest cuts are his, let him
but "hic"   195
The master cries "God bless you!"
double quick.
In short, he dotes upon him like a
fool;
Tartuffe's his hero, and he's the
villain's tool.
He quotes him with the wildest
admiration

And praises him on every least occasion.   200
Tartuffe, who knows a sucker when
he sees him,
Employs a hundred little arts to
please him;
He steals him blind, meanwhile, with
pious maxims,
While criticizing all the family's
actions.
Even that sneering jackanapes of a
boy   205
Who serves him as a page seems to
enjoy
The freedom of the house and has
the power
To lecture and correct us hour by
hour.
A handkerchief of mine drew his
complaints
Because he found it pressed in a
Book of Saints.   210

SCENE iii. ELMIRE, MARIANE, DAMIS,
CLÉANTE, *and* DORINE.

ELMIRE. You're lucky, brother, your
ears were not made sore
By her haranguing all the way to the
door.
But I saw my husband as I was
passing the stair;
I'll be in my room, if he wishes to
see me there.
CLÉANTE. Thanks. I'll wait, despite
your friendly warning,   215
And try at least to wish him a "Good
morning."

SCENE iv. CLÉANTE, DAMIS, *and*
DORINE.

DAMIS. Speak to him, if you will, about
Mariane.
You know I'm interested in her plan
To marry Valère. I fear my father's
delay
Is based on Tartuffe's dislike of the
wedding day.   220

If Valère and my sister marry, it may
  be
My own joy with his sister I may
  see
Quite soon...
CLÉANTE.   Here he comes.

SCENE v. ORGON, CLÉANTE, *and* DORINE.

ORGON.   Ah, good
  morning, brother.
CLÉANTE. Dear Orgon, I am glad to
  have another
  Chance to speak to you. The fields
  are drying...   225
ORGON. Forgive me, brother, but I'm
  dying
  To hear the latest news about the
  household
  From the greatest drawing room to
  the smallest mouse hole.

[*To* DORINE.]

  Has all gone happily since yester-
  day?
  How's everybody's health? Tell me,
  I pray!   230
DORINE. Madame was feverish and had
  to take
  A medicine to cure a vile headache.
ORGON. And Tartuffe?
DORINE.   Tartuffe? Healthy,
  stout and merry,
  Bright as paint and ruddy as a
  cherry.
ORGON. Poor man!
DORINE.   Last night, her head-
  ache grew so bad   235
  She scarce could stir out of her
  bed
  And could not eat a bit of dinner.
ORGON. And Tartuffe?
DORINE.   He ate—that
  well-fed sinner—
  A brace of good plump partridges,
  done brown,
  With a bottle of red wine to wash
  them down.   240
ORGON. Poor man!
DORINE.   She passed a tor-

tured, sleepless night
In endless pain; the morning's cold
  gray light
At last relieved her fever, but we sat
Beside her all night long; just think
  of that!
ORGON. And Tartuffe?
DORINE.   Replete and
  sleepy, satisfied,   245
  He drifted from the meal to his
  fireside,
  Crept thence into his warm and cozy
  bed
  And snored till dawn, the comfy
  sleepy-head.
ORGON. Poor man!
DORINE.   Madame, agreeing to
  our fond persuasions,
  Consented to the doctor's ministra-
  tions   250
  And, bled and physicked, felt some-
  what relieved.
ORGON. And Tartuffe?
DORINE.   Not, I must con-
  fess, unduly grieved
  By Madame's illness, but right
  valiantly
  Took arms against foul trouble's
  surging sea
  And drank some wine to replace the
  blood she'd lost.   255
ORGON. Poor man!
DORINE.   I'm happy to report
  the danger's past,
  And now I'll hasten to inform my
  mistress
  How pleased you are she's cured of
  her distress.

SCENE vi. ORGON *and* CLÉANTE.

CLÉANTE. Brother, she's laughing in
  your very face
  And, though I'm far from wishing
  you disgrace,   260
  I must say that she's right in her
  estimation.
  Who ever saw such a mad infatuation?

Is it possible this man has charmed
  you so
That you can forget all else for him,
  and go
Running about to do his commands?
  I swear   265
I've never seen such nonsense...
ORGON.   Stop right there;
  For you don't know the man of whom
  you speak.
CLÉANTE. All right, then. I don't know
  him, if you like,
  But I know various things that I
  have heard.
ORGON. To know him is to love him,
  take my word.   270
  I model myself on him whenever I
  can;
  He is a man who...well, in short, a
  man.
  Whoever follows his precepts lives in
  peace
  And sees the rest of the world as so
  much dross.
  Yes, I have changed since he came
  into my life;   275
  He's taught me not to waste my love
  on my wife
  Or on any mortal thing; what's more,
  I could see my children turned away
  from my door,
  Thanks to him, without the least
  concern.
CLÉANTE. These are surely humane
  truths to learn!   280
ORGON. Ah, if you could have seen him
  when at first
  We met, in the days when my life
  was still accursed!
  Each day in church he came and, if
  you please,
  Fell with a crash before me to his
  knees.
  He drew the attention of everybody
  there   285
  With the ardency and loudness of his
  prayer.
  He sighed, stretched flatly forth on
  his abdomen,

And kissed the floor with every pass-
  ing moment.
When I departed, he ran along before
  me.
And lightly sprinkled holy water o'er
  me.   290
I made inquiries of his servant, and
  he
Told me of who he was, and his
  poverty
Described so movingly, I could not
  choose
But offer gifts to him, which he'd
  refuse,
Forever crying, "No, no, it's too
  much;   295
I am unworthy, no, I dare not
  touch
A penny of it!" And, if I persisted,
He'd give it to the poor. Oh, he
  assisted
Many a one that way. Chaste
  Heaven, at last,
Moved me to take him in here as my
  guest.   300
Since then, all prospers. Sternly he
  reproves
All sinful and suspect behavior,
  moves
Particularly to guard my sacred
  honor
Where my wife's concerned. He keeps
  upon her
A most strict watch, and is indeed
  more jealous   305
Of all those coxcombs and conceited
  fellows
Who hang around her than *I* am, I
  feel;
You'd scarce believe the extent of his
  pious zeal.
One day he killed a flea with too
  much pique,
Then scourged himself and fasted for
  a week.   310
CLÉANTE. Brother, I swear, there's
  something wrong with your head.
  Are you laughing at me with all this
  that you've said?

What does it mean? This madness
worries me...
ORGON. Your language, brother, savors
of heresy.
Your thinking's somewhat tainted by
that vice,   315
And, as I've had to warn you once
or twice,
You're liable to a judgment on your
head.
CLÉANTE. To think like you is worse
than being dead.
You voluntary blind men always call
The rest of us "freethinkers," where-
as all   320
We're guilty of is scorning empty
shows
And faithlessness. And now do you
suppose
Your veiled denunciations frighten
me?
My heart is open for all men to see.
I am no dupe of formalistic panders;
Religion, like the throne, has false
pretenders.   326
And as the truly brave aren't always
those
Who trumpet loudest or with gaudy
shows
Paint their performance, so the true
devout
Don't always pray the loudest or go
about   330
With piously exaggerated ges-
tures;
True worth does not reside in out-
ward vestures,
Hypocrisy too often masks religion,
And men like you confuse life's true
condition
By judging that the mask must be
the face;   335
But don't you see such judgment's
a disgrace?
The shadow, not the substance, is
your God;
The false coin's what you worship,
not the good.
Man must be, indeed, a curious crea-

ture
Who can't obey the simple laws of
nature.   340
Reason seems to hem him in too
tightly,
And so he never plays his part quite
rightly.
He ruins every act by exaggeration
In trying to advance in estimation.
And, brother, by the way, a word to
the wise...   345
ORGON. Well, you must be a scholar in
disguise,
For clearly all the wisdom of the
ages
Has found its home in you; the
greatest sages
Are nothing unto you—you are a
Cato,
A Socrates, a Zeno, or a Plato!   350
CLÉANTE. I'm not a doctor of philoso-
phy,
And all life's wisdom doesn't reside
in me.
My science lies in being able to see
Distinctions between truth and fal-
sity.
And as I know of nothing more com-
mendable   355
Than the honest piety of depend-
able
And devoted holy men, so too I find
Nothing's worse than those whose
double mind
Betrays true holiness, those hypo-
crites
Upon whose subtle faces triumph sits
In smiling sacrilegious impu-
dence,   361
Whose lives are nothing but one long
pretense
Of piousness, the while they make a
mock
Of all that's good, and while they
fleece the flock
Of silly sheep by various devices 365
Designed to line their pockets; all
their vices
Masquerade as virtue; on their way

To Heaven they contrive to jest and
  play
In secrecy, maintaining the disguise
Of holiness by lifting up their eyes
In pious, zealous ardor; who, in
  short,   371
While living in the luxury of Court,
Dryly preach abstinence, plain living,
And retirement; who, without mis-
  giving,
Can reconcile their vices and their
  zeal;   375
Passionate, revengeful, they con-
  ceal
Their petty jealousies beneath the
  cloak
Of piety and goodness and invoke
God's name to consecrate their evils,
So bold and fearless are these subtle
  devils.   380
They place themselves upon the side
  of Heaven
And assassinate their foes with a
  sacred weapon.
This modern age, I fear, too rankly
  teems
With such pretenders, but although
  it seems
Hard to detect them, still true piety
Is never really difficult to see: 386
Look at Ariston, look at Périandre,
Oronte, Alcidamas, Polydore, and
  Clitandre.
No one would dare deny to them the
  title
Of honesty in any true recital   390
Of virtue's servants; never do they
  show
This ostentatious righteousness or go
Meddling into other folk's affairs
And giving themselves these smug
  and holy airs.
Their goodness is direct and free and
  simple   395
And only by their own benign exam-
  ple
Do they ever even so much as ven-
  ture
To subject others unto moral cen-
sure.
They do not trust the face that evil
  shows
But are the first to think the best of
  those   400
Whom lying slander villainously
  attacks.
We find no intrigues or no secret
  pacts
Among them; virtue's what they're
  interested in;
They love the sinner, though they
  hate the sin.
Above all, they're embarrassed to dis-
  close   405
Toward Heaven greater zeal than
  Heaven shows
Toward them. Such people truly
  share my heart.
ORGON. And have you finally spoken all
  your part?
CLÉANTE. Yes.
ORGON.   Your servant, sir. I bid
  you a good day.
CLÉANTE. A moment, brother. Please
  don't run away.   410
Do you recall your promise to
  Valère?
ORGON. Yes.
CLÉANTE.   And that you'd blessed the
  happy, loving pair?
ORGON. That's true.
CLÉANTE.   Why, then, is there
  this great delay?
ORGON. I don't know.
CLÉANTE.   You're   planning
  for another day?
ORGON. Perhaps.
CLÉANTE.   You mean you'd break
  your word?   415
ORGON. I don't say that.
CLÉANTE.   From   what
  I've heard,
You have no reason to delay things
  thus.
ORGON. That depends.
CLÉANTE.   There   certainly
  should be no fuss.
ORGON. I suppose not.

CLÉANTE.   What shall I tell
  Valère?
ORGON. Whatever you please.
CLÉANTE.   But don't you care   420
  To make your wishes clear?
ORGON.   I care
  Only to do what Heaven wills.

CLÉANTE.   Come, now,
  You gave the lad your sacred vow.
ORGON. Farewell.   [*Exits.*]
CLÉANTE.   I fear the worst in this
  affair.
  I must speak further quickly with
  Valère.   425

ACT II

SCENE i. ORGON *and* MARIANE.

ORGON. Mariane.
MARIANE.   Father?
ORGON.   Come closer;
  let me speak
  To you.
MARIANE [*to* ORGON, *who is peering
  off stage*]. What is it there that
  you seek?
ORGON. I'm looking to see if anyone's
  eavesdropping.
  This is a likely place for tricksy
  snooping.
  There now. All's well. Now then, my
  dear,   5
  There's something that I wish for
  you to hear;
  You know I've always held you in
  my heart.
MARIANE. You've always played a lov-
  ing father's part.
ORGON. Well said! And to deserve that
  love, my treasure,
  You should think of nothing but your
  father's pleasure.   10
MARIANE. I hope I never merit your
  reproof.
ORGON. Splendid! Tell me, what do you
  think of Tartuffe?
MARIANE. Who, I?
ORGON.   You. Take care with
  your answer, pray.
MARIANE. Alas! I'll say whatever you
  wish me to say.

[DORINE *enters quietly and stands
behind* ORGON *without his seeing her.*]

SCENE ii. ORGON, MARIANE, *and*
DORINE.

ORGON. Ah, wisely spoken. Then say,
  my dearest dove,   15
  He has inspired your heart with
  tender love
  And that the crown of joy upon your
  life
  Descends the day that you become
  his wife.
MARIANE. What?
ORGON.   Eh?
MARIANE.   What did you say?
ORGON.   Me?
MARIANE.   Heavens above!
  Who is it that's inspired my heart
  with love?   20
  Who'll place the crown of joy upon
  my life
  The day that I agree to be his wife?
ORGON. Tartuffe.
MARIANE.   But, father, I feel
  nothing of the sort.
  Would you have me betray the truth
  of my true heart?
ORGON. But I *want* it to be true. It
  should suffice   25
  That my wishes in this matter are
  precise.
MARIANE. What? You wish...?
ORGON.   I intend, you see,
  To firmly unite Tartuffe to my family
  By marrying him to you. With that
  in view,
  I'm resolved this marriage must...
    [*Sees* DORINE.] Ha! You!   30

Your curiosity must be a powerful passion
To make you come and eavesdrop in this fashion.

DORINE. I must say, sir, I don't know whether I can
Tell whether the rumor arose by careful plan
Or accident, but when somebody spoke   35
Of such a marriage, I treated it all as a joke.

ORGON. And what is so incredible, I pray?

DORINE. I'm sorry. I can't believe a word that you say.

ORGON. I know how to make you believe it, I'll tell you that.

DORINE. Ha! What a tale! You're talking through your hat!   40

OREGON. I'm telling you what will very soon prove true.

DORINE. Nonsense!

ORGON.   Now, daughter, I mean what I say, I'm warning you.

DORINE. Ha, ha! Don't believe him! He's only laughing!

ORGON. I tell you...

DORINE.   What stuff! Get out! You must be chaffing!

ORGON. I warn you now, take care; my anger's rising!   45

DORINE. Well, I must say, it's surely most surprising.
Are we to believe a man as wise as you
With that splendid beard and eyes of baby blue
Would be so big a fool...

ORGON.   Now listen here!
You're taking certain liberties, my dear,   50
Which do not please me at all, I can't deny.

DORINE. Come, let's speak calmly, sir, if we can, and try
To understand each other. Of course, you're joking.
Your daughter to marry a bigot, whose manner of speaking
Would scarce melt butter? And explain, if you can,   55
What such an alliance would bring to you, a man
Of notable wealth—to corrupt your daughter's love
By marrying her off to a beggar...

ORGON.   That's enough!
I tell you that's the reason I revere him.
His poverty is honest. If you could hear him   60
Spurning worldly wealth and vulgar rank
As gross deceptions, then, my girl, you'd thank
Your father for marrying you to a saint,
A man who never has a word of complaint,
Whatever his woes. But with my modest aid   65
He'll soon regain the splendid role he played
In happier days. He once owned property
And was a landed squire in his home county.

DORINE. Yes, so he says; I say his vanity
Does not sort well with all his piety.   70
When you set up in business as a saint,
You shouldn't boast and brag without restraint.
Humility and love and true devotion
Are strange bedmates, indeed, for gross ambition.
Why be so haughty? But I see that you   75
Don't care at all for this. Then let's turn to
His person, not his claims to noble rank;
Doesn't it make you sometimes shudder or shrink
To think of a hypocritical fool
Like that corrupting the innocent soul   80

Of a girl like this? Stop and consider
The consequences, if you commit
her
To such a loathesome and revolting
marriage.
You'd better save your breath to cool
your porridge
Than try to lecture a young and
ardent wife 85
Who's bound by marriage to a hate-
ful life.
Those husbands who wear horns upon
their heads
Have driven their wives away from
their weary beds
By their stupidities; and woe to
those fathers
Who make such marriages for their
poor daughters! 90
Beware of driving her to be a wife.
ORGON. It's nice of you to tell me
about life!
DORINE. You could do worse than follow my advice.
ORGON. I'm sure these learned strictures
are very nice.
But, daughter, you will do what I
command. 95
Obey your father: that's the law of
the land.
At one time, true, I'd pledged you
to Valère,
But now I'm much disturbed by
what I hear
Of that young man: free-thinking,
playing cards, and such.
DORINE. And next you'll say you don't
see him in church 100
Like those who go for advertising's
sake.
ORGON. May I remind you that I didn't
make
A special request for *your* precise
advice.
I don't intend to speak to you more
than twice.
The other man of whom we speak,
I say, 105
Has made his peace with Heaven.
That's the way

To build a marriage rich in every
blessing.
You'll love each other. There'll be
no transgressing.
You'll coo and gurgle like two doting
turtles
And grow to be the happiest of
mortals. 110
You'll make of him whatever you
wish to make.
DORINE. She'll furnish him with horns
within a week.
ORGON. What? What's that?
DORINE. He's got the head for it,
And I fear the melancholy aspect of
his planet,
Despite your daughter's virtue, will
prove too strong. 115
ORGON. *I* say stop interrupting and hold
your tongue!
Mind your business; stop this dam-
nable meddling.
DORINE. I'm only trying to stop your
foolish fiddling.
ORGON. That's very kind of you. Now
please be silent.
DORINE. If I didn't love you, sir...
ORGON. I'm growing violent. 120
DORINE. I want to help you, sir, despite
your ire.
ORGON. Ha!
DORINE. It's true. Believe me, I
can't bear
All the mocking you'd be subject to.
ORGON. You won't shut up?
DORINE. Whatever else, I'm true,
True-blue, to my employer all the
way. 125
ORGON. Serpent! Silence! The next
word you say...!
DORINE. A holy man like you, in such
a temper?
ORGON. You plague me so, I find I
can't remember
What I started to say. Not one more
squawk!
DORINE. All right, but I can think, if
I can't talk. 130
ORGON. Think, if you like, but see that
you don't dare

To utter a word. [*to* MARIANE] I'll
grant you that Valère
Is a handsome chap...
DORINE.   It drives me
simply crazy
Not to be able to speak.
ORGON.   Though no fop or daisy,
Tartuffe has looks...
DORINE.   Indeed! To stop
a clock.   135
ORGON. And, too, he comes of very
ancient stock.
His other gifts...
DORINE.   Oh, you fortunate girl!
If I were forced to marry such a
churl,
I'd have my sweet revenge already
planned
And prove a woman always has at
hand   140
Those weapons that will give her the
last hit.
ORGON. You won't obey my orders? Is
that it?
DORINE. What's your trouble? I'm not
talking to you.
ORGON. To whom, pray tell?
DORINE.   Why, to
myself, that's who.
ORGON [*aside*]. *Eh bien*. There's only
one recourse in such a case   145
And that's to give her a slap across
the face.

[*Raises his hand to give her a blow, but
whenever he looks at her, she stands
mute and motionless.*]

ORGON. Daughter, you ought to think
well of my scheme;
Tartuffe's the answer to a maiden's
dream. [*to* DORINE]
Why don't you speak?
DORINE.   I've nothing
more to say.
ORGON. Go on. One little word.
DORINE.   Thanks, not today.   150
ORGON. I'm all ready for you.
DORINE.   I'm not *that* dumb.
ORGON [*to* MARIANE]. It's not that I
want my daughter under my

thumb,
But you must learn to accept a
father's rule.
DORINE [*fleeing*]. I'd die before I'd
marry that fat fool!

[ORGON *tries to slap her but misses and
falls down as she runs out.*]

ORGON. I can't live any longer with that
pest   155
Or I'll suffer the sin of anger. I must
rest.
I'm not in any state to go on with
our talk.
Excuse me while I go and take a
walk.

[*Exit* ORGON. DORINE *re-enters cautiously.*]

SCENE iii. MARIANE *and* DORINE.

DORINE. Mariane—ye gods—have you
nothing to say?
And must I play the part that you
should play?   160
A proposition utterly absurd,
And yet you don't defend yourself
with a word!
MARIANE. His power is absolute. What
can I do?
DORINE.   Tell him that a girl
wants you to.
MARIANE. What?
DORINE.   Tell him that a girl
can't love by proxy,   165
And when it comes to marrying a
foxy
And bigoted old hypocrite—*mon
Dieu!*—
Your wishes ought to count for some-
thing, too.
If he loves Tartuffe dearer than a
brother,
Then—Devil take it!—Let them
marry each other!   170
MARIANE. I know, but father is so over-
bearing,
I don't dare raise my voice within
his hearing.

DORINE. Look here. Let's think this through. Valère, you know,
Has offered you his hand. Is that not so?
MARIANE. Stop it, Dorine! Of course I love Valère   175
More than words can tell, and I can't bear
To think of looking at another lover;
But I've repeated all this ten times over.
DORINE. I'm sometimes doubtful of such a coy admission
And wonder if you're merely feigning passion.   180
MARIANE. You do me wrong in doubting me, my dear.
I'd thought that you believed I was sincere.
DORINE. In short, you love the boy?
MARIANE.   Oh, yes, with passion!
DORINE. And it would seem he loves you in like fashion?
MARIANE. I think so.
DORINE.   And the way to happiness   185
For both of you is marriage?
MARIANE.   Yes, oh, yes!
DORINE. And what about Tartuffe, love's adversary?
MARIANE. I'll kill myself, if that seems necessary.
DORINE. Oh, fine! "I'll kill myself," the maid replied.
The answer to life's grief is suicide.   190
A sovereign cure! It makes me mad clear through
To hear that kind of crazy talk from you.
MARIANE. Good heavens, what a temper! There you go!
You don't much sympathize with others' woe.
DORINE. I don't much sympathize with those who drivel,   195
Like you; then, when the test comes, shrivel.
MARIANE. You know I've always been a timid sort.

DORINE. But love demands a strong, courageous heart.
MARIANE. Loyalty to Valère's my firm intent,
But he must ask, and gain, Papa's consent.   200
DORINE. But if your father is an utter goof
Who's so infatuated with Tartuffe
He'll break the promise that he's pledged you to,
What is there left for poor Valère to do?
MARIANE. If I confess my true scorn for Tartuffe,   205
Won't I reveal unconsciously the truth
Of my affections? Though I love Valère,
Should I abandon modesty and dare
To flaunt my love for all the world to see?
DORINE. Oh, never mind. At least it's clear to me   210
You really want to be Madame Tartuffe,
And I was wrong to offer my reproof.
Why should I argue with two loving hearts?
The match would be ideal on both your parts.
Monsieur Tartuffe! a pretty pouter pigeon!   215
Tartuffe the Great! A man of high position!
A lucky girl she is who is his wife!
She royally has fixed herself for life.
Every day, each hour, you hear his praises
Sung by choirs in half a dozen places;   220
His ears are red as is the richest rose,
Only surpassed in glory by his nose.
MARIANE. Oh, God!
DORINE.   What ecstasy will fill your loving breast
When you go home to share his little nest.
MARIANE. Stop this agonizing talk! Not one more word!   225

I cannot stand it any more. I've
heard
Enough. Tell me how I can escape
his clutches.
DORINE. A daughter should obey her
father's wishes,
Although he choose a monkey for
her mate.
I'd like to help, but really, it's too
late.   230
Just think, you'll have a splendid
horse and carriage
To help you ease the boredom of
your marriage.
You can go calling on aunts, uncles,
cousins,
Whom you'll find round the city by
the dozens.
You'll call upon the Lord High
Mayoress   235
And on the tax-collector's wife, no
less,
Who'll seat you on a stool, the place
of honor,
And might invite you to stay on for
dinner;
A round of balls—as much as once
a year—
Two bagpipes for a band, some watery
beer;   240
Perhaps a puppet show, complete
with monkey.
However, if your husband...
MARIANE.   Oh, that donkey!
Dorine, for heaven's sake, I need
advice.
DORINE. You must excuse me.
MARIANE.   Please,
I've asked you twice.
DORINE. To punish you, this marriage
must go through.   245
MARIANE. Dorine!
DORINE.   No!
MARIANE.   I'll speak to
father, as you wish me to.
DORINE. You've made your choice. It's
clear Tartuffe's your man.
MARIANE. No more, Dorine. I've done
all that I can.
My tears and sighs don't even leave

you ruffled.
DORINE. As far as I'm concerned,
you'll be Tartuffled.   250
MARIANE. Since my unhappiness can't
move your heart,
I must surrender to despair and start
To search out methods of escaping
life:
A little vial of poison or a knife.
DORINE. Here, here, come back. I'll
put aside my ire   255
And help you to attain your true
desire.
MARIANE. Dorine, if they insist on
martyring me,
I'll simply die. I'll end my life. You'll
see
DORINE. Don't worry. We can find a
way to spare
Your life, I'm sure. But look, here
comes Valère.   260

[*Enter* VALÈRE. *He speaks at first
jestingly.*]

SCENE iv. VALÈRE, MARIANE, *and*
DORINE.

VALÈRE. Mademoiselle, a story's reached
my ears
Confirming all my wildest doubts and
fears.
MARIANE. What's that?
VALÈRE.   You're marrying Tartuffe.
MARIANE.   That's true.
My father wishes...What else can
I do?
VALÈRE. Your father, mademoiselle...
MARIANE. Has changed his mind.   265
Tartuffe's the man for whom I am
designed.
VALÈRE. Is he serious?
MARIANE.   As serious as
serious can be.
He just was urging this affair to me.
VALÈRE. What's your opinion of this
serious prank,
Pray tell?

MARIANE. I just don't know.

VALÈRE. Well, at least, that's frank. 270
You don't know?

MARIANE. No.

VALÈRE. No?

MARIANE. What's your advice?

VALÈRE. Accept this splendid husband. Don't think twice.

MARIANE. That's your advice?

VALÈRE. Yes.

MARIANE. Really?

VALÈRE. Absolutely.
You must pursue this rare chance resolutely.

MARIANE. I'm much obliged to you for this sage counsel. 275

VALÈRE. No thanks are due. I scarcely strained a tonsil.

MARIANE. I'll ponder your advisements at my leisure.

VALÈRE. I gave the counsel but to give you pleasure.

DORINE [*aside*]. I wonder how this all is going to end?

VALÈRE. I owe you thanks for frankness, at least, my friend. 280
When you...

MARIANE. I beg you not to talk like that.
You told me in so many words I should accept
The man my father chose to pledge me to;
I'm saying that's what I intend to do;
I'm simply following your own advice. 285

VALÈRE. Don't fob me off with that antique device.
Before I ever spoke, your mind was fixed
And now you're seizing on some frivolous pretext
To justify your falsehood to my face.

MARIANE. Well put! Quite true.

VALÈRE. The plain facts of the case 290
Are that you've never loved me for a minute.

MARIANE. Think what you will, if you take pleasure in it.

VALÈRE. Pleasure? Ha! The hurt you've dealt my heart
Is deep, but I'll learn to make a second start
And find more sympathy and warmth than I do here. 295

MARIANE. I don't doubt that. What girl would not admire
Your character?

VALÈRE. Forget my character.
It's not so hot. I'm crooked as a barrister,
Blind as a fool in love, yes, even blinder,
But there's a girl somewhere who may be kinder 300
Than you. She'll take me on the rebound, if she must.

MARIANE. The loss is not so great. Somehow, I trust,
I'll manage to sustain it stoically.

VALÈRE. I'm sure you will comport yourself heroically.
And, as for me, it's never very pleasant 305
To find oneself forgotten. For the present,
I'll do my best to sigh, smile and forget,
Or, if I can't forget, pretend. And yet
There's something weak and pitiful and wilted
About a man who weeps when he's been jilted. 310

MARIANE. A lofty sentiment, indeed, if true.

VALÈRE. More people should approve it, as you do.
What! Would you have me keep within my heart
My love for you unchanging from the start,
See you go happy to another's arms 315
And not seek solace in a lady's charms?

MARIANE. Why, not at all! That's what
    I most desire—
A new romance to set your heart
    afire!
VALÈRE. You'd like that?
MARIANE.   Yes.
VALÈRE.   Enough of
    this detraction!
I'll try to give you instant satisfac-
    tion.   320

[*Starts to leave and returns through the
next few speeches.*]

MARIANE. Good.
VALÈRE.   Kindly remember that,
    for good or ill,
I follow your example.
MARIANE.   As you will.
VALÈRE. Your wishes are quite clear.
    I will comply.
MARIANE. Fine!
VALÈRE.   Enough. You get no
    more of me. Good-bye.
MARIANE. Excellent!
VALÈRE.   Eh?
MARIANE.   What?
VALÈRE.   I thought
    I heard my name.   325
MARIANE. You must be hearing things.
VALÈRE. This game
    Begins to weary me. Farewell.
MARIANE.   Adieu.
DORINE.   May I
Speak up now as a humble stander-by
And say I think you both are addled
And ought to have your backsides
    paddled?   330
Monsieur Valère!

[*She takes him by the arm; he feigns
resistance.*]

VALÈRE.   What do you want,
    Dorine?
DORINE. Come here!
VALÈRE.   No, no! I'm in a
    rage. You've seen
I'm doing what she wants. Don't
    interfere.
DORINE. Stop!
VALÈRE.   The matter is all settled,
    that's quite clear.

DORINE. Ha!
MARIANE.   My presence here clearly
    annoys someone.   335
It's wiser if I leave him quite alone.

[DORINE *leaves* VALÈRE *and runs to*
MARIANE.]

DORINE. Where are you going?
MARIANE.   Let me alone!
DORINE.   Come back!
MARIANE. No use, Dorine. You try
    another tack.
VALÈRE. It's clear it tortures her to
    look at me.
I'll just remove myself and set her
    free.   340
DORINE [*leaving* MARIANE *and running
    to* VALÈRE]. What the deuce?
What's all this that I hear?
Now stop this nonsense! Both of
    you come here!

[*She pulls at them, one with each
hand.*]

VALÈRE. What are you up to?
MARIANE.   What do
    you think you're doing?
DORINE. Trying to get you two to
    billing and cooing.
VALÈRE. You must be crazy, as far as
    I can see.   345
Didn't you hear the way she talked
    to me?
DORINE [*to* MARIANE]. You act as if
    you're going off your head.
MARIANE. Didn't you hear the awful
    things he said?
DORINE. You're crazy, both of you.
    [*to* VALÈRE] Now I am sure
The only thing she wants is to be
    yours.   350
    [*to* MARIANE] He loves you only;
    I'm prepared to swear
That marriage—and to you—is his
    desire.
MARIANE [*to* VALÈRE]. Why did you
    give me, then, your vile advice?
VALÈRE [*to* MARIANE]. Your asking
    for it wasn't exactly nice.
DORINE. I said you both were crazy.
    Give me your hand.   355
Yours, now.

VALÈRE.   Why give you my hand?
DORINE.   You'll understand
MARIANE. What *is* all this?
DORINE.   Just   this.
  You're both in love
  More than you're either of you con-
    scious of.
VALÈRE. Well, there's no harm—at least
  once in a while—
  In giving a man a little friendly
  smile.   360

[MARIANE *looks at* VALÈRE *and smiles feebly.*]

DORINE. The fact is, lovers are completely daft.
VALÈRE. *I've* reason to complain, you
  know. You laughed
  At me and scorned me with reproof
  Because I thought you'd said "Yes"
  to Tartuffe.
MARIANE. But you yourself...it really
  is a shame...   365
DORINE. Let's leave this issue for an-
  other time.
  The thing we need now is a cunning
  plan.
MARIANE. Speak up, Dorine. We'll do
  all that we can.
DORINE. There are a lot of tricks that
  we can play.
  Your father's bluffing, surely, but
  the way   370
  For you to get around him is to feign
  Complete compliance with his mad
  design,
  So that, in case of crisis, you can
  manage
  To keep postponing this unwelcome
  marriage.
  Time has many virtues; it can
  heal   375
  Many a wound that seems beyond
  repeal.
  And there are many tricks. Say you
  fell ill;
  No one can force you then against
  your will.
  Or maybe some dire omen greets
  your eyes:
  A funeral in the street (a grim
  surprise),   380
  A broken mirror, auguring the worst,
  A black cat, which suggests your life
  is cursed—
  A dozen dodges. But I would much
  rather
  You two would not be seen like this
  together.
  [*to* VALÈRE] Now go and use the
  help of all your friends   385
  To win the girl that clearly Fate
  intends
  For you. [*to* MARIANE] I'm sure
  you'll get your brother
  To help you, not to mention your
  stepmother.
  Good-bye!
VALÈRE [*to* MARIANE]. We all will do
  whatever we can do,
  But my best hope and love resides
  in you.   390
MARIANE. I don't know what my father
  may decide.
  I only know I'll not be Tartuffe's
  bride.
VALÈRE. You make me very happy. And
  if ever...
DORINE. Lovers are never tired. They
  talk forever.
  Come on, get going!
VALÈRE.   Farewell...
DORINE.   Oh,
  talk, talk, talk!   395
  You that way, and you this. Come
  on, now! Walk!

ACT III

SCENE i. DAMIS *and* DORINE.

DAMIS. Let Heaven strike me with a
  lightning bolt,
  Let all the world call me a rogue,
  a dolt;
  No talk of filial respect, no father's
  power
  Will hold me back; I'll act within
  the hour!

DORINE. For Heaven's sake, enough of
   this mad chatter;   5
Your father's merely talked about
   the matter.
Need I remind you that there's many
   a slip
Betwixt the smooth cup and the
   slippery lip?
DAMIS. I'll stop that fat conspirator's
   career;
I'll speak a word or two into his
   ear.   10
DORINE. Easy does it, boy; let your
   stepmother
Handle him, the way she does your
   father.
Tartuffe becomes like putty in her
   hands
And easily agrees to her demands.
I think he eyes her with a secret
   yen;   15
Lord knows, I hope that that's the
   case, for then
She'll come to interview him, for your
   sake,
Learn what his feelings are and make
Him understand what troubles will
   be brewing
If he continues as he has been
   doing.   20
His valet tells me that he's at his
   prayers;
No one can see him; he's alone up-
   stairs.
But he'll be coming down in a minute
   or two,
So beat it, please; I'll see what I
   can do.
DAMIS. I must be present when he
   talks to her.   25
DORINE. Never! Beat it!
DAMIS.   I won't speak or stir.
DORINE. Nonsense! I know how you
   fly off the handle,
And that's the surest way to snuff
   the candle.
Go on!
DAMIS. I promise I won't rage or shout.
DORINE. Oh, what a pest you are!
   Look, here he comes! Get out!   30

[DORINE *pushes him out.* TARTUFFE
enters and, seeing DORINE, *calls off
stage.*]

SCENE ii. TARTUFFE *and* DORINE.

TARTUFFE. [*Calls off stage.*] Put away
   my hair shirt and my scourge
And pray perpetually that Heaven
   may purge
Our souls of sin. If someone asks for
   me,
I've gone to bless the poor with
   charity.
DORINE [*aside*]. What hogwash! What
   a stupid thing to say!   35
TARTUFFE. What do you want?
DORINE.   I . . .
TARTUFFE [*drawing out a kerchief*].
   Wait! I pray,
Take this handkerchief before you
   speak.
DORINE. Why?
TARTUFFE.   Cover that bosom which
   demurely peeks
Above your bodice. Such forbidden
   sights
May well give rise to slightly carnal
   thoughts.   40
DORINE. You must be quite concupis-
   cently queasy
If a little flesh can make you so
   uneasy.
Of course, I don't know how you're
   stimulated
Put I'm not quite so easily elated.
Why, I could see you nude without
   a qualm;   45
In fact, I think I'd stay supremely
   calm.
TARTUFFE. A bit more modesty in
   speech, my dear,
Or I'll withdraw and leave you stand-
   ing here.
DORINE. No, I will go and leave you
   here alone,
But first, there's something that you
   should have known;   50
Madame Elmire will soon come into

view.
She'd like to have a word or two
with you.
TARTUFFE. Delighted!
DORINE [*aside*]. He leaps and
bleats just like a woolly lamb.
I'm right, he has a hankering for
madame.
TARTUFFE. She's coming soon?
DORINE. Yes, here
she comes this way; 55
I'll leave you two together, if I may.

[*Exit.*]

SCENE iii. ELMIRE *and* TARTUFFE.

TARTUFFE. May Heaven's grace,
madame, preserve you whole
And sound in mind, in body, and in
soul,
And bless your days according to the
prayers
Of one who's much concerned with
your affairs. 60
ELMIRE. I'm deeply grateful for your
pieties.
Let us sit down and chat more at
our ease.
TARTUFFE. I trust, madame, your fever's
not persisted?
ELMIRE. I'm feeling well; the fever's
quite arrested.
TARTUFFE. My poor and humble prayers
here in this place 65
Seem all too small to have brought
down such grace
Upon you from on high; yet I confess
My constant thoughts are of your
happiness.
ELMIRE. Your pious zeal is rather over-
powering.
TARTUFFE. Pray Heaven that the
heavens keep on showering 70
Blessings on you; I'd give my life
for yours.
ELMIRE. There's no need for such
drastic overtures.
But I'm indebted to you for your

prayers.
TARTUFFE. Dear lady, *any*thing to ease
your cares...

[DAMIS *enters unseen behind them.*]

ELMIRE. I wanted to speak privately
to you. 75
I'm glad we're here out of the public
view.
TARTUFFE. And so am I! Dear Heaven,
but it's sweet
To be beside you, madame, on this
seat.
This is a chance for which I've often
prayed;
It seems a stroke of luck that Fate
has made. 80
ELMIRE. I know, my friend, exactly
what you mean.
I've often longed for a chat like this,
unseen.
TARTUFFE. Oh, how I've prayed that
we could freely share
Our thoughts and words, that I could
boldly bare
My soul unto you, that I might
explain 85
My distaste for the friends you
entertain
Springs not from my dislike of your
devotion
To them, but rather from my own
profound emotion
Which fairly chokes me...
ELMIRE. Well, your zeal
Is something, sir, that you need not
conceal. 90
TARTUFFE [*taking her hand and
squeezing her fingers*]. How hard
I pray for you, and even harder...
ELMIRE. Ouch! You're hurting me!
TARTUFFE. Forgive my ardor!
I had no idea of hurting you, I
swear!
It's just...

[*Puts his hand on her knee.*]

ELMIRE. Your hand. What is it
doing there?
TARTUFFE. Just feeling the material;

it's nice!   95

ELMIRE. I'm ticklish. Please, don't make
    me ask you twice.

[*She moves her chair away;* TARTUFFE
*brings his closer. This continues
throughout the scene.*]

TARTUFFE. I am a great admirer of fine
    lace.
    The workmanship, the beauty, and
        the grace
    Of the design. What lovely decora-
        tion!

ELMIRE. Perhaps. But now, sir, to our
    conversation.   100
    I hear my husband wants to marry
        you
    To Mariane. Pray tell me, is that
        true?

TARTUFFE. He's mentioned it. But,
    lady, need I say
    That's not the joy I dream of night
        and day?
    It's elsewhere that I see the lovely
        fire   105
    Which blazes with the beauties I
        desire.

ELMIRE. You mean you don't love
    earthly things alone?

TARTUFFE. I mean, madame, my heart's
    not made of stone.

ELMIRE. I see. You mean your thoughts
    are turned to Heaven,
    Toward which your yearning spirit
        long has striven.   110

TARTUFFE. The love which draws us
    toward eternal beauty
    Does not release us from our earthly
        duty
    To love each other. Heaven often
        forms
    A vessel whose supernal beauty
        warms
    Our earthly blood. And such a one
        are you;   115
    My spirit soars when you come into
        view.
    Heaven's glories shine within your
        face;
    Your form and figure testify to Grace.

O perfect beauty, perfect in each
    feature!
In you I worship great creating
    Nature.   120
Fair goddess! wondrous woman; in
    your eyes
I see the will of Heaven and am wise.
At first I trembled, lest my sacred
    passion
For you prove false, a hindrance to
    salvation,
Perhaps—who knows?—a horrid
    stratagem   125
Of the Evil One, a trap to catch
    me in.
I even thought to flee in foolish
    fashion,
But then I came to see that such a
    passion,
Inspired by Heaven as it is, un-
    doubtedly,
Need not be inconsistent with true
    modesty.   130
And so I gave my eager heart full
    rein.
I know I should not hope that you
    will deign
To smile with condescension on my
    suit;
But still, when Heaven calls, dare
    man be mute?
In you is all my hope, my good, my
    peace;   135
In you rests my damnation or release.
I may taste bliss or be tormented
    still;
It all will be according to your will.

ELMIRE. This is indeed a gallant decla-
    ration.
    I must confess, though, to some
        consternation.   140
    You should have steeled your feel-
        ings somewhat better;
    Why, what would happen if my hus-
        band ever
    Heard words like this from such a
        pious man? . . .

TARTUFFE. Though I am pious, I am
    still a man,
    An erring, mortal man, and when

your beauties 145
Flame on my sight, all my religious duties
Grow somewhat blurred. I know such an appraisal
May shock you somewhat. Still, I'm not an angel.
And if you view my conduct with alarm,
You must accuse your own bewitching charm. 150
Since I first viewed your beauty's flawless art,
You've been the sovereign of my secret heart.
My poor soul struggled, but alas! in vain
Against your distant beauty and disdain;
In vain, in vain my fasting, prayers and tears. 155
Each soft breeze blew your sweet name to my ears.
How long I've sought to say this with my eyes;
Now hear it in my words and in my sighs.
And if you look with pity and compassion
Upon this poor unworthy slave of passion, 160
If you consent to bring me consolation
And bring about my yearning soul's salvation,
I'll swear to you with most profound emotion
Unending service and a true devotion.
And in my hands be sure a lady's honor 165
Is safe, no danger that there'll come upon her
The smallest breath of scandal. These young sparks
That ladies dote on are unsafe. Their larks,
Their jokes, their boasts about the wars of love
Leave ladies' reputations not above 170
Reproach, and many ladies have been tarnished
By faithless gallants whose careers have furnished
Examples of betrayal and deceit.
But fear me not, dear lady; I'm discreet.
The care a man like me takes of his name 175
Is guarantee that you need fear no shame;
You buy, if you accept my heart, my dear,
Love without scandal, pleasure without fear.

ELMIRE. I'm fascinated; and your rhetoric
Effectively removes all the inveterate 180
Fears I might have felt; but don't *you* fear
That I might speak a word in Orgon's ear
About your strange behavior here today?
If I did, what do you think he'd say?

TARTUFFE. I know you are too merciful and good 185
And that my love is not misunderstood.
Pity for human frailty will excuse
My overardent voicing of such views.
Although I yearn toward the True and Good,
Still I am human, merely flesh and blood. 190

ELMIRE. Another woman might, indeed, repeat
This story; but I too can be discreet.
I'll not tell Orgon of your strange behavior;
In turn I'll beg of you a certain favor:
I want you to speak boldly and declare 195
That you support the marriage of Valère
And Mariane, that you renounce the

claim
By which you would usurp another's
name,
And...

SCENE iv. ELMIRE, DAMIS, *and* TAR-
TUFFE.

DAMIS [*emerging*]. No, madame, no!
This news must come to light!
I've been this while concealed there,
within sight   200
And hearing. Heaven's favor led me
there
To trap this hypocrite in his own
snare
And place within my hands at last
the power
Of sweet revenge. Aha! Within the
hour
I'll undeceive my father and he'll
know   205
The gross sins of that fat Lothario!
ELMIRE. No, Damis, it's enough if he
repents.
I'll count that a sufficient recompense.
I've promised it; don't make me
break a vow.
No nasty scenes; I'm willing to
allow   210
The whole affair to pass and not
displease
My husband's ears with such absurd-
ities.
DAMIS. You may have reason, madame,
to be lenient,
But I do not consider it convenient
To lose this chance of pricking his
fat bubble   215
And plunging him up to the ears in
trouble.
His sanctimonious impudence too
long
Has stirred up trouble in our home;
too long
He's bilked my father, led him by
the nose.
And now with vengeance sure, do
you suppose   220

I'll overlook my opportunity?
It is a grace that Heaven's conferred
on me.
Now and henceforth I am Heaven's
debtor,
And Heaven knows when I will find
a better
Chance to give this slippery fox a
jolt.   225
If I passed up this chance, I'd be
a dolt.
ELMIRE. Damis...
DAMIS.   I must do what I
think is justified.
I've never felt so richly satisfied.
Please don't deter me. Try to under-
stand
My joy in holding vengeance in
my hand.   230
I'll have full satisfaction, I vow,
And see, here comes my opportunity,
right now.

SCENE v. ORGON, ELMIRE, DAMIS, *and*
TARTUFFE.

DAMIS [*continuing to* ORGON, *who
enters*]. Father, I've got a bit of
a surprise
For you; some news to open up your
eyes.
Your kindnesses have here been well
repaid;   235
This gentleman, behind your back,
has made
Proposals to madame which cast upon
her
A curious light and work to your
dishonor.
In short, I've just surprised this
monstrous beast
In making love to her and, sir, he
ceased   240
Only when I spoke. Madame implored
I spare you this recital, but I've
stored
A thirst for vengeance in my hungry
heart,
And I don't choose to play a forgiv-

ing part.

ELMIRE. I think a wife ought never to annoy 245
Her husband with such silly tales. My boy,
A woman likes to handle such affairs
In her own way, so that nobody shares
The knowledge of the circumstances. You'd be
Silent now if you were ruled by me. [*Exit.*] 250

SCENE vi. ORGON, DAMIS, *and* TAR-TUFFE.

ORGON. Oh, gracious Heavens! Can I trust my ears?

TARTUFFE. Alas, the case is just as it appears:
I am a sinner lost in deep iniquity,
One who would let mere physical propinquity
Corrupt his holy purposes and stain 255
His spotless shield of honor; don't refrain
From heaping censure on me. I'm a beast.
My life's a mass of crime; there's not the least
Extenuation possible for me.
Heaven has contrived all this, I see, 260
As punishment for my most rank misdeeds
And Heaven has ordained that no one pleads
For me. Let no man speak. Let me be driven
Out of your house, out of the sight of Heaven.

ORGON [*to* DAMIS]. Traitor! How do you dare, with nasty lies, 265
To bring the innocent tears into his eyes?

DAMIS. Don't tell me all this blubber-ing and bluster
Is going to make you think...

ORGON. Be silent, monster!

TARTUFFE. Ah, let him speak! How wrongly you accuse him!
Believe his words! It's wrong if you refuse him 270
Your trusting ears. Why put your faith in me?
How do you know what sort of man I might be?
Brother, how can you trust my out-ward seeming?
Perhaps when you look at me you're merely dreaming.
No, no, my outward semblance may deceive; 275
Within, I am far worse than you believe.
Although I commonly pass for a man of virtue,
You sadly let my outer surface cheat you. [*to* DAMIS]
Speak, dear boy, call me a vile traitor,
Perfidious, a liar, betrayer 280
Of friendship's trust; call me the vilest term
You can imagine; I'm lower than a worm. [*on his knees*]
Let me acknowledge here upon my knees
My horrid crimes. Condemn me, if you please.

ORGON. Brother, this is too much! [*to* DAMIS] So—your heart 285
Remains unmoved?

DAMIS. He's merely play-ing a part!

ORGON. Silence, scoundrel! [*to* TAR-TUFFE] My brother, I beg you, stand! [*to* DAMIS]
Rascal!

DAMIS. He can...

ORGON. Silence!

DAMIS. Don't you understand?

ORGON. Just one more word, and I'll punch you in the nose!

TARTUFFE. Do not be angry, brother. Do you suppose 290
I would not rather suffer indignity
Than have him suffer the slightest scratch for me?

ORGON [*to* DAMIS]. Ingrate!

TARTUFFE.   Leave him
in peace! See, I'm kneeling
To ask you for his pardon.

ORGON.   Oh, what feeling!

[*Falling on his knees and embracing*
TARTUFFE.]

Observe his goodness!

DAMIS.   But...

ORGON.   Peace!

DAMIS.   But, I...

ORGON.   Quiet! 295
I understand why you're raising all
   this riot.
You hate him, all of you: my faithful
   wife,
My children, servants—why, upon
   my life!
It's a conspiracy to drive this saint
Out of my house. And this absurd
   complaint   300
Against him doesn't move me, not
   a whit.
I'll stand with him forever; you can
   sit
And spin your lies; I'll hasten with
   my plan
To marry this wronged saint to
   Mariane.

DAMIS. You think you'll force her into
   such a plight?   305

ORGON. Yes, and, to spite you all, this
   very night!
Oh, I defy you! Defy you, do you
   hear?
I'll show you, mark my words, who's
   master here!
Take back your wicked words, you
   monster, and entreat
His pardon. I command you, fall at
   his feet!   310

DAMIS. What? Fall at the feet of this
   repulsive liar?

ORGON. Ah, you resist my will? You've
   roused my ire!
Give me a stick, a stick! Don't hold
   me back!
Out of my sight! I'll deal you such
   a crack

Your ears will ring! Out! Out of my
   place!   315

DAMIS. All right, I'll go, but...

ORGON.   Don't
   let me see your face!
Reptile, I'll remove you from my
   will!
Take my curse, and go—wherever
   you will.   [*Exit* DAMIS.]

SCENE vii. ORGON *and* TARTUFFE.

ORGON [*continuing, to* TARTUFFE].
Think of offering such insults to
   you!

TARTUFFE. May Heaven pardon him,
   as I would do.   320
Ah, could you know how bitterly I
   suffer
To hear such words spoken to my
   brother...

ORGON. Alas!

TARTUFFE.   Merely to think of such
   ingratitude
Makes my heart ache. Words so
   rough and crude
Fill my soul with a horror that's so
   deep   325
I can do nothing but beat my breast
   and weep!

ORGON. [*Runs to the door where he has
   driven* DAMIS.] Villain! I'm sorry
   I didn't knock you down
When I had the chance! Liar
   Monster! Clown!

TARTUFFE. Brother, compose yourself.
   Don't be distressed.
Let's have no more of this. I think it
   best   330
That I should leave your home, dear
   friend, right now.
I'll never return to bother you, I vow.

ORGON. You're jesting!

TARTUFFE.   No, no, they all
   hate me here.
They'd even question my sincerity,
   I fear.

ORGON. Do you think I listen to any-

thing they say?   335
TARTUFFE. But they'll go on with their
    tales, day after day.
  These stories that today have left
      you grieved
  Tomorrow may be readily believed.
ORGON. Oh, never, brother, never!
TARTUFFE.   Brother, a wife
  May sway a husband's mind and rule
      his life.   340
ORGON. You shall not go! Never! I will
    not hear it!
TARTUFFE. Well, I'll remain, to mortify
    my spirit.
  Still, if you desired it...
ORGON.   Oh!
TARTUFFE.   Well, no more.
  I'll not behave as I have done before.
  Honor is delicate, and, like Caesar's
      wife,   345
  I must be past suspicion. On my life,
  I'll flee the presence of madame and
      call...
ORGON. No, you'll attend her, to defy

them all.
  My one desire now is to fully spite
      them;
  You must be with her constantly—
      we'll fight them,   350
  Fire with fire, slander with suspicion,
  To keep their tongues a-wagging. In
      addition,
  I'm firm resolved that you must be
      my heir.
  I'll change my will today, and I'll
      declare
  That all my wealth is yours by legal
      right.   355
  I tell you, brother, I take more
      delight
  In you, my heir, than in all my
      family.
TARTUFFE. May Heaven's will be done
    eternally.
ORGON. Come, let's change the docu-
    ment; meanwhile,
  Let the jealous choke on their own
      bile!   360

ACT IV

SCENE i. CLÉANTE *and* TARTUFFE.

CLÉANTE. Everywhere I go I hear this
    story;
  It's one that doesn't add unto your
      glory;
  And I am glad, sir, I've run into you
  So I can tell you briefly what my
      view
  Of the matter is. I won't weigh right
      and wrong;   5
  In any case, the evidence is strong.
  But let's assume the tale Damis
      propounded
  Was false, and the whole thing was
      unfounded.
  Should not a Christian pardon the
      mistake,
  Turning the other cheek for charity's
      sake?   10
  Should such a quarrel, by purpose or
      by chance

  Be cause for Damis' disinheritance?
  In perfect frankness, sir, let me
      repeat:
  The story's spreading; everyone you
      meet
  Is talking of it. Look at what you've
      done!   15
  It's not too late for father and for son
  To reconcile; if you promote this
      union,
  You'll bring yourself back into good
      opinion.
TARTUFFE. Alas, how happy I would
    be, if this could be!
  God knows, my heart of rancor is
      quite free.   20
  I would not harm him, bless you, if
      I could;
  I long with all my heart to do him
      good.
  But Heaven's will doesn't always fit
      my heart;

If he returns to the house, I must depart.
No, no, I couldn't stay with him in this place,   25
Not without a sense of complete disgrace;
It would be an intolerable situation;
Why, people might accuse me of calculation.
They'd say I was pretending, as a ruse, sir,
False charity to silence my accuser.   30
They'd say I kept him here beneath surveillance
Merely to ensure his guilty silence.

CLÉANTE. Your statements have some plausibility,
But still it all sounds quite farfetched to me.
Since when are you the self-appointed judge   35
Of who must cringe beneath great Heaven's scourge?
Let God decide on matters of election
And let him implement his own correction.
And he who's moved by Heaven, not his humors,
Should not be sensitive to idle rumors.   40
No need, I'm sure, for fearing idle tongues
When you act truly to correct great wrongs,
And he who would take justice in his hands
Should first be sure he's tuned to God's commands.

TARTUFFE. My one desire's to be obedient   45
To God, whenever it's expedient.
But, after Damis' recent rude behavior,
I'd not forgive him, no, were I the Savior.

CLÉANTE. And does God order you to punish him
By aiding and abetting Orgon's whim   50
To disinherit him? And does God know
How you will profit by his overthrow?

TARTUFFE. No one who's plumbed the true depths of my spirit
Could think a thing like that of me, or fear it.
The riches of this world are dross to me;   55
Their gleaming superficiality
Does not seduce me; and if I accept
Something of the wealth Orgon has kept
Hidden away, my motives are quite pure:
To keep it out of the hands of an evildoer,   60
Someone who might, alas! make evil use
Of it, or squander it without excuse;
How better, then, to give it to one who swore he
Would dedicate its use to Heaven's glory?

CLÉANTE. Your reasons are somewhat sophistical,   65
If not, indeed, a trifle egotistical.
Why not let Damis have his proper wealth,
As long as you have liberty and health?
Better, indeed, to let the lad misuse it
Than countenance the rumor you'd abuse it   70
For your own purposes. I'm amazed
You could have heard this plan and not have raised
Your voice in protest. As far as I'm aware,
God doesn't condone defrauding a son and heir.
And if God in truth your heart has steeled   75
Against Damis, then why not quit the field
As any honorable adversary should
And leave the house to him? I'm sure I would.
Believe me, sir, it does you no great credit

To have this story spread, and if
you let it   80
Gain further credence, your basic
piety
Will seem...

TARTUFFE.   Excuse me, sir, it's half-
past three;
I must retire to prayers and medita-
tions;
I leave you with my best felicitations.

[*Exit.*]

SCENE ii. ELMIRE, MARIANE, CLÉANTE,
and DORINE.

DORINE. Sir, can't you help her soul
gain some relief,   85
For she is suffering a most cruel grief?
This hateful marriage pledge her
father's made
Has sickened her poor heart, and it's
betrayed
Her fondest hopes. He's coming now.
Let's try
To undermine this project on the
sly,   90
And unite this poor maid and Valère.

[*Enter* ORGON.]

SCENE iii. ORGON, ELMIRE, MARIANE,
CLÉANTE, *and* DORINE.

ORGON. I'm glad to find you all assem-
bled here. [*to* MARIANE]
There's something in this deed to
make you smile,
And I'll reveal it in a little while.
MARIANE. Father, I call on Heaven,
which knows my grief!   95
Look in your heart and offer me relief
From this oppressive sorrow; oh,
relax
The rights of fatherhood, I pray.
Don't tax
My frail forbearance, so that I must
cry
In bitter protest unto God on high. 100

Don't make a senseless tragedy
Out of that life which you have given
me.
Though you forbid my wedding the
one I love,
At least, I beg, by all the powers
above,
Don't bring me to this miserable
estate   105
By forcing me to marry one I hate.
Don't drive me to an act of blind
despair
By bringing all your legal powers to
bear.
ORGON [*aside*]. Be strong, my heart!
Don't yield to human frailty!
MARIANE. I'm not distressed by your
continued loyalty   110
To him. Give him your wealth, if
that's what you want to do
And, if that's not enough, why, take
mine too.
Give him all that I have; it cannot
worsen
My grief. But don't consign to him
my person!
Just spare me that. Then, when the
deed is done,   115
Let me retire to spend my life as a
nun.
ORGON. You think, by waxing weepy
and despondent,
And talking crazily about a convent,
You'll frighten me? Get up! I say,
the more
Your heart recoils, the more you'll
answer for.   120
So mortify your senses by your
yielding
Meekly to the power that I'm wield-
ing.
DORINE. But what...?
ORGON.   Be silent!
Speak when you're spoken to!
I don't want to hear a syllable out
of you!
CLÉANTE. If you'll permit me to offer
some advice...   125
ORGON. Your words, dear brother, al-
ways are quite nice,

And your advice is always full of
merit,
So much so, I'd prefer just not to
hear it.
ELMIRE [*to* ORGON]. Seeing all this, I
find myself struck dumb.
I can't believe how blind you have
become.   130
You must be hypnotized, or else
insane,
To doubt our word about this recent
scene.
ORGON. I believe your words, dear, one
by one,
And I know how fond you are of my
rascal son.
Clearly you were afraid to disavow 135
The fraud he tried to perpetrate just
now.
And you were, I must protest, a shade
too calm;
A woman in your place should have
showed alarm.
ELMIRE. Should a woman's honor be
so stirred
If someone offers her a wicked
word?   140
And does a mere suggestion then
require
Denunciations and a tongue of fire?
Why, all I do is laugh at such
advances;
To me, they're unimportant circum-
stances.
I try to wear my virtue modestly   145
And not like some protesting prudes
I see
Whose virtue comes full-armed with
teeth and claws
Ready to scratch and bite at the
slightest cause.
Heaven preserve me from such
purity!
True Virtue needs no arms and need
not be   150
Masked by scowls. A firm and simple
"No"
Will tell unwelcome lovers where to
go.

ORGON. You needn't try to make a
dupe of me.
ELMIRE. I can't believe your gullibility!
Could I shake your blind, unthinking
faith   155
By making you witness to the truth?
ORGON. Witness?
ELMIRE.   Yes.
ORGON.   Nonsense!
ELMIRE.   Suppose
I show you the fact before your very
eyes?
ORGON. Balderdash!
ELMIRE.   Oh, what a man!
It's too absurd!
You obviously won't believe a
word.   160
Suppose we could place you here
concealed
Where you could see what would be
revealed,
And you saw the truth? Then what
would you do?
ORGON. I'd say in that case...well,
I'd say "Pooh pooh!"
For it cannot be.
ELMIRE.   You've been too
long unwise,   165
And you've accused me for too long
of telling lies.
Now, for my satisfaction and your
proof,
I'll make you witness to the living
truth.
ORGON. I'll take you up on that! Let's
see your scheme.
The truth will be far stranger than
you dream.   170
ELMIRE [*to* DORINE]. Send him in here.
DORINE. He's clever as a fox
And he won't be easily trapped within
a box.
ELMIRE. Some men are easily fooled by
infatuation;
Such blindness must be cured by
illumination.
Have him come down. [*to* CLÉANTE
and MARIANE] And, you two,
please go.   175

[*Exeunt* DORINE, CLÉANTE, *and* MARI-
ANE.]

SCENE iv. ELMIRE *and* ORGON.

ELMIRE [*continuing, to* ORGON]. See
that table? There's your place—
below.
ORGON. What?
ELMIRE.   You'll have to hide
yourself, that's clear.
ORGON. But why beneath the table?
ELMIRE.   Get under here!
I have my plan; you'll see how it
works out;
Under the table, quick, and when
you're set,   180
Not a whisper. Don't make any
comments.
ORGON. I must say, I'm most patient
with your nonsense.
Well, let me see you wiggle out of
this one.
ELMIRE. Remember, there are one or
two conditions:
Since this is a rather ticklish situa-
tion,   185
I must behave according to the
occasion;
Pray don't be scandalized if I seem
to behave
Quite forwardly; I do it for you, to
save
Your sanity; some questions I may
ask
Are merely traps to tempt him to
unmask,   190
And if I smile upon his lewd desires
It's merely to arouse his amorous
fires.
Remember: for your sake and his
confusion
I have consented here in this seclu-
sion
To meet with him. The action will
subside   195
As soon as you feel fully satisfied.
Your task will be, concealed there
as you are,
To call a halt if things have gone
too far.
A husband, after all, should shield
his wife
From the unpleasant perils of this
life;   200
You are the master in the house, and
your will
Should be obeyed...Sh! Here he
comes! Be still!

SCENE v. TARTUFFE, ELMIRE, *and*
ORGON. ORGON *is under the table.*

TARTUFFE. They said, dear lady, you
were waiting here.
ELMIRE. Yes. I've a secret for your
private ear.
But close that door first, please, and
peep   205
About the room. Let's not be caught
asleep.

[TARTUFFE *shuts the door and looks
about.*]

ELMIRE. We certainly don't want again,
you know,
The sort of scene we had a while ago.
That was most disagreeable, it's true,
And I was in a panic because of
you.   210
You saw I did my best to keep him
quiet.
But he was clearly determined to
raise a riot.
Of course, I was so alarmed—I was
nearly dead!—
I didn't think to deny the things he'd
said.
But, Heaven be praised, it all worked
out ideally   215
And everything is understood—yes,
really!
Your reputation's so strong, it cannot
fall,
And my husband does not suspect
you, not at all.

In fact, to still the voice of slander, he
Wants us to be together con-
tinually.   220
So now we're able to be sequestered here
Behind locked doors and free of blame or fear,
And I can reveal what my true feel-ings are
About you, sir—but perhaps I go too far.
TARTUFFE. This talk is rather baffling, I'll admit;   225
You've changed, madame, since the last time we met.
ELMIRE. Why, if you're angry at my earlier rebuff,
You don't know women's hearts quite well enough.
You don't know what our hearts are trying to speak
When our defense seems languid, slow, and weak.   230
And ever our modesty must make a show
Of struggling valiantly to overthrow
Our feelings, which, the while we're yielding,
We blush to find our words have been revealing.
At first we fight against them, but our tender   235
Sighs betray our swift complete sur-render.
For honor's sake, we put our hearts on trial
And promise everything with a denial.
I fear I'm speaking much too honestly
And overlooking proper modesty. 240
But, since I'm speaking frankly, don't you see
Why I didn't struggle to restrain Damis?
And would I, pray, so graciously, so long,
Have listened to your offer, and so long
Have let you pour your heart out in full measure   245

If the affair did not afford me pleasure?
And when I argued with such force and courage
To get you to renounce your coming marriage
Why would my claims have been so strongly pressed
Except for my own selfish interest? 250
In short, I feared this marriage might divide
A heart I wanted whole, and near my side.
TARTUFFE. Ah, madame, it gives me joy extreme
To hear such words from you. It's like a dream!
Their honey pours into my tortured brain;   255
Their liquid sweetness flows through every vein.
My aim's to please you, all things else above;
My heart's beatitude lies in your love.
And yet I hope you'll not think me suspicious
To dare to doubt my joys are so delicious.   260
I could almost suspect a sly arrange-ment
To get me to break off my late engagement.
And so, madame, to put the matter bluntly,
And much as I enjoy your lovely company,
I'll dare to doubt your tender words until   265
Some tangible favors indicate your will,
Implanting in my wavering soul a faith
That your dear bounty's not a vagrant wraith.
ELMIRE [*coughing to warn* ORGON].
What do you mean? Don't tell me that you think
You can rush love to its climax in a wink!   270

I've forced myself to make a rash
admission,
But now you'd add, I see, another
condition,
And you won't be satisfied until you
win
Love's final favors almost before you
begin.
TARTUFFE. The less one merits, the
less one dares to hope;   275
Where talk is cheap, each parish
priest's a Pope.
One easily mistrusts a promised bliss
And can't believe it till it's really his.
Knowing how little I am worthy of
you,
I doubt I'll ever be allowed to love
you.   280
In short, madame, I'll not believe a
word
Till facts confirm these promises I've
heard.
ELMIRE. Dear me! Your love is really
quite tyrannical.
I'd hate to think I'm being puri-
tanical,
But, mercy me! love drives men quite
insane,   285
So powerful and violent is its reign;
Can I not raise my hands in weak
defense?
Is there no way to curb your violence?
Take pity on a lady, sir, and send
her
Reprieve. Complete, abject sur-
render   290
Is frightening, you know, and it may
cost
You a regard you'd rather not have
lost.
TARTUFFE. If you receive my homage
with compassion,
Then why withhold love's tangible
expression?
ELMIRE. But, if I consent, won't Heaven
be offended?   295
This is your constant theme, and I
commend it.
TARTUFFE. Pooh! If Heaven's all that's
worrying you,

I'll take care of that, and easily too;
I can remove such obstacles with
ease.
ELMIRE. And yet they threaten us so
with Heaven's decrees!   300
TARTUFFE. I can banish such super-
stitious fear.
There is an art, you know, in making
clear
Heaven's will, and though Heaven
may proscribe
Certain joys, a bit of a spiritual
bribe
Can clear the path sometimes. There
is science   305
Of loosening the conscience so com-
pliance
Is easy, and the evil of an action
Is rectified to Heaven's satisfaction.
I'll teach you all these secrets; you
will see.
But you must put your confidence
in me.   310
Content my longings, lady; do not
fear.
The risk is mine; don't hesitate, my
dear. [ELMIRE *coughs.*]
TARTUFFE. You have a nasty cough...
ELMIRE. It's most distressing.
TARTUFFE. I have some cough drops.
Try one, with my blessing.
ELMIRE. I've had this cough for weeks,
would you believe it?   315
I fear that all your cough drops can't
relieve it.
TARTUFFE. Very annoying.
ELMIRE.   Yes, it's quite severe.
TARTUFFE. Well, at least I can dispel
your fear.
Your secret is known to us alone,
And evil's not evil until it's known   320
To the world at large, and, as for
sin,
To sin in silence is not to sin.
ELMIRE. [*Coughs.*] In short, I see that
I shall have to yield
And, fleeing, leave you master of the
field
Of my poor honor, for I can't con-
vince   325

A man who demands such tangible
evidence.
I must admit I fear to go so far,
But who cares what my foolish
scruples are?
And since I'm driven to it cruelly
By one who seems to find my pleas
unduly   330
Quibbling and demands complete con-
viction
I must decide to render satisfaction
Unto his claims. If there is any crime
In such consent, it's clear the blame's
not mine.
Surely I am not responsible.   335
TARTUFFE. Of course not, lady! Why
the thought's impossible!
ELMIRE. But first, please open the door
—but not too wide—
And see if my husband's lurking there
outside.
TARTUFFE. Pooh! Why worry about
dolts like those?
He's the type you can lead around
by the nose,   340
The type to abet our little intimacies;
Why, we can make him believe what-
ever we please.
ELMIRE. All the same, I'd feel much
more secure
If you'd take a look around just to
be sure.   [*Exit* TARTUFFE.]

SCENE vi. ORGON *and* ELMIRE.

ORGON [*emerging from under the
table*]. Such wickedness is incon-
ceivable!   345
I'm thunderstruck! It's unbelievable!
ELMIRE. What, crawling out so soon?
Don't be absurd!
Creep in again and wait. You haven't
heard
A fraction yet. Wait, and you'll cor-
rect your
Ideas further, and it won't be mere
conjecture.   350
ORGON. Nothing more wicked has ever
come out of hell!

ELMIRE. Don't be too quick to believe
the tales they tell
About him. Perhaps you are mistaken
And you've let your faith be far too
lightly shaken...

[*As* TARTUFFE *re-enters,* ELMIRE *quickly hides* ORGON *behind her.*]

SCENE vii. TARTUFFE, ELMIRE, *and*
ORGON.

TARTUFFE. Everything's working out,
madame, for the best.   355
The coast is clear. It seems that
Heaven has blessed
This moment. My senses are de-
lighted...

[*As he advances to embrace* ELMIRE,
*she steps aside, and he walks into the
arms of* ORGON.]

ORGON. Hold on a minute! Don't get
so excited!
Don't let your passions carry you
away!
Aha! You pious soul, you thought to
betray   360
Your benefactor by seducing his wife,
Wedding his daughter and fixing
yourself for life!
I've long suspected that some day I
would see
You're not all that you're cracked up
to be.
But now I've seen enough, yes, and
I've heard   365
More than enough. No, not another
word.
ELMIRE [*to* TARTUFFE]. It's not my
manner to tease and betray,
But I've been forced to treat you in
this way.
TARTUFFE [*to* ORGON]. What, can you
believe...?
ORGON.   Let no more be said.
Get out of here before I lose my
head.   370

TARTUFFE. I only sought...
ORGON.   To secret-
   ly seduce my spouse!
   I know. This minute—get out of
   my house!
TARTUFFE. But, just a moment—*you*
   are the one to leave.
   This house belongs to me, I do
   believe.
   There's no use trying to pick a
   quarrel with me   375
   On such a poor excuse. You wait!
   You'll see!
   You're in a poor position to evict
   me,
   When *you're* the one to pack and
   leave—and quickly!
   I have the power to avenge offended
   Heaven;
   Please be gone by quarter past
   eleven.   [*Exit.*]   380

SCENE viii. ELMIRE *and* ORGON.

ELMIRE. What's he talking about? It's
   all a bluff.
ORGON. I wish it were. I fear he's
   serious enough.
ELMIRE. What is it?
ORGON.   This is a pretty
   mess, indeed.
   I made a great mistake when I gave
   him that deed.
ELMIRE. A deed?
ORGON.   Yes, and it's signed
   and sealed.   385
   But there may be even more to be
   revealed.
ELMIRE. What's that?
ORGON.   I'll tell you later;
   first, I want to see
   If my strongbox still is where it used
   to be.

ACT V

SCENE i. ORGON *and* CLÉANTE.

CLÉANTE. Where are you going?
ORGON.   I don't know.
CLÉANTE.   It's clear
   We need to talk about this dreadful
   affair.
ORGON. The strongbox mainly weighs
   upon my mind,
   More than all the other matters com-
   bined.
CLÉANTE. This strongbox is an im-
   portant mystery?   5
ORGON. It has a most unusual history.
   My good friend Argas gave it to me
   in trust,
   Impressing on me, come what may,
   I must
   Keep it a secret; his life, his property
   Depended on that box he gave to
   me.   10
CLÉANTE. Then why, pray tell, did you
   give it to Tartuffe?
ORGON. I know, dear brother; I merit
   your reproof.
   I hoped to keep my conscience easy,
   though,
   And he persuaded me to let it go
   By telling me that, in case of investi-
   gation,   15
   I might deny then any imputation
   Of guilty knowledge and could take
   an oath
   That would not be contrary to the
   truth.
CLÉANTE. I must confess, I fear you're
   on the rocks.
   The deed of gift, the transfer of the
   box—   20
   I speak the truth, I cannot deal in
   lies—
   To put the matter gently, were most
   unwise.
   With these as evidence, it's clear he's
   got you
   Exactly where he wants you. You
   forgot you
   Were dealing with a man of many
   schemes;   25
   You never should have pushed him
   to extremes.

ORGON. Oh! Under such an outward show of piety
To hide such wickedness and impropriety!
To think I rescued him from sheer disgrace!
From now on, I renounce the human race.   30
Henceforth I'll shun them utterly and call
Myself a fool if I don't hate them all!
CLÉANTE. Now there you go, flying off the handle!
Won't you ever learn to burn the candle
At just one end? You waver wildly, brother,   35
From one grotesque extreme back to the other.
You see your error now and recognize
That you were taken in by pious lies,
But why correct your error and confusion
By falling into greater disillusion   40
And lump all mankind in one category
As though that told the full facts of the story?
Because a rascal cuts truth on the bias,
Pretending to be holy, good, and pious,
You would conclude that Chaos is upon us   45
And that the human race has turned dishonest.
Let the freethinkers think that, if they choose,
But learn to separate the external views
From the inner truth. And then don't rush away
Too hastily, but keep to the middle way.   50
Try not to be the dupe of charlatans,
But don't brand truly pious men as harlequins.
And if you must make one or the other choice,
Then let excessive leniency be your vice.

SCENE ii. ORGON, CLÉANTE, and DAMIS.

DAMIS. Father, is it true this brazen rogue,   55
Forgetting all the favors you've bestowed,
Has grown presumptuous and threatens
To use your benefits against you as his weapons?
ORGON. My son, I'm sorry to say it's all too true.
DAMIS. Give me the word, and I'll run him through and through   60
With a carving knife. One should never waver
Before the impudence of that soul-saver!
I'll fix him so he'll never bother us again!
CLÉANTE. Ah, that's the speech of youth. But now and then
It's necessary to be more composed.   65
We're men, not beasts; the course that you've proposed
Is surely no way to resolve the matter.

SCENE iii. MADAME PERNELLE, ORGON, ELMIRE, CLÉANTE, MARIANE, DAMIS, *and* DORINE.

MME. PERNELLE. Good Heavens, what's the meaning of all this chatter?
ORGON. Strange things indeed I've seen with my own eyes,
And a strange and most unpleasant kind of surprise!   70
I rescue a man from abject poverty,
Give him my home, my daughter, my property,
Treat him, in short, better than my brother,
Crown every benefit I give him with another,
And what is my reward, upon my life?   75

He seeks beneath my nose to seduce
my wife,
And, still not fully satisfied with
this,
He dares to use against me my own
gifts,
Trying to bring me down by using
the hold
I've given him by my kindness, and
he's bold   80
Enough to kick me from under this
roof that's covered him
And leave me in the gutter where I
discovered him!
DORINE. The poor man!
MME. PERNELLE.   My son, I can't
imagine
He could behave in such a fashion.
ORGON. What!
MME. PERNELLE. People always envy
pious men.   85
ORGON. Do I have to tell you all of
this again?
MME. PERNELLE. I know that people
here don't love him;
I know they're all quite jealous of
him.
ORGON. And what's that got to do with
this affair?
MME. PERNELLE. When you were a boy,
I warned you to take care,   90
For virtue's always slandered by a
lie;
Though envy perishes, the envious
won't die.
ORGON. I don't see how any of this is
apropos.
MME. PERNELLE. Liars will tirelessly
spread their lies, you know.
ORGON. I tell you I saw it all with my
very own eyes!   95
MME. PERNELLE. Ah, alas! that this
world is so full of lies!
ORGON. You'll make me sin through
anger. For the last time,
I tell you I *saw* his shameless attempt
at crime!
MME. PERNELLE. This world is ever
full of slanderous tongues
Ready to make up tales of imagined

wrongs.   100
ORGON. What you are saying is absolute
nonsense!
I *saw* the man! He hasn't the slight-
est defense!
I *saw* him try to do it! Do I have
to yell
The simple truth in your ear or ring
a bell?
MME. PERNELLE. Mercy me! Appear-
ances often deceive.   105
Don't be overly rash in what you
believe.
ORGON. You're driving me crazy!
MME. PERNELLE.   False suspicion
Is common to one in your condi-
tion.
ORGON. Then he piously sought to im-
prove my life
By making infamous love to my
wife?   110
MME. PERNELLE. You need *facts* to
support an accusation
Which might destroy a good man's
reputation.
ORGON. *Facts?* How in the hell can I
be more factual
Than to catch the scoundrel in the
actual
Act of...no, you almost made me
say it.   115
MME. PERNELLE. If there's evil in him,
he doesn't betray it,
Not by the slightest glance or sneer;
I just can't believe these stories I
hear.
ORGON. Good Lord, I'm so mad I could
jump on my hat!
If you weren't my mother, I'd do
worse than that!   120
DORINE [*to* ORGON]. You wouldn't
believe a word we'd say;
Now turn about, I'm afraid, is fair
play.
CLÉANTE. We're wasting time here
babbling like silly sheep;
When the wolf is on the prowl, one
shouldn't sleep.
How are we going to meet that
scoundrel's scheme?   125

DAMIS. He wouldn't have the nerve! He wouldn't dream...!

ELMIRE. I really doubt if he'd take legal action
Merely to obtain his satisfaction.

CLÉANTE. Don't be too sure. He's got tricks up his sleeve,
And we know he's slyer than anyone dare believe.   130
For less than this, men have served a spell
With bread and water in a prison cell.
And I repeat, since we know what his weapons are,
You made a mistake in pushing him so far.

ORGON. All right, all right, but what else could I do?   135
His impudence simply angered me through and through.

CLÉANTE. I wish with all my heart we could arrange
Some kind of fair and equitable exchange.

ELMIRE. If I had known he held such trumps in hand,
I'd have thought twice about the trick I planned.   140

[M. LOYAL *appears at the door;* DORINE *goes to meet him.*]

SCENE iv. ORGON, MADAME PERNELLE, ELMIRE, MARIANE, CLÉANTE, DAMIS, DORINE, *and* MONSIEUR LOYAL.

ORGON. Who's that fellow? Tell him to go away.
I'm in no state to deal with callers today.

M. LOYAL. Sister, good morning. Your master, pray, where is he?
I must speak to him at once.

DORINE.   He's busy.
He can't see anyone, I fear.   145

M. LOYAL. I shouldn't like to intrude upon him here.
But I don't think my business will upset him;

He can hear my news, if you will let him.

DORINE. Your name?

M. LOYAL.   Just say I've come to bring him proof
Of the warm regard of Monsieur Tartuffe.   150

DORINE [*to* ORGON]. He is a messenger, and quite soft-spoken,
From our old friend. He says he brings a token
Of Tartuffe's regard.

CLÉANTE.   You'd better see
Who he is and what his news can be.

ORGON. Maybe he's coming to offer apologies.   155
Should I greet him politely and put him at his ease?

CLÉANTE. Speak softly, but don't vouchsafe any admission.
If he offers peace, though—better listen.

M. LOYAL. Greetings, good sir! May Heaven confound your foes
And shower you with love and sweet repose!   160

ORGON [*to* CLÉANTE]. A most polite beginning! An indication
He wants a reconciliation.

M. LOYAL. Your family's interests have long been mine.
I served your worthy father many a time.

ORGON. I beg your pardon, sir, but to my shame   165
I must confess I don't recall your name.

M. LOYAL. My name is Loyal. I too have a confession.
I am a process-server by profession.
For forty years it's been my pride and joy
To hold that honorable office, man and boy.   170
You asked my business here, sir? This is it:
To serve upon you this judicial writ.

ORGON. What!

M. LOYAL.   Now, please, let's talk without unseemly friction.
It's just a little notice of eviction.

You and your family must get out, 175
Remove your goods and furniture,
  and in about—
Let's say, an hour—sooner, if you
  could.
ORGON. What, leave my house!
M. LOYAL.   If you
  would be so good.
This house belongs, as you are well
  aware,
To good Monsieur Tartuffe. A deed
  I bear   180
Attests unto the fact beyond dispute,
So please don't force him, good sir,
  to bring suit
And call upon the law in his defense.
DAMIS. I'm simply staggered by such
  insolence!
M. LOYAL. Young man, my business
  here is not with you,   185
But with your father, a good man
  and true,
Who knows his legal duties, you may
  trust us,
And wouldn't dream of contravening
  justice.
ORGON. But...
M. LOYAL.   Yes, I know that not for
  a fortune
Would you protest or would you
  importune   190
The court to contradict its stern
  commands
And remove this writ from out of
  your hands.
DAMIS. You might get a wholesome
  beating on the end
Of your black and gloomy coat, my
  friend!
M. LOYAL. Sir, bid your son be silent
  and retire.   195
I'd hate to have to report his ire
And his threats of violence and fits
  of pique.
DORINE [*aside*]. He says his name is
  Loyal? I'd say, Sneak.
M. LOYAL. I have a great respect for
  honesty,
And I agreed to serve this writ, you
  see,   200
Just to oblige you and to give you

pleasure,
For others might not execute the
  seizure
Of your goods with such considera-
  tion
As I, who feel for you such admi-
  ration.
ORGON. What could be worse, or could
  be a greater crime   205
Than evicting a man?
M. LOYAL.   But, you see,
  I'm giving you time.
I will suspend till tomorrow, if you
  need
Some extra time, the service of the
  deed.
I'll merely come, with a dozen of
  my men,
To quietly spend the night with you,
  and then   210
I'll ask you to deliver to me the keys
Of the house before you go to bed,
  if you please.
Please be assured, we'll not trouble
  your repose;
It's just a matter of form, you know
  how it goes.
Tomorrow morning early you'll move
  out   215
All your furniture. I've picked some
  stout
And husky fellows; you'll find they're
  quite discreet,
As well as skilled at moving things
  out on the street.
No one, I think, could possibly act
  more fairly,
Nor put the matter before you more
  sincerely,   220
And as I'm giving you all this kind
  assistance
I must beg you to offer no resistance.
ORGON [*aside*]. How happy I would be
  to give my last
Hundred louis for the chance to blast
This monster of pure impudence and
  clout   225
Him violently and squarely on the
  snout!
CLÉANTE. Easy, don't lose your head.
DAMIS. Oh, I insist.

Just one punch. I've got an itching
  fist.
DORINE. That noble back, monsieur,
  seems to demand
A good sound beating from a lady's
  hand.   230
M. LOYAL. Beware, my dear; the law
  makes no distinction
Regarding sex when it comes to legal
  action.
CLÉANTE. No more of this, sir; what-
  ever the law allows,
Just give us the writ, and then get
  out of the house.
M. LOYAL. *Au revoir*, gentlemen! May
  God content you!   [*Exit.*] 235

SCENE v. ORGON, MADAME PERNELLE,
ELMIRE, CLÉANTE, MARIANE, DAMIS,
and DORINE.

ORGON. May He confound you and the
  man who sent you!

[*To* MME. PERNELLE.]

Well, Mother, tell me, was I right
About this monster who is your
  delight?
MME. PERNELLE. I'm flabbergasted! I
  can't believe my ears!
DORINE. Well, maybe it's all better
  than it appears.   240
His goal is good; he's doing all he
  can
To demonstrate how he loves his
  fellow man.
He knows the soul's corrupted by the
  love
Of money, so he'll lovingly remove
Temptation from his friends, for their
  salvation.   245
ORGON. Oh, shut up! Stop this bicker-
  ing! Damnation!
CLÉANTE. Let's try to think of the
  proper course to take.
ELMIRE. Let's tell the world he's a
  hyprocritical fake.
These despicable tricks he has
  employed

Would render any contract null and
  void.   250
Public opinion, once his deeds are
  known,
Will surely rise, and its power will
  be shown.

SCENE vi. VALÈRE, ORGON, MADAME
PERNELLE, ELMIRE, CLÉANTE, MARI-
ANE, DAMIS, *and* DORINE.

VALÈRE. I'm sorry, sir, to cause you any
  distress,
But I feel obliged to by the present
  mess
You're in; a very old and trusted
  friend   255
Who knows my interest has dared to
  send
Me word of your affairs, in violation
Of that high secrecy belonging to
  his station.
The news he sends is bitter, curt, and
  tight:
Your only possible recourse is
  flight.   260
He who has swindled you of every-
  thing.
Has made an accusation to the
  King,
And has supported his charges, sad
  to relate,
With the strongbox of an outlaw of
  the state,
The which he found, he says, in your
  possession.   265
Proof of your most traitorous trans-
  gression.
I don't know whether you're innocent
  or not,
But you're ordered to be arrested on
  the spot,
And Tartuffe himself has been com-
  mended
And charged to see that you are
  apprehended.   270
CLÉANTE. Thus armed might assists
  him in his schemes
And helps him realize his evil dreams.

ORGON. Oh, that man is wicked past man's thought!

VALÈRE. Any delay will be fatal, so I've brought
My carriage round to whisk you safely away   275
And a thousand louis to help you on your way.
So don't waste time; this is a fearful blow;
Escape is the only answer that I know.
I'll find you a hiding place with another friend
And I'll stay by your side until the end.   280

ORGON. I owe so much to your kind consideration,
But that can wait for a happier occasion;
I only pray that Heaven gives me the power
To fitly remember your goodness in this hour.
Good-bye, my friends...

CLÉANTE.   Hurry! No delays! Don't fear,   285
We'll take care of everything right here.

[*Enter* TARTUFFE *and a* POLICE OFFICER. *As* ORGON *starts to exit*, TARTUFFE *seizes him.*]

SCENE vii. TARTUFFE, *a* POLICE OFFICER, MADAME PERNELLE, ORGON, ELMIRE, CLÉANTE, MARIANE, VALÈRE, DAMIS, *and* DORINE.

TARTUFFE. Here now, good sir! Don't run away so fast!
A lodging's ready for you. No need for haste.
I take you prisoner, in the name of the King.

ORGON. Villain, you are guilty of everything;   290
You duped me into listening to your counsel
So that you might bring about my utter downfall!

TARTUFFE. I will not flinch, although you rave quite wildly.
Heaven has taught me to suffer insults mildly.

CLÉANTE. So these are the lessons your religion has given!   295

DAMIS. How impudently he plays with the name of Heaven!

TARTUFFE. You cannot move me by your enmity;
To do my duty means everything to me.

MARIANE. Much glory you will draw from this affair,
And maybe more honor than even you can bear!   300

TARTUFFE. Glory only accrues unto an action
Blessed and commanded by the royal sanction.

ORGON. Have you forgotten it was my charity
That rescued you from the depths of poverty?

TARTUFFE. True, you helped me with an occasional loan,   305
But my highest duty is to the royal throne.
This sacred and compelling obligation
Extinguishes all small considerations
Of petty gratitude. Upon my life,
I place it ahead of children, family, or wife!   310

ELMIRE. Impostor!

DORINE.   This treacherous, sly snake would
Twist and mock all values we hold sacred!

CLÉANTE. But if this noble and religious zeal
Is quite as perfect as you'd have us feel,
How is it that it waited to appear   315
Till you were caught embracing Madame here?
Why did you delay your denunciation
Till you were trapped in that curious situation?

I won't allege, though it might have
    played a part,
That deed of gift from the goodness
    of his heart,   320
But why accept the money, then and
    later,
Of a man whom you denounce now
    as a traitor?

TARTUFFE [*to the* POLICE OFFICER].
    Deliver me, monsieur, from attacks
    like these
And execute your orders, if you
    please.

OFFICER. Yes, I've delayed too long
    now, at the best;   325
And, aptly enough, you're the one
    who makes the request.
So here's the order: kindly follow me
To the prison cell that is your home
    to be.

TARTUFFE. Who, me?

OFFICER.   Yes, you.

TARTUFFE.   What do
    you mean? You must be insane!

OFFICER. You're not the one to whom
    I must explain. [*to* ORGON] 330
You've had a nasty scare, but, praised
    be God,
Our present King is an enemy of
    fraud;
His eyes can penetrate his subjects'
    hearts
And he's not deluded by a trickster's
    arts.
His great spirit, mighty, calm, and
    wise,   335
Watches his kingdom with discerning
    eyes.
Charlatans and practicers of treason
Cannot delude or shake his sovereign
    reason.
To worthy men he gives due recom-
    pense,
Yet he's not blind to fraud and false
    pretense.   340
His love for truth, however, does not
    eclipse
The horror one should feel for
    hypocrites.
Tartuffe was not the type who could

hoodwink him:
The King is more perceptive than
    men think him.   344
Immediately and subtly he divined
The vile conniving of an evil mind.
This man betrayed himself by his
    accusation
And by a process of due retribution
The King identified him as a thief
With a criminal record almost past
    belief,   350
A man of various names, whose
    numerous crimes
Have been recorded a good many
    times.
In short, His Majesty found so
    abhorrent
This man's career, that it was ample
    warrant
For his arrest. This additional
    crime   355
Only sealed his fate. That's why I'm
With him today. The King com-
    manded me
To accompany him today and see
What impudence he would dare as
    a last evasion.
Now I shall force him to make you
    reparation,   360
Seizing the powers that he might
    have destroyed;
The King declares the contract null
    and void
Which might have made Tartuffe
    your legal heir
And he pardons that transgression
    where
You erred but to protect a friend. 365
Thus he rewards you, thus does he
    commend
Your past fidelity in the civil wars,
Proving his heart remembers and
    rewards
A loyal subject; like the King of
    paradise,
He's mindful more of virtue than of
    vice.   370

DORINE. May Heaven be praised!

MME. PERNELLE.   Ah,
    I'm so relieved!

ELMIRE. All's well again!
MARIANE.   This scarcely
   can be believed!
ORGON [*to* TARTUFFE]. So now we've
   got you, villain...

[*The* OFFICER *drags* TARTUFFE *away*.]

SCENE viii. MADAME PERNELLE, ORGON,
ELMIRE, MARIANE, CLÉANTE, VALÈRE,
DAMIS, *and* DORINE.

CLÉANTE.   Please; moderation.
   Don't yield to an unworthy exulta-
   tion.
   Leave the wretched man to his
      wretched fate;   375
   He's already bowed beneath the heavy
      weight

Of his own remorse. Why not hope,
   rather,
That his heart may undergo a change,
   dear brother,
And by progressing to better from
   the worse, he
May move the King to temper justice
   with mercy,   380
The while you kneel before the royal
   throne
To beg that Tartuffe's fate might be
   like your own.
ORGON. Well said, indeed. So let us, at
   his feet,
Thank him for his kindness and
   entreat
Mercy for our enemies. This done, 385
There's one more crown of joy left
   to be won,
And that's for me to happily declare
Mariane shall be the bride of Valère.

Arms and the Man

The themes and genre of George Bernard Shaw's *Arms and the Man* are implied in its title, which echoes the opening lines of Virgil's *Aeneid,* "Of arms and the man I sing." Shaw's play, like Virgil's epic, deals with the twin themes of love and war. But the setting of the play—not Carthage and Italy but late nineteenth-century Bulgaria, a Gilbert and Sullivan country to Englishmen of the time—suggests a less than heroic mode. Where Virgil "sang," heightening his discourse to suit the grandeur of his subject and characters, Shaw satirizes, letting his characters heighten *their* discourse but now and again introducing a scratchy, mock-heroic discord of his own. What remains of the Virgilian epic is merely an epic pretentiousness in the characters. Except, of course, for Bluntschli, who like Tartuffe intrudes his way into a family circle. But whereas the pious Tartuffe, welcomed by Orgon as a friend, turns out to be an enemy, the official enemy of the Bulgarians turns out to be a savior to the Petkoffs. What he saves them from is not terribly ominous, merely the likelihood of evaporating in the rarefied atmosphere of high romance. But accomplishing even this much, especially in a world so devoted to verbal and attitudinal vaporizings, has something of the heroic about it, or so Shaw (1856–1950) ironically implies when he insinuates Bluntschli into the company of "the man" Aeneas at the end of the play: "What a man! Is he a man!" (p. 363).

Mock-heroic specializes in perspective by incongruity, in seeing one thing from the perspective of another—specifically, in seeing the grand, the ideal, and the higher in terms of the trivial, the real, and the lower. The effect is to diminish and deflate. Bluntschli is the major deflator in the play. It is he who sets military conquest in the perspective of self-preservation by preferring chocolate bars to ammunition, who sacrifices the sentiments of romance to the exigencies of wartime travel by pawning the cloak Raina had given him, and who refuses to let the conventions of dueling disguise the lethal fact beneath by choosing for his weapon against Sergius a machinegun. What Bluntschli throws into relief is the discrepancy between form and content, style and meaning, that is basic to the mock-heroic mode. Certainly the Petkoff family and Sergius are impassioned devotees of high style and manner at the expense of meaning and matter. There is the library, so grandly and frequently announced and so thinly stocked; the "fashionable tea gown" worn by Catherine on all occasions; and the impressive electric bell, which along with newspapers and occidental furnishings is part of a Western European style considered chic by the Petkoffs. This concern for stylization takes its most obvious form in the physical posturings of Raina and Sergius. We first encounter Raina languishing on her balcony, dreamily gazing at the snowy Balkans, and thoroughly enjoying the notion of herself languishing on her balcony dreamily gazing at the snowy Balkans. Sergius' unrelenting sense of honor is so welded to his poses that he has only to fold his arms for everyone to know that a principle is beginning to petrify within him.

In a play whose central characters are impostors trying to pass themselves off as something considerably higher than they are, the plot necessarily revolves around recognition scenes in which recognition means primarily exposure. Sergius' cavalry charge, his reunion with Raina, and Raina's admission of lying are the major exposures. Rebelling against the unheroics of military combat—"soldiering," Petkoff says, "has to be a trade like any other trade"—Sergius sets off across the battlefield "flourishing like a drum major." At a gallop he is all style, the perfect embodiment of headstrong romantic individuality; but as Bluntschli reveals to Raina, it is style devoid of sense, the charge having been little more than an attempt at suicide in which the pistol misfired. Sergius and Raina are no less stylized in the drawing room or garden, especially during the scene in Act II when they are reunited. While he "posts himself with conscious dignity against the rail of the steps," she waits out of sight listening for the right dramatic moment to make an entrance. They approach one another, bow, and separate with all the mannered self-consciousness of a pair of ballroom dancers. The "higher love" is expressed not only choreographically but linguistically. Their dialogue is based on the genteel cliché, verbal petals plucked no doubt from the paper-covered novels in the library and wafted back and forth between them: "You have been out in the world, on the field of battle, able to prove yourself there worthy of any woman in the world"..."Dearest, all my deeds have been yours"..."never been absent from my thoughts a moment," etc. Unfortunately, as Sergius reveals to Louka, the professional poseur must work as hard as the professional athlete. The higher love is a "fatiguing thing to keep up for any length of time. One feels the need of some relief after it." And so he turns from the exhaustiveness of the high style to the deftness of the low style in turning from the mistress to the servant. Finally, Raina's admission of lying is an exposure of a similar mock-heroic sort: "I! I!!!... How did you find me out?"

Thus throughout the play Shaw's satire is generated by the abrasive contact between high romance and low realism, and the major action would seem to be the comic fall of Sergius and Raina toward the authentic values represented in Bluntschli. But precisely what those values are is not clear. Near the end of the play, the deflation of Sergius and Raina seems complete. Raina says to Bluntschli, "I daresay you think us a couple of grown-up babies, don't you?" But is that all there is to Sergius' and Raina's romanticism? Immediately after Raina confesses her habit of lying and of cultivating "the noble attitude and the thrilling voice" Bluntschli confesses that he does not find her posing unattractive: "It's part of your youth: part of your charm...I'm your infatuated admirer." As for Sergius, his code of honor is silly enough, but he can both disregard it, by apologizing to Louka, and stick to it, by acknowledging her his fiance. Even his cavalry charge has a certain appeal when compared to proper soldiering, which he defines as "the coward's art of attacking mercilessly when you are strong, and keeping out of harm's way when you are weak."

What this suggests is that the center of values in the play is not reached simply by sweeping romance and the high style aside in favor of blunt realism. In fact, Bluntschli has his unattractive side, too. Sergius says he has no "magnetism," that he is less a man than a "machine," and he replies, "Quite true, quite true. I always was that sort of a chap. I'm very sorry." Yet later on Bluntschli admits that his "incurably romantic disposition" has spoiled all his chances in life. Is this convincing? Has he revealed his romantic side in the play? He is obviously not a romantic of the early Sergius and Raina variety. Nor is he a realist of the

Nicola type, for whom realism simply means lack of principle and who is thus a good candidate for the title of machine. Perhaps Shaw's stage directions for Bluntschli's final speech are a good index of the values he embodies. His greeting Raina's acceptance of him "with a boyish laugh of delight" associates him with her own youth and charm, but his glancing at his watch in the next instant and suddenly becoming "businesslike" associates him with Nicola. Obviously, a fusion of the two is required. Lacking a firm sense of practical reality, the romantic spirit drifts blithely beyond purpose and meaning. But without an impulse to idealize, or even romantically to rebel against the plainness of plain facts, man becomes debased into a kind of mechanism—efficient, practical, and empty.

Arms and the Man

ACT I

Night: A lady's bedchamber in Bulgaria, in a small town near the Dragoman Pass, late in November in the year 1885. Through an open window with a little balcony a peak of the Balkans, wonderfully white and beautiful in the starlit snow, seems quite close at hand, though it is really miles away. The interior of the room is not like anything to be seen in the west of Europe. It is half rich Bulgarian, half cheap Viennese. Above the head of the bed, which stands against a little wall cutting off the left-hand corner of the room, is a painted wooden shrine, blue and gold, with an ivory image of Christ, and a light hanging before it in a pierced metal ball suspended by three chains. The principal seat, placed towards the other side of the room and opposite the window, is a Turkish ottoman. The counterpane and hangings of the bed, the window curtains, the little carpet, and all the ornamental textile fabrics in the room are oriental and gorgeous; the paper on the walls is occidental and paltry. The washstand, against the wall on the side nearest the ottoman and window, consists of an enamelled iron basin with a pail beneath it in a painted metal frame, and a single towel on the rail at the side. The dressing table, between the bed and the window, is a common pine table, covered with a cloth of many colours, with an expensive toilet mirror on it. The door is on the side nearest the bed; and there is a chest of drawers between. This chest of drawers is also covered by a variegated native cloth; and on it there is a pile of paper-backed novels, a box of chocolate creams, and a miniature easel with a large photograph of an extremely handsome officer, whose lofty bearing and magnetic glance can be felt even from the portrait. The room is lighted by a candle on the chest of drawers, and another on the dressing table with a box of matches beside it. The window is hinged doorwise and stands wide open. Outside, a pair of wooden shutters, opening outwards, also stand open. On the balcony a young lady, intensely conscious of the romantic beauty of the night, and of the fact that her own youth and beauty are part of it, is gazing at the snowy Balkans. She is in her nightgown, well covered by a long mantle of furs, worth, on a moderate estimate, about three times the furniture of the room.

Her reverie is interrupted by her mother, CATHERINE PETKOFF, a woman over forty, imperiously energetic, with magnificent black hair and eyes, who might be a very splendid specimen of the wife of a mountain farmer, but is determined to be a Viennese lady, and to that end wears a fashionable tea gown on all occasions.

CATHERINE [*entering hastily, full of good news*]. Raina! [*She pronounces it Rah-eena, with the stress on the ee.*] Raina! [*She goes to the bed, expecting to find* RAINA *there.*] Why, where—? [RAINA *looks into the*

Reprinted by permission of The Shaw Estate, The Public Trustee, and The Society of Authors.

room.] Heavens, child! are you out in the night air instead of in your bed? Youll catch your death. Louka told me you were asleep.

RAINA [*dreamily*]. I sent her away. I wanted to be alone. The stars are so beautiful! What is the matter?

CATHERINE. Such news! There has been a battle.

RAINA [*her eyes dilating*]. Ah! [*She comes eagerly to* CATHERINE.]

CATHERINE. A great battle at Slivnitza! A victory! And it was won by Sergius.

RAINA [*with a cry of delight*]. Ah! [*They embrace rapturously.*] Oh, mother! [*then, with sudden anxiety*] Is father safe?

CATHERINE. Of course! he sends me the news. Sergius is the hero of the hour, the idol of the regiment.

RAINA. Tell me, tell me. How was it? [*ecstatically*] Oh, mother! mother! mother!

[*She pulls her mother down on the ottoman; and they kiss one another frantically.*]

CATHERINE [*with surging enthusiasm*]. You cant guess how splendid it is. A cavalry charge! think of that! He defied our Russian commanders—acted without orders—led a charge on his own responsibility—headed it himself—was the first man to sweep through their guns. Cant you see it, Raina: our gallant splendid Bulgarians with their swords and eyes flashing, thundering down like an avalanche and scattering the wretched Serbs and their dandified Austrian officers like chaff. And you! you kept Sergius waiting a year before you would be betrothed to him. Oh, if you have a drop of Bulgarian blood in your veins, you will worship him when he comes back.

RAINA. What will he care for my poor little worship after the acclamations of a whole army of heroes? But no matter: I am so happy! so proud! [*She rises and walks about excitedly.*] It proves that all our ideas were real after all.

CATHERINE [*indignantly*]. Our ideas real! What do you mean?

RAINA. Our ideas of what Sergius would do. Our patriotism. Our heroic ideals. I sometimes used to doubt whether they were anything but dreams. Oh, what faithless little creatures girls are! When I buckled on Sergius's sword he looked so noble: it was treason to think of disillusion or humiliation or failure. And yet—and yet—[*She sits down again suddenly.*] Promise me youll never tell him.

CATHERINE. Dont ask me for promises until I know what I'm promising.

RAINA. Well, it came into my head just as he was holding me in his arms and looking into my eyes, that perhaps we only had our heroic ideas because we are so fond of reading Byron and Pushkin, and because we were so delighted with the opera that season at Bucharest. Real life is so seldom like that! indeed never, as far as I knew it then. [*remorsefully*] Only think, mother: I doubted him: I wondered whether all his heroic qualities and his soldiership might not prove mere imagination when he went into a real battle. I had an uneasy fear that he might cut a poor figure there beside all those clever officers from the Tsar's court.

CATHERINE. A poor figure! Shame on you! The Serbs have Austrian officers who are just as clever as the Russians; but we have beaten them in every battle for all that.

RAINA [*laughing and snuggling against her mother*]. Yes: I was only a prosaic little coward. Oh, to think that it was all true! that Sergius is just as splendid and noble as he looks! that the world is really a glorious world for women who can see its glory and men who can act its romance! What happiness! what unspeakable fulfilment!

[*They are interrupted by the entry of* LOUKA, *a handsome proud girl in a pretty Bulgarian peasant's dress with double apron, so defiant that her servility to* RAINA *is almost insolent. She is afraid of* CATHERINE, *but even with her goes as far as she dares.*]

LOUKA. If you please, madam, all the windows are to be closed and the shutters made fast. They say there may be shooting in the streets. [RAINA *and* CATHERINE *rise together, alarmed.*] The Serbs are being chased right back through the pass; and they say they may run into the town. Our cavalry will be after them; and our people will be ready for them, you may be sure, now theyre running away.

[*She goes out on the balcony, and pulls the outside shutters to; then steps back into the room.*]

CATHERINE [*businesslike, housekeeping instincts aroused*]. I must see that everything is made safe downstairs.

RAINA. I wish our people were not so cruel. What glory is there in killing wretched fugitives?

CATHERINE. Cruel! Do you suppose they would hesitate to kill you—or worse?

RAINA [*to* LOUKA]. Leave the shutters so that I can just close them if I hear any noise.

CATHERINE [*authoritatively, turning on her way to the door*]. Oh no, dear: you must keep them fastened. You would be sure to drop off to sleep and leave them open. Make them fast, Louka.

LOUKA. Yes, madam.

[*She fastens them.*]

RAINA. Dont be anxious about me. The moment I hear a shot, I shall blow out the candles and roll myself up in bed with my ears well covered.

CATHERINE. Quite the wisest thing you can do, my love. Goodnight.

RAINA. Goodnight. [*Her emotion comes back for a moment.*] Wish me joy. [*They kiss.*] This is the happiest night of my life—if only there are no fugitives.

CATHERINE. Go to bed, dear; and dont think of them.   [*She goes out.*]

LOUKA [*secretly to* RAINA]. If you would like the shutters open, just give them a push like this. [*She pushes them: they open: she pulls them to again.*] One of them ought to be bolted at the bottom; but the bolt's gone.

RAINA [*with dignity, reproving her*]. Thanks, Louka; but we must do what we are told. [LOUKA *makes a grimace.*] Goodnight.

LOUKA [*carelessly*]. Goodnight.

[*She goes out, swaggering.*]

[RAINA, *left alone, takes off her fur cloak and throws it on the ottoman. Then she goes to the chest of drawers, and adores the portrait there with feelings that are beyond all expression. She does not kiss it or press it to her breast, or shew it any mark of bodily affection; but she takes it in her hands and elevates it, like a priestess.*]

RAINA [*looking up at the picture*]. Oh, I shall never be unworthy of you any more, my soul's hero: never, never, never. [*She replaces it reverently. Then she selects a novel from the little pile of books. She turns over the leaves dreamily; finds her page; turns the book inside out at it; and, with a happy sigh, gets into bed and prepares to read herself to sleep. But before abandoning herself to fiction, she raises her eyes once more, thinking of the blessed reality, and murmurs:*] My hero! my hero!

[*A distant shot breaks the quiet of the night. She starts, listening; and two shots, much nearer, follow, startling her so that she scrambles out of bed, and hastily blows out the candle on the chest of drawers. Then, putting her fingers in her ears, she runs to the dressing table, blows out the light there, and hurries back to bed in the dark, nothing being visible but the glimmer of the light in the pierced ball before the image, and the starlight seen through the slits at the top of the shutters. The firing breaks out again: there is a startling fusillade quite close at hand. Whilst it is still echoing, the shutters disappear, pulled open from without; and for an instant the rectangle of snowy starlight flashes out with the figure of a man silhouetted in black upon it. The shutters close immediately; and the room is dark again. But the silence is now broken by the sound of panting. Then there is a scratch; and the flame of a match is seen in the middle of the room.]*

RAINA [*crouching on the bed*]. Who's there? [*The match is out instantly.*] Who's there? Who is that?

A MAN'S VOICE [*in the darkness, subduedly, but threateningly*]. Sh—sh! Dont call out; or youll be shot. Be good; and no harm will happen to you. [*She is heard leaving her bed, and making for the door.*] Take care: it's no use use trying to run away.

RAINA. But who—

THE VOICE [*warning*]. Remember: if you raise your voice my revolver will go off. [*commandingly*] Strike a light and let me see you. Do you hear. [*Another moment of silence and darkness as she retreats to the chest of drawers. Then she lights a candle; and the mystery is at an end. He is a man of about 35, in a deplorable plight, bespattered with mud and blood and snow, his belt and the strap of his revolver case keeping together the torn ruins of the blue tunic of a Serbian artillery officer. All that the candlelight and* his unwashed unkempt condition make it possible to discern is that he is of middling stature and undistinguished appearance, with strong neck and shoulders, roundish obstinate looking head covered with short crisp bronze curls, clear quick eyes and good brows and mouth, hopelessly prosaic nose like that of a strong minded baby, trim soldierlike carriage and energetic manner, and with all his wits about him in spite of his desperate predicament: even with a sense of the humor of it, without, however, the least intention of trifling with it or throwing away a chance. Reckoning up what he can guess about* RAINA, *her age, her social position, her character, and the extent to which she is frightened, he continues, more politely but still most determinedly.*] Excuse my disturbing you; but you recognize my uniform? Serb! If I'm caught I shall be killed. [*menacingly*] Do you understand that?

RAINA. Yes.

THE MAN. Well, I dont intend to get killed if I can help it. [*still more formidably*] Do you understand that?

[*He locks the door quickly but quietly.*]

RAINA [*disdainfully*]. I suppose not. [*She draws herself up superbly, and looks him straight in the face, adding, with cutting emphasis:*] Some soldiers, I know, are afraid to die.

THE MAN [*with grim goodhumor*]. All of them, dear lady, all of them, believe me. It is our duty to live as long as we can. Now, if you raise an alarm—

RAINA [*cutting him short*]. You will shoot me. How do you know that *I* am afraid to die?

THE MAN [*cunningly*]. Ah; but suppose I dont shoot you, what will happen then? A lot of your cavalry will burst into this pretty room of yours and slaughter me here like a pig; for I'll fight like a demon: they shant get me into the street to amuse themselves with: I know what they are. Are you prepared to receive that sort of company in your present undress? [RAINA, *suddenly conscious of her nightgown, instinctively shrinks and gathers it more closely about her neck. He watches her and adds pitilessly:*] Hardly presentable, eh? [*She turns to the ottoman. He raises his pistol instantly, and cries*] Stop! [*She stops.*] Where are you going?

RAINA [*with dignified patience*]. Only to get my cloak.

THE MAN [*passing swiftly to the ottoman and snatching the cloak*]. A good idea! I'll keep the cloak; and youll take care that nobody comes in and sees you without it. This is a better weapon than the revolver: eh?

[*He throws the pistol down on the ottoman.*]

RAINA [*revolted*]. It is not the weapon of a gentleman!

THE MAN. It's good enough for a man with only you to stand between him and death. [*As they look at one another for a moment,* RAINA *hardly able to believe that even a Serbian officer can be so cynically and selfishly unchivalrous, they are startled by a sharp fusillade in the street. The chill of imminent death hushes the* MAN'S *voice as he adds:*] Do you hear? If you are going to bring those blackguards in on me you shall receive them as you are.

[*Clamor and disturbance. The pursuers in the street batter at the house door, shouting* "Open the door! Open the door! Wake up, will you!" *A man servant's voice calls to them angrily from within* "This is Major Petkoff's house: you cant come in here;" *but a renewal of the clamor, and a torrent of blows on the door, end with his letting a chain down with a clank, followed by a rush*

of heavy footsteps and a din of triumphant yells, dominated at last by the voice of CATHERINE, *indignantly addressing an officer with* "What does this mean, sir? Do you know where you are?" *The noise subsides suddenly.*]

LOUKA [*outside, knocking at the bedroom door*]. My lady! my lady! get up quick and open the door. If you dont they will break it down.

[*The fugitive throws up his head with the gesture of a man who sees that it is all over with him, and drops the manner he has been assuming to intimidate* RAINA.]

THE MAN [*sincerely and kindly*]. No use, dear: I'm done for. [*flinging the cloak to her*] Quick! wrap yourself up: theyre coming.

RAINA. Oh, thank you.

[*She wraps herself up with intense relief.*]

THE MAN [*between his teeth*]. Dont mention it.

RAINA [*anxiously*]. What will you do?

THE MAN [*grimly*]. The first man in will find out. Keep out of the way; dont look. It wont last long; but it will not be nice.

[*He draws his sabre and faces the door, waiting.*]

RAINA [*impulsively*]. I'll help you. I'll save you.

THE MAN. You cant.

RAINA. I can. I'll hide you. [*She drags him towards the window.*] Here! behind the curtains.

THE MAN [*yielding to her*]. Theres just half a chance, if you keep your head.

RAINA [*drawing the curtain before him*]. S-sh!

[*She makes for the ottoman.*]

THE MAN [*putting out his head*]. Remember—

RAINA [*running back to him*]. Yes?

THE MAN.—nine soldiers out of ten are born fools.

RAINA. *Oh!*

[*She draws the curtain angrily before him.*]

THE MAN [*looking out at the other side*]. If they find me, I promise you a fight: a devil of a fight.

[*She stamps at him. He disappears hastily. She takes off her cloak, and throws it across the foot of the bed. Then, with a sleepy, disturbed air, she opens the door. LOUKA enters excitedly.*]

LOUKA. One of those beasts of Serbs has been seen climbing up the water-pipe to your balcony. Our men went to search for him; and they are so wild and drunk and furious. [*She makes for the other side of the room to get as far from the door as possible.*] My lady says you are to dress at once and to—

[*She sees the revolver lying on the ottoman, and stops, petrified.*]

RAINA [*as if annoyed at being disturbed*]. They shall not search here. Why have they been let in?

CATHERINE [*coming in hastily*]. Raina, darling, are you safe? Have you seen anyone or heard anything?

RAINA. I heard the shooting. Surely the soldiers will not dare come in here?

CATHERINE. I have found a Russian officer, thank Heaven: he knows Sergius. [*speaking through the door to someone outside*] Sir: will you come in now. My daughter will receive you.

[*A young Russian OFFICER, in Bulgarian uniform, enters, sword in hand.*]

THE OFFICER [*with soft feline politeness and stiff military carriage*]. Good evening, gracious lady. I am sorry to intrude; but there is a Serb hiding on the balcony. Will you and the gracious lady your mother please to withdraw whilst we search?

RAINA [*petulantly*]. Nonsense, sir: you can see that there is no one on the balcony.

[*She throws the shutters wide open and stands with her back to the curtain where the man is hidden, pointing to the moonlit balcony. A couple of shots are fired right under the window; and a bullet shatters the glass opposite RAINA, who winks and gasps, but stands her ground; whilst CATHERINE screams, and the OFFICER, with a cry of "Take care!" rushes to the balcony.*]

THE OFFICER [*on the balcony, shouting savagely down to the street*]. Cease firing there, you fools: do you hear? Cease firing, damn you! [*He glares down for a moment; then turns to RAINA, trying to resume his polite manner.*] Could anyone have got in without your knowledge? Were you asleep?

RAINA. No: I have not been to bed.

THE OFFICER [*impatiently coming back into the room*]. Your neighbors. have their heads so full of runaway Serbs that they see them everywhere. [*politely*] Gracious lady: a thousand pardons. Goodnight.

[*Military bow, which RAINA returns coldly. Another to CATHERINE, who follows him out. RAINA closes the shutters, She turns and sees LOUKA, who has been watching the scene curiously.*]

RAINA. Dont leave my mother, Louka, until the soldiers go away.

[*LOUKA glances at RAINA, at the ottoman, at the curtain; then purses her lips secretively, laughs insolently, and goes out. RAINA, highly offended by this demonstration, follows her to the door, and shuts it behind her with a slam, locking it violently. The man immediately steps out from behind the curtain, sheathing his sabre. Then, dismissing the danger from his mind in a businesslike way, he comes affably to RAINA.*]

THE MAN. A narrow shave; but a

miss is as good as a mile. Dear young lady: your servant to the death. I wish for your sake I had joined the Bulgarian army instead of the other one. I am not a native Serb.

RAINA [*haughtily*]. No: you are one of the Austrians who set the Serbs on to rob us of our national liberty, and who officer their army for them. We hate them!

THE MAN. Austrian! not I. Dont hate me, dear young lady. I am a Swiss, fighting merely as a professional soldier. I joined the Serbs because they came first on the road from Switzerland. Be generous: youve beaten us hollow.

RAINA. Have I not been generous?

THE MAN. Noble! Heroic! But I'm not saved yet. This particular rush will soon pass through; but the pursuit will go on all night by fits and starts. I must take my chance to get off in a quiet interval. [*pleasantly*] You dont mind my waiting just a minute or two, do you?

RAINA [*putting on her most genteel society manner*]. Oh, not at all. Wont you sit down?

THE MAN. Thanks.

[*He sits on the foot of the bed. RAINA walks with studied elegance to the ottoman and sits down. Unfortunately she sits on the pistol, and jumps up with a shriek. The man, all nerves, shies like a frightened horse to the other side of the room.*]

THE MAN [*irritably*]. Dont frighten me like that. What is it?

RAINA. Your revolver! It was staring that officer in the face all the time. What an escape!

THE MAN [*vexed at being unnecessarily terrified*]. Oh, is that all?

RAINA [*staring at him rather superciliously as she conceives a poorer and poorer opinion of him, and feels proportionately more and more at her ease*]. I am sorry I frightened

you. [*She takes up the pistol and hands it to him.*] Pray take it to protect yourself against me.

THE MAN [*grinning wearily at the sarcasm as he takes the pistol*]. No use, dear young lady: theres nothing in it. It's not loaded.

[*He makes a grimace at it, and drops it disparagingly into his revolver case.*]

RAINA. Load it by all means.

THE MAN. Ive no ammunition. What use are cartridges in battle? I always carry chocolate instead; and I finished the last cake of that hours ago.

RAINA [*outraged in her most cherished ideals of manhood*]. Chocolate! Do you stuff your pockets with sweets— like a schoolboy—even in the field?

THE MAN [*grinning*]. Yes: isnt it contemptible? [*hungrily*] I wish I had some now.

RAINA. Allow me. [*She sails away scornfully to the chest of drawers, and returns with the box of confectionery in her hand.*] I am sorry I have eaten them all except these.

[*She offers him the box.*]

THE MAN [*ravenously*]. Youre an angel! [*He gobbles the contents.*] Creams! Delicious! [*He looks anxiously to see whether there are any more. There are none: he can only scrape the box with his fingers and suck them. When that nourishment is exhausted he accepts the inevitable with pathetic goodhumor, and says, with grateful emotion:*] Bless you, dear lady! You can always tell an old soldier by the inside of his holsters and cartridge boxes. The young ones carry pistols and cartridges: the old ones, grub. Thank you. [*He hands back the box. She snatches it contemptuously from him and throws it away. He shies again, as if she had meant to strike him.*] Ugh! Dont do things so suddenly, gracious lady. It's mean to revenge yourself because I frightened you just now.

RAINA [*loftily*]. Frighten me! Do you know, sir, that though I am only a woman, I think I am at heart as brave as you.

THE MAN. I should think so. You havnt been under fire for three days as I have. I can stand two days without shewing it much; but no man can stand three days: I'm as nervous as a mouse. [*He sits down on the ottoman, and takes his head in his hands.*] Would you like to see me cry?

RAINA [*alarmed*]. No.

THE MAN. If you would, all you have to do is to scold me just as if I were a little boy and you my nurse. If I were in camp now, theyd play all sorts of tricks on me.

RAINA [*a little moved*]. I'm sorry. I wont scold you. [*Touched by the sympathy in her tone, he raises his head and looks gratefully at her: she immediately draws back and says stiffly:*] You must excuse me: our soldiers are not like that.

[*She moves away from the ottoman.*]

THE MAN. Oh yes they are. There are only two sorts of soldiers: old ones and young ones. Ive served fourteen years: half of your fellows never smelt powder before. Why, how is it that youve just beaten us? Sheer ignorance of the art of war, nothing else. [*indignantly*] I never saw anything so unprofessional.

RAINA [*ironically*]. Oh! was it unprofessional to beat you?

THE MAN. Well, come! is it professional to throw a regiment of cavalry on a battery of machine guns, with the dead certainty that if the guns go off not a horse or man will ever get within fifty yards of the fire? I couldnt believe my eyes when I saw it.

RAINA [*eagerly turning to him, as all her enthusiasm and her dreams of glory rush back on her*]. Did you see the great cavalry charge? Oh, tell me about it. Describe it to me.

THE MAN. You never saw a cavalry charge, did you?

RAINA. How could I?

THE MAN. Ah, perhaps not. No: of course not! Well, it's a funny sight. It's like slinging a handful of peas against a window pane: first one comes; then two or three close behind him; and then all the rest in a lump.

RAINA [*her eyes dilating as she raises her clasped hands ecstatically*]. Yes, first One! the bravest of the brave!

THE MAN [*prosaically*]. Hm! you should see the poor devil pulling at his horse.

RAINA. Why should he pull at his horse?

THE MAN [*impatient of so stupid a question*]. It's running away with him, of course: do you suppose the fellow wants to get there before the others and be killed? Then they all come. You can tell the young ones by their wildness and their slashing. The old ones come bunched up under the number one guard: they know that theyre mere projectiles, and that it's no use trying to fight. The wounds are mostly broken knees, from the horses cannoning together.

RAINA. Ugh! But I dont believe the first man is a coward. I know he is a hero!

THE MAN [*goodhumoredly*]. Thats what youd have said if youd seen the first man in the charge today.

RAINA [*breathless, forgiving him everything*]. Ah, I knew it! Tell me. Tell me about him.

THE MAN. He did it like an operatic tenor. A regular handsome fellow, with flashing eyes and lovely moustache, shouting his warcry and charging like Don Quixote at the windmills. We did laugh.

RAINA. You dared to laugh!

THE MAN. Yes; but when the sergeant ran up as white as a sheet, and told us theyd sent us the wrong ammunition, and that we couldnt fire a round for the next ten minutes, we laughed at the other side of our mouths. I never felt so sick in my life; though Ive been in one or two very tight places. And I hadnt even a revolver cartridge: only chocolate. We'd no bayonets: nothing. Of course, they just cut us to bits. And there was Don Quixote flourishing like a drum major, thinking he'd done the cleverest thing ever known, whereas he ought to be courtmartialled for it. Of all the fools ever let loose on a field of battle, that man must be the very maddest. He and his regiment simply committed suicide; only the pistol missed fire: thats all.

RAINA [*deeply wounded, but steadfastly loyal to her ideals*]. Indeed! Would you know him again if you saw him?

THE MAN. Shall I ever forget him!

[*She again goes to the chest of drawers. He watches her with a vague hope that she may have something more for him to eat. She takes the portrait from its stand and brings it to him.*]

RAINA. That is a photograph of the gentleman—the patriot and hero— to whom I am betrothed.

THE MAN [*recognizing it with a shock*]. I'm really very sorry. [*looking at her*] Was it fair to lead me on? [*He looks at the portrait again.*] Yes: thats Don Quixote: not a doubt of it. [*He stifles a laugh.*]

RAINA [*quickly*]. Why do you laugh?

THE MAN [*apologetic, but still greatly tickled*]. I didnt laugh, I assure you. At least I didnt mean to. But when I think of him charging the windmills and imagining he was doing the finest thing—

[*He chokes with suppressed laugher.*]

RAINA [*sternly*]. Give me back the portrait, sir.

THE MAN [*with sincere remorse*]. Of course. Certainly. I'm really very sorry. [*He hands her the picture. She deliberately kisses it and looks him straight in the face before returning to the chest of drawers to replace it. He follows her, apologizing.*] Perhaps I'm quite wrong, you know: no doubt I am. Most likely he had got wind of the cartridge business somehow, and knew it was a safe job.

RAINA. That is to say, he was a pretender and a coward! You did not dare say that before.

THE MAN [*with a comic gesture of despair*]. It's no use, dear lady: I cant make you see it from the professional point of view.

[*As he turns away to get back to the ottoman, a couple of distant shots threaten renewed trouble.*]

RAINA [*sternly, as she sees him listening to the shots*]. So much the better for you!

THE MAN [*turning*]. How?

RAINA. You are my enemy; and you are at my mercy. What would I do if I were a professional soldier?

THE MAN. Ah, true, dear young lady: youre always right. I know how good youve been to me: to my last hour I shall remember those three chocolate creams. It was unsoldierly; but it was angelic.

RAINA [*coldly*]. Thank you. And now I will do a soldierly thing. You cannot stay here after what you have just said about my future husband; but I will go out on the balcony and see whether it is safe for you to climb down into the street.

[*She turns to the window.*]

THE MAN [*changing countenance*]. Down that waterpipe! Stop! Wait! I cant! I darent! The very thought of it makes me giddy. I came up it fast enough with death behind me. But to face it now in cold blood—! [*He sinks on the ottoman.*] It's no use: I give up: I'm beaten. Give the alarm.

[*He drops his head on his hands in the deepest dejection.*]

RAINA [*disarmed by pity*]. Come: dont be disheartened. [*She stoops over him almost maternally: he shakes his head.*] Oh, you are a very poor soldier: a chocolate cream soldier! Come, cheer up! it takes less courage to climb down than to face capture: remember that.

THE MAN [*dreamily, lulled by her voice*]. No: capture only means death; and death is sleep: oh, sleep, sleep, sleep, undisturbed sleep! Climbing down the pipe means doing something—exerting myself—thinking! Death ten times over first.

RAINA [*softly and wonderingly, catching the rhythm of his weariness*]. Are you as sleepy as that?

THE MAN. Ive not had two hours undisturbed sleep since I joined. I havnt closed my eyes for forty-eight hours.

RAINA [*at her wit's end*]. But what am I to do with you?

THE MAN [*staggering up, roused by her desperation*]. Of course, I must do something. [*He shakes himself; pulls himself together; and speaks with rallied vigor and courage.*] You see, sleep or no sleep, hunger or no hunger, tired or not tired, you can always do a thing when you know it must be done. Well, that pipe must be got down: [*He hits himself on the chest.*] do you hear that, you chocolate cream soldier?

[*He turns to the window.*]

RAINA [*anxiously*]. But if you fall?

THE MAN. I shall sleep as if the stones were a feather bed. Goodbye.

[*He makes boldly for the window; and his hand is on the shutter when there is a terrible burst of firing in the street beneath.*]

RAINA [*rushing to him*]. Stop! [*She seizes him recklessly, and pulls him quite round.*] Theyll kill you.

THE MAN [*coolly, but attentively*]. Never mind: this sort of thing is all in my day's work. I'm bound to take my chance. [*decisively*] Now do what I tell you. Put out the candle; so that they shant see the light when I open the shutters. And keep away from the window, whatever you do. If they see me theyre sure to have a shot at me.

RAINA [*clinging to him*]. Theyre sure to see you: it's bright moonlight. I'll save you. Oh, how can you be so indifferent! You want me to save you, dont you?

THE MAN. I really dont want to be troublesome. [*She shakes him in her impatience.*] I am not indifferent, dear young lady, I assure you. But how is it to be done?

RAINA. Come away from the window. [*She takes him firmly back to the middle of the room. The moment she releases him he turns mechanically towards the window again. She seizes him and turns him back, exclaiming:*] Please! [*He becomes motionless, like a hypnotized rabbit, his fatigue gaining fast on him. She releases him, and addresses him patronizingly.*] Now listen. You must trust to our hospitality. You do not yet know in whose house you are. I am a Petkoff.

THE MAN. A pet what?

RAINA [*rather indignantly*]. I mean that I belong to the family of the Petkoffs, the richest and best known in our country.

THE MAN. Oh yes, of course. I beg your pardon. The Petkoffs, to be sure. How stupid of me!

RAINA. You know you never heard of

them until this moment. How can you stoop to pretend!

THE MAN. Forgive me: I'm too tired to think; and the change of subject was too much for me. Dont scold me.

RAINA. I forgot. It might make you cry. [*He nods, quite seriously. She pouts and then resumes her patronizing tone.*] I must tell you that my father holds the highest command of any Bulgarian in our army. He is [*proudly*] a Major.

THE MAN [*pretending to be deeply impressed*]. A Major! Bless me! Think of that!

RAINA. You shewed great ignorance in thinking that it was necessary to climb up the balcony because ours is the only private house that has two rows of windows. There is a flight of stairs inside to get up and down by.

THE MAN. Stairs! How grand! You live in great luxury indeed, dear young lady.

RAINA. Do you know what a library is?

THE MAN. A library? A roomful of books?

RAINA. Yes. We have one, the only one in Bulgaria.

THE MAN. Actually a real library! I should like to see that.

RAINA [*affectedly*]. I tell you these things to shew you that you are not in the house of ignorant country folk who would kill you the moment they saw your Serbian uniform, but among civilized people. We go to Bucharest every year for the opera season; and I have spent a whole month in Vienna.

THE MAN. I saw that, dear young lady. I saw at once that you knew the world.

RAINA. Have you ever seen the opera of Ernani?

THE MAN. Is that the one with the devil in it in red velvet, and a soldiers' chorus?

RAINA [*contemptuously*]. No!

THE MAN [*stifling a heavy sigh of weariness*]. Then I dont know it.

RAINA. I thought you might have remembered the great scene where Ernani, flying from his foes just as you are tonight, takes refuge in the castle of his bitterest enemy, an old Castilian noble. The noble refuses to give him up. His guest is sacred to him.

THE MAN [*quickly, waking up a little*]. Have your people got that notion?

RAINA [*with dignity*]. My mother and I can understand that notion, as you call it. And if instead of threatening me with your pistol as you did you had simply thrown yourself as a fugitive on our hospitality, you would have been as safe as in your father's house.

THE MAN. Quite sure?

RAINA [*turning her back on him in disgust*]. Oh, it is useless to try to make you understand.

THE MAN. Dont be angry: you see how awkward it would be for me if there was any mistake. My father is a very hospitable man: he keeps six hotels; but I couldnt trust him as far as that. What about your father?

RAINA. He is away as Slivnitza fighting for his country. I answer for your safety. There is my hand in pledge of it. Will that reassure you?

[*She offers him her hand.*]

THE MAN [*looking dubiously at his own hand*]. Better not touch my hand, dear young lady. I must have a wash first.

RAINA [*touched*]. That is very nice of you. I see that you are a gentleman.

THE MAN [*puzzled*]. Eh?

RAINA. You must not think I am surprised. Bulgarians of really good standing—people in our position— wash their hands nearly every day. So you see I can appreciate your delicacy. You may take my hand.

[*She offers it again.*]

THE MAN [*kissing it with his hands behind his back*]. Thanks, gracious young lady: I feel safe at last. And now would you mind breaking the news to your mother? I had better not stay here secretly longer than is necessary.

RAINA. If you will be so good as to keep perfectly still whilst I am away.

THE MAN. Certainly.

[*He sits down on the ottoman. RAINA goes to the bed and wraps herself in the fur cloak. His eyes close. She goes to the door. Turning for a last look at him, she sees that he is dropping off to sleep.*]

RAINA [*at the door*]. You are not going asleep, are you? [*He murmurs inarticulately: she runs to him and shakes him.*] Do you hear? Wake up: you are falling asleep.

THE MAN. Eh? Falling aslee—? Oh no: not the least in the world: I was only thinking. It's all right: I'm wide awake.

RAINA [*severely*]. Will you please stand up while I am away. [*He rises reluctantly.*] All the time, mind.

THE MAN [*standing unsteadily*]. Certainly. Certainly: you may depend on me.

[*RAINA looks doubtfully at him. He smiles weakly. She goes reluctantly, turning again at the door, and almost catching him in the act of yawning. She goes out.*]

THE MAN [*drowsily*]. Sleep, sleep, sleep, sleep, slee—[*The words trail off into a murmur. He wakes again with a shock on the point of falling.*] Where am I? Thats what I want to know: where am I? Must keep awake. Nothing keeps me awake except danger: remember that: [*intently*] danger, danger, danger, dan—[*trailing off again: another shock*] Wheres danger? Mus' find it. [*He starts off vaguely round the room in search of it.*] What am I looking for? Sleep—danger—dont know. [*He stumbles against the bed.*] Ah yes: now I know. All right now. I'm to go to bed, but not to sleep. Be sure not to sleep, because of danger. Not to lie down either, only sit down. [*He sits on the bed. A blissful expression comes into his face.*] Ah!

[*With a happy sigh he sinks back at full length; lifts his boots into the bed with a final effort; and falls fast asleep instantly.*]

[CATHERINE *comes in, followed by* RAINA.]

RAINA [*looking at the ottoman*]. He's gone! I left him here.

CATHERINE. Here! Then he must have climbed down from the—

RAINA [*seeing him*]. Oh! [*She points.*]

CATHERINE [*scandalized*]. Well! [*She strides to the bed, RAINA following until she is opposite her on the other side.*] He's fast asleep. The brute!

RAINA [*anxiously*]. Sh!

CATHERINE [*shaking him*]. Sir! [*shaking him again, harder*] Sir!! [*vehemently, shaking very hard*] Sir!!!

RAINA [*catching her arm*]. Dont, mamma; the poor darling is worn out, Let him sleep.

CATHERINE [*letting him go, and turning amazed to* RAINA]. The poor darling! Raina!!!

[*She looks sternly at her daughter.* THE MAN *sleeps profoundly.*]

ACT II

The sixth of March, 1886. In the garden of MAJOR PETKOFF'S *house. It is a fine spring morning: the garden looks fresh and pretty. Beyond the paling the tops of a couple of minarets can be seen, shewing that there is a valley there, with the little town in it. A few miles further the Balkan mountains rise and shut in the landscape. Looking towards them from within the garden, the side of the house is seen on the left, with a garden door reached by a little flight of steps. On the right the stable yard, with its gateway, encroaches on the garden. There are fruit bushes along the paling and house, covered with washing spread out to dry. A path runs by the house, and rises by two steps at the corner, where it turns out of sight. In the middle, a small table, with two bent wood chairs at it is laid for breakfast with Turkish coffee pot, cups, rolls, etc.; but the cups have been used and the bread broken. There is a wooden garden seat against the wall on the right.*

LOUKA, *smoking a cigaret, is standing between the table and the house, turning her back with angry disdain on a man servant who is lecturing her. He is a middle-aged man of cool temperament and low but clear and keen intelligence, with the complacency of the servant who values himself on his rank in servitude, and the imperturbability of the accurate calculator who has no illusions. He wears a white Bulgarian costume: jacket with embroidered border, sash, wide knickerbockers, and decorated gaiters. His head is shaved up to the crown, giving him a high Japanese forehead. His name is* NICOLA.

NICOLA. Be warned in time, Louka: mend your manners. I know the mistress. She is so grand that she never dreams that any servant could dare be disrespectful to her; but if she once suspects that you are defying her, out you go.

LOUKA. I do defy her. I will defy her. What do I care for her?

NICOLA. If you quarrel with the family, I never can marry you. It's the same as if you quarrelled with me!

LOUKA. You take her part against me, do you?

NICOLA [*sedately*]. I shall always be dependent on the good will of the family. When I leave their service and start a shop in Sofia, their custom will be half my capital: their bad word would ruin me.

LOUKA. You have no spirit. I should like to catch them saying a word against me!

NICOLA [*pityingly*]. I should have expected more sense from you, Louka. But youre young: youre young!

LOUKA. Yes; and you like me the better for it, dont you? But I know some family secrets they wouldnt care to have told, young as I am. Let them quarrel with me if they dare!

NICOLA [*with compassionate superiority*]. Do you know what they would do if they heard you talk like that?

LOUKA. What could they do?

NICOLA. Discharge you for untruthfulness. Who would believe any stories you told after that? Who would give you another situation? Who in this house would dare be seen speaking to you ever again? How long would your father be left on his little farm? [*She impatiently throws away the end of her cigaret, and stamps on it.*] Child: you dont know the power such high people have over the like of you and me when we try to rise out of our poverty against them. [*He goes close to her and lowers his voice.*] Look at me, ten years in their service. Do you think I know no secrets? I know things about the mistress that she wouldnt have the master know for a thousand levas.* I know things about him that she wouldnt let him hear the last of for six months if I blabbed them to her. I know things about Raina that would break off her match with Sergius if—

LOUKA [*turning on him quickly*]. How do you know? I never told you!

NICOLA [*opening his eyes cunningly*]. So thats your little secret, is it? I thought it might be something like that. Well, you take my advice and be respectful; and make the mistress feel that no matter what you know or dont know, she can depend on you to hold your tongue and serve the family faithfully. Thats what they like; and thats how youll make most out of them.

LOUKA [*with searching scorn*]. You have the soul of a servant, Nicola.

NICOLA [*complacently*]. Yes: thats the secret of success in service.

[*A loud knocking with a whip handle on a wooden door is heard from the stable yard.*]

MALE VOICE OUTSIDE. Hollo! Hollo there! Nicola!

LOUKA. Master! back from the war!

NICOLA [*quickly*]. My word for it, Louka, the war's over. Off with you and get some fresh coffee.

[*He runs out into the stable yard.*]

LOUKA [*as she collects the coffee pot and cups on the tray, and carries it into the house*]. Youll never put the soul of a servant into me.

[MAJOR PETKOFF *comes from the stable yard, followed by* NICOLA. *He is a cheerful, excitable, insignificant, unpolished man of about 50, naturally unambitious except as to his income*

and his importance in local society, but just now greatly pleased with the military rank which the war has thrust on him as a man of consequence in his town. The fever of plucky patriotism which the Serbian attack roused in all the Bulgarians has pulled him through the war; but he is obviously glad to be home again.*]

PETKOFF [*pointing to the table with his whip*]. Breakfast out here, eh?

NICOLA. Yes, sir. The mistress and Miss Raina have just gone in.

PETKOFF [*sitting down and taking a roll*]. Go in and say Ive come; and get me some fresh coffee.

NICOLA. It's coming, sir.

[*He goes to the house door.* LOUKA, *with fresh coffee, a clean cup, and a brandy bottle on her tray, meets him.*]

Have you told the mistress?

LOUKA. Yes: she's coming.

[NICOLA *goes into the house.* LOUKA *brings the coffee to the table.*]

PETOKOFF. Well: the Serbs havnt run away with you, have they?

LOUKA. No, sir.

PETKOFF. Thats right. Have you brought me some cognac?

LOUKA [*putting the bottle on the table*]. Here, sir.

PETKOFF. Thats right.

[*He pours some into his coffee.*]

[CATHERINE, *who, having at this early hour made only a very perfunctory toilet, wears a Bulgarian apron over a once brilliant but now half worn-out dressing gown, and a colored handkerchief tied over her thick black hair, comes from the house with Turkish slippers on her bare feet, looking astonishingly handsome and stately under all the circumstances.* LOUKA *goes into the house.*]

CATHERINE. My dear Paul: what a surprise for us! [*She stoops over the

* The *lev* was about a cent.

back of his chair to kiss him.] Have they brought you fresh coffee?

PETKOFF. Yes: Louka's been looking after me. The war's over. The treaty was signed three days ago at Bucharest; and the decree for our army to demobilize was issued yesterday.

CATHERINE [*springing erect, with flashing eyes*]. Paul: have you let the Austrians force you to make peace?

PETKOFF [*submissively*]. My dear: they didnt consult me. What could *I* do? [*She sits down and turns away from him.*] But of course we saw to it that the treaty was an honorable one. It declares peace—

CATHERINE [*outraged*]. Peace!

PETKOFF [*appeasing her*].—but not friendly relations: remember that. They wanted to put that in; but I insisted on its being struck out. What more could I do?

CATHERINE. You could have annexed Serbia and made Prince Alexander* Emperor of the Balkans. Thats what I would have done.

PETKOFF. I dont doubt it in the least, my dear. But I should have had to subdue the whole Austrian Empire first; and that would have kept me too long away from you. I missed you greatly.

CATHERINE [*relenting*]. Ah!

[*She stretches her hand affectionately across the table to squeeze his.*]

PETKOFF. And how have you been, my dear?

CATHERINE. Oh, my usual sore throats: thats all.

PETKOFF [*with conviction*]. That comes from washing your neck every day. Ive often told you so.

CATHERINE. Nonsense, Paul!

PETKOFF [*over his coffee and cigaret*]. I dont believe in going too far with these modern customs. All this washing cant be good for the health: it's

not natural. There was an Englishman at Philippopolis who used to wet himself all over with cold water every morning when he got up. Disgusting! It all comes from the English: their climate makes them so dirty that they have to be perpetually washing themselves. Look at my father! he never had a bath in his life; and he lived to be ninety-eight, the healthiest man in Bulgaria. I dont mind a good wash once a week to keep up my position; but once a day is carrying the thing to a ridiculous extreme.

CATHERINE. You are a barbarian at heart still, Paul. I hope you behaved yourself before all those Russian officers.

PETKOFF. I did my best. I took care to let them know that we have a library.

CATHERINE. Ah; but you didnt tell them that we have an electric bell in it? I have had one put up.

PETKOFF. Whats an electric bell?

CATHERINE. You touch a button; something tinkles in the kitchen; and then Nicola comes up.

PETKOFF. Why not shout for him?

CATHERINE. Civilized people never shout for their servants. Ive learnt that while you were away.

PETKOFF. Well, I'll tell you something Ive learnt too. Civilized people dont hang out their washing to dry where visitors can see it; so youd better have all that [*indicating the clothes on the bushes*] put somewhere else.

CATHERINE. Oh, thats absurd, Paul: I dont believe really refined people notice such things.

SERGIUS [*knocking at the stable gates*]. Gate, Nicola!

PETKOFF. Theres Sergius. [*shouting*] Hollo, Nicola!

CATHERINE. Oh, dont shout, Paul: it really isnt nice.

PETKOFF. Bosh! [*He shouts louder than before.*] Nicola!

---

* Alexander of Battenburg, ruler of Bulgaria at the time.

NICOLA [*appearing at the house door*]. Yes, sir.

PETKOFF. Are you deaf? Dont you hear Major Saranoff knocking? Bring him round this way.

[*He pronounces the name with the stress on the second syllable: Sarahnoff.*]

PETKOFF. You must talk to him, my dear, until Raina takes him off our hands. He bores my life out about our not promoting him. Over my head, if you please.

CATHERINE. He certainly ought to be promoted when he marries Raina. Besides, the country should insist on having at least one native general.

PETKOFF. Yes; so that he could throw away whole brigades instead of regiments. It's no use, my dear: he hasnt the slightest chance of promotion until we're quite sure that the peace will be a lasting one.

NICOLA [*at the gate, announcing*]. Major Sergius Saranoff!

[*He goes into the house and returns presently with a third chair, which he places at the table. He then withdraws.*]

[MAJOR SERGIUS SARANOFF, *the original of the portrait in* RAINA'S *room, is a tall romantically handsome man, with the physical hardihood, the high spirit, and the susceptible imagination of an untamed mountaineer chieftain. But his remarkable personal distinction is of a characteristically civilized type. The ridges of his eyebrows, curving with an interrogative twist round the projections at the outer corners; his jealously observant eye; his nose, thin, keen, and apprehensive in spite of the pugnacious high bridge and large nostril; his assertive chin would not be out of place in a Parisian salon, shewing that the clever imaginative barbarian has an acute critical faculty which has been thrown into intense activity by the arrival of western civilization in the Balkans. The result is precisely what the advent of* nineteenth century thought first produced in England: to wit, Byronism. By his brooding on the perpetual failure, not only of others, but of himself, to live up to his ideals; by his consequent cynical scorn for humanity; by his jejune credulity as to the absolute validity of his concepts and the unworthiness of the world in disregarding them; by his wincings and mockeries under the sting of the petty disillusions which every hour spent among men brings to his sensitive observation, he has acquired the half tragic, half ironic air, the mysterious moodiness, the suggestion of a strange and terrible history that has left nothing but undying remorse, by which Childe Harold fascinated the grandmothers of his English contemporaries. It is clear that here or nowhere is* RAINA'S *ideal hero.* CATHERINE *is hardly less enthusiastic about him than her daughter, and much less reserved in shewing her enthusiasm. As he enters from the stable gate, she rises effusively to greet him.* PETKOFF *is distinctly less disposed to make a fuss about him.*]

PETKOFF. Here already, Sergius! Glad to see you.

CATHERINE. My dear Sergius!

[*She holds out both her hands.*]

SERGIUS [*kissing them with scrupulous gallantry*]. My dear mother, if I may call you so.

PETKOFF [*drily*]. Mother-in-law, Sergius: mother-in-law! Sit down; and have some coffee.

SERGIUS. Thank you: none for me.

[*He gets away from the table with a certain distaste for* PETKOFF'S *enjoyment of it, and posts himself with conscious dignity against the rail of the steps leading to the house.*]

CATHERINE. You look superb. The campaign has improved you, Sergius. Everybody here is mad about you. We were all wild with enthusiasm about that magnificent cavalry charge.

SERGIUS [*with grave irony*]. Madam: it was the cradle and the grave of my military reputation.

CATHERINE. How so?

SERGIUS. I won the battle the wrong way when our worthy Russian generals were losing it the right way. In short, I upset their plans, and wounded their self-esteem. Two Cossak colonels had their regiments routed on the most correct principles of scientific warfare. Two major-generals got killed strictly according to military etiquette. The two colonels are now major-generals; and I am still a simple major.

CATHERINE. You shall not remain so, Sergius. The women are on your side; and they will see that justice is done you.

SERGIUS. It is too late. I have only waited for the peace to send in my resignation.

PETKOFF [*dropping his cup in his amazement*]. Your resignation!

CATHERINE. Oh, you must withdraw it!

SERGIUS [*with resolute measured emphasis, folding his arms*]. I never withdraw.

PETKOFF [*vexed*]. Now who could have supposed you were going to do such a thing?

SERGIUS [*with fire*]. Everyone that knew me. But enough of myself and my affairs. How is Raina; and where is Raina?

RAINA [*suddenly coming round the corner of the house and standing at the top of the steps in the path*]. Raina is here.

[*She makes a charming picture as they turn to look at her. She wears an under-dress of pale green silk, draped with an overdress of thin ecru canvas embroidered with gold. She is crowned with a dainty eastern cap of gold tinsel. SERGIUS goes impulsively to meet her. Posing regally, she presents her hand:*]

he drops chivalrously on one knee and kisses it.]

PETKOFF [*aside to CATHERINE, beaming with parental pride*]. Pretty, isn't it? She always appears at the right moment.

CATHERINE [*impatiently*]. Yes; she listens for it. It is an abominable habit.

[SERGIUS *leads* RAINA *forward with splendid gallantry. When they arrive at the table, she turns to him with a bend of the head: he bows; and thus they separate, he coming to his place and she going behind her father's chair.*]

RAINA [*stooping and kissing her father*]. Dear father! Welcome home!

PETKOFF [*patting her cheek*]. My little pet girl.

[*He kisses her. She goes to the chair left by* NICOLA *for* SERGIUS, *and sits down.*]

CATHERINE. And so youre no longer a soldier, Sergius.

SERGIUS. I am no longer a soldier. Soldiering, my dear madam, is the coward's art of attacking mercilessly when you are strong, and keeping out of harm's way when you are weak. That is the whole secret of successful fighting. Get your enemy at a disadvantage; and never, on any account, fight him on equal terms.

PETKOFF. They wouldnt let us make a fair stand-up fight of it. However, I suppose soldiering has to be a trade like any other trade.

SERGIUS. Precisely. But I have no ambition to shine as a tradesman; so I have taken the advice of that bagman of a captain that settled the exchange of prisoners with us at Pirot, and given it up.

PETKOFF. What! that Swiss fellow? Sergius: Ive often thought of that exchange since. He over-reached us about those horses.

SERGIUS. Of course he over-reached us.

His father was a hotel and livery stable keeper; and he owed his first step to his knowledge of horse-dealing. [*with mock enthusiasm*] Ah, he was a soldier: every inch a soldier! If only I had bought the horses for my regiment instead of foolishly leading it into danger, I should have been a field-marshal now!

CATHERINE. A Swiss? What was he doing in the Serbian army?

PETKOFF. A volunteer, of course: keen on picking up his profession. [*chuckling*] We shouldnt have been able to begin fighting if these foreigners hadnt shewn us how to do it: we knew nothing about it; and neither did the Serbs. Egad, thered have been no war without them!

RAINA. Are there many Swiss officers in the Serbian Army?

PETKOFF. No. All Austrians, just as our officers were all Russians. This was the only Swiss I came across. I'll never trust a Swiss again. He humbugged us into giving him fifty ablebodied men for two hundred worn out chargers. They werent even eatable!

SERGIUS. We were two children in the hands of that consummate soldier, major: simply two innocent little children.

RAINA. What was he like?

CATHERINE. Oh, Raina, what a silly question!

SERGIUS. He was like a commercial traveller in uniform. Bourgeois to his boots!

PETKOFF [*grinning*]. Sergius: tell Catherine that queer story his friend told us about how he escaped after Slivnitza. You remember. About his being hid by two women.

SERGIUS [*with bitter irony*]. Oh yes: quite a romance! He was serving in the very battery I so unprofessionally charged. Being a thorough soldier, he ran away like the rest of them, with our cavalry at his heels. To escape their sabres he climbed a waterpipe and made his way into the bedroom of a young Bulgarian lady. The young lady was enchanted by his persuasive commercial traveller's manners. She very modestly entertained him for an hour or so, and then called in her mother lest her conduct should appear unmaidenly. The old lady was equally fascinated; and the fugitive was sent on his way in the morning, disguised in an old coat belonging to the master of the house, who was away at the war.

RAINA [*rising with marked stateliness*]. Your life in the camp has made you coarse, Sergius. I did not think you would have repeated such a story before me. [*She turns away coldly.*]

CATHERINE [*also rising*]. She is right, Sergius. If such women exist, we should be spared the knowledge of them.

PETKOFF. Pooh! nonsense! what does it matter?

SERGIUS [*ashamed*]. No, Petkoff: I was wrong. [*to* RAINA, *with earnest humility*] I beg your pardon. I have behaved abominably. Forgive me, Raina. [*She bows reservedly.*] And you too, madam. [CATHERINE *bows graciously and sits down. He proceeds solemnly, again addressing* RAINA.] The glimpses I have had of the seamy side of life during the last few months have made me cynical; but I should not have brought my cynicism here: least of all into your presence, Raina. I—

[*Here, turning to the others, he is evidently going to begin a long speech when the* MAJOR *interrupts him.*]

PETKOFF. Stuff and nonsense, Sergius! Thats quite enough fuss about nothing: a soldier's daughter should be able to stand up without flinching to a little strong conversation. [*He rises.*] Come: it's time for us to get to business. We have to make up our minds how those three regiments are to get back to Philippopolis: theres no forage for them on the Sofia route. [*He goes towards the house.*] Come along.

[SERGIUS *is about to follow him when* CATHERINE *rises and intervenes.*]

CATHERINE. Oh, Paul, cant you spare Sergius for a few moments? Raina has hardly seen him yet. Perhaps I can help you to settle about the regiments.

SERGIUS [*protesting*]. My dear madam, impossible: you—

CATHERINE [*stopping him playfully*]. You stay here, my dear Sergius: theres no hurry. I have a word or two to say to Paul. [SERGIUS *instantly bows and steps back.*] Now, dear [*taking* PETKOFF'S *arm*]: come and see the electric bell.

PETKOFF. Oh, very well, very well.

[*They go into the house together affectionately.* SERGIUS, *left alone with* RAINA, *looks anxiously at her, fearing that she is still offended. She smiles, and stretches out her arms to him.*]

SERGIUS [*hastening to her*]. Am I forgiven?

RAINA [*placing her hands on his shoulders as she looks up at him with admiration and worship*]. My hero! My king!

SERGIUS. My queen!

[*He kisses her on the forehead.*]

RAINA. How I have envied you, Sergius! You have been out in the world, on the field of battle, able to prove yourself there worthy of any woman in the world; whilst I have had to sit at home inactive—dreaming—useless—doing nothing that could give me the right to call myself worthy of any man.

SERGIUS. Dearest: all my deeds have been yours. You inspired me. I have

gone through the war like a knight in a tournament with his lady looking down at him!

RAINA. And you have never been absent from my thoughts for a moment. [*very solemnly*] Sergius: I think we two have found the higher love. When I think of you, I feel that I could never do a base deed, or think an ignoble thought.

SERGIUS. My lady and my saint!

[*He clasps her reverently.*]

RAINA [*returning his embrace*]. My lord and my—

SERGIUS. Sh—sh! Let me be the worshipper, dear. You little know how unworthy even the best man is of a girl's pure passion!

RAINA. I trust you. I love you. You will never disappoint me, Sergius. [LOUKA *is heard singing within the house. They quickly release each other.*] I cant pretend to talk indifferently before her: my heart is too full.

[LOUKA *comes from the house with her tray. She goes to the table, and begins to clear it, with her back turned to them.*]

I will get my hat; and then we can go out until lunch time. Wouldnt you like that?

SERGIUS. Be quick. If you are away five minutes, it will seem five hours.

[RAINA *runs to the top of the steps, and turns there to exchange looks with him and wave him a kiss with both hands. He looks after her with emotion for a moment; then turns slowly away, his face radiant with the loftiest exaltation. The movement shifts his field of vision, into the corner of which there now comes the tail of* LOUKA'S *double apron. His attention is arrested at once. He takes a stealthy look at her, and begins to twirl his moustache mischievously, with his left hand akimbo on his hip. Finally, striking the ground with his heels in something of a cavalry swagger, he strolls over to the other side of the table, opposite her, and says:*]

Louka: do you know what the higher love is?

LOUKA [*astonished*]. No, sir.

SERGIUS. Very fatiguing thing to keep up for any length of time, Louka. One feels the need of some relief after it.

LOUKA [*innocently*]. Perhaps you would like some coffee, sir?

[*She stretches her hand across the table for the coffee pot.*]

SERGIUS [*taking her hand*]. Thank you, Louka.

LOUKA [*pretending to pull*]. Oh, sir, you know I didnt mean that. I'm surprised at you!

SERGIUS [*coming clear of the table and drawing her with him*]. I am surprised at myself, Louka. What would Sergius, the hero of Slivnitza, say if he saw me now? What would Sergius, the apostle of the higher love, say if he saw me now? What would the half dozen Sergiuses who keep popping in and out of this handsome figure of mine say if they caught us here? [*letting go her hand and slipping his arm dexterously round her waist*] Do you consider my figure handsome, Louka?

LOUKA. Let me go, sir. I shall be disgraced. [*She struggles: he holds her inexorably.*] Oh, will you let go?

SERGIUS [*looking straight into her eyes*]. No.

LOUKA. Then stand back where we cant be seen. Have you no common sense?

SERGIUS. Ah! thats reasonable.

[*He takes her into the stableyard gateway, where they are hidden from the house.*]

LOUKA [*plaintively*]. I may have been seen from the windows: Miss Raina is sure to be spying about after you.

SERGIUS [*stung: letting her go*]. Take

care, Louka. I may be worthless enough to betray the higher love; but do not you insult it.

LOUKA [*demurely*]. Not for the world, sir, I'm sure. May I go on with my work, please, now?

SERGIUS [*again putting his arm round her*]. You are a provoking little witch, Louka. If you were in love with me, would you spy out of windows on me?

LOUKA. Well, you see, sir, since you say you are half a dozen different gentlemen all at once, I should have a great deal to look after.

SERGIUS [*charmed*]. Witty as well as pretty. [*He tries to kiss her.*]

LOUKA [*avoiding him*]. No: I dont want your kisses. Gentlefolk are all alike: you making love to me behind Miss Raina's back; and she doing the same behind yours.

SERGIUS [*recoiling a step*]. Louka!

LOUKA. It shews how little you really care.

SERGIUS [*dropping his familiarity, and speaking with freezing politeness*]. If our conversation is to continue, Louka, you will please remember that a gentleman does not discuss the conduct of the lady he is engaged to with her maid.

LOUKA. It's so hard to know what a gentleman considers right. I thought from your trying to kiss me that you had given up being so particular.

SERGIUS [*turning from her and striking his forehead as he comes back into the garden from the gateway*]. Devil! devil!

LOUKA. Ha! ha! I expect one of the six of you is very like me, sir; though I am only Miss Raina's maid.

[*She goes back to her work at the table, taking no further notice of him.*]

SERGIUS [*speaking to himself*]. Which of the six is the real man? thats the question that torments me. One of them is a hero, another a buffoon, another a humbug, another perhaps a bit of a blackguard. [*He pauses, and looks furtively at* LOUKA *as he adds, with deep bitterness:*] And one, at least, is a coward: jealous, like all cowards. [*He goes to the table.*] Louka.

LOUKA. Yes?

SERGIUS. Who is my rival?

LOUKA. You shall never get that out of me, for love or money.

SERGIUS. Why?

LOUKA. Never mind why. Besides, you would tell that I told you; and I should lose my place.

SERGIUS [*holding out his right hand in affirmation*]. No! on the honor of a—[*He checks himself; and his hand drops, nerveless, as he concludes sardonically:*]—of a man capable of behaving as I have been behaving for the last five minutes. Who is he?

LOUKA. I dont know. I never saw him. I only heard his voice through the door of her room.

SERGIUS. Damnation! How dare you?

LOUKA [*retreating*]. Oh, I mean no harm: youve no right to take up my words like that. The mistress knows all about it. And I tell you that if that gentleman ever comes here again, Miss Raina will marry him, whether he likes it or not. I know the difference between the sort of manner you and she put on before one another and the real manner.

[SERGIUS *shivers as if she had stabbed him. Then, setting his face like iron, he strides grimly to her, and grips her above the elbows with both hands.*]

SERGIUS. Now listen you to me.

LOUKA [*wincing*]. Not so tight: youre hurting me.

SERGIUS. That doesn't matter. You have stained my honor by making me a party to your eavesdropping. And you have betrayed your mistress.

LOUKA [*writhing*]. Please—

SERGIUS. That shews that you are an abominable little clod of common clay, with the soul of a servant.

[*He lets her go as if she were an unclean thing, and turns away, dusting his hands of her, to the bench by the wall, where he sits down with averted head, meditating gloomily.*]

LOUKA [*whimpering angrily with her hands up her sleeves, feeling her bruised arms*]. You know how to hurt with your tongue as well as with your hands. But I dont care, now Ive found out that whatever clay I'm made of, youre made of the same. As for her, she's a liar; and her fine airs are a cheat; and I'm worth six of her.

[*She shakes the pain off hardily; tosses her head; and sets to work to put the things on the tray. He looks doubtfully at her. She finishes packing the tray, and laps the cloth over the edges, so as to carry all out together. As she stoops to lift it, he rises.*]

SERGIUS. Louka! [*She stops and looks defiantly at him.*] A gentleman has no right to hurt a woman under any circumstances. [*with profound humility, uncovering his head*] I beg your pardon.

LOUKA. That sort of apology may satisfy a lady. Of what use is it to a servant?

SERGIUS [*rudely crossed in his chivalry, throws it off with a bitter laugh, and says slightingly*]. Oh! you wish to be paid for the hurt!

[*He puts on his shako, and takes some money from his pocket.*]

LOUKA [*her eyes filling with tears in spite of herself*]. No: I want my hurt made well.

SERGIUS [*sobered by her tone*]. How?

[*She rolls up her left sleeve; clasps her arm with the thumb and fingers of her right hand; and looks down at the bruise. Then she raises her head and looks straight at him. Finally, with a superb gesture, she presents her arm to be kissed. Amazed, he looks at her; at the arm; at her again; hesitates; and then, with shuddering intensity, exclaims "Never!" and gets away as far as possible from her.*

Her arm drops. Without a word, and with unaffected dignity, she takes her tray, and is approaching the house when RAINA *returns, wearing a hat and jacket in the height of the Vienna fashion of the previous year, 1885.* LOUKA *makes way proudly for her, and then goes into the house.*]

RAINA. I'm ready. Whats the matter? [*gaily*] Have you been flirting with Louka?

SERGIUS [*hastily*]. No, no. How can you think such a thing?

RAINA [*ashamed of herself*]. Forgive me, dear: it was only a jest. I am so happy today.

[*He goes quickly to her, and kisses her hand remorsefully.* CATHERINE *comes out and calls to them from the top of the steps.*]

CATHERINE [*coming down to them*]. I am sorry to disturb you, children; but Paul is distracted over those three regiments. He doesnt know how to send them to Philippopolis; and he objects to every suggestion of mine. You must go and help him, Sergius. He is in the library.

RAINA [*disappointed*]. But we are just going out for a walk.

SERGIUS. I shall not be long. Wait for me just five minutes.

[*He runs up the steps to the door.*]

RAINA [*following him to the foot of the steps and looking up at him with timid coquetry*]. I shall go round and wait in full view of the library windows. Be sure you draw father's attention to me. If you are a moment longer than five minutes, I shall go

in and fetch you, regiments or no regiments.

SERGIUS [*laughing*]. Very well.

[*He goes in.*]

[RAINA *watches him until he is out of her sight. Then, with a perceptible relaxation of manner, she begins to pace up and down the garden in a brown study.*]

CATHERINE. Imagine their meeting that Swiss and hearing the whole story! The very first thing your father asked for was the old coat we sent him off in. A nice mess you have got us into!

RAINA [*gazing thoughtfully at the gravel as she walks*]. The little beast!

CATHERINE. Little beast! What little beast?

RAINA. To go and tell; Or, if I had him here, I'd cram him with chocolate creams till he couldnt ever speak again!

CATHERINE. Dont talk such stuff. Tell me the truth, Raina. How long was he in your room before you came to me?

RAINA [*whisking round and recommencing her march in the opposite direction*]. Oh, I forget.

CATHERINE. You cannot forget! Did he really climb up after the soldiers were gone; or was he there when that officer searched the room?

RAINA. No. Yes: I think he must have been there then.

CATHERINE. You think! Oh, Raina! Raina! Will anything ever make you straightforward? If Sergius finds out, it will be all over between you.

RAINA [*with cool impertinence*]. Oh, I know Sergius is your pet. I sometimes wish you could marry him instead of me. You would just suit him. You would pet him, and spoil him, and mother him to perfection.

CATHERINE [*opening her eyes very widely indeed*]. Well, upon my word!

RAINA [*capriciously: half to herself*]. I always feel a longing to do or say something dreadful to him—to shock his propriety—to scandalize the five senses out of him. [*to* CATHERINE, *perversely*] I dont care whether he finds out about the chocolate cream soldier or not. I half hope he may.

[*She again turns and strolls flippantly away up the path to the corner of the house.*]

CATHERINE. And what should I be able to say to your father, pray?

RAINA [*over her shoulder, from the top of the two steps*]. Oh, poor father! As if he could help himself!

[*She turns the corner and passes out of sight.*]

CATHERINE [*looking after her, her fingers itching*]. Oh, if you were only ten years younger!

[LOUKA *comes from the house with a salver, which she carries hanging down by her side.*]

Well?

LOUKA. Theres a gentleman just called, madam. A Serbian officer.

CATHERINE [*flaming*]. A Serb! And how dare he—[*checking herself bitterly*] Oh, I forgot. We are at peace now. I suppose we shall have them calling every day to pay their compliments. Well: if he is an officer why dont you tell your master? He is in the library with Major Saranoff. Why do you come to me?

LOUKA. But he asks for you, madam. And I dont think he knows who you are: he said the lady of the house. He gave me this little ticket for you.

[*She takes a card out of her bosom; puts it on the salver; and offers it to* CATHERINE.]

CATHERINE [*reading*]. "Captain Bluntschli"? Thats a German name.

LOUKA. Swiss, madam, I think.

CATHERINE [*with a bound that makes* LOUKA *jump back*]. Swiss! What is he like?

LOUKA [*timidly*]. He has a big carpetbag, madam.

CATHERINE. Oh Heavens! he's come to return the coat. Send him away: say we're not at home: ask him to leave his address and I'll write to him. Oh stop: that will never do. Wait! [*She throws herself into a chair to think it out.* LOUKA *waits.*] The master and Major Saranoff are busy in the library, arnt they?

LOUKA. Yes, madam.

CATHERINE [*decisively*]. Bring the gentleman out here at once. [*peremptorily*] And be very polite to him. Dont delay. Here [*impatiently snatching the salver from her*]: leave that here; and go straight back to him.

LOUKA. Yes, madam [*going*].

CATHERINE. Louka!

LOUKA [*stopping*]. Yes, madam.

CATHERINE. Is the library door shut?

LOUKA. I think so, madam.

CATHERINE. If not, shut it as you pass through.

LOUKA. Yes, madam [*going*].

CATHERINE. Stop. [LOUKA *stops.*] He will have to go that way [*indicating the gate of the stable yard*]. Tell Nicola to bring his bag here after him. Dont forget.

LOUKA [*surprised*]. His bag?

CATHERINE. Yes: here: as soon as possible. [*vehemently*] Be quick!

[LOUKA *runs into the house.* CATHERINE *snatches her apron off and throws it behind a bush. She then takes up the salver and uses it as a mirror, with the result that the handkerchief tied round her head follows the apron. A touch to her hair and a shake to her dressing gown make her presentable.*]

Oh, how? how? how can a man be such a fool! Such a moment to select!

[LOUKA *appears at the door of the house, announcing* "Captain Bluntschli." *She stands aside at the top of the steps to let him pass before she goes in again. He is the man of the midnight adventure in* RAINA'S *room, clean, well brushed, smartly uniformed, and out of trouble, but still unmistakably the same man. The moment* LOUKA'S *back is turned,* CATHERINE *swoops on him with impetuous, urgent, coaxing appeal.*]

Captain Bluntschli: I am very glad to see you; but you must leave this house at once. [*He raises his eyebrows.*] My husband has just returned with my future son-in-law; and they know nothing. If they did, the consequences would be terrible. You are a foreigner: you do not feel our national animosities as we do. We still hate the Serbs: the effect of the peace on my husband has been to make him feel like a lion baulked of his prey. If he discovers our secret, he will never forgive me; and my daughter's life will hardly be safe. Will you, like the chivalrous gentleman and soldier you are, leave at once before he finds you here?

BLUNTSCHLI [*disappointed, but philosophical*]. At once, gracious lady. I only came to thank you and return the coat you lent me. If you will allow me to take it out of my bag and leave it with your servant as I pass out, I need detain you no further.

[*He turns to go into the house.*]

CATHERINE [*catching him by the sleeve*]. Oh, you must not think of going back that way. [*coaxing him across to the stable gates*] This is the shortest way out. Many thanks. So glad to have been of service to you. Good-bye.

BLUNTSCHLI. But my bag?

CATHERINE. It shall be sent on. You will leave me your address.

BLUNTSCHLI. True. Allow me.

[*He takes out his cardcase, and stops to write his address, keeping* CATHERINE *in an agony of impatience. As he hands her the card,* PETKOFF, *hatless, rushes from the house in a fluster of hospitality, followed by* SERGIUS.]

PETKOFF [*as he hurries down the steps*]. My dear Captain Bluntschli—

CATHERINE. Oh Heavens!

[*She sinks on the seat against the wall.*]

PETKOFF [*too preoccupied to notice her as he shakes* BLUNTSCHLI'S *hand heartily*]. Those stupid people of mine thought I was out here, instead of in the—haw!—library. [*He cannot mention the library without betraying how proud he is of it.*] I saw you through the window. I was wondering why you didnt come in. Saranoff is with me: you remember him, dont you?

SERGIUS [*saluting humorously, and then offering his hand with great charm of manner*]. Welcome, our friend the enemy!

PETKOFF. No longer the enemy, happily. [*rather anxiously*] I hope youve called as a friend, and not about horses or prisoners.

CATHERINE. Oh, quite as a friend, Paul. I was just asking Captain Bluntschli to stay to lunch; but he declares he must go at once.

SERGIUS [*sardonically*]. Impossible, Bluntschli. We want you here badly. We have to send on three cavalry regiments to Philippopolis; and we dont in the least know how to do it.

BLUNTSCHLI [*suddenly attentive and businesslike*]. Philippopolis? The forage is the trouble, I suppose.

PETKOFF [*eagerly*]. Yes: thats it. [*to* SERGIUS] He sees the whole thing at once.

BLUNTSCHLI. I think I can shew you how to manage that.

SERGIUS. Invaluable man! Come along!

[*Towering over* BLUNTSCHLI, *he puts*

his hand on his shoulder and takes him to the steps, PETKOFF *following*.]

[RAINA *comes from the house as* BLUNTSCHLI *puts his foot on the first step*.]

RAINA. Oh! The chocolate cream soldier!

[BLUNTSCHLI *stands rigid,* SERGIUS, *amazed, looks at* RAINA, *then at* PET-KOFF, *who looks back at him and then at his wife*.]

CATHERINE [*with commanding presence of mind*]. My dear Raina, dont you see that we have a guest here? Captain Bluntschli: one of our new Serbian friends.

[RAINA *bows:* BLUNTSCHLI *bows*.]

RAINA. How silly of me! [*She comes down into the centre of the group, between* BLUNTSCHLI *and* PETKOFF.] I made a beautiful ornament this morning for the ice pudding; and that stupid Nicola has just put down a pile of plates on it and spoilt it. [*to* BLUNTSCHLI, *winningly*] I hope you didn't think that you were the chocolate cream soldier, Captain Bluntschli.

BLUNTSCHLI [*laughing*]. I assure you I did. [*stealing a whimsical glance at her*] Your explanation was a relief.

PETKOFF [*suspiciously, to* RAINA]. And since when, pray, have you taken to cooking?

CATHERINE. Oh, whilst you were away. It is her latest fancy.

PETKOFF [*testily*]. And has Nicola taken to drinking? He used to be careful enough. First he shews Captain Bluntschli out here when he knew quite well I was in the library; and then he goes downstairs and breaks Raina's chocolate soldier. He must—

[NICOLA *appears at the top of the steps with the bag. He descends; places it respectfully before* BLUNTSCHLI; *and*

waits for further orders. General amazement.* NICOLA, *unconscious of the effect he is producing, looks perfectly satisfied with himself. When* PETKOFF *recovers his power of speech, he breaks out at him with:*]

Are you mad, Nicola?

NICOLA [*taken aback*]. Sir?

PETKOFF. What have you brought that for?

NICOLA. My lady's orders, major. Louka told me that—

CATHERINE [*interrupting him*]. My orders! Why should I order you to bring Captain Bluntschli's luggage out here? What are you thinking of, Nicola?

NICOLA [*after a moment's bewilderment, picking up the bag as he addresses* BLUNTSCHLI *with the very perfection of servile discretion*]. I beg your pardon, captain, I am sure. [*to* CATHERINE] My fault, madam: I hope youll overlook it.

[*He bows, and is going to the steps with the bag, when* PETKOFF *addresses him angrily*.]

PETKOFF. Youd better go and slam that bag, too, down on Miss Raina's ice pudding! [*This is too much for* NICOLA. *The bag drops from his hand almost on his master's toes, eliciting a roar of:*] Begone, you butter-fingered donkey.

NICOLA [*snatching up the bag, and escaping into the house*]. Yes, major.

CATHERINE. Oh, never mind, Paul: dont be angry.

PETKOFF [*blustering*]. Scoundrel! He's got out of hand while I was away. I'll teach him. Infernal blackguard! The sack next Saturday! I'll clear out the whole establishment—

[*He is stifled by the caresses of his wife and daughter, who hang round his neck, petting him*].

CATHERINE.
RAINA. } [*together*]

Now, now, now, it mustnt be angry.
Wow, wow, wow: not on your first
He meant no harm. Be good to
day at home. I'll make another ice
please me, dear. Sh-sh-sh-sh!
pudding. Tch-ch-ch!

PETKOFF [*yielding*]. Oh well, never
mind. Come, Bluntschli: lets have no
more nonsense about going away. You
know very well youre not going back
to Switzerland yet. Until you do go
back youll stay with us.

RAINA. Oh, do, Captain Bluntschli.

PETKOFF [*to* CATHERINE]. Now, Catherine: it's of you he's afraid. Press

him: and he'll stay.

CATHERINE. Of course I shall be only
too delighted if [*appealingly*] Captain Bluntschli really wishes to stay.
He knows my wishes.

BLUNTSCHLI [*in his driest military
manner*]. I am at madam's orders.

SERGIUS [*cordially*]. That settles it!

PETKOFF [*heartily*]. Of course!

RAINA. You see you must stay.

BLUNTSCHLI [*smiling*]. Well, if I must,
I must.

[*Gesture of despair from* CATHERINE.]

ACT III

*In the library after lunch. It is not
much of a library. Its literary equipment consists of a single fixed shelf
stocked with old paper covered novels,
broken backed, coffee stained, torn and
thumbed; and a couple of little hanging
shelves with a few gift books on them:
the rest of the wall space being occupied by trophies of war and the chase.
But it is a most comfortable sitting
room. A row of three large windows
shews a mountain panorama, just now
seen in one of its friendliest aspects in
the mellowing afternoon light. In the
corner next the right-hand window a
square earthenware stove, a perfect
tower of glistening pottery, rises nearly
to the ceiling and guarantees plenty of
warmth. The ottoman is like that in
RAINA's room, and similarly placed;
and the window seats are luxurious with
decorated cushions. There is one object,
however, hopelessly out of keeping with
its surroundings. This is a small kitchen
table, much the worse for wear, fitted
as a writing table with an old canister
full of pens, an eggcup filled with ink,
and a deplorable scrap of heavily used
pink blotting paper.
At the side of this table, which stands
to the left of anyone facing the*

window, BLUNTSCHLI *is hard at work
with a couple of maps before him, writing orders. At the head of it sits* SER-
GIUS, *who is supposed to be also at
work, but is actually gnawing the
feather of a pen, and contemplating*
BLUNTSCHLI's *quick, sure businesslike
progress with a mixture of envious irritation at his own incapacity and awestruck
wonder at an ability which seems to
him almost miraculous, though its
prosaic character forbids him to esteem
it. The* MAJOR *is comfortably established on the ottoman, with a newspaper
in his hand and the tube of his hookah
within easy reach.* CATHERINE *sits at
the stove, with her back to them, em-
broidering.* RAINA, *reclining on the
divan, is gazing in a daydream out at
the Balkan landscape, with a neglected
novel in her lap.
The door is on the same side as the
stove, farther from the window. The
button of the electric bell is at the
opposite side, behind* BLUNTSCHLI.

PETKOFF [*looking up from his paper
to watch how they are getting on at
the table*]. Are you sure I cant help
in any way, Bluntschli?

BLUNTSCHLI [*without interrupting his*

writing or looking up]. Quite sure, thank you. Saranoff and I will manage it.

SERGIUS [*grimly*]. Yes: we'll manage it. He finds out what to do; draws up the orders; and I sign em. Division of labor! [BLUNTSCHLI *passes him a paper.*] Another one? Thank you. [*He plants the paper squarely before him; sets his chair carefully parallel to it; and signs with his cheek on his elbow and his protruded tongue following the movements of his pen.*] This hand is more accustomed to the sword than to the pen.

PETKOFF. It's very good of you, Bluntschli: it is indeed, to let yourself be put upon in this way. Now are you quite sure I can do nothing?

CATHERINE [*in a low warning tone*]. You can stop interrupting, Paul.

PETKOFF [*starting and looking round at her*]. Eh? Oh! Quite right, my love: quite right. [*He takes his newspaper up again, but presently lets it drop.*] Ah, you havnt been campaigning, Catherine: you dont know how pleasant it is for us to sit here, after a good lunch, with nothing to do but enjoy ourselves. Theres only one thing I want to make me thoroughly comfortable.

CATHERINE. What is that?

PETKOFF. My old coat. I'm not at home in this one: I feel as if I were on parade.

CATHERINE. My dear Paul, how absurd you are about that old coat! It must be hanging in the blue closet where you left it.

PETKOFF. My dear Catherine, I tell you Ive looked there. Am I to believe my own eyes or not? [CATHERINE *rises and crosses the room to press the button of the electric bell.*] What are you shewing off that bell for? [*She looks at him majestically, and silently resumes her chair and her needlework.*] My dear: if you think the obstinacy of your sex can make

a coat out of two old dressing gowns of Raina's, your waterproof, and my mackintosh, youre mistaken. Thats exactly what the blue closet contains at present.

[NICOLA *presents himself.*]

CATHERINE. Nicola: go to the blue closet and bring your master's old coat here: the braided one he wears in the house.

NICOLA. Yes, madame. [*He goes out.*]

PETKOFF. Catherine.

CATHERINE. Yes, Paul.

PETKOFF. I bet you any piece of jewellery you like to order from Sofia against a week's housekeeping money that the coat isnt there.

CATHERINE. Done, Paul!

PETKOFF [*excited by the prospect of a gamble*]. Come: heres an opportunity for some sport. Wholl bet on it? Bluntschli: I'll give you six to one.

BLUNTSCHLI [*imperturbably*]. It would be robbing you, major. Madame is sure to be right.

[*Without looking up, he passes another batch of papers to* SERGIUS.]

SERGIUS [*also excited*]. Bravo, Switzerland! Major: I bet my best charger against an Arab mare for Raina that Nicola finds the coat in the blue closet.

PETKOFF [*eagerly*]. Your best char—

CATHERINE [*hastily interrupting him*]. Dont be foolish, Paul. An Arabian mare will cost you 50,000 levas.

RAINA [*suddenly coming out of her picturesque revery*]. Really, mother, if you are going to take the jewellery, I dont see why you should grudge me my Arab.

[NICOLA *comes back with the coat, and brings it to* PETKOFF, *who can hardly believe his eyes.*]

CATHERINE. Where was it, Nicola?

NICOLA. Hanging in the blue closet, madame.

PETKOFF. Well, I am d—

CATHERINE [*stopping him*]. Paul!

PETKOFF. I could have sworn it wasnt there. Age is beginning to tell on me. I'm getting hallucinations. [*to* NICOLA] Here: help me to change. Excuse me, Bluntschli. [*He begins changing coats,* NICOLA *acting as valet.*] Remember: I didnt take that bet of yours, Sergius. Youd better give Raina that Arab steed yourself, since youve roused her expectations. Eh, Raina? [*He looks round at her; but she is again rapt in the landscape. With a little gush of parental affection and pride, he points her out to them, and says:*] She's dreaming, as usual.

SERGIUS. Assuredly she shall not be the loser.

PETKOFF. So much the better for her. *I* shant come off so cheaply, I expect.

[*The change is now complete.* NICOLA *goes out with the discarded coat.*]

Ah, now I feel at home at last.

[*He sits down and takes his newspaper with a grunt of relief.*]

BLUNTSCHLI [*to* SERGIUS, *handing a paper*]. Thats the last order.

PETKOFF [*jumping up*]. What! Finished?

BLUNTSCHLI. Finished.

PETKOFF [*with childlike envy*]. Havnt you anything for me to sign?

BLUNTSCHLI. Not necessary. His signature will do.

PETKOFF [*inflating his chest and thumping it*]. Ah well, I think weve done a thundering good day's work. Can I do anything more?

BLUNTSCHLI. You had better both see the fellows that are to take these. [SERGIUS *rises.*] Pack them off at once; and shew them that Ive marked on the orders the time they should hand them in by. Tell them that if they stop to drink or tell stories— if theyre five minutes late, theyll have the skin taken off their backs.

SERGIUS [*stiffening indignantly*]. I'll say so. [*He strides to the door.*] And if one of them is man enough to spit in my face for insulting him, I'll buy his discharge and give him a pension. [*He goes out.*]

BLUNTSCHLI [*confidentially*]. Just see that he talks to them properly, major, will you?

PETKOFF [*officiously*]. Quite right, Bluntschli, quite right. I'll see to it. [*He goes to the door importantly, but hesitates on the threshold.*] By the bye, Catherine, you may as well come too. Theyll be far more frightened of you than of me.

CATHERINE [*putting down her embroidery*]. I daresay I had better. You would only splutter at them.

[*She goes out,* PETKOFF *holding the door for her and following her.*]

BLUNTSCHLI. What an army! They make cannons out of cherry trees, and the officers send for their wives to keep discipline!

[*He begins to fold and docket the papers.* RAINA, *who has risen from the divan, marches slowly down the room with her hands clasped behind her, and looks mischievously at him.*]

RAINA. You look ever so much nicer than when we last met. [*He looks up, surprised.*] What have you done to yourself?

BLUNTSCHLI. Washed; brushed; good night's sleep and breakfast. Thats all.

RAINA. Did you get back safely that morning?

BLUNTSCHLI. Quite, thanks.

RAINA. Were they angry with you for running away from Sergius's charge?

BLUNTSCHLI. [*grinning*] No: they were glad; because theyd all just run away themselves.

RAINA [*going to the table, and leaning over it towards him*]. It must have made a lovely story for them: all that about me and my room.

BLUNTSCHLI. Capital story. But I only told it to one of them: a particular friend.

RAINA. On whose discretion you could absolutely rely?

BLUNTSCHLI. Absolutely.

RAINA. Hm! He told it all to my father and Sergius the day you exchanged the prisoners.

[*She turns away and strolls carelessly across to the other side of the room.*]

BLUNTSCHLI [*deeply concerned, and half incredulous*]. No! You dont mean that, do you?

RAINA [*turning, with sudden earnestness*]. I do indeed. But they dont know that it was in this house you took refuge. If Sergius knew, he would challenge you and kill you in a duel.

BLUNTSCHLI. Bless me! then dont tell him.

RAINA. Please be serious, Captain Bluntschli. Can you not realize what it is to me to deceive him? I want to be quite perfect with Sergius: no meanness, no smallness, no deceit. My relation to him is the one really beautiful and noble part of my life. I hope you can understand that.

BLUNTSCHLI [*skeptically*]. You mean that you wouldnt like him to find out that the story about the ice pudding was a—a—a—You know.

RAINA [*wincing*]. Ah, dont talk of it in that flippant way. I lied: I know it. But I did it to save your life. He would have killed you. That was the second time I ever uttered a falsehood. [BLUNTSCHLI *rises quickly and looks doubtfully and somewhat severely at her.*] Do you remember the first time?

BLUNTSCHLI. I! No. Was I present?

RAINA. Yes; and I told the officer who was searching for you that you were not present.

BLUNTSCHLI. True. I should have remembered it.

RAINA [*greatly encouraged*]. Ah, it is natural that you should forget it first. It cost you nothing: it cost me a lie! A lie!

[*She sits down on the ottoman, looking straight before her with her hands clasped around her knee.* BLUNTSCHLI, *quite touched, goes to the ottoman with a particularly reassuring and considerate air, and sits down beside her.*]

BLUNTSCHLI. My dear young lady, dont let this worry you. Remember: I'm a soldier. Now what are the two things that happen to a soldier so often that he comes to think nothing of them? One is hearing people tell lies: [RAINA *recoils.*] the other is getting his life saved in all sorts of ways by all sorts of people.

RAINA [*rising in indignant protest*]. And so he becomes a creature incapable of faith and of gratitude.

BLUNTSCHLI [*making a wry face*]. Do you like gratitude? I dont. If pity is akin to love, gratitude is akin to the other thing.

RAINA. Gratitude! [*turning on him*] If you are incapable of gratitude you are incapable of any noble sentiment. Even animals are grateful. Oh, I see now exactly what you think of me! You were not surprised to hear me lie. To you it was something I probably did every day! every hour! That is how men think of women.

[*She paces the room tragically.*]

BLUNTSCHLI [*dubiously*]. Theres reason in everything. You said youd told only two lies in your whole life. Dear young lady: isnt that rather a short allowance? I'm quite a straightforward man myself; but it wouldnt last me a whole morning.

RAINA [*staring haughtily at him*]. Do you know, sir, that you are insulting me?

BLUNTSCHLI. I cant help it. When you strike that noble attitude and speak in that thrilling voice, I admire you; but I find it impossible to believe a single word you say.

RAINA [*superbly*]. Captain Bluntschli!

BLUNTSCHLI [*unmoved*]. Yes?

RAINA [*standing over him, as if she could not believe her senses*]. Do you mean what you said just now? Do you know what you said just now?

BLUNTSCHLI. I do.

RAINA [*gasping*]. I! I!!! [*She points to herself incredulously, meaning "I, Raina Petkoff, tell lies!" He meets her gaze unflinchingly. She suddenly sits down beside him, and adds, with a complete change of manner from the heroic to a babyish familiarity:*] How did you find me out?

BLUNTSCHLI [*promptly*]. Instinct, dear young lady. Instinct, and experience of the world.

RAINA [*wonderingly*]. Do you know, you are the first man I ever met who did not take me seriously?

BLUNTSCHLI. You mean, dont you, that I am the first man that has ever taken you quite seriously?

RAINA. Yes: I suppose I do mean that. [*cosily, quite at her ease with him*] How strange it is to be talked to in such a way! You know, Ive always gone on like that.

BLUNTSCHLI. You mean the—?

RAINA. I mean the noble attitude and the thrilling voice. [*They laugh together.*] I did it when I was a tiny child to my nurse. She believed in it. I do it before my parents. They believe in it. I do it before Sergius. He believes in it.

BLUNTSCHLI. Yes: he's a little in that line himself, isnt he?

RAINA [*startled*]. Oh! Do you think so?

BLUNTSCHLI. You know him better than I do.

RAINA. I wonder—I wonder is he? If I thought that—! [*discouraged*] Ah, well: what does it matter? I suppose, now youve found me out, you despise me.

BLUNTSCHLI [*warmly, rising*]. No, my dear young lady, no, no, no a thousand times. It's part of your youth: part of your charm. I'm like all the rest of them: the nurse, your parents, Sergius: I'm your infatuated admirer.

RAINA [*pleased*]. Really?

BLUNTSCHLI [*slapping his breast smartly with his hand, German fashion*]. Hand aufs Herz! Really and truly.

RAINA [*very happy*]. But what did you think of me for giving you my portrait?

BLUNTSCHLI [*astonished*]. Your portrait! You never gave me your portrait.

RAINA [*quickly*]. Do you mean to say you never got it?

BLUNTSCHLI. No. [*He sits down beside her, with renewed interest, and says, with some complacency:*] When did you send it to me?

RAINA [*indignantly*]. I did not send it to you. [*She turns her head away, and adds, reluctantly:*] It was in the pocket of that coat.

BLUNTSCHLI [*pursing his lips and rounding his eyes*]. Oh-o-oh! I never found it. It must be there still.

RAINA [*springing up*]. There still! for my father to find the first time he puts his hand in his pocket! Oh, how could you be so stupid?

BLUNTSCHLI [*rising also*]. It doesnt matter: I suppose it's only a photograph: how can he tell who it was intended for? Tell him he put it there himself.

RAINA [*bitterly*]. Yes: that is so clever! isnt it? [*distractedly*] Oh! what shall I do?

BLUNTSCHLI. Ah, I see. You wrote something on it. That was rash.

RAINA [*vexed almost to tears*]. Oh, to have done such a thing for you, who care no more—except to laugh at me —oh! Are you sure nobody has touched it?

BLUNTSCHLI. Well, I cant be quite sure. You see, I couldnt carry it about with me all the time: one cant take much luggage on active service.

RAINA. What did you do with it?

BLUNTSCHLI. When I got through to Pirot I had to put it in safe keeping somehow. I thought of the railway cloak room; but thats the surest place to get looted in modern warfare. So I pawned it.

RAINA. Pawned it!!!

BLUNTSCHLI. I know it doesn't sound nice; but it was much the safest plan. I redeemed it the day before yesterday. Heaven only knows whether the pawnbroker cleared out the pockets or not.

RAINA [*furious: throwing the words right into his face*]. You have a low shopkeeping mind. You think of things that would never come into a gentleman's head.

BLUNTSCHLI [*phlegmatically*]. Thats the Swiss national character, dear lady. [*He returns to the table.*]

RAINA. Oh, I wish I had never met you.

[*She flounces away, and sits at the window fuming.*]

[LOUKA *comes in with a heap of letters and telegrams on her salver, and crosses, with her bold free gait, to the table. Her left sleeve is looped up to the shoulder with a brooch, shewing her naked arm, with a broad gilt bracelet covering the bruise.*]

LOUKA [*to* BLUNTSCHLI]. For you. [*She empties the salver with a fling on the table.*] The messenger is waiting.

[*She is determined not to be civil to an enemy, even if she must bring him his letters.*]

BLUNTSCHLI [*to* RAINA]. Will you excuse me: the last postal delivery that reached me was three weeks ago. These are the subsequent accumulations. Four telegrams: a week old. [*He opens one.*] Oho! Bad news!

RAINA [*rising and advancing a little remorsefully*]. Bad news?

BLUNTSCHLI. My father's dead.

[*He looks at the telegram with his lips pursed, musing on the unexpected change in his arrangements.* LOUKA *crosses herself hastily.*]

RAINA. Oh, how very sad!

BLUNTSCHLI. Yes: I shall have to start for home in an hour. He has left a lot of big hotels behind him to be looked after. [*He takes up a fat letter in a long blue envelope.*] Here's a whacking letter from the family solicitor. [*He puts out the enclosures and glances over them.*] Great Heavens! Seventy! Two hundred! [*in a crescendo of dismay*] Four hundred! Four thousand! Nine thousand six hundred!!! What on earth am I to do with them all?

RAINA [*timidly*]. Nine thousand hotels?

BLUNTSCHLI. Hotels! nonsense. If you only knew! Oh, it's too ridiculous! Excuse me: I must give my fellow orders abouts starting.

[*He leaves the room hastily, with the documents in his hand.*]

LOUKA [*knowing instinctively that she can annoy* RAINA *by disparaging* BLUNTSCHLI]. He has not much heart, that Swiss. He has not a word of grief for his poor father.

RAINA [*bitterly*]. Grief! A man who has been doing nothing but killing people for years! What does he care? What does any soldier care?

[*She goes to the door, restraining her tears with difficulty.*]

LOUKA. Major Saranoff has been fighting too; and he has plenty of heart left.

[RAINA, *at the door, draws herself up haughtily and goes out.*]

Aha I thought you wouldnt get much feeling out of your soldier.

[*She is following* RAINA *when* NICOLA

enters with an armful of logs for the stove.]

NICOLA [*grinning amorously at her*]. Ive been trying all the afternoon to get a minute alone with you, my girl. [*His countenance changes as he notices her arm.*] Why, what fashion is that of wearing your sleeve, child?

LOUKA [*proudly*]. My own fashion.

NICOLA. Indeed! If the mistress catches you, she'll talk to you.

[*He puts the logs down, and seats himself comfortably on the ottoman.*]

LOUKA. Is that any reason why you should take it on yourself to talk to me?

NICOLA. Come! dont be so contrary with me. Ive some good news for you. [*She sits down beside him. He takes out some paper money. LOUKA, with an eager gleam in her eyes, tries to snatch it; but he shifts it quickly to his left hand, out of her reach.*] See! a twenty leva bill! Sergius gave me that, out of pure swagger. A fool and his money are soon parted. Theres ten levas more. The Swiss gave me that for backing up the mistress's and Raina's lies about him. He's no fool, he isnt. You should have heard old Catherine downstairs as polite as you please to me, telling me not to mind the Major being a little impatient; for they knew what a good servant I was—after making a fool and a liar of me before them all! The twenty will go to our savings; and you shall have the ten to spend if youll only talk to me so as to remind me I'm a human being. I get tired of being a servant occasionally.

LOUKA. Yes: sell your manhood for 30 levas, and buy me for 10! [*rising scornfully*] Keep your money. You were born to be a servant. I was not. When you set up your shop you will only be everybody's servant instead of somebody's servant.

[*She goes moodily to the table and seats herself regally in* SERGIUS's *chair.*]

NICOLA [*picking up his logs, and going to the stove*]. Ah, wait til you see. We shall have our evenings to ourselves; and I shall be master in my own house, I promise you.

[*He throws the logs down and kneels at the stove.*]

LOUKA. You shall never be master in mine.

NICOLA [*turning, still on his knees, and squatting down rather forlornly on his calves, daunted by her implacable disdain*]. You have a great ambition in you, Louka. Remember: if any luck comes to you, it was I that made a woman of you.

LOUKA. You!

NICOLA [*scrambling up and going to her*]. Yes, me. Who was it made you give up wearing a couple of pounds of false black hair on your head and reddening your lips and cheeks like any other Bulgarian girl! I did. Who taught you to trim your nails, and keep your hands clean, and be dainty about yourself, like a fine Russian lady! Me: do you hear that? me! [*She tosses her head defiantly; and he turns away, adding more coolly:*] Ive often thought that if Raina were out of the way, and you just a little less of a fool and Sergius just a little more of one, you might come to be one of my grandest customers, instead of only being my wife and costing me money.

LOUKA. I believe you would rather be my servant than my husband. You would make more out of me. Oh, I know that soul of yours.

NICOLA [*going closer to her for greater emphasis*]. Never you mind my soul; but just listen to my advice. If you want to be a lady, your present behavior to me wont do at all, unless when we're alone. It's too sharp and impudent; and impudence is a sort of familiarity: it shews affection for me. And don't you try being high and mighty with me, either. Youre like all country girls: you think it's genteel to treat a servant the way I treat a stableboy. Thats only your ignorance; and dont you forget it. And dont be so ready to defy everybody. Act as if you expected to have your own way, not as if you expected to be ordered about. The way to get on as a lady is the same as the way to get on as a servant: youve got to know your place: thats the secret of it. And you may depend on me to know my place if you get promoted. Think over it, my girl. I'll stand by you: one servant should always stand by another.

LOUKA [*rising impatiently*]. Oh, I must behave in my own way. You take all the courage out of me with your cold-blooded wisdom. Go and put those logs in the fire: thats the sort of thing you understand.

[*Before* NICOLA *can retort,* SERGIUS *comes in. He checks himself a moment on seeing* LOUKA; *then goes to the stove.*]

SERGIUS [*to* NICOLA]. I am not in the way of your work, I hope.

NICOLA [*in a smooth, elderly manner*]. Oh no, sir: thank you kindly. I was only speaking to this foolish girl about her habit of running up here to the library whenever she gets a chance, to look at the books. Thats the worst of her education, sir: it gives her habits above her station. [*to* LOUKA] Make that table tidy, Louka, for the Major.

[*He goes out sedately.*]

[LOUKA, *without looking at* SERGIUS, *pretends to arrange the papers on the table. He crosses slowly to her, and studies the arrangement of her sleeve reflectively.*]

SERGIUS. Let me see: is there a mark there? [*He turns up the bracelet and sees the bruise made by his grasp. She stands motionless, not looking at him: fascinated, but on her guard.*] Ffff! Does it hurt?

LOUKA. Yes.

SERGIUS. Shall I cure it?

LOUKA [*instantly withdrawing herself proudly, but still not looking at him*]. No. You cannot cure it now.

SERGIUS [*masterfully*]. Quite sure?

[*He makes a movement as if to take her in his arms.*]

LOUKA. Dont trifle with me, please. An officer should not trifle with a servant.

SERGIUS [*indicating the bruise with a merciless stroke of his forefinger*]. That was no trifle, Louka.

LOUKA [*flinching; then looking at him for the first time*]. Are you sorry?

SERGIUS [*with measured emphasis, folding his arms*]. I am never sorry.

LOUKA [*wistfully*]. I wish I could believe a man could be as unlike a woman as that. I wonder are you really a brave man?

SERGIUS [*unaffectedly, relaxing his attitude*]. Yes: I am a brave man. My heart jumped like a woman's at the first shot; but in the charge I found that I was brave. Yes: that at least is real about me.

LOUKA. Did you find in the charge that the men whose fathers are poor like mine were any less brave than the men who are rich like you?

SERGIUS [*with bitter levity*]. Not a bit. They all slashed and cursed and yelled like heroes. Psha! the courage to rage and kill is cheap. I have an English bull terrier who has as much of that sort of courage as the whole Bulgarian nation, and the whole Russian nation at its back. But he lets my groom thrash him, all the same. Thats your soldier all over! No, Louka: your poor men can cut throats; but they are afraid of their officers; they put up with insults and blows; they stand by and see one another punished like children: aye, and help to do it when they are ordered. And the officers!!! Well [*with a short harsh laugh*] *I* am an officer. Oh, [*fervently*] give me the man who will defy to the death any power on earth or in heaven that sets itself up against his own will and conscience: he alone is the brave man.

LOUKA. How easy it is to talk! Men never seem to me to grow up: they all have schoolboy's ideas. You dont know what true courage is.

SERGIUS [*ironically*]. Indeed! I am willing to be instructed.

[*He sits on the ottoman, sprawling magnificently.*]

LOUKA. Look at me! How much am I allowed to have my own will? I have to get your room ready for you: to sweep and dust, to fetch and carry. How could that degrade me if it did not degrade you to have it done for you? But [*with subdued passion*] if I were Empress of Russia, above everyone in the world, then!! Ah then, though according to you I could shew no courage at all, you should see, you should see.

SERGIUS. What would you do, most noble Empress?

LOUKA. I would marry the man I loved, which no other queen in Europe has the courage to do. If I loved you, though you would be as far beneath me as I am beneath you, I would dare to be the equal of my inferior. Would you dare as much if you loved me? No: if you felt the beginnings of love for me you would not let it grow. You would not dare: you would marry a rich man's daughter because you would be afraid of what other people would say of you.

SERGIUS [*bounding up*]. You lie: it is

not so, by all the stars! If I loved you, and I were the Tsar himself, I would set you on the throne by my side. You know that I love another woman, a woman as high above you as heaven is above earth. And you are jealous of her.

LOUKA. I have no reason to be. She will never marry you now. The man I told you of has come back. She will marry the Swiss.

SERGIUS [*recoiling*]. The Swiss!

LOUKA. A man worth ten of you. Then you can come to me; and I will refuse you. You are not good enough for me. [*She turns to the door.*]

SERGIUS [*springing after her and catching her fiercely in his arms*]. I will kill the Swiss; and afterwards I will do as I please with you.

LOUKA [*in his arms, passive and steadfast*]. The Swiss will kill you, perhaps. He has beaten you in love. He may beat you in war.

SERGIUS [*tormentedly*]. Do you think I believe that she—she! whose worst thoughts are higher than your best ones, is capable of trifling with another man behind my back?

LOUKA. Do you think she would believe the Swiss if he told her now that I am in your arms?

SERGIUS [*releasing her in despair*]. Damnation! Oh, damnation! Mockery! mockery everywhere! everything I think is mocked by everything I do. [*He strikes himself frantically on the breast.*] Coward! liar! fool! Shall I kill myself like a man, or live and pretend to laugh at myself? [*She again turns to go.*] Louka! [*She stops near the door.*] Remember: you belong to me.

LOUKA [*turning*]. What does that mean? an insult?

SERGIUS [*commandingly*]. It means that you love me, and that I have had you here in my arms, and will perhaps have you there again. Whether that is an insult I neither know nor care: take it as you please. But [*vehemently*] I will not be a coward and a trifler. If I choose to love you, I dare marry you, in spite of all Bulgaria. If these hands ever touch you again, they shall touch my affianced bride.

LOUKA. We shall see whether you dare keep your word. And take care. I will not wait long.

SERGIUS [*again folding his arms and standing motionless in the middle of the room*]. Yes: we shall see. And you shall wait my pleasure.

[BLUNTSCHLI, *much preoccupied, with his papers still in his hand, enters, leaving the door open for* LOUKA *to go out. He goes across to the table, glancing at her as he passes.* SERGIUS, *without altering his resolute attitude, watches him steadily.* LOUKA *goes out, leaving the door open.*]

BLUNTSCHLI [*absently, sitting at the table as before, and putting down his papers*]. Thats a remarkable looking young woman.

SERGIUS [*gravely, without moving*]. Captain Bluntschli.

BLUNTSCHLI. Eh?

SERGIUS. You have deceived me. You are my rival. I brook no rivals. At six o'clock I shall be in the drilling-ground on the Klissoura road, alone, on horseback, with my sabre. Do you understand?

BLUNTSCHLI [*staring, but sitting quite at his ease*]. Oh, thank you: thats a cavalry man's proposal. I'm in the artillery; and I have the choice of weapons. If I go, I shall take a machine gun. And there shall be no mistake about the cartridges this time.

SERGIUS [*flushing, but with deadly coldness*]. Take care, sir. It is not our custom in Bulgaria to allow invitations of that kind to be trifled with.

BLUNTSCHLI [*warmly*]. Pooh! dont talk to me about Bulgaria. You dont know what fighting is. But have it your own way. Bring your sabre along. I'll meet you.

SERGIUS [*fiercely delighted to find his opponent a man of spirit*]. Well said, Switzer. Shall I lend you my best horse?

BLUNTSCHLI. No: damn your horse! thank you all the same, my dear fellow.

[RAINA *comes in, and hears the next sentence.*]

I shall fight you on foot. Horseback's too dangerous; I dont want to kill you if I can help it.

RAINA [*hurrying forward anxiously*]. I have heard what Captain Bluntschli said, Sergius. You are going to fight. Why? [SERGIUS *turns away in silence, and goes to the stove, where he stands watching her as she continues, to* BLUNTSCHLI:] What about?

BLUNTSCHLI. I dont know: he hasnt told me. Better not interfere, dear young lady. No harm will be done: Ive often acted as sword instructor. He wont be able to touch me; and I'll not hurt him. It will save explanations. In the morning I shall be off home; and youll never see me or hear of me again. You and he will then make it up and live happily ever after.

RAINA [*turning away deeply hurt, almost with a sob in her voice*]. I never said I wanted to see you again.

SERGIUS [*striding forward*]. Ha! That is a confession.

RAINA [*haughtily*]. What do you mean?

SERGIUS. You love that man!

RAINA [*scandalized*]. Sergius!

SERGIUS. You allow him to make love to you behind my back, just as you treat me as your affianced husband behind his. Bluntschli: you knew our relations; and you deceived me. It is for that that I call you to account, not for having received favors *I* never enjoyed.

BLUNTSCHLI [*jumping up indignantly*]. Stuff! Rubbish! I have received no favors. Why, the young lady doesnt even know whether I'm married or not.

RAINA [*forgetting herself*]. Oh! [*collapsing on the ottoman*] Are you?

SERGIUS. You see the young lady's concern, Captain Bluntschli. Denial is useless. You have enjoyed the privilege of being received in her own room, late at night—

BLUNTSCHLI [*interrupting him pepperily*]. Yes, you blockhead! she received me with a pistol at her head. Your cavalry were at my heels. I'd have blown out her brains if she'd uttered a cry.

SERGIUS [*taken aback*]. Bluntschli! Raina: is this true?

RAINA [*rising in wrathful majesty*]. Oh, how dare you, how dare you?

BLUNTSCHLI. Apologize, man: apologize.

[*He resumes his seat at the table.*]

SERGIUS [*with the old measured emphasis, folding his arms*]. I never apologize!

RAINA [*passionately*]. This is the doing of that friend of yours, Captain Bluntschli. It is he who is spreading this horrible story about me.

[*She walks about excitedly.*]

BLUNTSCHLI. No: he's dead. Burnt alive!

RAINA [*stopping, shocked*]. Burnt alive!

BLUNTSCHLI. Shot in the hip in a woodyard. Couldnt drag himself out. Your fellows shells set the timber on fire and burnt him, with half a dozen other poor devils in the same predicament.

RAINA. How horrible!

SERGIUS. And how ridiculous! Oh, war! war! the dream of patriots and heroes! A fraud, Bluntschli. A hollow sham, like love.

RAINA [*outraged*]. Like love! You say that before me!

BLUNTSCHLI. Come, Saranoff: that matter is explained.

SERGIUS. A hollow sham, I say. Would you have come back here if nothing had passed between you except at the muzzle of your pistol? Raina is mistaken about your friend who was burnt. He was not my informant.

RAINA. Who then? [*suddenly guessing the truth*] Ah, Louka! my maid! my servant! You were with her this morning all that time after—after— Oh, what sort of god is this I have been worshipping! [*He meets her gaze with sardonic enjoyment of her disenchantment. Angered all the more, she goes closer to him, and says, in a lower, intenser tone:*] Do you know that I looked out of the window as I went upstairs, to have another sight of my hero; and I saw something I did not understand then. I know now that you were making love to her.

SERGIUS [*with grim humor*]. You saw that?

RAINA. Only too well.

[*She turns away, and throws herself on the divan under the centre window, quite overcome.*]

SERGIUS [*cynically*]. Raina: our romance is shattered. Life's a farce.

BLUNTSCHLI [*to* RAINA, *whimsically*]. You see: he's found himself out now.

SERGIUS [*going to him*]. Bluntschli: I have allowed you to call me a blockhead. You may now call me a coward as well. I refuse to fight you. Do you know why?

BLUNTSCHLI. No; but it doesnt matter. I didnt ask the reason when you cried on; and I dont ask the reason now that you cry off. I'm a professional soldier I fight when I have to, and am very glad to get out of it when

I havnt to. Youre only an amateur: you think fighting's an amusement.

SERGIUS [*sitting down at the table, nose to nose with him*]. You shall hear the reason all the same, my professional. The reason is that it takes two men—real men—men of heart, blood and honor—to make a genuine combat. I could no more fight with you than I could make love to an ugly woman. Youve no magnetism: youre not a man: youre a machine.

BLUNTSCHLI [*apologetically*]. Quite true, quite true. I always was that sort of chap. I'm very sorry.

SERGIUS. Psha!

BLUNTSCHLI. But now that youve found that life isnt a farce, but something quite sensible and serious, what further obstacle is there to your happiness?

RAINA [*rising*]. You are very solicitous about my happiness and his. Do you forget his new love—Louka? It is not you that he must fight now, but his rival, Nicola.

SERGIUS. Rival!!

[*Bounding half across the room.*]

RAINA. Dont you know that theyre engaged?

SERGIUS. Nicola! Are fresh abysses opening? Nicola!!

RAINA [*sarcastically*]. A shocking sacrifice, isnt it? Such beauty! such intellect! such modesty! wasted on a middle-aged servant man. Really, Sergius, you cannot stand by and allow such a thing. It would be unworthy of your chivalry.

SERGIUS [*losing all self-control*]. Viper! Viper!

[*He rushes to and fro, raging.*]

BLUNTSCHLI. Look here, Saranoff: youre getting the worst of this.

RAINA [*getting angrier*]. Do you realize what he has done, Captain Bluntschli? He has set this girl as a spy on us; and her reward is that he makes love to her.

SERGIUS. False! Monstrous!

RAINA. Monstrous! [*confronting him*] Do you deny that she told you about Captain Bluntschli being in my room?

SERGIUS. No; but—

RAINA [*interrupting*]. Do you deny that you were making love to her when she told you?

SERGIUS. No; but I tell you—

RAINA [*cutting him short contemptuously*]. It is unnecessary to tell us anything more. That is quite enough for us.

[*She turns away from him and sweeps majestically back to the window.*]

BLUNTSCHLI [*quietly, as* SERGIUS, *in an agony of mortification, sinks on the ottoman, clutching his averted head between his fists*]. I told you you were getting the worst of it, Saranoff.

SERGIUS. Tiger cat!

RAINA [*running excitedly to* BLUNTSCHLI]. You hear this man calling me names, Captain Bluntschli?

BLUNTSCHLI. What else can he do, dear lady? He must defend himself somehow. Come [*very persuasively*]: dont quarrel. What good does it do?

[RAINA, *with a gasp, sits down on the ottoman, and after a vain effort to look vexedly at* BLUNTSCHLI, *falls a victim to her sense of humor, and actually leans back babyishly against the writhing shoulder of* SERGIUS.]

SERGIUS. Engaged to Nicola! Ha! ha! Ah well, Bluntschli, you are right to take this huge imposture of a world coolly.

RAINA [*quaintly to* BLUNTSCHLI, *with an intuitive guess at his state of mind*]. I daresay you think us a couple of grown-up babies, dont you?

SERGIUS [*grinning savagely*]. He does:

he does. Swiss civilization nursetending Bulgarian barbarism, eh?

BLUNTSCHLI [*blushing*]. Not at all, I assure you. I'm only very glad to get you two quieted. There! there! let's be pleasant and talk it over in a friendly way. Where is this other young lady?

RAINA. Listening at the door, probably.

SERGIUS [*shivering as if a bullet had struck him, and speaking with quiet but deep indignation*]. I will prove that that, at least, is a calumny.

[*He goes with dignity to the door and opens it. A yell of fury bursts from him as he looks out. He darts into the passage, and returns dragging in* LOUKA, *whom he flings violently against the table, exclaiming:*]

Judge her, Bluntschli. You, the cool impartial man: judge the eavesdropper.

[LOUKA *stands her ground, proud and silent.*]

BLUNTSCHLI [*shaking his head*]. I mustnt judge her. I once listened myself outside a tent when there was a mutiny brewing. It's all a question of the degree of provocation. My life was at stake.

LOUKA. My love was at stake. I am not ashamed.

RAINA [*contemptuously*]. Your love! Your curiosity, you mean.

LOUKA [*facing her and returning her contempt with interest*]. My love, stronger than anything you can feel, even for your chocolate cream soldier.

SERGIUS [*with quick suspicion, to* LOUKA]. What does that mean?

LOUKA [*fiercely*]. I mean—

SERGIUS [*interrupting her slightingly*]. Oh, I remember: the ice pudding. A paltry taunt, girl!

[MAJOR PETKOFF *enters, in his shirtsleeves.*]

PETKOFF. Excuse my shirtsleeves, gentlemen. Raina: somebody has been wearing that coat of mine: I'll swear it. Somebody with a differently shaped back. It's all burst open at the sleeve. Your mother is mending it. I wish she'd make haste: I shall catch cold. [*He looks more attentively at them.*] Is anything the matter?

RAINA. No.

[*She sits down at the stove, with a tranquil air.*]

SERGIUS. Oh no.

[*He sits down at the end of the table, as at first.*]

BLUNTSCHLI [*who is already seated*]. Nothing. Nothing.

PETKOFF [*sitting down on the ottoman in his old place*]. Thats all right. [*He notices* LOUKA.] Anything the matter, Louka?

LOUKA. No, sir.

PETKOFF [*genially*]. Thats all right. [*He sneezes.*] Go and ask your mistress for my coat, like a good girl, will you?

[NICOLA *enters with the coat.* LOUKA *makes a pretence of having business in the room by taking the little table with the hookah away to the wall near the windows.*]

RAINA [*rising quickly as she sees the coat on* NICOLA'S *arm*]. Here it is, papa. Give it to me, Nicola; and do you put some more wood on the fire.

[*She takes the coat, and brings it to the* MAJOR, *who stands up to put it on.* NICOLA *attends to the fire.*]

PETKOFF [*to* RAINA, *teasing her affectionately*]. Aha! Going to be very good to poor old papa just for one day after his return from the wars, eh?

RAINA [*with solemn reproach*]. Ah, how can you say that to me, father?

PETKOFF. Well, well, only a joke, little one. Come: give me a kiss. [*She kisses him.*] Now give me the coat.

RAINA. No: I am going to put it on

for you. Turn your back. [*He turns his back and feels behind him with his arms for the sleeves. She dexterously takes the photograph from the pocket and throws it on the table before* BLUNTSCHLI, *who covers it with a sheet of paper under the very nose of* SERGIUS, *who looks on amazed, with his suspicions roused in the highest degree. She then helps* PETKOFF *on with his coat.*] There, dear! Now are you comfortable?

PETKOFF. Quite, little love. Thanks. [*He sits down; and* RAINA *returns to her seat near the stove.*] Oh, by the bye, Ive found something funny. Whats the meaning of this? [*He puts his hand into the picked pocket.*] Eh? Hallo! [*He tries the other pocket.*] Well, I could have sworn —! [*Much puzzled, he tries the breast pocket.*] I wonder—[*trying the original pocket*] Where can it—? [*He rises, exclaiming:*] Your mother's taken it!

RAINA [*very red*]. Taken what?

PETKOFF. Your photograph, with the inscription: "Raina, to her Chocolate Cream Soldier: a Souvenir." Now you know theres something more in this than meets the eye; and I'm going to find it out. [*shouting*] Nicola!

NICOLA [*coming to him*]. Sir!

PETKOFF. Did you spoil any pastry of Miss Raina's this morning?

NICOLA. You heard Miss Raina say that I did, sir.

PETKOFF. I know that, you idiot. Was it true?

NICOLA. I am sure Miss Raina is incapable of saying anything that is not true, sir.

PETKOFF. Are you? Then I'm not. [*turning to the others*] Come: do you think I dont see it all? [*He goes to* SERGIUS, *and slaps him on the shoulder.*] Sergius: youre the chocolate cream soldier, arnt you?

SERGIUS [*starting up*]. I! A chocolate cream soldier! Certainly not.

PETKOFF. Not! [*He looks at them. They are all very serious and very conscious.*] Do you mean to tell me that Raina sends things like that to other men?

SERGIUS [*enigmatically*]. The world is not such an innocent place as we used to think, Petkoff.

BLUNTSCHLI [*rising*]. It's all right, major. I'm the chocolate cream soldier. [PETKOFF *and* SERGIUS *are equally astonished.*] The gracious young lady saved my life by giving me chocolate creams when I was starving: shall I ever forget their flavour! My late friend Stolz told you the story at Pirot. I was the fugitive.

PETKOFF. You! [*He gasps.*] Sergius: do you remember how those two women went on this morning when we mentioned it? [SERGIUS *smiles cynically.* PETKOFF *confronts* RAINA *severely.*] Youre a nice young woman, arnt you?

RAINA [*bitterly*]. Major Saranoff has changed his mind. And when I wrote that on the photograph, I did not know that Captain Bluntschli was married.

BLUNTSCHLI [*startled into vehement protest*]. I'm not married.

RAINA [*with deep reproach*]. You said you were.

BLUNTSCHLI. I did not. I positively did not. I never was married in my life.

PETKOFF [*exasperated*]. Raina: will you kindly inform me, if I am not asking too much, which of these gentlemen you are engaged to?

RAINA. To neither of them. This young lady [*introducing* LOUKA, *who faces them all proudly*] is the object of Major Saranoff's affections at present.

PETKOFF. Louka! Are you mad, Sergius? Why, this girl's engaged to Nicola.

NICOLA. I beg your pardon, sir. There is a mistake. Louka is not engaged to me.

PETKOFF. Not engaged to you, you scoundrel! Why, you had twenty-five levas from me on the day of your betrothal; and she had that gilt bracelet from Miss Raina.

NICOLA [*with cool unction*]. We gave it out so, sir. But it was only to give Louka protection. She had a soul above her station; and I have been no more than her confidential servant. I intend, as you know, sir, to set up a shop later on in Sofia; and I look forward to her custom and recommendation should she marry into the nobility.

[*He goes out with impressive discretion, leaving them all staring after him.*]

PETKOFF [*breaking the silence*]. Well, I am—hm!

SERGIUS. This is either the finest heroism or the most crawling baseness. Which is it, Bluntschli?

BLUNTSCHLI. Never mind whether it's heroism or baseness. Nicola's the ablest man Ive met in Bulgaria. I'll make him manager of a hotel if he can speak French and German.

LOUKA [*suddenly breaking out at SERGIUS*]. I have been insulted by everyone here. You set them the example. You owe me an apology.

[*SERGIUS, like a repeating clock of which the spring has been touched, immediately begins to fold his arms.*]

BLUNTSCHLI [*before he can speak*]. It's no use. He never apologizes.

LOUKA. Not to you, his equal and his enemy. To me, his poor servant, he will not refuse to apologize.

SERGIUS [*approvingly*]. You are right. [*He bends his knee in his grandest manner.*] Forgive me.

LOUKA. I forgive you. [*She timidly gives him her hand, which he kisses.*] That touch makes me your affianced wife.

SERGIUS [*springing up*]. Ah! forgot that.

LOUKA [*coldly*]. You can withdraw if you like.

SERGIUS. Withdraw! Never! You belong to me.

[*He puts his arm about her.*]

[*CATHERINE comes in and finds LOUKA in SERGIUS's arms, with all the rest gazing at them in bewildered astonishment.*]

CATHERINE. What does this mean?

[*SERGIUS releases LOUKA.*]

PETKOFF. Well, my dear, it appears that Sergius is going to marry Louka instead of Raina. [*She is about to break out indignantly at him: he stops her by exclaiming testily:*] Dont blame me: Ive nothing to do with it.

[*He retreats to the stove.*]

CATHERINE. Marry Louka! Sergius: you are bound by your word to us!

SERGIUS [*folding his arms*]. Nothing binds me.

BLUNTSCHLI [*much pleased by this piece of common sense*]. Saranoff: your hand. My congratulations. These heroics of yours have their practical side after all. [*to LOUKA*] Gracious young lady: the best wishes of a good Republican!

[*He kisses her hand, to RAINA's great disgust, and returns to his seat.*]

CATHERINE. Louka: you have been telling stories.

LOUKA. I have done Raina no harm.

CATHERINE [*haughtily*]. Raina!

[*RAINA, equally indignant, almost snorts at the liberty.*]

LOUKA. I have a right to call her Raina: she calls me Louka. I told Major Saranoff she would never marry him if the Swiss gentleman came back.

BLUNTSCHLI [*rising, much surprised*]. Hallo!

LOUKA [*turning to RAINA*]. I thought

you were fonder of him than of Sergius. You know best whether I was right.

BLUNTSCHLI. What nonsense! I assure you, my dear major, my dear madame, the gracious young lady simply saved my life, nothing else. She never cared two straws for me. Why, bless my heart and soul, look at the young lady and look at me. She, rich, young, beautiful, with her imagination full of fairy princes and noble natures and cavalry charges and goodness knows what! And I, a commonplace Swiss soldier who hardly knows what a decent life is after fifteen years of barracks and battles: a vagabond, a man who has spoiled all his chances in life through an incurably romantic disposition, a man—

SERGIUS [*starting as if a needle had pricked him and interrupting* BLUNTSCHLI *in incredulous amazement*]. Excuse me, Bluntschli: what did you say had spoiled your chances in life?

BLUNTSCHLI [*promptly*]. An incurably romantic disposition. I ran away from home twice when I was a boy. I went into the army instead of into my father's business. I climbed the balcony of this house when a man of sense would have dived into the nearest cellar. I came sneaking back here to have another look at the young lady when any other man of my age would have sent the coat back—

PETKOFF. My coat!

BLUNTSCHLI.—yes: thats the coat I mean—would have sent it back and gone quietly home. Do you suppose I am the sort of fellow a young girl falls in love with? Why, look at our ages! I'm thirty-four: I dont suppose the young lady is much over seventeen. [*This estimate produces a marked sensation, all the rest turning and staring at one another. He proceeds innocently.*] All that adventure which

was life or death to me, was only a schoolgirl's game to her—chocolate creams and hide and seek. Heres the proof! [*He takes the photograph from the table.*] Now, I ask you, would a woman who took the affair seriously have sent me this and written on it "Raina, to her Chocolate Cream Soldier: a Souvenir"?

[*He exhibits the photograph triumphantly, as if it settled the matter beyond all possibility of refutation.*]

PETKOFF. Thats what I was looking for. How the deuce did it get there?

[*He comes from the stove to look at it, and sits down on the ottoman.*]

BLUNTSCHLI [*to* RAINA, *complacently*]. I have put everything right, I hope, gracious young lady.

RAINA [*going to the table to face him*]. I quite agree with your account of yourself. You are a romantic idiot. [BLUNTSCHLI *is unspeakably taken aback.*] Next time, I hope you will know the difference between a schoolgirl of seventeen and a woman of twenty-three.

BLUNTSCHLI [*stupefied*]. Twenty-three!

[RAINA *snaps the photograph contemptuously from his hand; tears it up; throws the pieces in his face; and sweeps back to her former place.*]

SERGIUS [*with grim enjoyment of his rival's discomfiture*]. Bluntschli: my one last belief is gone. Your sagacity is a fraud, like everything else. You have less sense than even I!

BLUNTSCHLI [*overwhelmed*]. Twenty-three! Twenty-three! [*He considers.*] Hm! [*swiftly making up his mind and coming to his host*] In that case, Major Petkoff, I beg to propose formally to become a suitor for your daughter's hand, in place of Major Saranoff retired.

RAINA. You dare!

BLUNTSCHLI. If you were twenty-three when you said those things to me this afternoon, I shall take them seriously.

CATHERINE [*loftily polite*]. I doubt, sir, whether you quite realize either my daughter's position or that of Major Sergius Saranoff, whose place you propose to take. The Petkoffs and the Saranoffs are known as the richest and most important families in the country. Our position is almost historical: we can go back for twenty years.

PETKOFF. Oh, never mind that, Catherine. [*to* BLUNTSCHLI] We should be most happy, Bluntschli, if it were only a question of your position; but hang it, you know, Raina is accustomed to a very comfortable establishment. Sergius keeps twenty horses.

BLUNTSCHLI. But who wants twenty horses? We're not going to keep a circus.

CATHERINE [*severely*]. My daughter, sir, is accustomed to a first-rate stable.

RAINA. Hush, mother: youre making me ridiculous.

BLUNTSCHLI. Oh well, if it comes to a question of an establishment, here goes! [*He darts impetuously to the table; seizes the papers in the blue envelope; and turns to* SERGIUS.] How many horses did you say?

SERGIUS. Twenty, noble Switzer.

BLUNTSCHLI. I have two hundred horses. [*They are amazed.*] How many carriages?

SERGIUS. Three.

BLUNTSCHLI. I have seventy. Twenty-four of them will hold twelve inside, besides two on the box, without counting the driver and conductor. How many tablecloths have you?

SERGIUS. How the deuce do I know?

BLUNTSCHLI. Have you four thousand?

SERGIUS. No.

BLUNTSCHLI. I have. I have nine thousand six hundred pairs of sheets and blankets, with two thousand four hundred eider-down quilts. I have ten thousand knives and forks, and the same quantity of dessert spoons. I have three hundred servants. I have six palatial establishments, besides two livery stables, a tea garden, and a private house. I have four medals for distinguished services; I have the rank of an officer and the standing of a gentleman; and I have three native languages. Shew me any man in Bulgaria that can offer as much!

PETKOFF [*with childish awe*]. Are you Emperor of Switzerland?

BLUNTSCHLI. My rank is the highest known in Switzerland: I am a free citizen.

CATHERINE. Then, Captain Bluntschli, since you are my daughter's choice—

RAINA [*mutinously*]. He's not.

CATHERINE [*ignoring her*].— I shall not stand in the way of her happiness. [PETKOFF *is about to speak.*] That is Major Petkoff's feeling also.

PETKOFF. Oh, I shall be only too glad. Two hundred horses! Whew!

SERGIUS. What says the lady?

RAINA [*pretending to sulk*]. The lady says that he can keep his tablecloths and his omnibuses. I am not here to be sold to the highest bidder.

[*She turns her back on him.*]

BLUNTSCHLI. I wont take that answer. I appealed to you as a fugitive, a beggar, and a starving man. You accepted me. You gave me your hand to kiss, your bed to sleep in, and your roof to shelter me.

RAINA. I did not give them to the Emperor of Switzerland.

BLUNTSCHLI. Thats just what I say. [*He catches her by the shoulders and turns her face-to-face with him.*] Now tell us whom you did give them to.

RAINA [*succumbing with a shy smile*]. To my chocolate cream soldier.

BLUNTSCHLI [*with a boyish laugh of delight*]. Thatll do. Thank you. [*He looks at his watch and suddenly becomes businesslike.*] Time's up, major. Youve managed those regiments so well that youre sure to be asked to get rid of some of the infantry of the Timok division. Send them home by way of Lom Palanka.

Saranoff: dont get married until I come back: I shall be here punctually at five in the evening on Tuesday fortnight. Gracious ladies [*his heels click*] good evening.

[*He makes them a military bow, and goes.*]

SERGIUS. What a man! Is he a man?

Entertaining Mr. Sloane

A play whose hero beats an old man to death and is then blackmailed by his victim's nymphomaniacal daughter and homosexual son into dividing himself semiannually between them would not at first glance seem destined for comedy. Thus a number of dramatic critics, a bit puzzled by the midcentury vogue of plays featuring spectacular violence and moral decadence, have called up such terms as "dark comedy," "black comedy," and "theater of cruelty" to account for what seems a new dramatic form. Despite crime and immorality, however, *Entertaining Mr. Sloane* is a humorous, even a conventional play—conventional not in the social but in the literary sense, by virtue of Joe Orton's heavy reliance on the traditional elements of comic form.

Although Aristotle assigned crime to tragedy and folly to comedy, comic dramatists, especially those with satiric intentions, have always tended to push human foolishness to the edge of criminality and sometimes over it. For comic crimes to remain comic, however, they need to be insulated against the emotional involvement and moral disapproval of the audience. Therefore they usually take a nonviolent form, eschewing murders and rapes in favor of relieving victims of their money by fraud or of their wives and daughters by ingenious seduction. Like Macheath in Gay's *The Beggar's Opera*, many comic heroes are romantic outlaws who prey on members of the Establishment. What we would not normally approve of in real life the comic vision makes perversely attractive. The hero, though rascally, is after all a lover, and his victims, though respectable, are misers, domestic tyrants, or simply old, which in comedy is very nearly a crime itself. The intrusion of the youthful adventurer into the family circle for money, maiden, or mistress is thus made to suggest a liberation of life and love from the clogs of moral and social inhibitions.

This movement from a closed to an open society is reflected in the overall form of *Entertaining Mr. Sloane,* which is based on the gradual transformation of a household dominated by Kemp and the events of twenty years ago into a freer social grouping centering in the cyclical interchange of the youthful Sloane. The rather unorthodox social adjustment that constitutes the happy ending can come about only when Kemp has been done away with. He stands as a threatening obstacle to the fulfillment of desire, a wintry "superannuated old prat" who is associated (perhaps even in his nearsightedness) with the church and the law, much, for instance, as Malvolio is in Shakespeare's *Twelfth Night.* Malvolio, who winds up being thrust into a dark cell and treated as a madman, is merely one of a long line of Kemp's comic predecessors who pay almost as dearly as he for their anticomic spirit. Not his death perhaps but at least his maltreatment is sanctioned by comic convention. And because of the comic buffers placed around it, even his death does not engage our feelings at a moral level. It is a bit difficult to respond with moral horror to a murder that is immediately preceded by the murderer's tweaking his victim's ear and followed by his saying solicitously

"Wakey, wakey." Despite Sloane's attempts beforehand to menace Kemp, he seems not really to have intended murdering him and, in fact, is very nearly as victimized by the murder as Kemp himself. For these reasons we are inclined to be somewhat indulgent about the murderer's going free at the end of the play. His escape from legal punishment seems more than compensated for when he is reduced to a kind of sexual ping-pong ball to be batted back and forth between Kath and Ed. In a humorously distorted fashion, Orton (1933–1967) has incorporated into his denouement the developments that characterize the endings of both romantic and satiric comedy (see the introduction to comedy). From satiric comedy is derived the idea of punishment catching up with the offender (as in *Tartuffe,* but with a difference), and from romantic comedy an eccentric liberalizing of sexual relations as the traditional boy-wins-girl is transformed into girl-and-boy-win-boy.

That is not to say, however, that *Entertaining Mr. Sloane* is entirely light-hearted. As a satiric commentary on modern British life, it seems to explore a process of moral decline through the three phases from Kemp, to Ed and Kath, to Sloane. The aged Kemp is rigidly puritannical, refusing on moral grounds to speak to Ed for twenty years after catching him "committing some kind of felony." In the next generation, moral and social conventions do not control but instead screen the behavior of Ed and Kath. They are apparently capable of countenancing any kind of conduct in themselves or others so long as it can be filtered through the purifying clichés of respectability. In its most humorous form, their tolerance consists in either refusing to see what they do not want to see or in simply asking to be lied to. And finally, as a member of the third generation, potentially the son of Kath, Sloane is wholly amoral. Making no moral or intellectual distinction between true and false, real and unreal, he can ingenuously admit to anything, no matter how damning, or, on the other hand, lie with perfect ease and grace. In general he specializes in confessions, perhaps because as an orphan in a welfare state he has discovered that all evil can be attributed not to him but to his environment and background ("I need...understanding"; or, "You're bad"—"I'm an orphan"). Thus he is eternally innocent and indeed may well feel so in a society whose major business is to keep him innocent either by sentimentally forgiving or cold-bloodedly discounting what he does.

Entertaining Mr. Sloane

KATH
SLOANE

KEMP
ED

ACT I

A room. Evening. KATH *enters followed by* SLOANE.

KATH. This is my lounge.
SLOANE. Would I be able to use this room? Is it included?
KATH. Oh, yes, [*Pause.*] You mustn't imagine it's always like this. You ought to have rung up or something. And then I'd've been prepared.
SLOANE. The bedroom was perfect.
KATH. I never showed you the toilet.
SLOANE. I'm sure it will be satisfactory.

[*He walks round the room examining the furniture. Stops by the window.*]

KATH. I should change them curtains. Those are our winter ones. The summer ones are more of a chintz. [*Laughs.*] The walls need re-doing. The Dadda has trouble with his eyes. I can't ask him to do any work involving ladders. It stands to reason.

[*Pause.*]

SLOANE. I can't give you a decision right away.
KATH. I don't want you to. [*Pause.*] What do you think? I'd be happy to have you. [*Silence.*]
SLOANE. Are you married?

KATH. [*Pause.*] I was. I had a boy... killed in very sad circumstances. It broke my heart at the time. I got over it though. You do, don't you?

[*Pause.*]

SLOANE. A son?
KATH. Yes.
SLOANE. You don't look old enough.

[*Pause.*]

KATH. I don't let myself go like some of them you may have noticed. I'm just over...As a matter of fact I'm forty-one. [*Pause.*]
SLOANE [*briskly*]. I'll take the room.
KATH. Will you?
SLOANE. I'll bring my things over tonight. It'll be a change from my previous.
KATH. Was it bad?
SLOANE. Bad?
KATH. As bad as that?
SLOANE. You've no idea.
KATH. I don't suppose I have. I've led a sheltered life.
SLOANE. Have you been a widow long?
KATH. Yes a long time. My husband was a mere boy. [*with a half-laugh*] That sounds awful doesn't it?
SLOANE. Not at all.
KATH. I married out of school. I surprised everyone by the suddenness of it. [*Pause.*] Does that sound as if I had to get married.
SLOANE. I'm broadminded.

KATH. I should've known better. You won't breathe a word?

SLOANE. You can trust me.

KATH. My brother would be upset if he knew I told you. [*Pause.*] Nobody knows around here. The people in the nursing home imagined I *was* somebody. I didn't disillusion them.

SLOANE. You were never married then?

KATH. No.

SLOANE. What about—I hope you don't think I'm prying?

KATH. I wouldn't for a minute. What about—?

SLOANE. . . . the father?

KATH. [*Pause.*] We always planned to marry. But there were difficulties. I was very young and he was even younger. I don't believe we would have been allowed.

SLOANE. What happened to the baby?

KATH. Adopted.

SLOANE. By whom?

KATH. That I could not say. My brother arranged it.

SLOANE. What about the kid's father?

KATH. He couldn't do anything.

SLOANE. Why not?

KATH. His family objected. They were very nice but he had a duty you see. [*Pause.*] As I say, if it'd been left to him I'd be his widow today. [*Pause.*] I had a last letter. I'll show you some time. [*Silence.*] D'you like flock or foam rubber in your pillow?

SLOANE. Foam rubber.

KATH. You need a bit of luxury, don't you? I bought the Dadda one but he can't stand them.

SLOANE. I can.

KATH. You'll live with us then as one of the family?

SLOANE. I never had no family of my own.

KATH. Didn't you?

SLOANE. No, I was brought up in an orphanage.

KATH. You have the air of lost wealth.

SLOANE. That's remarkable. My parents, I believe, *were* extremely wealthy people.

KATH. Did Dr. Barnardo give you a bad time?

SLOANE. No. It was the lack of privacy I found most trying. [*Pause.*] And the lack of real love.

KATH. Did you never know your mamma?

SLOANE. Yes.

KATH. When did they die?

SLOANE. I was eight. [*Pause.*] They passed away together.

KATH. How shocking.

SLOANE. I've an idea that they had a suicide pact. Couldn't prove it of course.

KATH. Of course not. [*Pause.*] With a nice lad like you to take care of you'd think they'd've postponed it. [*Pause.*] Criminals, were they?

SLOANE. From what I remember they were respected. You know, H.P. debts. Bridge. A little light gardening. The usual activities of a cultured community. [*Silence.*] I respect their memory.

KATH. Do you? How nice.

SLOANE. Every year I pay a visit to their grave. I take sandwiches. Make a day of it. [*Pause.*] The graveyard is situated in pleasant surroundings so it's no hardship. [*Pause.*] Tomb an' all.

KATH. Marble? [*Pause.*] Is there an inscription?

SLOANE. Perhaps you'd come with me this trip?

KATH. We'll see.

SLOANE. I go in the autumn. I clean the leaves off the monument. As a tribute.

KATH. Any relations?

SLOANE. None.

KATH. Poor boy. Alone in the world. Like me.

SLOANE. You're not alone.

KATH. I am. [*Pause.*] Almost alone. [*Pause.*] If I'd been allowed to keep my boy I'd not be. [*Pause.*] You're almost the same age as he would be. You've got the same refinement.

SLOANE [*slowly*]. I need...understanding.

KATH. You do don't you. Here let me take your coat [*She helps him off with his coat.*] You've got a delicate skin. [*She touches his neck. His cheek. He shudders a little. Pause. She kisses his cheek.*] Just a motherly kiss. A real mother's kiss. [*Silence. She lifts his arms and folds them about her.*] You'll find me very sentimental. I upset easy. [*His arms are holding her.*] When I hear of... tragedies happening to perfect strangers. There are so many ruined lives. [*She puts her head on his shoulder.*] You must treat me gently when I'm in one of my moods.

[*Silence.*]

SLOANE [*clearing his throat*]. How much are you charging? I mean—I've got to know.

[*He drops his arms. She moves away.*]

KATH. We'll come to some arrangement. A cup of tea?

SLOANE. Yes I don't mind.

KATH. I'll get you one.

SLOANE. Can I have a bath?

KATH. Now?

SLOANE. Later would do.

KATH. You must do as you think fit.

[*A door slams.* KEMP'S *voice is heard off.*]

KEMP. You there?

KATH. [*Calls.*] I'm in here. Don't stand about. Sit down. Go on. We don't charge. [SLOANE *sits on the settee.*] That's a lovely shade of blue on your woolley. I'll fetch you one down later that I knitted for my brother.

[KEMP *enters.*]

[*loudly*] We have a visitor, Dadda.

KEMP. Eh?

KATH. A visitor.

[KEMP *stares, lifts his glasses and stares again.*]

KEMP. It's Eddie.

KATH. You are the limit. You show me up no end. It isn't Eddie. [*Pause.*] You behave like a sick child. I'm just about tired of it. Afraid to have a guest or a friend in the house. You put them off, Dadda. Let him shake your hand. Go on.

[KEMP *shakes* SLOANE'S *hand.*]

KEMP. What's he want then?

KATH. Mr. Sloane is going to stay with us.

KEMP. Stay with us?

KATH. That's what I said.

KEMP. He can't. We've no room.

KATH. Make an effort will you? What will the gentleman think? He'll think you're a rude old man. [*She exchanges looks with* SLOANE.] I'm going to have to apologize for your boorish attitude. Do you feel embarrassed, Mr. Sloane?

SLOANE. It's alright.

KATH. No, it isn't. [*to* KEMP] Pull yourself together! [*Silence.*] Can I trust you to behave yourself while I get something to eat? [KEMP *does not answer.*] Entertain Mr. Sloane now. Give him the benefit of your experience. [*Pause.*] You want to learn manners. That's what you want. [*She picks up a basket of provisions from the floor.*] I'm a good mind to give you no tea. [*to* SLOANE] I'd not care to wonder what you must think of us. [*She takes a packet of crumpets from the basket. Hands it to* KEMP.] Here, toast these. Give yourself something to do.

[KATH *exits.* KEMP *goes to fire. Begins to toast crumpets.*]

SLOANE. Haven't we met before?

KEMP. Not to my knowledge.

SLOANE. Your face is familiar. Have I seen your photo in the paper? In connection with some event?

KEMP. No.

SLOANE. Do you pop into the pub at the end of the road?

KEMP. I don't drink.

SLOANE. Are you a churchgoer?

KEMP. Not at the moment. I used to be. In the old days I'd knock up the Vicar at all hours. But then I lost touch.

SLOANE. I've seen you somewhere. I very rarely forget a face.

KEMP. You've got me confused with another person.

SLOANE. Perhaps.

KEMP. Forget it, son. I'm not seen about much.

SLOANE. [*Pause.*] You don't resent my being in the house, do you?

KEMP. Not at all.

SLOANE. I thought you did. Just now.

KEMP. No.

SLOANE. This seems a nice place. Friendly atmosphere. [*Pause.*] How many children have you?

KEMP. Two.

SLOANE. Is your daughter married?

KEMP. She was. Had a terrible time. Kiddy died.

SLOANE. You have a son, don't you?

KEMP. Yes, but we're not on speaking terms.

SLOANE. How long is it?

KEMP. Twenty years.

SLOANE. 'Strewth!

KEMP. You perhaps find that hard to believe?

SLOANE. I do actually. Not speaking for twenty years. That's coming it a bit strong.

KEMP. I may have exchanged a few words.

SLOANE. I can believe that.

KEMP. He was a good boy. Played some amazing games as a youth. Won every goal at football one season. Sport mad, he was. [*Pause.*] Then one day, shortly after his seventeenth birthday, I had cause to return home unexpected and found him committing some kind of felony in the bed-room.

SLOANE. Is that straight?

KEMP. I could never forgive him.

SLOANE. A puritan are you?

KEMP. Yes.

SLOANE. That kind of thing happens often, I believe. For myself I usually lock the door.

KEMP. I'd removed the lock.

SLOANE. Anticipating some such tendencies on his part?

KEMP. I'd done it as a precautionary measure.

SLOANE. There are fascinating possibilities in this situation. I'd get it down on paper if I were you.

[*He goes to the window.*]

KEMP. Admiring the view?

SLOANE. A perfect skyline you've got here. Lord Snowdon would give you something for a shot of that. Stunning it is. Stunning. Was this house a speculation?

KEMP. Not exactly.

SLOANE. Who built it then? Was he a mad financier? The bloke who conceived the idea of building a house in the midst of a rubbish dump?

KEMP. It was intended to be the first of a row.

SLOANE. Go on. What happened?

KEMP. They gave up.

SLOANE. Lost interest?

KEMP. There were financial restrictions.

SLOANE. What a way to carry on!

KEMP. We've tried putting in complaints, but it's no good. Look at it out there. An eyesore. You may admire it. I don't. A woman came all the way from Woolwich yesterday. A special trip she made in order to dump a bedstead. I told her, what do you want to saddle us with your filthy mess for? Came over in a shooting brake. She was an old woman. Had her daughter with her. Fouling the countryside with their litter.

SLOANE. What you want is someone

with pull on the council.

KEMP. If my boss were here I'd go to him.

SLOANE. Wealthy was he?

KEMP. He had holdings in some trust. He didn't go into details with me.

SLOANE. How old was he?

KEMP. Forty.

SLOANE. Early middle age.

KEMP. Yes.

SLOANE. Dead is he?

KEMP. Yes.

SLOANE. Did he die for his country?

KEMP. No. He was murdered. On the unsolved crimes file, he is.

SLOANE. A murderer not brought to justice. That's a sobering thought. [*Pause.*] Why can't they find the murderer? Didn't they advertise?

KEMP. Yes. They took a piece in the local paper.

SLOANE. How long ago was all this?

KEMP. Two years.

SLOANE. Do they have any clue to the murderer's identity?

KEMP. He was a young man with very smooth skin.

SLOANE. [*Pause.*] Was your boss a small man?

KEMP. Yes. Wavy hair. Wore a tweed tie.

SLOANE. What was his profession?

KEMP. He was a photographer. Specialized in views of the river.

SLOANE. You were employed in his service?

KEMP. Yes. As a general handyman. [*Pause.*] We gave the murderer a lift on the night of the crime.

SLOANE. [*Pause.*] You saw him then?

KEMP. Yes.

SLOANE. Why didn't you go to the police?

KEMP. I can't get involved in that type of case. I might get my name in the papers.

SLOANE. I see your point of view. [*Pause.*] They won't find the killer now.

KEMP. I should very much doubt it.

SLOANE. No, the scent's gone cold. [*He watches* KEMP *in silence.*] Have you ever toasted a crumpet before?

KEMP. Yes.

SLOANE. I thought it was your first time from the way you're messing that about. [KEMP *does not reply.*]

KEMP. [*Pause.*] Come here.

SLOANE. Why?

KEMP. I want to look at you.

SLOANE. What for?

KEMP. I think we have met before.

SLOANE. No, Pop. I'm convinced we haven't. I must have been getting you mixed up with a man called Fergusson. He had the same kind of way with him. Trustworthy.

KEMP. You think that?

SLOANE. Yes. [*Laughs.*]

KEMP. [*Pause.*] Fetch me a plate, will you?

SLOANE. Where from?

KEMP. The dresser. Back there.

[SLOANE *goes to the dresser. Fetches a plate. Comes to* KEMP, *bends down to give him the plate.* KEMP *seizes* SLOANE's *arm, pulls him towards him.*]

SLOANE. What's this?

KEMP. We have met before! I knew we had.

SLOANE. I've never met you.

KEMP. On my life. I remember.

SLOANE. Your eyes aren't good.

KEMP. I could still identify you.

SLOANE. [*Pause.*] Identify me?

KEMP. If it was necessary.

SLOANE. How could it be necessary?

KEMP. It might be.

SLOANE. Do lay off, Pop. You couldn't identify a herring on a plate!

KEMP. Don't speak to me like that, sonny. You'll find yourself in trouble.

SLOANE. Go on, you superannuated old prat!

KEMP. I'll have somebody to you. See if I don't. [SLOANE *turns away.*]

SLOANE. Why don't you shut your mouth and give your arse a chance? [KEMP *lunges at* SLOANE *with the toasting fork.* SLOANE *gives a squeal of pain.*] Oh, you bleeding maniac! My leg. My leg.

KEMP. You provoked me!

SLOANE. [*Sinks into an armchair.*] I'll be in a wheelchair for life. [*Examines his leg.*] Oh, you cow. I'm covered in blood! Call somebody! Go on!

[KEMP *goes to the door, shouting:*]

KEMP. Kathy! Kathy!

[KATH *runs on, drying her hands on her apron, sees* SLOANE, *screams.*]

KATH. What've you done?

KEMP. It wasn't intentional. [KEMP *comes forward. She shoos him away.*] Is there pain?

SLOANE. I can't move.

KATH. Are you hurt bad?

SLOANE. He's got an artery. I must be losing pints. Oh, Christ!

KATH. Come on. You'll be better on the settee. [*He allows her to guide him over. She settles him.*] What happened? Did he attack you? He's never shown signs before.

KEMP. I thought he was further off. I can't judge distances.

KATH. Let Mr. Sloane speak for himself.

SLOANE. He ought to be in Colney Hatch. He's a slate off. Throwing things about.

KATH. Throw them did he?

SLOANE. I don't know what he did.

KATH. I'm ashamed of you, Dadda. Really ashamed. I think you behave very badly. Lie down, Mr. Sloane. [*to* KEMP] Go and get the Dettol and some water. Make yourself useful. [KEMP *shuffles off.*] I never realized he was antagonistic to you, Mr. Sloane. Perhaps he's jealous. We were getting on so well. [*Pause.*] Is it hurting you?

SLOANE. Can you get a bandage?

KATH. I will.

[*She goes to the sideboard and rummages in a drawer. Rummages again.*

Repeat. Second drawer. Takes out and places on top of the sideboard a Boots folder containing snapshots and negatives, a reel of cotton, a piece of unfinished knitting, a tattered knitting pattern, a broken china figure, a magazine, a doorknob and several pieces of silk.]

SLOANE [*calling impatiently*]. There's blood running on your settee. You'll have a stain, I can see it coming.

[KATH *runs back with a piece of silk. She lifts his leg. Spreads the silk under the bloody patch.*]

KATH. This'll do. It's a piece of material my brother brought back. It's good stuff. I was intending to make a blouse but there's not enough.

SLOANE. What's he doing with that Dettol? Is he gone to Swansea for it?

KATH [*shouting*]. What are you doing, Dadda? He gets that thick. [*Goes to sideboard.* KEMP *enters with a bottle of Dettol. She takes it from him.*] You done enough damage for one day. Make yourself scarce. [*He shuffles off.*] And don't be eating anything out there.

[*She pushes past him. Returns with a saucepan full of water. After hunting in sideboard finds a torn towel. Comes to* SLOANE. *Kneels.*]

KATH. What a lovely pair of shoes you got.

[*Unlacing his shoes, she takes them off and places them under the settee.*]

SLOANE. I think I'm going to spew. [KATH *hastily holds the saucepan under him.*] No. I'll be alright.

KATH. I wonder, Mr. Sloane, if you'd take your trousers off? I hope you don't think there's anything behind the request. [*She looks at him. He unloosens his belt.*] I expect you guessed as much before I asked. If you'll lift up I'll pull them off. [*She tugs the trousers free. SLOANE tucks the tail of his shirt between his legs.*] That's right. [*Pause.*] Where is it then?

SLOANE. Here.

[*Pointing and lifting his leg.*]

KATH. He attacked you from behind? If you ask me it's only a deep scratch. [*Pause.*] I don't think we require outside assistance. [*Pause.*] Don't be embarrassed, Mr. Sloane. I'd the upbringing a nun would envy and that's the truth. Until I was fifteen I was more familiar with Africa than my own body. That's why I'm so pliable. [*Applies Dettol.*]

SLOANE. Ouch!

KATH. Just the thing for the germs. [*Pause.*] You've a skin on you like a princess. Better than on those tarts you see dancing about on the telly. Don't mind me saying so. [*Pause.*] I like a lad with a smooth body. [*Stops dabbing his leg. Takes up the bandage. Rises. Fetches a pair of scissors. Cuts bandage. Ties it round SLOANE's leg.*] Isn't it strange that the hairs on your legs should be dark?

SLOANE. Eh?

KATH. Attractive though.

SLOANE. Dark?

KATH. Yes. You being a blond.

SLOANE. Oh, yes.

KATH. Nature's a funny thing.

[*Ring on the doorbell.*]

SLOANE. Who's that?

KATH. Keep your voice down. [*Pause.*] It's probably her from the shops. I'll not answer it. She's only got one subject for talk.

SLOANE. She'll hear.

KATH. Not if you keep your voice down. [*Prolonged ringing.*]

SLOANE. What about Pop?

KATH. He won't answer. I don't want her in here. She tells everybody her business. And if she found me in this predicament she'd think all kinds of things. [*Pause.*] Her daughter's involved in a court case at the moment. Tells every detail. The details are endless. I suffer as she recounts. Oh, Mr. Sloane, if I'd only been born without ears. [*Silence. She finishes tying the bandages and squats on her haunches looking up at him. Pause.*] Is that bandage too tight?

SLOANE. No.

KATH. I wouldn't want to restrict your circulation.

SLOANE. It's O.K.

[*She picks up his trousers.*]

KATH. I'll sponge these, and there's a nick in the material. I'll fix it. [*She puts Dettol, bandage, etc. into the sideboard.*] This drawer is my medicine cabinet, dear. If you want an occasional aspirin help yourself. [*She comes back. He lies full length; she smiles. Silence. Confidentially.*] I've been doing my washing today and I haven't a stitch on...except my shoes...I'm in the rude under this dress. I tell you because you're bound to have noticed...[*Silence. SLOANE attempts to reach his trouser pocket.*] Don't move, dear. Not yet. Give the blood time to steady itself. [*SLOANE takes a nylon stocking from between cushions of settee.*] I wondered where I'd left it.

SLOANE. Is it yours?

KATH. Yes. You'll notice the length? I've got long legs. Long, elegant legs. [*She kicks out her leg.*] I could give one or two of them a surprise. [*Pause.*] My look is quite different when I'm in private. [*She leans over him.*] You can't see through this dress can you? I been worried for fear of embarrassing you. [*SLOANE lifts his hand and touches the point where he judges her nipple to be. She leaps back.*] Mr. Sloane—don't betray your trust.

SLOANE. I just thought—

KATH. I know what you thought. You wanted to see if my titties were all my own. You're all the same. [*Smirks.*] I must be careful of you. Have me naked on the floor if I give you a chance. If my brother was to know . . . [*Pause.*] . . . he's such a possessive man. [*Silence. She stands up.*] Would you like to go to bed?

SLOANE. It's early.

KATH. You need rest. You've had a shock. [*Pause.*] I'll bring your supper to your room.

SLOANE. What about my case?

KATH. The Dadda will fetch it. [*Pause.*] Can you get up the stairs on your own?

SLOANE. Mmmmm.

[*She motions him back. Stands in front of him.*]

KATH. Just a minute. [*Calls.*] Dadda! [*Pause.*] Dadda!

[KEMP *appears in the doorway.*]

KEMP. What?

KATH. Turn your face away. Mr. Sloane is passing. He has no trousers on. [*quietly to* SLOANE] You know the room?

SLOANE. Yes.

[*Silence.* SLOANE *exits.*]

KATH [*calling after him*]. Have a bath if you want to, dear. Treat the conveniences as if they were your own. [*Turns to* KEMP.] I want an explanation.

KEMP. Yes. Kathy . . .

KATH. Don't Kathy me.

KEMP. But he upset me.

KATH. Upset you? A grown man?

KEMP. I've seen him before.

KATH. You've seen the milkman before. That's no cause to thrown the shears at him.

KEMP. I didn't throw them.

KATH. Oh? I heard different. [*She picks

up her handbag and takes out money.*] Go and fetch his case. It'll be about 5d. on the bus. [*Presses the money into his hand.*] The address is 39 St. Hilary's Crescent.

KEMP. Where's that?

KATH [*losing her temper*]. By the Co-op! Behave yourself.

KEMP. A teetotal club on the corner is there?

KATH. That's the one. Only it closed. [*Pause.*] Can you find it?

KEMP. I expect so.

[*There is a noise of tapping.* KATH *goes to the window.*]

KATH [*over her shoulder*]. It's Eddie.

KEMP. What's that?

KATH [*speaking to someone outside*]. Why don't you come round the right way?

ED [*outside the window*]. I rang the bell but you was out.

KATH. Are you coming in?

ED. I'll be round.

[*She closes the window.*]

KATH. It's Eddie.

KEMP. I'm not going to talk to him!

KATH. I don't expect he wants you to.

KEMP. He knows I'm in always on Friday. [*Pause.*] I'm signing nothing you can tell him that.

KATH. Tell him what?

KEMP. That I'm not signing nothing.

ED [*entering*]. Is he still on about that? What's the matter with you? [KEMP *does not reply.*] Always on about something.

KEMP. I'm not speaking to him.

ED [*patiently*]. Go on, get out of it afore I kicks you out. Make me bad you do. With your silly, childish ways. [KEMP *does not reply.*]

KATH. Do what I told you, Dadda. Try not to lose yourself. Follow the railings. Then ask somebody.

[KEMP *exits.* KATH *dips towel in saucepan, begins to sponge bloody patch on *settee.* ED *watches her. Takes a drag of his cigarette.*]

ED. What's this I heard about you?

KATH. What?

ED. Listening are you?

KATH. Yes, Eddie, I'm listening.

ED. You've got a kid staying here.

KATH. No...

ED. Don't lie to me.

KATH. He's a guest. He's not a lodger.

ED. Who told you to take in lodgers?

[*Pause.*]

KATH. I needed a bit extra.

ED. I'll give you the money.

KATH. I'm taking Dadda away next year. [*Pause.*]

ED. I don't want men hanging around.

KATH. He's a nice young man.

ED. You know what these fellows are— young men with no fixed abode.

KATH. No.

ED. You know what they say about landladies?

KATH. No, Eddie.

ED. They say they'd sleep with a broom handle in trousers; that's what they say.

KATH [*uneasy*]. I'm not like that.

ED. You're good-natured though. They mistake it.

KATH. This young man is quite respectable.

ED. You've got to realize my position. I can't have my sister keeping a common kip. Some of my associates are men of distinction. They think nothing of tipping a fiver. That sort of person. If they realized how my family carry on I'd be banned from the best places. [*Pause.*] And another thing...you don't want them talking about you. An' I can't guarantee my influence will keep them quiet. Nosey neighbours and scandal. Oh, my word, the looks you'll get. [*Pause.*] How old is he?

KATH. He's young.

ED. These fellows sleep with their land-ladies automatic. Has he made suggestions? Suggested you bring him supper in bed?

KATH. No.

ED. That's what they do. Then they take advantage.

KATH. Mr. Sloane is superior to that.

ED. Where did you find him?

KATH. In the library.

ED. Picked him up, did you?

KATH. He was having trouble. With his rent. [*Pause.*] His landlady was unscrupulous.

ED. How long have you been going with him?

KATH. He's a good boy. [ED *sees trousers, picks them up.*] It was an accident.

ED. Had the trousers off him already I see. [*He balls his fist and punches her upper arm gently.*] Don't let me down, darlin'. [*Pause.*] Where is he?

KATH. Upstairs.

ED. You fetch him.

KATH. He hurt his leg.

ED. I want to see him.

KATH. He's resting. [*Pause.*] Ed, you won't tell him to go?

ED [*brushing her aside*]. Go and fetch him.

KATH. I'm not misbehaving. Ed, if you send him away I shall cry.

ED [*raising his voice*]. Let's have less of it. I'll decide. [*She exits. He calls after her.*] Tell him to put his trousers on. [*Picks up trousers and flings them after her.*] Cantering around the house with a bare bum. Good job I come when I did. [*Pause.*] Can't leave you alone for five minutes.

KATH [*off*]. Mr. Sloane! Would you step down here for a minute? My brother would like to meet you. [*Re-enters.*] He's trustworthy. Visits his parents once a month. Asked me to go with him. You couldn't object to a visit to a graveyard? The sight of the tombs would deter any looseness. [*She sniffs. Shrugs. Picks through the junk on the sideboard, finds a sweet and puts in in her mouth.*] He hasn't any mamma of his own. I'm to be his mamma. He's an orphan. Eddie, he wouldn't do wrong. Please don't send him away.

ED. It'd crease me if you misbehaved again. I got responsibilities.

KATH. Let him stay.

ED. Kid like that. Know what they'll say don't you? [*Pause.*]

KATH. He's cultured, Ed. He's informed. [ED *turns and lights another cigarette from the butt of the one he is smoking. Opens the window. Throws the butt out.* SLOANE *enters.*] This is my brother, Mr. Sloane. He expressed a desire to meet you.

[ED *turns, faces* SLOANE.]

ED. I...my sister was telling me about you. [*Pause.*] My sister was telling me about you being an orphan, Mr. Sloane.

SLOANE [*smiling*]. Oh, yes?

ED. Must be a rotten life for a kid. You look well on it though.

SLOANE. Yes.

ED. I could never get used to sleeping in cubicles. Was it a mixed home?

SLOANE. Just boys.

ED. Ideal. How many to a room?

SLOANE. Eight.

ED. Really? Same age were they? Or older?

SLOANE. The ages varied by a year or two.

ED. Oh well, you had compensations then. Keep you out of mischief, eh? [*Laughs.*] Well your childhood wasn't unhappy?

SLOANE. No.

ED. Sounds as though it was a happy atmosphere. [*Pause.*] Got anything to do, Kath?

KATH. No.

ED. No beds to make?

KATH. I made them this morning.

ED. Maybe you forgot to change the pillowslips?

KATH [*going*]. Eddie don't let me be

upset will you.   [*She exits.*]

ED. I must apologize for her behaviour. She's not in the best of health.

SLOANE. She seems all right.

ED. You can't always go on appearances. She's...well I wouldn't say unbalanced. No, that'd be going too far. She suffers from migraine. That's why it'd be best if you declined her offer of a room.

SLOANE. I see.

ED. When are you going?

SLOANE. But I like it here.

ED. I daresay you do. The fact is my sister's taking on too many responsibilities. She's a charming woman as a rule. Charming. I've no hesitation in saying that. Lost her husband. And her little kid. Tell you did she?

SLOANE. She mentioned it.

ED [*wary*]. What did she say?

SLOANE. Said she married young.

ED. She married a mate of mine—a valiant man—we were together in Africa.

SLOANE. In the army?

ED. You're interested in the army, eh? Soldiers, garrison towns, etc. Does that interest you?

SLOANE. Yes.

ED. Good, excellent. How old are you?

SLOANE. Seventeen.

ED. Married?

SLOANE. No.

ED. [*Laughs.*] Wise man, eh? Wise man. [*Pause.*] Girl friends?

SLOANE. No.

ED. No. You're a librarian?

SLOANE. No.

ED. I thought she said—

SLOANE. I help out at Len's...the tobacconist. Give him a hand. I'm not employed there.

ED. I was told you were.

SLOANE. I help out. On Saturdays.

ED. I see. I've been mistaken. [*Silence.*] Well, as I just said...I don't think it'd suit you. What with one thing and another. [*Pause.*] To show there's no hard feelings I'll make it worth your while. Call it a gift.

SLOANE. That's decent of you.

ED. Not at all. [*Pause.*] I'd like to give you a little present. Anything you care to name. Within reason.

SLOANE. What's within reason?

ED. [*Laughs.*] Well . . . no . . . Jags. [*Laughs.*]...no sports cars. I'm not going as far as that.

SLOANE [*relaxing*]. I was going to suggest an Aston Martin.

[ED *walks from the window looking for an ashtray. He does not find one.*]

ED. I wish I could give you one, boy. I wish I could. [*He stubs out his cigarette into a glass seashell on the sideboard.*] Are you a sports fan? Eh? Fond of sport? You look as though you might be. Look the— outdoor type, I'd say.

SLOANE. I am.

ED. I'd say you were. That's what struck me when you walked in. That's what puzzled me. She gave me the impression you were...well, don't be offended...I had the notion you were a shop assistant.

SLOANE. Never worked in a shop in my life.

ED. No. [*Pause.*] I see you're not that type. You're more of a...as you might say...the fresh air type.

SLOANE. I help out on Saturdays for a mate of mine. Len. You might know him. Lifeguard at the baths one time. Nice chap.

ED. You're fond of swimming?

SLOANE. I like a plunge now and then.

ED. Bodybuilding?

SLOANE. We had a nice little gym at the orphanage. Put me in all the teams they did. Relays...[ED *looks interested.*]...soccer...[ED *nods.*]... pole vault,...long distance...[ED *opens his mouth.*]...hundred yards, discus, putting the shot. [ED *rubs his hands together.*] Yes, yes. I'm an all rounder. A great all rounder. In anything you care to mention. Even in

life. [ED *lifts up a warning finger.*] ...yes I like a good work out now and then.

ED. I used to do a lot of that at one time. With my mate...we used to do all what you've just said. [*Pause.*] We were young. Innocent too. [*Shrugs. Pats his pocket. Takes out a packet of cigarettes. Smokes.*] All over now. [*Pause.*] Developing your muscles, eh? And character. [*Pause.*] I...well, well. [*breathless*] A little body-builder are you? I bet you are ...[*slowly*]...do you...[*shy*] exercise regular?

SLOANE. As clockwork.

ED. Good, good. Stripped?

SLOANE. Fully.

ED. Complete. [*striding to the window*] How invigorating.

SLOANE. And I box. I'm a bit of a boxer.

ED. Ever done any wrestling?

SLOANE. On occasions.

ED. So, so.

SLOANE. I've got a full chest. Narrow hips. My biceps are—

ED. Do you wear leather...next to the skin? Leather jeans, say? Without... aah...

SLOANE. Pants?

ED. [*Laughs.*] Get away! [*Pause.*] The question is are you clean living? You may as well know I set great store by morals. Too much of this casual bunking up nowadays. Too many lads being ruined by birds. I don't want you messing about with my sister.

SLOANE. I wouldn't.

ED. Have you made overtures to her?

SLOANE. No.

ED. Would you?

SLOANE. No.

ED. Not if circumstances were ripe?

SLOANE. Never.

ED. Does she disgust you?

SLOANE. Should she?

ED. It would be better if she did, boy. Women are like banks, breaking and entering is a serious business.

SLOANE. I've no interest in her. [*Pause.*]

ED. I've a certain amount of influence. Friends with money. I've two cars. Judge for yourself. I generally spend my holidays in places where the bints have got rings through their noses. [*Pause.*] Give me your word you're not vaginolatrous?

SLOANE. I'm not.

ED. [*Pause.*] I'll believe you. Can you drive?

SLOANE. Yes.

ED. I might let you be my chauffeur.

SLOANE. Would you?

ED. [*Laughs.*] We'll see...I could get you a uniform. Boots, pants, a guaranteed hundred per cent no imitation jacket...an...er...a white brushed nylon teeshirt...with a little leather cap. [*Laughs.*] Like that? [SLOANE *nods. Silence.*] Kip here a bit. Till we get settled. Come and see me. We'll discuss salary arrangements and any other business. Here's my card. [*He gives* SLOANE *a card.*] Have you seen my old dad? Wonderful for his age. [*Pause.*] Call her in will you? [SLOANE *exits.*]

SLOANE [*off*]. I think you're wanted.

[*Re-enters.*]

ED. You'll find me a nice employer. [*Pause.*] When you come to see me we must have a drink. A talk.

SLOANE. What about?

ED. Life. Sport. Love. Anything you care to name. Don't forget.

SLOANE. I'm looking forward to it.

ED. Do you drink?

SLOANE. When I'm not in training.

ED. You aren't in training at the moment, are you?

SLOANE. No.

ED. I wouldn't want you to break your training. Drinking I don't mind. Drugs I abhor. You'll get to know all my habits.

[KATH *enters.*]

KATH. What do you want?

ED. A word with you afore I go.

KATH. Are you staying, Mr. Sloane?

ED. 'Course he's staying.

KATH. Alright is it?

ED. He's going to work for me.

KATH. [*Pause.*] He isn't going away is he?

ED. Offered him a job I have. I want a word with my sister, Sloane. Would you excuse us?

[SLOANE *nods, smiles and turns to go.*]

KATH [*as he exits*]. Have a meal, Mr. Sloane. You'll find a quarter of boiled ham. Help yourself. You better have what's left 'cause I see he's been wolfing it. An' you heard me ask him to wait di'n't you? I told him.

[*Exit* SLOANE. *Silence.*]

ED. You picked a nice lad there. Very nice. Clean. No doubt upright. A sports enthusiast. All the proper requisites. Don't take any money from him. I'll pay.

KATH. Can I buy him a shirt?

ED. What do you want to do that for?

KATH. His own mamma can't.

ED. He can buy his own clothes. Making yourself look ridiculous. [*Pause.*]

KATH. When it's Christmas can I buy him a little gift?

ED. No.

KATH. Send him a card?

ED. Why?

KATH. I'd like to. I'd show you beforehand. [*Pause.*] Can I go to his mamma's grave?

ED. If you want. [*Pause.*] He'll laugh at you.

KATH. He wouldn't, Eddie. [*Silence.*]

ED. I must go. I'll have a light meal. Take a couple of nembutal and then bed. I shall be out of town tomorrow.

KATH. Where?

ED. In Aylesbury. I shall dress in a quiet suit. Drive up in the motor. The Commissionaire will spring forward. There in that miracle of glass and concrete my colleagues and me will have a quiet drink before the business of the day.

KATH. Are your friends nice?

ED. Mature men.

KATH. No ladies? [*Pause.*]

ED. What are you talking about? I live in a world of top decisions. We've not time for ladies.

KATH. Ladies are nice at a gathering.

ED. We don't want a lot of half-witted tarts.

KATH. They add colour and gaiety.

ED. Frightening everyone with their clothes. [*Pause.*]

KATH. I hope you have a nice time. Perhaps one day you'll invite me to your hotel.

ED. I might.

KATH. Show me round.

ED. Yes.

KATH. Is it exquisitely furnished? High up?

ED. Very high. I see the river often. [*A door slams.*] Persuade the old man to speak to me.

KEMP [*off*]. Is he gone?

KATH. Speak to him Dadda. He's something to ask you. [*Silence.*]

ED [*petulant*]. Isn't it incredible! I'm his only son. He won't see me. [*He goes to the door. Speaks through.*] I want a word with you. [*Pause.*] Is he without human feelings? [*Pause. Brokenly.*] He won't speak to me. Has he no heart?

KATH. Come again.

ED. I'll get my lawyer to send a letter. If it's done legal he'll prove amenable. Give us a kiss. [*He kisses her. Pats her bottom.*] Be a good girl now.

[*Exit.*]

KATH. Cheerio. [*Pause.*] I said Cheerio. [*Door slams. KATH goes to door.*] Why don't you speak to him?

[KEMP *enters. He does not reply.*]

He invited me to his suite. The luxury takes your breath away.

Money is no object. A waitress comes with the tea. [*Pause.*] I'm going to see him there one day. Speak to him Dadda.

KEMP. No.

KATH. Please.

KEMP. Never.

KATH. Let me phone saying you changed your mind.

KEMP. No.

KATH. Let me phone.

KEMP. No.

KATH [*tearfully*]. Oh, Dadda, you are unfair. If you don't speak to him, he won't invite me to his suite. It's a condition. I won't be able to go. You found that address?

KEMP. I got lost, though.

KATH. Why didn't you ask? [*Pause.*] You had a tongue in your head. Oh, Dadda, you make me so angry with your silly ways. [*Pause.*] What was the house like?

KEMP. I didn't notice.

KATH. He said it was a hovel. A boy like him shouldn't be expected to live with the rougher elements. Do you know, Dadda, he has skin the like of which I never felt before. And he confesses to being an orphan. His story is so sad. I wept when I heard it. You know how soft-hearted I am.

[*Silence.*]

KEMP. I haven't been feeling well lately.

KATH. No. Have you seen the optician?

KEMP. My eyes are getting worse, much worse!

KATH. Without a word of a lie you are like a little child.

KEMP. I'm all alone.

KATH. You have me.

KEMP. He may take you away.

KATH. Where to?

KEMP. Edinburgh.

KATH. Too cold.

KEMP. Or Bournemouth. You always said you'd go somewhere with palms.

KATH. I'd always consult you first.

KEMP. You'd put me in a home. [*Pause.*] Would you be tempted?

[*Silence.*]

KATH. You ought to consult an oculist. See your oculist at once. [*Pause.*] Go to bed. I'll bring you a drinkie. In the morning you'll feel different.

KEMP. You don't love me.

KATH. I've never stopped loving you.

KEMP. I'm going to die, Kath...I'm dying.

KATH [*angrily*]. You've been at that ham haven't you? Half a jar of pickles you've put away. Don't moan to me if you're up half the night with the tummy ache. I've got no sympathy for you.

KEMP. Goodnight then.

[*She watches him out of the door. Looks through into the kitchen.*]

KATH. Alright, Mr. Sloane? Help yourself...alright?

[*She comes back into the room. Takes table lamp and puts it on to small table beside settee. Switches it on. Pulls window curtains shut. Switches on gramophone. Pulls curtains in alcove and disappears behind them. The gramophone is heard playing, suddenly the needle slips over a groove, cuts across the record. The automatic change switches record off. KATH pokes her head from behind curtain and stares at gramophone. Disappears again. She can be heard singing. She comes from behind curtain dressed in a thin negligee. Picks up aerosol spray, sprays room. Goes to door.*]

KATH. Have you finished, Mr. Sloane, dear?

SLOANE [*off*]. Ugh.

KATH. You have? I'm so glad. I don't want to disturb you at your food. Come into the lounge if you wish.

[*She sees the knitting on the sideboard, puts down aerosol spray, picks up knitting.*]

KATH. I'm just at a quiet bit of knitting before I go to bed. [SLOANE *enters, wiping his mouth.*] A lovely piece of ham, wasn't it?

SLOANE. Lovely.

KATH. I'll give you a splendid breakfast in the morning. [*She realizes that there is only one needle in the knitting. Searches in the junk and finds the other. Takes it to the settee. SLOANE sits on one end. Pause.*] Isn't this room gorgeous?

SLOANE. Yes.

KATH. That vase over there comes from Bombay. Do you have any interest in that part of the world?

SLOANE. I like Dieppe.

KATH. Ah...it's all the same. I don't suppose they know the difference themselves. Are you comfortable? Let me plump your cushion. [*She plumps a cushion behind his head. Laughs lightly.*] I really by rights should ask you to change places. This light is showing me up. [*Pause.*] I blame it on the manufacturers. They make garments so thin nowadays you'd think they intended to provoke a rape. [*Pause.*] Sure you're comfy?

[*She leans over him.* SLOANE *pulls her hand towards him. She laughs, half in panic.*]

SLOANE. You're a teaser 'ent you?

[*She breaks away.*]

KATH. I hope I'm not. I was trying to find the letter from my little boy's father. I treasure it. But I seem to have mislaid it. I found a lot of photos though.

SLOANE. Yes.

KATH. Are you interested in looking through them?

[*She brings the snapshots over.*]

SLOANE. Are they him?

KATH. My lover.

SLOANE. Bit blurred.

KATH. It brings back memories. He reminds me of you. [*Pause.*] He too was handsome and in the prime of manhood. Can you wonder I fell. [*Pause.*] I wish he were here now to love and protect me. [*She leans her arm on his shoulder. Shows him another snap.*] This is me. I was young then.

SLOANE. Smart.

KATH. Yes my hair was nice.

SLOANE. Yes.

KATH. An' this . . . I don't know whether I ought to let you see it. [SLOANE *attempts to seize it.*] Now then! [*He takes it from her.*]

SLOANE. A seat in a wood?

KATH. That seat is erected to the memory of Mrs. Gwen Lewis. She was a lady who took a lot of trouble with invalids. [*Pause.*] It was near that seat that my baby was thought of.

SLOANE. On that seat?

KATH [*shyly*]. Not on it exactly. Nearby . . .

SLOANE. In the bushes? . . . [*She giggles.*]

KATH. Yes. [*Pause.*] He was rough with me.

SLOANE. Uncomfortable, eh?

KATH. I couldn't describe my feelings. [*Pause.*] I don't think the fastening on this thing I'm wearing will last much longer. [*The snapshots slip from her hand.*] There! You've knocked the photos on the floor. [*Pause; he attempts to move; she is almost on top of him.*] Mr. Sloane . . . [*She rolls on to him.*] You should wear more clothes, Mr. Sloane. I believe you're as naked as me. And there's no excuse for it. [*Silence.*] I'll be your mamma. I need to be loved. Gently. Oh! I shall be so ashamed in the morning. [*She switches off the light.*] What a big heavy baby you are. Such a big heavy baby.

ACT II

Some months later. Morning. SLOANE *is lying on the settee. A newspaper covers his face.* KATH *enters. Looks at the settee.*

SLOANE. Where you been?

KATH. Shopping, dear. Did you want me?

SLOANE. I couldn't find you.

[KATH *goes to the window. Takes off her headscarf.*]

KATH. What's Eddie doing?

SLOANE. A bit of servicing.

KATH. But that's your job. [SLOANE *removes the newspaper.*] He shouldn't do your work.

SLOANE. I was on the beer. My guts is playing up.

KATH. Poor boy. [*Pause.*] Go and help him. For mamma's sake.

SLOANE. I may in a bit.

KATH. He's a good employer. Studies your interests. You want to think of his position. He's proud of it. Now you're working for him his position is your position. [*Pause.*] Go and give him a hand.

SLOANE. No.

KATH. Are you too tired?

SLOANE. Yes.

KATH. We must make allowances for you. You're young. [*Pause.*] You're not taking advantage are you?

SLOANE. No.

KATH. I know you aren't. When you've had a drinkie go and help him.

SLOANE. If you want. [*Pause.*]

KATH. Did mamma hear you were on the razzle.

SLOANE. Yes.

KATH. Did you go up West? You were late coming home. [*Pause.*] Very late.

SLOANE. Three of my mates and me had a night out.

KATH. Are they nice boys?

SLOANE. We have interests in common.

KATH. They aren't roughs are they? Mamma doesn't like you associating with them.

SLOANE. Not on your life. They're gentle. Refined youths. Thorpe, Beck and Doolan. We toured the nighteries in the motor.

KATH. Was Ed with you?

SLOANE. No.

KATH. Did you ask him? He would have come.

SLOANE. He was tired. A hard day yesterday.

KATH. Ask him next time. [*Pause.*]

SLOANE. We ended up at a fabulous place. Soft music, pink shades, lovely atmosphere.

KATH. I hope you behaved yourself.

SLOANE. One of the hostesses give me her number. Told me to ring her.

KATH. Take no notice of her. She might not be nice.

SLOANE. Not nice?

KATH. She might be a party girl.

[*Pause.*]

SLOANE. What exactly do you mean?

KATH. Mamma worries for you.

SLOANE. You're attempting to run my life.

KATH. Is baby cross?

SLOANE. You're developing distinctly possessive tendencies.

KATH. You can get into trouble saying that.

SLOANE. A possessive woman.

KATH. A mamma can't be possessive.

SLOANE. Can't she?

KATH. You know she can't. You're being naughty.

SLOANE. Never heard of a possessive mum?

KATH. Stop it. It's rude. Did she teach you to say that?

SLOANE. What?

KATH. What you just said. [SLOANE *makes no reply*.] You're spoiling yourself in my eyes, Mr. Sloane. You won't ring this girl will you?

SLOANE. I haven't decided.

KATH. Decide now. To please me. I don't know what you see in these girls. You have your friends for company.

SLOANE. They're boys.

KATH. What's wrong with them? You can talk freely. Not like with a lady.

SLOANE. I don't want to talk [*Pause.*]

KATH. She might be after your money.

SLOANE. I haven't got any.

KATH. But Eddie has. She might be after his.

SLOANE. Look, you're speaking of a very good class bird.

KATH. I have to protect you, baby, because you're easily led.

SLOANE. I like being led. [*Pause.*] I need to be let out occasionally. Off the lead. [*Pause.*]

KATH. She'll make you ill.

SLOANE. Shut it. [*Pause.*] Make me ill!

KATH. Girls do.

SLOANE. How dare you. Making filthy insinuations. I won't have it. You disgust me you do. Standing there without your teeth. Why don't you get smartened up? Get a new rig-out.

[*Pause.*]

KATH. Do I disgust you?

SLOANE. Yes.

KATH. Honest?

SLOANE. And truly. You horrify me. [*Pause.*] You think I'm kidding. I'll give up my room if you don't watch out.

KATH. Oh, no!

SLOANE. Clear out.

KATH. Don't think of such drastic action. I'd never forgive myself if I drove you away. [*Pause.*] I won't any more. [*He attempts to rise.* KATH *takes his hand.*] Don't go dear. Stay with me while I collect myself. I've been upset and I need comfort. [*Silence.*] Are you still disgusted?

SLOANE. A bit.

[*She takes his hand, presses it to her lips.*]

KATH. Sorry, baby. Better?

SLOANE. Mmmm. [*Silence.*]

KATH. How good you are to me.

KEMP. [*Enters. He carries a stick. Taps his way to the sideboard.*] My teeth, since you mentioned the subject, Mr. Sloane, are in the kitchen in Stergene. Usually I allow a good soak overnight. But what with one thing and another I forgot. Otherwise I would never be in such a state. [*Pause.*] I hate people who are careless with their dentures. [*Opens a drawer.*] Seen my tablets?

KATH. If you're bad go to bed.

KEMP. I need one a my pills.

[*He picks his way through the junk.* SLOANE *goes over to him.*]

SLOANE. What you want?

KEMP. Let me alone.

SLOANE. Tell me what you want.

KEMP. I don't want no help. [*Pause.*] I'm managing.

SLOANE. Let me know what you want and I'll look for it.

KEMP. I can manage.

[SLOANE *goes back to the settee. Silence.*]

KATH. What a lot of foreigners there are about lately. I see one today. Playing the accordion. They live in a world of their own these people.

KEMP. Coloured?

KATH. No.

KEMP. I expect he was. They do come over here. Raping people. It's a problem. Just come out a jail had he?

KATH. I really didn't stop long enough

to ask. I just commented on the tune he was playing.

KEMP. Oh, they're all for that.

[KATH *leans over* SLOANE.]

KATH. Mamma has something special to say to you.

SLOANE. All for that. [SLOANE *touches her hair.*] What?

KATH [*to* KEMP *louder*]. I don't think he was dark enough to be coloured, Dadda. Honestly I don't.

KEMP. They should send them back.

SLOANE. What's your news?

KATH. Can't you guess?

SLOANE. No.

KATH. I know you can't.

KEMP. You should've put in a complaint.

KATH. Oh, no Dadda.

KEMP. Playing his bloody music in the street.

KATH. What language! You should be a splendid example to us. Instead of which you carry on like a common workman. Don't swear like that in my presence again.

[*Silence.* SLOANE *attempts to grab her shopping bag. She rises.* SLOANE *touches her up. She grunts. Smacks his hand.*]

KEMP. What's up?

KATH. Nothing. Aren't the tulips glorious this year by the municipal offices? What a brave showing. They must spend a fortune.

SLOANE. What have you brought me?

KATH. Mamma is going to have a . . .

[*Makes a rocking motion with her arms.*]

SLOANE. What? [*Pause.*] What?

KATH. A little—[*Looks over to* KEMP. *Makes the motion of rocking a baby in her arms. Purses her lips. Blows a kiss.* SLOANE *sits up. Points to himself. She nods her head. Presses her mouth to his ear; whispers.*] A baby brother.

KEMP. What are you having?

KATH. A...bath, Dadda. You know that woman from the shops? [*Pause.*] You wouldn't believe what a ridiculous spectacle she's making of herself.

KEMP. Oh.

KATH [*to* SLOANE]. 'Course it's ever so dangerous at my age. But doctor thinks it'll be alright.

SLOANE. Sure?

KATH. I was worried in case you'd be cross.

SLOANE. We mustn't let anyone know.

KATH. It's our secret. [*Pause.*] I'm excited.

KEMP. Are you having it after tea, Kath?

KATH. Why?

KEMP. I thought of having one as well. Are you there?

KATH. Yes.

KEMP. Have you seen them pills?

KATH. Have I seen his pills? They're where you left them I expect. [*She goes to the sideboard. Finds bottle. Gives it to* KEMP.] How many you had today?

KEMP. Two.

KATH. They're not meant to be eaten like sweets you know.   [*He exits.*] I been to the Register Office.

SLOANE. What for?

KATH. To enquire about the licence.

SLOANE. Who?

KATH. You.

SLOANE. Who to?

KATH. Me. Don't you want to? You wouldn't abandon me? Leave me to face the music.

SLOANE. What music?

KATH. When Eddie hears.

SLOANE. He mustn't hear.

KATH. Baby, how can we stop him?

SLOANE. He'd kill me. I'd be out of a job.

KATH. I suppose we couldn't rely on him employing you any longer.

SLOANE. Don't say anything. I'll see a man I know.

KATH. What? But I'm looking forward to having a new little brother.

SLOANE. Out of the question.

KATH. Please...

SLOANE. No. In any case I couldn't marry you. I'm not the type. And all things being equal I may not be living here much longer.

KATH. Aren't you comfy in your bed?

SLOANE. Yes.

[KATH *folds her arms round him. Kisses his head.*]

KATH. We could marry in secret. Couldn't you give me something, baby? So's I feel in my mind we were married.

SLOANE. What like?

KATH. A ring. Or a bracelet. You got a nice locket. I noticed it. Make me a present of that.

SLOANE. I can't do that.

KATH. As a token of your esteem. So's I feel I belong to you.

SLOANE. It belonged to my mum.

KATH. I'm your mamma now.

SLOANE. No.

KATH. Go on.

SLOANE. But it was left to me.

KATH. You mustn't cling to old memories. I shall begin to think you don't love mamma.

SLOANE. I do.

KATH. Then give me that present. [*She unhooks the chain.*] Ta.

SLOANE. I hate parting with it.

KATH. I'll wear it for ever.

[ED *enters. Stands smoking a cigarette. Turns. Exits. Re-enters with a cardboard box.*]

ED. This yours?

[KATH *goes over. Looks in the box.*]

KATH. It's my gnome.

ED. They just delivered it.

KATH. The bad weather damaged him. His little hat come off. I sent him to the Gnomes' hospital to be repaired.

ED. Damaged, was he?

KATH. Yes.

ED. Well, well. [*Pause.*] It's monkey weather out there.

SLOANE. I wasn't cold.

ED. You're young. Healthy. Don't feel the cold, do you?

SLOANE. No.

ED. Not at all?

SLOANE. Sometimes.

ED. Not often. [*Pause.*] I expect it's all that orange juice.

KATH. Mr. Sloane was coming out, Eddie. I assure you.

ED. I know that. I can trust him.

KATH. You've a lovely colour. Let me feel your hand. Why it's freezing. You feel his hand Mr. Sloane.

ED. He doesn't want to feel my hand. [*Pause.*] When you're ready, boy, we'll go.

SLOANE. Check the oil?

ED. Mmm.

SLOANE. Petrol?

ED. Mmm. [*Pause.*] Down, en it?

SLOANE. Down?

ED. From yesterday. We filled her up yesterday.

SLOANE. Did we? Was it yesterday?

ED. Mmm. [*Pause.*] We used a lot since then.

SLOANE. You ought to get yourself a new car. It eats petrol. [*Pause.*]

ED. Maybe you're right. You didn't use it last night did you?

SLOANE. Me?

ED. I thought you might have.

SLOANE. No.

ED. Funny. [*Silence.*]

KATH. I see a woolly in Boyce's, Mr. Sloane. I'm giving it you as a birthday present.

ED. What do you want to do that for?

KATH. Mr. Sloane won't mind.

ED. Chucking money about.

KATH. Mr. Sloane doesn't mind me. He's one of the family.

ED. Hark at it. Shove up, boy. [SLOANE *moves.* ED *sits next to him.*] You didn't use my motor last night then?

SLOANE. No.

ED. That's all I wanted. As long as you're telling the truth, boy. [*He takes* SLOANE's *hand.*] You've an honest hand. Square. What a grip you got.

SLOANE. I'm improving.

ED. Yes, I can tell that. You've grown bolder since we met. Bigger and bolder. Don't get too bold will you? Eh? [*Laughs.*] I'm going to buy you something for your birthday as well.

SLOANE. Can I rely on it?

ED. Aah.

SLOANE. Will it be expensive?

ED. Very. I might consider lashing out a bit and buying you a...um, er, aahhh...

SLOANE. Thank you. Thank you.

ED. Don't thank me. Thank yourself. You deserve it.

SLOANE. I think I do.

ED. I think you do. Go and put that box in the kitchen.

KATH. It's no trouble, Eddie.

ED. Let the boy show you politeness.

KATH. But he does. Often. He's often polite to me.

[SLOANE *picks up the box and exits.*]

I never complain. [*Pause.*]

ED. Where was he last night?

KATH. He watched the telly. A programme where people guessed each other's names.

ED. What else?

KATH. Nothing else.

ED. He used the car last night.

KATH. No. [*Pause.*]

ED. If he's not careful he can have his cards.

KATH. He's only young.

ED. Joy-riding in my motor.

KATH. He's a good boy.

ED. Act your age. [*Pause.*] Encouraging him. I've watched you. What you want to keep him in here for all morning?

KATH. I didn't want him here. I told him to go and help you.

ED. You did? And he wouldn't?

KATH. No. Yes.

ED. What do you mean?

KATH. I thought it was his rest period, Eddie. You do give him a rest sometimes. I know 'cause you're a good employer. [*She sits beside him.*]

ED. What do I pay him for?

KATH. To keep him occupied, I suppose. [ED *makes no reply.*]

ED [*at last, irritated*]. You're a pest, you are.

KATH. I'm sorry. [*He glances at her.*]

ED. Keeping him in when he ought to be at work. How do you expect him to work well with you messing about?

KATH. He was just coming.

ED. Taking him from his duty. Wasting my money.

KATH. I won't any more.

ED. It's too late. I'll pay him off. Not satisfactory.

KATH. No.

ED. Not the type of person that I had expected.

KATH. He likes his work.

ED. He can go elsewhere.

KATH. He's a great help to me. I shall cry if he goes away. [*Pause.*] I shall have to take a sedative.

ED. I'll find someone else for you.

KATH. No.

ED. An older man. With more maturity.

KATH. I want my baby.

ED. Your what?

KATH. I'm his mamma and he appreciates me. [*Pause.*] He told me.

ED. When? When?

KATH. I can't remember.

ED. He loves you?

KATH. No, I didn't say that. But he calls me mamma. I love him 'cause I have no little boy of my own. And if you send him away I shall cry like the time you took my real baby.

ED. You were wicked then.

KATH. I know.

ED. Being rude. Ruining my little mate. Teaching him nasty things. That's

why I sent it away. [*Pause.*] You're not doing rude things with this kiddy, are you, like you did with Tommy?

KATH. No.

ED. Sure?

KATH. I love him like a mamma.

ED. I can't trust you.

KATH. I'm a trustworthy lady.

ED. Allowing him to kip here was a mistake. [*Silence.*]

KATH. I never wanted to do rude things. Tommy made me.

ED. Liar!

KATH. Insisted. Pestered me he did. All summer.

ED. You're a liar.

KATH. Am I?

ED. He didn't want anything to do with you. He told me that.

KATH. You're making it up.

ED. I'm not.

KATH. He loved me.

ED. He didn't.

KATH. He wanted to marry me.

ED. Marry you? You're a ridiculous figure and no mistake.

KATH. He'd have married me only his folks were against it.

ED. I always imagined you were an intelligent woman. I find you're not.

KATH. He said they was.

ED. Did he? When?

KATH. When the stork was coming.

ED. [*Laughs.*] Well, well. Fancy you remembering. You must have a long memory.

KATH. I have.

ED. Let me disillusion you.

KATH. Don't hurt me, Eddie.

ED. You need hurting you do. Mr. and Mrs. Albion Bolter were quite ready to have you marry Tommy.

KATH. No they wasn't.

ED. Allow me to know.

KATH. [*Pause.*] He wouldn't have lied, Ed. You're telling stories.

ED. I'm not.

KATH. But he said it was 'cause I was poor. [*Pause.*] I couldn't fit into the social background demanded of him. His duty came between us.

ED. You could have been educated. Gone to beauty salons. Learned to speak well.

KATH. No.

ED. They wanted you to marry him. Tommy and me had our first set-to about it. You should have heard the language he used to me.

KATH. I was loved. How can you say that?

ED. Forget it.

KATH. He sent me the letter I treasure.

ED. I burned it. [*Pause.*]

KATH. It was his last words to me.

ED. And that kiddy out there. I'm not having him go the same way.

[KATH *goes to the window.*]

KATH. Did you burn my letter?

ED. Yes. [*Pause.*] And that old photo as well. I thought you was taking an unhealthy interest in the past.

KATH. The photo as well?

ED. You forget it.

KATH. I promised to show it to someone. I wondered why I couldn't find it.

ED. You wicked girl.

KATH. I'm not wicked. I think you're wicked.

[*She sniffs without dignity.* ED *lights a cigarette. Looks at her.*]

ED. While I'm at it I'll get the old man to look at those papers. [*Pause.*] Get my case in will you. [*She does not reply. He stands up. Exits. Returns with brief case.*] I made a mark where he's to sign. On the dotted line. [*Laughs.*] I'll be glad when it's over. To use an expression foreign to my nature—I'll be bloody glad. [*He stares at* KATH *as she continues to cry. He glances at* KATH. *Turns away. Pause.*] Quit bawling, will you? [KATH *blows her nose on the edge of her apron.*] You should be like me. You'd have something to cry over

then, if you got responsibilities like me. [*Silence.*] Haven't you got a hankie? You don't want the boy to see you like that. [*Silence.* SLOANE *enters.*] Put it away did you?

SLOANE. Yes.

ED. That's a good boy. [*Pause.*]

KATH. Mr. Sloane.

SLOANE. What?

KATH. Can I call you Boy?

SLOANE. I don't think you'd better.

KATH. Why not?

ED. I'm his employer see. He knows that you're only his landlady.

[SLOANE *smiles.*]

KATH. I don't mean in front of strangers. [*Pause.*] I'd be sparing with the use of the name.

ED. No! [*Sharply.*] Haven't you got anything to do? Standing there all day.   [KATH *exits.*] Getting fat as a pig she is.

SLOANE. Is she?

ED. Not noticed?

SLOANE. No.

ED. I have.

SLOANE. How old is she?

ED. Forty-one. [*Shrugs.*] Forty-two. She ought to slim. I'd advise that.

SLOANE. She's . . .

ED. She's like a sow. Though she is my sister.

SLOANE. She's not bad.

ED. No?

SLOANE. I don't think so.

[ED *goes to the window. Stands. Lost. Pause.*]

ED. Where was you last night?

SLOANE. I told you—

ED. I know what you told me. A pack of lies. D'you think I'm an idiot or something?

SLOANE. No.

ED. I want the truth.

SLOANE. I went for a spin. I had a headache.

ED. Where did you go?

SLOANE. Along the A40.

ED. Who went with you?

SLOANE. Nobody.

ED. Are you being entirely honest?

[*Pause.*]

SLOANE. Three mates come with me.

ED. They had headaches too?

SLOANE. I never asked.

ED. Cheeky. [*Pause.*] Who are they? Would I want them in my motor?

SLOANE. You'd recognize Harry Thorpe. Small, clear complexioned, infectious good humour.

ED. I might.

SLOANE. Harry Beck I brought up one night. A Wednesday it was. But Doolan no. You wouldn't know him.

ED. Riding round in my motor all night eh?

SLOANE. I'd challenge that.

ED. What type of youth are they?

SLOANE. Impeccable taste. Buy their clothes up West.

ED. Any of them wear lipstick?

SLOANE. Certainly not.

ED. You'd notice would you? [*He throws over a lipstick.*] What's this doing in the back of the motor?

[*Silence.*]

SLOANE. [*Laughs.*] Oh...you jogged my memory...yes...Doolan's married...an' we took his wife along.

ED. Can't you do better than that.

SLOANE. Straight up.

ED [*emotionally*]. Oh, boy...Taking birds out in my motor.

SLOANE. Would you accept an unconditional apology?

ED. Telling me lies.

SLOANE. It won't happen again.

ED. What are your feelings towards me?

SLOANE. I respect you.

ED. Is that the truth?

SLOANE. Honest.

ED. Then why tell me lies?

SLOANE. That's only your impression.

[*Pause.*]

ED. Was this an isolated incident?

SLOANE. This is the first time.

ED. Really.

SLOANE. Yes. Can you believe me?

[*Pause.*]

ED. I believe you. I believe you're regretting the incident already. But don't repeat it. [*Silence.*] Or next time I won't be so lenient. [*Pause.*] I think the time has come for us to make a change.

SLOANE. In what way?

ED. I need you on tap.

SLOANE. Mmmmn... [*Pause.*]

ED. At all hours. In case I have to make a journey to a distant place at an unexpected and inconvenient time of the night. In a manner of speaking it's urgent.

SLOANE. Of course.

ED. I got work to do. [*Pause.*] I think it would be best if you leave here today.

SLOANE. It might be.

ED. Give it a trial. [*Pause.*] You see my way of looking at it?

SLOANE. Sure.

ED. And you shouldn't be left with her. She's no good. No good at all. A crafty tart she is. I could tell you things about—the way these women carry on. [*Pause.*] Especially her. [*Opens window. Throws cigarette out.*] These women do you no good. I can tell you that. [*Feels in his coat pocket. Takes out a packet of mints. Puts one in his mouth. Pause.*] One of sixteen come up to me the other day—which is a thing I never expected, come up to me and said she'd been given my address. I don't know whether it was a joke or something. You see that sort of thing...

SLOANE. Well...?

ED. You could check it.

SLOANE. I'd be pleased.

ED. Certainly. I got feelings.

SLOANE. You're sensitive. You can't be bothered.

ED. You got it wrong when you says that. I seen birds all shapes and sizes and I'm most certainly not... um...ah...sensitive.

SLOANE. No?

ED. I just don't give a monkey's fart.

SLOANE. It's a legitimate position.

ED. But I can deal with them same as you.

SLOANE. I'm glad to hear it.

ED. What's your opinion of the way these women carry on? [*Pause.*]

SLOANE. I feel...how would you say?

ED. Don't you think they're crude?

SLOANE. Occasionally. In a way.

ED. You never know where you are with half of them.

SLOANE. All the same it's necessary.

ED. Ah well you're talking of a different subject entirely. It's necessary. Occasionally. But it's got to be kept within bounds.

SLOANE. I'm with you there. All the way.

ED. [*Laughs.*] I've seen funny things happen and no mistake. The way these birds treat decent fellows. I hope you never get serious with one. What a life. Backache, headache or her mum told her never to when there's an 'R' in the month. [*Pause. Stares from window.*] How do you feel then?

SLOANE. On the main points we agree.

ED. Pack your bags.

SLOANE. Now?

ED. Immediate.

SLOANE. Will I get a rise in pay?

ED. A rise?

SLOANE. My new situation calls for it.

ED. You already had two.

SLOANE. They were tokens. I'd like you to upgrade my salary. How about a little car?

ED. That's a bit [*Laughs.*] of an unusual request en it?

SLOANE. You could manage it.

ED. It all costs money. I tell you what —I'll promise you one for Christmas.

SLOANE. This year?

ED. Or next year.

SLOANE. It's a date.

ED. You and me. That's the life, boy. Without doubt I'm glad I met you.

SLOANE. Are you?

ED. I see you had possibilities from the start. You had an air. [*Pause.*] A way with you.

SLOANE. Something about me.

ED. That's it. The perfect phrase. Personality.

SLOANE. Really?

ED. That's why I don't want you living here. Wicked waste. I'm going to tell you something. Prepare to raise your eyebrows.

SLOANE. Yes.

ED. She had a kiddy once.

SLOANE. Go on.

ED. That's right. On the wrong side of the blanket.

SLOANE. Your sister?

ED. I had a mate. What times we had. Fished. Swam. Rolled home pissed at two in the morning. We were innocent I tell you. Until she came on the scene. [*Pause.*] Teaching him things he shouldn't a done. It was over... gone...finished. [*Clears his throat.*] She got him to put her in the family way—that's what I always maintain. Nothing was the same after. Not ever. A typical story.

SLOANE. Sad, though.

ED. Yes it is. I should say. Of course in a way of looking at it it laid the foundation of my success. I put him to one side which was difficult because he was alluring. I managed it though. Got a grip on myself. And finally became a success. [*Pause.*] That's no mean achievement, is it?

SLOANE. No.

ED. I'm proud.

SLOANE. Why shouldn't you be?

ED. I'm the possesser of two bank accounts. Respected in my own right. And all because I turned my back on him. Does that impress you?

SLOANE. It impresses me.

ED. I have no hesitation in saying that it was worth it. None.

[*The door opens slowly;* KEMP *stands waiting, staring in, listening.*]

SLOANE. What is it, Pop?

[KEMP *enters the room, listens, backs to the door. Stops.*]

KEMP. Is Ed there with you? [*Pause.*] Ed?

ED [*with emotion*]. Dad... [*He goes to* KEMP, *puts an arm round his shoulder.*] What's come over you? [KEMP *clutches* ED'S *coat, almost falls to his knees.* ED *supports him.*] Don't kneel to me. I forgive you. I'm the one to kneel.

KEMP. No, no.

ED. Pat me on the head. Pronounce a blessing. Forgive and forget eh? I'm sorry and so are you.

KEMP. I want a word with you. [*He squints in* SLOANE'S *direction.*] Something to tell you.

ED. Words, Dad. A string of words. We're together again. [*Pause.*]

KEMP. Tell him to go.

ED. Dad, what manners you got. How rude you've become.

KEMP. I got business to discuss.

SLOANE. He can speak in front of me, can't he, Ed?

ED. I've no secrets from the boy.

KEMP. It's personal.

SLOANE. I'd like to stay Ed... in case...

KEMP. I'm not talking in front of him.

SLOANE. Pop... [*Laughs.*] ... Ed will tell me afterwards. See if he doesn't.

[*Pause.*]

KEMP. I want to talk in private.

[ED *nods at the door;* SLOANE *shrugs.*]

SLOANE. Give in to him eh, Ed? [*Laughs.*] You know, Pop... well... [*Pause.*] O.K. have it your own way.

[SLOANE *exits.*]

KEMP. Is he gone?

ED. What's the matter with you?

KEMP. That kid—who is he?

ED. He's lived here six months. Where have you been?

KEMP. What's his background?

ED. He's had a hard life, Dad. Struggles. I have his word for it. An orphan deserves our sympathy.

KEMP. You like him?

ED. One of the best. [*Silence.*]

KEMP. He comes to my room at night.

ED. He's being friendly.

KEMP. I can't get to sleep. He talks all the time.

ED. Give an example of his conversation. What does he talk about?

KEMP. Goes on and on. [*Pause.*] And he makes things up about me. [*He rolls up his sleeve, shows a bruise.*] Give me a thumping he did.

ED. When? [*Pause.*] Can't you remember?

KEMP. Before the weekend.

ED. Did you complain?

KEMP. I can't sleep for worry. He comes in and stands by my bed in the dark. In his pyjamas. [*Pause.*]

ED. I'll have a word with him.

[KEMP *lifts his trouser leg, pulls down his sock, shows an Elastoplast.*]

KEMP. He kicked me yesterday.

[SLOANE *appears in the doorway.*]

SLOANE. There's a man outside wants a word with you, Pop. [*Pause.*] Urgent he says.

KEMP. Tell him to wait.

SLOANE. How long?

KEMP. Tell him to wait will you?

SLOANE. It's urgent.

KEMP. What's his name?

SLOANE. Grove. Or Greeves, I don't know.

KEMP. I don't know nobody called that.

SLOANE. He's on about the... [*Pause.*] ...whether he can dump something. You'd better see him.

[KEMP *swings round, tries to bring* SLOANE *into focus.*]

KEMP. Oh . . . [ED *nods, winks.*]

ED. In a minute, boy.

[SLOANE *closes door, exits. Silence.*]

ED. Dad . . .

KEMP. He's in bed with her most nights. People talk. The woman from the shop spotted it first. Four months gone, she reckons. [*Pause.*]

ED. That's interesting.

KEMP. She's like the side of a house lately. It's not what she eats. [*Silence.*] Shall I tell you something else?

ED. Don't. [*Pause.*]

KEMP. He's got it in for me.

ED. . . . .don't—tell me anything—

KEMP. It's because I'm a witness. To his crime.

ED. What crime?

[SLOANE *enters carrying a suitcase. Puts it on the table. Opens it.*]

SLOANE. Man en half creating, Pop. You ought to see to him. Jones or Greeves or whatever his name is. He's out the back.

ED. Go and see to him, Dad.

[SLOANE *exits.*]

See this man, Dad. Go on.

KEMP. There's no man there.

ED. How do you know? You haven't been and looked have you?

KEMP. It's a blind. [*Pause.*] Let me tell you about the boy.

ED. I don't want to hear. [*Pause.*] I'm surprised to find you spreading stories about the kiddy. Shocked.

[SLOANE *returns with a pile of clothes.*]

That's slander. You'll find yourself in queer street. [SLOANE *begins to pack the case.*] Apologize. [KEMP *shakes his head.*] The old man's got

something to say to you, boy.

SLOANE [*smiling*]. Oh, yes?

ED [*to* KEMP]. Haven't you? [*Pause.*] Do you talk to him much? Is he talkative at night?

SLOANE. We have the odd confab sometimes. As I dawdle over my cocoa.

ED. You go and talk to that man, Dad. See if you can't get some sense into him. Dumping their old shit back of the house.

[*They watch* KEMP *exit. Silence.*]

He's just been putting in a complaint.

SLOANE. About me?

ED. I can't take it serious. He more or less said you . . . well, in so many words he said . . .

SLOANE. Really?

ED. Did you ever kick him?

SLOANE. Sometimes. He understands.

ED. An' he said . . . Is she pregnant?

[*Pause.*]

SLOANE. Who?

ED. Deny it, boy. Convince me it isn't true.

SLOANE. Why?

ED. So's I—[*Pause.*] Lie to me.

SLOANE. Why should I?

ED. It's true then? Have you been messing with her?

SLOANE. She threw herself at me.

[*Silence.*]

ED. What a little whoreson you are. You little whoreson. You are a little whoreson and no mistake. I'm put out, boy. Choked. [*Pause.*] What attracted you? Did she give trading stamps? You're like all these layabouts. Kiddies with no fixed abode.

SLOANE. I put up a fight.

ED. She had your cherry?

SLOANE. No.

ED. Not the first time?

SLOANE. No.

ED. Or the second?

SLOANE. No.

ED. Dare I go on?

SLOANE. It's my upbringing. Lack of training. No proper parental control.

ED. I'm sorry for you.

SLOANE. I'm glad of that. I wouldn't want to upset you.

ED. That does you credit.

SLOANE. You've no idea what I've been through. [*Pause.*] I prayed for guidance.

ED. I'd imagine the prayer for your situation would be hard to come by. [*Pause.*] Did you never think of locking your bedroom door?

SLOANE. She'd think I'd gone mad.

ED. Why didn't you come to me?

SLOANE. It's not the kind of thing I could.

ED. I'd've been your confessor.

SLOANE. It gathered momentum.

ED. You make her sound like a washing machine. When did you stop?

SLOANE. I haven't stopped.

ED. Not stopped yet?

SLOANE. Here, lay off.

ED. What a ruffian.

SLOANE. I got my feelings.

ED. You were stronger than her. Why didn't you put up a struggle?

SLOANE. I was worn out. I was overwrought. Nervous. On edge. [*Pause.*]

ED. You're a constant source of amazement, boy, a never-ending tale of infamy. I'd hardly credit it. A kid of your age. Joy-riding in a expensive car, a woman pregnant. My word, you're unforgivable. [*Pause.*] I don't know whether I'm qualified to pronounce judgement. [*Pause.*]

SLOANE. I'm easily led. I been dogged by bad luck.

ED. You've got to learn to live a decent life sometime, boy. I blame the way you are on emotional shock. So perhaps [*Pause.*] we ought to give you another chance.

SLOANE. That's what I says.

ED. Are you confused?

SLOANE. I shouldn't be surprised.

ED. Never went to church? Correct me if I'm wrong.

SLOANE. You got it, Ed. Know me better than I know myself.

ED. Your youth pleads for leniency and, by God, I'm going to give it. You're pure as the Lamb. Purer.

SLOANE. Am I forgiven?

ED. Will you reform?

SLOANE. I swear it...Ed, speak a few words of forgiveness. [*Pause.*] Pity me.

ED. I do.

SLOANE. Forgive this once. Oh, Ed, you're a pal.

ED. Am I?

SLOANE. One of my mates.

ED. Is that a fact? How refreshing to hear you say it.

SLOANE. You've a generous nature.

ED. You could say that. I don't condemn out of hand like some. But do me a favour—avoid the birds in future. That's what's been your trouble.

SLOANE. It has.

ED. She's to blame.

SLOANE. I've no hesitation in saying that.

ED. Why conform to the standards of the cowshed? [*Pause.*] It's a thing you grow out of. With me behind you, boy, you'll grow out of it.

SLOANE. Thanks.

ED. Your hand on it. [SLOANE *holds out his hand.* ED *takes it, holds it for a long time, searches* SLOANE's *face.*] I think you're a good boy. [*Silence.*] I knew there must be some reasonable explanation for your otherwise inexplicable conduct. I'll have a word with the old man.

SLOANE. Gets on my nerves he does.

ED. Has he been tormenting you?

SLOANE. I seriously consider leaving as a result of the way he carries on.

ED. Insults?

SLOANE. Shocking. Took a dislike to me he did the first time he saw me.

ED. Take no notice.

SLOANE. I can't make him out.

Ed. Stubborn.

Sloane. That's why I lose my temper.

Ed. I sympathize. [*Pause.*]

Sloane. He deserves a good belting.

Ed. You may have something there.

Sloane. I thought you might be against me for that.

Ed. No.

Sloane. I thought you might have an exaggerated respect for the elderly.

Ed. Not me.

Sloane. I've nothing against him. [*Pause.*] But he's lived so long he's more like an old bird than a bloke. How is it such a father has such a son? A mystery. [*Pause.*] Certainly is. [Ed *pats his pockets.*] Out of fags again are you?

Ed. Yes.

Sloane. Give them up. Never be fully fit, Ed. [Ed *smiles, shakes his head.*] Are you going to the shop?

Ed. Yes.

Sloane. *Good.* [*Silence.*] How long will you be?

Ed. Five minutes. Maybe ten.

Sloane. Mmmmn. [*Pause.*] Well, while you're gone I'm going to have a word with Pop.

Ed. Good idea.

Sloane. See if we can't find an area of agreement. I'll hold out the hand of friendship an' all that. I'm willing to forget the past. If he is. [*Silence.*] I'd better have a word with him. Call him.

Ed. Me?

Sloane. No good me asking him anything is there?

Ed. I don't know whether we're speaking.

Sloane. Gone funny again has he?

[Ed *goes to the door, opens it, looks out. Calls.*]

Ed. Dad! [*Pause.*] I want a word with you.

Kemp [*off*]. What's that? [*Pause.*]

Ed. Me—me—I want to see you. [*He closes the door.*] He gets worse.

[*Silence.*] Appeal to his better nature. Say you're upset. Wag your finger, perhaps. I don't want you to be er, well...at each other's throats, boy. Let's try...and...well be friends. [*Pause.*] I've the fullest confidence in your ability. [*Pause.*] Yes...well I'm going out now. [*Pause.*]...it's a funny business en it?...I mean... well, it's a ticklish problem. [*Pause.*] Yes...it is.

[*Exit.* Sloane *sits, waits. Pause.* Kemp *enters.* Sloane *rises, steps behind* Kemp, *bangs door.* Kemp *swings round, backs.*]

Kemp. Ed? [*Pause.*] Where's Ed?

[Sloane *takes hold of* Kemp's *stick, pulls it away from him.* Kemp *struggles.* Sloane *wrenches the stick from his hand. Leads* Kemp *to a chair.*]

Sloane. Sit down, Pop.

Kemp [*Turns to go.* Sloane *pushes him into the chair.*] Ed's not here. Gone for a walk. What you been saying about me?

Kemp. Nothing, sonnie.

Sloane. What have you told him? What were you going to tell him?

Kemp. I—[*Pause.*] Business.

Sloane. What kind of business? [Kemp *does not reply.*] Told him she's up the stick did you? [*No reply.*] Why did you tell him?

Kemp. He's her brother. He ought to know.

Sloane. Fair enough.

Kemp. Got to know sometime.

Sloane. Right. [*Silence.*] What else did you tell him? [Kemp *attempts to rise,* Sloane *pushes him back.*] Did you say anything else? [Kemp *attempts to rise.*] Eh?

Kemp. No.

Sloane. Were you going to?

Kemp. Yes.

Sloane. Why?

Kemp. You're a criminal.

Sloane. Who says I am?

KEMP. I know you are. You killed my old boss. I know it was you.

SLOANE. Your vision is faulty. You couldn't identify nobody now. So long after. You said so yourself.

KEMP. I got to go. [*Pause.*] I'm expecting delivery of a damson tree.

SLOANE. Sit still! [*Silence.*] How were you going to identify me?

KEMP. I don't have to. They got fingerprints.

SLOANE. Really?

KEMP. All over the shop.

SLOANE. It was an accident, Pop. I'm innocent. You don't know the circumstances...

KEMP. Oh...I know...

SLOANE. But you don't.

KEMP. You murdered him.

SLOANE. Accidental death. [*Pause.*]

KEMP. No, sonnie...no.

SLOANE. You're pre-judging my case.

KEMP. You're bad.

SLOANE. I'm an orphan.

KEMP. Get away from me. Leave me alone.

[SLOANE *puts the stick into* KEMP's *hand.*]

SLOANE. I trust you, Pop. Listen. Keep quiet. [*Silence.*] It's like this see. One day I leave the Home. Stroll along. Sky blue. Fresh air. They'd found me a likeable permanent situation. Canteen facilities. Fortnight's paid holiday. Overtime? Time and a half after midnight. A staff dance each year. What more could one wish to devote one's life to? I certainly loved that place. The air round Twickenham was like wine. Then one day I take a trip to the old man's grave. Hic Jacets in profusion. Ashes to ashes. Alas the fleeting. A few press-ups on a tomb belonging to a family name of Cavaneagh. The sun was declining when I left the graveyard. I thumbs a lift from a geyser who promises me a bed. Gives me a bath. And a meal. Very friendly. All

you could wish he was, photographer. He shows me one or two experimental studies. An experience for the retina and no mistake. He wanted to photo me. For certain interesting features I had that he wanted the exclusive right of preserving. You know how it is. I didn't like to refuse. No harm in it I suppose. But then I got to thinking...I knew a kid once called MacBride that happened to. Oh, yes...so when I gets to think of this I decide I got to do something about it. And I gets up in the middle of the night looking for the film see. He has a lot of expensive equipment about in his studio see. Well it appears that he gets the wrong idea. Runs in. Gives a shout. And the long and the short of it is I loses my head which is a thing I never ought to a done with the worry of them photos an' all. And I hits him. I hits him. [*Pause.*] He must have had a weak heart. Something like that I should imagine. Definitely should have seen his doctor before that. I wasn't to know was I? I'm not to blame. [*Silence.*]

KEMP. He was healthy. Sound as a bell.

SLOANE. How do you know?

KEMP. He won cups for it. Looked after himself.

SLOANE. A weak heart.

KEMP. Weak heart my arse. You murdered him.

SLOANE. He fell.

KEMP. He was hit from behind.

SLOANE. I had no motive.

KEMP. The equipment.

SLOANE. I never touched it.

KEMP. You meant to.

SLOANE. Not me, Pop. [*Laughs.*] Oh, no.

KEMP. Liar...lying little bugger. I knew what you was from the start.

[*Pause.*]

SLOANE. What are you going to do? Are you going to tell Ed? [KEMP *makes no reply.*] He won't believe you. [KEMP *makes no reply.*] He'll think you're raving.

KEMP. No...you're finished.

[*He attempts to rise.* SLOANE *pushes him back.* KEMP *raises his stick;* SLOANE *takes it from him.*]

SLOANE. You can't be trusted I see. I've lost faith in you. [*Throws stick out of reach.*] Irresponsible. Can't give you offensive weapons.

KEMP. Ed will be back soon.

[*Rises to go.*]

SLOANE. He will.

KEMP. I'm seeing him then.

SLOANE. Are you threatening me? Do you feel confident? Is that it? [*Stops. Clicks his tongue. Pause. Leans over and straightens* KEMP's *tie.*] Ed and me are going away. Let's have your word you'll forget it. [KEMP *does not reply.*] Pretend you never knew. Who was he? No relation. Hardly a friend. An employer. You won't bring him back by hanging me. [KEMP *does not*

reply.] Where's your logic? Can I have a promise you'll keep your mouth shut?

KEMP. No. [SLOANE *twists* KEMP's *ear.*] Ugh! Aaah...

SLOANE. You make me desperate. I've nothing to lose you see. One more chance, Pop. Are you going to give me away?

KEMP. I'll see the police.

SLOANE. You don't know what's good for you. [*He knocks* KEMP *behind the settee. Kicks him.*] You bring this on yourself. [*He kicks him again.*] All this could've been avoided. [KEMP *half-rises, groans, collapses on to floor. Pause.* SLOANE *kicks him gently with the toe of his boot.*] Eh then. Wake up. [*Pause.*] Wakey, wakey. [*Silence. He goes to the door and calls.*] Ed! [*Pause.*] Ed!

[KATH *comes to the door. He pushes her back.*]

KATH [*off*]. What's happened?

SLOANE. Where's Ed? Not you! I want Ed!

ACT III

Door slams off.

ED. What is it?

[ED *enters.* KATH *struggles in doorway with* SLOANE. SLOANE *gives up; she enters.*]

SLOANE. Some kind of attack.

ED. What did you do? [*He kneels.*]

KATH. If only there were some spirits in the house. Unfortunately I don't drink myself. [*She loosens* KEMP's *collar.*] Somebody fetch his tablets.

[*Nobody moves.*]

ED. He's reviving.

KATH. Speak to me, Dadda. [*Pause.*] He's been off his food for some time. [*Pause.*] He's cut his lip.

[ED *lifts* KEMP.]

ED. Can you walk?

KEMP [*muttering*]. Go away...

ED. I'll carry you upstairs. [KATH *opens the door, stands in the passage.*] He'll be better in a bit. Is his bed made?

KATH. Yes. Let him lie still and he'll get his feelings back.

[ED *exits with* KEMP.]

[*Slowly.*] Mr. Sloane, did you strike the Dadda?

SLOANE. Yes.

KATH. You admit it? Did he provoke you?

SLOANE. In a way.

KATH. What a thing to do. Hit an old

man. It's not like you. You're usually
so gentle.

SLOANE. He upset me.

KATH. He can be aggravating I know,
but you shouldn't resort to violence,
dear. [*Pause.*] Did he insult you?
[*Pause.*] Was it a bad word?
[*Pause.*] I don't expect you can tell
me what it was. I'd blush.

SLOANE. I hit him several times.

KATH. You're exaggerating. You're not
that type of young man. [*Pause.*]
But don't do it again. Mamma
wouldn't like it.

[ED *enters.*]

Is he alright?

ED. Yes.

KATH. I'll go up to him.

ED. He's asleep.

KATH. Sleeping off the excitement, is
he?   [*Exit.*]

ED [*taking* SLOANE *aside*]. How hard
did you hit him?

SLOANE. Not hard.

ED. You don't know your own strength,
boy. Using him like a punchbag.

SLOANE. I've told you—

ED. He's dead.

SLOANE. Dead? His heart.

ED. Whatever it was it's murder, boy.
You'll have some explaining to do.

[ED *lights a cigarette.* KATH *enters with
a carpet sweeper, begins to sweep.*]

KATH. I'd take up a toffee, but he only
gets them stuck round his teeth.

ED. You're not usually at a loss, surely?
You can conjure up an idea or two.

KATH. Let Mr. Sloane regain his com-
posure, Ed. Let him collect his
thoughts. Forget the incident.

[*She goes upstage, begins to hum* "The
Indian Love Call." SLOANE *looks at* ED.
ED *smiles, shakes his head.*]

ED. That isn't possible, I'm afraid.

KATH. He meant no harm.

ED. What are you doing?

KATH. My housework. I musn't neglect
my chores.

ED. Can't you find a better time than
this?

KATH. It's my usual time. Guess what's
for dinner, Mr. Sloane.

SLOANE. I'm not hungry.

ED. He doesn't want any.

KATH. Guess what mamma's prepared?

ED. Let him alone! All you think of is
food. He'll be out of condition before
long. As gross as you are.

KATH. Is he upset?

ED. Tell her.

SLOANE. I'm really upset.

ED. Turned your stomach, has it?

KATH. Will you feel better by this
afternoon?

SLOANE. I don't know.

ED. He's worried.

KATH. The Dadda won't say anything,
dear, if that's what's on your mind.
He'll keep quiet. [*Pause.*] That new
stove cooks excellent, Eddie.

ED. Does it?

KATH. Yes. I cooked a lovely egg
yesterday. Mr. Sloane had it. I think
they ought to have put the grill different though. I burned my hand.

ED. You want to look what you're
doing.

KATH. It's awkwardly placed.

ED. Cooking with your eyes shut.

KATH. [*Pause.*] You haven't guessed
yet what's for dinner. Three guesses.
Go on.

SLOANE. I don't know!

KATH. Chips.

SLOANE. Really?

KATH. And peas. And two eggs.

SLOANE. I don't give a sod what's for
dinner!

ED. Don't use those tones to my relations, Sloane. Behave yourself for a
change. [*He lights a cigarette.*]

SLOANE. Can I see you outside?

ED. What do you want to see me outside for?

SLOANE. To explain.

ED. There's nothing to explain.

SLOANE. How I came to be involved in
this situation.

[KATH *puts the Ewbank away.*]

ED. I don't think that would be advisable. Some things will have to be sorted out. A check on your excesses is needed.

SLOANE. Are you sure he's——?

ED. As forty Dodos. I tried the usual methods of ascertaining; no heartbeats, no misting on my cigarette case. The finest legal brains in the country can't save you now.

[KATH *re-enters.*]

SLOANE. I feel sick.

KATH. It's the weather.

SLOANE. No.

KATH. Take a pill or something. I had some recommended me the other day. [*Opens a drawer, searches. She finds the tablets, shakes out two into her hand. Offers them to* SLOANE.] Take them with a glass of water. Swallow them quick. They'll relieve the symptoms.

SLOANE. I don't want them! [*He knocks them from her hand.*] I don't want pills!   [*Exits.*]

KATH. He's bad, isn't he?

ED. A very bad boy.

[KATH *picks up one tablet, searches for the other, gives up.*]

KATH. Somebody will tread on them. That's the reason for these stains. Things get into the pile. The Dadda dropped a pickled walnut and trod it into the rug yesterday. If only we had a dog we wouldn't have so much bother.

ED. You're not having a dog.

KATH. Eddie, is Mr. Sloane ill?

ED. He may be.

KATH. He looks pale. I wonder if he isn't sickening for something.

ED. He might have to go away. Something has happened which makes his presence required elsewhere.

KATH. Where?

ED. I'm not sure. Not for certain.

KATH. Is he in trouble?

ED. Dead trouble.

KATH. It was an accident surely?

ED. You know then?

KATH. The Dadda told me about it. Mr. Sloane was unfortunate. He was joking, I expect.

ED. He never jokes.

KATH. No, he's remarkably devoid of a sense of fun. Dadda was full of it.

ED. I don't understand you.

KATH. Oh, I said he had no proof. I didn't waste my energy listening to him. Sometimes I think he makes up these things to frighten me. He ought to curb his imagination.   [*Exits.*]

ED. I should have asked for references. I can see that now. The usual credentials would have avoided this. An attractive kid, so disarming, too— to tell me lies and—

[KATH *enters carrying a china figure.*]

KATH. This shepherdess is a lovely piece of chinawork. She comes up like new when I give her a wash. [ED *looks at her.*] The crack spoils it, though. I should have it mended professionally.

[*She exits, re-enters with a large vase.*]

Dadda gets up to some horrible pranks lately. [*Shakes vase.*] Throwing things in my best vase now. The habits of the elderly are beyond the pale.

[*She exits with vase.* SLOANE *enters, glances at* ED. ED *does not look up.*]

SLOANE. Accept my apology, Ed. Sorry I was rude, but my nerves won't stand much more, I can tell you. [*Begins to pack.*] She's got two of my shirts in the wash. Good ones. [*Opens sideboard, takes out cardigan.*] Can't risk asking her for them. [*Looks under sideboard, finds canvas shoes. Holding up razor.*] She's been using this again. I can tell. That's not hygienic, is it?

ED. What are you doing?

SLOANE. Packing.

ED. Why?

SLOANE. I'm going away.

ED. Where?

SLOANE. With you.

ED. No, boy. Not with me.

SLOANE. It was settled.

ED. I can't allow you to take up abode in Dulverton Mansions now.

SLOANE. Why not?

ED. What a fantastic person you are. You've committed a murder.

SLOANE. An accident.

ED. Murder.

SLOANE. Those pills were undermining his constitution. Ruining his health. He couldn't have lasted much longer.

ED. Attacking a defenceless old man!

SLOANE. He had his stick.

ED. He wasn't strong enough to use it.

SLOANE. I blame that on the pills. Who prescribed them?

ED. His doctor.

SLOANE. Reputable is he?

ED. He's on the register. What more do you want?

SLOANE. You'll find medical evidence agrees with my theory.

ED. The pills had nothing to do with it. You've no excuse. None.

SLOANE. What kind of life is it at his age?

ED. You've abused my trust.

SLOANE. I did him a service in a manner of speaking.

ED. You'll have to face the authorities.

SLOANE. Look, I'm facing no one.

ED. You've no choice.

SLOANE. I'll decide what choice I have.

ED. Get on the blower and call the law. We're finished.

SLOANE. You wouldn't put me away, would you?

ED. Without a qualm.

SLOANE. You're my friend.

ED. No friend of thugs.

SLOANE. He died of heart failure. You can't ruin my life. I'm impressionable. Think what the nick would do to me. I'd pick up criminal connections.

ED. You already got criminal connec-

tions.

SLOANE. Not as many as I would have.

ED. That's a point in your favour.

SLOANE. Give me a chance.

ED. You've had several.

SLOANE. One more.

ED. I've given you chances. Expected you to behave like a civilized human being.

SLOANE. Say he fell downstairs.

ED. What kind of person does that make me?

SLOANE. A loyal friend.

ED. You'll get me six months. More than that. Depends on the judge.

SLOANE. What a legal system. Say he fell.

ED. Aiding and abetting.

SLOANE. Fake the evidence.

ED. You're completely without morals, boy. I hadn't realized how depraved you were. You murder my father. Now you ask me to help you evade justice. Is that where my liberal principles have brought me?

SLOANE. You've got no principles.

ED. No principles? Oh, you really have upset me now. Why am I interested in your welfare? Why did I give you a job? Why do thinking men everywhere show young boys the straight and narrow? Flash cheque-books when delinquency is mentioned? Support the scout movement? Principles, boy, bleeding principles. And don't you dare say otherwise or you'll land in serious trouble.

SLOANE. Are you going to help me?

ED. No.

SLOANE. We must find a basis for agreement.

ED. There can be no agreement. I'm a citizen of this country. My duty is clear. You must accept responsibility for your actions.

[SLOANE *sits beside* ED. *Lays a hand on his knee.*]

SLOANE. I accept responsibility.

ED. Do you?

SLOANE. Fully.

ED. Good. Remove that hand will you?

SLOANE. Certainly.

ED. What you just said about no principles—that's really upset me. Straight. Really upset me.

SLOANE. Sorry, Eddie, sorry.

ED. One thing I wanted to give you—my principles. Oh, I'm disillusioned. I feel I'm doing no good at all.

SLOANE. I'm very bad. Only you can help me on the road to a useful life. [*Pause.*] A couple of years ago I met a man similar to yourself. Same outlook on life. A dead ringer for you as far as physique went. He was an expert on the adolescent male body. He'd completed an exhaustive study of his subject before I met him. During the course of one magical night he talked to me of his principles— offered me a job if I would accept them. Like a fool I turned him down. What an opportunity I lost, Ed. If you were to make the same demands I'd answer loudly in the affirmative.

[*Pause.*]

ED. You mean that?

SLOANE. In future you'd have nothing to complain of.

ED. You really mean what you say?

SLOANE. Let me live with you. I'd wear my jeans out in your service. Cook for you.

ED. I eat out.

SLOANE. Bring you your tea in bed.

ED. Only women drink tea in bed.

SLOANE. You bring me my tea in bed then. Any arrangement you fancy.

[KATH *screams loudly offstage. Pause. Screams again nearer. She enters.*]

KATH. Ed!

ED. Come here.

KATH. Ed, I must—[ED *takes her arm; she pulls back.*] It's Dadda—he's dead. Come quick.

ED. Sit down. [*to* SLOANE] Bring the car round. We'll fetch the doctor.

KATH. Eddie, he's dead!

ED. I know, we know. We didn't want to upset you.   [SLOANE *exits.*]

KATH. I can't believe it. He was in perfect health.

ED. He was ill.

KATH. Was he?

ED. You told me he was.

KATH. I didn't believe it. I only took his word for it.

ED. Didn't he say he was ill?

KATH. Often. I took no notice. You know how he is. I thought he was having me on.

ED. He was telling the truth.

[KATH *begins to sniff.*]

KATH. Poor Dadda. How he must have suffered. I'm truly ashamed of myself. [*She wipes her eyes on her apron.*] It's all the health scheme's fault. Will I have to send his pension book in?

ED. Yes.

KATH. I thought I would.

ED. Now listen—

KATH. Eddie.

ED. —carefully to what I say. [*He passes a hand across his mouth.*] When the doctor comes what are you going to tell him?

KATH. Me?

ED. He'll want to know.

KATH. I'll say Dadda had an attack. He passed away suddenly.

ED. What about the cuts on his face?

KATH. He was rude to Mr. Sloane, Eddie. Provoked him.

ED. They won't wear that.

KATH. Won't they? [*Pause.*] I shall never get in my black. I've put on weight since we buried mamma.

ED. They'll get the boy for murder.

KATH. They'd never do that would they?

ED. They'll hang him. [*Pause.*]

KATH. Hang him?

ED. They might. I'm not sure. I get confused by the changes in the law.

KATH. Is it bad?

ED. Awful. You wouldn't see him again. You understand?

KATH. The Dadda was rude. He said a rude word about me.

ED. That's no excuse in the eyes of the law. You must say he fell downstairs.

KATH. I couldn't.

ED. I would never suggest deceiving the authorities under normal circumstances. But we have ourselves to think of. I'm in a funny position. I pay his wages. That's a tricky situation.

KATH. Is it?

ED. I'm compromised. My hands are tied. If the situation was different I might say something. Depend on it.

KATH. Wouldn't they make an exception? If we gave him a good character?

ED. He hasn't got a good character.

KATH. We could say he had.

ED. That would be perjury.

KATH. He has nice manners when he wants. I've seen them.

ED. I feel bad doing this. You see the position? He went too far. But he did it out of respect for you. That's some consideration.

KATH. He did it out of love for me?

ED. You should be grateful. No doubt of that. [*Pause.*] Do you polish that lino?

KATH. Eh?

ED. On the stairs?

KATH. No, never. I have to think of the Dadda.

ED. Go and polish them.

KATH. Doctor will be cross.

ED. Let him be.

KATH. He'll think I'm silly. He'll think I caused Dadda's fall.

ED. It doesn't matter as long as he thinks it was an accident.

[KATH *bites her lip, considers.*]

KATH. Shall I put Dadda's new shoes on him?

ED. Now you're using your initiative. Slippy are they?

KATH. He only wore them once.

ED. Good girl.

[SLOANE *enters.*]

SLOANE. Ready? Come on then.

[ED *nods to* KATH, *waiting. She looks from one to the other. Notices the case.*]

KATH. Why is he taking his case?

ED. He's coming with me. He can't stay here.

KATH. Why not?

ED. They'll suspect. [*Pause.*]

KATH. When is he coming back?

ED. Day after next.

KATH. He doesn't need that big case.

[*She exits.*]

ED. Get in the car, boy.

SLOANE. How about my shirts?

ED. I'll see about buying a couple.

KATH [*off*]. Why is he taking his clothes?

[KATH *returns.*]

ED. What are you on about?

KATH. I've just checked. They aren't in the laundry basket.

ED. Snooping around. Don't you trust me?

KATH. You're taking him away.

SLOANE. We thought I ought to live in.

KATH. Do you want to leave?

SLOANE. I'll be back when this has blown over.

KATH. Why are you leaving your mamma? There's no need for him to go away, Eddie. Doctor knows he lives here.

ED. He'll instigate proceedings.

KATH. Doctors don't do that. He wants to stay.

ED. Ask him. [*to* SLOANE] Do you want to stay?

SLOANE. No.

ED. The question is answered.

KATH. Ed—

ED. Send a wire—

KATH. I've something to tell you. [*She lifts her apron. Shyly.*] I've a bun in the oven.

ED. You've a whole bloody baker's shop in the oven from the look of that.

KATH. Mr. Sloane was nice to me. Aren't you shocked?

ED. No, it's what I expect of you.

KATH. Aren't you angry with Mr. Sloane?

ED. I'm angry with you.

KATH. Are you?

ED. Mr. Sloane's already explained.

KATH. What did he explain?

ED. How you carried on.

KATH. I didn't carry on! What a wicked thing to say.

ED. Seducing him.

KATH. Did he say that?

ED. Told me the grisly details.

[*Silence.*]

KATH. Mr. Sloane, dear, take back your locket.

ED. What locket?

KATH. He gave me a locket. [*She takes off the locket.* SLOANE *attempts to take it.*] I don't believe he'd take it if you weren't here, Ed. [*She puts the locket back. To* SLOANE.] How could you behave so bad. Accusing me of seducing you.

SLOANE. But you did!

KATH. That's neither here nor there. Using expressions like that. Making yourself cheap. [SLOANE *turns to the suitcase.*] I see the truth of the matter. He's been at you. Isn't that like him?

ED. He wants to come with me.

KATH. Let him decide for himself.

ED. He's got problems. Needs a man's hand on his shoulder.

KATH. I'm afraid you're unduly influencing him.

ED. You've been found out.

KATH. Found out?

ED. Exposed.

KATH. Rubbish!

ED. Making a spectacle of yourself. Corrupting a kid young enough to be your son.

KATH. He loves me.

ED. Prove it.

KATH. A woman knows when she's loved.

ED. I blame myself for letting him stay. Knowing your character.

KATH. My character will stand analysis.

ED. You're older than him.

KATH. I'm a benign influence. A source of good.

ED. You spoil him.

KATH. Who tucks him up at night? And he likes my cooking. He won't deny that.

ED. No.

KATH. See I'm right.

ED. I can't argue with you.

KATH. You can't.

ED. You don't make sense.

KATH. I do.

ED. You have no logical train of thought.

KATH. What is that?

ED. No power of argument.

KATH. I keep his trousers pressed nice. He's been smarter since I knew him.

ED. He's lost with you.

KATH. I gave him everything.

ED. No backbone. Spineless.

KATH. He's lovely with me. Charming little baby he is.

ED. No, he's soft. You softened him up.

KATH. I gave him three meals a day. Porridge for breakfast. Meat and two veg. for dinner. A fry for tea. And cheese for supper. What more could he want?

ED. Freedom.

KATH. He's free with me.

ED. You're immoral.

KATH. It's natural.

ED. He's clean-living by nature; that's every man's right.

KATH. What are you going to give him?

ED. The world.

[KATH *comes round the case, looks in.*]

KATH. The state of this case. Mr. Sloane, dear, you can't even pack. See how he needs me in the smallest things? Can't manage without a woman.

ED. Let him try.

KATH. Women are necessary.

ED. Granted.

KATH. Where's your argument?

ED. In limited doses.

KATH. You're silly, Eddie, silly...

ED. Let him choose. Let's have it in black and white, boy.

SLOANE. I'm going with Ed.

[ED *nods, smacks* SLOANE'S *shoulder, laughs.*]

KATH. Is it the colour of the curtains in your room?

SLOANE. No.

KATH. Is it because I'm pregnant?

SLOANE. No. Better opportunities. A new life.

KATH. You vowed you loved me.

SLOANE. Never for a second.

KATH. I was kind to you.

SLOANE. Yes.

KATH. Are you grateful?

SLOANE. I paid.

KATH. I paid too. Baby on the way. Reputation ruined.

SLOANE. You had no reputation.

KATH. Is that what he's taught you?

ED. I taught him nothing. He was innocent until you got your maulers on to him.

KATH. He'd packed the experience of a lifetime into a few short years.

ED. Pure in heart he was. He wouldn't know where to put it.

KATH. I attracted him instantly.

ED. You couldn't attract a blind man.

KATH. He wanted to marry me.

ED. What a bride!

KATH. We were to ask your consent.

ED. Look in the glass, lady. Let's enjoy a laugh. [*He takes her to the mirror.*] What do you see?

KATH. Me.

ED. What are you?

KATH. My hair is nice. Natural. I'm mature, but still able to command a certain appeal.

ED. You look like death! [*She shakes him off. He drags her back to mirror.*] Flabby mouth. Wrinkled neck. Puffy hands.

KATH. It's baby coming.

ED. Sagging tits. You cradle-snatcher.

KATH. He said I was a Venus. I held him in my arms.

ED. What a martyrdom!

KATH. He wanted for nothing. I loved him sincerely.

ED. Your appetite appalled him.

KATH. I loved him.

ED. Insatiable.

KATH [*to* SLOANE]. Baby, my little boy...

ED. He aches at every organ.

KATH. ... mamma forgives you.

ED. What have you to offer? You're fat and the crows-feet under your eyes would make you an object of terror. Pack it in, I tell you. Sawdust up to the navel. You've nothing to lure any man.

KATH. Is that the truth, Mr. Sloane?

SLOANE. More or less.

KATH. Why didn't you tell me?

ED. How could he tell you? You showed him the gate of Hell every night. He abandoned Hope when he entered there.

[KATH *snaps the suitcase shut.*]

KATH. Mr. Sloane, I believed you were a good boy. I find you've deceived me.

SLOANE. You deceived yourself.

KATH. Perhaps. [*She holds out her hand.*] Kiss my hand, dear, in the manner of the theatre. [*He kisses her hand.*] I shall cry.

[*She feels for a handkerchief.*]

ED. On with the waterworks.

KATH. I'm losing you for ever.

SLOANE. I'll pop round.

KATH. I'll not be able to bear it.

SLOANE. You'll have the baby.

KATH. I shall die of it, I'm sure.

ED. What a cruel performance you're giving. Like an old tart grinding to her climax.

[SLOANE *kisses* KATH's *cheek.*]

KATH. Baby... [*She holds him close. Looks at* ED *over* SLOANE's *shoulder.*] Before you go, Mr. Sloane, we must straighten things out. The Dadda's death was a blow to me.

SLOANE. Ed can vouch for me. You can support his story.

KATH. What story?

SLOANE. The old man fell downstairs.

KATH. I shall never under any circumstances allow anyone to perjure me. It was murder.

[SLOANE *releases her. Pause.*]

SLOANE. He was ill.

KATH. Ah, you know as well as I he was perfectly healthy this morning.

SLOANE. Ed will give me an alibi.

KATH. He wasn't there, dear. Respect the truth always. It's the least you can do under the circumstances.

SLOANE. He'll say he was a witness.

KATH. It's not in accordance with my ideas of morality.

SLOANE. Look—mamma...see—

KATH. When doctor comes he'll want to know things. Are you asking me to deceive our G.P.? He's an extremely able man. He'll notice discrepancies. And then where will we be? He'd make his report and mamma would be behind bars. I'm sure that isn't your idea. Is it?

SLOANE. Ed is supporting me.

KATH. He must decide for himself. I won't practice a falsehood.

SLOANE. You're not going back on your word?

KATH. You know how I go to pieces under cross-examination.

SLOANE. Make an effort.

KATH. Who for?

SLOANE. Me.

KATH. You won't be here.

SLOANE. I'll come and see you.

KATH. No. Call me names if you wish, but I won't tell stories. I'm a firm believer in truth.

ED. Look...Kathy—Say you were out when the accident occurred.

KATH. No.

ED. Down the shops.

KATH. But I wasn't.

ED. You didn't see him fall.

KATH. I would have heard him.

ED. Say you were out of range.

KATH. No.

ED. Forget the whole business.

KATH. No.

ED. Go to the police then. What will you achieve? Nothing. This boy was carried away by the exuberance of youth. He's under age.

[KATH *hands the suitcase to* ED.]

KATH. You struck the Dadda down in cold blood, Mr. Sloane. In the course of conversations before his death he told me one or two things of interest.

SLOANE. Concerning whom?

KATH. We talked only of you. I could hardly give credence to the report of your crimes. I didn't believe the old man. I'm paid for it now.

ED. The last word, eh? Using your whore's prerogative?

KATH. Stay with me.

SLOANE. No.

KATH. Hold me tight again.

SLOANE. No.

KATH. There's no need to go away, dear. Don't make me unhappy.

SLOANE. I'm going with Ed.

KATH. I was never subtle, Mr. Sloane ...If you go with Eddie I'll tell the police.

SLOANE. If I stay here he'll do the same.

ED. It's what is called a dilemma, boy. You are on the horns of it. [*Silence.*]

KATH. You see how things are, Mr. Sloane?

[SLOANE *smacks her face; she screams.*]

ED. What are you doing?

SLOANE. Leave her to me.

KATH. Don't attempt to threaten me.

ED. There's no suggestion of threats.

KATH. What's he doing then?

ED. Let her alone, boy.

SLOANE. Keep out of this! [ED *lays a hand on* SLOANE's *shoulder, tries to pull him away from* KATH. SLOANE *turns, shoves* ED *from him.*] Did you hear what I said? Keep out of it!

ED. Don't be violent. No violence at any cost. [SLOANE *gets* KATH *into a corner; struggles with her.*] What's this exhibition for? This is gratuitous violence. Give over both of you!

[SLOANE *shakes* KATH.]

SLOANE. Support me, you mare! Support me!

KATH. Make him stop! I shall be sick. He's upsetting my insides.

[ED *runs round.*]

ED. What did you want to provoke him for?

[SLOANE *shakes* KATH *harder. She screams.*]

KATH. My teeth! [*She clasps a hand over her mouth.*] My teeth! [SLOANE *flings her from him. She crawls round the floor searching.*] He's broke my teeth! Where are they?

ED. Expensive equipment gone west now see! I'm annoyed with you, boy. Seriously annoyed. Giving us the benefit of your pauperism. Is this what we listen to the Week's Good Cause for? A lot of vicars and actresses making appeals for cash gifts to raise hooligans who can't control themselves? I'd've given my cheque to the anti-Jewish League if I'd known.

KATH [*reaching under the settee*]. I'll still forgive and forget.

ED. Coming in here as a lodger. Raised in a charity home. The lack of common courtesy in some people is appalling.

SLOANE. She's won! The bitch has won!

[*He grips* ED's *arm.* ED *shrugs him away.*]

ED. We'll discuss the matter.

SLOANE. We need action not discussion. Persuade her. Cut her throat, but persuade her!

ED. Don't use that tone of voice to me, boy. I won't be dictated to. Perhaps we can share you.

SLOANE. Deal with her.

ED. We'll think of something.

SLOANE. She must be primed. Get her evidence correct.

ED. Don't worry. I'm in perfect control of the situation.

SLOANE. You're in control of nothing! Where are your influential friends? Ring them, we need protection.

KATH. It's his nerves. He doesn't know what he's doing.

ED. Put your teeth in will you? Sitting there with them in your hand.

KATH. He's broke them.

ED. They're only chipped. Go on, turn your back.

[KATH *puts her teeth in.*]

KATH. What are we going to do, Eddie?

ED. Stand up. We can't conduct a serious discussion from that position.

KATH. Help me up, Mr. Sloane. Thank you, baby. See, Ed, he hasn't lost respect for me.

ED. An arrangement to suit all tastes. That is what's wanted.

KATH. I don't want to lose my baby.

ED. You won't lose him.

KATH. But—

[ED *holds up a hand.*]

ED. What are your main requirements? I take it there's no question of making an honest woman of you. You don't demand the supreme sacrifice?

SLOANE. I'm not marrying her!

ED. Calm down, will you?

SLOANE. Remember our agreement.

ED. I'm keeping it in mind, boy.

SLOANE. Don't saddle me with her for life.

KATH. He's close to tears. Isn't he sweet?

ED. Yes, he's definitely attractive in adversity. Really, boy, what with one thing and another...I warned you against women, didn't I? They land you in impossible predicaments of this nature.

SLOANE. You can solve it, Ed.

ED. You believe that, do you? I hope so. Marriage is a non-starter then?

KATH. He's led me on.

ED. Are you repentant now? Truly ashamed of yourself?

SLOANE. I am.

ED. You aren't going to press your claims are you? Even if he thee worshipped with his body, his mind would be elsewhere. And a wife cannot testify against her husband.

KATH. Can't she?

ED. No, a minor point.

KATH. I don't mind about marriage as long as he doesn't leave me.

ED. Fine. [*Pause.*] I think, boy, you'd better go and wait in the car. Keep the engine running. I won't be long. I want a private talk with my sister.

SLOANE. Is it going to be O.K.?

ED. Well...perhaps.

SLOANE. I'll be grateful.

ED. Will you?

SLOANE. Eternally.

ED. Not eternally, boy. Just a few years.

[*He pats* SLOANE *on the shoulder.* SLOANE *exits.*]

What will the story be?

KATH. Like you said—he fell downstairs.

ED. That will explain the cuts and bruises. You'd better say you were out. Stick to that. You know nothing. I'll manage the doctor.

KATH. Yes, Ed.

ED. Can I trust you?

KATH. Yes.

ED. Then let's have no more threats. You'll support him?

KATH. As long as he stays here.

ED. You've had him six months; I'll have him the next six. I'm not robbing you of him permanently.

KATH. Aren't you?

ED. No question of it. [*Pause.*] As long as you're prepared to accept the idea of partnership.

KATH. For how long?

ED. As long as the agreement lasts.

KATH. How long is that?

ED. By the half-year.

KATH. That's too long, dear. I get so lonely.

ED. I've got no objections if he visits you from time to time. Briefly. We could put it in the contract. Fair enough?

KATH. Yes.

ED. I'd bring him over myself in the car. Now, you'll be more or less out of action for the next three months. So shall we say till next March? Agreed?

KATH. Perfect, Eddie. It's very clever of you to have thought of such a lovely idea.

ED. Put it down to my experience at the conference table. [*Car sounds off.*]

KATH. Can he be present at the birth of his child?

ED. You're not turning him into a midwife.

KATH. It deepens the relationship if the father is there.

ED. It's all any reasonable child can expect if the dad is present at the conception. Let's hear no more of it. Give me that locket.

KATH. It was his present to me.

ED. You'll get it back in March. [*She hands him the locket. He puts it on.*] And behave yourself in future. I'm not having you pregnant every year. I'll have a word with him about it. [*He kisses her cheek, pats her bottom.*] Be a good girl.

KATH. Yes, Ed.

Ed. Well, it's been a pleasant morning. See you later.

[*He exits. The front door slams.* KATH *goes to the sideboard and rummages in drawer; takes out a sweet, unwraps it and puts it into her mouth. Sits on settee.*]

Tragicomedy and Open Form

Introduction

Though types of plays are nearly as various as fish from the whale to the spiny-finned wrasse, critics usually fit them into three bins, comedies, tragedies, and leftovers, the first two much more discussed than the third. Aristotle passed judgment on hybrids by conspicuous silence; Cicero and Horace found them repulsive to nature, like human heads on the bodies of lions. In the Renaissance the particular mixture "tragicomedy" (a reversal form beginning as apparent tragedy and ending as comedy) was relatively short lived and even at the height of its popularity was distrusted by those who preferred having their heroes either joyfully married or sorrowfully slain. Recently, a historian concluded that tragicomedy proper came on the scene late and expired early. Plays that are neither distinctly tragic nor comic, however, are not rare nor are they new. Both the Greeks and Shakespeare wrote them, and such plays as the miracle and morality plays of the medieval "cycles" and heroic modes like Dryden's and Racine's would require trimming to fit conventional tragic or comic molds—not to mention the plays of Brecht, Williams, O'Neill, Beckett, Ionesco, Pirandello, Genet, and their predecessors Strindberg and Chekhov, which until recently dominated serious contemporary theater.

Though the term tragicomedy is often used to describe these plays, it suggests that the playwright intentionally sets out to blend one set of ingredients under another as under an egg beater, which is obviously not what happens in plays conceived of as distinct dramatic modes from the outset. Since critics and playwrights often consider comedy and tragedy as poles between which other forms are located, however, that very expectation sometimes produces mixtures of tragic and comic conventions and double plots, one strand high or dignified and the other low or comic, or one happily concluded and the other unhappily. In such mixtures as Shakespeare's history and problem plays, certain scenes often mirror others ironically, resulting in a *reciprocity* between tragedy and comedy or an antithetical mode that juxtaposes clowns and kings, pathos and humor. Characters may take part in two quite different actions (like Prince Hal in *1 Henry IV*) or in a diversity of actions that make for a diversity of *reactions* in the audience as well as for complexity of character. Hence mixed plots, whether purposely tragicomic or distinct and independent types, make it unlikely that the completion of one element will be the completion of all others. Or if all plot elements are resolved, as in *The Visit*, key people in the play may not realize fully what has happened, and their ignorance leaves an unresolved gap between them and the audience.

The complexity of action in mixed forms does not usually include the jostling incongruities by which seriousness explodes in farce. The slipping and falling of mixed-form characters may be humorous or ironic if we see it approaching from their blind sides, but the audience shares their injuries too much to laugh easily. Nor is their complexity merely a matter of intrigue, as the multiple schemes of *The Alchemist* are, for instance; rather, it is a complexity of cross-reference, discordant values, implication, character, and mood, like that of *The Cherry Orchard* and *1 Henry IV*. The comic element is either limited to minor characters or to embarrassments of major characters compatible with a degree of seriousness (like Lopakhin's clumsiness in *The Cherry Orchard*). Actually, comic humors and side-shows are usually limited even in comedy by the plots to which they are loosely relevant. Though clowning may not be directed to a particular purpose in advancing the action (a buffoon is always in a sense out of line), it is normally directed *against* something or deflates values that someone takes seriously. Both social expectation and artistic form require that a comedy sooner or later set aside laughable irrelevance and restore normalcy. But in mixed forms, the humor, though less likely to dissolve in laughter, is engrained; it is more incurable. The ending is not a purged, single state that accounts for all plot elements and returns to a world of common sense but a continued uneasy marriage of seriousness and comic incongruity, the antitheses of mood and character having implicitly derived from the basically incorrigible reality that the play imitates. The metaphysical farce of Beckett's *Waiting for Godot,* for instance, contrasts the vaudeville antics of two tramps with the seriousness of their plight, and they remain both as funny and as lost at the end as they have been all along. It would be misleading to say that Beckett's aim is to fuse tragic and comic conventions. Instead he uses them to work new awareness of the inartistic and mystifying forces that govern the action. Like Ionesco's anti-play *The Chairs* and other modern mixed forms, the play discredits conventional dramatic forms. Its aim is thus not to make the audience cry through laughter (as *comedie larmoyante* does) but to sharpen the audience's critical awareness of the play as an entertaining means of passing time while one waits for Godot.

Since so many modern and some older experiments in dramatic form fall outside the normal range of tragicomic reciprocity, let us call them open or indeterminate forms on the basis of their avoidance of plot symmetry and completion and begin with an examination of the implications of that openness for dramatic convention.

Open and Closed Dramatic Form   That married couples do not live happily ever after—unchanged by disease, quarrels, and old age—and that disaster in the real world does not assume the gratifying aesthetic form it has in tragedy has always been as apparent to dramatists as to other men. But those who write tragicomic mixtures and explore antithetical actions obviously feel more decisively that aesthetic forms that conclude too neatly and proceed with too great an inevitability falsify reality. In open or mixed drama, powers like Godot who can define a character's place once and for all fail to make their timely appearances: the characters feel permanently out of sorts, unable to define themselves by any summary action or even communicate effectively with the Godots who lead them on. Like Beckett's hero in the novel *The Unnamable* who concludes, "I don't know, I'll never know, in the silence you don't know, you must go on, I can't go on, I'll go on," some corner of their minds remains unemployed, in excess of the action, which leaves their feelings, too, detached from coherent purpose. Lacking final purpose, they cannot progress through passion to perception.

In contrast, in tragedy (as Jean Anouilh writes in *Antigone*) "nothing is in doubt and everyone's destiny is known. That makes for tranquillity": tranquility and simplicity of a kind. Caught in the machinery of his own acts or destiny, a tragic protagonist is not allowed to contemplate certain kinds of alternatives that may occur to the nonheroic characters of Chekhov or Brecht. He commits himself to an action completed in the play, which prevents his deciding part way through that he had better turn back. Like Anouilh's Antigone, who says in defiance of the way-things-are, "I want everything of life, I do; and I want it now! I want it total, complete," he is therefore relatively single-minded and strong-willed. Even Macbeth, Hamlet, and T. S. Eliot's Becket (*Murder in the Cathedral*), who vacillate a good deal, eventually commit themselves to a fatal course of action. We have difficulty imagining a fully tragic hero who does otherwise: Lear, for instance, no longer shattered by the discovery that children can be ungrateful, perhaps taking the Fool's advice and sitting comfortably before his daughters' fires; or Othello getting an annulment and conceding that, after all, infidelity is not chaos; Coriolanus deciding that if playing the politician before the mob is the only way to get elected, he'll have to go through with it.

In indeterminate plays, on the other hand, time and change undermine romantic absolutism and values that demand total commitment. The protagonist confronts a sea of alternatives, in the grammar of maybe rather than willed imperatives. He not only hesitates to commit himself, he has no way to; the action available to him cannot alter his environment significantly. He is reduced as his scene expands, his passion and will eroded by compromise, skepticism, and new shades of awareness. Neither death nor marriage is a consummation, only a change of condition.

In this openness, he is also unlike comic types such as the Seducer, the Glutton, or the Miser, which cannot range outside the motives allotted them (someone caught in an embarrassing position behind the closet door is forcibly summed up, for the moment, by his situation); and he is further unlike the prince and princess archetypes of romantic comedy, who tend to classify everything as either marriage-and-final-happiness or obstacle-to-marriage things. Though perhaps more obvious than the average unmasking, the recognition scene of Shakespeare's *As You Like It* is typical of what happens to both romantic protagonists and their comic counterparts:

DUKE SENIOR. If there be truth in sight, you are my daughter.
ORLANDO. If there be truth in sight, you are my Rosalind.
PHEBE. If sight and shape be true
    Why then, my love adieu!
ROSALIND. I'll have no father, if you be not he;
    I'll have no husband, if you be not he;
    Nor ne'er love woman, if you be not she.
HYMEN. Peace, ho! I bar confusion.
    'Tis I must make conclusion
        Of these most strange events.

In this manner Shakespeare brings to a ritual close various searches for accurate labels. After all maskings and intrigues are finished, truth is simply and plainly visible, both for the central pairs and for the humorous lovers who settle for less. Secure in his blessings, each sums up what he wishes in the titles daughter, husband, Rosalind. Hymen's task is indeed to "bar confusion" and "make conclusion." In contrast to this conclusiveness, indeterminate plays point toward some encroaching mystification, or perhaps something known but uncontrollable. What remains offstage beyond the limits of the represented action may become as important as the present-tense concern of the play, whose motives are buried in the past or directed toward a future too distant to be dramatized. The hero and heroine are presented, say, some fifteen years after marriage and have gradually come to realize that marriages are contracted in social terms none too clear and that the outcome is unforeseeable.

Open forms may also abandon the distinction between minor and major characters, between central and secondary actions, so clear in romance comedy and tragedy. In Chekhov, for instance, the movement of the play is not that of a single plot sweeping to a crisis and resolution (though it does have both a crisis and a resolution of sorts) but a choppy interaction of small movements, as a multiplicity of characters run against one another. Our involvement in a given character's plight is thus counterchecked by those who claim equal interest and sympathy, and we are forced to rise to the detached and ironic perspective of the playwright outside the ensemble. There are obviously many degrees of countercheck, as there are degrees of retardation of an action or obstacles to main characters. Shakespeare limits the openness of *1 Henry IV*, for instance, by centering interest in the prince, whose career is the connective matter of the play but is held back by trouble in the kingdom and his own truancy. (If Falstaff's criticism of honor and ambition represented the play's viewpoint, it would cease to matter whether or not the prince becomes what he sets out to be; our identification with the central hero would be jarred loose. Though he might eventually enact the role of king, it would seem a pretense, and the audience's perspective would transcend his. As it is, however, Falstaff qualifies our view of the kingship without constituting an equal counteraction.) Forms more completely open than this generally leave us detached enough from the concluding speeches to consider values and future possibilities not summed up in them, and we cannot leave the theater or put down the text with the singleness of response that tragic and comic catharsis foster.

Tragicomedy and the History Play   Comic and tragic plots often *prefigure* the true identity of the central figures during the course of the action. ("Everyone's destiny is known," as Anouilh says.) Tragicomedies in the sense of reversal plays that begin ominously but end happily (or *tragedia di lieto fin*) are equally definitive eventually, but they progress through a *misleading* prediction that prepares the characters for a startling reversal: a protagonist reported to have cast himself over a fatally high cliff (in despair over love) is discovered at a critical moment to have made friends with a bush on the way down and is now ready for marriage. The effect of false prediction and reversal is not so much to force the form open or even create a reciprocity of tragedy and comedy as to make for an even more definitive ending insofar as someone who has just escaped a large fall does not ponder the problems of the next thirty years. Moreover, a last minute reversal suggests that a miraculous force, either a god's or a hero's, has the kind of ultimate control over destiny that makes for closed forms.

A *tragedia di lieto fin,* then, might often be said to pass through a curse to a New Gospel blessing. Its affinities with religious ritual, by which divine and human purpose are united in one plot, are often explicit. In dramatizing scriptural events from Noah to the resurrection, for instance, medieval cycle plays make up a tragicomedy depicting Christian history in several parts. They begin with apparent tragedies such as Noah's flood or Herod's seeking of the Christ child and proceed to the good news of salvation. (The *felix culpa,* or fortunate fall, in which sin and death lead to redeemed life is basically a tragicomic concept.) As we have seen, the *Quem Quaeritis* trope, one of the early cycle plays, compresses a hint of the total movement of that tragicomedy into a single dramatic encounter:

QUESTION OF THE ANGELS. Whom seek ye in the sepulchre, O followers of Christ?
ANSWER OF THE MARYS. Jesus of Nazareth, which was crucified, O celestial ones.
ANGELS.   He is not here; he is risen, just as he foretold. Go, announce that he is risen
from the sepulchre.

The action seems momentarily headed for tragedy as the logical culmination of Adam's curse. But the reversal comes as the oracle said it would ("just as he foretold"), the fuller Christian context of which is readily supplied by the audience both from scripture and from surrounding church ceremonies. That the blessings extend to the audience is suggested by the final command, "Go, announce (to the church members) that he is risen." Similarly, in Calderon's *Devotion to the Cross,* all temporal disasters are translated into salvation for the hero, whose devotion to the cross frees him from the secular scramble. Earth remains a confused shambles, but his soul escapes.

As we suggested earlier, the difference between these sequential mixtures of tragedy and comedy and indeterminate forms is essentially that one involves a progression from one state to another while the other presents us with a permanent antithesis. If an open play dose have a reversal, it is likely to consist of the new knowledge of the protagonist, who has not heretofore realized the true nature of his plight. The difference will be clear if we imagine Beckett's *Waiting for Godot* offering a first messenger who announces to the tramps "Godot is dead, weep for him," and then a second who corrects him, "Godot is risen and blesses you, for the last shall be first" (a reversal form). As it is, the two messengers who do appear say much the same thing: no news from Godot, keep waiting. Thus, left without clear tidings on their road leading nowhere, the tramps anticipate, talk, cajole their fates, but remain unable to act, impotent, incurable. Godot retreats into a vague combination of father, employer, bureaucrat, and feudal lord—anything but the effective end-term or *deus ex machina* required to reverse their downward path. Perhaps one reason that he does not appear is that he could not clarify anything if he did; he cannot offer an ultimate station or remake the tramps' metaphysical condition or produce a long lost brother to clap them on the back and welcome them into the upper middle class. In problem forms the shoe, unlike the glass slipper, never fits. (Beckett makes literal application of this incompatibility of character and event, giving one of the tramps an odd-size boot that changes even the nature of its oddness from day to day.)

The chief difference between history plays and either conventional plays or comparatively more open forms is that their main concern is the hero's relationship with the collective community or realpolitik: the action of the central figure gives the play relatively defined limits, but the play also looks backward and forward in history and outward into the social body for its motives. It thus scatters the focus among subjects who suffer or rejoice at different rates, for different causes, and for different durations. The nodal points at which the characters are brought together are forms of large scale public pageantry, usually either battles or state ceremonies, short-lived in themselves but implicitly able to influence the future. The tension between our desire to see the emergence of a healthy society and the famines, crises, revolutions, and evolutions that history offers is never quite resolved. A conclusive reversal for one is likely to be gain for another. In this respect the history play is a cousin to modern plays of dispersed focus and antitheses of mood and value. It is not surprising to find Brecht, Pirandello, Strindberg, and others exploring variations of the form but making the ceremonies of state a kind of masquerade rather than enactments of genuine communal order.

Mood and Dramatic Counterpoint   Let us return to the idea of dispersed interest and antithetical structure. Any of the conclusive forms we have mentioned —tragedy, comedy, and tragedy-averted—place obstacles in the way of the main action that retard and complicate it, and such obstacles may amount to subplots and counterthemes. But only when the audience is led to spread its sympathy among characters in both primary and secondary actions do we have a genuine mixed and unresolved effect. The ruin of a Shylock or setting aside of a Falstaff for whom our sympathy is limited is not enough to undermine the blessings that the main characters are granted. As Johnson suggests with respect to the tragicomic structure of Shakespeare's plays, the passions may be "interrupted in their progress," but they are not dislocated as they are in the jarring confusions of indeterminate modes. Conventional forms are normally clear about who is to win and who is to lose, and with whom we are to take sides.

This is true even if the subplot parodies the main plot, as Falstaff parodies both Hotspur and the kingly dignity of Henry IV. In such a parody what appears solemn at one juncture is played with burlesque in another, but the contrast may serve only to prevent the audience from sinking into an uncritical identity with the official powers. In fully indeterminate modes on the other hand, morality and immorality, success and failure, honor and the burlesque of honor break loose from readily definable values. Two tramps talking of inconsequential matters may hold the center of the stage from which weightier affairs have been banished. The basic counterpoint of such forms is not that of main plot and subplot or even the kind of tragicomic reciprocity that Sean O'Casey describes as a dialectic of joy and sorrow; it is the more basic interplay of expectation and nonfulfillment, hope for a discovery of meaning and purpose in an action—but a discovery instead of mystery or absurdity. The questions posed by Ionesco's people who turn into rhinoceroses or Beckett's tramps are rudimentary questions of being and existence. Given the skepticism of the play and the breakdown of communication among the characters, no social order can take shape, and thus in a sense no play can form as coherent social interaction. The conventional connections between protagonist and antagonist, main plot and subplot, are replaced by an interplay of illusion and reality, or position and mere role playing.

The effect of such counterpoint is as far reaching on mood as it is on plot. As in Sean O'Casey's *The Plough and the Stars,* it juxtaposes diverse emotions. "Even where one lies dead," O'Casey writes, "laughter is often heard in the next room. There's no tragedy that isn't tinged with humor, no comedy that hasn't its share of tragedy." Dr. Johnson's concept of Shakespeare is similar:

> Shakespeare's plays are not in the rigorous and critical sense either tragedies or comedies, but compositions of a distinct kind; exhibiting the real state of sublunary nature, which partakes of good and evil, joy and sorrow, mingled with endless variety of proportion and innumerable modes of combination; and expressing the course of the world, in which the loss of one is the gain of another; in which, at the same time, the reveller is hasting to his wine, and the mourner burying his friend; in which the malignity of one is sometimes defeated by the frolick of another; and many mischiefs and many benefits are done and hindered without design.

For a strict neo-classicist this was an accurate account of even Shakespeare's main comedies and tragedies. For us it is still an accurate account of his problem plays. For instance, in *Troilus and Cressida* the audience is forced further from the hero than it would be from a normal comic or tragic protagonist. As Troilus abandons his belief in "truth's simplicity," he carries the play into a confusion of values that keeps the audience at a respectful distance. He says of Cressida, who has betrayed him:

> If beauty have a soul, this is not she.
> If souls guide vows, if vows are sanctimony,
> If sanctimony be the gods' delight,
> If there be rule in unity itself,
> This is not she.
> ....
> The bonds of heaven are slipp'd, dissolv'd, and loos'd;
> And with another knot, five-finger tied,
> The fractions of her faith, orts of her love,
> The fragments, scraps, the bits and greasy relics
> Of her o'er eaten-faith, are bound to Diomed.
>   (V.ii.138–60)

If indeed vows were sanctimony, it might be possible for the Trojans to form a perimeter of defense around those who incorporate it. But what is "below" in a fragmentary state remains untranslatable into universal "bonds of heaven." Hence the play reflects the "fragments, scraps, the bits and greasy relics" of unfaithful lovers and unprincipled politicians, and we realize that Shakespeare cannot allow Troilus either the honor of a tragic death or a comic (romance) marriage. As we last see him, Troilus is committed to continued war, and in an epilogue Pandarus suggests that the diseases of the play are those of the audience, which will carry them into the street.

Or consider Cressida's lament as she is taken from the Trojans. "O you immortal gods!" she apostrophizes in the high mode, "I will not go":

> I'll go in and weep,
> Tear my bright hair and scratch my praised cheeks,
> Crack my clear voice with sobs and break my heart
> With sounding Troilus. I will not go from Troy.

We are clearly meant to realize that her stand is partly laughable. As "bright hair," "praised cheeks," "clear voice," and the broken heart (and their serial listing) indicate, she is thinking of public accounts of her beauty, performances before the mirror, and her present style; straining too much for tragic gestures, she passes into melodrama. As the audience can perhaps guess from the posturing, she *will* leave Troy behind, with quite short memories and scarcely a tear. But then again, since the betrayal has serious repercussions at least for Troilus, the irony also has a bitter taste, appropriate to a play cast partly in the mood of Thersites, the "deformed and scurrilous Greek" who fingers the lust and greed around him too comfortably. The reaction of the audience is necessarily complex, both at the time of Cressida's speech and in retrospect.

Character and Alienation   As might be expected, the style of dialogue and other means of demonstrating character become inconclusive in such forms. Chekhov's people, for instance, form and dissolve duets and ensembles fluidly, as they search for some common ground and find, instead, merely crossing biases. In other modern dramatists, main characters often remain outsiders, letting others (perhaps under some variation of mass hypnosis) join public spectacles and become herds of rhinoceroses or chickens of a feather. The title character of Anouilh's play *Ardele,* for instance, never appears on stage among those who have respectability in common but speaks from behind locked doors. Her isolation indicates not only aloofness from social scheming but also incommunicable character, which may or may not be genuine but in either case is not available to those on stage. Like Godot, she is an invisible power, incapable of emerging and setting the players in order. Inconclusiveness of plot is thus matched by an undemonstrated quality of character and a social disequilibrium that contributes to its incapacity to find a social function.

Perhaps the most conspicuous tactician of the technique of alienation in recent times has been Bertolt Brecht. Though Beckett, Ionesco, Genet, and others offer more extreme examples of indeterminate form and anti-plays, Brecht has proceeded more methodically in evolving a theory of the theater to match its practice. To Brecht as to Shakespeare in *Troilus and Cressida,* the theater is a satiric medium designed to distance the audience from the characters, whom as a Marxist he finds to be bourgeois roleplayers. Hence he seeks for ways to *talk about* as well as *enact* character, including such devices as the narration of parables and the summary of scenes in progress on painted signs. Believing that a critical audience demands a scientific exposure of human inconsistencies, he jettisons both the dim half-lights and colors of the impressionist theater and the naturalistic method of the Russian director Stanislavsky, the one presupposing psychic tones and depths in the individual mind, the other an uncritical acceptance of people as they are, in all their squalor and greed. Instead, he floods the stage with white light and makes the source of light visible. He asks the actors to report on character as a mimic might demonstrate an event to someone absent when it happened, implying as they proceed, "this is the way your soldiers, your profiteers, and your brigands behave."

By means of these devices, Brecht aims to "historify" the action and anatomize the past as it is being represented. (His original term for plays of historification was "epic" theater.) He thus gives the theater a stronger narrative past tense than is normal and allows ample opportunity for satiric commentary. The play becomes a dialectical instrument (as he later called it), both *mimicry* and the demonstration of a *thesis,* a projection of what is or has been against a clear suggestion of what ought to be.

These techniques of alienation are related to another aspect of indeterminate plays widely used by other writers as well as Brecht: the mixing of fantasy, realism, and allegory. Historical narrative leads to sprawling, episodic structures, but it can be drawn together with parables, symbolic fantasies, and allegorical incidents in the manner of morality plays. Unlike traditional morality plays, however, open forms such as Ionesco's and Brecht's do not reward virtue and punish vice. Their rearrangements of reality stop short of improving on it. Though they pose basic moral questions, they are likely to leave them doubtful or resolve issues in ways offensive to justice. At the end of Dürrenmatt's *The Visit,* for instance, the play's money goddess forces the citizens of a small town to take part in hollow rites devoted to her, to seal their attainment of prosperity with a sacrifice of their humanity. The discrepancy between the official roles they enact and the inner reality does not permit their emergence into a healthy social organism. What in a conventional comedy or tragedy might be taken as relief over the removal of danger to the community is an ironic display of oblivious self-concern. The final scene is a mixture of allegory, Brecht-like satire, dreamlike fantasy, and social realism, the total effect of which is again to make us rise above the limited awareness of the characters and reinterpret the prosperity of a typical western European town from outside.

As forms of alienation and satire, open plays point up the difficulties of writing conventional tragedy and comedy without some concept of human dignity and individual worth on which to found a social order. Their suspended enigmas, multiplicity of ironies and points of view, mixtures of bitterness and gaiety, tangled and confused conversation, and exposure of foolishness make them a highly intellectual theater having quite different functions from plays that enact the commonly accepted values of more unified social orders.

Everyman

Everyman dates from around the close of the fifteenth century and marks a relatively late stage in the movement of drama from the precincts of the church to the secular theater. Its strongest affinities are with homiletic literature, its moral being plainly set forth in the opening speech of the messenger and summed up in a final admonition, "how transitory be all our day." Put abstractly, this *memento mori* appears to offer little latitude for dramatic entertainment and even less for drama's normal business of complication, intrigue, and unraveling. But the play is more than a dry illustration of vice and virtue: it employs a dramatic method and builds toward a climax that defines the relative value of the inner and external forces that Everyman confronts in his trial.

Structurally, the ordeal of Everyman after Death's summons follows the familiar pattern of the separation of true from false friends under an experience that throws new light on all customary institutions and values. The light is harshly truthful and so the friends are naturally not anxious to expose themselves to it. But they desert Everyman not so much because they are treacherous as because by definition they cannot go where he must. The purpose of the play is to demonstrate which ones can, and thus to argue implicitly that what they represent should constitute one's goals while living. Most surprising, perhaps, is the last minute desertion of everything that could be called character and intellect. Everyman requires only the knowledge that leads directly to moral purgation, which does not include science, art, or industry (all preparations for a career among life's goods and services). Only Good Deeds goes all the way.

This evaluation of means by the end causes a complete disjunction between temporal and eternal life, and this disjunction underlies the dramatic shock of the play. Unlike the reversal of tragedy, its main change of state comes early in the play; its impact on Everyman thus suggests tragedy carried beyond the normal conclusion until a redefinition of the hero's destiny converts it into comedy. Everyman's shock does touch upon some of the deeper hiding places of his ego, however, and like many allegories, *Everyman* reinforces it with a traumatic, dreamlike progression. (*Pilgrim's Progress,* for instance, begins with a dream: "As I walked through the wilderness of this world," Christian says, "I lighted on a certain place where was a Den, and I laid me down in that place to sleep; and, as I slept, I dreamed a dream.") The flattened style and matter-of-fact method of the play do less than they might in this mode, but the play does suggest an inherent anxiety that gives weight to the semi-choral lamentations of the hero (no doubt more powerful to a fifteenth-century audience than to a modern reader).

Unlike the mystifying dream-shapes of some allegories, the tormentors of Everyman are eventually controlled and assigned a definite nomenclature: they are after all the familiar shapes of Prodigality, Vice, Worldly Wisdom, and Goods.

Our anxiety over Everyman's apparently tragic summons gives way to relief at his escape from them. That relief is perhaps qualified by an awareness of its expense, but the angel's promise for the future clearly outweighs the loss of Everyman's fair-weather cousins.

Everyman

MESSENGER
GOD: ADONAI
DEATH
EVERYMAN
FELLOWSHIP
COUSIN
KINDRED
GOODS
GOOD DEEDS

KNOWLEDGE
CONFESSION
BEAUTY
STRENGTH
DISCRETION
FIVE WITS
ANGEL
DOCTOR

*Here beginneth a treatise how the High
Father of Heaven sendeth Death to
summon every creature to come and
give account of their lives in this world,
and is in manner of a moral play.*

[*Enter* MESSENGER *to speak prologue.*]

MESSENGER. I pray you all give your
    audience,
  And hear this matter with reverence,
  By figure a moral play—
  The *Summoning of Everyman* called
    it is,
  That of our lives and ending shows 5
  How transitory we be all day.
  This matter is wondrous precious,
  But the intent of it is more gracious,
  And sweet to bear away.
  The story saith:—Man, in the begin-
    ning,   10
  Look well, and take good heed to
    the ending,
  Be you never so gay!
  Ye think sin in the beginning full
    sweet,
  Which in the end causeth the soul
    to weep,

  When the body lieth in clay.   15
  Here shall you see how Fellowship
    and Jollity,
  Both Strength, Pleasure, and Beauty,
  Will fade from thee as flower in May.
  For ye shall hear how our Heaven
    King
  Calleth Everyman to a general reck-
    oning.   20
  Give audience, and hear what he
    doth say.   [*Exit.*]

[GOD *speaketh from above.*]

GOD. I perceive, here in my majesty,
  How that all creatures be to me
    unkind,
  Living without dread in worldly pros-
    perity.
  Of ghostly sight the people be so
    blind,   25—
  Drowned in sin, they know me not
    for their God.
  In worldly riches is all their mind,
  They fear not my rightwiseness, the
    sharp rod;
  My love that I showed when I for
    them died
  They forget clean, and shedding of
    my blood red;   30

From Anthology of English Drama Before
Shakespeare, *edited by Robert B. Heilman,
published by Holt, Rinehart and Winston.*

25 *ghostly sight:* spiritual insight.

I hanged between two, it cannot be
denied;
To get them life I suffered to be dead;
I healed their feet, with thorns hurt
was my head.
I could do no more than I did, truly;
And now I see the people do clean
forsake me.   35
They use the seven deadly sins dam-
nable;
As pride, covetise, wrath, and lechery,
Now in the world be made com-
mendable;
And thus they leave of angels the
heavenly company.
Every man liveth so after his own
pleasure,   40
And yet of their life they be nothing
sure.
I see the more that I them forbear
The worse they be from year to year;
All that liveth appaireth fast.
Therefore I will, in all the haste,   45
Have a reckoning of every man's
person;
For, and I leave the people thus alone
In their life and wicked tempests,
Verily they will become much worse
than beasts;
For now one would by envy another
up eat;   50
Charity they all do clean forget.
I hoped well that every man
In my glory should make his man-
sion,
And thereto I had them all elect;
But now I see, like traitors deject,   55
They thank me not for the pleasure
that I to them meant,
Nor yet for their being that I them
have lent.
I proffered the people great multitude
of mercy,
And few there be that asketh it
heartily;
They be so cumbered with worldly
riches,   60

That needs on them I must do justice,
On every man living, without fear.
Where art thou, Death, thou mighty
messenger?

[*Enter* DEATH.]

DEATH. Almighty God, I am here at
your will,
Your commandment to fulfill.   65
GOD. Go thou to Everyman,
And show him, in my name,
A pilgrimage he must on him take,
Which he in no wise may escape;
And that he bring with him a sure
reckoning   70
Without delay or any tarrying.
DEATH. Lord, I will in the world go
run over all,
And cruelly out search both great
and small.   [GOD *withdraws*.]
Every man will I beset that liveth
beastly
Out of God's laws, and dreadeth not
folly.   75
He·that loveth riches I will strike
with my dart,
His sight to blind, and from heaven
to depart,
Except that alms be his good friend,
In hell for to dwell, world without
end.
Lo, yonder I see Everyman walk-
ing;   80
Full little he thinketh on my coming;
His mind is on fleshly lusts and his
treasure;
And great pain it shall cause him
to endure
Before the Lord, Heaven King.
Everyman, stand still! Whither art
thou going   85
Thus gaily? Hast thou thy Maker
forgot?
EVERYMAN. Why askest thou?
Wouldst thou wete?
DEATH. Yea, sir, I will show you;
In great haste I am sent to thee   90
From God out of his Majesty.

---

44 *appaireth:* declines. 46 *reckoning:* doom
or judgment, balancing of the "book of count",
the goal of Everyman's summoning. 47 *and:* if.

88 *wete:* know.

EVERYMAN. What, sent to me?

DEATH. Yea, certainly.

    Though thou have forgot him here,

    He thinketh on thee in the heavenly

      sphere,   95

    As, ere we depart, thou shalt know.

EVERYMAN. What desireth God of me?

DEATH. That shall I show thee;

    A reckoning he will needs have

    Without any longer respite.   100

EVERYMAN. To give a reckoning longer

    leisure I crave;

    This blind matter troubleth my wit.

DEATH. On thee thou must take a long

    journey;

    Therefore thy book of count with

      thee thou bring;

    For turn again thou cannot by no

      way.   105

    And look thou be sure of thy reck-

      oning,

    For before God thou shalt answer and

      show

    Thy many bad deeds, and good but

      a few,

    How thou hast spent thy life, and

      in what wise,

    Before the Chief Lord of paradise. 110

    Have ado that we were in that way,

    For, wete thou well, thou shalt make

    none attorney.

EVERYMAN. Full unready I am such

    reckoning to give.

    I know thee not. What messenger

    art thou?

DEATH. I am Death, that no man

    dreadeth.   115

    For every man I 'rest, and no man

    spareth;

    For it is God's commandment

    That all to me should be obedient.

EVERYMAN. O Death! thou comest when

    I had thee least in mind!

    In thy power it lieth me to save,   120

    Yet of my goods will I give thee, if

    thou will be kind;

---

103 *On:* upon. 111 *Have ado:* hustle. 112
wete: know; *make none attorney:* make no
one speak for you.

    Yea, a thousand pound shalt thou

    have,

    If thou defer this matter till another

    day.

DEATH. Everyman, it may not be, by

    no way!

    I set not by gold, silver, nor riches, 125

    Nor by pope, emperor, king, duke,

    nor princes.

    For, and I would receive gifts great,

    All the world I might get;

    But my custom is clean contrary.

    I give thee no respite. Come hence,

    and not tarry.   130

EVERYMAN. Alas! shall I have no longer

    respite?

    I may say Death giveth no warning.

    To think on thee, it maketh my

    heart sick,

    For all unready is my book of

    reckoning.

    But twelve year and I might have

    abiding,   135

    My counting-book I would make so

    clear,

    That my reckoning I should not need

    to fear.

    Wherefore, Death, I pray thee, for

    God's mercy,

    Spare me till I be provided of remedy.

DEATH. Thee availeth not to cry, weep,

    and pray;   140

    But haste thee lightly that thou

    were gone that journey,

    And prove thy friends if thou can.

    For wete thou well the tide abideth

    no man;

    And in the world each living creature

    For Adam's sin must die of nature. 145

EVERYMAN. Death, if I should this

    pilgrimage take,

    And my reckoning surely make,

    Show me, for saint charity,

    Should I not come again shortly?

DEATH. No, Everyman; and thou be

    once there,   150

    Thou mayst never more come here,

    Trust me verily.

EVERYMAN. O gracious God, in the high

    seat celestial,

Have mercy on me in this most
 need!
Shall I have no company from this
 vale terrestrial   155
Of mine acquaintance that way me to
 lead?
DEATH. Yea, if any be so hardy,
That would go with thee and bear
 thee company.
Hie thee that thou were gone to
 God's magnificence,
Thy reckoning to give before his
 presence.   160
What! weenest thou thy life is given
 thee,
And thy worldly goods also?
EVERYMAN. I had weened so, verily.
DEATH. Nay, nay; it was but lent thee;
For, as soon as thou art gone,   165
Another a while shall have it, and
 then go therefrom
Even as thou hast done.
Everyman, thou art mad! Thou hast
 thy wits five,
And here on earth will not amend
 thy life;
For suddenly I do come.   170
EVERYMAN. O wretched caitiff! whither
 shall I flee,
That I might 'scape endless sorrow?
Now, gentle Death, spare me till
 tomorrow,
That I may amend me
With good advisement.   175
DEATH. Nay, thereto I will not consent,
Nor no man will I respite,
But to the heart suddenly I shall
 smite
Without any advisement.
And now out of thy sight I will me
 hie;   180
See thou make thee ready shortly,
For thou mayst say this is the day
That no man living may 'scape away.

[*Exit* DEATH.]

EVERYMAN. Alas! I may well weep with

sighs deep.
Now have I no manner of com-
 pany   185
To help me in my journey and me
 to keep;
And also my writing is full unready.
How shall I do now for to excuse
 me?
I would to God I had never been
 gete!
To my soul a full great profit it had
 be;   190
For now I fear pains huge and great.
The time passeth; Lord, help, that
 all wrought.
For though I mourn it availeth
 naught.
The day passeth, and is almost a-go;
I wot not well what for to do.   195
To whom were I best my complaint
 to make?
What if I to Fellowship thereof
 spake,
And showed him of this sudden
 chance?
For in him is all mine affiance,
We have in the world so many a
 day   200
Been good friends in sport and play.
I see him yonder, certainly;
I trust that he will bear me com-
 pany;
Therefore to him will I speak to ease
 my sorrow.
Well met, good Fellowship, and good
 morrow!   205

[FELLOWSHIP *speaketh.*]

FELLOWSHIP. Everyman, good morrow,
 by this day!
Sir, why lookest thou so piteously?
If any thing be amiss, I pray thee
 me say,
That I may help to remedy.
EVERYMAN. Yea, good Fellowship,
 yea,   210
I am in great jeopardy.

---

161 *weenest:* think. 171 *caitiff!:* scoundrel.
179 *advisement:* warning.

189 *gete:* begot. 195 *wot:* know. 199 *affiance:*
trust.

FELLOWSHIP. My true friend, show to me your mind;
I will not forsake thee to my life's end
In the way of good company.
EVERYMAN. That was well spoken, and lovingly.   215
FELLOWSHIP. Sir, I must needs know your heaviness;
I have pity to see you in any distress;
If any have you wronged, ye shall revenged be,
Though I on the ground be slain for thee
Though that I know before that I should die.   220
EVERYMAN. Verily, Fellowship, gramercy.
FELLOWSHIP. Tush! by thy thanks I set not a straw!
Show me your grief, and say no more.
EVERYMAN. If I my heart should to you break,
And then you to turn your mind from me,   225
And would not me comfort when you hear me speak,
Then should I ten times sorrier be.
FELLOWSHIP. Sir, I say as I will do, indeed.
EVERYMAN. Then be you a good friend at need;
I have found you true here before.   230
FELLOWSHIP. And so ye shall evermore;
For, in faith, and thou go to hell,
I will not forsake thee by the way!
EVERYMAN. Ye speak like a good friend. I believe you well;
I shall deserve it, and I may.   235
FELLOWSHIP. I speak of no deserving, by this day!
For he that will say and nothing do
Is not worthy with good company to go;
Therefore show me the grief of your mind,
As to your friend most loving and kind.   240
EVERYMAN. I shall show you how it is:

Commanded I am to go a journey,
A long way, hard and dangerous,
And give a strict count without delay
Before the high judge, Adonai.   245
Wherefore, I pray you, bear me company,
As ye have promised, in this journey.
FELLOWSHIP. That is matter indeed! Promise is duty;
But, and I should take such a voyage on me,
I know it well, it should be to my pain.   250
Also it maketh me afeared, certain.
But let us take counsel here as well as we can,
For your words would fright a strong man.
EVERYMAN. Why, ye said if I had need, Ye would me never forsake, quick nor dead,   255
Though it were to hell, truly.
FELLOWSHIP. So I said, certainly,
But such pleasures be set aside, the sooth to say.
And also, if we took such a journey, When should we come again?   260
EVERYMAN. Nay, never again till the day of doom.
FELLOWSHIP. In faith, then will not I come there!
Who hath you these tidings brought?
EVERYMAN. Indeed, Death was with me here.
FELLOWSHIP. Now, by God that all hath bought,   265
If Death were the messenger,
For no man that is living today
I will not go that loath journey—
Nor for the father that begat me!
EVERYMAN. Ye promised otherwise, pardie.   270
FELLOWSHIP. I wot well I said so, truly;
And yet if thou wilt eat, and drink, and make good cheer,
Or haunt to women the lusty company,

---

271 *wot:* know.

I would not forsake you while the day
is clear,
Trust me verily!   275
EVERYMAN. Yea, thereto ye would be
ready;
To go to mirth, solace, and play,
Your mind will sooner apply
Than to bear me company in my
long journey.
FELLOWSHIP. Now, in good faith, I
will not that way.   280
But and thou wilt murder, or any
man kill,
In that I will help thee with a good
will!
EVERYMAN. O, that is a simple advice
indeed!
Gentle fellow, help me in my neces-
sity;
We have loved long, and now I
need,   285
And now, gentle Fellowship, remem-
ber me!
FELLOWSHIP. Whether ye have loved
me or no,
By Saint John, I will not with thee
go.
EVERYMAN. Yet, I pray thee, take the
labor, and do so much for me
To bring me forward, for saint
charity,   290
And comfort me till I come without
the town.
FELLOWSHIP. Nay, and thou would give
me a new gown,
I will not a foot with thee go;
But, and thou had tarried, I would
not have left thee so.
And as now God speed thee in thy
journey,   295
For from thee I will depart as fast
as I may.
EVERYMAN. Whither away, Fellowship?
Will you forsake me?
FELLOWSHIP. Yea, by my fay, to God
I betake thee.
EVERYMAN. Farewell, good Fellowship!
For thee my heart is sore;

Adieu forever! I shall see thee no
more.   300
FELLOWSHIP. In faith, Everyman, fare-
well now at the end!
For you I will remember that parting is mourning.

[Exit FELLOWSHIP.]

EVERYMAN. Alack! shall we thus depart
indeed
(Ah, Lady, help!) without any more
comfort?
Lo, Fellowship forsaketh me in my
most need.   305
For help in this world wither shall
I resort?
Fellowship here before with me would
merry make,
And now little sorrow for me doth
he take.
It is said, "In prosperity men friends
may find,
Which in adversity be full un-
kind."   310
Now whither for succor shall I flee,
Sith that Fellowship hath forsaken
me?
To my kinsmen I will, truly,
Praying them to help me in my
necessity;
I believe that they will do so,   315
For "kind will creep where it may
not go."
I will go say, for yonder I see them
go.
Where be ye now, my friends and
kinsmen?

[*Enter* KINDRED *and* COUSIN.]

KINDRED. Here be we now, at your
commandment.
Cousin, I pray you show us your
intent   320
In any wise, and do not spare.
COUSIN. Yea, Everyman, and to us
declare
If ye be disposed to go any wither,
For, wete you well, we will live and
die together.

---

298 *betake:* leave.

316 *go:* walk.   317 *say:* try.

KINDRED. In wealth and woe we will with you hold,   325
For over his kin a man may be bold.
EVERYMAN. Gramercy, my friends and kinsmen kind.
Now shall I show you the grief of my mind.
I was commanded by a messenger
That is a high king's chief officer;   330
He bade me go a pilgrimage, to my pain,
And I know well I shall never come again;
Also I must give a reckoning straight,
For I have a great enemy that hath me in wait,
Which intendeth me for to hinder.   335
KINDRED. What account is that which ye must render?
That would I know.
EVERYMAN. Of all my works I must show
How I have lived, and my days spent;
Also of ill deeds that I have used   340
In my time, sith life was me lent;
And of all virtues that I have refused.
Therefore I pray you go thither with me,
To help to make mine account, for saint charity.
COUSIN. What, to go thither? Is that the matter?   345
Nay, Everyman, I had liefer fast bread and water
All this five year and more.
EVERYMAN. Alas, that ever I was bore!
For now shall I never be merry
If that you forsake me.   350
KINDRED. Ah, sir, what! Ye be a m rry man!
Take good heart to you, and make no moan.
But one thing I warn you, by Saint Anne,
As for me, ye shall go alone.
EVERYMAN. My Cousin, will you not with me go?   355

COUSIN. No, by our Lady! I have the cramp in my toe.
Trust not to me; for, so God me speed,
I will deceive you in your most need.
KINDRED. It availeth not us to tice.
Ye shall have my maid with all my heart;   360
She loveth to go to feasts, there to be nice,
And to dance, and abroad to start;
I will give her leave to help you in that journey,
If that you and she may agree.
EVERYMAN. Now show me the very effect of your mind.   365
Will you go with me, or abide behind?
KINDRED. Abide behind? Yea, that will I, and I may!
Therefore farewell till another day.
                    [*Exit* KINDRED.]
EVERYMAN. How should I be merry or glad?
For fair promises men to me make,   370
But when I have most need, they me forsake.
I am deceived; that maketh me sad.
COUSIN. Cousin Everyman, farewell now,
For verily I will not go with you;
Also of mine own life an unready reckoning   375
I have to account; therefore I make tarrying.
Now, God keep thee, for now I go.
                    [*Exit* COUSIN.]
EVERYMAN. Ah, Jesus! is all come hereto?
Lo, fair words maketh fools fain;
They promise and nothing will do certain.   380
My kinsmen promised me faithfully
For to abide with me steadfastly,
And now fast away do they flee.
Even so Fellowship promised me.
What friend were best me of to provide?   385

---

334 *hath me in wait:* lies in wait for me.   359 *tice:* entice.   379 *fain:* glad.

I lose my time here longer to abide.
Yet in my mind a thing there is:
All my life I have loved riches;
If that my Goods now help me might,
He would make my heart full
    light.   390
I will speak to him in this distress.
Where art thou, my Goods and riches?
GOODS [*from within*]. Who calleth me?
    Everyman? What, hast thou haste?
I lie here in corners, trussed and
    piled so high,
And in chests I am locked so fast, 395
Also sacked in bags—thou mayst see
    with thine eye—
I cannot stir; in packs low I lie.
What would ye have? Lightly me say.
EVERYMAN. Come hither, Goods, in all
    the haste thou may.
For of counsel I must desire thee. 400

[*Enter* GOODS.]

GOODS. Sir, and ye in the world have
    sorrow or adversity,
That can I help you to remedy
    shortly.
EVERYMAN. It is another disease that
    grieveth me;
In this world it is not, I tell thee so.
I am sent for another way to go, 405
To give a strict count general
Before the highest Jupiter of all;
And all my life I have had joy and
    pleasure in thee;
Therefore I pray thee go with me,
For, peradventure, thou mayst before
    God Almighty   410
My reckoning help to clean and
    purify;
For it is said ever among,
That "money maketh all right that
    is wrong."
GOODS. Nay, Everyman; I sing another
    song,
I follow no man in such voyages; 415
For, and I went with thee,
Thou shouldst fare much the worse
    for me;
For because on me thou did set thy
    mind,

Thy reckoning I have made blotted
    and blind,
That thine account thou cannot make
    truly;   420
And that hast thou for the love of
    me.
EVERYMAN. That would grieve me full
    sore,
When I should come to that fearful
    answer.
Up, let us go thither together.
GOODS. Nay, not so! I am too brittle,
    I may not endure;   425
I will follow no man one foot, be ye
    sure.
EVERYMAN. Alas! I have thee loved,
    and had great pleasure
All my life-days on goods and trea-
    sure.
GOODS. That is to thy damnation, with-
    out lesing!
For my love is contrary to the love
    everlasting.   430
But if thou had me loved moderately
    during,
As to the poor to give part of me,
Then shouldst thou not in this dolor
    be,
Nor in this great sorrow and care.
EVERYMAN. Lo, now was I deceived
    ere I was ware,   435
And all I may wyte my spending of
    time.
GOODS. What, weenest thou that I am
    thine?
EVERYMAN. I had weened so.
GOODS. Nay, Everyman, I say no;
As for a while I was lent thee, 440
A season thou hast had me in pros-
    perity.
My condition is man's soul to kill;
If I save one, a thousand I do spill;
Weenest thou that I will follow thee
From this world? Nay, verily. 445
EVERYMAN. I had weened otherwise.
GOODS. Therefore to thy soul Goods is
    a thief;

---

429 *lesing:* lying. 435 *ware:* aware, wary.
436 *wyte:* blame.

For when thou art dead, this is my
guise—
Another to deceive in the same wise
As I have done thee, and all to his
soul's reprief.   450
EVERYMAN. O false Goods, curséd thou
be!
Thou traitor to God, that hast de-
ceived me
And caught me in thy snare.
GOODS. Marry! thou brought thyself
in care,
Whereof I am right glad.   455
I must needs laugh, I cannot be sad.
EVERYMAN. Ah, Goods, thou hast had
long my heartly love;
I gave thee that which should be
the Lord's above.
But wilt thou not go with me indeed?
I pray thee truth to say.   460
GOODS. No, so God me speed!
Therefore farewell, and have good
day.   [*Exit* GOODS.]
EVERYMAN. O, to whom shall I make
my moan
For to go with me in that heavy
journey?
First Fellowship said he would with
me gone;   465
His words were very pleasant and
gay,
But afterward he left me alone.
Then spake I to my kinsmen, all in
despair,
And also they gave me words fair,
They lacked no fair speaking,   470
But all forsook me in the ending.
Then went I to my Goods, that I
loved best,
In hope to have comfort, but there
had I least;
For my Goods sharply did me tell
That he bringeth many into hell.   475
Then of myself I was ashamed,
And so I am worthy to be blamed;
Thus may I well myself hate.
Of whom shall I now counsel take?
I think that I shall never speed   480

Till that I go to my Good Deeds.
But alas! she is so weak
That she can neither go nor speak.
Yet will I venture on her now.
My Good Deeds, where be you?   485

[GOOD DEEDS *speaks from the ground.*]

GOOD DEEDS. Here I lie, cold in the
ground.
Thy sins hath me sore bound,
That I cannot stir.
EVERYMAN. O Good Deeds! I stand in
fear;
I must you pray of counsel,   490
For help now should come right well.
GOOD DEEDS. Everyman, I have under-
standing
That ye be summoned account to
make
Before Messias, of Jerusalem King;
And you do by me, that journey with
you will I take.   495
EVERYMAN. Therefore I come to you
my moan to make;
I pray you that ye will go with me.
GOOD DEEDS. I would full fain, but I
cannot stand, verily.
EVERYMAN. Why, is there anything on
you fall?
GOOD DEEDS. Yea, sir, I may thank
you of all;   500
If ye had perfectly cheered me,
Your book of count full ready had
be.
Look, the books of your works and
deeds eke;
Ah, see how they lie under the feet,
To your soul's heaviness.   505
EVERYMAN. Our Lord Jesus help me!
For one letter here I cannot see.
GOOD DEEDS. There is a blind reckon-
ing in time of distress!
EVERYMAN. Good Deeds, I pray you,
help me in this need,
Or else I am forever damned in-
deed;   510

---

448 *guise:* practice. 450 *reprief:* reproof.

495 *do by me:* do as I say. 498 *fain:* gladly.
499 *on you fall:* befalls you. 500 *of all:* for
all. 501 *cheered:* encouraged. 503 *eke:* also.

Therefore help me to make my
reckoning
Before the Redeemer of all thing,
That King is, and was, and ever shall.
GOOD DEEDS. Everyman, I am sorry of
your fall,
And fain would I help you, and I
were able.   515
EVERYMAN. Good Deeds, your counsel
I pray you give me.
GOOD DEEDS. That shall I do verily;
Though that on my feet I may not
go,
I have a sister that shall with you
also,
Called Knowledge, which shall with
you abide,   520
To help you to make that dreadful
reckoning.

[*Enter* KNOWLEDGE.]

KNOWLEDGE. Everyman, I will go with
thee, and be thy guide
In thy most need to go by thy side.
EVERYMAN. In good condition I am
now in everything,
And am wholly content with this
good thing;   525
Thanked be God my Creator.
GOOD DEEDS. And when he hath
brought thee there,
Where thou shalt heal thee of thy
smart,
Then go you with your reckoning and
your Good Deeds together
For to make you joyful at heart 530
Before the blesséd Trinity.
EVERYMAN. My Good Deeds, gramercy!
I am well content, certainly,
With your words sweet.
KNOWLEDGE. Now go we together
lovingly   535
To Confession, that cleansing river.
EVERYMAN. For joy I weep; I would
we were there!
But, I pray you, give me cognition
Where dwelleth that holy man, Con-
fession.
KNOWLEDGE. In the house of salva-
tion;   540
We shall find him in that place,

That shall us comfort, by God's
grace.

[KNOWLEDGE *leads* EVERYMAN *to* CON-
FESSION.]

Lo, this is Confession. Kneel down
and ask mercy,
For he is in good conceit with God
almighty.
EVERYMAN [*kneeling*]. O glorious
fountain, that all uncleanness doth
clarify,   545
Wash from me the spots of vice
unclean,
That on me no sin may be seen.
I come, with Knowledge, for my
redemption,
Redempt with hearty and full con-
trition;
For I am commanded a pilgrimage
to take,   550
And great accounts before God to
make.
Now, I pray you, Shrift, mother of
salvation.
Help my Good Deeds for my piteous
exclamation.
CONFESSION. I know your sorrow well,
Everyman.
Because with Knowledge ye come to
me,   555
I will you comfort as well as I can,
And a precious jewel I will give thee,
Called penance, voider of adversity;
Therewith shall your body chastised
be,
With abstinence, and perseverance
in God's service.   560
Here shall you receive that scourge of
me. [*Gives* EVERYMAN *a scourge.*]
Which is penance strong, that ye
must endure
To remember thy Savior was scourg-
ed for thee
With sharp scourges, and suffered it
patiently;
So must thou ere thou 'scape that
painful pilgrimage.   565
Knowledge, keep him in this voyage,

544 *conceit:* esteem.

And by that time Good Deeds will
be with thee.
But in any wise be seeker of mercy,
For your time draweth fast, and ye
will saved be;
Ask God mercy, and He will grant
truly;   570
When with the scourge of penance
man doth him bind,
The oil of forgiveness then shall he
find.   [*Exit* CONFESSION.]
EVERYMAN. Thanked be God for his
gracious work!
For now I will my penance begin;
This hath rejoiced and lighted my
heart,   575
Though the knots be painful and
hard within.
KNOWLEDGE. Everyman, look your
penance that ye fulfill,
What pain that ever it to you be,
And Knowledge shall give you coun-
sel at will
How your account ye shall make
clearly. [EVERYMAN *kneels*.]   580
EVERYMAN. O eternal God! O heavenly
figure!
O way of rightwiseness! O goodly
vision!
Which descended down in a virgin
pure
Because he would Everyman redeem,
Which Adam forfeited by his dis-
obedience.   585
O blesséd Godhead! elect and high
divine,
Forgive me my grievous offense;
Here I cry thee mercy in this
presence.
O ghostly treasure! O ransomer and
redeemer!
Of all the world hope and conduc-
tor,   590
Mirror of joy, and founder of mercy,
Which illumineth heaven and earth
thereby,
Hear my clamorous complaint, though
it late be.
Receive my prayers; unworthy in
this heavy life.
Though I be a sinner most abomi-

nable,   595
Yet let my name be written in
Moses' table.
O Mary! pray to the Maker of all
thing,
Me for to help at my ending,
And save me from the power of my
enemy,
For Death assaileth me strongly. 600
And, Lady, that I may by means of
thy prayer
Of your Son's glory to be partner,
By the means of his passion I it
crave;
I beseech you, help my soul to save.

[*He rises.*]

Knowledge, give me the scourge of
penance.   605
My flesh therewith shall give a
quittance.
I will now begin, if God give me
grace.
KNOWLEDGE. Everyman, God give you
time and space.
Thus I bequeath you in the hands
of our Savior,
Now may you make your reckoning
sure.   610
EVERYMAN. In the name of the Holy
Trinity,
My body sore punished shall be.

[*Scourges himself.*]

Take this, body, for the sin of the
flesh;
Also thou delightest to go gay and
fresh,
And in the way of damnation thou
did me bring;   615
Therefore suffer now strokes of
punishing.
Now of penance I will wade the
water clear,
To save me from purgatory, that
sharp fire.

[GOOD DEEDS *rises from floor.*]

---

606 *quittance:* aquittance.

GOOD DEEDS. I thank God, now I can walk and go,
And am delivered of my sickness and woe.   620
Therefore with Everyman I will go, and not spare;
His good works I will help him to declare.
KNOWLEDGE. Now, Everyman, be merry and glad!
Your Good Deeds cometh now, ye may not be sad;
Now is your Good Deeds whole and sound,   625
Going upright upon the ground.
EVERYMAN. My heart is light, and shall be evermore.
Now will I smite faster than I did before.
GOOD DEEDS. Everyman, pilgrim, my special friend,
Blessèd be thou without end.   630
For thee is prepared the eternal glory.
Ye have me made whole and sound,
Therefore I will bide by thee in every stound.
EVERYMAN. Welcome, my Good Deeds; now I hear thy voice,
I weep for very sweetness of love.   635
KNOWLEDGE. Be no more sad, but ever rejoice;
God seeth thy living in his throne above.
Put on this garment to thy behoof,
Which is wet with your tears,
Or else before God you may it miss,   640
When you to your journey's end come shall.
EVERYMAN. Gentle Knowledge, what do ye it call?
KNOWLEDGE. It is the garment of sorrow;
From pain it will you borrow;
Contrition it is   645
That getteth forgiveness;
It pleaseth God passing well.

GOOD DEEDS. Everyman, will you wear it for your heal?

[EVERYMAN *puts on garment of contrition.*]

EVERYMAN. Now blessèd be Jesu, Mary's Son,
For now have I on true contrition.   650
And let us go now without tarrying;
Good Deeds, have we clear our reckoning?
GOOD DEEDS. Yea, indeed I have it here.
EVERYMAN. Then I trust we need not fear.
Now, friends, let us not part in twain.   655
KNOWLEDGE. Nay, Everyman, that will we not, certain.
GOOD DEEDS. Yet must thou lead with thee
Three persons of great might.
EVERYMAN. Who should they be?
GOOD DEEDS. Discretion and Strength they hight,   660
And thy Beauty may not abide behind.
KNOWLEDGE. Also ye must call to mind
Your Five Wits as for your counselors.
GOOD DEEDS. You must have them ready at all hours.
EVERYMAN. How shall I get them hither?   665
KNOWLEDGE. You must call them all together,
And they will hear you incontinent.
EVERYMAN. My friends, come hither and be present;
Discretion, Strength, my Five Wits, and Beauty.

[*Enter* DISCRETION, STRENGTH, FIVE WITS, *and* BEAUTY.]

BEAUTY. Here at your will we be all ready.   670
What will ye that we should do?

---

633 *bide:* stay; *stound:* hour.

660 *hight:* are named.

GOOD DEEDS. That ye would with
Everyman go,
And help him in his pilgrimage.
Advise you, will ye with him or not
in that voyage?
STRENGTH. We will bring him all
thither,   675
To his help and comfort, ye may
believe me.
DISCRETION. So will we go with him
all together.
EVERYMAN. Almighty God, lovéd may
thou be!
I give thee laud that I have hither
brought
Strength, Discretion, Beauty, and
Five Wits. Lack I naught;   680
And my Good Deeds, with Knowl-
edge clear,
All be in company at my will here.
I desire no more to my business.
STRENGTH. And I, Strength, will by you
stand in distress,
Though thou would in battle fight
on the ground.   685
FIVE WITS. And though it were through
the world round,
We will not depart for sweet nor
sour.
BEAUTY. No more will I, unto death's
hour,
Whatsoever thereof befall.
DISCRETION. Everyman, advise you first
of all;   690
Go with a good advisement and
deliberation.
We all give you virtuous monition
That all shall be well.
EVERYMAN. My friends, hearken what
I will tell:
I pray God reward you in his heav-
enly sphere.   695
Now hearken, all that be here,
For I will make my testament
Here before you all present:
In alms half my goods I will give
with my hands twain
In the way of charity, with good
intent,   700
And the other half still shall remain;

I it bequeath to be returned there
it ought to be.
This I do in despite of the fiend of
hell,
To go quite out of his peril
Ever after and this day.   705
KNOWLEDGE. Everyman, hearken what
I say;
Go to priesthood, I you advise,
And receive of him in any wise
The holy sacrament and ointment
together;
Then shortly see ye turn again
hither;   710
We will all abide you here.
FIVE WITS. Yea, Everyman, hie you
that ye ready were.
There is no emperor, king, duke, nor
baron,
That of God hath commission
As hath the least priest in the world
being;   715
For of the blesséd sacraments pure
and benign
He beareth the keys, and thereof
hath the cure
For man's redemption—it is ever
sure—
Which God for our soul's medicine
Gave us out of his heart with great
pain,   720
Here in this transitory life, for thee
and me.
The blesséd sacraments seven there
be:
Baptism, confirmation, with priest-
hood good,
And the sacrament of God's precious
flesh and blood,
Marriage, the holy extreme unction,
and penance.   725
These seven be good to have in re-
membrance,
Gracious sacraments of high divinity.
EVERYMAN. Fain would I receive that
holy body
And meekly to my ghostly father I
will go.

---

729 *ghostly:* spiritual.

FIVE WITS. Everyman, that is the best
    that ye can do.   730
God will you to salvation bring,
For priesthood exceedeth all other
    thing;
To us Holy Scripture they do teach,
And converteth man from sin, heaven
    to reach;
God hath to them more power
    given,   735
Than to any angel that is in heaven.
With five words he may consecrate
God's body in flesh and blood to
    make,
And handleth his Maker between his
    hands.
The priest bindeth and unbindeth all
    bands,   740
Both in earth and in heaven;
Thou ministers all the sacraments
    seven;
Though we kissed thy feet, thou
    wert worthy;
Thou art the surgeon that cureth sin
    deadly:
No remedy we find under God   745
But all only priesthood.
Everyman, God gave priests that
    dignity,
And setteth them in his stead among
    us to be;
Thus be they above angels, in degree.

                    [*Exit* EVERYMAN.]

KNOWLEDGE. If priests be good, it is
    so, surely.   750
But when Jesus hanged on the cross
    with great smart,
There he gave out of his blessed
    heart
The same sacrament in great tor-
    ment.
He sold them not to us, that Lord
    omnipotent.
Therefore Saint Peter the Apostle
    doth say   755
That Jesus' curse hath all they
Which God their Savior do buy or
    sell,
Or they for any money do take or
    tell.

Sinful priests giveth the sinners exam-
    ple bad;
Their children sitteth by other men's
    fires, I have heard;   760
And some haunteth women's company
With unclean life, as lusts of lechery.
These be with sin made blind.
FIVE WITS. I trust to God no such may
    we find.
Therefore let us priesthood honor, 765
And follow their doctrine for our
    souls' succor.
We be their sheep, and they shep-
    herds be
By whom we all be kept in surety.
Peace! for yonder I see Everyman
    come,
Which hath made true satisfac-
    tion.   770
GOOD DEEDS. Methinketh it is he in-
    deed.

[*Re-enter* EVERYMAN.]

EVERYMAN. Now Jesu be your alder
    speed.
I have received the sacrament for
    my redemption,
And then mine extreme unction.
Blesséd be all they that counseled
    me to take it!   775
And now, friends, let us go without
    longer respite.
I thank God that ye have tarried so
    long.
Now set each of you on this rod
    your hand,
And shortly follow me.
I go before, there I would be. God
    be our guide.   780
STRENGTH. Everyman, we will not from
    you go,
Till ye have done this voyage long.
DISCRETION. I, Discretion, will bide by
    you also.
KNOWLEDGE. And though this pilgrim-
    age be never so strong,
I will never part you fro.   785
Everyman, I will be as sure by thee

---

772 *be your alder speed:* be comfort to all of
you. 778 *rod:* cross.

As ever I did by Judas Maccabee.

[They go together to the grave.]

EVERYMAN. Alas! I am so faint I may not stand,
My limbs under me do fold.
Friends, let us not turn again to this land,   790
Not for all the world's gold;
For into this cave must I creep
And turn to earth, and there to sleep.
BEAUTY. What, into this grave? Alas!
EVERYMAN. Yea, there shall you consume, more and less.   795
BEAUTY. And what, should I smother here?
EVERYMAN. Yea, by my faith, and never more appear.
In this world live no more we shall,
But in heaven before the highest Lord of all.
BEAUTY. I cross out all this; adieu, by Saint John!   800
I take my cap in my lap and am gone.
EVERYMAN. What, Beauty, whither will ye?
BEAUTY. Peace! I am deaf. I look not behind me,
Not and thou would give me all the gold in thy chest. *[Exit BEAUTY.]*
EVERYMAN. Alas, whereto may I trust?   805
Beauty goeth fast away from me;
She promised with me to live and die.
STRENGTH. Everyman, I will thee also forsake and deny.
Thy game liketh me not at all.
EVERYMAN. Why, then ye will forsake me all?   810
Sweet Strength, tarry a little space.
STRENGTH. Nay, sir, by the rood of grace,
I will hie me from thee fast,
Though thou weep till thy heart to-brast.
EVERYMAN. Ye would ever bide by me, ye said.   815

STRENGTH. Yea, I have you far enough conveyed.
Ye be old enough, I understand,
Your pilgrimage to take on hand.
I repent me that I hither came.
EVERYMAN. Strength, you to displease I am to blame;   820
Yet promise is debt, this ye well wot.
STRENGTH. In faith, I care not!
Thou art but a fool to complain.
You spend your speech and waste your brain;
Go, thrust thee into the ground.   825

[Exit STRENGTH.]

EVERYMAN. I had weened surer I should you have found.
He that trusteth in his Strength
She him deceiveth at the length.
Both Strength and Beauty forsaketh me,
Yet they promised me fair and lovingly.   830
DISCRETION. Everyman, I will after Strength be gone;
As for me I will leave you alone.
EVERYMAN. Why, Discretion, will ye forsake me?
DISCRETION. Yea, in faith, I will go from thee;
For when Strength goeth before   835
I follow after evermore.
EVERYMAN. Yet, I pray thee, for the love of the Trinity,
Look in my grave once piteously.
DISCRETION. Nay, so nigh will I not come.
Farewell, everyone!   840

[Exit DISCRETION.]

EVERYMAN. O all thing faileth, save God alone—
Beauty, Strength, and Discretion;
For when Death bloweth his blast,
They all run from me full fast.
FIVE WITS. Everyman, my leave now of thee I take;   845
I will follow the other, for here I thee forsake.
EVERYMAN. Alas! then may I wail and weep,

---

814 *to-brast:* shatters.

For I took you for my best friend.
FIVE WITS. I will no longer thee keep;
Now farewell, and there an end. 850

[*Exit* FIVE WITS.]

EVERYMAN. O Jesu, help! All hath
forsaken me!
GOOD DEEDS. Nay, Everyman; I will
bide with thee,
I will not forsake thee indeed;
Thou shalt find me a good friend at
need.
EVERYMAN. Gramercy, Good Deeds!
Now may I true friends see. 855
They have forsaken me, every one;
I loved them better than my Good
Deeds alone.
Knowledge, will ye forsake me also?
KNOWLEDGE. Yea, Everyman, when ye
to death shall go;
But not yet, for no manner of
danger. 860
EVERYMAN. Gramercy, Knowledge, with
all my heart.
KNOWLEDGE. Nay, yet I will not from
hence depart
Till I see where ye shall be come.
EVERYMAN. Methink, alas, that I must
be gone
To make my reckoning and my debts
pay, 865
For I see my time is nigh spent away.
Take example, all ye that this do
hear or see,
How they that I loved best do for-
sake me,
Except my Good Deeds that bideth
truly.
GOOD DEEDS. All earthly things is but
vanity. 870
Beauty, Strength, and Discretion do
man forsake,
Foolish friends and kinsmen, that
fair spake,
All fleeth save Good Deeds, and that
am I.
EVERYMAN. Have mercy on me, God
most mighty;
And stand by me, thou Mother and
Maid, holy Mary! 875

GOOD DEEDS. Fear not, I will speak
for thee.
EVERYMAN. Here I cry God mercy!
GOOD DEEDS. Short our end, and
'minish our pain.
Let us go and never come again.
EVERYMAN. Into thy hands, Lord, my
soul I commend. 880
Receive it, Lord, that it be not lost.
As thou me boughtest, so me defend,
And save me from the fiend's boast,
That I may appear with that blesséd
host
That shall be saved at the day of
doom. 885
In manus tuas—of might's most
Forever—*commendo spiritum meum.*

[EVERYMAN *and* GOOD DEEDS *descend
into the grave.*]

KNOWLEDGE. Now hath he suffered that
we all shall endure;
The Good Deeds shall make all sure.
Now hath he made ending. 890
Methinketh that I hear angels sing
And make great joy and melody
Where Everyman's soul received shall
be.
ANGEL [*within*]. Come, excellent elect
spouse to Jesu!
Here above thou shalt go 895
Because of thy singular virtue.
Now the soul is taken the body fro,
Thy reckoning is crystal clear.
Now shalt thou into the heavenly
sphere,
Unto the which all ye shall come 900
That liveth well before the day of
doom.

[*Exit* KNOWLEDGE. *Enter* DOCTOR *for
epilogue.*]

DOCTOR. This moral men may have in
mind;
Ye hearers, take it of worth, old and
young,
And forsake Pride, for he deceiveth
you in the end,

886–7 *In manus tuas commendo spiritum
meum:* I commend my spirit to your hands.

And remember Beauty, Five Wits,
Strength, and Discretion,   905
They all at the last do Everyman
forsake,
Save his Good Deeds there doth he
take.
But beware, and they be small
Before God he hath no help at all.
None excuse may be there for Every-
man.   910
Alas, how shall he do then?
For, after death, amends may no
man make,
For then mercy and pity doth him
forsake.
If his reckoning be not clear when
he doth come,
God will say, "*Ite, maledicti, in ignem
aeternum.*"   915
And he that hath his account whole
and sound,
High in heaven he shall be crowned.
Unto which place God bring us all
thither,
That we may live body and soul
together.
Thereto help the Trinity!   920
Amen, say ye, for saint charity.

---

915 *Ite, maledicti, in ignem aeternum:* Go
cursed ones, into eternal fire.

1 Henry IV

Although *1 Henry IV* represents many events of the reign of Henry the Fourth (1399–1413) much as they happened, William Shakespeare (1564–1616) reorganizes and improves on them in the interests of dramatic coherence. He reduces the age of Hotspur to make him more pointedly comparable to the prince and to create a dramatic contrast that history, in its untidiness, neglected to do. As a counterpart to chivalric honor and serious affairs of state, he adds the subplot of Falstaff and the thieves, tempters of the prince and lovers of other people's purses. These two changes give the prince a model of high honor and bravery on one side and a "villainous abominable misleader of youth" on the other. Together with a compression of time and diverse events, they make for thematic tightness, a structural symmetry that produces many analogies among scenes, and ultimately a sense of dramatic completion when the prince successfully deals with Falstaff and Hotspur and returns to his father's side.

As psychoanalysts have pointed out (particularly Ernst Kris in *Psychoanalytic Explorations in Art*), they also establish certain psychological tensions that are resolved along with the political problems. The analogous pairs of characters produce several divided-father images: the prince has two fathers, Falstaff and Henry IV (whom the mock interview associates together), one delightful but irresponsible, the other stern and forbidding, and ultimately he takes a third for guide, Chief Justice, who replaces both of the others; the king has several sons; Hotspur stands between a weak father (Northumberland) and a scheming uncle (Worcester), who are jointly responsible for his disaster. Thus Shakespeare traces the motives of civil war in the fundamental conflicts of families that underlie all social orders and especially societies with strong men and family succession at the center.

Since the prince participates in most of the main actions, predicts his own emergence as king, and makes good his word in battle, he is naturally the focus of both the personal and the political conflict. His threefold task is to free the kingship of its curse, reform or get rid of Falstaff, and transfer Hotspur's chivalric honors to himself as credentials for the kingship. He accomplishes all three of these goals on the battlefield, demonstrating the strength if not the rightness of the king's party, bringing about Falstaff's promise to live better, and transforming what in Hotspur has been an illegal, egocentric quest for glory into the legitimate chivalry of the heir apparent. Thus the battlefield is to the history play (in matters of recognition and unmaskings) what drawing rooms and marriages are to comedy: the unravelling is there effected by the prince's sword and explained in the formal speeches of rivals as they take leave of each other or seal their new contracts in proper high fashion. The future course of the collective society under the kingly succession stems from the realignments symbolized in its pageantry and duels.

Hal's major battlefield achievement is not an emergence from the schemes of the Boar's Head Tavern into the bright world of Hotspur's values, however. Rather, it is a discovery of just balance between indulgence in private life—whether Falstaff's sensual indulgence or Hotspur's quest for personal glory—and public duty. Such a balance is implicitly the discovery of a compromise between irresponsibility and arbitrary stifling of what fathers call rebellion in the interest of what they call solid order. Whereas Hotspur and Falstaff avoid all government incompatible with honor (in one) and a love of wit and wine (in the other), the prince learns to subordinate himself to politics.

Our opinion of the prince probably both suffers and gains from this subordination: like all executives and warriors, he must shrink in some ways to expand in others. Likewise Falstaff, having translated himself from an entertaining and harmless robber of the king's highway to a man of public counsel and military authority (of sorts), would have to abandon much of himself to "live cleanly as a nobleman should do" (V. iv.166) as he promises. Though not a severe test of loyalty to common sense and morality, the prince's final sacrifice of him in Part 2 is hard for most critics to accept because it touches something deeper than duty: the same source of individual rebellion that perennially divides children against fathers and fathers against their own self-discipline. Certainly no fully comic world would require that Falstaff buckle down (or in). Paradoxically, the prince becomes father to Falstaff, chastizing him and sending him to the corner. This ultimate reversal of roles is rehearsed in the tavern scene of Part 1 when Hal plays the king, is further practiced at Shrewsbury when he says farewell to the "dead" Falstaff in summary and abrupt terms, and finally becomes a reality when he banishes Falstaff at the end of Part 2. Falstaff may spring up as though reborn claiming personal victory over the representatives of courage and honor, but he is still doomed.

But more is involved in the relationship between Falstaff's comedy and the prince's serious politics than the disciplining of one to accommodate the other, and if we are aware of the play's form we can perhaps clarify both their sacrifices. The opening scenes make clear that of the play's three plots, one is primary and two are counterplots. The primary plot is aimed at ridding the kingdom of its insurgents and insuring an uncompromised transfer of the crown— obviously not possible unless Hotspur is controlled and the prince is liberated from Falstaff. The respective plots of Hotspur, Falstaff, and the prince are kept apart by serial representation in distinct scenes and held together by analogies and cross references. They converge for the first time on the battlefield. Given the *subordination* of the counterplots, we are led to expect seriousness and relevance to become ascendant at Shrewsbury, and this expectation would be seriously jolted if Falstaff were allowed to get out of hand. As it turns out, Shakespeare allows him to be at least as eloquent as Hotspur in talking about war and much more successful in acting on his principles: he lives while Hotspur dies. When the various standards of value converge and are tested against the needs of a healthy kingship, we are not excessively disappointed at Falstaff's fate if we have allowed the logic of the form to work as it should. Falstaff carries clowning into the mouth of cannons (substituting sack for pistols) and survives, but at the same time the prince proves his detachment from him.

Before the battle, then, we have ample indications of the prince's control over the values he must subordinate and transform: his satire of Hotspur near the beginning of II. iv ("Fie on this quiet life; I want work!") suggests that he can already pocket up Percy, and the counterintrigue against Falstaff's robbery (in the buckram farce) shows that he can participate in the comic world of wit and joking without being committed to it. In forecasting Falstaff's banishment, as in the earlier soliloquy, he extricates himself from the comic intrigue and confirms his historical role behind the mask of the truant. By these indications of ascendancy, he frees himself and the main plot from the necessary deflation of Falstaff's comic fortune and from the destructive rivalry that the various factions direct against the king.

The prince's range of language matches his participation in, yet detachment from, the subplots in that he speaks the dialect of several groups from the heavily punning (prose) idiom of Falstaff to the dignified verse of the court but is personally committed only to the programmatic and ceremonial language of the future king (who is to use it *ceremonially* as display and *persuasively* as a means of moving others to action). If his ascendancy is not to be a total reversal of what he has seemed—if it is to unite the diverse elements of the kingdom in a single nation—he must preserve something of his Falstaffian education. The ideal polity is nationalistic for Shakespeare and therefore broadly encompassing rather than narrowly feudal and divisive as Hotspur would have it. (Hotspur's own camp, not all of which makes it to the battle, threatens to subdivide.) Hence the prince continues to talk in *2 Henry IV* with his "brothers" in a style that draws them together in a national effort, and in *1 Henry IV* makes a gesture in that direction by playing along with Falstaff's pretence to have killed Hotspur. His participation in this byplay is a counterpart in action to the brotherliness of his later rhetoric. It demonstrates again the history play's capacity to take some comedy under its wing.

Like the prince, each of the major characters must adjust to the requirements of the nation or be excluded from the society that emerges when rebels and clowns are subdued. From the standpoint of the prince's success in bringing disparate types into the national unity, *1 Henry IV* might be a civil or political *comedy;* but given the burden of the political themes, the nature of the ending, and the distinct generic shape that history plays assumed in the 1590's, it would probably be better to think of it as an indeterminate mode whose diversity of characters and byplay spreads beyond traditional dramatic forms. Its climax, though a form of unmasking, is obviously unlike that of Shakespearean comedy in which lovers meet and marry: the right side wins and ends the "intestine shock / And curious close of civil butchery," but a reconciled father and son are different from a brave new society of young people headed for a wedding banquet. Besides, Shakespeare's audiences knew that further trials awaited both the king and his son—and that eventually the early death of Henry V and a weak Henry VI would bring the long War of the Roses. Even in terms of the immediate plot, Shakespeare leaves a nagging problem for the king's party: Northumberland and Scroop remain at large and lead us toward *2 Henry IV,* in which many old wounds reopen as though they had never healed.

In contrast to comedy, then, the plot is a civil rather than a marriage plot, and history proves too undisciplined to assume the kind of order that the pairings of characters, the ritual victories, and the rise of the fairy-tale prince seem to want to create. It necessarily gives us a social order different from that of either comedy or tragedy and, in doing so, both mirrors the facts of history and teaches us how to regard them, informed by and formulating them.

The History of Henry IV

[Part One]

KING HENRY THE FOURTH
HENRY, PRINCE OF WALES ⎫ the King's
JOHN OF LANCASTER ⎭ sons
EARL OF WESTMORELAND
SIR WALTER BLUNT
THOMAS PERCY, EARL OF WORCESTER
HENRY PERCY, EARL OF NORTHUMBERLAND
HENRY PERCY ("HOTSPUR") his son
EDMUND MORTIMER, EARL OF MARCH
RICHARD SCROOP, ARCHBISHOP OF YORK
ARCHIBALD, EARL OF DOUGLAS
OWEN GLENDOWER
SIR RICHARD VERNON
SIR JOHN FALSTAFF

SCENE. England and Wales

SIR MICHAEL   a friend of the ARCHBISHOP
  OF YORK
POINS
GADSHILL
PETO
BARDOLPH
FRANCIS   a waiter
LADY PERCY   HOTSPUR'S wife and MOR-
  TIMER'S sister
LADY MORTIMER   GLENDOWER'S daughter
  and MORTIMER'S wife
MISTRESS QUICKLY   hostess of the tavern
SHERIFF, VINTNER, CHAMBERLAIN, TWO
  CARRIERS, OSTLER, MESSENGERS, TRAV-
  ELERS, ATTENDANTS

ACT I

SCENE i. [London. The palace.]

Enter the KING, LORD JOHN OF LAN-
CASTER, EARL OF WESTMORELAND, [SIR
WALTER BLUNT,] with others.

KING. So shaken as we are, so wan
    with care,
  Find we a time for frighted peace to
    pant
  And breathe short-winded accents of
    new broils
  To be commenced in stronds afar
    remote.
  No more the thirsty entrance of this
    soil   5
  Shall daub her lips with her own

children's blood,
  No more shall trenching war channel
    her fields,
  Nor bruise her flow'rets with the
    armed hoofs
  Of hostile paces. Those opposed eyes
  Which, like the meteors of a troubled
    heaven,   10
  All of one nature, of one substance
    bred,
  Did lately meet in the intestine shock
  And furious close of civil butchery,
  Shall now in mutual well-beseeming
    ranks

I.i.4 stronds: shores.

11 of one substance: i.e., all English.   12
intestine: internal.   13 close: hand to hand.
14 mutual: interdependent.

437

March all one way and be no more
  opposed   15
Against acquaintance, kindred, and
  allies.
The edge of war, like an ill-sheathed
  knife,
No more shall cut his master. There-
  fore, friends,
As far as to the sepulcher of Christ—
Whose soldier now, under whose
  blessed cross   20
We are impressed and engaged to
  fight—
Forthwith a power of English shall
  we levy,
Whose arms were molded in their
  mother's womb
To chase these pagans in those holy
  fields
Over whose acres walked those blessed
  feet   25
Which fourteen hundred years ago
  were nailed
For our advantage on the bitter cross.
But this our purpose now is twelve-
  month old,
And bootless 'tis to tell you we will
  go.
Therefore we meet not now. Then let
  me hear   30
Of you, my gentle cousin Westmore-
  land,
What yesternight our council did
  decree
In forwarding this dear expedience.
WESTMORELAND. My liege, this haste
  was hot in question
And many limits of the charge set
  down   35
But yesternight; when all athwart
  there came
A post from Wales, loaden with heavy
  news,
Whose worst was that the noble

Mortimer,
Leading the men of Herefordshire to
  fight
Against the irregular and wild Glen-
  dower,   40
Was by the rude hands of that
  Welshman taken,
A thousand of his people butchered;
Upon whose dead corpse there was
  such misuse,
Such beastly shameless transforma-
  tion
By those Welsh women done, as may
  not be   45
Without much shame retold or spoken
  of.
KING. It seems then that the tidings
  of this broil
Brake off our business for the Holy
  Land.
WESTMORELAND. This, matched with
  other, did, my gracious lord;
For more uneven and unwelcome
  news   50
Came from the north, and thus it did
  import:
On Holy-rood Day the gallant Hot-
  spur there,
Young Harry Percy, and brave
  Archibald,
That ever-valiant and approved Scot,
At Holmedon met, where they did
  spend   55
A sad and bloody hour;
As by discharge of their artillery
And shape of likelihood the news
  was told;
For he that brought them, in the
  very heat
And pride of their contention did
  take horse,   60
Uncertain of the issue any way.
KING. Here is a dear, a true industrious
  friend,
Sir Walter Blunt, new lighted from
  his horse,

21 *impressed:* pressed into service. 22 *power:*
army. 29 *bootless:* needless. 33 *dear expedience:* valued and important undertaking.
34 *hot in question:* hotly debated. 35 *limits
of the charge:* either assigning of duties or
fixing of costs. 37 *post:* messenger.

50 *uneven:* disturbing. 52 *Holy-rood Day:*
Holy Cross Day, September 14. 55 *Holmedon:*
Humbleton. 58 *shape of likelihood:* prob-
ability. 59 *them:* news. 60 *pride:* height.

Stained with the variation of each
soil
Betwixt that Holmedon and this seat
of ours,   65
And he hath brought us smooth and
welcome news.
The Earl of Douglas is discomfited;
Ten thousand bold Scots, two and
twenty knights,
Balked in their own blood did Sir
Walter see
On Holmedon's plains. Of prisoners,
Hotspur took   70
Mordake, Earl of Fife and eldest son
To beaten Douglas, and the Earl of
Athol,
Of Murray, Angus, and Menteith.
And is not this an honorable spoil?
A gallant prize? Ha, cousin, is it
not?   75
WESTMORELAND. In faith it is. A con-
quest for a prince to boast of.
KING. Yea, there thou mak'st me sad,
and mak'st me sin
In envy that my Lord Northumber-
land
Should be the father to so blest a
son:
A son who is the theme of honor's
tongue,   80
Amongst a grove the very straightest
plant;
Who is sweet fortune's minion and
her pride;
Whilst I, by looking on the praise of
him,
See riot and dishonor stain the brow
Of my young Harry. O that it could
be proved   85
That some night-tripping fairy had
exchanged
In cradle clothes our children where
they lay,
And called mine Percy, his Planta-
genet!
Then would I have his Harry, and

he mine.
But let him from my thoughts. What
think you, coz,   90
Of this young Percy's pride? The
prisoners
Which he in this adventure hath sur-
prised
To his own use he keeps, and sends
me word
I shall have none but Mordake, Earl
of Fife.
WESTMORELAND. This is his uncle's
teaching, this is Worcester,   95
Malevolent to you in all aspects,
Which makes him prune himself and
bristle up
The crest of youth against your
dignity.
KING. But I have sent for him to
answer this;
And for this cause awhile we must
neglect   100
Our holy purpose to Jerusalem.
Cousin, on Wednesday next our coun-
cil we
Will hold at Windsor, so inform the
lords:
But come yourself with speed to us
again,
For more is to be said and to be
done   105
That out of anger can be uttered.
WESTMORELAND. I will, my liege.

Exeunt.

SCENE ii. [*London. The* PRINCE'S *lodging.*]

Enter PRINCE OF WALES *and* SIR JOHN
FALSTAFF.

FALSTAFF. Now, Hal, what time of day
is it, lad?
PRINCE. Thou art so fat-witted with
drinking of old sack, and unbutton-

---

69 *Balked:* stopped, piled up. 82 *minion:*
favorite. 88 *Plantagenet:* Henry's family
dynasty.

90 *coz:* cousin. 92 *surprised:* captured. 96
Malevolent...aspects: evil-willed, like a malign
star whose "aspect" betokens ill. 97 *prune:*
preen. 106 *uttered:* talked about in public.
I.ii.4 *sack:* wine.

ing thee after supper, and sleep- 5
ing upon benches after noon, that
thou hast forgotten to demand that
truly which thou wouldest truly
know. What a devil hast thou to do
with the time of the day? Unless 10
hours were cups of sack, and minutes
capons, and clocks the tongues of
bawds, and dials the signs of leaping
houses, and the blessed sun himself
a fair hot wench in flame-colored 15
taffeta, I see no reason why thou
shouldst be so superfluous to demand
the time of the day.

FALSTAFF. Indeed you come near me
now, Hal; for we that take purses 20
go by the moon and the seven stars,
and not by Phoebus, he, that wand'r-
ing knight so fair. And I prithee,
sweet wag, when thou art a king, as,
God save the Grace—Majesty I 25
should say, for grace thou wilt have
none—

PRINCE. What, none?

FALSTAFF. No, by my troth; not so
much as will serve to be prologue 30
to an egg and butter.

PRINCE. Well, how then? Come, roundly, roundly.

FALSTAFF. Marry, then, sweet wag,
when thou art king, let not us 35
that are squires of the night's body
be called thieves of the day's beauty.
Let us be Diana's foresters, gentlemen of the shade, minions of the
moon; and let men say we be 40
men of good government, being governed, as the sea is, by our noble and
chaste mistress the moon, under
whose countenance we steal.

PRINCE. Thou sayest well, and it 45
holds well too; for the fortune of us
that are the moon's men doth ebb
and flow like the sea, being governed
as the sea is by the moon. As, for
proof now: a purse of gold most 50
resolutely snatched on Monday night
and most dissolutely spent on Tuesday morning; got with swearing "Lay
by," and spent with crying "Bring
in"; now in as low an ebb as 55
the foot of the ladder, and by and by
in as high a flow as the ridge of the
gallows.

FALSTAFF. By the Lord, thou say'st
true, lad—and is not my hostess 60
of the tavern a most sweet wench?

PRINCE. As the honey of Hybla, my old
lad of the castle—and is not a buff
jerkin a most sweet robe of durance?

FALSTAFF. How now, how now, mad 65
wag? What, in thy quips and thy
quiddities? What a plague have I to
do with a buff jerkin?

PRINCE. Why, what a pox have I to do
with my hostess of the tavern? 70

FALSTAFF. Well, thou hast called her
to a reckoning many a time and oft.

PRINCE. Did I ever call for thee to
pay thy part?

FALSTAFF. No; I'll give thee thy 75
due, thou hast paid all there.

PRINCE. Yea, and elsewhere, so far as
my coin would stretch; and where it
would not, I have used my credit.

FLASTAFF. Yea, and so used it that, 80
were it not here apparent that thou
art heir apparent—But I prithee,

---

13 *dials:* sundials. 13–14 *leaping houses:*
brothels. 19 *come near me:* hit the mark.
21 *seven stars:* Pleiades. 22 *Phoebus:* sun.
34 *Marry:* a mild oath. 36–37 *squires...
beauty:* pun on night-knight and perhaps
beauty-booty. Falstaff says in effect, "When
you become king, let us not abandon our
present night life for daytime activity." The
king-sun association is reinforced later. 38
Diana: goddess of the moon and the hunt for
"booty". 39 *minions:* favorites.

46 *holds well:* continues well ("if you pursue
the metaphor further"). 54–55 *"Bring in":*
serve the drinks and food. 62 *Hybla:* place
in Sicily known for good honey. 63 *castle:*
Oldcastle was Falstaff's name in the source
play, *The Famous Victories of Henry V,* and
the name of a brothel in London. 63–64 *buff
jerkin:* leather jacket. 64 *durance:* of lasting
quality, also like a prison sentence since the
uniform of the sheriff was of buff jerkin and
"durance" means "imprisonment." 67 *quiddities:* jokes and puns. 69 *pox:* the "plague"
of brothels. 72 *reckoning:* called to account,
to an adding of the bill.

sweet wag, shall there be gallows standing in England when thou art king? And resolution thus fubbed 85 as it is with the rusty curb of old father Antic the law? Do not thou, when thou art king, hang a thief.

PRINCE. No; thou shalt.

FALSTAFF. Shall I? O rare! By the 90 Lord, I'll be a brave judge.

PRINCE. Thou judgest false already. I mean, thou shalt have the hanging of the thieves and so become a rare hangman. 95

FALSTAFF. Well, Hal, well; and in some sort it jumps with my humor as well as waiting in the court, I can tell you.

PRINCE. For obtaining of suits? 100

FALSTAFF. Yea, for obtaining of suits, whereof the hangman hath no lean wardrobe. 'Sblood, I am as melancholy as a gib-cat or a lugged bear.

PRINCE. Or an old lion, or a lover's 105 lute.

FALSTAFF. Yea, or the drone of a Lincolnshire bagpipe.

PRINCE. What sayest thou to a hare, or the melancholy of Moorditch? 110

FALSTAFF. Thou hast the most unsavory similes, and art indeed the most comparative, rascalliest, sweet young prince. But, Hal, I prithee trouble me no more with vanity. I would 115 to God thou and I knew where a commodity of good names were to be bought. An old lord of the council rated me the other day in the street about you, sir, but I marked 120 him not; and yet he talked very wisely, but I regarded him not; and

yet he talked wisely, and in the street too.

PRINCE. Thou didst well, for wis- 125 dom cries out in the streets, and no man regards it.

FALSTAFF. O, thou hast damnable iteration, and art indeed able to corrupt a saint. Thou hast done 130 much harm upon me, Hal—God forgive thee for it! Before I knew thee, Hal, I knew nothing; and now am I, if a man should speak truly, little better than one of the wicked. 135 I must give over this life, and I will give it over! By the Lord, an I do not, I am a villain! I'll be damned for never a king's son in Christendom.

PRINCE. Where shall we take a 140 purse tomorrow, Jack?

FALSTAFF. 'Zounds, where thou wilt, lad! I'll make one. An I do not, call me villain and baffle me.

PRINCE. I see a good amendment 145 of life in thee—from praying to purse-taking.

FALSTAFF. Why, Hal, 'tis my vocation, Hal. 'Tis no sin for a man to labor in his vocation. 150

Enter Poins.

Poins! Now shall we know if Gadshill have set a match. O, if men were to be saved by merit, what hole in hell were hot enough for him? This is the most omnipotent villain that 155 ever cried "Stand!" to a true man.

PRINCE. Good morrow, Ned.

POINS. Good morrow, sweet Hal. What says Monsieur Remorse? What says

---

85 *resolution...fubbed:* (the robbers') courage cheated of its reward. 87 *Antic:* clown. 91 *brave:* striking. 97 *jumps with my humor:* agrees with me. 100 *suits:* petitions to the court, and clothes. 103 *'Sblood:* God's blood, a mild oath. 104 *gib-cat:* tomcat; *lugged:* baited. 107 *drone:* base pipe of a bagpipe. 109 *hare:* thought to be melancholy. 110 *Moorditch:* a London drainage ditch. 112–13 *comparative:* wont to make comparisons. 117 *commodity:* supply. 119 *rated:* chided.

125–26 *wisdom cries out...:* Proverbs I: 20–24. 129 *iteration:* way of quoting (and applying) scripture. 137 *an:* if. 142 *'Zounds:* by God's wounds. 144 *baffle:* hang inverted (like those punished for perjuring themselves). 152 *set a match:* arrange a meeting. 153 *merit:* in speaking of the wicked, his vocation, and salvation by merit, Falstaff makes use of current Puritan terms to justify his own "calling" and to condemn others in mock seriousness. 156 *true:* square and trustworthy.

Sir John Sack and Sugar? Jack, 160
how agrees the devil and thee about
thy soul, that thou soldest him on
Good Friday last for a cup of
Madeira and a cold capon's leg?

PRINCE. Sir John stands to his 165
word, the devil shall have his bargain; for he was never yet a breaker
of proverbs. He will give the devil
his due.

POINS. Then art thou damned for 170
keeping thy word with the devil.

PRINCE. Else he had been damned for
cozening the devil.

POINS. But, my lads, my lads, tomorrow
morning, by four o'clock early, 175
at Gad's Hill! There are pilgrims
going to Canterbury with rich offerings, and traders riding to London
with fat purses. I have vizards for
you all; you have horses for 180
yourselves. Gadshill lies tonight in
Rochester. I have bespoke supper
tomorrow night in Eastcheap. We
may do it as secure as sleep. If you
will go, I will stuff your purses 185
full of crowns; if you will not, tarry
at home and be hanged!

FALSTAFF. Hear ye, Yedward: if I
tarry at home and go not, I'll hang
you for going. 190

POINS. You will, chops?

FALSTAFF. Hal, wilt thou make one?

PRINCE. Who, I rob? I a thief? Not I,
by my faith.

FALSTAFF. There's neither honesty, 195
manhood, nor good fellowship in thee,
nor thou cam'st not of the blood
royal if thou darest not stand for
ten shillings.

PRINCE. Well then, once in my 200
days I'll be a madcap.

FALSTAFF. Why, that's well said.

PRINCE. Well, come what will, I'll tarry
at home.

FALSTAFF. By the Lord, I'll be a 205
traitor then, when thou art king.

PRINCE. I care not.

POINS. Sir John, I prithee, leave the
Prince and me alone. I will lay him
down such reasons for this 210
adventure that he shall go.

FALSTAFF. Well, God give thee the
spirit of persuasion and him the ears
of profiting, that what thou speakest
may move and what he hears 215
may be believed, that the true prince
may (for recreation sake) prove a
false thief; for the poor abuses of
the time want countenance. Farewell;
you shall find me in Eastcheap. 220

PRINCE. Farewell, thou latter spring!
Farewell, All-hallown summer!

[*Exit* FALSTAFF.]

POINS. Now, my good sweet honey
lord, ride with us tomorrow. I have
a jest to execute that I cannot 225
manage alone. Falstaff, Bardolph,
Peto, and Gadshill shall rob those
men that we have already waylaid;
yourself and I will not be there; and
when they have the booty, if 230
you and I do not rob them, cut this
head off from my shoulders.

PRINCE. How shall we part with them
in setting forth?

POINS. Why, we will set forth 235
before or after them and appoint
them a place of meeting, wherein it
is at our pleasure to fail; and then
will they adventure upon the exploit
themselves, which they shall 240
have no sooner achieved, but we'll
set upon them.

PRINCE. Yea, but 'tis like that they
will know us by our horses, by our
habits, and by every other ap- 245
pointment, to be ourselves.

---

160 *Sack and Sugar:* sweetened wine. 173
cozening: cheating. 176 *Gad's Hill:* site of
frequent robberies on the road from London
to Rochester. 179 *vizards:* masks. 183 *Eastcheap:* London street and district. 188 *Yedward:* Edward. 191 *chops:* porky. 198 *royal:*
a ten-shilling coin; *stand for:* pass for or contest for.

---

219 *countenance:* protection. 222 *All-hallown:*
late autumn when, as for Falstaff in his old
age, spring seems to come again. 245 *habits:*
clothes. 245–46 *appointment:* equipment.

POINS. Tut! Our horses they shall not see—I'll tie them in the wood; our vizards we will change after we leave them; and, sirrah, I have cases 250 of buckram for the nonce, to immask our noted outward garments.

PRINCE. Yea, but I doubt they will be too hard for us.

POINS. Well, for two of them, I 255 know them to be as true-bred cowards as ever turned back; and for the third, if he fight longer than he sees reason, I'll forswear arms. The virtue of this jest will be the incom- 260 prehensible lies that this same fat rogue will tell us when we meet at supper: how thirty, at least, he fought with; what wards, what blows, what extremities he endured; and in 265 the reproof of this lives the jest.

PRINCE. Well, I'll go with thee. Provide us all things necessary and meet me tomorrow night in Eastcheap. There I'll sup. Farewell. 270

POINS. Farewell, my lord. *Exit.*

PRINCE. I know you all, and will awhile uphold
The unyoked humor of your idleness.
Yet herein will I imitate the sun,
Who doth permit the base contagious clouds 275
To smother up his beauty from the world,
That, when he please again to be himself,
Being wanted, he may be more wond'red at
By breaking through the foul and ugly mists
Of vapors that did seem to strangle him. 280
If all the year were playing holidays,
To sport would be as tedious as to work;
But when they seldom come, they wished-for come,
And nothing pleaseth but rate accidents.
So when this loose behavior I throw off 285
And pay the debt I never promised,
By how much better than my word I am,
By so much shall I falsify men's hopes;
And, like bright metal on a sullen ground,
My reformation, glitt'ring o'er my fault, 290
Shall show more goodly and attract more eyes
Than that which hath no foil to set it off.
I'll so offend to make offense a skill,
Redeeming time when men think least I will. *Exit.*

SCENE iii. [*Windsor. The council chamber.*]

Enter the KING, NORTHUMBERLAND, WORCESTER, HOTSPUR, SIR WALTER BLUNT, *with others.*

KING. My blood hath been too cold and temperate,
Unapt to stir at these indignities,
And you have found me, for accordingly
You tread upon my patience; but be sure
I will from henceforth rather be myself, 5
Mighty and to be feared, than my condition,

---

250 *sirrah:* a form of address implying condescension. 250–51 *cases...nonce:* coverings of coarse linen for the purpose. 253 *doubt:* fear. 260–61 *incomprehensible:* inordinate. 264 *wards:* warding off of blows. 266 *reproof:* disproof. 273 *humor:* tendency, inherent disposition. 275 *contagious:* pestilence spreading. 278 *wanted:* missed.

284 *accidents:* incidents. 289 *sullen:* dull. 292 *foil:* contrast. 294 *Redeeming time:* cf. Ephesians V.15–16: "See then that ye walk circumspectly, not as fools, but as wise. Redeeming the time, because the days are evil." I.iii.3 *found me:* found me out. 6 *condition:* "I will be my kingly self rather than my natural weakened condition."

Which hath been smooth as oil, soft
as young down,
And therefore lost that title of respect
Which the proud soul ne'er pays but
to the proud.
WORCESTER. Our house, my sovereign
liege, little deserves   10
The scourge of greatness to be used
on it—
And that same greatness too which
our own hands
Have holp to make so portly.
NORTHUMBERLAND.   My lord—
KING. Worcester, get thee gone, for I
do see   .
Danger and disobedience in thine
eye.   15
O, sir, your presence is too bold and
peremptory,
And majesty might never yet endure
The moody frontier of a servant
brow.
You have good leave to leave us:
when we need
Your use and counsel, we shall send
for you.   *Exit* WORCESTER. 20
You were about to speak.
NORTHUMBERLAND.   Yea, my
good lord.
Those prisoners in your Highness'
name demanded
Which Harry Percy here at Holme-
don took,
Were, as he says, not with such
strength denied
As is delivered to your Majesty. 25
Either envy, therefore, or misprision
Is guilty of this fault, and not my
son.
HOTSPUR. My liege, I did deny no
prisoners.
But I remember, when the fight was
done,
When I was dry with rage and ex-
treme toil,   30
Breathless and faint, leaning upon

my sword,
Came there a certain lord, neat and
trimly dressed,
Fresh as a bridegroom, and his chin
new reaped
Showed like a stubble land at harvest
home.
He was perfumed like a milliner, 35
And 'twixt his finger and his thumb
he held
A pouncet box, which ever and anon
He gave his nose, and took't away
again;
Who therewith angry, when it next
came there,
Took it in snuff; and still he smiled
and talked;   40
And as the soldiers bore dead bodies
by,
He called them untaught knaves, un-
mannerly,
To bring a slovenly unhandsome
corse
Betwixt the wind and his nobility.
With many holiday and lady terms 45
He questioned me, amongst the rest
demanded
My prisoners in your Majesty's
behalf.
I then, all smarting with my wounds
being cold,
To be so pest'red with a popingay,
Out of my grief and my impatience 50
Answered neglectingly, I know not
what—
He should, or he should not; for he
made me mad
To see him shine so brisk, and smell
so sweet,
And talk so like a waiting gentle-
woman
Of guns and drums and wounds—
God save the mark!—   55

---

33 *reaped:* clipped. 37 *pouncet box:* snuff
box. 39 *Who:* his nose. 40 *Took it in snuff:*
"took offense" and "snuffed" the perfume. 43
corse: corpse. 45 *holiday:* dainty, choice.
49 *popingay:* parrot. 50 *grief:* discomfort.
55 *God save the mark:* usually a term of
blessing, here used ironically.

---

13 *holp:* helped; *portly:* dignified. 26 *misprision:* misunderstanding. 30 *dry:* the
"humor" of fire has dried him out.

And telling me the sovereignest thing
  on earth
Was parmacity for an inward bruise,
And that it was great pity, so it was,
This villainous saltpeter should be
  digged
Out of the bowels of the harmless
  earth,   60
Which many a good tall fellow had
  destroyed
So cowardly, and but for these vile
  guns,
He would himself have been a soldier.
This bald unjointed chat of his, my
  lord,
I answered indirectly, as I said,   65
And I beseech you, let not his report
Come current for an accusation
Betwixt my love and your high
  Majesty.
BLUNT. The circumstance considered,
  good my lord,
Whate'er Lord Harry Percy then had
  said   70
To such a person, and in such a
  place,
At such a time, with all the rest
  retold,
May reasonably die, and never rise
To do him wrong, or any way impeach
What then he said, so he unsay it
  now.   75
KING. Why, yet he doth deny his
  prisoners,
But with proviso and exception,
That we at our own charge shall
  ransom straight
His brother-in-law, the foolish Morti-
  mer;
Who, on my soul, hath willfully
  betrayed   80
The lives of those that he did lead
  to fight
Against that great magician, damned
  Glendower—

Whose daughter, as we hear, that
  Earl of March
Hath lately married. Shall our coffers,
  then,
Be emptied to redeem a traitor
  home?   85
Shall we buy treason, and indent
  with fears
When they have lost and forfeited
  themselves?
No, on the barren mountains let him
  starve!
For I shall never hold that man my
  friend
Whose tongue shall ask me for one
  penny cost   90
To ransom home revolted Mortimer.
HOTSPUR. Revolted Mortimer?
He never did fall off, my sovereign
  liege,
But by the chance of war. To prove
  that true
Needs no more but one tongue for
  all those wounds,   95
Those mouthed wounds, which val-
  iantly he took
When on the gentle Severn's sedgy
  bank,
In single opposition hand to hand,
He did confound the best part of an
  hour
In changing hardiment with great
  Glendower.   100
Three times they breathed, and three
  times did they drink,
Upon agreement, of swift Severn's
  flood;
Who then affrighted with their bloody
  looks
Ran fearfully among the trembling
  reeds
And hid his crisp head in the hollow
  bank,   105
Bloodstained with these valiant com-
  batants.

---

57 *parmacity:* spermaceti, fatty substance from sperm whales used as medicine. 61 *tall:* stalwart. 67 *current:* pass from hand to hand as acceptable currency and become a running current between them.

86 *indent:* covenant; *fears:* fearful ones turned traitor. 99 *confound:* mix it up. 100 *changing hardiment:* exchanging blows. 101 *breathed:* rested. 105 *crisp:* curled, rippled.

Never did bare and rotten policy
Color her working with such deadly
wounds;
Nor never could the noble Mortimer
Receive so many, and all willingly.   110
Then let not him be slandered with
revolt.
KING. Thou dost belie him, Percy, thou
dost belie him!
He never did encounter with Glen-
dower.
I tell thee, he durst as well have met
the devil alone
As Owen Glendower for an enemy.   115
Art thou not ashamed? But, sirrah,
henceforth
Let me not hear you speak of
Mortimer.
Send me your prisoners with the
speediest means,
Or you shall hear in such a kind
from me
As will displease you. My Lord
Northumberland,   120
We license your departure with your
son.
Send us your prisoners, or you will
hear of it.

Exit KING, [*with* BLUNT, *and train*].

HOTSPUR. And if the devil come and
roar for them,
I will not send them. I will after
straight
And tell him so, for I will ease my
heart,   125
Albeit I make a hazard of my head.
NORTHUMBERLAND. What, drunk with
choler? Stay, and pause awhile.
Here comes your uncle.

Enter WORCESTER.

HOTSPUR.   Speak of Mortimer?
'Zounds, I will speak of him, and let
my soul
Want mercy if I do not join with
him!   130
Yea, on his part I'll empty all these
veins,
And shed my dear blood drop by
drop in the dust,
But I will lift the downtrod Mortimer
As high in the air as this unthankful
king,
As this ingrate and cank'red Boling-
broke.   135
NORTHUMBERLAND. Brother, the King
hath made your nephew mad.
WORCESTER. Who struck this heat up
after I was gone?
HOTSPUR. He will forsooth have all
my prisoners;
And when I urged the ransom once
again
Of my wife's brother, then his cheek
looked pale,   140
And on my face he turned an eye
of death,
Trembling even at the name of
Mortimer.
WORCESTER. I cannot blame him. Was
not he proclaimed
By Richard that dead is, the next
of blood?
NORTHUMBERLAND. He was, I heard
the proclamation: 145
And then it was when the unhappy
king
(Whose wrongs in us God pardon!)
did set forth
Upon his Irish expedition;
From whence he intercepted did
return
To be deposed, and shortly mur-
dered.   150
WORCESTER. And for whose death we
in the world's wide mouth
Live scandalized and foully spoken
of.
HOTSPUR. But soft, I pray you, did
King Richard then

---

107 *policy:* strategem.   111 *revolt:* treason.
112 *belie:* misrepresent.   116 *sirrah:* equivalent to "boy" as a slighting address.   127
choler: anger.

135 *ingrate and cank'red:* ungrateful and
ulcerous or all-devouring.   141 *eye of death:*
perhaps threatening death, perhaps deathly
afraid.   147 *wrongs in us:* our wrongs toward
him.

Proclaim my brother Edmund Mor-
timer
Heir to the crown?
NORTHUMBERLAND.   He did, myself did
hear it.   155
HOTSPUR.   Nay, then I cannot blame
his cousin king,
That wished him on the barren
mountains starve.
But shall it be that you, that set
the crown
Upon the head of this forgetful man,
And for his sake wear the detested
blot   160
Of murderous subornation—shall it
be
That you a world of curses undergo,
Being the agents or base second
means,
The cords, the ladder, or the hang-
man rather?
O, pardon me that I descend so
low   165
To show the line and the predicament
Wherein you range under this subtle
king!
Shall it for shame be spoken in these
days,
Or fill up chronicles in time to come,
That men of your nobility and
power   170
Did gage them both in an unjust
behalf
(As both of you, God pardon it,
have done)
To put down Richard, that sweet
lovely rose,
And plant this thorn, this canker
Bolingbroke?
And shall it in more shame be further
spoken   175
That you are fooled, discarded, and
shook off
By him for whom these shames ye

underwent?
No, yet time serves wherein you
may redeem
Your banished honors and restore
yourselves
Into the good thoughts of the world
again;   180
Revenge the jeering and disdained
contempt
Of this proud king, who studies day
and night
To answer all the debt he owes to
you
Even with the bloody payment of
your deaths.
Therefore I say—
WORCESTER.   Peace, cousin, say
no more;   185
And now I will unclasp a secret book,
And to your quick-conceiving dis-
contents
I'll read you matter deep and danger-
ous,
As full of peril and adventurous
spirit
As to o'erwalk a current roaring
loud   190
On the unsteadfast footing of a
spear.
HOTSPUR. If he fall in, good night, or
sink, or swim!
Send danger from the east unto the
west,
So honor cross it from the north to
south,
And let them grapple. O, the blood
more stirs   195
To rouse a lion than to start a hare!
NORTHUMBERLAND.   Imagination of
some great exploit
Drives him beyond the bounds of
patience.
HOTSPUR. By heaven, methinks it were
an easy leap
To pluck bright honor from the pale-
faced moon,   200
Or dive into the bottom of the deep,

---

161 *subornation:* conspiracy. 166 *line:* tether
wherein they "range" and breeding or mettle;
predicament: "state of being" and "quandry."
171 *gage:* covenant.   174 *canker:* dog-rose
with a suggestion as in line 135 above of cancerous sore.

---

187 *quick-conceiving:* alert. 192 *or sink, or
swim:* whether he sinks or swims a short
while, one who falls in is lost.

Where fathom line could never touch
the ground,
And pluck up drowned honor by the
locks,
So he that doth redeem her thence
might wear
Without corrival all her dignities;　　　　　　　　　　　　　205
But out upon this half-faced fellowship!

WORCESTER. He apprehends a world of
figures here,
But not the form of what he should
attend.
Good cousin, give me audience for
a while.

HOTSPUR. I cry you mercy.　　　　210

WORCESTER. Those same noble Scots
that are your prisoners—

HOTSPUR. I'll keep them all.
By God, he shall not have a Scot of
them!
No, if a Scot would save his soul, he
shall not.
I'll keep them, by this hand!

WORCESTER.　　　You start away　215
And lend no ear unto my purposes.
Those prisoners you shall keep.

HOTSPUR.　　　Nay, I will! That's flat!
He said he would not ransom Mor-
timer,
Forbade my tongue to speak of
Mortimer,
But I will find him when he lies
asleep,　　　　　　　　　　　　220
And in his ear I'll hollo "Mortimer."
Nay, I'll have a starling shall be
taught to speak
Nothing but "Mortimer," and give
it him
To keep his anger still in motion.

WORCESTER. Hear you, cousin, a word.

HOTSPUR. All studies here I solemnly
defy　　　　　　　　　　　　226

Save how to gall and pinch this
Bolingbroke;
And that same sword-and-buckler
Prince of Wales,
But that I think his father loves him
not
And would be glad he met with some
mischance,　　　　　　　　　　230
I would have him poisoned with a
pot of ale.

WORCESTER. Farewell, kinsman: I'll
talk to you
When you are better tempered to
attend.

NORTHUMBERLAND. Why, what a wasp-
stung and impatient fool
Art thou to break into this woman's
mood,　　　　　　　　　　　235
Tying thine ear to no tongue but
thine own!

HOTSPUR. Why, look you, I am whipped
and scourged with rods,
Nettled, and stung with pismires,
when I hear
Of this vile politician, Bolingbroke.
In Richard's time—what do you call
the place?　　　　　　　　　　240
A plague upon it! It is in Gloucestershire;
'Twas where the madcap duke his
uncle kept,
His uncle York—where I first bowed
my knee
Unto this king of smiles, this Bolingbroke—
'Sblood!—when you and he came
back from Ravenspurgh—　　245

NORTHUMBERLAND. At Berkeley Castle.

HOTSPUR. You say true.
Why, what a candy deal of courtesy
This fawning greyhound then did
proffer me!
"Look when his infant fortune came
to age,"　　　　　　　　　　250
And "gentle Harry Percy," and "kind

---

205 *corrival:* compeer, rival.　206 *out upon:*
away with; *half-faced:* divided, incomplete.
207 *figures:* metaphors, insubstantial fantasies.
210 *cry you mercy:* beg your pardon.　214
Scot: small payment.　226 *studies:* interests;
defy: reject.

228 *sword-and-buckler:* low-bred.　238 *pismires:* ants.　242 *kept:* lived.　245 *Ravenspurgh:* seacoast town in York.　248 *candy
deal:* sweet bit.

cousin"—

O, the devil take such cozeners!—
God forgive me!

Good uncle, tell your tale; I have
done.

WORCESTER. Nay, if you have not, to
it again.

We will stay your leisure.

HOTSPUR.   I have done, i' faith. 255

WORCESTER. Then once more to your
Scottish prisoners:

Deliver them up without their ransom
straight,

And make the Douglas' son your only
mean

For powers in Scotland—which, for
divers reasons

Which I shall send you written, be
assured   260

Will easily be granted. [*to* NORTH-
UMBERLAND] You, my lord,

Your son in Scotland being thus
employed,

Shall secretly into the bosom creep

Of that same noble prelate well-
beloved,

The Archbishop.   265

HOTSPUR. Of York, is it not?

WORCESTER. True; who bears hard

His brother's death at Bristow, the
Lord Scroop.

I speak not this in estimation,

As what I think might be, but what
I know   270

Is ruminated, plotted, and set down,

And only stays but to behold the
face

Of that occasion that shall bring it
on.

HOTSPUR. I smell it. Upon my life, it
will do well.

NORTHUMBERLAND. Before the game is
afoot thou still let'st slip.   275

HOTSPUR. Why, it cannot choose but

be a noble plot.

And then the power of Scotland and
of York

To join with Mortimer, ha?

WORCESTER.   And so they shall.

HOTSPUR. In faith, it is exceedingly
well aimed.

WORCESTER. And 'tis no little reason
bids us speed   280

To save our heads by raising of a
head;

For, bear ourselves as even as we
can,

The King will always think him in
our debt,

And think we think ourselves un-
satisfied,

Till he hath found a time to pay us
home.   285

And see already how he doth begin

To make us strangers to his looks
of love.

HOTSPUR. He does, he does! We'll be
revenged on him.

WORCESTER. Cousin, farewell. No further go in this

Than I by letters shall direct your
course.   290

When time is ripe, which will be
suddenly,

I'll steal to Glendower and Lord
Mortimer,

Where you and Douglas, and our
pow'rs at once,

As I will fashion it, shall happily
meet,

To bear our fortunes in our own
strong arms,   295

Which now we hold at much uncertainty.

NORTHUMBERLAND.   Farewell, good
brother. We shall thrive, I trust.

HOTSPUR. Uncle, adieu. O, let the hours
be short

Till fields and blows and groans applaud our sport!   *Exeunt.*

---

252 *cozeners:* rogues. 268 *Bristow:* Bristol;
the Lord Scroop: William Scrope, Earl of
Wiltshire, whom Henry had executed. 269
estimation: guess or rumor. 275 *let'st slip:*
let the hounds loose (on the scent).

---

281 *head:* army. 285 *pay us home:* i.e., with
a final stroke. 291 *suddenly:* immediately.

ACT II

SCENE i. [*Rochester. An inn yard.*]

[*Enter a* CARRIER *with a lantern in his hand.*]

FIRST CARRIER. Heigh-ho! An it be not four by the day, I'll be hanged. Charles' wain is over the new chimney, and yet our horse not packed. What, ostler! 5

OSTLER. [*within*] Anon, anon.

FIRST CARRIER. I prithee, Tom, beat Cut's saddle, put a few flocks in the point; poor jade is wrung in the withers out of all cess. 10

Enter another CARRIER.

SECOND CARRIER. Peas and beans are as dank here as a dog, and that is the next way to give poor jades the bots. This house is turned upside down since Robin Ostler died. 15

FIRST CARRIER. Poor fellow never joyed since the price of oats rose; it was the death of him.

SECOND CARRIER. I think this be the most villainous house in all London road for fleas, I am stung like a tench. 20

FIRST CARRIER. Like a tench? By the mass, there is ne'er a king christen could be better bit than I have been since the first cock. 25

SECOND CARRIER. Why, they will allow us ne'er a jordan, and then we leak in your chimney, and your chamberlye breeds fleas like a loach. 30

FIRST CARRIER. What, ostler! Come away and be hanged! Come away!

SECOND CARRIER. I have a gammon of bacon and two razes of ginger, to be delivered as far as Charing Cross. 35

FIRST CARRIER. God's body! The turkeys in my pannier are quite starved. What, ostler! A plague on thee, hast thou never an eye in thy head? Canst not hear? And 'twere not as good deed as drink to break the pate on thee, I am a very villain. Come, and be hanged! Hast no faith in thee? 40

Enter GADSHILL.

GADSHILL. Good morrow, carriers, what's o'clock? 45

FIRST CARRIER. I think it be two o'clock.

GADSHILL. I prithee lend me thy lantern to see my gelding in the stable. 50

FIRST CARRIER. Nay, by God, soft! I know a trick worth two of that, i' faith.

GADSHILL. I pray thee lend me thine.

SECOND CARRIER. Ay, when? Canst tell? Lend me thy lantern, quoth he? Marry, I'll see thee hanged first! 55

GADSHILL. Sirrah carrier, what time do you mean to come to London?

SECOND CARRIER. Time enough to go to bed with a candle, I warrant thee. Come, neighbor Mugs, we'll call up the gentlemen, they will along with company, for they have great charge. *Exeunt* [CARRIERS]. 60–65

GADSHILL. What, ho! Chamberlain!

Enter CHAMBERLAIN.

CHAMBERLAIN. "At hand, quoth pickpurse."

GADSHILL. That's even as fair as "at

II.i.1 *Carrier:* transporter. *2 by the day:* A.M. 3 *Charles' wain:* the Great Bear. 7 *beat:* pound into softness. 8–9 *flocks in the point:* wool in the pommel (for padding). 9–10 *wrung in the withers:* galled at the shoulders. 10 *out of all cess:* excessively. 13 *next:* nearest. 14 *bots:* worms. 22 *tench:* red-spotted fish. 23 *By the mass:* a mild oath. 26 *first cock:* midnight. 28 *jordan:* chamberpot. 29 *chimney:* fireplace. 29–30 *chamber-lye:* urine. 30 *loach:* fast-breeding fish.

33 *gammon:* haunch. 34 *razes:* roots. 42 *pate:* head. 60–61 *Time...candle:* an evasion. 65 *charge:* luggage. 66 *Chamberlain:* room servant. 67 *"At hand":* "Here I am" (and ready with a quick hand to pick purses). 69 *even as fair:* just as believable.

hand, quoth the chamberlain"; 70
for thou variest no more from picking
of purses than giving direction doth
from laboring: thou layest the plot
how.

CHAMBERLAIN. Good morrow, 75
Master Gadshill. It holds current that
I told you yesternight: there's a
franklin in the Wild of Kent hath
brought three hundred marks with
him in gold, I heard him tell it 80
to one of his company last night
at supper—a kind of auditor, one
that hath abundance of charge too,
God knows what. They are up already
and call for eggs and butter, 85
they will away presently.

GADSHILL. Sirrah, if they meet not
with Saint Nicholas' clerks, I'll give
thee this neck.

CHAMBERLAIN. No, I'll none of it; 90
I pray thee keep that for the hangman; for I know thou worshippest
Saint Nicholas as truly as a man
of falsehood may.

GADSHILL. What talked thou to me 95
of the hangman? If I hang, I'll make
a fat pair of gallows; for if I hang,
old Sir John hangs with me, and
thou knowest he is no starveling. Tut!
There are other Trojans that 100
thou dream'st not of, the which for
sport sake are content to do the
profession some grace; that would
(if matters should be looked into)
for their own credit sake make 105
all whole. I am joined with no foot-
landrakers, no long-staff sixpenny
strikers, none of these mad mustachio
purple-hued maltworms; but with
nobility and tranquillity, burgo- 110
masters and great oneyers, such as
can hold in, such as will strike sooner
than speak, and speak sooner than
drink, and drink sooner than pray—
and yet, 'zounds, I lie, for they 115
pray continually to their saint, the
commonwealth, or rather, not pray
to her, but prey on her, for they
ride up and down on her and make
her their boots. 120

CHAMBERLAIN. What, the commonwealth their boots? Will she hold out
water in foul way?

GADSHILL. She will, she will! Justice
hath liquored her. We steal as 125
in a castle, cocksure. We have the
receipt of fernseed, we walk invisible.

CHAMBERLAIN. Nay, by my faith, I
think you are more beholding to the
night than to fernseed for your 130
walking invisible.

GADSHILL. Give me thy hand. Thou
shalt have a share in our purchase,
as I am a true man.

CHAMBERLAIN. Nay, rather let me 135
have it, as you are a false thief.

GADSHILL. Go to; "homo" is a common
name to all men. Bid the ostler bring
my gelding out of the stable. Farewell, you muddy knave. *Exeunt.* 140

SCENE ii. [*The highway, near Gad's
Hill.*]

Enter PRINCE, POINS, *and* PETO, *etc.*

POINS. Come, shelter, shelter! I have
removed Falstaff's horse, and he frets
like a gummed velvet.

PRINCE. Stand close. [*They step aside.*]

Enter FALSTAFF.

---

76 *current:* true.   78 *franklin:* land owner;
Wild: weald, open country.   79 *three hundred
marks:* equivalent to £200 Elizabethan currency.   88 *Saint Nicholas' clerks:* highwaymen.
100 *Trojans:* good fellows.   106–7 *foot-land-
rakers:* foot-loose thieves.   107–8 *long-staff
sixpenny strikers:* small-time highwaymen
armed with staffs to unhorse victims.   109
purple-hued maltworms: red-nosed drunkards.

111 *oneyers:* ones.   112 *hold in:* keep mum.
120 *boots:* booty, spoils.   123 *foul way:* muddy
roads.   125 *liquored:* waterproofed.   127
receipt of fernseed: recipe of fernseed, thought
to make one invisible.   133 *purchase:* ironic
for plunder.   II.ii.3 *gummed:* when stripped
away, gum roughens ("frets") the velvet it
has stiffened.

FALSTAFF. Poins! Poins, and be 5
hanged! Poins!

PRINCE. [*comes forward*] Peace, ye
fat-kidneyed rascal! What a brawling
dost thou keep!

FALSTAFF. Where's Poins, Hal? 10

PRINCE. He is walked up to the top of
the hill; I'll go seek him. [*Steps aside.*]

FALSTAFF. I am accursed to rob in that
thief's company. The rascal hath removed my horse and tied him I 15
know not where. If I travel but four
foot by the squire further afoot, I
shall break my wind. Well, I doubt
not but to die a fair death for all
this, if I scape hanging for killing 20
that rogue. I have forsworn his company hourly any time this two and
twenty years, and yet I am bewitched
with the rogue's company. If the
rascal have given me medicines 25
to make me love him, I'll be hanged.
It could not be else: I have drunk
medicines. Poins! Hal! A plague
upon you both! Bardolph! Peto! I'll
starve ere I'll rob a foot further. 30
And 'twere not as good a deed as
drink to turn true man and to leave
these rogues, I am the veriest varlet
that ever chewed with a tooth. Eight
yards of uneven ground is three- 35
score and ten miles afoot with me,
and the stony-hearted villains know
it well enough. A plague upon it when
thieves cannot be true one to another! [*They whistle.*] Whew! 40
A plague upon you all! Give me my
horse, you rogues! Give me my horse
and be hanged!

PRINCE. [*comes forward*] Peace, ye
fat-guts! Lie down, lay thine ear 45
close to the ground, and list if thou
canst hear the tread of travelers.

FALSTAFF. Have you any levers to lift
me up again, being down? 'Sblood,
I'll not bear mine own flesh so 50
far afoot again for all the coin in
thy father's exchequer. What a plague

mean ye to colt me thus?

PRINCE. Thou liest, thou art not colted,
thou art uncolted. 55

FALSTAFF. I prithee, good Prince Hal,
help me to my horse, good king's
son.

PRINCE. Out, ye rogue! Shall I be your
ostler? 60

FALSTAFF. Hang thyself in thine own
heir-apparent garters! If I be ta'en,
I'll peach for this. And I have not
ballads made on you all, and sung
to filthy tunes, let a cup of sack 65
be my poison. When a jest is so
forward—and afoot too—I hate it.

Enter GADSHILL [*and* BARDOLPH].

GADSHILL. Stand!

FALSTAFF. So I do, against my will.

POINS. O, 'tis our setter; I know 70
his voice. [*Comes forward.*] Bardolph, what news?

BARDOLPH. Case ye, case ye! On with
your vizards! There's money of the
King's coming down the hill; 'tis 75
going to the King's exchequer.

FALSTAFF. You lie, ye rogue! 'Tis going
to the King's tavern.

GADSHILL. There's enough to make us
all— 80

FALSTAFF. To be hanged.

PRINCE. Sirs, you four shall front them
in the narrow lane; Ned Poins and
I will walk lower: if they scape from
your encounter, then they light 85
on us.

PETO. How many be there of them?

GADSHILL. Some eight or ten.

FALSTAFF. 'Zounds, will they not rob us?

PRINCE. What, a coward, Sir John 90
Paunch?

FALSTAFF. Indeed, I am not John of
Gaunt your grandfather, but yet no
coward, Hal.

---

17 *squire:* measure.

---

53 *colt:* trick. 63 *peach:* "rat" on him,
impeach him. 70 *setter:* either a confederate
or an informer. 73 *Case ye:* disguise yourselves. 92–93 *John of Gaunt:* Falstaff puns
on the name since Hal himself is thin.

PRINCE. Well, we leave that to the 95
proof.

POINS. Sirrah Jack, thy horse stands
behind the hedge. When thou need'st
him, there thou shalt find him. Farewell and stand fast. 100

FALSTAFF. Now cannot I strike him, if
I should be hanged.

PRINCE. [*aside to* POINS] Ned, where
are our disguises?

POINS. [*aside to* PRINCE] Here, 105
hard by. Stand close.

[*Exeunt* PRINCE *and* POINS.]

FALSTAFF. Now, my masters, happy
man be his dole, say I. Every man
to his business.

Enter the TRAVELERS.

TRAVELER. Come, neighbor. The 110
boy shall lead our horses down the
hill; we'll walk afoot awhile and ease
our legs.

THIEVES. Stand!

TRAVELER. Jesus bless us! 115

FALSTAFF. Strike! Down with them!
Cut the villains' throats! Ah, whoreson caterpillars! Bacon-fed knaves!
They hate us youth. Down with
them! Fleece them! 120

TRAVELER. O, we are undone, both we
and ours forever!

FALSTAFF. Hang ye, gorbellied knaves,
are ye undone? No, ye fat chuffs;
I would your store were here! 125
On, bacons, on! What, ye knaves,
young men must live. You are grand
jurors, are ye? We'll jure ye, faith!

Here they rob them and bind them.
Exeunt.

Enter the PRINCE *and* POINS [*dis-*
guised].

---

96 *proof:* test. 106 *hard by:* nearby. 107–8
happy...dole: good fortune. 117–18 *whore-*
son caterpillars: bastardly parasites. 123
gorbellied: fat. 124 *chuffs:* misers. 125 *store:*
riches. 126 *bacons:* fat men. 127–28 *grand*
jurors: men of enough wealth to serve as
jurors.

PRINCE. The thieves have bound the
true men. Now could thou and I 130
rob the thieves and go merrily to
London, it would be argument for
a week, laughter for a month, and
a good jest forever.

POINS. Stand close! I hear them 135
coming. [*They stand aside.*]

Enter the THIEVES *again.*

FALSTAFF. Come, my masters, let us
share, and then to horse before day.
And the Prince and Poins be not
two arrant cowards, there's no 140
equity stirring. There's no more valor
in that Poins than in a wild duck.

PRINCE. Your money!

POINS. Villains!

{ *As they are sharing, the* PRINCE *and*
{ POINS *set upon them. They all run*
{ *away, and Falstaff, after a blow or*
{ *two, runs away too, leaving the*
{ *booty behind them.*

PRINCE. Got with much ease. Now 145
merrily to horse. The thieves are all
scattered, and possessed with fear so
strongly that they dare not meet
each other: each takes his fellow for
an officer. Away, good Ned. Fal- 150
staff sweats to death and lards the
lean earth as he walks along. Were't
not for laughing, I should pity him.

POINS. How the fat rogue roared!

Exeunt.

SCENE iii. [*Northumberland. Warkworth*
Castle.]

Enter HOTSPUR *solus, reading a letter.*

HOTSPUR. "But, for mine own part, my
lord, I could be well contented to
be there, in respect of the love I
bear your house." He could be con-

---

132 *be argument:* make conversation. 140
arrant: through and through. 140–41 *no equity*
stirring: no justice left. II.iii.s.d. *solus:*
alone. 4 *house:* family.

tented—why is he not then? In 5
respect of the love he bears our
house! He shows in this he loves his
own barn better than he loves our
house. Let me see some more. "The
purpose you undertake is danger- 10
ous"—why, that's certain! 'Tis dangerous to take a cold, to sleep, to
drink; but I tell you, my lord fool, out
of this nettle, danger, we pluck this
flower, safety. "The purpose 15
you undertake is dangerous, the
friends you have named uncertain,
the time itself unsorted, and your
whole plot too light for the counter-
poise of so great an opposi- 20
tion." Say you so, say you so? I say
unto you again, you are a shallow,
cowardly hind, and you lie. What
a lack-brain is this! By the Lord,
our plot is a good plot as ever 25
was laid; our friends true and constant: a good plot, good friends, and
full of expectation; an excellent plot,
very good friends. What a frosty-
spirited rogue is this! Why, my 30
Lord of York commends the plot and
the general course of the action.
'Zounds, and I were now by this
rascal, I could brain him with his
lady's fan. Is there not my 35
father, my uncle, and myself; Lord
Edmund Mortimer, my Lord of York,
and Owen Glendower? Is there not,
besides, the Douglas? Have I not all
their letters to meet me in arms 40
by the ninth of the next month, and
are they not some of them set forward already? What a pagan rascal
is this, an infidel! Ha! you shall see
now, in very sincerity of fear 45
and cold heart will he to the King
and lay open all our proceedings. O,
I could divide myself and go to
buffets for moving such a dish of
skim milk with so honorable an 50

action! Hang him, let him tell the
King! We are prepared. I will set
forward tonight.

Enter his LADY.

How now, Kate? I must leave you
within these two hours.

LADY. O my good lord, why are you
   thus alone?   55
For what offense have I this fortnight
   been
A banished woman from my Harry's
   bed?
Tell me, sweet lord, what is't that
   takes from thee
Thy stomach, pleasure, and thy
   golden sleep?
Why dost thou bend thine eyes upon
   the earth,   60
And start so often when thou sit'st
   alone?
Why hast thou lost the fresh blood
   in thy cheeks
And given my treasures and my
   rights of thee
To thick-eyed musing and cursed
   melancholy?
In thy faint slumbers I by thee have
   watched,   65
And heard thee murmur tales of iron
   wars,
Speak terms of manage to thy bound-
   ing steed,
Cry "Courage! To the field!" And
   thou hast talked
Of sallies and retires, of trenches,
   tents,
Of palisadoes, frontiers, parapets, 70
Of basilisks, of cannon, culverin,
Of prisoners' ransom, and of soldiers
   slain,
And all the currents of a heady fight.

---

59 *stomach:* appetite. 64 *thick-eyed musing
and cursed:* dim-sighted (perhaps from weeping) and peevish. 67 *manage:* training
(manège) or putting a horse through his paces.
70 *palisadoes:* barrier of stakes; *frontiers:*
outer defenses; *parapets:* walls. 71 *basilisks,
culverin:* cannons. 73 *currents:* tides of battle; *heady:* violent.

---

18 *unsorted:* ill-chosen. 23 *hind:* rustic. 31
Lord of York: Archbishop of York. 48–49
divide...buffets: fight myself.

Thy spirit within thee hath been so
at war,
And thus hath so bestirred thee in
thy sleep,   75
That beads of sweat have stood upon
thy brow
Like bubbles in a late-disturbed
stream,
And in thy face strange motions have
appeared,
Such as we see when men restrain
their breath
On some great sudden hest. O, what
portents are these?   80
Some heavy business hath my lord
in hand,
And I must know it, else he loves
me not.
HOTSPUR. What, ho!

[*Enter a* SERVANT.]

Is Gilliams with the packet gone?
SERVANT. He is, my lord, an hour ago.
HOTSPUR. Hath Butler brought   85
those horses from the sheriff?
SERVANT. One horse, my lord, he
brought even now.
HOTSPUR. What horse? A roan, a crop-
ear, is it not?   90
SERVANT. It is, my lord.
HOTSPUR. That roan shall be my
throne. Well, I will back him straight.
O Esperance! Bid Butler lead him
forth into the park.   95

[*Exit* SERVANT.]

LADY. But hear you, my lord.
HOTSPUR. What say'st thou, my lady?
LADY. What is it carries you away?
HOTSPUR. Why, my horse, my love—
my horse!   100
LADY. Out, you mad-headed ape! A
weasel hath not such a deal of spleen
as you are tossed with. In faith, I'll
know your business, Harry, that I
will! I fear my brother Mortimer   105

doth stir about his title and hath
sent for you to line his enterprise;
but if you go—
HOTSPUR. So far afoot, I shall be
weary, love.   110
LADY. Come, come, you paraquito,
answer me directly unto this question that I ask. In faith, I'll break
thy little finger, Harry, and if thou
wilt not tell me all things true.   115
HOTSPUR. Away, away, you trifler!
Love? I love thee not;
I care not for thee, Kate. This is no
world
To play with mammets and to tilt
with lips.
We must have bloody noses and
cracked crowns,
And pass them current too. Gods me,
my horse!   120
What say'st thou, Kate? What
wouldst thou have with me?
LADY. Do you not love me? Do you
not indeed?
Well, do not then; for since you love
me not,
I will not love myself. Do you not
love me?
Nay, tell me if you speak in jest
or no.   125
HOTSPUR. Come, wilt thou see me
ride?
And when I am a-horseback, I will
swear
I love thee infinitely. But hark you,
Kate:
I must not have you henceforth ques-
tion me
Whither I go, nor reason where-
about.   130
Whither I must, I must, and—to
conclude,
This evening must I leave you, gentle
Kate.

---

80 *hest:* injunction. 94 *Esperance:* hope (the
Percy motto is *Esperance en dieu*). 102
spleen: wilfullness.

107 *line:* strengthen. 111 *paraquito:* parrot.
118 *mammets:* dolls; *tilt:* duel. 119 *crowns:*
"heads" and "coins," which must be passed as
"currency," as the present crowned head
(Henry IV) is passing himself off as real coin.
120 *Gods me:* God save me.

I know you wise—but yet no farther
   wise
Than Harry Percy's wife; constant
   you are—
But yet a woman; and for se-
   crecy,   135
No lady closer—for I well believe
Thou wilt not utter what thou dost
   not know,
And so far will I trust thee, gentle
   Kate—

LADY. How? So far?

HOTSPUR. Not an inch further. But
   hark you, Kate: 140
Whither I go, thither shall you go
   too;
Today will I set forth, tomorrow you.
Will this content you, Kate?

LADY.   It must of force.

Exeunt.

SCENE iv. [*Eastcheap. The tavern.*]

[*Enter* PRINCE *and* POINS.]

PRINCE. Ned, prithee come out of that
fat room and lend me thy hand to
laugh a little.

POINS. Where hast been, Hal?

PRINCE. With three or four logger-   5
heads amongst three or fourscore
hogsheads. I have sounded the very
bass string of humility. Sirrah, I am
sworn brother to a leash of drawers
and can call them all by their   10
christen names, as Tom, Dick, and
Francis. They take it already upon
their salvation that, though I be put
Prince of Wales, yet I am the king
of courtesy, and tell me flatly I   15
am no proud Jack like Falstaff, but
a Corinthian, a lad of mettle, a good
boy (by the Lord, so they call me!),
and when I am King of England I
shall command all the good lads   20
in Eastcheap. They call drinking
deep, dyeing scarlet; and when you
breathe in your watering, they cry
"hem!" and bid you play it off. To
conclude, I am so good a pro-   25
ficient in one quarter of an hour
that I can drink with any tinker in
his own language during my life. I
tell thee, Ned, thou hast lost much
honor that thou wert not with me   30
in this action. But, sweet Ned—to
sweeten which name of Ned, I give
thee this pennyworth of sugar,
clapped even now into my hand by
an under-skinker, one that never   35
spake other English in his life than
"Eight shillings and sixpence," and
"You are welcome," with this shrill
addition, "Anon, anon, sir! Score a
pint of bastard in the Half-   40
moon," or so—but, Ned, to drive
away the time till Falstaff come, I
prithee do thou stand in some by-
room while I question my puny
drawer to what end he gave me   45
the sugar; and do thou never leave
calling "Francis!" that his tale to
me may be nothing but "Anon!"
Step aside, and I'll show thee a
precedent.   50

POINS. Francis!

PRINCE. Thou art perfect.

POINS. Francis! [POINS *steps aside.*]

Enter [FRANCIS, *a*] *drawer.*

FRANCIS. Anon, anon, sir. Look down
into the Pomgarnet, Ralph.   55

PRINCE. Come hither, Francis.

FRANCIS. My lord?

---

143 *of force:* of necessity. II.iv.s.d. *tavern:*
probably the Boar's Head. 2 *fat:* stuffy. 5–6
loggerheads: blockheads. 9 *leash:* three, as
three hounds were usually tied to one leash;
drawers: tapsters. 16 *Jack:* fellow. 17
Corinthian: gay fellow.

21–22 *drinking deep, dyeing scarlet:* turning
one's face red by drink and perhaps supplying
urine for dyers, as J. Dover Wilson suggests.
23 *breathe...watering:* breathe while drinking. 24 *play it off:* quaff. 35 *under-skinker:*
subordinate tapster. 39 *Score:* charge. 40
bastard: sweet Spanish wine. 40–41 *Half-
moon:* a room in the inn. 50 *precedent:*
example. 55 *Pomgarnet:* Pomegranate, a
room in the inn.

PRINCE. How long hast thou to serve, Francis?

FRANCIS. Forsooth, five years, and 60 as much as to—

POINS. [*within*] Francis!

FRANCIS. Anon, anon, sir.

PRINCE. Five year! By'r Lady, a long lease for the clinking of pewter. 65 But, Francis, darest thou be so valiant as to play the coward with thy indenture and show it a fair pair of heels and run from it?

FRANCIS. O Lord, sir, I'll be sworn 70 upon all the books in England I could find in my heart—

POINS. [*within*] Francis!

FRANCIS. Anon, sir.

PRINCE. How old art thou, Francis? 75

FRANCIS. Let me see: about Michaelmas next I shall be—

POINS. [*within*] Francis!

FRANCIS. Anon, sir. Pray stay a little, my lord. 80

PRINCE. Nay, but hark you, Francis. For the sugar thou gavest me— 'twas a pennyworth, was't not?

FRANCIS. O Lord! I would it had been two! 85

PRINCE. I will give thee for it a thousand pound. Ask me when thou wilt, and thou shalt have it.

POINS. [*within*] Francis!

FRANCIS. Anon, anon. 90

PRINCE. Anon, Francis? No, Francis; but tomorrow, Francis; or, Francis, a Thursday; or indeed, Francis, when thou wilt. But, Francis—

FRANCIS. My lord? 95

PRINCE. Wilt thou rob this leathern-jerkin, crystal-button, not-pated, agate-ring, puke-stocking, caddis-garter, smooth-tongue, Spanish-pouch? 100

FRANCIS. O Lord, sir, who do you mean?

PRINCE. Why then, your brown bastard

is your only drink; for look you, Francis, your white canvas doublet will sully. In Barbary, sir, it 105 cannot come to so much.

FRANCIS. What, sir?

POINS. [*within*] Francis!

PRINCE. Away, you rogue! Dost thou not hear them call? 110

Here they both call him. The drawer stands amazed, not knowing which way to go.

Enter VINTNER.

VINTNER. What, stand'st thou still, and hear'st such a calling? Look to the guests within.   [*Exit* FRANCIS.] My lord, old Sir John, with half a dozen more, are at the door. 115 Shall I let them in?

PRINCE. Let them alone awhile, and then open the door. [*Exit* VINTNER.] Poins!

POINS. [*within*] Anon, anon, sir. 120

Enter POINS.

PRINCE. Sirrah, Falstaff and the rest of the thieves are at the door. Shall we be merry?

POINS. As merry as crickets, my lad. But hark ye; what cunning 125 match have you made with this jest of the drawer? Come, what's the issue?

PRINCE. I am now of all humors that have showed themselves humors 130 since the old days of goodman Adam to the pupil age of this present twelve o'clock at midnight.

[*Enter* FRANCIS.]

What's o'clock, Francis?

FRANCIS. Anon, anon, sir. [*Exit.*] 135

PRINCE. That ever this fellow should

---

59 *serve:* i.e., as an apprentice. 68 *indenture:* contract. 76 *Michaelmas:* September 29. 96–100 *rob...Spanish-pouch:* steal from this inn-keeper, thus bedecked.

105–6 *In Barbary...much:* probably intended as nonsense. 110s.d. *Vintner:* the innkeeper. 128 *issue:* outcome. 129–33 *I...midnight:* "I am prepared for all manner of frolic that men have tried between the beginning of time and now."

have fewer words than a parrot, and yet the son of a woman! His industry is upstairs and downstairs, his eloquence the parcel of a reckoning. 140 I am not yet of Percy's mind, the Hotspur of the North: he that kills me some six or seven dozen of Scots at a breakfast, washes his hands, and says to his wife, "Fie upon this 145 quiet life! I want work." "O my sweet Harry," says she, "how many hast thou killed today?" "Give my roan horse a drench," says he, and answers "Some fourteen," an 150 hour after, "a trifle, a trifle." I prithee call in Falstaff. I'll play Percy, and that damned brawn shall play Dame Mortimer his wife. "Rivo!" says the drunkard. Call in Ribs, call in 155 Tallow.

Enter FALSTAFF, [GADSHILL, BARDOLPH, *and* PETO; FRANCIS *follows with wine*].

POINS. Welcome, Jack. Where hast thou been?
FALSTAFF. A plague of all cowards, I say, and a vengeance too! Marry 160 and amen! Give me a cup of sack, boy. Ere I lead this life long, I'll sew netherstocks, and mend them and foot them too. A plague of all cowards! Give me a cup of sack, 165 rogue. Is there no virtue extant?

[*He drinketh.*]

PRINCE. Didst thou never see Titan kiss a dish of butter (pitiful-hearted⁻ Titan!) that melted at the sweet tale of the sun's? If thou didst, then 170 behold that compound.
FALSTAFF. You rogue, here's lime in this sack too! There is nothing but roguery to be found in villainous

man. Yet a coward is worse 175 than a cup of sack with lime in it— a villainous coward! Go thy ways, old Jack, die when thou wilt; if manhood, good manhood, be not forgot upon the face of the 180 earth, then am I a shotten herring. There lives not three good men unhanged in England; and one of them is fat, and grows old. God help the while! A bad world, I say. I 185 would I were a weaver; I could sing psalms or anything. A plague of all cowards, I say still!
PRINCE. How now, woolsack? What mutter you? 190
FALSTAFF. A king's son! If I do not beat thee out of thy kingdom with a dagger of lath and drive all thy subjects afore thee like a flock of wild geese, I'll never wear hair 195 on my face more. You Prince of Wales?
PRINCE. Why, you whoreson round man, what's the matter?
FALSTAFF. Are not you a coward? 200 Answer me to that—and Poins there?
POINS. 'Zounds, ye fat paunch, and ye call me coward, by the Lord, I'll stab thee.
FALSTAFF. I call thee coward? I'll 205 see thee damned ere I call thee coward, but I would give a thousand pound I could run as fast as thou canst. You are straight enough in the shoulders; you care not 210 who sees your back. Call you that backing of your friends? A plague upon such backing, give me them that will face me. Give me a cup of sack. I am a rogue if I drunk 215 today.
PRINCE. O villain, thy lips are scarce wiped since thou drunk'st last.
FALSTAFF. All is one for that. [*He*

---

140 *parcel of a reckoning:* quantity of a bill. 149 *drench:* dose of medicine. 153 *brawn:* boar. 154 *"Rivo":* apparently a drinker's oath. 159 *of:* on. 163 *netherstocks:* stockings. 169 *Titan:* sun. Falstaff and drink are a combination ("compound") like the sun melting a dish of butter. 172 *lime:* added to wine to make it clear.

181 *shotten herring:* a herring that has spawned and is therefore slim. 186–87 *sing psalms:* weavers were noted psalm singers and often Puritans—as much like Falstaff as slim herring are. 193 *dagger of lath:* wooden stage weapon.

drinketh.] A plague of all cow- 220
ards, still say I.

PRINCE. What's the matter?

FALSTAFF. What's the matter? There
be four of us here have ta'en a thousand pound this day morning. 225

PRINCE. Where is it, Jack, where is it?

FALSTAFF. Where is it? Taken from us
it is. A hundred upon poor four of
us!

PRINCE. What, a hundred, man? 230

FALSTAFF. I am a rogue if I were not
at half sword with a dozen of them
two hours together. I have scaped
by miracle. I am eight times thrust
through the doublet, four 235
through the hose; my buckler cut
through and through; my sword
hacked like a handsaw—*ecce signum!*
I never dealt better since I was a
man. All would not do. A plague 240
of all cowards! Let them speak. If
they speak more or less than truth,
they are villains and the sons of
darkness.

PRINCE. Speak, sirs. How was it? 245

GADSHILL. We four set upon some
dozen—

FALSTAFF. Sixteen at least, my lord.

GADSHILL. And bound them.

PETO. No, no, they were not bound. 250

FALSTAFF. You rogue, they were bound,
every man of them, or I am a Jew
else—an Ebrew Jew.

GADSHILL. As we were sharing, some
six or seven fresh men set upon 255
us—

FALSTAFF. And unbound the rest, and
then come in the other.

PRINCE. What, fought you with them
all? 260

FALSTAFF. All? I know not what you
call all, but if I fought not with
fifty of them, I am a bunch of rad-
ish! If there were not two or three
and fifty upon poor old Jack, 265

then am I no two-legged creature.

PRINCE. Pray God you have not
murd'red some of them.

FALSTAFF. Nay, that's past praying for.
I have peppered two of them. 270
Two I am sure I have paid, two
rogues in buckram suits. I tell thee
what, Hal—if I tell thee a lie, spit
in my face, call me horse. Thou
knowest my old ward: here I 275
lay, and thus I bore my point. Four
rogues in buckram let drive at me.

PRINCE. What, four? Thou saidst but
two even now.

FALSTAFF. Four, Hal. I told thee 280
four.

POINS. Ay, ay, he said four.

FALSTAFF. These four came all afront
and mainly thrust at me. I made me
no more ado but took all their 285
seven points in my target, thus.

PRINCE. Seven? Why, there were but
four even now.

FALSTAFF. In buckram?

POINS. Ay, four, in buckram suits. 290

FALSTAFF. Seven, by these hilts, or I
am a villain else.

PRINCE. [*aside to* POINS] Prithee let
him alone. We shall have more anon.

FALSTAFF. Dost thou hear me, Hal? 295

PRINCE. Ay, and mark thee too, Jack.

FALSTAFF. Do so, for it is worth the
list'ning to. These nine in buckram
that I told thee of—

PRINCE. So, two more already. 300

FALSTAFF. Their points being broken—

POINS. Down fell their hose.

FALSTAFF. Began to give me ground;
but I followed me close, came in,
foot and hand, and with a 305
thought seven of the eleven I paid.

PRINCE. O monstrous! Eleven buckram
men grown out of two!

FALSTAFF. But, as the devil would have

---

232 *at half sword:* at close quarters. 235
doublet: close-fitting garmet. 236 *hose:*
breeches. 238 *ecce signum:* behold the sign
(proof). 239 *dealt:* fought.

275 *ward:* fencing form. 284 *mainly:* with
might and main. 286 *target:* shield. 291 *by
these hilts:* by the cross formed by the sword
handle. 301 *points:* "swords" and, as Poins'
remark indicates, "laces" holding the breeches
up.

it, three misbegotten knaves in 310
Kendal green came at my back and
let drive at me; for it was so dark,
Hal, that thou couldest not see thy
hand.

PRINCE. These lies are like their 315
father that begets them—gross as a
mountain, open, palpable. Why, thou
clay-brained guts, thou knotty-pated
fool, thou whoreson obscene greasy
tallow-catch— 320

FALSTAFF. What, art thou mad? Art
thou mad? Is not the truth the truth?

PRINCE. Why, how couldst thou know
these men in Kendal green when it
was so dark thou couldst not 325
see thy hand? Come, tell us your
reason. What sayest thou to this?

POINS. Come, your reason, Jack, your
reason.

FALSTAFF. What, upon compul- 330
sion? 'Zounds, and I were at the
strappado or all the racks in the
world, I would not tell you on compulsion. Give you a reason on compulsion? If reasons were as 335
plentiful as blackberries, I would
give no man a reason upon compulsion, I.

PRINCE. I'll be no longer guilty of this
sin; this sanguine coward, this 340
bed-presser, this horseback-breaker,
this huge hill of flesh—

FALSTAFF. 'Sblood, you starveling, you
eel skin, you dried neat's tongue, you
bull's pizzle, you stockfish—O 345
for breath to utter what is like thee!
—you tailor's yard, you sheath, you
bowcase, you vile standing tuck!

PRINCE. Well, breathe awhile, and then
to it again; and when thou hast 350
tired thyself in base comparisons,
hear me speak but this.

---

318 *knotty-pated:* thick headed. 320 *tallow-
catch:* tub of lard. 232 *strappado:* an instrument of torture by which men were raised
and suddenly dropped part way to the ground
—to the end of a rope tying their hands
behind them. 340 *sanguine:* red-faced. 344
neat's tongue: ox tongue. 345 *pizzle:* penis;
stockfish: dried cod. 348 *tuck:* rapier.

POINS. Mark, Jack.

PRINCE. We two saw you four set on
four, and bound them and were 355
masters of their wealth. Mark now
how a plain tale shall put you down.
Then did we two set on you four
and, with a word, outfaced you from
your prize, and have it; yea, 360
and can show it you here in the
house. And, Falstaff, you carried
your guts away as nimbly, with as
quick dexterity, and roared for
mercy, and still run and roared, 365
as ever I heard bullcalf. What a
slave art thou to hack thy sword as
thou hast done, and then say it was
in fight! What trick, what device,
what starting hole canst thou 370
now find out to hide thee from this
open and apparent shame?

POINS. Come, let's hear, Jack. What
trick hast thou now?

FALSTAFF. By the Lord, I knew ye 375
as well as he that made ye. Why,
hear you, my masters. Was it for me
to kill the heir apparent? Should I
turn upon the true prince? Why,
thou knowest I am as valiant as 380
Hercules, but beware instinct. The
lion will not touch the true prince.
Instinct is a great matter. I was now
a coward on instinct. I shall think
the better of myself, and thee, 385
during my life—I for a valiant lion,
and thou for a true prince. But, by
the Lord, lads, I am glad you have
the money. Hostess, clap to the doors.
Watch tonight, pray tomorrow. 390
Gallants, lads, boys, hearts of gold,
all the titles of good fellowship come
to you! What, shall we be merry?
Shall we have a play extempore?

PRINCE. Content—and the argu- 395
ment shall be thy running away.

FALSTAFF. Ah, no more of that, Hal,
and thou lovest me!

Enter HOSTESS.

---

370 *starting hole:* hiding place. 390 *watch:*
(1) "be on guard" (against temptation) and
(2) "carouse." 395-96 *argument:* subject.

HOSTESS. O Jesu, my lord the Prince!

PRINCE. How now, my lady the 400 hostess? What say'st thou to me?

HOSTESS. Marry, my lord, there is a nobleman of the court at door would speak with you. He says he comes from your father. 405

PRINCE. Give him as much as will make him a royal man, and send him back again to my mother.

FALSTAFF. What manner of man is he?

HOSTESS. An old man. 410

FALSTAFF. What doth gravity out of his bed at midnight? Shall I give him his answer?

PRINCE. Prithee do, Jack.

FALSTAFF. Faith, and I'll send 415 him packing. [*Exit.*]

PRINCE. Now, sirs. By'r Lady, you fought fair; so did you, Peto; so did you, Bardolph. You are lions too, you ran away upon instinct, you will 420 not touch the true prince; no—fie!

BARDOLPH. Faith, I ran when I saw others run.

PRINCE. Faith, tell me now in earnest, how came Falstaff's sword so 425 hacked?

PETO. Why, he hacked it with his dagger, and said he would swear truth out of England but he would make you believe it was done in 430 fight, and persuaded us to do the like.

BARDOLPH. Yea, and to tickle our noses with speargrass to make them bleed, and then to beslubber our gar- 435 ments with it and swear it was the blood of true men. I did that I did not this seven year before—I blushed to hear his monstrous devices.

PRINCE. O villain! Thou stolest a 440 cup of sack eighteen years ago and wert taken with the manner, and ever since thou hast blushed extempore. Thou hadst fire and sword on

thy side, and yet thou ran'st 445 away. What instinct hadst thou for it?

BARDOLPH. My lord, do you see these meteors? Do you behold these exhalations? 450

PRINCE. I do.

BARDOLPH. What think you they portend?

PRINCE. Hot livers and cold purses.

BARDOLPH. Choler, my lord, if 455 rightly taken.

PRINCE. No, if rightly taken, halter.

Enter FALSTAFF.

Here comes lean Jack; here comes bare-bone. How now, my sweet creature of bombast? How long is't 460 ago, Jack, since thou sawest thine own knee?

FALSTAFF. My own knee? When I was about thy years, Hal, I was not an eagle's talent in the waist; I 465 could have crept into any alderman's thumb ring. A plague of sighing and grief, it blows a man up like a bladder. There's villainous news abroad. Here was Sir John Bracy from 470 your father: you must to the court in the morning. That same mad fellow of the north, Percy, and he of Wales that gave Amamon the bastinado, and made Lucifer cuck- 475 old, and swore the devil his true liegeman upon the cross of a Welsh hook—what a plague call you him?

POINS. Owen Glendower.

FALSTAFF. Owen, Owen—the same; 480 and his son-in-law Mortimer, and old Northumberland, and that sprightly Scot of Scots, Douglas, that

---

407 *royal man:* "noble" and "royal" both refer to Elizabethan coins. 411 *gravity:* wise old man. 442 *taken with the manner:* caught red-handed. 444 *fire:* a red face.

449–50 *meteors, exhalations:* Bardolph's pimples. 454 *Hot livers and cold purses:* drink fills the liver and empties the purse. 455 *choler:* anger. 457 *halter:* "hangman's collar" not "choler," the Prince asserts. 460 *bombast:* cotton padding. 465 *talent:* talon. 474–78 *Amamon...hook:* Falstaff suggests that Glendower beat the devil Amamon, gave Lucifer the horns of the cuckhold, and made the devil swear allegiance to him on the (non-existent) "cross" of a Walsh hook-shaped pike.

runs a-horseback up a hill perpendi-
cular—   485
PRINCE. He that rides at high speed
and with his pistol kills a sparrow
flying.
FALSTAFF. You have hit it.
PRINCE. So did he never the spar-   490
row.
FALSTAFF. Well, that rascal hath good
metal in him; he will not run.
PRINCE. Why, what a rascal art thou
then, to praise him so for running!   495
FALSTAFF. A-horseback, ye cuckoo! But
afoot he will not budge a foot.
PRINCE. Yes, Jack, upon instinct.
FALSTAFF. I grant ye, upon instinct.   500
Well, he is there too, and one Mordake, and a thousand bluecaps more.
Worcester is stol'n away tonight;
thy father's beard is turned white
with the news; you may buy   505
land now as cheap as stinking
mack'rel.
PRINCE. Why then, it is like, if there
come a hot June, and this civil buf-
feting hold, we shall buy   510
maidenheads as they buy hobnails,
by the hundreds.
FALSTAFF. By the mass, lad, thou sayest
true; it is like we shall have good
trading that way. But tell me,   515
Hal, art not thou horrible afeard?
Thou being heir apparent, could the
world pick thee out three such
enemies again as that fiend Douglas,
that spirit Percy, and that devil   520
Glendower? Art thou not horribly a-
fraid? Doth not thy blood thrill at it?
PRINCE. Not a whit, i' faith. I lack
some of thy instinct.
FALSTAFF. Well, thou wilt be hor-   525
ribly chid tomorrow when thou
comest to thy father. If thou love
me, practice an answer.
PRINCE. Do thou stand for my father
and examine me upon the parti-   530
culars of my life.
FALSTAFF. Shall I? Content. This chair

502 *bluecaps:* Scots.   522 *thrill:* tingle.

shall be my state, this dagger my
scepter, and this cushion my crown.
PRINCE. Thy state is taken for a   535
joined stool, thy golden scepter for
a leaden dagger, and thy precious
rich crown for a pitiful bald crown.
FALSTAFF. Well, and the fire of grace
be not quite out of thee, now   540
shalt thou be moved. Give me a cup
of sack to make my eyes look red,
that it may be thought I have wept;
for I must speak in passion, and I
will do it in King Cambyses'   545
vein.
PRINCE. Well, here is my leg.
FALSTAFF. And here is my speech. Stand
aside, nobility.
HOSTESS. O Jesu, this is excellent sport,
i' faith!
FALSTAFF. Weep not, sweet queen, for
trickling tears are vain.   550
HOSTESS. O, the Father, how he holds
his countenance!
FALSTAFF. For God's sake, lords, convey my tristful queen!
For tears do stop the floodgates of
her eyes.
HOSTESS. O Jesu, he doth it as like one
of these harlotry players as   555
ever I see!
FALSTAFF. Peace, good pintpot. Peace,
good tickle-brain. Harry, I do not
only marvel where thou spendest thy
time, but also how thou art ac-   560
companied. For though the camomile,
the more it is trodden on, the faster
it grows, so youth, the more it is
wasted, the sooner it wears. That
thou art my son I have partly   565
thy mother's word, partly my own

533 *state:* chair of state.   535 *Thy:* either
Falstaff's or Henry IV's (if the Prince is
imagined to address his father in an apos-
trophe).   545–46 *King Cambyses' vein:* i.e.,
in inflated style like that of the play *King
Cambyses.*   547 *leg:* a bow of obeisance.   551
holds his countenance: keeps a straight face.
552 *convey:* escort; *tristful:* sorrowful.   555
harlotry: ribald.   557 *pintpot:* beer seller.
558 *tickle-brain:* seller of strong liquor.   561
camomile: a creeping herb.

opinion, but chiefly a villainous trick
of thine eye and a foolish hanging
of thy nether lip that doth warrant
me. If then thou be son to me, 570
here lies the point: why, being son to
me, art thou so pointed at? Shall
the blessed sun of heaven prove a
micher and eat blackberries? A
question not to be asked. Shall 575
the son of England prove a thief and
take purses? A question to be asked.
There is a thing, Harry, which thou
hast often heard of, and it is known
to many in our land by the 580
name of pitch. This pitch (as ancient
writers do report) doth defile; so
doth the company thou keepest. For,
Harry, now I do not speak to thee
in drink, but in tears; not in 585
pleasure, but in passion; not in words
only, but in woes also: and yet there
is a virtuous man whom I have often
noted in thy company, but I know
not his name. 590
PRINCE. What manner of man, and it
like your Majesty?
FALSTAFF. A goodly portly man, i'
faith, and a corpulent; of a cheerful
look, a pleasing eye, and a most 595
noble carriage; and, as I think, his
age some fifty, or, by'r Lady, inclin-
ing to threescore; and now I remember me, his name is Falstaff. If that
man should be lewdly given, 600
he deceiveth me; for, Harry, I see
virtue in his looks. If then the tree
may be known by the fruit, as the
fruit by the tree, then, peremptorily
I speak it, there is virtue 605
in that Falstaff. Him keep with, the
rest banish. And tell me now, thou
naughty varlet, tell me where hast
thou been this month?
PRINCE. Dost thou speak like a 610
king? Do thou stand for me, and I'll
play my father.

FALSTAFF. Depose me? If thou dost it
half so gravely, so majestically, both
in word and matter, hang me 615
up by the heels for a rabbit-sucker
or a poulter's hare.
PRINCE. Well, here I am set.
FALSTAFF. And here I stand. Judge,
my masters. 620
PRINCE. Now, Harry, whence come you?
FALSTAFF. My noble lord, from Eastcheap.
PRINCE. The complaints I hear of 625
thee are grievous.
FALSTAFF. 'Sblood, my lord, they are
false! Nay, I'll tickle ye for a young
prince, i' faith.
PRINCE. Swearest thou, ungracious 630
boy? Henceforth ne'er look on me.
Thou art violently carried away from
grace. There is a devil haunts thee in
the likeness of an old fat man; a tun
of man is thy companion. Why 635
dost thou converse with that trunk
of humors, that bolting hutch of
beastliness, that swoll'n parcel of
dropsies, that huge bombard of sack,
that stuffed cloakbag of guts, 640
that roasted Manningtree ox with
the pudding in his belly, that reverend
vice, that gray iniquity, that father
ruffian, that vanity in years? Wherein is he good, but to taste sack 645
and drink it? Wherein neat and
cleanly, but to carve a capon and
eat it? Wherein cunning, but in craft?
Wherein crafty, but in villainy?
Wherein villainous, but in all 650
things? Wherein worthy, but in nothing?
FALSTAFF. I would your Grace would
take me with you. Whom means your
Grace? 655

---

567 *trick:* mannerism. 574 *micher:* truant;
eat blackberries: wander after blackberries.
604 *peremptorily:* positively.

616 *rabbit-sucker:* suckling rabbit. 628 *tickle
ye for:* amuse you as. 634 *tun:* hogshead.
637 *humors:* bodily fluids; *bolting hutch:*
sifting bin. 639 *bombard:* leather liquor jug.
641 *Manningtree:* a town in Essex where
large oxen were roasted. 643 *vice:* morality-
play character. 654 *take me with you:* tell
me what you mean.

PRINCE. That villainous abominable misleader of youth, Falstaff, that old white-bearded Satan.

FALSTAFF. My lord, the man I know.

PRINCE. I know thou dost.   660

FALSTAFF. But to say I know more harm in him than in myself were to say more than I know. That he is old, the more the pity, his white hairs do witness it; but that he   665 is, saving your reverence, a whore-master, that I utterly deny. If sack and sugar be a fault, God help the wicked! If to be old and merry be a sin, then many an old host   670 that I know is damned. If to be fat be to be hated, then Pharaoh's lean kine are to be loved. No, my good lord: banish Peto, banish Bardolph, banish Poins; but for sweet   675 Jack Falstaff, kind Jack Falstaff, true Jack Falstaff, valiant Jack Falstaff, and therefore more valiant being, as he is, old Jack Falstaff, banish not him   thy   Harry's   company,   680 banish not him thy Harry's company, banish plump Jack, and banish all the world!

PRINCE. I do, I will.

[*A knocking heard. Exeunt* HOSTESS, FRANCIS, *and* BARDOLPH.]

[*Enter* BARDOLPH, *running.*]

BARDOLPH. O, my lord, my lord!   685 The sheriff with a most monstrous watch is at the door.

FALSTAFF. Out, ye rogue! Play out the play, I have much to say in the behalf of that Falstaff.   690

Enter the HOSTESS.

HOSTESS. O Jesu, my lord, my lord!

PRINCE. Heigh, heigh, the devil rides upon a fiddlestick! What's the matter?

HOSTESS. The sheriff and all the   695 watch are at the door. They are come to search the house. Shall I let them in?

FALSTAFF. Dost thou hear, Hal? Never call a true piece of gold a coun-   700 terfeit. Thou art essentially made without seeming so.

PRINCE. And thou a natural coward without instinct.

FALSTAFF. I deny your major. If   705 you will deny the sheriff, so; if not, let him enter. If I become not a cart as well as another man, a plague on my bringing up! I hope I shall as soon be strangled with a halter   710 as another.

PRINCE. Go hide thee behind the arras. The rest walk up above. Now, my masters, for a true face and good conscience.   715

FALSTAFF. Both which I have had; but their date is out, and therefore I'll hide me.   [*Exit.*]

PRINCE. Call in the sheriff.

[*Exeunt all but the* PRINCE *and* PETO.]

Enter SHERIFF *and the* CARRIER.

Now, master sheriff, what is your will with me?   720

SHERIFF. First, pardon me, my lord. A hue and cry
Hath followed certain men unto this house.

PRINCE. What men?

SHERIFF. One of them is well known, my gracious lord—
A gross fat man.

CARRIER.   As fat as butter.   725

PRINCE. The man, I do assure you, is not here,
For I myself at this time have employed him.
And, sheriff, I will engage my word to thee
That I will by tomorrow dinner time

672–73 *Pharaoh's lean kine:* cows (Genesis 41:19–21).

701 *essentially made:* a genuine article (despite appearances).   705 *major:* major premise. 707 *cart:* hangman's cart.   712 *arras:* tapestry. 714 *true:* honest.   728 *engage my word:* give my oath.

Send him to answer thee, or any man, 730
For anything he shall be charged withal;
And so let me entreat you leave the house.

SHERIFF. I will, my lord. There are two gentlemen
Have in this robbery lost three hundred marks.

PRINCE. It may be so. If he have robbed these men, 735
He shall be answerable; and so farewell.

SHERIFF. Good night, my noble lord.

PRINCE. I think it is good morrow, is it not?

SHERIFF. Indeed, my lord, I think it be two o'clock. *Exit [with* CARRIER].

PRINCE. This oily rascal is known 740
as well as Paul's. Go call him forth.

PETO. Falstaff! Fast asleep behind the arras, and snorting like a horse.

PRINCE. Hark how hard he fetches breath. Search his pockets. 745

[*He searcheth his pocket and findeth certain papers.*]

What hast thou found?

PETO. Nothing but papers, my lord.

PRINCE. Let's see what they be. Read them.

[PETO *reads*]

"Item, A capon 2s. 2d. 750
Item, Sauce . . . . 4d.
Item, Sack two gallons. 5s. 8d.
Item, Anchovies and sack
after supper . . . . 2s. 6d.
Item, Bread . . . . .ob." 755

PRINCE. O monstrous! But one halfpennyworth of bread to this intolerable deal of sack! What there is else, keep close; we'll read it at more advantage. There let him sleep 760 till day. I'll to the court in the morning. We must all to the wars, and thy place shall be honorable. I'll procure this fat rogue a charge of foot, and I know his death will be a march 765 of twelve score. The money shall be paid back again with advantage. Be with me betimes in the morning, and so good morrow, Peto.

PETO. Good morrow, good my lord. 770

[*Exeunt.*]

ACT III

SCENE i. [*Wales. A room.*]

Enter HOTSPUR, WORCESTER, LORD MORTIMER, OWEN GLENDOWER.

MORTIMER. These promises are fair, the parties sure,
And our induction full of prosperous hope.

HOTSPUR. Lord Mortimer, and cousin Glendower, will you sit down? 5
And uncle Worcester. A plague upon it! I have forgot the map.

GLENDOWER. No, here it is. Sit, cousin Percy, sit, good cousin Hotspur, for by that name as oft as Lancaster 10
doth speak of you, his cheek looks

pale, and with a rising sigh he wisheth you in heaven.

HOTSPUR. And you in hell, as oft as he hears Owen Glendower spoke 15
of.

GLENDOWER. I cannot blame him. At my nativity
The front of heaven was full of fiery shapes
Of burning cressets, and at my birth
The frame and huge foundation of the earth 20

---

741 *Paul's:* St. Paul's Cathedral.

755 *ob.:* obolus, a halfpenny. 758 *deal:* quantity. 764 *charge of foot:* command of infantry. 766 *twelve score:* twelve score yards. 767 *advantage:* interest; *betimes:* early. III.i.2 *induction:* beginning. 18 *front:* forehead. 19 *cressets:* basket beacons.

Shaked like a coward.

HOTSPUR. Why, so it would have done
at the same season if your mother's
cat had but kittened, though yourself
had never been born.   25

GLENDOWER. I say the earth did shake
when I was born.

HOTSPUR. And I say the earth was not
of my mind,
If you suppose as fearing you it
shook.

GLENDOWER. The heavens were all on
fire, the earth did tremble.

HOTSPUR. O, then the earth shook to
see the heavens on fire,   30
And not in fear of your nativity.
Diseased nature oftentimes breaks
forth
In strange eruptions; oft the teeming
earth
Is with a kind of colic pinched and
vexed
By the imprisoning of unruly wind   35
Within her womb, which, for enlarge-
ment striving,
Shakes the old beldame earth and
topples down
Steeples and mossgrown towers. At
your birth
Our grandam earth, having this dis-
temp'rature,
In passion shook.

GLENDOWER.   Cousin, of many
men   40
I do not bear these crossings. Give
me leave
To tell you once again that at my
birth
The front of heaven was full of fiery
shapes,
The goats ran from the mountains,
and the herds
Were strangely clamorous to the
frighted fields.   45
These signs have marked me extraordinary,

And all the courses of my life do
show
I am not in the roll of common men.
Where is he living, clipped in with
the sea
That chides the banks of England,
Scotland, Wales,   50
Which calls me pupil or hath read
to me?
And bring him out that is but
woman's son
Can trace me in the tedious ways
of art
And hold me pace in deep experi-
ments.

HOTSPUR. I think there's no man speaks
better Welsh. I'll to dinner.   55

MORTIMER. Peace, cousin Percy; you
will make him mad.

GLENDOWER. I can call spirits from the
vasty deep.

HOTSPUR. Why, so can I, or so can
any man;
But will they come when you do
call for them?   60

GLENDOWER. Why, I can teach you,
cousin, to command the devil.

HOTSPUR. And I can teach thee, coz,
to shame the devil—
By telling truth. Tell truth and shame
the devil.
If thou have power to raise him,
bring him hither,   65
And I'll be sworn I have power to
shame him hence.
O' while you live, tell truth and
shame the devil!

MORTIMER. Come, come, no more of
this unprofitable chat.

GLENDOWER. Three times hath Henry
Bolingbroke made head
Against my power; thrice from the
banks of Wye   70
And sandy-bottomed Severn have I
sent him

---

36 *enlargement:* freedom.   37 *beldame:* grandmother.   39 *distemp'rature:* sickness.

49 *clipped in with:* embraced by.   51 *read
to:* taught.   53 *trace:* follow; *art:* magic.
54 *hold me pace:* keep pace with me.   54–55
speaks better Welsh: talks more nonsense.

Booteless home and weather-beaten
back.

HOTSPUR. Home without boots, and in
foul weather too?

How scapes he agues, in the devil's
name?

GLENDOWER. Come, here is the map.
Shall we divide our right   75
According to our threefold order
ta'en?

MORTIMER. The Archdeacon hath di-
vided it
Into three limits very equally.
England, from Trent and Severn
hitherto,
By south and east is to my part
assigned;   80
All westward, Wales beyond the
Severn shore,
And all the fertile land within that
bound,
To Owen Glendower; and, dear coz,
to you
The remnant northward lying off
from Trent.
And our indentures tripartite are
drawn,   85
Which being sealed interchangeably
(A business that this night may
execute),
Tomorrow, cousin Percy, you and I
And my good Lord of Worcester will
set forth
To meet your father and the Scottish
power,   90
As is appointed us, as Shrewsbury.
My father Glendower is not ready
yet,
Nor shall we need his help these
fourteen days.
[*to* GLENDOWER] Within that space
you may have drawn together
Your tenants, friends, and neighbor-
ing gentlemen.   95

GLENDOWER. A shorter time shall send
me to you, lords;

And in my conduct shall your ladies
come,
From whom you now must steal and
take no leave,
For there will be a world of water
shed
Upon the parting of your wives and
you.   100

HOTSPUR. Methinks my moiety, north
from Burton here,
In quantity equals not one of yours.
See how this river comes me crank-
ing in
And cuts me from the best of all my
land
A huge half moon, a monstrous cantle
out.   105
I'll have the current in this place
dammed up,
And here the smug and silver Trent
shall run
In a new channel fair and evenly.
It shall not wind with such a deep
indent
To rob me of so rich a bottom
here.   110

GLENDOWER. Not wind? It shall, it
must! You see it doth.

MORTIMER. Yea, but mark how he
bears his course, and runs me up
with like advantage on the   115
other side, gelding the opposed continent as much as on the other side
it takes from you.

WORCESTER. Yea, but a little charge
will trench him here
And on this north side win this cape
of land;   120
And then he runs straight and even.

HOTSPUR. I'll have it so, a little charge
will do it.

GLENDOWER. I'll not have it alt'red.

HOTSPUR. Will not you?   125

GLENDOWER. No, nor you shall not.

HOTSPUR. Who shall say me nay?

---

72 *Booteless:* without profit.   73 *agues:*
fevers.   78 *limits:* bounded parts.   85 *indentures tripartite:* three-party agreement.

101 *moiety:* share.   103 *cranking:* twisting.
105 *cantle:* chunk.   107 *smug:* smooth.   116
gelding: cutting.   116–17 *continent:* bank.
119 *charge:* expense.

GLENDOWER. Why, that will I.

HOTSPUR. Let me not understand you
then; speak it in Welsh.   130

GLENDOWER. I can speak English, lord,
as well as you;
For I was trained up in the English
court,
Where, being but young, I framed to
the harp
Many an English ditty lovely well,
And gave the tongue a helpful orna-
ment—   135
A virtue that was never seen in you.

HOTSPUR. Marry, and I am glad of it
with all my heart!
I had rather be a kitten and cry mew
Than one of these same meter ballad-
mongers.
I had rather hear a brazen canstick
turned   140
Or a dry wheel grate on the axletree,
And that would set my teeth nothing
on edge,
Nothing so much as mincing poetry.
'Tis like the forced gait of a shuffling
nag.

GLENDOWER. Come, you shall have
Trent turned.   145

HOTSPUR. I do not care. I'll give thrice
so much land
To any well-deserving friend;
But in the way of bargain, mark ye
me,
I'll cavil on the ninth part of a hair.
Are the indentures drawn? Shall we
be gone?   150

GLENDOWER. The moon shines fair;
you may away by night.
I'll haste the writer, and withal
Break with your wives of your
departure hence.
I am afraid my daughter will run
mad,
So much she doteth on her Mortimer.   *Exit.*   155

MORTIMER. Fie, cousin Percy, how you
cross my father!

HOTSPUR. I cannot choose. Sometime
he angers me
With telling me of the moldwarp and
the ant,
Of the dreamer Merlin and his pro-
phecies,
And of a dragon and a finless fish, 160
A clip-winged griffin and a moulten
raven,
A couching lion and a ramping cat,
And such a deal of skimble-skamble
stuff
As puts me from my faith. I tell you
what—
He held me last night at least nine
hours   165
In reckoning up the several devils'
names
That were his lackeys. I cried "hum,"
and "Well, got to!"
But marked him not a word. O, he is
as tedious
As a tired horse, a railing wife;
Worse than a smoky house. I had
rather live   170
With cheese and garlic in a windmill
far
Than feed on cates and have him
talk to me
In any summer house in Christen-
dom.

MORTIMER. In faith, he is a worthy
gentleman,
Exceedingly well read and profited 175
In strange concealments, valiant as
a lion,
And wondrous affable, and as bountiful
As mines of India. Shall I tell you,
cousin?

---

139 *meter ballad-mongers:* street performers.
140 *canstick turned:* candlestick turned on a
lathe. 143 *mincing:* affected. 152 *withal:*
meanwhile. 153 *Break with:* tell.

158 *moldwarp:* mole. 159 *Merlin:* the
Arthurian magician. 161 *griffin:* mythological
beast, part lion and part eagle. 162 *ramping:*
rearing. 163 *skimble-skamble:* senseless. 164
puts...faith: makes me a disbeliever. 172
cates: dainties. 175–76 *profited...conceal-
ments:* skilfull in magic.

He holds your temper in a high respect
And curbs himself even of his natural scope 180
When you come 'cross his humor. Faith, he does.
I warrant you that man is not alive
Might so have tempted him as you have done
Without the taste of danger and reproof.
But do not use it oft, let me entreat you. 185

WORCESTER. In faith, my lord, you are too willful-blame,
And since your coming hither have done enough
To put him quite besides his patience.
You must needs learn, lord, to amend this fault.
Though sometimes it show greatness, courage, blood— 190
And that's the dearest grace it renders you—
Yet oftentimes it doth present harsh rage,
Defect of manners, want of government,
Pride, haughtiness, opinion, and disdain;
The least of which haunting a nobleman 195
Loseth men's hearts, and leaves behind a stain
Upon the beauty of all parts besides,
Beguiling them of commendation.

HOTSPUR. Well, I am schooled. Good manners be your speed!
Here come our wives, and let us take our leave. 200

Enter GLENDOWER *with the* LADIES.

MORTIMER. This is the deadly spite that angers me—
My wife can speak no English, I no Welsh.

GLENDOWER. My daughter weeps; she'll not part with you,
She'll be a soldier too, she'll to the wars.

MORTIMER. Good father, tell her that she and my aunt Percy 205
Shall follow in your conduct speedily.

GLENDOWER *speaks to her in Welsh, and she answers him in the same.*

GLENDOWER. She is desperate here.
A peevish self-willed harlotry, one that no persuasion can do good upon.

The LADY *speaks in Welsh.*

MORTIMER. I understand thy looks. That pretty Welsh 210
Which thou pourest down from these swelling heavens
I am too perfect in; and, but for shame,
In such a parley should I answer thee.

The LADY *again in Welsh.*

I understand thy kisses, and thou mine,
And that's a feeling disputation. 215
But I will never be a truant, love,
Till I have learnt thy language; for thy tongue
Makes Welsh as sweet as ditties highly penned,
Sung by a fair queen in a summer's bow'r,
With ravishing division, to her lute. 220

GLENDOWER. Nay, if you melt, then will she run mad.

The LADY *speaks again in Welsh.*

MORTIMER. O, I am ignorance itself in this!

---

180 *scope:* predisposition. 181 *humor temperament.* 183 *tempted:* crossed. 186 *too willful-blame:* at fault for willfulness. 190 *blood:* spirit. 192 *present:* indicate. 193 *government:* self-discipline. 194 *opinion:* arrogance. 198 *Beguiling:* depriving. 199 *be your speed:* make you successful. 201 *spite:* annoyance.

208 *harlotry:* fool. 210 *Welsh:* language of tears. 211 *heavens:* eyes. 215 *disputation:* conversation. 218 *highly penned:* elegant. 220 *division:* melody.

GLENDOWER. She bids you on the wanton rushes lay you down
And rest your gentle head upon her lap,
And she will sing the song that pleaseth you   225
And on your eyelids crown the god of sleep,
Charming your blood with pleasing heaviness,
Making such difference 'twixt wake and sleep
As is the difference betwixt day and night
The hour before the heavenly harnessed team   230
Begins his golden progress in the east.
MORTIMER. With all my heart I'll sit and hear her sing.
By that time will our book, I think, be drawn.
GLENDOWER. Do so, and those musicians that shall play to you
Hang in the air a thousand leagues from hence,   235
And straight they shall be here: sit, and attend.
HOTSPUR. Come, Kate, thou art perfect in lying down. Come, quick, quick, that I may lay my head in thy lap.
LADY PERCY. Go, ye giddy goose.   240

The music plays.

HOTSPUR. Now I perceive the devil understands Welsh,
And 'tis no marvel he is so humorous,
By'r Lady, he is a good musician.
LADY PERCY. Then should you be nothing but musical,
For you are altogether governed by humors.   245
Lie still, ye thief, and hear the lady sing in Welsh.
HOTSPUR. I had rather hear Lady, my brach, howl in Irish.
LADY PERCY. Wouldst thou have thy head broken?   250

HOTSPUR. No.
LADY PERCY. Then be still.
HOTSPUR. Neither! 'Tis a woman's fault.
LADY PERCY. Now God help thee!
HOTSPUR. To the Welsh lady's bed. 255
LADY PERCY. What's that?
HOTSPUR. Peace! She sings.

Here the LADY *sings a Welsh song.*

Come, Kate, I'll have your song too.
LADY PERCY. Not mine, in good sooth.
HOTSPUR. Not yours, in good sooth? 260
Heart, you swear like a comfit-maker's wife. "Not you, in good sooth!" and "as true as I live!" and "as God shall mend me!" and "as sure as day!"   265
And givest such sarcenet surety for thy oaths
As if thou never walk'st further than Finsbury.
Swear me, Kate, like a lady as thou art,
A good mouth-filling oath, and leave "in sooth"
And such protest of pepper ginger-bread   270
To velvet guards and Sunday citizens. Come, sing.
LADY PERCY. I will not sing.
HOTSPUR. 'Tis the next way to turn tailor or be red-breast teacher. 275
And the indentures be drawn, I'll away within these two hours; and so come in when ye will.   [*Exit.*]
GLENDOWER. Come, come, Lord Mortimer. You are as slow
As hot Lord Percy is on fire to go.   280
By this our book is drawn; we'll but seal,
And then to horse immediately.
MORTIMER.   With all my heart.

Exeunt.

---

223 *wanton:* luxuriant.   230 *team:* sun's horses. 233 *book:* compact. 242 *humorous:* capricious. 248 *brach:* bitch-hound.

259 *sooth:* truth. 261–62 *comfit-maker's:* confectioner's. 266 *sarcenet:* flimsy ("silken"). 267 *Finsbury:* a resort near London. 271 *velvet guards:* those who wear velvet trim. 275 *tailor:* noted for singing; *red-breast teacher:* teacher of birds. 281 *this:* this time.

Scene ii. [*London. The palace.*]

Enter the King, Prince of Wales, *and others.*

KING. Lords, give us leave: the Prince
    of Wales and I
  Must have some private conference;
    but be near at hand,
  For we shall presently have need
    of you.   *Exeunt* Lords.
  I know not whether God will have
    it so
  For some displeasing service I have
    done,   5
  That, in his secret doom, out of my
    blood
  He'll breed revengement and a
    scourge for me;
  But thou dost in thy passages of life
  Make me believe that thou art only
    marked
  For the hot vengeance and the rod
    of heaven   10
  To punish my mistreadings. Tell me
    else,
  Could such inordinate and low
    desires,
  Such poor, such bare, such lewd,
    such mean attempts,
  Such barren pleasures, rude society,
  As thou art matched withal and
    grafted to,   15
  Accompany the greatness of thy
    blood
  And hold their level with thy princely
    heart?
PRINCE. So please your Majesty, I
    would I could
  Quit all offenses with as clear excuse
  As well as I am doubtless I can
    purge   20
  Myself of many I am charged withal.
  Yet such extenuation let me beg
  As, in reproof of many tales devised,
  Which oft the ear of greatness needs

    must hear
  By smiling pickthanks and base
    newsmongers,   25
  I may, for some things true wherein
    my youth
  Hath faulty wand'red and irregular,
  Find pardon on my true submission.
KING. God pardon thee! Yet let me
    wonder, Harry,
  At thy affections, which do hold a
    wing   30
  Quite from the flight of all thy
    ancestors.
  Thy place in council thou hast rudely
    lost,
  Which by thy younger brother is
    supplied,
  And art almost an alien to the hearts
  Of all the court and princes of my
    blood.   35
  The hope and expectation of thy time
  Is ruined, and the soul of every man
  Prophetically do forethink thy fall.
  Had I so lavish of my presence been,
  So common-hackneyed in the eyes
    of men,   40
  So stale and cheap to vulgar com-
    pany,
  Opinion, that did help me to the
    crown,
  Had still kept loyal to possession
  And left me in reputeless banishment
  A fellow of no mark nor likelihood.   45
  By being seldom seen, I could not
    stir
  But, like a comet, I was wond'red at;
  That men would tell their children,
    "This is he!"
  Others would say, "Where? Which
    is Bolingbroke?"
  And then I stole all courtesy from
    heaven,   50
  And dressed myself in such humility
  That I did pluck allegiance from
    men's hearts,

III.ii.6. *doom:* judgment; *blood:* heirs. 8
passages: deeds. 13 *bare:* low-born. 15
withal: with. 19 *Quit:* acquit. 20 *As well
as:* as. 23 *reproof:* refutation.

25 *pickthanks:* sycophants. 30 *affections:*
inclinations. 36 *time:* youth. 42 *Opinion:*
public opinion. 43 *to possession:* to the legal
king, Richard II.

Loud shouts and salutations from
their mouths
Even in the presence of the crowned
King.
Thus did I keep my person fresh
and new,   55
My presence, like a robe pontifical,
Ne'er seen but wond'red at; and so
my state,
Seldom but sumptuous, showed like
a feast
And won by rareness such solemnity.
The skipping King, he ambled up
and down   60
With shallow jesters and rash bavin
wits,
Soon kindled and soon burnt; carded
his state;
Mingled his royalty with cap'ring
fools;
Had his great name profaned with
their scorns
And gave his countenance, against
his name,   65
To laugh at gibing boys and stand
the push
Of every beardless vain comparative;
Grew a companion to the common
streets,
Enfeoffed himself to popularity;
That, being daily swallowed by men's
eyes,   70
They surfeited with honey and began
To loathe the taste of sweetness,
whereof a little
More than a little is by much too
much.
So, when he had occasion to be seen,
He was but as the cuckoo is in
June,   75
Heard, not regarded—seen, but with
such eyes
As, sick and blunted with com-
munity,
Afford no extraordinary gaze,

Such as is bent on sunlike majesty
When it shines seldom in admiring
eyes;   80
But rather drowsed and hung their
eyelids down,
Slept in his face, and rend'red such
aspect
As cloudy men use to their adver-
saries,
Being with his presence glutted,
gorged, and full.
And in that very line, Harry, standest
thou;   85
For thou hast lost thy princely
privilege
With vile participation. Not an eye
But is aweary of thy common sight,
Save mine, which hath desired to
see thee more;
Which now doth that I would not
have it do—   90
Make blind itself with foolish tender-
ness.
PRINCE. I shall hereafter, my thrice-
gracious lord,
Be more myself.
KING.   For all the world,
As thou art to this hour was Richard
then
When I from France set foot at
Ravenspurgh;   95
And even as I was then is Percy now.
Now, by my scepter, and my soul
to boot,
He hath more worthy interest to
the state
Than thou the shadow of succession;
For of no right, nor color like to
right,   100
He doth fill fields with harness in
the realm,
Turns head against the lion's armed
jaws,
And, being no more in debt to years
than thou,

---

61 *bavin:* brushwood. 62 *carded:* debased.
66 *stand the push:* tolerate the crowd's insults. 67 *comparative:* wit. 69 *Enfeoffed...
popularity:* gave himself to the mob. 77
community: commonness.

82 *in:* in front of. 83 *cloudy:* sullen. 87 *vile
participation:* indiscriminate fellowship. 98
interest: title. 100 *color:* resemblance. 101
harness: armor.

Leads ancient lords and reverend
bishops on
To bloody battles and to bruising
arms.   105
What never-dying honor hath he got
Against renowned Douglas! whose
high deeds,
Whose hot incursions and great name
in arms
Holds from all soldiers chief majority
And military title capital   110
Through all the kingdoms that
acknowledge Christ.
Thrice hath this Hotspur, Mars in
swathling clothes,
This infant warrior, in his enterprises
Discomfited great Douglas; ta'en him
once,
Enlarged him, and made a friend of
him,   115
To fill the mouth of deep defiance up
And shake the peace and safety of
our throne.
And what say you to this? Percy,
Northumberland,
The Archbishop's grace of York,
Douglas, Mortimer
Capitulate against us and are up. 120
But wherefore do I tell these news
to thee?
Why, Harry, do I tell thee of my
foes,
Which art my nearest and dearest
enemy?
Thou that art like enough, through
vassal fear,
Base inclination, and the start of
spleen,   125
To fight against me under Percy's
pay,
To dog his heels and curtsy at his
frowns,
To show how much thou art degen-
erate.
PRINCE. Do not think so, you shall

not find it so.
And God forgive them that so much
have swayed   130
Your Majesty's good thoughts away
from me.
I will redeem all this on Percy's head
And, in the closing of some glorious
day,
Be bold to tell you that I am your
son,
When I will wear a garment all of
blood,   135
And stain my favors in a bloody
mask,
Which, washed away, shall scour my
shame with it.
And that shall be the day, whene'er
it lights,
That this same child of honor and
renown,
This gallant Hotspur, this all-praised
knight,   140
And your unthought-of Harry chance
to meet.
For every honor sitting on his helm,
Would they were multitudes, and on
my head
My shames redoubled! For the time
will come
That I shall make this northern
youth exchange   145
His glorious deeds for my indignities.
Percy is but my factor, good my
lord,
To engross up glorious deeds on my
behalf;
And I will call him to so strict
account
That he shall render every glory
up,   150
Yea, even the slightest worship of
his time,
Or I will tear the reckoning from his
heart.
This in the name of God I promise
here;

109 *chief majority:* highest rank. 110 *capi-tal:* head. 115 *Enlarged:* freed. 116 *To... up:* shout defiance. 120 *Capitulate:* draw up agreements; *up:* up in arms.

136 *favors:* features. 147 *factor:* agent. 148 *engross:* store. 151 *worship:* honor; *time:* accumulated life.

The which if he be pleased I shall
   perform,
I do beseech your Majesty may
   salve   155
The long-grown wounds of my intemperance.
If not, the end of life cancels all
   bands,
And I will die a hundred thousand
   deaths
Ere break the smallest parcel of this
   vow.
KING. A hundred thousand rebels die
   in this!   160
Thou shalt have charge and sovereign trust herein.

Enter BLUNT.

How now, good Blunt? Thy looks are
   full of speed.
BLUNT. So hath the business that I
   come to speak of.
Lord Mortimer of Scotland hath sent
   word
That Douglas and the English rebels
   met   165
The eleventh of this month at
   Shrewsbury.
A mighty and a fearful head they are,
If promises be kept on every hand,
As ever off'red foul play in a state.
KING. The Earl of Westmoreland set
   forth today;   170
With him my son, Lord John of
   Lancaster:
For this advertisement is five days
   old.
On Wednesday next, Harry, you shall
   set forward;
On Thursday we ourselves will
   march. Our meeting
Is Bridgenorth; and, Harry, you
   shall march   175
Through Gloucestershire; by which
   account,
Our business valued, some twelve

days hence
Our general forces at Bridgenorth
   shall meet.
Our hands are full of business. Let's
   away:
Advantage feeds him fat while men
   delay.   *Exeunt.* 180

SCENE iii. [*Eastcheap. The tavern.*]

Enter FALSTAFF *and* BARDOLPH.

FALSTAFF. Bardolph, am I not fall'n
   away vilely since this last action?
   Do I not bate? Do I not dwindle?
   Why, my skin hangs about me like
   an old lady's loose gown! I am 5
   withered like an old apple-john. Well,
   I'll repent, and that suddenly, while
   I am in some liking. I shall be out
   of heart shortly, and then I shall
   have no strength to repent. And 10
   I have not forgotten what the inside
   of a church is made of, I am a
   peppercorn, a brewer's horse. The
   inside of a church! Company, villainous company, hath been the spoil 15
   of me.
BARDOLPH. Sir John, you are so fretful
   you cannot live long.
FALSTAFF. Why, there is it! Come, sing
   me a bawdy song, make me 20
   merry. I was as virtuously given as
   a gentleman need to be, virtuous
   enough: swore little, diced not above
   seven times a week, went to a bawdy
   house not above once in a 25
   quarter of an hour, paid money that
   I borrowed three or four times, lived
   well, and in good compass; and now
   I live out of all order, out of all
   compass.   30
BARDOLPH. Why, you are so fat, Sir
   John, that you must needs be out
   of all compass—out of all reasonable
   compass, Sir John.

---

157 *bands:* bonds. 159 *parcel:* part. 167 *head:* army. 172 *advertisement:* news. 175 *Bridgenorth:* a small town near Shrewsbury. 177 *valued:* assessed.

---

180 *him:* itself. III.iii.3 *bate:* waste away. 6 *apple-john:* withered apple. 13 *brewer's horse:* skinny nag. 28 *compass:* order.

FALSTAFF. Do thou amend thy 35
face, and I'll amend my life. Thou
art our admiral, thou bearest the
lantern in the poop—but 'tis in the
nose of thee: thou art the Knight
of the Burning Lamp. 40

BARDOLPH. Why, Sir John, my face
does you no harm.

FALSTAFF. No, I'll be sworn. I make
as good use of it as many a man doth
of a death's head or a memento 45
mori. I never see thy face but I think
upon hell fire and Dives that lived in
purple; for there he is in his robes,
burning, burning. If thou wert any
way given to virtue, I would 50
swear by thy face; my oath should
be "By this fire, that's God's angel."
But thou art altogether given over,
and wert indeed, but for the light in
thy face, the son of utter dark- 55
ness. When thou ran'st up Gad's Hill
in the night to catch my horse, if
I did not think thou hadst been an
ignis fatuus or a ball of wildfire,
there's no purchase in money. 60
O, thou art a perpetual triumph, an
everlasting bonfire light! Thou hast
saved me a thousand marks in links
and torches, walking with thee in the
night betwixt tavern and tavern; 65
but the sack that thou hast drunk
me would have bought me lights as
good cheap at the dearest chandler's
in Europe. I have maintained that
salamander of yours with fire any 70
time this two and thirty years. God
reward me for it!

BARDOLPH. 'Sblood, I would my face
were in your belly!

FALSTAFF. God-a-mercy! So should 75

---

37 *admiral:* flagship. 45 *death's head:* skull.
45–46 *memento mori:* reminder of death. 47
Dives: see Luke 16:19–31, in which Dives is
condemned for greed. 52 *angel:* angels often
appear as flames or are announced by flames.
59 *ignis fatuus:* will-o'-the-wisp; *wildfire:*
fireworks. 61 *triumph:* public celebration.
63 *links:* torches. 68 *good cheap:* cheaply;
chandler's: candle seller's. 70 *salamander:*
a lizard thought capable of surviving in fire.

I be sure to be heartburned.

Enter HOSTESS.

How now, Dame Partlet the hen?
Have you enquired yet who picked
my pocket?

HOSTESS. Why, Sir John, what do 80
you think, Sir John? Do you think
I keep thieves in my house? I have
searched, I have enquired, so has my
husband, man by man, boy by boy,
servant by servant. The tithe of 85
a hair was never lost in my house
before.

FALSTAFF. Ye lie, hostess. Bardolph
was shaved and lost many a hair,
and I'll be sworn my pocket was 90
picked. Go to, you are a woman, go!

HOSTESS. Who, I? No; I defy thee!
God's light, I was never called so in
mine own house before!

FALSTAFF. Go to, I know you well 95
enough.

HOSTESS. No, Sir John; you do not
know me, Sir John. I know you, Sir
John. You owe me money, Sir John,
and now you pick a quarrel to 100
beguile me of it. I bought you a
dozen of shirts to your back.

FALSTAFF. Dowlas, filthy dowlas! I
have given them away to bakers'
wives; they have made bolters 105
of them.

HOSTESS. Now, as I am a true woman,
holland of eight shillings an ell. You
owe money here besides, Sir John,
for your diet and by-drinkings, 110
and money lent you, four and twenty
pound.

FALSTAFF. He had his part of it; let
him pay.

HOSTESS. He? Alas, he is poor; 115
he hath nothing.

FALSTAFF. How? Poor? Look upon his

---

77 *Dame Partlet:* aggressively talkative hen.
85 *tithe:* tenth part. 89 *shaved...hair:* had
a venereal disease. 103 *Dowlas:* coarse linen.
105 *bolters:* sieves. 108 *holland:* fine linen;
ell: a yard and a quarter. 110 *by-drinkings:*
occasional drinks.

face. What call you rich? Let them
coin his nose, let them coin his
cheeks. I'll not pay a denier.   120
What, will you make a younker of
me? Shall I not take mine ease in
mine inn but I shall have my pocket
picked? I have lost a seal ring of
my grandfather's worth forty   125
mark.

HOSTESS. O Jesu, I have heard the
Prince tell him, I know not how oft,
that that ring was copper!

FALSTAFF. How? The Prince is a   130
Jack, a sneak-up. 'Sblood, and he
were here, I would cudgel him like
a dog if he would say so.

Enter the PRINCE [*and* POINS], *marching, and* FALSTAFF *meets them, playing
upon his truncheon like a fife.*

How now, lad? Is the wind in that
door, i' faith? Must we all   135
march?

BARDOLPH. Yea, two and two, Newgate
fashion.

HOSTESS. My lord, I pray you hear me.

PRINCE. What say'st thou, Mistress   140
Quickly? How doth thy husband?
I love him well, he is an honest man.

HOSTESS. Good my lord, hear me.

FALSTAFF. Prithee let her alone and
list to me.   145

PRINCE. What say'st thou, Jack?

FALSTAFF. The other night I fell asleep
here behind the arras and had my
pocket picked. This house is turned
bawdy house; they pick pockets.   150

PRINCE. What didst thou lose, Jack?

FALSTAFF. Wilt thou believe me, Hal,
three or four bonds of forty pound
apiece and a seal ring of my grandfather's.   155

PRINCE. A trifle, some eightpenny
matter.

HOSTESS. So I told him, my lord, and

I said I heard your Grace say so;
and, my lord, he speaks most   160
vilely of you, like a foulmouthed man
as he is, and said he would cudgel
you.

PRINCE. What! He did not?

HOSTESS. There's neither faith,   165
truth, nor womanhood in me else.

FALSTAFF. There's no more faith in
thee than in a stewed prune, nor no
more truth in thee than in a drawn
fox; and for womanhood, Maid   170
Marian may be the deputy's wife of
the ward to thee. Go, you thing,
go!

HOSTESS. Say, what thing, what thing?

FALSTAFF. What thing? Why, a thing
to thank God on.   175

HOSTESS. I am no thing to thank God
on, I would thou shouldst know it!
I am an honest man's wife, and,
setting thy knighthood aside, thou
art a knave to call me so.   180

FALSTAFF. Setting thy womanhood
aside, thou art a beast to say otherwise.

HOSTESS. Say, what beast, thou knave,
thou?   185

FALSTAFF. What beast? Why, an otter.

PRINCE. An otter, Sir John? Why an
otter?

FALSTAFF. Why, she's neither fish nor
flesh; a man knows not where   190
to have her.

HOSTESS. Thou art an unjust man in
saying so. Thou or any man knows
where to have me, thou knave, thou!

PRINCE. Thou say'st true, hostess,   195
and he slanders thee most grossly.

HOSTESS. So he doth you, my lord, and
said this other day you ought him
a thousand pound.

PRINCE. Sirrah, do I owe you a   200
thousand pound?

FALSTAFF. A thousand pound, Hal? A

---

120 *denier:* a French coin of little worth. 121
younker: easy mark. 131 *Jack:* common fellow; *sneak-up:* sneak. 133s.d. *truncheon:*
cudgel. 134–35 *Is...door:* "Is that how the
wind blows?" 137 *two and two:* chained
together like Newgate prisoners.

168 *stewed prune:* procuress. 169–70 *drawn
fox:* i.e., a fox drawn from his den and trying
to save his pups by guile. 170–71 *Maid
Marian...thee:* "a light woman is a pillar of
virtue next to you." 198 *ought:* owed.

million! Thy love is worth a million, thou owest me thy love.

HOSTESS. Nay, my lord, he called 205
you Jack and said he would cudgel you.

FALSTAFF. Did I, Bardolph?

BARDOLPH. Indeed, Sir John, you said so. 210

FALSTAFF. Yea, if he said my ring was copper.

PRINCE. I say 'tis copper. Darest thou be as good as thy word now?

FALSTAFF. Why, Hal, thou knowest, 215
as thou art but man, I dare; but as thou art Prince, I fear thee as I fear the roaring of the lion's whelp.

PRINCE. And why not as the lion?

FALSTAFF. The King himself is to 220
be feared as the lion. Dost thou think I'll fear thee as I fear thy father? Nay, and I do, I pray God my girdle break.

PRINCE. O, if it should, how would 225
thy guts fall about thy knees! But, sirrah, there's no room for faith, truth, nor honesty in this bosom of thine. It is all filled up with guts and. midriff. Charge an honest 230
woman with picking thy pocket? Why, thou whoreson, impudent, embossed rascal, if there were anything in thy pocket but tavern reckonings, memorandums of 235
bawdy houses, and one poor pennyworth of sugar candy to make thee long-winded—if thy pocket were enriched with any other injuries but these, I am a villain. And yet 240
you will stand to it; you will not pocket up wrong. Art thou not ashamed?

FALSTAFF. Dost thou hear, Hal? Thou knowest in the state of innocency 245
Adam fell, and what should poor Jack Falstaff do in the days of villainy? Thou seest I have more flesh than another man, and therefore more frailty. You confess then, 250

you picked my pocket?

PRINCE. It appears so by the story.

FALSTAFF. Hostess, I forgive thee, go make ready breakfast, love thy husband, look to thy servants, 255
cherish thy guests. Thou shalt find me tractable to any honest reason. Thou seest I am pacified still. Nay, prithee be gone. *Exit* HOSTESS.
Now, Hal, to the news at court. 260
For the robbery, lad—how is that answered?

PRINCE. O my sweet beef, I must still be good angel to thee. The money is paid back again. 265

FALSTAFF. O, I do not like that paying back! 'Tis a double labor.

PRINCE. I am good friends with my father, and may do anything.

FALSTAFF. Rob me the exchequer 270
the first thing thou doest, and do it with unwashed hands too.

BARDOLPH. Do, my lord.

PRINCE. I have procured thee, Jack, a charge of foot. 275

FALSTAFF. I would it had been of horse. Where shall I find one that can steal well? O for a fine thief of the age of two and twenty or thereabouts! I am heinously unprovided. 280
Well, God be thanked for these rebels, they offend none but the virtuous: I laud them, I praise them.

PRINCE. Bardolph!

BARDOLPH. My lord? 285

PRINCE. Go bear this letter to Lord John of Lancaster, to my brother John; this to my Lord of Westmoreland.

[*Exit* BARDOLPH.]

Go, Peto, to horse, to horse; for thou and I
Have thirty miles to ride yet ere dinner time. [*Exit* PETO.]
Jack, meet me tomorrow in the Temple Hall 290

---

223 *girdle:* belt. 233 *embossed:* swollen.

272 *with unwashed hands:* quickly, without taking time to wash. 275 *charge of foot:* company of infantry.

At two o'clock in the afternoon.
There shalt thou know thy charge,
and there receive
Money and order for their furniture.
The land is burning, Percy stands
on high,

And either we or they must lower
lie.   [*Exit.*]   295
FALSTAFF. Rare words! Brave world!
Hostess, my breakfast, come.
O, I could wish this tavern were my
drum!   [*Exit.*]

ACT IV

SCENE i. [*The rebel camp, near Shrewsbury.*]

Enter HOTSPUR, WORCESTER, *and*
DOUGLAS.

HOTSPUR. Well said, my noble Scot. If
speaking truth
In this fine age were not thought
flattery,
Such attribution should the Douglas
have
As not a soldier of this season's
stamp
Should go so general current through
the world.   5
By God, I cannot flatter, I do defy
The tongues of soothers! But a
braver place
In my heart's love hath no man than
yourself.
Nay, task me to my word; approve
me, lord.
DOUGLAS.   Thou   art   the   king   of
honor.   10
No man so potent breathes upon the
ground
But I will beard him.

Enter one with letters.

HOTSPUR.   Do so, and 'tis well.—
What letters hast thou there?—I can
but thank you.
MESSENGER. These letters come from
your father.

HOTSPUR. Letters from him? Why
comes he not himself?   15
MESSENGER. He cannot come, my lord,
he is grievous sick.
HOTSPUR. 'Zounds! How has he the
leisure to be sick
In such a justling time? Who leads
his power?
Under whose government come they
along?
MESSENGER. His letters bears his mind,
not I, my lord.   20
WORCESTER. I prithee tell me, doth he
keep his bed?
MESSENGER. He did, my lord, four days
ere I set forth,
And at the time of my departure
thence
He was much feared by his physi-
cians.
WORCESTER. I would the state of time
had first been whole   25
Ere he by sickness had been visited.
His health was never better worth
than now.
HOTSPUR. Sick now? Droop now? This
sickness doth infect
The very lifeblood of our enterprise.
'Tis catching hither, even to our
camp.   30
He writes me here that inward sick-
ness—
And that his friends by deputation
Could not so soon be drawn; nor did
he think it meet
To lay so dangerous and dear a trust
On any soul removed but on his
own.   35

---

293 *furniture:* armor. 296 *brave:* splendid.
297 *drum:* place to gather troops. IV.i.3
attribution: honor. 4 *season's stamp:* recent
coinage. 6 *defy:* despise. 7 *soothers:* flatterers; *braver:* better. 9 *task:* try. 12 *beard:*
affront.

---

18 *justling:* hustling. 24 *feared:* feared for.
33 *meet:* suitable, proper.

Yet doth he give us bold advertise-
ment,
That with our small conjunction we
should on,
To see how fortune is disposed to us;
For, as he writes, there is no quail-
ing now,
Because the King is certainly pos-
sessed   40
Of all our purposes. What say you
to it?
WORCESTER. Your father's sickness is
a maim to us.
HOTSPUR. A perilous gash, a very limb
lopped off.
And yet, in faith, it is not! His
present want
Seems more than we shall find it.
Were it good   45
To set the exact wealth of all our
states
All at one cast? To set so rich a
main
On the nice hazard of one doubtful
hour?
It were not good; for therein should
we read
The very bottom and the soul of
hope,   50
The very list, the very utmost bound
Of all our fortunes.
DOUGLAS.   Faith, and so we should.
Where now remains a sweet rever-
sion,
We may boldly spend upon the hope
of what is to come in.
A comfort of retirement lives in
this.   55
HOTSPUR. A rendezvous, a home to fly
unto,
If that the devil and mischance look
big
Upon the maidenhead of our affairs.
WORCESTER. But yet I would your

father had been here.
The quality and hair of our at-
tempt   60
Brooks no division. It will be thought
By some that know not why he is
away,
That wisdom, loyalty, and mere dislike
Of our proceedings kept the Earl
from hence.   64
And think how such an apprehension
May turn the tide of fearful faction
And breed a kind of question in our
cause.
For well you know we of the off'ring
side
Must keep aloof from strict arbitra-
ment,
And stop all sight holes, every loop
from whence   70
The eye of reason may pry in
upon us.
This absence of your father's draws
a curtain
That shows the ignorant a kind of
fear
Before not dreamt of.
HOTSPUR.   You strain too far.
I rather of his absence make this
use: 75
It lends a luster and more great
opinion,
A larger dare to our great enterprise,
Than if the Earl were here; for men
must think,
If we, without his help, can make
a head
To push against a kingdom, with his
help   80
We shall o'erturn it topsy-turvy
down.
Yet all goes well; yet all our joints
are whole.
DOUGLAS. As heart can think. There is
not such a word
Spoke of in Scotland as this term
of fear.

37 *conjunction:* combined powers. 40 *possessed:* informed. 44 *want:* absence. 46 *set:*
stake. 47 *main:* "stake" and "force." 48
nice: closely balanced. 51 *list:* limit. 53
reversion: future inheritance. 57 *big:* dan-
gerously.

60 *hair:* nature. 61 *Brooks:* tolerates. 68
off'ring: attacking. 69 *strict arbitrament:*
close examination. 72 *draws:* draws aside.
76 *opinion:* reputation. 79 *head:* army.

Enter Sir Richard Vernon.

Hotspur. My cousin Vernon, welcome,
by my soul.   85
Vernon. Pray God my news be worth
a welcome, lord.
   The Earl of Westmoreland, seven
   thousand strong,
   Is marching hitherwards; with him
   Prince John.
Hotspur. No harm. What more?
Vernon.   And
   further, I have learned
   The King himself in person is set
   forth,   90
   Or hitherwards intended speedily,
   With strong and mighty preparation.
Hotspur. He shall be welcome too.
   Where is his son,
   The nimble-footed madcap Prince of
   Wales,
   And his comrades, that daffed the
   world aside   95
   And bid it pass?
Vernon.   All furnished, all in arms;
   All plumed like estridges that with
   the wind
   Bated like eagles having lately
   bathed;
   Glittering in golden coats like images;
   As full of spirit as the month of
   May   100
   And gorgeous as the sun at mid-
   summer;
   Wanton as youthful goats, wild as
   young bulls.
   I saw young Harry with his beaver
   on,
   His cushes on his thighs, gallantly
   armed,
   Rise from the ground like feathered
   Mercury,   105
   And vaulted with such ease into his
   seat
   As if an angel dropped down from
   the clouds

To turn and wind a fiery Pegasus
And witch the world with noble
horsemanship.
Hotspur. No more, no more! Worse
than the sun in March,   110
This praise doth nourish agues. Let
them come.
They come like sacrifices in their
trim,
And to the fire-eyed maid of smoky
war
All hot and bleeding will we offer
them.
The mailed Mars shall on his altars
sit   115
Up to the ears in blood. I am on fire
To hear this rich reprisal is so nigh,
And yet not ours. Come, let me taste
my horse,
Who is to bear me like a thunderbolt
Against the bosom of the Prince of
Wales.   120
Harry to Harry shall, hot horse to
horse,
Meet, and ne'er part till one drop
down a corse.
O that Glendower were come!
Vernon.   There is more news.
I learned in Worcester, as I rode
along,
He cannot draw his power this four-
teen days.   125
Douglas. That's the worst tidings that
I hear of yet.
Worcester. Ay, by my faith, that
bears a frosty sound.
Hotspur. What may the King's whole
battle reach unto?
Vernon. To thirty thousand.
Hotspur.   Forty let it be.
My father and Glendower being both
away,   130
The powers of us may serve so great
a day.
Come, let us take a muster speedily.

---

95 *daffed:* thrust. 97 *estridges:* ostriches. 98
Bated: shook. 99 *images:* statues. 102 *Wanton:* playful. 103 *beaver:* lower part of a face
guard of a helmet. 104 *cushes:* thigh armor.

108 *wind:* wheel; *Pegasus:* mythological flying horse. 109 *witch:* bewitch, enthrall. 111
agues: chills and fevers. 113 *maid:* Bellona,
Roman goddess of war. 115 *mailed:* armed.
117 *reprisal:* prize. 128 *battle:* battle force.

Doomsday is near. Die all, die merrily.
DOUGLAS. Talk not of dying. I am out
of fear
Of death or death's hand for this one
half year.   *Exeunt.* 135

SCENE ii. [*A road near Coventry.*]

Enter FALSTAFF [*and*] BARDOLPH.

FALSTAFF. Bardolph, get thee before to
Conventry; fill me a bottle of sack.
Our soldiers shall march through.
We'll to Sutton Co'fil' tonight.
BARDOLPH. Will you give me money, 5
captain?
FALSTAFF. Lay out, lay out.
BARDOLPH. This bottle makes an angel.
FALSTAFF. And if it do, take it for thy
labor; and if it make twenty, 10
take them all; I'll answer the coinage.
Bid my lieutenant Peto meet me at
town's end.
BARDOLPH. I will, captain. Farewell.

Exit.

FALSTAFF. If I be not ashamed of 15
my soldiers, I am a soused gurnet.
I have misused the King's press
damnably. I have got, in exchange
of a hundred and fifty soldiers, three
hundred and odd pounds. I press 20
me none but good householders,
yeomen's sons; inquire me out contracted bachelors, such as had been
asked twice on the banes—such a
commodity of warm slaves as 25
had as lief hear the devil as a drum,
such as fear the report of a caliver
worse than a struck fowl or a hurt

wild duck. I pressed me none but
such   toasts-and-butter,   with 30
hearts in their bellies no bigger than
pins' heads, and they have bought
out their services; and now my whole
charge consists of ancients, corporals,
lieutenants, gentlemen of com- 35
panies—slaves as ragged as Lazarus
in the painted cloth, where the glutton's dogs licked his sores; and such
as indeed were never soldiers, but
discarded unjust serving men, 40
younger sons to younger brothers,
revolted tapsters, and ostlers trade-
fall'n; the cankers of a calm world
and a long peace; ten times more
dishonorable ragged than an old 45
fazed ancient; and such have I to
fill up the rooms of them as have
bought out their services that you
would think that I had a hundred
and fifty tattered prodigals lately 50
come from swine-keeping, from eating
draff and husks. A mad fellow met
me on the way, and told me I had
unloaded all the gibbets and pressed
the dead bodies. No eye hath 55
seen such scarecrows. I'll not march
through Coventry with them, that's
flat. Nay, and the villains march wide
betwixt the legs, as if they had gyves
on, for indeed I had the most 60
of them out of prison. There's not
a shirt and a half in all my company,
and the half shirt is two napkins
tacked together and thrown over the
shoulders like a herald's coat 65
without sleeves; and the shirt, to say
the truth, stol'n from my host at
Saint Albans, or the red-nose inn-
keeper of Daventry. But that's all

IV.ii.4. *Sutton Co'fil:* Sutton-Coldfield, a small
town near Shrewsbury, the scene of the battle.
7 *Lay out:* pay. 8 *angel:* about ten shillings.
9 *do:* "if the bottle is 'coining' (rather than
costing) you angels, you may keep them."
11 *answer:* guarantee. 16 *soused gurnet:*
pickled fish. 17 *press:* draft. 24 *twice on the
banes:* announced twice in banns an intent to
be married (three were usually required). 25
commodity: parcel. 27 *caliver:* musket.

30 *toasts-and-butter:* softies. 34 *ancients:*
flag bearers. 35–36 *gentlemen of companies:*
low-ranking officers. 37 *painted cloth:* wall
hanging, depicting the resurrected Lazarus
(Luke 16:19–31). 42 *revolted:* runaway. 42–
43 *trade-fall'n:* unemployed. 43 *cankers:*
sores. 46 *fazed ancient:* frayed flag. 52 *draff:*
swill. 54 *gibbets:* poles used for gallows. 59
gyves: fetters.

one; they'll find linen enough on 70
every hedge.

Enter the PRINCE [*and the*] LORD OF
WESTMORELAND.

PRINCE. How now, blown Jack? How
now, quilt?

FALSTAFF. What, Hal? How now, mad
wag? What a devil dost thou in 75
Warwickshire? My good Lord of
Westmoreland, I cry you mercy. I
thought your honor had already been
at Shrewsbury.

WESTMORELAND. Faith, Sir John, 80
'tis more than time that I were there,
and you too, but my powers are there
already. The King, I can tell you,
looks for us all, we must away all
night.   85

FALSTAFF. Tut, never fear me: I am
as vigilant as a cat to steal cream.

PRINCE. I think, to steal cream indeed,
for thy theft hath already made thee
butter. But tell me, Jack, whose 90
fellows are these that come after?

FALSTAFF. Mine, Hal, mine.

PRINCE. I did never see such pitiful
rascals.

FALSTAFF. Tut, tut, good enough 95
to toss; food for powder, food for
powder, they'll fill a pit as well as
better. Tush, man, mortal men,
mortal men.

WESTMORELAND. Ay, but, Sir John, 100
methinks they are exceeding poor
and bare, too beggarly.

FALSTAFF. Faith, for their poverty, I
know not where they had that, and
for their bareness, I am sure 105
they never learned that of me.

PRINCE. No, I'll be sworn, unless you
call three fingers in the ribs bare.
But, sirrah, make haste. Percy is
already in the field.   *Exit.* 110

FALSTAFF. What, is the King en-
camped?

WESTMORELAND. He is, Sir John. I fear
we shall stay too long.

FALSTAFF. Well, to the latter end 115
of a fray and the beginning of a
feast fits a dull fighter and a keen
guest.   *Exeunt.*

SCENE iii. [*The rebel camp, near
Shrewsbury.*]

Enter HOTSPUR, WORCESTER, DOUGLAS
VERNON.

HOTSPUR. We'll fight with him tonight.

WORCESTER.   It may not be.

DOUGLAS. You give him then advantage.

VERNON.   Not a whit.

HOTSPUR. Why say you so? Looks he
not for supply?

VERNON. So do we.

HOTSPUR.   His is certain, ours
is doubtful.

WORCESTER. Good cousin, be advised;
stir not tonight.   5

VERNON. Do not, my lord.

DOUGLAS.   You do not counsel well.
You speak it out of fear and cold
heart.

VERNON. Do me no slander, Douglas.
By my life—
And I dare well maintain it with my
life—
If well-respected honor bid me on, 10
I hold as little counsel with weak
fear
As you, my lord, or any Scot that
this day lives.
Let it be seen tomorrow in the battle
Which of us fears.

DOUGLAS.   Yea, or tonight.

VERNON.   Content.

HOTSPUR. Tonight, say I.   15

VERNON. Come, come, it may not be.
I wonder much, being men of such
great leading as you are,
That you foresee not what impediments

---

71 *hedge:* improvised clothesline. 72 *blown:*
puffed out and winded. 84 *away:* be on the
way. 96 *toss:* stick on a pike.

IV.iii.3 *supply:* reinforcement. 17 *leading:*
leadership.

Drag back our expedition. Certain
  horse
Of my cousin Vernon's are not yet
  come up.   20
Your uncle Worcester's horse came
  but today;
And now their pride and mettle is
  asleep
Their courage with hard labor tame
  and dull,
That not a horse is half the half
  of himself.
HOTSPUR. So are the horses of the
  enemy   25
In general journey-bated and brought
  low.
The better part of ours are full of
  rest.
WORCESTER. The number of the King
  exceedeth ours.
For God's sake, cousin, stay till all
  come in.

The trumpet sounds a parley.

Enter SIR WALTER BLUNT.

BLUNT. I come with gracious offers
  from the King,   30
If you vouchsafe me hearing and
  respect.
HOTSPUR. Welcome, Sir Walter Blunt,
  and would to God
You were of our determination.
Some of us love you well; and even
  those some
Envy your great deservings and good
  name,   35
Because you are not of our quality,
But stand against us like an enemy.
BLUNT. And God defend but still I
  should stand so,
So long as out of limit and true rule
You stand against anointed maj-
  esty.   40
But to my charge. The King hath
  sent to know
The nature of your griefs, and where-
  upon
You conjure from the breast of civil
  peace
Such bold hostility, teaching his
  duteous land
Audacious cruelty. If that the
  King   45
Have any way your good deserts
  forgot,
Which he confesseth to be manifold,
He bids you name your griefs, and
  with all speed
You shall have your desires with
  interest,
And pardon absolute for yourself and
  these   50
Herein misled by your suggestion.
HOTSPUR. The King is kind, and well
  we know the King
Knows at what time to promise, when
  to pay.
My father and my uncle and myself
Did give him that same royalty he
  wears;   55
And when he was not six and twenty
  strong,
Sick in the world's regard, wretched
  and low,
A poor unminded outlaw sneaking
  home,
My father gave him welcome to the
  shore;
And when he heard him swear and
  vow to God   60
He came but to be Duke of Lan-
  caster,
To sue his livery and beg his peace,
With tears of innocency and terms
  of zeal,
My father, in kind heart and pity
  moved,
Swore him assistance, and performed
  it too.   65
Now when the lords and barons of
  the realm
Perceived Northumberland did lean
  to him,

---

19 *expedition:* progress. 26 *journey-bated:*
travel-wearied. 33 *determination:* conviction.
36 *quality:* party. 38 *defend:* forbid. 39
limit: propriety.

62 *sue...peace:* plead for his due right and
forgiveness.

The more and less came in with cap
and knee,
Met him in boroughs, cities, villages,
Attended him on bridges, stood in
lanes,   70
Laid gifts before him, proffered him
their oaths,
Gave him their heirs as pages, fol-
lowed him
Even at the heels in golden multi-
tudes.
He presently, as greatness knows
itself,
Steps me a little higher than his
vow   75
Made to my father, while his blood
was poor,
Upon the naked shore at Ravens-
purgh;
And now, forsooth, takes on him to
reform
Some certain edicts and some strait
decrees
That lie too heavy on the common-
wealth;   80
Cries out upon abuses, seems to weep
Over his country's wrongs; and by
this face,
This seeming brow of justice, did
he win
The hearts of all that he did angle
for;
Proceeded further—cut me off the
heads   85
Of all the favorites that the absent
king
In deputation left behind him here
When he was personal in the Irish
war.
BLUNT. Tut! I came not to hear this.
HOTSPUR.   Then to the point.
In short time after, he deposed the
King;   90
Soon after that deprived him of his
life;

And in the neck of that tasked the
whole state;
To make that worse, suff'red his
kinsman March
(Who is, if every owner were well
placed,
Indeed his king) to be engaged in
Wales,   95
There without ransom to lie forfeited;
Disgraced me in my happy victories,
Sought to entrap me by intelligence;
Rated mine uncle from the council
board;
In rage dismissed my father from the
court;   100
Broke oath on oath, committed wrong
on wrong;
And in conclusion drove us to seek
out
This head of safety, and withal to pry
Into his title, the which we find
Too indirect for long continuance. 105
BLUNT. Shall I return this answer to
the King?
HOTSPUR. Not so, Sir Walter. We'll
withdraw awhile.
Go to the King; and let there be
impawned
Some surety for a safe return again,
And in the morning early shall mine
uncle   110
Bring him our purposes; and so
farewell.
BLUNT. I would you would accept of
grace and love.
HOTSPUR. And may be so we shall.
BLUNT.   Pray God you do.

[*Exeunt.*]

SCENE iv. [*York. The* ARCHBISHOP'S
palace.]

Enter [*the*] ARCHBISHOP OF YORK
[*and*] SIR MICHAEL.

---

68 *with cap and knee:* with respect and obeisance. 70 *lanes:* i.e., forming lanes for him to
pass through. 74 *knows itself:* feels its power.
79 *strait:* strict. 88 *personal:* personally
involved.

92 *in the neck of that:* immediately; *tasked:*
taxed. 98 *intelligence:* spying. 99 *Rated:*
chastized. 103 *head:* army; *withal:* meanwhile.

ARCHBISHOP. Hie, good Sir Michael; bear this sealed brief
With winged haste to the Lord Marshal;
This to my cousin Scroop; and all the rest
To whom they are directed. If you knew
How much they do import, you would make haste.   5
SIR MICHAEL. My good lord, I guess their tenor.
ARCHBISHOP. Like enough you do.
Tomorrow, good Sir Michael, is a day
Wherein the fortune of ten thousand men
Must bide the touch; for, sir, at Shrewsbury,   10
As I am truly given to understand,
The King with mighty and quick-raised power
Meets with Lord Harry; and I fear, Sir Michael,
What with the sickness of Northumberland,
Whose power was in the first proportion,   15
And what with Owen Glendower's absence thence,
Who with them was a rated sinew too
And comes not in, overruled by prophecies—
I fear the power of Percy is too weak
To wage an instant trial with the King.   20
SIR MICHAEL. Why, my good lord, you need not fear;
There is Douglas and Lord Mortimer.
ARCHBISHOP. No, Mortimer is not there.
SIR MICHAEL. But there is Mordake, Vernon, Lord Harry Percy,
And there is my Lord of Worcester, and a head   25
Of gallant warriors, noble gentlemen.
ARCHBISHOP. And so there is; but yet the King hath drawn
The special head of all the land together—
The Prince of Wales, Lord John of Lancaster,
The noble Westmoreland and warlike Blunt,   30
And many moe corrivals and dear men
Of estimation and command in arms.
SIR MICHAEL. Doubt not, my lord, they shall be well opposed.
ARCHBISHOP. I hope no less, yet needful 'tis to fear;
And, to prevent the worst, Sir Michael, speed.   35
For if Lord Percy thrive not, ere the King
Dismiss his power, he means to visit us,
For he hath heard of our confederacy,
And 'tis but wisdom to make strong against him.
Therefore make haste. I must go write again   40
To other friends; and so farewell, Sir Michael.   *Exeunt.*

ACT V

SCENE i. [*The* KING's *camp, near Shrewsbury.*]

Enter the KING, PRINCE OF WALES, LORD JOHN OF LANCASTER, EARL OF WESTMORELAND, SIR WALTER BLUNT, FALSTAFF.

KING. How bloodily the sun begins to peer
Above yon busky hill! The day looks pale
At his distemp'rature.
PRINCE.   The southern wind

IV.iv.1 *brief:* letter. 10 *bide the touch:* endure the test. 15 *proportion:* magnitude. 17 *rated sinew:* valued strength.

31 *moe corrivals:* more associates; *dear:* honored. V.i.2 *busky:* bushy. 3 *his distemp'rature:* the sun's sickness.

Doth play the trumpet to his purposes
And by his hollow whistling in the
leaves   5
Foretells a tempest and a blust'ring
day.
KING. Then with the losers let it
sympathize,
For nothing can seem foul to those
that win.

The trumpet sounds. Enter WORCESTER
[*and* VERNON].

How now, my Lord of Worcester?
'Tis not well
That you and I should meet upon
such terms   10
As now we meet. You have deceived
our trust
And made us doff our easy robes of
peace
To crush our old limbs in ungentle
steel.
This is not well, my lord; this is not
well.
What say you to it? Will you again
unknit   15
This churlish knot of all-abhorred
war,
And move in that obedient orb again
Where you did give a fair and
natural light,
And be no more an exhaled meteor,
A prodigy of fear, and a portent 20
Of broached mischief to the unborn
times?
WORCESTER. Hear me, my liege.
For mine own part, I could be well
content
To entertain the lag-end of my life
With quiet hours, for I protest   25
I have not sought the day of this
dislike.
KING. You have not sought it! How
comes it then?
FALSTAFF. Rebellion lay in his way,
and he found it.

PRINCE. Peace, chewet, peace!
WORCESTER. It pleased your Majesty
to turn your looks   30
Of favor from myself and all our
house;
And yet I must remember you, my
lord,
We were the first and dearest of your
friends.
For you my staff of office did I break
In Richard's time, and posted day
and night   35
To meet you on the way and kiss
your hand
When yet you were in place and in
account
Nothing so strong and fortunate as I.
It was myself, my brother, and his
son
That brought you home and boldly
did outdare   40
The dangers of the time. You swore
to us,
And you did swear that oath at
Doncaster,
That you did nothing purpose 'gainst
the state,
Nor claim no further than your new-
fall'n right,
The seat of Gaunt, dukedom of
Lancaster.   45
To this we swore our aid. But in
short space
It rained down fortune show'ring on
your head,
And such a flood of greatness fell
on you—
What with our help, what with the
absent King,
What with the injuries of a wanton
time,   50
The seeming sufferances that you had
borne,
And the contrarious winds that held
the King
So long in his unlucky Irish wars

---

4 *his purposes:* the sun's portents. 16 *churlish:*
intractable. 17 *orb:* orbit. 19 *exhaled:*
vaporous. 21 *broached:* public.

29 *chewet:* jackdaw (chatterer). 32 *remember:* remind. 35 *posted:* hastened. 52 *contrarious:* adverse.

That all in England did repute him
  dead—
And from this swarm of fair advan-
  tages   55
You took occasion to be quickly
  wooed
To gripe the general sway into your
  hand;
Forgot your oath to us at Doncaster;
And, being fed by us, you used us so
As that ungentle gull, the cuckoo's
  bird,   60
Useth the sparrow—did oppress our
  nest,
Grew by our feeding to so great a
  bulk
That even our love durst not come
  near your sight
For fear of swallowing; but with
  nimble wing
We were enforced for safety sake
  to fly   65
Out of your sight and raise this
  present head;
Whereby we stand opposed by such
  means
As you yourself have forged against
  yourself
By unkind usage, dangerous counte-
  nance,
And violation of all faith and troth 70
Sworn to us in your younger enter-
  prise.
KING. These things, indeed, you have
  articulate,
Proclaimed at market crosses, read
  in churches,
To face the garment of rebellion
With some fine color that may
  please the eye   75
Of fickle changelings and poor dis-
  contents,
Which gape and rub the elbow at
  the news

Of hurlyburly innovation.
And never yet did insurrection want
Such water colors to impaint his
  cause,   80
Nor moody beggars, starving for a
  time
Of pell-mell havoc and confusion.
PRINCE. In both your armies there is
  many a soul
Shall pay full dearly for this en-
  counter,
If once they join in trial. Tell your
  nephew   85
The Prince of Wales doth join with
  all the world
In praise of Henry Percy. By my
  hopes,
This present enterprise set off his
  head,
I do not think a braver gentleman,
More active-valiant or more valiant-
  young,   90
More daring or more bold, is now
  alive
To grace this latter age with noble
  deeds.
For my part, I may speak it to my
  shame,
I have a truant been to chivalry;
And so I hear he doth account me
  too.   95
Yet this before my father's majesty—
I am content that he shall take the
  odds
Of his great name and estimation,
And will, to save the blood on either
  side,
Try fortune with him in a single
  fight.   100
KING. And, Prince of Wales, so dare
  we venture thee;
Albeit, considerations infinite
Do make against it. No, good
  Worcester, no!
We love our people well; even those
  we love

---

57 *gripe:* grasp. 60 *gull...bird:* the cuckoos
hatch out in the nests of other birds, whom
they then push out. 69 *dangerous:* menacing.
72 *articulate:* set forth. 73 *face:* trim. 77
rub the elbow: show pleasure.

---

78 *hurlyburly innovation:* wild revolution. 88
set...head: not charged against him. 96 *this
before:* "this (I'll say) in front of."

That are misled upon your cousin's
part;   105
And, will they take the offer of our
grace,
Both he, and they, and you, yea,
every man
Shall be my friend again, and I'll
be his.
So tell your cousin, and bring me
word
What he will do. But if he will not
yield,   110
Rebuke and dread correction wait
on us,
And they shall do their office. So be
gone.
We will not now be troubled with
reply.
We offer fair; take it advisedly.

Exit WORCESTER [*with* VERNON].

PRINCE. It will not be accepted, on my
life.   115
The Douglas and the Hotspur both
together
Are confident against the world in
arms.
KING. Hence, therefore, every leader
to his charge;
For, on their answer, will we set on
them,
And God befriend us as our cause is
just!   120

Exeunt. Manent PRINCE [*and*] FAL-
STAFF.

FALSTAFF. Hal, if thou see me down
in the battle and bestride me, so!
'Tis a point of friendship.
PRINCE. Nothing but a colossus can do
thee that friendship. Say thy   125
prayers, and farewell.
FALSTAFF. I would 'twere bedtime, Hal,
and all well.
PRINCE. Why, thou owest God a death.

[*Exit.*]

FALSTAFF. 'Tis not due yet: I   130
would be loath to pay him before his
day. What need I be so forward with
him that calls not on me? Well, 'tis
no matter; honor pricks me on. Yea,
but how if honor prick me off   135
when I come on? How then? Can
honor set to a leg? No. Or an arm?
No. Or take away the grief of a
wound? No. Honor hath no skill in
surgery then? No. What is   140
honor? A word. What is in that word
honor? What is that honor? Air—
a trim reckoning! Who hath it? He
that died a Wednesday. Doth he feel
it? No. Doth he hear it? No. 'Tis 145
insensible then? Yea, to the dead.
But will it not live with the living?
No. Why? Detraction will not suffer
it. Therefore I'll none of it. Honor
is a mere scutcheon—and so   150
ends my catechism.   *Exit.*

SCENE ii. [*The rebel camp, near Shrewsbury.*]

Enter WORCESTER [*and*] SIR RICHARD
VERNON.

WORCESTER. O no, my nephew must not
know, Sir Richard,
The liberal and kind offer of the
King.
VERNON. 'Twere best he did.
WORCESTER.   Then are
we all undone.
It is not possible, it cannot be,
The King should keep his word in
loving us.   5
He will suspect us still and find a
time
To punish this offense in other faults.
Supposition all our lives shall be
stuck full of eyes;

---

106 *grace:* pardon. 111 *wait on:* attend.
120s.d. *Manent:* remain. 122 *so:* so be it.

134 *pricks:* "spurs on" and "checks off a
casualty list." 143 *trim:* fine. 146 *insensible:*
not perceptible. 148 *Detraction:* slander. 150
scutcheon: escutcheon, or shield decorated
with a coat of arms. V.ii.8 *Supposition:*
suspicion.

For treason is but trusted like the
fox,
Who, never so tame, so cherished
and locked up,   10
Will have a wild trick of his
ancestors.
Look how we can, or sad or merrily,
Interpretation will misquote our
looks,
And we shall feed like oxen at a stall,
The better cherished still the nearer
death.   15
My nephew's trespass may be well
forgot;
It hath the excuse of youth and heat
of blood,
And an adopted name of privilege—
A hare-brained Hotspur, governed by
a spleen.
All his offenses live upon my head   20
And on his father's. We did train
him on;
And, his corruption being ta'en from
us,
We, as the spring of all, shall pay
for all.
Therefore, good cousin, let not Harry
know,
In any case, the offer of the King. 25

Enter HOTSPUR [*and* DOUGLAS].

VERNON. Deliver what you will, I'll
say 'tis so.
Here comes your cousin.
HOTSPUR.   My uncle is returned.
Deliver up my Lord of West-
moreland.
Uncle, what news?
WORCESTER. The King will bid you
battle presently.   30
DOUGLAS. Defy him by the Lord of
Westmoreland.
HOTSPUR. Lord Douglas, go you and
tell him so.
DOUGLAS. Marry, and shall, and very

willingly.   *Exit.*
WORCESTER. There is no seeming mercy
in the King.
HOTSPUR. Did you beg any? God
forbid!   35
WORCESTER. I told him gently of our
grievances,
Of his oath-breaking, which he
mended thus,
By now forswearing that he is forsworn.
He calls us rebels, traitors, and will
scourge
With haughty arms this hateful name
in us.   40

Enter DOUGLAS.

DOUGLAS. Arm, gentlemen, to arms, for
I have thrown
A brave defiance in King Henry's
teeth,
And Westmoreland, that was engaged,
did bear it;
Which cannot choose but bring him
quickly on.
WORCESTER. The Prince of Wales step-
ped forth before the King   45
And, nephew, challenged you to single
fight.
HOTSPUR. O, would the quarrel lay
upon our heads,
And that no man might draw short
breath today
But I and Harry Monmouth! Tell
me, tell me,
How showed his tasking? Seemed it
in contempt?   50
VERNON. No, by my soul. I never in
my life
Did hear a challenge urged more
modestly,
Unless a brother should a brother
dare
To gentle exercise and proof of arms.
He gave you all the duties of a
man;   55
Trimmed up your praises with a
princely tongue;

11 *trick:* mannerism or wile. 12 *or:* either
...or. 19 *spleen:* temper. 21 *train:* lure. 28
Westmoreland: the hostage whom Henry IV
gave in guarantee of Worcester and Vernon's
safety.

43 *engaged:* given as hostage. 50 *tasking:*
challenge. 55 *duties:* honors.

Spoke your deservings like a chron-
icle;
Making you ever better than his
praise
By still dispraising praise valued with
you;
And, which became him like a prince
indeed,   60
He made a blushing cital of himself,
And chid his truant youth with such
a grace
As if he mast'red there a double spirit
Of teaching and of learning instantly.
There did he pause; but let me tell
the world,   65
If he outlive the envy of this day,
England did never owe so sweet a
hope,
So much misconstrued in his wanton-
ness.

HOTSPUR. Cousin, I think thou art
enamored
On his follies. Never did I hear   70
Of any prince so wild a liberty.
But be he as he will, yet once ere
night
I will embrace him with a soldier's
arm,
That he shall shrink under my
courtesy.
Arm, arm with speed! And, fellows,
soldiers, friends,   75
Better consider what you have to do
Than I, that have not well the gift
of tongue,
Can lift your blood up with persua-
sion.

Enter a MESSENGER.

MESSENGER. My lord, here are letters
for you.
HOTSPUR. I cannot read them now.— 80
O gentlemen, the time of life is short!
To spend that shortness basely were
too long
If life did ride upon a dial's point,

Still ending at the arrival of an hour.
And if we live, we live to tread on
kings;   85
If die, brave death, when princes die
with us!
Now for our consciences, the arms
are fair,
When the intent of bearing them is
just.

Enter another [MESSENGER].

MESSENGER. My lord, prepare. The
King comes on apace.
HOTSPUR. I thank him that he cuts me
from my tale,   90
For I profess not talking: only this—
Let each man do his best; and here
draw I
A sword whose temper I intend to
stain
With the best blood that I can meet
withal
In the adventure of this perilous
day.   95
Now, Esperance! Percy! and set on.
Sound all the lofty instruments of
war,
And by that music let us all embrace;
For, heaven to earth, some of us
never shall
A second time do such a courtesy. 100

*Here they embrace. The trumpets
sound.* [*Exeunt.*]

SCENE iii. [*Shrewsbury. The battlefield.*]

The KING *enters with his power.
Alarum to the battle.* [*Exeunt.*] *Then
enter* DOUGLAS, *and* SIR WALTER
BLUNT [*disguised as the* KING].

BLUNT. What is thy name, that in
battle thus thou crossest me?
What honor dost thou seek upon my
head?

---

59 *valued with:* compared (himself) with. 61
cital: recital. 64 *instantly:* simultaneously.
67 *owe:* own. 83 *dial's point:* hand of a clock.

---

84 *Still:* forever. 96 *Esperance:* hope. 97
lofty instruments: drums and trumpets.

DOUGLAS. Know then my name is
Douglas,

And I do haunt thee in the battle
thus

Because some tell me that thou art
a king.   5

BLUNT. They tell thee true.

DOUGLAS. The Lord of Stafford dear
today hath bought

Thy likeness, for instead of thee,
King Harry,

This sword hath ended him: so shall
it thee,

Unless thou yield thee as my prisoner.   10

BLUNT. I was not born a yielder, thou
proud Scot;

And thou shalt find a king that will
revenge

Lord Stafford's death.

[*They fight.* DOUGLAS *kills* BLUNT.
Then enter HOTSPUR.

HOTSPUR. O Douglas, hadst thou fought
at Holmedon thus,

I never had triumphed upon a
Scot.   15

DOUGLAS. All's done, all's won: here
breathless lies the King.

HOTSPUR. Where?

DOUGLAS. Here.

HOTSPUR. This, Douglas? No. I know
this face full well.

A gallant knight he was, his name
was Blunt;   20

Semblably furnished like the King
himself.

DOUGLAS. A fool go with thy soul,
whither it goes!

A borrowed title hast thou bought
too dear:

Why didst thou tell me that thou
wert a king?

HOTSPUR. The King hath many marching in his coats.   25

DOUGLAS. Now, by my sword, I will
kill all his coats;

I'll murder all his wardrobe, piece

by piece,

Until I meet the King.

HOTSPUR.   Up and away!
Our soldiers stand full fairly for the
day.   [*Exeunt.*]

[*Alarum. Enter* FALSTAFF *solus.*]

FALSTAFF. Though I could scape 30
shot-free at London, I fear the shot
here. Here's no scoring but upon the
pate. Soft! Who are you? Sir Walter
Blunt. There's honor for you! Here's
no vanity! I am as hot as molten 35
lead, and as heavy too. God keep lead
out of me. I need no more weight
than mine own bowels. I have led
my rag-of-muffins where they are
peppered. There's not three of 40
my hundred and fifty left alive, and
they are for the town's end, to beg
during life. But who comes here?

[*Enter the* PRINCE.]

PRINCE. What, stands thou idle here?
Lend me thy sword.

Many a nobleman lies stark and
stiff   45

Under the hoofs of vaunting enemies,
whose deaths are yet unrevenged. I
prithee lend me thy sword.

FALSTAFF. O Hal, I prithee give me
leave to breathe awhile. Turk 50
Gregory never did such deeds in
arms as I have done this day. I have
paid Percy, I have made him sure.

PRINCE. He is indeed, and living to kill
thee.

I prithee lend me thy sword.   55

FALSTAFF. Nay, before God, Hal, if
Percy be alive, thou gets not my
sword; but take my pistol if thou
wilt.

---

29 *fairly:* in good position.   31 *shot-free:*
scot-free.   32 *scoring:* tabulating the bill,
striking with the sword.   40 *peppered:* (1)
sprinkled with shot and (2) killed.   50–51
Turk Gregory: "Turk" meant "ruthless," and
both Pope Gregory VII and Gregory XIII
qualified in Shakespeare's time as the per-
sonification of ruthlessness.   53 *paid:* sent
him to his reckoning.

V.iii.21 *Semblably furnished:* outfitted like.

PRINCE. Give it me. What, is it in   60
the case?

FALSTAFF. Ay, Hal. 'Tis hot, 'tis hot.
There's that will sack a city.

[The PRINCE *draws it out and finds it
to be a bottle of sack.]*

PRINCE. What, is it a time to jest and
dally now?   65

He throws the bottle at him. Exit.

FALSTAFF. Well, if Percy be alive, I'll
pierce him. If he do come in my way,
so; if he do not, if I come in his
willingly, let him make a carbonado
of me. I like not such grinning   70
honor as Sir Walter hath. Give me
life; which if I can save, so; if not,
honor comes unlooked for, and there's
an end.   *[Exit.]*

SCENE iv. *[Shrewsbury. The battlefield.]*

Alarum. Excursions. Enter the KING,
the PRINCE, LORD JOHN OF LANCASTER,
EARL OF WESTMORELAND.

KING. I prithee, Harry, withdraw thyself, thou bleedest too much.
Lord John of Lancaster, go you with
him.

JOHN. Not I, my lord, unless I did
bleed too.

PRINCE. I beseech your Majesty make
up,
Lest your retirement do amaze your
friends.   5

KING. I will do so. My Lord of Westmoreland, lead him to his tent.

WESTMORELAND. Come, my lord, I'll
lead you to your tent.

PRINCE. Lead me, my lord? I do not
need your help;
And God forbid a shallow scratch
should drive   10

The Prince of Wales from such a
field as this,
Where stained nobility lies trodden
on,
And rebels' arms triumph in mas-
sacres!

JOHN. We breathe too long. Come,
cousin Westmoreland,
Our duty this way lies. For God's
sake, come.   15

[Exeunt LANCASTER *and* WESTMORE-
LAND.]

PRINCE. By God, thou hast deceived
me, Lancaster!
I did not think thee lord of such a
spirit.
Before, I loved thee as a brother,
John,
But now I do respect thee as my soul.

KING. I saw him hold Lord Percy at
the point   20
With lustier maintenance than I did
look for
Of such an ungrown warrior.

PRINCE. O, this boy lends mettle to us
all!   *Exit.*

[Enter DOUGLAS.]

DOUGLAS. Another king? They grow
like Hydra's heads.
I am the Douglas, fatal to all those   25
That wear those colors on them.
What art thou
That counterfeit'st the person of a
king?

KING. The King himself, who, Douglas,
grieves at heart
So many of his shadows thou hast
met,
And not the very King. I have two
boys   30
Seek Percy and thyself about the
field;
But, seeing thou fall'st on me so
luckily,

---

69 *carbonado:* meat sliced ready for broiling.
V.iv.s.d. *Excursions:* sorties.   4 *make up:*
pull in.   5 *amaze:* dismay.

14 *breathe:* rest.   21 *lustier maintenance:*
hardier endurance.   24 *Hydra:* a many-headed
monster that grew new heads when old ones
were cut off.

I will assay thee, and defend thyself.

DOUGLAS. I fear thou art another counterfeit;

And yet, in faith, thou bearest thee like a king.   35

But mine I am sure thou art, whoe'er thou be,

And thus I win thee.

They fight, the KING *being in danger.*
Enter PRINCE OF WALES.

PRINCE. Hold up thy head, vile Scot, or thou art like

Never to hold it up again. The spirits

Of valiant Shirley, Stafford, Blunt are in my arms.   40

It is the Prince of Wales that threatens thee,

Who never promiseth but he means to pay. *They fight:* DOUGLAS *flieth.*

Cheerly, my lord. How fares your Grace?

Sir Nicholas Gawsey hath for succor sent,

And so hath Clifton. I'll to Clifton straight.   45

KING. Stay and breathe awhile.

Thou hast redeemed thy last opinion,

And showed thou mak'st some tender of my life,

In this fair rescue thou hast brought to me.

PRINCE. O God, they did me too much injury   50

That ever said I heark'ned for your death.

If it were so, I might have let alone

The insulting hand of Douglas over you,

Which would have been as speedy in your end

As all the poisonous potions in the world,   55

And saved the treacherous labor of your son.

KING. Make up to Clifton; I'll to Sir Nicholas Gawsey.   *Exit.*

[*Enter* HOTSPUR.]

HOTSPUR. If I mistake not, thou art Harry Monmouth.

PRINCE. Thou speak'st as if I would deny my name.

HOTSPUR. My name is Harry Percy.   60

PRINCE. Why, then I see a very valiant rebel of the name.

I am the Prince of Wales, and think not, Percy,

To share with me in glory any more.

Two stars keep not their motion in one sphere,

Nor can one England brook a double reign   65

Of Harry Percy and the Prince of Wales.

HOTSPUR. Nor shall it, Harry, for the hour is come

To end the one of us; and would to God

Thy name in arms were now as great as mine!

PRINCE. I'll make it greater ere I part from thee,   70

And all the budding honors on thy crest

I'll crop to make a garland for my head.

HOTSPUR. I can no longer brook thy vanities. *They fight.*

Enter FALSTAFF.

FALSTAFF. Well said, Hal! To it, Hal! Nay, you shall find no boy's play   75 here, I can tell you.

Enter DOUGLAS. *He fighteth with* FALSTAFF, [*who*] *falls down as if he were dead.* [*Exit* DOUGLAS.] *The* PRINCE *killeth* PERCY.

HOTSPUR. O Harry, thou hast robbed me of my youth!

I better brook the loss of brittle life

Than those proud titles thou hast won of me.

---

33 *assay:* try.   47 *opinion:* reputation.   48 *tender:* regard.

64 *sphere:* orbit.   65 *brook:* tolerate.   73 *vanities:* empty words.

They wound my thoughts worse than
thy sword my flesh.   80
But thoughts, the slaves of life, and
life, time's fool,
And time, that takes survey of all
the world,
Must have a stop. O, I could pro-
phesy,
But that the earthy and cold hand
of death
Lies on my tongue. No, Percy, thou
art dust,   85
And food for— [*Dies.*]
PRINCE. For worms, brave Percy. Fare
thee well, great heart.
Ill-weaved ambition, how much art
thou shrunk!
When that this body did contain a
spirit,
A kingdom for it was too small a
bound;   90
But now two paces of the vilest earth
Is room enough. This earth that bears
thee dead
Bears not alive so stout a gentleman.
If thou wert sensible of courtesy,
I should not make so dear a show
of zeal.   95
But let my favors hide thy mangled
face;
And, even in thy behalf, I'll thank
myself
For doing these fair rites of tender-
ness.
Adieu, and take thy praise with thee
to heaven.
Thy ignominy sleep with thee in the
grave,   100
But not rememb'red in thy epitaph.

He spieth FALSTAFF *on the ground.*

What, old acquaintance? Could not
all this flesh
Keep in a little life? Poor Jack,
farewell!
I could have better spared a better
man.

O, I should have a heavy miss of
thee   105
If I were much in love with vanity.
Death hath not struck so fat a deer
today,
Though many dearer, in this bloody
fray.
Emboweled will I see thee by-and-by;
Till then in blood by noble Percy
lie.   *Exit.*   110

FALSTAFF *riseth up.*

FALSTAFF. Emboweled? If thou em-
bowel me today, I'll give you leave to
powder me and eat me too tomorrow.
'Sblood, 'twas time to counterfeit, or
that hot termagant Scot had paid   115
me scot and lot too. Counterfeit? I
lie; I am no counterfeit. To die is to
be a counterfeit, for he is but the
counterfeit of a man who hath not the
life of a man; but to counterfeit   120
dying when a man thereby liveth, is
to be no counterfeit, but the true and
perfect image of life indeed. The
better part of valor is discretion, in
the which better part I have   125
saved my life. 'Zounds, I am afraid of
this gunpowder Percy, though he be
dead How if he should counterfeit
too, and rise? By my faith, I am
afraid he would prove the   130
better counterfeit. Therefore I'll make
him sure; yea, and I'll swear I killed
him. Why may not he rise as well as
I? Nothing confutes me but eyes,
and nobody sees me. Therefore,   135
sirrah [*stabs him*], with a new wound
in your thigh, come you along with me.

He takes up HOTSPUR *on his back.*
Enter PRINCE [*and*] JOHN OF LAN-
CASTER.

PRINCE. Come, brother John; full
bravely hast thou fleshed

---

93 *stout:* brave. 95 *dear:* sincere. 96 *favors:*
plumes.

105 *heavy miss:* sorrowful and weighty loss.
108 *dearer:* of more value. 109 *Emboweled:*
disemboweled for burial. 113 *powder:* salt.
115 *termagant:* hot-headed. 116 *scot and lot:*
in full.

Thy maiden sword.

JOHN.   But, soft! whom
      have we here?
   Did you not tell me this fat man
      was dead?   140
PRINCE. I did; I saw him dead,
   Breathless and bleeding on the
      ground. Art thou alive,
   Or is it fantasy that plays upon our
      eyesight?
   I prithee speak. We will not trust
      our eyes
   Without our ears. Thou art not what
      thou seem'st.   145
FALSTAFF. No, that's certain, I am not
   a double man; but if I be not Jack
   Falstaff, then am I a Jack. There
   is Percy. If your father will do me
   any honor, so; if not, let him   150
   kill the next Percy himself. I look
   to be either earl or duke, I can assure
   you.
PRINCE. Why, Percy I killed myself,
   and saw thee dead!   155
FALSTAFF. Didst thou? Lord, Lord, how
   this world is given to lying. I grant
   you I was down, and out of breath,
   and so was he; but we rose both at
   an instant and fought a long   160
   hour by Shrewsbury clock. If I may
   be believed, so; if not, let them that
   should reward valor bear the sin upon
   their own heads. I'll take it upon my
   death, I gave him this wound   165
   in the thigh. If the man were alive
   and would deny it, 'zounds! I would
   make him eat a piece of my sword.
JOHN. This is the strangest tale that
   ever I heard.
PRINCE. This is the strangest fellow,
   brother John.   170
   Come, bring your luggage nobly on
      your back.
   For my part, if a lie may do thee
      grace,
   I'll gild it with the happiest terms I
   have. *A retreat is sounded.*

The trumpet sounds retreat; the day
   is ours.
Come, brother, let us to the highest
   of the field,   175
To see what friends are living, who
   are dead.

Exeunt [PRINCE HENRY *and* PRINCE
JOHN].

FALSTAFF. I'll follow, as they say, for
   reward. He that rewards me, God
   reward him. If I do grow great, I'll
   grow less; for I'll purge, and   180
   leave sack, and live cleanly, as nobleman should do.

            Exit [*bearing off the body*].

SCENE v. [*Shrewsbury. The battlefield.*]

The trumpets sound. Enter the KING,
PRINCE OF WALES, LORD JOHN OF
LANCASTER, EARL OF WESTMORELAND,
with WORCESTER *and* VERNON *prisoners.*

KING. Thus ever did rebellion find
      rebuke.
   Ill-spirited Worcester, did not we
      send grace,
   Pardon, and terms of love to all of
      you?
   And wouldst thou turn our offers
      contrary?
   Misuse the tenor of thy kinsman's
      trust?   5
   Three knights upon our party slain
      today,
   A noble earl, and many a creature
      else
   Had been alive this hour,
   If like a Christian thou hadst truly
      borne
   Betwixt our armies true intelli-
      gence.   10
WORCESTER. What I have done my
      safety urged me to;

----

147 *double man:* a ghost and twofold man;
Jack: scoundrel. 172 *grace:* favor.

180 *purge:* "purify myself" (morally and
physically). V.v.2 *grace:* forgiveness. 10 *intelligence:* information.

And I embrace this fortune patiently,
Since not to be avoided it falls on me.
KING. Bear Worcester to the death, and
    Vernon too;
Other   offenders   we   will   pause
    upon.   15

[*Exeunt* WORCESTER *and* VERNON,
guarded.]

How goes the field?
PRINCE. The noble Scot, Lord Douglas,
    when he saw
The fortune of the day quite turned
    from him,
The noble Percy slain, and all his
    men
Upon the foot of fear, fled with the
    rest;   20
And falling from a hill, he was so
    bruised
That the pursuers took him. At my
    tent
The Douglas is, and I beseech your
    Grace
I may dispose of him.
KING.   With all my heart.
PRINCE. Then, brother John of Lan-
    caster, to you   25
This honorable bounty shall belong.
Go to the Douglas and deliver him
Up to his pleasure, ransomless and
free.
His valors shown upon our crests
    today
Have taught us how to cherish such
    high deeds,   30
Even in the bosom of our adversaries.
JOHN. I thank your Grace for this high
    courtesy,
Which I shall give away immediately.
KING. Then this remains, that we
    divide our power.
You, son John, and my cousin West-
    moreland,   35
Towards York shall bend you with
    your dearest speed
To meet Northumberland and the
    prelate Scroop,
Who, as we hear, are busily in arms.
Myself and you, son Harry, will
    towards Wales
To fight with Glendower and the
    Earl of March.   40
Rebellion in this land shall lose his
    sway,
Meeting the check of such another
    day;
And since this business so fair is
    done,
Let us not leave till all our own be
    won.   *Exeunt.*

The Cherry Orchard

As we suggested in the general introduction, the selling and cutting of the orchard in *The Cherry Orchard* is the central example of the play's main concern: the transfer of power from an old aristocratic family to a representative bourgeois, the businessman Lopakhin. The basic causes of this central action lie in the pervasive uncertainty and spiritual emptiness of the characters, in a paralysis of the individual will that demands a new concept of dramatic method and dialogue transaction. The people of such a society, Anton Chekhov (1860–1904) says, are neither heroic nor villainous, merely average; they spend their hours "eating, drinking, running after women or men, talking nonsense." The focus shifts from character to character and prevents anyone from becoming central. The irony of the play derives largely from the balancing of those who rise against those who fall—and from the common plight and indignities that all characters suffer. Such progress as Chekhov's people manage comes at the expense of much that is good (the replacing of the old loyal servant Fiers with the impudent Yasha, for instance). Although Lopakhin's goals might seem to make the transfer of power a triumph of productivity and common sense over hopeless procrastination and waste, sympathy with Gaev and Mme. Ranevsky quickly counterbalances whatever sympathy we have with him. Though Lopakhin's work is finally begun at the end of the play, and the distant goals of Anya and Trofimov perhaps seem closer than they were then, none of these plans promises to get very far.

This equilibrium between pathetic and comic elements is merely one aspect of the play's general crisscrossing of motives and moods. It is complemented by an ironic use of dramatic expectation generally and the conventions of melodramatic mortgage-forclosure plots specifically. The arrival of the family, the climactic exchange of the estate, and the departure are just enough action to convince the audience that it has seen a play. Chekhov exploits these patterns to gain insight into both the emptiness of his characters' lives and the falsity of conventional dramatic methods, which *because* they are dramatic must depart from the norm of "eating, drinking, talking nonsense." He purposely *dissipates* the dramatic effects of the foreclosure, for instance, staging the actual buying offstage and then making the critical encounter fizzle as it plunges into the ambivalent depths of Lopakhin's past and the emotional currents of those who hear the news. At each key point something like a vacuum reasserts itself: it reduces the action to farce or directs our attention outward beyond the normal completion of the action to vistas that engulf the immediate concerns of the play. This extension of the action is its main significance, the thing that lies masked, the hidden clause in the social contract.

Typical of Chekhov's handling of the intrusion of that hidden element is his treatment of the catalyst Lopakhin. In a melodrama we could easily imagine Lopakhin becoming a villainous forecloser, or perhaps in a local-man-makes-good comedy, an enterprising hero. In *The Cherry Orchard* he is obviously neither of these; nor is he an average man making a moral decision that might bring into focus the various strands of his life or clarify the place of the serf-born entrepreneur around whom a new social order might take shape. Though in one sense he causes the ruin of the family—at least he buys the estate and cuts down the trees—he himself is part of the old times and does all he can to forewarn his victims. His motives are not only complex but virtually self-cancelling; as he presses forward to realize his dream, half of him hangs back. It is when he enters with ownership in hand that the play appears to be approaching what the audience can at last call genuine drama, a showdown. But Chekhov teases our expectations: as Lopakhin makes his entry, Varya, the one he is expected to marry, hits him with a stick (intending to hit Epikhodov). He narrates his achievement clumsily, among copious apologies to the family, which despite ample warning is dismayed. His joy is gradually poisoned by his awareness of them. He finds his purchase dreamlike and uncertain: "I'm asleep, it's only a dream, an illusion"—and then the phrase that tells us that we are once again in the presence of the vacuum, "It's the fruit of imagination, wrapped in the fog of the unknown" (III). (For once his sense of reality corresponds to that of Varya, who says of their potential marriage, "I think that it will all come to nothing. He's a busy man. I'm not his affair...there's nothing in it at all, it's all like a dream.") He recovers momentarily and celebrates his new name and power: "Come and look at Ermolai Lopakhin laying his axe to the cherry orchard, come and look at the trees falling! We'll build villas here, and our grandsons and great-grandsons will see a new life." But he speaks with increasing irony and soon lapses into melancholy; the moment dissipates in weeping. It is not surprising after this that Lopakhin cannot bring himself to propose to Varya (though once again Chekhov prepares us for a definite climax). When the two of them are closeted for a hurried moment, words simply won't come. Not even marriage is to be salvaged from the confusion and general scattering of the family (which continues with intermittent shouts while they talk). The trivialities of weather fill in for declarations of love, and the vacancies of their dialogue speak more tellingly than the substance.

In one of Chekhov's skillful balancings of character (there are several of them in the play), Lopakhin is pitted against Trofimov, who would remake society not by middle-class enterprise but by infusing it with ideals. Trofimov may seem to represent the play's greatest future hope, but the cross fire to which Chekhov exposes him shows him to be as ineffectual as he is enthusiastic. A shabby middle age is beginning to cover his youth. Not only does he lack position and concrete prospects but he gives no clear indication of going anywhere except back to the same ideas. If Marxist revolutionaries of the future are implicit in him, Chekhov buries them too deeply beneath Trofimov's pompous front to offer much encouragement. Trofimov is also above romance, which removes the possibility of a marriage with Anya and the beginning of a new generation. His most momentous act in the play is a search for galoshes—which, when located, prove to be none too sightly or durable. He is depressed as often as exhilarated and is both in regular cycles. Mme. Ranevsky finds it relatively easy to deflate his confidence with a few harsh truths—following which he falls clumsily down stairs.

In view of the dwindling of his and Lopakhin's prospects and the general decline of the fortunes of everyone to whom we are not indifferent, we are perhaps justified in rephrasing our concept of the play's central plot as a transfer of *illusory* power, merely the main instance of which is Lopakhin's purchase. Although several people prophesy improvement in human fortunes, none of them can be said to speak for the play, and in each case something immediately intrudes that twists the dream grotesquely or comically. What remains is a commitment to activity and whatever local consolations it brings. Work, for instance, is a weapon against confusion, a way to pass the time (both here and in *Uncle Vanya*). But it, too, is ambiguous: it is a limited instrument to use against an unlimited or at least indefinite void, and its goals have a habit of receding out of reach. As it is with work, so it is with all *action* and *suffering*, which cannot pass through crisis to clarification. The immediate contact that each character has with reality is too intangible to yield strong moments of perception. Each ends trying merely to get back where he started, barely hanging on (like Fiers), or being cut down like the orchard: Mme. Ranevsky returns to Paris to the same man who has consumed her (spilling money is typical of her waste); Gaev takes an uninspiring job in a bank; and Trofimov goes forth to collect more ideas.

Spilled *words* are part of the same difficulty, much talk being spent to little purpose because the distance between people is as vast as the distance between reality and dream-ideals. It is true that several characters experience warm enthusiasm for each other on the basis of a common nostalgia or a seemingly glowing future, but the bond always proves as impermanent as the vision. In pursuing a means of staging this nonculminating tangle, Chekhov invented an unusual kind of dialogue in which people talk and sometimes answer each other but seldom keep company. They rhapsodize or lament in each other's presence, responding whenever two of them hit upon the same topic, but for the most part they turn inward, forward, or backward to their private dreams.

In the opening scene, for instance, Dunyasha, ignoring the mood of her companion Anya, laughs, kisses her in greeting, and reveals that her impatience over their arrival is due not so much to a desire to see Anya as to her own state of excitement, for she has news: "The clerk, Epikhodov, proposed to me after Easter." We may appear to have promising material for a comedy here, this being the first of the several potential marriages that could conceivably create a fertile new life. But Epikhodov is scarcely one to generate excitement in Anya, used to Paris and tired from lack of sleep. She replies, "Always the same... (*Puts her hair straight*) I've lost all my hairpins." Startling as this intrusion of triviality seems, Dunyasha takes no offense, perhaps because Anya's response registers no more with her than the proposal from Epikhodov registers with Anya.

This dialogue is typical: like the handling of critical scenes, it arouses expectations and then dashes them. The second act is a skillful progression of relevant irrelevance, of apparently disjunctive sequences of character groupings and speeches that despite their apparent randomness add up to a statement on the encroaching of the new order (symbolized by the industrial town in the distance), the encroaching chill against which Fiers tries to protect his master, and the emptiness of the various age groups and classes (all of these summed up in the awkward music of Epikhodov and the breaking of the cosmic string). The gentle emotions of evening are disrupted by the sinister movement of time, as Gaev's rhetoric in celebration of an imaginary transcendental nature breaks apart against what nature is. The act ends with a typical maimed ceremony as the shouts of Varya interrupt the idealistic dreaming of Trofimov and Anya.

The ending of the play, a pause in the flow of disjunctive moments, is perhaps the most effective of the play's broken social rites. It is marked by the cutting of the trees and the repeated sound of the breaking string, as though the creation and the orchard were coming down together. But just as it may seem that the action is concluding operatically, with sweet parting, we realize that each is taking merely another faltering step in pursuit of private mirages, while the axes chip away freely at Mme. Ranevsky's personal history (her truth) to build Lopakhin's intangible future. Neither what is lost nor what is gained in the reversal has the elevation of tragic suffering or enlightenment.

The Cherry Orchard

A COMEDY IN FOUR ACTS

LUBOV ANDREYEVNA RANEVSKY (MME. RANEVSKY) *a landowner*
ANYA *her daughter, aged seventeen*
VARYA (BARBARA) *her adopted daughter, aged twenty-seven*
LEONID ANDREYEVITCH GAEV MME. RANEVSKY'S *brother*
ERMOLAI ALEXEYEVITCH LOPAKHIN *a merchant*
PETER SERGEYEVITCH TROFIMOV *a student*
BORIS BORISOVITCH SIMEONOV-PISCHIN *a landowner*

CHARLOTTA IVANOVNA *a governess*
SIMEON PANTELEYEVITCH EPIKHODOV *a clerk*
DUNYASHA (AVDOTYA FEDOROVNA) *a maid-servant*
FIERS *an old footman, aged eighty-seven*
YASHA *a young footman*
A TRAMP
A STATION-MASTER
POST OFFICE CLERK
GUESTS
A SERVANT

The action takes place on MME. RANEVSKY'S *estate.*

ACT I

A room which is still called the nursery. One of the doors leads into ANYA'S *room. It is close on sunrise. It is May. The cherry trees are in flower, but it is chilly in the garden. There is an early frost. The windows of the room are shut.* DUNYASHA *comes in with a candle, and* LOPAKHIN *with a book in his hand.*

LOPAKHIN. The train's arrived, thank God. What's the time?

DUNYASHA. It will soon be two. [*Blows out candle.*] It is light already.

LOPAKHIN. How much was the train late? Two hours at least. [*Yawns and stretches himself.*] I have made a rotten mess of it! I came here on purpose to meet them at the station, and then overslept myself...in my chair. It's a pity. I wish you'd wakened me.

DUNYASHA. I thought you'd gone away. [*listening*] I think I hear them coming.

LOPAKHIN. [*Listens.*] No....They've got to collect their luggage and so on. ...[*Pause.*] Lubov Andreyevna has been living abroad for five years; I don't know what she'll be like now. ...She's a good sort—an easy, simple person. I remember when I was a boy of fifteen, my father, who is dead —he used to keep a shop in the village here—hit me on the face with his fist, and my nose bled....We had gone into the yard together for something or other, and he was a little drunk. Lubov Andreyevna, as I re-

From Six Famous Plays *by Anton Tchekov, translated by Julius West. Copyright* © *by Gerald Duckworth & Co. Ltd. Reprinted by permission of Gerald Duckworth & Co. Ltd.*

member her now, was still young, and very thin, and she took me to the washstand here in this very room, the nursery. She said, "Don't cry, little man, it'll be all right in time for your wedding." [*Pause.*] "Little man".... My father was a peasant, it's true, but here I am in a white waistcoat and yellow shoes...a pearl out of an oyster. I'm rich now, with lots of money, but just think about it and examine me, and you'll find I'm still a peasant down to the marrow of my bones. [*Turns over the pages of his book.*] Here I've been reading this book, but I understood nothing. I read and fell asleep. [*Pause.*]

DUNYASHA. The dogs didn't sleep all night; they know that they're coming.

LOPAKHIN. What's up with you, Dunyasha...?

DUNYASHA. My hands are shaking. I shall faint.

LOPAKHIN. You're too sensitive, Dunyasha. You dress just like a lady, and you do your hair like one too. You oughtn't. You should know your place.

EPIKHODOV. [*Enters with a bouquet. He wears a short jacket and brilliantly polished boots, which squeak audibly. He drops the bouquet as he enters, then picks it up.*] The gardener sent these; says they're to go into the dining room.

[*Gives the bouquet to* DUNYASHA.]

LOPAKHIN. And you'll bring me some kvass.

DUNYASHA. Very well.   [*Exit.*]

EPIKHODOV. There's a frost this morning—three degrees, and the cherry trees are all in flower. I can't approve of our climate. [*Sighs.*] I can't. Our climate is indisposed to favor us even this once. And, Ermolai Alexeyevitch, allow me to say to you, in addition, that I bought myself some boots two days ago, and I beg to assure you that they squeak in a per-

fectly unbearable manner. What shall I put on them?

LOPAKHIN. Go away. You bore me.

EPIKHODOV. Some misfortune happens to me every day. But I don't complain; I'm used to it, and I can smile.

[DUNYASHA *comes in and brings* LOPAKHIN *some kvass.*]

I shall go. [*Knocks over a chair.*] There.... [*triumphantly*] There, you see, if I may use the word, what circumstances I am in, so to speak. It is even simply marvelous.   [*Exit.*]

DUNYASHA. I may confess to you, Ermolai Alexeyevitch, that Epikhodov has proposed to me.

LOPAKHIN. Ah!

DUNYASHA. I don't know what to do about it. He's a nice young man, but every now and again, when he begins talking, you can't understand a word he's saying. I think I like him. He's madly in love with me. He's an unlucky man; every day something happens. We tease him about it. They call him "two-and-twenty troubles."

LOPAKHIN. [*Listens.*] There they come, I think.

DUNYASHA. They're coming! What's the matter with me? I'm cold all over.

LOPAKHIN. There they are, right enough. Let's go and meet them. Will she know me? We haven't seen each other for five years.

DUNYASHA [*excited*]. I shall faint in a minute....Oh, I'm fainting!

[*Two carriages are heard driving up to the house.* LOPAKHIN *and* DUNYASHA *quickly go out. The stage is empty. A noise begins in the next room.* FIERS, *leaning on a stick, walks quickly across the stage; he has just been to meet* LUBOV ANDREYEVNA. *He wears an old-fashioned livery and a tall hat. He is saying something to himself, but not a word of it can be made out. The noise behind the stage gets louder and louder. A voice is heard:* "Let's go in there."

Enter LUBOV ANDREYEVNA, ANYA, *and* CHARLOTTA IVANOVNA *with a little dog on a chain and all dressed in traveling clothes,* VARYA *in a long coat and with a kerchief on her head.* GAEV, SIMEONOV-PISCHIN, LOPAKHIN, DUN-YASHA *with a parcel and an umbrella, and a servant with luggage—all cross the room.*]

ANYA. Let's come through here. Do you remember what this room is, mother?
LUBOV [*joyfully, through her tears*]. The nursery!
VARYA. How cold it is! My hands are quite numb. [*to* LUBOV ANDRE-YEVNA] Your rooms, the white one and the violet one, are just as they used to be, mother.
LUBOV. My dear nursery, oh, you beautiful room.... I used to sleep here when I was a baby. [*Kisses her brother,* VARYA, *then her brother again.*] And Varya is just as she used to be, just like a nun. And I knew Dunyasha. [*Kisses her.*]
GAEV. The train was two hours late. There now; how's that for punctuality?
CHARLOTTA [*to* PISCHIN]. My dog eats nuts too.
PISCHIN [*astonished*]. To think of that, now!

[*All go out except* ANYA *and* DUNYA-SHA.]

DUNYASHA. We did have to wait for you! [*Takes off* ANYA's *cloak and hat.*]
ANYA.... I didn't get any sleep for four nights on the journey.... I'm awfully cold.
DUNYASHA. You went away during Lent, when it was snowing and frosty, but now? Darling! [*Laughs and kisses her.*] We did have to wait for you, my joy, my pet.... I must tell you at once, I can't bear to wait a minute.
ANYA [*tired*]. Something else now ...?
DUNYASHA. The clerk, Epikhodov, pro-

posed to me after Easter.
ANYA. Always the same.... [*Puts her hair straight.*] I've lost all my hair-pins. ...

[*She is very tired and even staggers as she walks.*]

DUNYASHA. I don't know what to think about it. He loves me, he loves me so much!
ANYA. [*Looks into her room; in a gentle voice:*] My room, my windows, as if I'd never gone away. I'm at home! Tomorrow morning I'll get up and have a run in the garden.... Oh, if I could only get to sleep! I didn't sleep the whole journey, I was so bothered.
DUNYASHA. Peter Sergeyevitch came two days ago.
ANYA [*joyfully*]. Peter!
DUNYASHA. He sleeps in the bath house, he lives there. He said he was afraid he'd be in the way. [*Looks at her pocketwatch.*] I ought to wake him, but Barbara Mihailovna told me not to. "Don't wake him," she said.

[*Enter* VARYA, *a bunch of keys on her belt.*]

VARYA. Dunyasha, some coffee, quick. Mother wants some.
DUNYASHA. This minute. [*Exit.*]
VARYA. Well, you've come, glory be to God. Home again. [*caressing her*] My darling is back again! My pretty one is back again!
ANYA. I did have an awful time, I tell you.
VARYA. I can just imagine it!
ANYA. I went away in Holy Week; it was very cold then. Charlotta talked the whole way and would go on performing her tricks. Why did you tie Charlotta on to me?
VARYA. You couldn't go alone, darling, at seventeen!
ANYA. We went to Paris; it's cold there and snowing. I talk French perfectly horribly. My mother lives on the fifth

floor. I go to her, and find her there with various Frenchmen, women, an old abbé with a book, and everything in tobacco smoke and with no comfort at all. I suddenly became very sorry for mother—so sorry that I took her head in my arms and hugged her and wouldn't let her go. Then mother started hugging me and crying. . . .

VARYA [*weeping*]. Don't say any more, don't say any more. . . .

ANYA. She's already sold her villa near Mentone; she's nothing left, nothing. And I haven't a copeck left either; we only just managed to get here. And mother won't understand! We had dinner at a station; she asked for all the expensive things, and tipped the waiters one rouble each. And Charlotta too. Yasha wants his share too—it's too bad. Mother's got a footman now, Yasha; we've brought him here.

VARYA. I saw the wretch.

ANYA. How's business? Has the interest been paid?

VARYA. Not much chance of that.

ANYA. Oh God, oh God. . . .

VARYA. The place will be sold in August.

ANYA. O God. . . .

LOPAKHIN. [*Looks in at the door and moos.*] Moo!. . .   [*Exit.*]

VARYA [*through her tears*]. I'd like to. . . . [*Shakes her fist.*]

ANYA. [*Embraces* VARYA, *softly:*] Varya, has he proposed to you? [VARYA *shakes her head.*] But he loves you. . . . Why don't you make up your minds? Why do you keep on waiting?

VARYA. I think that it will all come to nothing. He's a busy man. I'm not his affair. . .he pays no attention to me. Bless the man, I don't want to see him. . . . But everybody talks about our marriage, everybody congratulates me, and there's nothing in it at all, it's all like a dream. [*in an-other tone*] You've got a brooch like a bee.

ANYA [*sadly*]. Mother bought it. [*Goes into her room and talks lightly, like a child.*] In Paris I went up in a balloon!

VARYA. My darling's come back, my pretty one's come back! [DUNYASHA *has already returned with the coffee-pot and is making the coffee.*] I go about all day, looking after the house, and I think all the time, if only you could marry a rich man, then I'd be happy and would go away somewhere by myself, then to Kiev. . .to Moscow, and so on, from one holy place to another. I'd tramp and tramp. That would be splendid!

ANYA. The birds are singing in the garden. What time is it now?

VARYA. It must be getting on for three. Time you went to sleep, darling. [*Goes into* ANYA's *room.*] Splendid!

[*Enter* YASHA *with a plaid shawl and a traveling bag.*]

YASHA. [*crossing the stage; politely:*] May I go this way?

DUNYASHA. I hardly knew you, Yasha. You have changed abroad.

YASHA. Hm. . .and who are you?

DUNYASHA. When you went away I was only so high. [*showing with her hand*] I'm Dunyasha, the daughter of Theodore Kozoyedov. You don't remember!

YASHA. Oh, you little cucumber!

[*Looks round and embraces her. She screams and drops a saucer.* YASHA *goes out quickly.*]

VARYA. [*in the doorway; in an angry voice:*] What's that?

DUNYASHA [*through her tears*]. I've broken a saucer.

VARYA. It may bring luck.

ANYA [*coming out of her room*]. We must tell mother that Peter's here.

VARYA. I told them not to wake him.

ANYA [*thoughtfully*]. Father died six

years ago, and a month later my brother Grisha was drowned in the river—such a dear little boy of seven! Mother couldn't bear it; she went away, away, without looking round.... [*Shudders.*] How I understand her; if only she knew! And Peter Trofimov was Grisha's tutor, he might tell her....

[*Enter* FIERS *in a short jacket and white waistcoat.*]

FIERS. [*Goes to the coffeepot, nervously:*] The mistress is going to have some food here.... [*Puts on white gloves.*] Is the coffee ready? [*to* DUNYASHA, *severely*] You! Where's the cream?

DUNYASHA. Oh, dear me...!

[*Rapid exit.*]

FIERS [*fussing round the coffeepot*]. Oh, you bungler.... [*Murmurs to himself.*] Back from Paris...the master went to Paris once...in a carriage.... [*Laughs.*]

VARYA. What are you talking about, Fiers?

FIERS. I beg your pardon? [*joyfully*] The mistress is home again. I've lived to see her! Don't care if I die now. ...[*Weeps with joy.*]

[*Enter* LUBOV ANDREYEVNA, GAEV, LOPAKHIN, *and* SIMEONOV-PISCHIN, *the latter in a long jacket of thin cloth and loose trousers.* GAEV, *coming in, moves his arms and body about as if he is playing billiards.*]

LUBOV. Let me remember now. Red into the corner! Twice into the center!

GAEV. Right into the pocket! Once upon a time you and I used both to sleep in this room, and now I'm fifty-one; it does seem strange.

LOPAKHIN. Yes, time does go.

GAEV. Who does?

LOPAKHIN. I said that time does go.

GAEV. It smells of patchouli here.

ANYA. I'm going to bed. Good night, mother. [*Kisses her.*]

LUBOV. My lovely little one. [*Kisses her hand.*] Glad to be at home? I can't get over it.

ANYA. Good night, uncle.

GAEV. [*Kisses her face and hands.*] God be with you. How you do resemble your mother! [*to his sister*] You were just like her at her age, Luba.

[ANYA *gives her hand to* LOPAKHIN *and* PISCHIN *and goes out, shutting the door behind her.*]

LUBOV. She's awfully tired.

PISCHIN. It's a very long journey.

VARYA [*to* LOPAKHIN *and* PISCHIN]. Well, sirs, it's getting on for three, quite time you went.

LUBOV. [*Laughs.*] You're just the same as ever, Varya. [*Draws her close and kisses her.*] I'll have some coffee now, then we'll all go. [FIERS *lays a cushion under her feet.*] Thank you, dear. I'm used to coffee. I drink it day and night. Thank you, dear old man. [*Kisses* FIERS.]

VARYA. I'll go and see if they've brought in all the luggage. [*Exit.*]

LUBOV. Is it really I who am sitting here? [*Laughs.*] I want to jump about and wave my arms. [*Covers her face with her hands.*] But suppose I'm dreaming! God knows I love my own country, I love it deeply; I couldn't look out of the railway carriage, I cried so much. [*through her tears*] Still, I must have my coffee. Thank you, Fiers. Thank you, dear old man. I'm so glad you're still with us.

FIERS. The day before yesterday.

GAEV. He doesn't hear well.

LOPAKHIN. I've got to go off to Kharkov by the five o'clock train. I'm awfully sorry! I should like to have a look at you, to gossip a little. You're as fine looking as ever.

PISCHIN. [*Breathes heavily.*] Even finer looking...dressed in Paris fashions ...confound it all.

LOPAKHIN. Your brother, Leonid Andreyevitch, says I'm a snob, a usurer, but that is absolutely nothing to me. Let him talk. Only I do wish you would believe in me as you once did, that your wonderful, touching eyes would look at me as they did before. Merciful God! My father was the serf of your grandfather and your own father, but you—you more than anybody else—did so much for me once upon a time that I've forgotten everything and love you as if you belonged to my family...and even more.

LUBOV. I can't sit still, I'm not in a state to do it. [*Jumps up and walks about in great excitement.*] I'll never survive this happiness....You can laugh at me; I'm a silly woman.... My dear little cupboard. [*Kisses cupboard.*] My little table.

GAEV. Nurse has died in your absence.

LUBOV. [*Sits and drinks coffee.*] Yes, bless her soul. I heard by letter.

GAEV. And Anastasius has died too. Peter Kosoy has left me and now lives in town with the commissioner of police.

[*Takes a box of sugar candy out of his pocket and sucks a piece.*]

PISCHIN. My daughter, Dashenka, sends her love.

LOPAKHIN. I want to say something very pleasant, very delightful, to you. [*Looks at his watch.*] I'm going away at once, I haven't much time...but I'll tell you all about it in two or three words. As you already know, your cherry orchard is to be sold to pay your debts, and the sale is fixed for August 22; but you needn't be alarmed, dear madam, you may sleep in peace; there's a way out. Here's my plan. Please attend carefully! Your estate is only thirteen miles from the town, the railway runs by, and if the cherry orchard and the land by the river are broken up into building lots and are then leased off for villas you'll get at least twenty-five thousand roubles a year profit out of it.

GAEV. How utterly absurd!

LUBOV. I don't understand you at all, Ermolai Alexeyevitch.

LOPAKHIN. You will get twenty-five roubles a year for each dessiatin from the leaseholders at the very least, and if you advertise now I'm willing to bet that you won't have a vacant plot left by the autumn; they'll all go. In a word, you're saved. I congratulate you. Only, of course, you'll have to put things straight, and clean up....For instance, you'll have to pull down all the old buildings, this house, which isn't any use to anybody now, and cut down the old cherry orchard...

LUBOV. Cut it down? My dear man, you must excuse me, but you don't understand anything at all. If there's anything interesting or remarkable in the whole province, it's this cherry orchard of ours.

LOPAKHIN. The only remarkable thing about the orchard is that it's very large. It only bears fruit every other year, and even then you don't know what to do with it; nobody buys any.

GAEV. This orchard is mentioned in the "Encyclopædic Dictionary."

LOPAKHIN. [*Looks at his watch.*] If we can't think of anything and don't make up our minds to anything, then on August 22 both the cherry orchard and the whole estate will be up for auction. Make up your mind! I swear there's no other way out, I'll swear it again.

FIERS. In the old days, forty or fifty years back, they dried the cherries, soaked them and pickled them, and made jam of them, and it used to happen that...

GAEV. Be quiet, Fiers.

FIERS. And then we'd send the dried cherries off in carts to Moscow and Kharkov. And money! And the dried cherries were soft, juicy, sweet, and nicely scented...They knew the way....

LUBOV. What was the way?

FIERS. They've forgotten. Nobody remembers.

PISCHIN [*to* LUBOV ANDREYEVNA]. What about Paris? Eh? Did you eat frogs?

LUBOV. I ate crocodiles.

PISCHIN. To think of that, now.

LOPAKHIN. Up to now in the villages there were only the gentry and the laborers, and now the people who live in villas have arrived. All towns now, even small ones, are surrounded by villas. And it's safe to say that in twenty years' time the villa resident will be all over the place. At present he sits on his balcony and drinks tea, but it may well come to pass that he'll begin to cultivate his patch of land, and then your cherry orchard will be happy, rich, splendid....

GAEV [*angry*]. What rot!

[*Enter* VARYA *and* YASHA.]

VARYA. There are two telegrams for you, little mother. [*Picks out a key and noisily unlocks an antique cupboard.*] Here they are.

LUBOV. They're from Paris.... [*Tears them up without reading them.*] I've done with Paris.

GAEV. And do you know, Luba, how old this case is? A week ago I took out the bottom drawer; I looked and saw figures burnt out in it. That case was made exactly a hundred years ago. What do you think of that? What? We could celebrate its jubilee. It hasn't a soul of its own, but still, say what you will, it's a fine bookcase.

PISCHIN [*astonished*]. A hundred years. ...Think of that!

GAEV. Yes...it's a real thing. [*handling it*] My dear and honored case! I congratulate you on your existence, which has already for more than a hundred years been directed toward the bright ideals of good and justice;

your silent call to productive labor has not grown less in the hundred years [*weeping*] during which you have upheld virtue and faith in a better future to the generations of our race, educating us up to ideals of goodness and to the knowledge of a common consciousness. [*Pause.*]

LOPAKHIN. Yes.

LUBOV. You're just the same as ever, Leon.

GAEV [*a little confused*]. Off the white on the right, into the corner pocket. Red ball goes into the middle pocket!

LOPAKHIN. [*Looks at his watch.*] It's time I went.

YASHA [*giving* LUBOV ANDREYEVNA *her medicine*]. Will you take your pills now?

PISCHIN. You oughtn't to take medicines, dear madam; they do you neither harm nor good.... Give them here, dear madam. [*Takes the pills, turns them out into the palm of his hand, blows on them, puts them into his mouth, and drinks some kvass.*] There!

LUBOV [*frightened*]. You're off your head!

PISCHIN. I've taken all the pills.

LOPAKHIN. Gormandizer! [*All laugh.*]

FIERS. They were here in Easter week and ate half a pailful of cucumbers. ...[*Mumbles.*]

LUBOV. What's he driving at?

VARYA. He's been mumbling away for three years. We're used to that.

YASHA. Senile decay.

[CHARLOTTA IVANOVNA *crosses the stage, dressed in white: She is very thin and tightly laced, has a lorgnette at her waist.*]

LOPAKHIN. Excuse me, Charlotta Ivanovna, I haven't said "How do you do" to you yet. [*Tries to kiss her hand.*]

CHARLOTTA. [*Takes her hand away.*] If you let people kiss your hand, then they'll want your elbow, then your shoulder, and then...

LOPAKHIN. My luck's out today! [*All laugh.*] Show us a trick, Charlotta Ivanovna!

LUBOV ANDREYEVNA. Charlotta, do us a trick.

CHARLOTTA. It's not necessary. I want to go to bed.   [*Exit.*]

LOPAKHIN. We shall see each other in three weeks. [*Kisses* LUBOV ANDRE-YEVNA's *hand.*] Now, goodbye. It's time to go. [*to* GAEV] See you again. [*Kisses* PISCHIN.] Au revoir. [*Gives his hand to* VARYA, *then to* FIERS *and to* YASHA.] I don't want to go away. [*to* LUBOV ANDREYEVNA] If you think about the villas and make up your mind, then just let me know, and I'll raise a loan of 50,000 roubles at once. Think about it seriously.

VARYA [*angrily*]. Do go, now!

LOPAKHIN. I'm going, I'm going....

[*Exit.*]

GAEV. Snob. Still, I beg pardon.... Varya's going to marry him, he's Varya's young man.

VARYA. Don't talk too much, uncle.

LUBOV. Why not, Varya? I should be very glad. He's a good man.

PISCHIN. To speak the honest truth... he's a worthy man.... And my Dashenka...also says that...she says lots of things. [*Snores but wakes up again at once.*] But still, dear madam, if you could lend me... 240 roubles...to pay the interest on my mortgage tomorrow...

VARYA [*frightened*]. We haven't got it, we haven't got it!

LUBOV. It's quite true. I've nothing at all.

PISCHIN. I'll find it all right. [*Laughs.*] I never lose hope. I used to think, "Everything's lost now. I'm a dead man," when, lo and behold, a railway was built over my land...and they paid me for it. And something else will happen today or tomorrow. Dashenka may win 20,000 roubles... she's got a ticket.

LUBOV. The coffee's all gone, we can go to bed.

FIERS. [*brushing* GAEV's *trousers; in an insistent tone:*] You've put on the wrong trousers again. What am I to do with you?

VARYA [*quietly*]. Anya's asleep. [*Opens window quietly.*] The sun has risen already; it isn't cold. Look, little mother: what lovely trees! And the air! The starlings are singing!

GAEV. [*Opens the other window.*] The whole garden's white. You haven't forgotten, Luba? There's that long avenue going straight, straight, like a stretched strap; it shines on moonlight nights. Do you remember? You haven't forgotten?

LUBOV. [*Looks out into the garden.*] Oh, my childhood, days of my innocence! In this nursery I used to sleep; I used to look out from here into the orchard. Happiness used to wake with me every morning, and then it was just as it is now; nothing has changed. [*Laughs from joy.*] It's all, all white! Oh, my orchard! After the dark autumns and the cold winters, you're young again, full of happiness, the angels of heaven haven't left you.... If only I could take my heavy burden off my breast and shoulders, if I could forget my past!

GAEV. Yes, and they'll sell this orchard to pay off debts. How strange it seems!

LUBOV. Look, there's my dead mother going in the orchard...dressed in white! [*Laughs from joy.*] That's she.

GAEV. Where?

VARYA. God bless you, little mother.

LUBOV. There's nobody there; I thought I saw somebody. On the right, at the turning by the summer house, a white little tree bent down, looking just like a woman.

[*Enter* TROFIMOV *in a worn student uniform and spectacles.*]

What a marvelous garden! White masses of flowers, the blue sky....

TROFIMOV. Lubov Andreyevna! [*She looks round at him.*] I only want to show myself, and I'll go away. [*Kisses her hand warmly.*] I was told to wait till the morning, but I didn't have the patience.

[LUBOV ANDREYEVNA *looks surprised.*]

VARYA [*crying*]. It's Peter Trofimov.
TROFIMOV. Peter Trofimov, once the tutor of your Grisha.... Have I changed so much?

[LUBOV ANDREYEVNA *embraces him and cries softly.*]

GAEV [*confused*]. That's enough, that's enough, Luba.
VARYA. [*Weeps.*] But I told you, Peter, to wait till tomorrow.
LUBOV. My Grisha...my boy...Grisha ...my son.
VARYA. What are we to do, little mother? It's the will of God.
TROFIMOV [*softly, through his tears*]. It's all right, it's all right.
LUBOV [*still weeping*]. My boy's dead; he was drowned. Why? Why, my friend? [*softly*] Anya's asleep in there. I am speaking so loudly, making such a noise.... Well, Peter? What's made you look so bad? Why have you grown so old?
TROFIMOV. In the train an old woman called me a decayed gentleman.
LUBOV. You were quite a boy then, a nice little student, and now your hair is not at all thick and you wear spectacles. Are you really still a student?

[*Goes to the door.*]

TROFIMOV. I suppose I shall always be a student.
LUBOV. [*Kisses her brother, then* VARYA.] Well, let's go to bed. ... And you've grown older, Leonid.
PISCHIN. [*Follows her.*] Yes, we've got to go to bed.... Oh, my gout! I'll stay the night here. If only, Lubov Andreyevna, my dear, you could get me 240 roubles tomorrow morning—
GAEV. Still the same story.
PISCHIN. Two hundred and forty roubles...to pay the interest on the mortgage.

LUBOV. I haven't any money, dear man.
PISCHIN. I'll give it back...it's a small sum....
LUBOV. Well, then, Leonid will give it to you.... Let him have it, Leonid.
GAEV. By all means; hold out your hand.
LUBOV. Why not? He wants it; he'll give it back.

[LUBOV ANDREYEVNA, TROFIMOV, PISCHIN, *and* FIERS *go out.* GAEV, VARYA, *and* YASHA *remain.*]

GAEV. My sister hasn't lost the habit of throwing money about. [*to* YASHA] Stand off, do; you smell of poultry.
YASHA. [*Grins.*] You are just the same as ever, Leonid Andreyevitch.
GAEV. Really? [*to* VARYA] What's he saying?
VARYA [*to* YASHA]. Your mother's come from the village; she's been sitting in the servants' room since yesterday, and wants to see you....
YASHA. Bless the woman!
VARYA. Shameless man.
YASHA. A lot of use there is in her coming. She might have come tomorrow just as well. [*Exit.*]
VARYA. Mother hasn't altered a scrap, she's just as she always was. She'd give away everything, if the idea only entered her head.
GAEV. Yes.... [*Pause.*] If there's any illness for which people offer many remedies, you may be sure that particular illness is incurable, I think. I work my brains to their hardest. I've several remedies, very many, and that really means I've none at all. It would be nice to inherit a fortune from somebody, it would be nice to marry our Anya to a rich man, it would be nice to go to Yaroslav and try my luck with my aunt the Countess. My aunt is very, very rich.
VARYA. [*Weeps.*] If only God helped us.
GAEV. Don't cry. My aunt's very rich, but she doesn't like us. My sister, in

the first place, married an advocate, not a noble. . . . [ANYA *appears in the doorway.*] She not only married a man who was not a noble, but she behaved herself in a way which cannot be described as proper. She's nice and kind and charming, and I'm very fond of her, but say what you will in her favor and you still have to admit that she's wicked; you can feel it in her slightest movements.

VARYA. [*Whispers.*] Anya's in the doorway.

GAEV. Really? [*Pause.*] It's curious, something's got into my right eye... I can't see properly out of it. And on Thursday, when I was at the District Court...

[*Enter* ANYA.]

VARYA. Why aren't you in bed, Anya?

ANYA. Can't sleep. It's no good.

GAEV. My darling! [*Kisses* ANYA's *face and hands.*] My child. . . . [*crying*] You're not my niece, you're my angel, you're my all. . . . Believe in me, believe...

ANYA. I do believe in you, uncle. Everybody loves you and respects you... but, uncle dear, you ought to say nothing, no more than that. What were you saying just now about my mother, your own sister? Why did you say those things?

GAEV. Yes, yes. [*Covers his face with her hand.*] Yes, really, it was awful. Save me, my God! And only just now I made a speech before a bookcase...it's so silly! And only when I'd finished I knew how silly it was.

VARYA. Yes, uncle dear, you really ought to say less. Keep quiet, that's all.

ANYA. You'd be so much happier in yourself if you only kept quiet.

GAEV. All right, I'll be quiet. [*Kisses their hands.*] I'll be quiet. But let's talk business. On Thursday I was in the District Court, and a lot of us met there together, and we began to talk of this, that, and the other, and

now I think I can arrange a loan to pay the interest into the bank.

VARYA. If only God would help us!

GAEV. I'll go on Tuesday. I'll talk to you about it again. [*to* VARYA] Don't howl. [*to* ANYA] Your mother will have a talk to Lopakhin; he, of course, won't refuse...And when you've rested you'll go to Yaroslav to the Countess, your grandmother. So you see, we'll have three irons in the fire, and we'll be safe. We'll pay up the interest. I'm certain. [*Puts some sugar candy into his mouth.*] I swear on my honor, on anything you will, that the estate will not be sold! [*excitedly*] I swear on my happiness! Here's my hand. You may call me a dishonorable wretch if I let it go to auction! I swear by all I am!

ANYA. [*She is calm again and happy.*] How good and clever you are, uncle. [*Embraces him.*] I'm happy now! I'm happy! All's well!

[*Enter* FIERS.]

FIERS [*reproachfully*]. Leonid Andreyevitch, don't you fear God? When are you going to bed?

GAEV. Soon, soon. You go away, Fiers. I'll undress myself. Well, children, bye-bye...! I'll give you the details tomorrow, but let's go to bed now. [*Kisses* ANYA *and* VARYA.] I'm a man of the eighties. . . . People don't praise those years much, but I can still say that I've suffered for my beliefs. The peasants don't love me for nothing, I assure you. We've got to learn to know the peasants! We ought to learn how. . . .

ANYA. You're doing it again, uncle!

VARYA. Be quiet, uncle!

FIERS [*angrily*]. Leonid Andreyevitch!

GAEV. I'm coming, I'm coming. . . . Go to bed now. Off two cushions into the middle! I turn over a new leaf. . . .

[*Exit.* FIERS *goes out after him.*]

ANYA. I'm quieter now. I don't want to go to Yaroslav, I don't like grandmother; but I'm calm now, thanks to uncle. [*Sits down.*]

VARYA. It's time to go to sleep. I'll go. There's been an unpleasantness here while you were away. In the old servants' part of the house, as you know, only the old people live—little old Efim and Polya and Evstigney, and Karp as well. They started letting some tramps or other spend the night there—I said nothing. Then I heard that they were saying that I had ordered them to be fed on peas and nothing else; from meanness, you see.... And it was all Evstigney's doing.... Very well, I thought, if that's what the matter is, just you wait. So I call Evstigney....[*Yawns.*] He comes. "What's this," I say, "Evstigney, you old fool...." [*Looks

at ANYA.*] Anya dear! [*Pause.*] She's dropped off.... [*Takes ANYA's arm.*] Let's go to bye-bye.... Come along! ...[*Leads her.*] My darling's gone to sleep! Come on....

[*They go. In the distance, the other side of the orchard, a shepherd plays his pipe. TROFIMOV crosses the stage and stops on seeing VARYA and ANYA.*]

Sh! She's asleep, asleep. Come on, dear.

ANYA [*quietly, half asleep*]. I'm so tired...all the bells...uncle, dear! Mother and uncle!

VARYA. Come on, dear, come on!

[*They go into ANYA's room.*]

TROFIMOV [*moved*]. My sun! My spring!

ACT II

In a field. An old, crooked shrine, which has been long abandoned; near it a well and large stones, which apparently are old tombstones, and an old garden seat. The road is seen to GAEV's estate. On one side rise dark poplars, behind them begins the cherry orchard. In the distance is a row of telegraph poles, and far, far away on the horizon are the indistinct signs of a large town, which can only be seen on the finest and clearest days. It is close on sunset. CHARLOTTA, YASHA, and DUNYASHA are sitting on the seat; EPIKHODOV stands by and plays on a guitar; all seem thoughtful. CHARLOTTA wears a man's old peaked cap; she has unslung a rifle from her shoulders and is putting to rights the buckle on the strap.

CHARLOTTA [*thoughtfully*]. I haven't a real passport. I don't know how old I am, and I think I'm young. When I was a little girl my father and mother used to go round fairs and give very good performances and I used to do the *salto mortale* and various little

things. And when papa and mamma died a German lady took me to her and began to teach me. I liked it. I grew up and became a governess. And where I came from and who I am, I don't know.... Who my parents were—perhaps they weren't married —I don't know. [*Takes a cucumber out of her pocket and eats.*] I don't know anything. [*Pause.*] I do want to talk, but I haven't anybody to talk to...I haven't anybody at all.

EPIKHODOV. [*Plays on the guitar and sings:*]
"What is this noisy earth to me,
What matter friends and foes?"
I do like playing on the mandolin!

DUNYASHA. That's a guitar, not a mandolin.

[*Looks at herself in a little mirror and powders herself.*]

EPIKHODOV. For the enamored madman, this is a mandolin. [*Sings:*]
"Oh that the heart was warmed,
By all the flames of love returned!"

[YASHA *sings too.*]

CHARLOTTA. These people sing terribly.
...Foo! Like jackals.

DUNYASHA [*to* YASHA]. Still, it must be nice to live abroad.

YASHA. Yes, certainly. I cannot differ from you there.

[*Yawns and lights a cigar.*]

EPIKHODOV. That is perfectly natural. Abroad everything is in full complexity.

YASHA. That goes without saying.

EPIKHODOV. I'm an educated man, I read various remarkable books, but I cannot understand the direction I myself want to go—whether to live or to shoot myself, as it were. So, in case, I always carry a revolver about with me. Here it is.

[*Shows a revolver.*]

CHARLOTTA. I've done. Now I'll go. [*Slings the rifle.*] You, Epikhodov, are a very clever man and very terrible; women must be madly in love with you. Brrr! [*going*] These wise ones are all so stupid. I've nobody to talk to. I'm always alone, alone; I've nobody at all...and I don't know who I am or why I live.

[*Exit slowly.*]

EPIKHODOV. As a matter of fact, independently of everything else, I must express my feeling, among other things, that fate has been as pitiless in her dealings with me as a storm is to a small ship. Suppose, let us grant, I am wrong; then why did I wake up this morning, to give an example, and behold an enormous spider on my chest, like that. [*Shows with both hands.*] And if I do drink some kvass, why is it that there is bound to be something of the most indelicate nature in it, such as a beetle? [*Pause.*] Have you read Buckle? [*Pause.*] I should like to

trouble you, Avdotya Fedorovna, for two words.

DUNYASHA. Say on.

EPIKHODOV. I should prefer to be alone with you. [*Sighs.*]

DUNYASHA [*shy*]. Very well, only first bring me my little cloak....It's by the cupboard. It's a little damp here.

EPIKHODOV. Very well...I'll bring it. ...Now I know what to do with my revolver.

[*Takes guitar and exit, strumming.*]

YASHA. Two-and-twenty troubles! A silly man, between you and me and the gatepost. [*Yawns.*]

DUNYASHA. I hope to goodness he won't shoot himself. [*Pause.*] I'm so nervous, I'm worried. I went into service when I was quite a little girl, and now I'm not used to common life, and my hands are white, white as a lady's. I'm so tender and so delicate now, respectable and afraid of everything. ...I'm so frightened. And I don't know what will happen to my nerves if you deceive me, Yasha.

YASHA. [*Kisses her.*] Little cucumber! Of course, every girl must respect herself; there's nothing I dislike more than a badly behaved girl.

DUNYASHA. I'm awfully in love with you; you're educated, you can talk about everything. [*Pause.*]

YASHA. [*Yawns.*] Yes. I think this: if a girl loves anybody, then that means she's immoral. [*Pause.*] It's nice to smoke a cigar out in the open air.... [*Listens.*] Somebody's coming. It's the mistress, and people with her. [DUNYASHA *embraces him suddenly.*] Go to the house, as if you'd been bathing in the river; go by this path, or they'll meet you and will think I've been meeting you. I can't stand that sort of thing.

DUNYASHA. [*Coughs quietly.*] My head's aching because of your cigar.

[*Exit.* YASHA *remains, sitting by the*

shrine. Enter Lubov Andreyevna, Gaev, *and* Lopakhin.]

Lopakhin. You must make up your mind definitely—there's no time to waste. The question is perfectly plain. Are you willing to let the land for villas or no? Just one word, yes or no? Just one word!

Lubov. Who's smoking horrible cigars here? [*Sits.*]

Gaev. They built that railway; that's made this place very handy. [*Sits.*] Went to town and had lunch...red in the middle! I'd like to go in now and have just one game.

Lubov. You'll have time.

Lopakhin. Just one word! [*imploringly*] Give me an answer!

Gaev. [*Yawns.*] Really!

Lubov. [*Looks in her purse.*] I had a lot of money yesterday, but there's very little today. My poor Varya feeds everybody on milk soup to save money, in the kitchen the old people only get peas, and I spend recklessly. [*Drops the purse, scattering gold coins.*] There, they are all over the place.

Yasha. Permit me to pick them up.

[*Collects the coins.*]

Lubov. Please do, Yasha. And why did I go and have lunch there?...A horrid restaurant with band and tablecloths smelling of soap....Why do you drink so much, Leon? Why do you eat so much? Why do you talk so much? You talked again too much today in the restaurant, and it wasn't at all to the point—about the seventies and about decadents. And to whom? Talking to the waiters about decadents!

Lopakhin. Yes.

Gaev. [*Waves his hand.*] I can't be cured, that's obvious.... [*irritably to* Yasha] What's the matter? Why do you keep twisting about in front of me?

Yasha. [*Laughs.*] I can't listen to your voice without laughing.

Gaev [*to his sister*]. Either he or I...

Lubov. Go away, Yasha; get out of this....

Yasha. [*Gives purse to* Lubov Andreyevna.] I'll go at once. [*hardly able to keep from laughing*] This minute. ... [*Exit.*]

Lopakhin. That rich man Deriganov is preparing to buy your estate. They say he'll come to the sale himself.

Lubov. Where did you hear that?

Lopakhin. They say so in town.

Gaev. Our Yaroslav aunt has promised to send something, but I don't know when or how much.

Lopakhin. How much will she send? A hundred thousand roubles? Or two, perhaps?

Lubov. I'd be glad of ten or fifteen thousand.

Lopakhin. You must excuse my saying so, but I've never met such frivolous people as you before, or anybody so unbusinesslike and peculiar. Here I am telling you in plain language that your estate will be sold, and you don't seem to understand.

Lubov. What are we to do? Tell us, what?

Lopakhin. I tell you every day. I say the same thing every day. Both the cherry orchard and the land must be leased off for villas and at once, immediately—the auction is staring you in the face: Understand! Once you do definitely make up your minds to the villas, then you'll have as much money as you want and you'll be saved.

Lubov. Villas and villa residents—it's so vulgar, excuse me.

Gaev. I entirely agree with you.

Lopakhin. I must cry or yell or faint. I can't! You're too much for me! [*to* Gaev] You old woman!

Gaev. Really!

Lopakhin. Old woman! [*Going out.*]

Lubov [*frightened*]. No, don't go away, do stop; be a dear. Please.

Perhaps we'll find some way out!

LOPAKHIN. What's the good of trying to think!

LUBOV. Please don't go away. It's nicer when you're here.... [*Pause.*] I keep on waiting for something to happen, as if the house is going to collapse over our heads.

GAEV [*thinking deeply*]. Double in the corner...across the middle....

LUBOV. We have been too sinful....

LOPAKHIN. What sins have you committed?

GAEV. [*Puts candy into his mouth.*] They say that I've eaten all my substance in sugar candies. [*Laughs.*]

LUBOV. Oh, my sins.... I've always scattered money about without holding myself in, like a madwoman, and I married a man who made nothing but debts. My husband died of champagne—he drank terribly—and to my misfortune, I fell in love with another man and went off with him, and just at that time—it was my first punishment, a blow that hit me right on the head—here, in the river...my boy was drowned, and I went away, quite away, never to return, never to see this river again.... I shut my eyes and ran without thinking, but *he* ran after me...without pity, without respect. I bought a villa near Mentone because *he* fell ill there, and for three days I knew no rest either by day or night; the sick man wore me out, and my soul dried up. And last year, when they had sold the villa to pay my debts, I went away to Paris, and there he robbed me of all I had and threw me over and went off with another woman. I tried to poison myself.... It was so silly, so shameful.... And suddenly I longed to be back in Russia, my own land, with my little girl.... [*Wipes her tears.*] Lord, Lord be merciful to me, forgive me my sins! Punish me no more! [*Takes a telegram out of her pocket.*] I had this today from Paris.... He begs my forgiveness, he implores me to return.... [*Tears it up.*] Don't I hear music? [*Listens.*]

GAEV. That is our celebrated Jewish band. You remember—four violins, a flute, and a double bass.

LUBOV. So it still exists? It would be nice if they came along some evening.

LOPAKHIN. [*Listens.*] I can't hear.... [*Sings quietly.*] "For money will the Germans make a Frenchman of a Russian." [*Laughs.*] I saw such an awfully funny thing at the theater last night.

LUBOV. I'm quite sure there wasn't anything at all funny. You oughtn't to go and see plays, you ought to go and look at yourself. What a gray life you lead, what a lot you talk unnecessarily.

LOPAKHIN. It's true. To speak the straight truth, we live a silly life. [*Pause.*] My father was a peasant, an idiot, he understood nothing, he didn't teach me, he was always drunk, and always used a stick on me. In point of fact, I'm a fool and an idiot too. I've never learned anything, my handwriting is bad, I write so that I'm quite ashamed before people, like a pig!

LUBOV. You ought to get married, my friend.

LOPAKHIN. Yes...that's true.

LUBOV. Why not to our Varya? She's a nice girl.

LOPAKHIN. Yes.

LUBOV. She's quite homely in her ways, works all day, and, what matters most, she's in love with you. And you've liked her for a long time.

LOPAKHIN. Well? I don't mind...she's a nice girl. [*Pause.*]

GAEV. I'm offered a place in a bank. Six thousand roubles a year.... Did you hear?

LUBOV. What's the matter with you! Stay where you are....

[*Enter* FIERS *with an overcoat.*]

FIERS [*to* GAEV]. Please, sir, put this on, it's damp.
GAEV [*putting it on*]. You're a nuisance, old man.
FIERS. It's all very well.... You went away this morning without telling me. [*Examining* GAEV.]
LUBOV. How old you've grown, Fiers!
FIERS. I beg your pardon?
LOPAKHIN. She says you've grown very old!
FIERS. I've been alive a long time. They were already getting ready to marry me before your father was born.... [*Laughs.*] And when the Emancipation came I was already first valet. Only I didn't agree with the Emancipation and remained with my people. ...[*Pause.*] I remember everybody was happy, but they didn't know why.
LOPAKHIN. It was very good for them in the old days. At any rate, they used to beat them.
FIERS [*not hearing*]. Rather. The peasants kept their distance from the masters and the masters kept their distance from the peasants, but now everything's all anyhow and you can't understand anything.
GAEV. Be quiet, Fiers. I've got to go to town tomorrow. I've been promised an introduction to a general who may lend me money on a bill.
LOPAKHIN. Nothing will come of it. And you won't pay your interest, don't you worry.
LUBOV. He's talking rubbish. There's no general at all.

[*Enter* TROFIMOV, ANYA, *and* VARYA.]

GAEV. Here they are.
ANYA. Mother's sitting down here.
LUBOV [*tenderly*]. Come, come, my dears.... [*embracing* ANYA *and* VARYA] If you two only knew how much I love you. Sit down next to me, like that. [*All sit down.*]

LOPAKHIN. Our eternal student is always with the ladies.
TROFIMOV. That's not your business.
LOPAKHIN. He'll soon be fifty, and he's still a student.
TROFIMOV. Leave off your silly jokes!
LOPAKHIN. Getting angry, eh, silly?
TROFIMOV. Shut up, can't you.
LOPAKHIN. [*Laughs.*] I wonder what you think of me?
TROFIMOV. I think, Ermolai Alexeyevitch, that you're a rich man, and you'll soon be a millionaire. Just as the wild beast which eats everything it finds is needed for changes to take place in matter, so you are needed too. [*All laugh.*]
VARYA. Better tell us something about the planets, Peter.
LUBOV ANDREYEVNA. No, let's go on with yesterday's talk!
TROFIMOV. About what?
GAEV. About the proud man.
TROFIMOV. Yesterday we talked for a long time but we didn't come to anything in the end. There's something mystical about the proud man, in your sense. Perhaps you are right from your point of view, but if you take the matter simply, without complicating it, then what pride can there be, what sense can there be in it, if a man is imperfectly made, physiologically speaking, if in the vast majority of cases he is coarse and stupid and deeply unhappy? We must stop admiring one another. We must work, nothing more.
GAEV. You'll die, all the same.
TROFIMOV. Who knows? And what does it mean—you'll die? Perhaps a man has a hundred senses, and when he dies only the five known to us are destroyed and the remaining ninety-five are left alive.
LUBOV. How clever of you, Peter!
LOPAKHIN [*ironically*]. Oh, awfully!
TROFIMOV. The human race progresses, perfecting its powers. Everything that

is unattainable now will some day be near at hand and comprehensible, but we must work, we must help with all our strength those who seek to know what fate will bring. Meanwhile in Russia only a very few of us work. The vast majority of those intellectuals whom I know seek for nothing, do nothing, and are at present incapable of hard work. They call themselves intellectuals, but they use "thou" and "thee" to their servants, they treat the peasants like animals, they learn badly, they read nothing seriously, they do absolutely nothing, about science they only talk, about art they understand little. They are all serious, they all have severe faces, they all talk about important things. They philosophize, and at the same time, the vast majority of us, ninety-nine out of a hundred, live like savages, fighting and cursing at the slightest opportunity, eating filthily, sleeping in the dirt, in stuffiness, with fleas, stinks, smells, moral filth, and so on....And it's obvious that all our nice talk is only carried on to distract ourselves and others. Tell me, where are those creches we hear so much of? and where are those reading rooms? People only write novels about them; they don't really exist. Only dirt, vulgarity, and Asiatic plagues really exist....I'm afraid, and I don't at all like serious faces; I don't like serious conversations. Let's be quiet sooner.

LOPAKHIN. You know, I get up at five every morning, I work from morning till evening, I am always dealing with money—my own and other people's —and I see what people are like. You've only got to begin to do anything to find out how few honest, honorable people there are. Sometimes, when I can't sleep, I think: "Oh Lord, you've given us huge forests, infinite fields, and endless horizons, and we, living here, ought really to be giants."

LUBOV. You want giants, do you?... They're only good in stories, and even there they frighten one.

[EPIKHODOV *enters at the back of the stage playing his guitar.*]

ANYA [*thoughtfully*]. Epikhodov's there.

GAEV. The sun's set.

TROFIMOV. Yes.

GAEV [*not loudly, as if declaiming*]. O Nature, thou art wonderful, thou shinest with eternal radiance! Oh, beautiful and indifferent one, thou whom we call mother, thou containest in thyself existence and death, thou livest and destroyest....

VARYA [*entreatingly*]. Uncle, dear!

ANYA. Uncle, you're doing it again!

TROFIMOV. You'd better double the red into the middle.

GAEV. I'll be quiet, I'll be quiet.

[*They all sit thoughtfully. It is quiet. Only the mumbling of* FIERS *is heard. Suddenly a distant sound is heard as if from the sky, the sound of a breaking string, which dies away sadly.*]

LUBOV. What's that?

LOPAKHIN. I don't know. It may be a bucket fallen down a well somewhere. But it's some way off.

GAEV. Or perhaps it's some bird...like a heron.

TROFIMOV. Or an owl.

LUBOV. [*Shudders.*] It's unpleasant, somehow. [*A pause.*]

FIERS. Before the misfortune the same thing happened. An owl screamed and the samovar hummed without stopping.

GAEV. Before what misfortune?

FIERS. Before the Emancipation.

[*A pause.*]

LUBOV. You know, my friends, let's go in; it's evening now. [*to* ANYA] You've tears in your eyes....What is it, little girl? [*Embraces her.*]

ANYA. It's nothing, mother.

TROFIMOV. Someone's coming.

[*Enter a* TRAMP *in an old white peaked cap and overcoat. He is a little drunk.*]

TRAMP. Excuse me, may I go this way straight through to the station?

GAEV. You may. Go along this path.

TRAMP. I thank you from the bottom of my heart. [*Hiccups.*] Lovely weather.... [*Declaims.*] My brother, my suffering brother.... Come out on the Volga, you whose groans...[*to* VARYA] Mademoiselle, please give a hungry Russian thirty copecks....

[VARYA *screams, frightened.*]

LOPAKHIN [*angrily*]. There's manners everybody's got to keep!

LUBOV [*with a start*]. Take this... here you are.... [*Feels in her purse.*] There's no silver.... It doesn't matter, here's gold.

TRAMP. I am deeply grateful to you!

[*Exit. Laughter.*]

VARYA [*frightened*]. I'm going, I'm going.... Oh, little mother, at home there's nothing for the servants to eat, and you gave him gold.

LUBOV. What is to be done with such a fool as I am! At home I'll give you everything I've got. Ermolai Alexeye-vitch, lend me some more!...

LOPAKHIN. Very well.

LUBOV. Let's go, it's time. And Varya, we've settled your affair; I congratulate you.

VARYA [*crying*]. You shouldn't joke about this, mother.

LOPAKHIN. Oh, feel me, get thee to a nunnery.

GAEV. My hands are all trembling; I haven't played billiards for a long time

LOPAKHIN. Oh, feel me, nymph, remember me in thine orisons.

LUBOV. Come along; it'll soon be suppertime.

VARYA. He did frighten me. My heart is beating hard.

LOPAKHIN. Let me remind you, ladies and gentlemen, on August 22 the cherry orchard will be sold. Think of that!...Think of that!...

[*All go out except* TROFIMOV *and* ANYA.]

ANYA. [*Laughs.*] Thanks to the tramp who frightened Barbara, we're alone now.

TROFIMOV. Varya's afraid we may fall in love with each other and won't get away from us for days on end. Her narrow mind won't allow her to understand that we are above love. To escape all the petty and deceptive things which prevent our being happy and free, that is the aim and meaning of our lives. Forward! We go irresistibly on to that bright star which burns there, in the distance! Don't lag behind, friends!

ANYA [*clapping her hands*]. How beautifully you talk! [*Pause.*] It is glorious here today!

TROFIMOV. Yes, the weather is wonderful.

ANYA. What have you done to me, Peter? I don't love the cherry orchard as I used to. I loved it so tenderly, I thought there was no better place in the world than our orchard.

TROFIMOV. All Russia is our orchard. The land is great and beautiful, there are many marvelous places in it. [*Pause.*] Think, Anya, your grandfather, your great-grandfather, and all your ancestors were serf owners, they owned living souls; and now, doesn't something human look at you from every cherry in the orchard, every leaf and every stalk? Don't you hear voices...? Oh, it's awful, your orchard is terrible; and when in the evening or at night you walk through the orchard, then the old bark on the trees sheds a dim light and the old cherry trees seem to be dreaming of all that was a hundred, two hundred years ago, and are oppressed by their heavy visions. Still, at any rate, we've left those two hundred years behind us. So far we've gained nothing at all—we don't yet know what the past is to be to us—we only philosophize, we complain that we are dull, or we drink vodka. For it's so clear that in order to begin to live in the present we must first redeem the past, and that can only be done by suffering, by strenuous, uninterrupted labor. Understand that, Anya.

ANYA. The house in which we live has long ceased to be our house; I shall go away. I give you my word.

TROFIMOV. If you have the housekeeping keys, throw them down the well and go away. Be as free as the wind.

ANYA [*enthusiastically*]. How nicely you said that!

TROFIMOV. Believe me, Anya, believe me! I'm not thirty, yet, I'm young, I'm still a student, but I have undergone a great deal! I'm as hungry as the winter, I'm ill, I'm shaken. I'm as poor as a beggar, and where haven't I been—fate has tossed me everywhere! But my soul is always my own; every minute of the day and the night it is filled with unspeakable presentiments. I know that happiness is coming, Anya, I see it already...

ANYA [*thoughtful*]. The moon is rising.

[EPIKHODOV *is heard playing the same sad song on his guitar. The moon rises. Somewhere by the poplars* VARYA *is looking for* ANYA *and calling,* "Anya, where are you?"]

TROFIMOV. Yes, the moon has risen. [*Pause.*] There is happiness, there it comes; it comes nearer and nearer; I hear its steps already. And if we do not see it we shall not know it, but what does that matter? Others will see it!

THE VOICE OF VARYA. Anya! Where are you?

TROFIMOV. That's Varya again! [*angry*] Disgraceful!

ANYA. Never mind. Let's go to the river. It's nice there.

TROFIMOV. Let's go.   [*They go out.*]

THE VOICE OF VARYA. Anya! Anya!

ACT III

A reception room cut off from a drawing room by an arch. Chandelier lighted. A Jewish band, the one mentioned in Act II, is heard playing in another room. Evening. In the drawing room the grand rond *is being danced. Voice of* SIMEONOV PISCHIN: *"Promenade a une paire!" Dancers come into the reception room; the first pair are* PISCHIN *and* CHARLOTTA IVANOVNA; *the second,* TROFIMOV *and* LUBOV ANDREYEVNA; *the third,* ANYA *and the* POST OFFICE CLERK; *the fourth,* VARYA *and the* STATION-MASTER, *and so on.* VARYA *is crying gently and wipes away her tears as she dances.* DUNYASHA *is in the last pair. They go off into the* drawing room, PISCHIN *shouting,* "Grand rond, balancez;" *and* "Les cavaliers à genou et remerciez vos dames!" FIERS, *in a dresscoat, carries a tray with seltzer water across. Enter* PISCHIN *and* TROFIMOV *from the drawing room.*

PISCHIN. I'm full-blooded and have already had two strokes; it's hard for me to dance, but, as they say, if you're in Rome, you must do as Rome does. I've got the strength of a horse. My dead father, who liked a joke, peace to his bones, used to say, talking of our ancestors, that the ancient stock of the Simeonov-

Pischins was descended from that identical horse that Caligula made a senator.... [*Sits.*] But the trouble is, I've no money! A hungry dog only believes in meat. [*Snores and wakes up again immediately.*] So I...only believe in money....

TROFIMOV. Yes. There is something equine about your figure.

PISCHIN. Well...a horse is a fine animal...you can sell a horse.

[*Billiard playing can be heard in the next room.* VARYA *appears under the arch.*]

TROFIMOV [*teasing*]. Madame Lopakhin! Madame Lopakhin!

VARYA [*angry*]. Decayed gentleman!

TROFIMOV. Yes, I am a decayed gentleman, and I'm proud of it!

VARYA [*bitterly*]. We've hired the musicians, but how are they to be paid?   [*Exit.*]

TROFIMOV. If the energy which you, in the course of your life, have spent in looking for money to pay interest had been used for something else, then, I believe, after all, you'd be able to turn everything upside down.

PISCHIN. Nietzsche...a philosopher... a very great, a most celebrated man ...a man of enormous brain, says in his books that you can forge banknotes.

TROFIMOV. And have you read Nietzsche?

PISCHIN. Well...Dashenka told me. Now I'm in such a position, I wouldn't mind forging them...I've got to pay 310 roubles the day after tomorrow...I've got 130 already. ...[*Feels his pockets, nervously.*] I've lost the money! The money's gone! [*crying*] Where's the money? [*joyfully*] Here it is behind the lining...I even began to perspire.

[*Enter* LUBOV ANDREYEVNA *and* CHARLOTTA IVANOVNA.]

LUBOV [*humming a Caucasian dance*]. Why is Leonid away so long? What's he doing in town? [*to* DUNYASHA] Dunyasha, give the musicians some tea.

TROFIMOV. Business is off, I suppose,

LUBOV. And the musicians needn't have come, and we needn't have got up this ball.... Well, never mind....

[*Sits and sings softly.*]

CHARLOTTA. [*Gives a pack of cards to* PISCHIN.] Here's a pack of cards, think of any one card you like.

PISCHIN. I've thought of one.

CHARLOTTA. Now shuffle. All right, now. Give them here, oh my dear Mr. Pischin. *Ein, zwei, drei!* Now look and you'll find it in your coattail pocket.

PISCHIN. [*Takes a card out of his coattail pocket.*] Eight of spades, quite right! [*surprised*] Think of that now!

CHARLOTTA. [*Holds the pack of cards on the palm of her hand. To* TROFIMOV:] Now tell me quickly. What's the top card?

TROFIMOV. Well, the queen of spades.

CHARLOTTA. Right! [*to* PISCHIN] Well now? What card's on top?

PISCHIN. Ace of hearts.

CHARLOTTA. Right! [*Claps her hands, the pack of cards vanishes.*] How lovely the weather is today. [*A mysterious woman's voice answers her, as if from under the floor,* "Oh yes, it's lovely weather, madam."] You are so beautiful, you are my ideal. [VOICE: "You, madam, please me very much too."]

STATION-MASTER. [*Applauds.*] Madame ventriloquist, bravo!

PISCHIN [*surprised*]. Think of that, now! Delightful, Charlotta Ivanovna ...I'm simply in love....

CHARLOTTA. In love? [*shrugging her shoulders*] Can you love? *Guter Mensch aber schlechter Musikant.*

TROFIMOV. [*Slaps* PISCHIN *on the shoulder.*] Oh, you horse!

CHARLOTTA. Attention please, here's another trick. [*Takes a shawl from a chair.*] Here's a very nice plaid shawl, I'm going to sell it. . . . [*Shakes it.*] Won't anybody buy it?

PISCHIN [*astonished*]. Think of that now!

CHARLOTTA. *Ein, zwei, drei.*

[*She quickly lifts up the shawl, which is hanging down.* ANYA *is standing behind it; she bows and runs to her mother, hugs her, and runs back to the drawing room amid general applause.*]

LUBOV. [*Applauds.*] Bravo, bravo!

CHARLOTTA. Once again! *Ein, zwei, drei!*

[*Lifts the shawl.* VARYA *stands behind it and bows.*]

PISCHIN [*astonished*]. Think of that, now.

CHARLOTTA. The end!

[*Throws the shawl at* PISCHIN, *curtsies, and runs into the drawing room.*]

PISCHIN. [*Runs after her.*] Little wretch. . . . What? Would you? [*Exit.*]

LUBOV. Leonid hasn't come yet. I don't understand what he's doing so long in town! Everything must be over by now. The estate must be sold; or, if the sale never came off, then why does he stay so long?

VARYA. [*Tries to soothe her.*] Uncle has bought it. I'm certain of it.

TROFIMOV [*sarcastically*]. Oh, yes!

VARYA. Grandmother sent him her authority for him to buy it in her name and transfer the debt to her. She's doing it for Anya. And I'm certain that God will help us and uncle will buy it.

LUBOV. Grandmother sent fifteen thousand roubles from Yaroslav to buy the property in her name—she won't trust us—and that wasn't even enough to pay the interest. [*Covers her face with her hands.*] My fate will be settled today, my fate. . . .

TROFIMOV [*teasing* VARYA]. Madame Lopakhin!

VARYA [*angry*]. Eternal student! He's already been expelled twice from the university.

LUBOV. Why are you getting angry, Varya? He's teasing you about Lopakhin, well what of it? You can marry Lopakhin if you want to, he's a good, interesting man. . . . You needn't if you don't want to; nobody wants to force you against your will, my darling.

VARYA. I do look at the matter seriously, little mother, to be quite frank. He's a good man, and I like him.

LUBOV. Then marry him. I don't understand what you're waiting for.

VARYA. I can't propose to him myself, little mother. People have been talking about him to me for two years now, but he either says nothing, or jokes about it. I understand. He's getting rich, he's busy, he can't bother about me. If I had some money, even a little, even only a hundred roubles, I'd throw up everything and go away. I'd go into a convent.

TROFIMOV. How nice!

VARYA [*to* TROFIMOV]. A student ought to have sense! [*gently, in tears*] How ugly you are now, Peter, how old you've grown! [*to* LUBOV ANDREYEVNA, *no longer crying*] But I can't go on without working, little mother. I want to be doing something every minute.

[*Enter* YASHA.]

YASHA [*nearly laughing*]. Epikhodov's broken a billiard cue!   [*Exit.*]

VARYA. Why is Epikhodov here? Who said he could play billiards? I don't understand these people.   [*Exit.*]

LUBOV. Don't tease her, Peter, you see that she's quite unhappy without that.

TROFIMOV. She takes too much on herself, she keeps on interfering in other people's business. The whole summer she's given no peace to me or to Anya, she's afraid we'll have a romance all to ourselves. What has it to do with her? As if I'd ever given her grounds to believe I'd stoop to such vulgarity! We are above love.

LUBOV. Then I suppose I must be beneath love. [*in agitation*] Why isn't Leonid here? If I only knew whether the estate is sold or not! The disaster seems to me so improbable that I don't know what to think, I'm all at sea...I may scream...or do something silly. Save me, Peter. Say something, say something.

TROFIMOV. Isn't it all the same whether the estate is sold today or isn't? It's been all up with it for a long time; there's no turning back, the path's grown over. Be calm, dear, you shouldn't deceive yourself; for once in your life at any rate you must look the truth straight in the face.

LUBOV. What truth? You see where truth is, and where untruth is, but I seem to have lost my sight and see nothing. You boldly settle all important questions, but tell me, dear, isn't it because you're young, because you haven't had time to suffer till you settled a single one of your questions? You boldly look forward, isn't it because you cannot foresee or expect anything terrible, because so far life has been hidden from your young eyes? You are bolder, more honest, deeper than we are, but think only, be just a little magnanimous, and have mercy on me. I was born here, my father and mother lived here, my grandfather too, I love this house. I couldn't understand my life without that cherry orchard, and if it really must be sold, sell me with it! [*Embraces* TROFIMOV, *kisses his forehead.*] My son was drowned here. ...[*Weeps.*] Have pity on me, good, kind man.

TROFIMOV. You know I sympathize with all my soul.

LUBOV. Yes, but it ought to be said differently, differently.... [*Takes another handkerchief, a telegram falls on the floor.*] I'm so sick at heart today, you can't imagine. Here it's so noisy, my soul shakes at every sound. I shake all over, and I can't go away by myself, I'm afraid of the silence. Don't judge me harshly, Peter...I loved you, as if you belonged to my family. I'd gladly let Anya marry you, I swear it, only dear, you ought to work, finish your studies. You don't do anything, only fate throws you about from place to place, it's so odd.... Isn't it true? Yes? And you ought to do something to your beard to make it grow better. [*Laughs.*] You are funny!

TROFIMOV [*picking up telegram*]. I don't want to be a Beau Brummel.

LUBOV. This telegram's from Paris. I get one every day. Yesterday and today. That wild man is ill again, he's bad again.... He begs for forgiveness, and implores me to come, and I really ought to go to Paris to be near him. You look severe, Peter, but what can I do, my dear, what can I do; he's ill, he's alone, unhappy, and who's to look after him, who's to keep him away from his errors, to give him his medicine punctually? And why should I conceal it and say nothing about it; I love him, that's plain, I love him, I love him. ...That love is a stone round my neck; I'm going with it to the bottom, but I love that stone and can't live without it. [*Squeezes* TROFIMOV's *hand.*] Don't think hardly of me, Peter, don't say anything to me, don't say...

TROFIMOV [*weeping*]. For God's sake forgive my speaking candidly, but that man has robbed you!

LUBOV. No, no, no, you oughtn't to say that! [*Stops her ears.*]

TROFIMOV. But he's a wretch, you alone

don't know it! He's a petty thief, a nobody....

LUBOV [*angry, but restrained*]. You're twenty-six or twenty-seven, and still a schoolboy of the second class!

TROFIMOV. Why not!

LUBOV. You ought to be a man, at your age you ought to be able to understand those who love. And you ought to be in love yourself, you must fall in love! [*angry*] Yes, yes! You aren't pure, you're just a freak, a queer fellow, a funny growth....

TROFIMOV [*in horror*]. What is she saying!

LUBOV. "I'm above love!" You're not above love, you're just what our Fiers calls a bungler. Not to have a mistress at your age!

TROFIMOV [*in horror*]. This is awful! What is she saying? [*Goes quickly up into the drawing room, clutching his head.*] It's awful...I can't stand it, I'll go away. [*Exit, but returns at once.*] All is over between us!

[*Exit.*]

LUBOV. [*Shouts after him.*] Peter, wait! Silly man, I was joking! Peter! [*Somebody is heard going out and falling downstairs noisily. ANYA and VARYA scream; laughter is heard immediately.*] What's that?

[*ANYA comes running in, laughing.*]

ANYA. Peter's fallen downstairs!

[*Runs out again.*]

LUBOV. This Peter's a marvel.

[*The STATION-MASTER stands in the middle of the drawing room and recites "The Magdalen" by Tolstoy. He is listened to, but he has only delivered a few lines when a waltz is heard from the front room, and the recitation is stopped. Everybody dances. TROFIMOV, ANYA, VARYA, and LUBOV ANDREYEVNA come in from the front room.*]

LUBOV. Well, Peter...you pure soul... I beg your pardon...let's dance.

[*She dances with PETER. ANYA and VARYA dance.*]

[*FIERS enters and stands his stick by a side door. YASHA has also come in and looks on at the dance.*]

YASHA. Well, grandfather?

FIERS. I'm not well. At our balls some time back, generals and barons and admirals used to dance, and now we send for post office clerks and the station-master, and even they come as a favor. I'm very weak. The dead master, the grandfather, used to give everybody sealing wax when anything was wrong. I've taken sealing wax every day for twenty years, and more; perhaps that's why I still live.

YASHA. I'm tired of you, grandfather. [*Yawns.*] If you'd only hurry up and kick the bucket.

FIERS. Oh you...bungler! [*Mutters.*]

[*TROFIMOV and LUBOV ANDREYEVNA dance in the reception room, then into the sitting room.*]

LUBOV. *Merci*. I'll sit down. [*Sits.*] I'm tired.

[*Enter ANYA.*]

ANYA [*excited*]. Somebody in the kitchen was saying just now that the cherry orchard was sold today.

LUBOV. Sold to whom.

ANYA. He didn't say to whom. He's gone mad.

[*Dances out into the reception room with TROFIMOV.*]

YASHA. Some old man was chattering about it a long time ago. A stranger!

FIERS. And Leonid Andreyevitch isn't here yet, he hasn't come. He's wearing a light, *demi-saison* overcoat. He'll catch cold. Oh these young fellows.

LUBOV. I'll die of this. Go and find out, Yasha, to whom it's sold.

YASHA. Oh, but he's been gone a long time, the old man. [*Laughs.*]

LUBOV [*slightly vexed*]. Why do you laugh? What are you glad about?

YASHA. Epikhodov's too funny. He's a silly man. Two-and-twenty troubles.

LUBOV. Fiers, if the estate is sold, where will you go?

FIERS. I'll go wherever you order me to go.

LUBOV. Why do you look like that? Are you ill? I think you ought to go to bed. . . .

FIERS. Yes. . . [*with a smile*] I'll go to bed, and who'll hand things round and give orders without me? I've the whole house on my shoulders.

YASHA [*to* LUBOV ANDREYEVNA]. Lubov Andreyevna! I want to ask a favor of you, if you'll be so kind! If you go to Paris again, then please take me with you. It's absolutely impossible for me to stop here. [*looking round; in an undertone:*] What's the good of talking about it, you see for yourself that this is an uneducated country, with an immoral population, and it's so dull. The food in the kitchen is beastly, and here's this Fiers walking about mumbling various inappropriate things. Take me with you, be so kind!

[*Enter* PISCHIN.]

PISCHIN. I come to ask for the pleasure of a little waltz, dear lady. . . . [LUBOV ANDREYEVNA *goes to him.*] But all the same, you wonderful woman, I must have 180 little roubles from you. . . . I must. . . . [*They dance.*] 180 little roubles. . . . [*They go through into the drawing room.*]

YASHA. [*Sings softly.*]
   "Oh, will you understand
   My soul's deep restlessness?"

[*In the drawing room a figure in a gray top hat and in baggy check trousers is waving its hands and jumping about; there are cries of* "Bravo, Charlotta Ivanovna!"]

DUNYASHA. [*Stops to powder her face.*] The young mistress tells me to dance —there are a lot of gentlemen, but few ladies—and my head goes round when I dance, and my heart beats, Fiers Nicolaevitch; the post office clerk told me something just now which made me catch my breath.

[*The music grows faint.*]

FIERS. What did he say to you?

DUNYASHA. He says, "You're like a little flower."

YASHA. [*Yawns.*] Impolite. . . . [*Exit.*]

DUNYASHA. Like a little flower. I'm such a delicate girl; I simply love words of tenderness.

FIERS. You'll lose your head.

[*Enter* EPIKHODOV.]

EPIKHODOV. You, Avdotya Fedorovna, want to see me no more than if I was some insect. [*Sighs.*] Oh, life!

DUNYASHA. What do you want?

EPIKHODOV. Undoubtedly, perhaps, you may be right. [*Sighs.*] But, certainly, if you regard the matter from the aspect, then you, if I may say so, and you must excuse my candidness, have absolutely reduced me to a state of mind. I know my fate, every day something unfortunate happens to me, and I've grown used to it a long time ago, I even look at my fate with a smile. You gave me your word, and though I . . .

DUNYASHA. Please, we'll talk later on, but leave me alone now. I'm meditating now. [*Plays with her fan.*]

EPIKHODOV. Every day something unfortunate happens to me, and I, if I may so express myself, only smile, and even laugh.

[VARYA *enters from the drawing room.*]

VARYA. Haven't you gone yet, Simeon? You really have no respect for anybody. [*to* DUNYASHA] You go away, Dunyasha. [*to* EPIKHODOV] You play billiards and break a cue, and walk about the drawing room as if you were a visitor!

EPIKHODOV. You cannot, if I may say so, call me to order.

VARYA. I'm not calling you to order, I'm only telling you. You just walk about from place to place and never do your work. Goodness only knows why we keep a clerk.

EPIKHODOV [*offended*]. Whether I work, or walk about, or eat, or play billiards, is only a matter to be settled by people of understanding and my elders.

VARYA. You dare to talk to me like that! [*furious*] You dare? You mean that I know nothing? Get out of this! This minute!

EPIKHODOV [*nervous*]. I must ask you to express yourself more delicately.

VARYA [*beside herself*]. Get out this minute. Get out!

[*He goes to the door; she follows.*]

Two-and-twenty troubles! I don't want any sign of you here! I don't want to see anything of you! [EPIKHODOV *has gone out; his voice can be heard outside:* "I'll make a complaint against you."] What, coming back? [*Snatches up the stick left by* FIERS *by the door.*] Go...go...go. I'll show you.... Are you going? Are you going? Well, then take that.

[*She hits out as* LOPAKHIN *enters.*]

LOPAKHIN. Much obliged.

VARYA [*angry but amused*]. I'm sorry.

LOPAKHIN. Never mind. I thank you for my pleasant reception.

VARYA. It isn't worth any thanks. [*Walks away, then looks back, and asks gently.*] I didn't hurt you, did I?

LOPAKHIN. No, not at all. There'll be an enormous bump, that's all.

VOICES FROM THE DRAWING ROOM. Lopakhin's returned! Ermolai Alexeyevitch!

PISCHIN. Now we'll see what there is to see and hear what there is to hear.

...[*Kisses* LOPAKHIN.] You smell of cognac, my dear, my soul. And we're all having a good time.

[*Enter* LUBOV ANDREYEVNA.]

LUBOV. Is that you, Ermolai Alexeyevitch? Why were you so long? Where's Leonid?

LOPAKHIN. Leonid Andreyevitch came back with me, he's coming....

LUBOV [*excited*]. Well, what? Is it sold? Tell me?

LOPAKHIN [*confused, afraid to show his pleasure*]. The sale ended up at four o'clock.... We missed the train, and had to wait till half-past nine. [*Sighs heavily.*] Ooh! My head's going round a little.

[*Enter* GAEV; *in his right hand he carries things he has bought, with his left he wipes away his tears.*]

LUBOV. Leon, what's happened? Leon, well? [*impatiently, in tears*] Quick, for the love of God....

GAEV. [*Says nothing to her, only waves his hand; to* FIERS, *weeping:*] Here, take this.... Here are anchovies, herrings from Kertch.... I've had no food today.... I have had a time! [*The door from the billiard room is open; the clicking of the balls is heard, and* YASHA'S *voice,* "Seven, eighteen!" GAEV'S *expression changes, he cries no more.*] I'm awfully tired. Let me change my clothes, Fiers.

[*Goes out through the drawing room;* FIERS *after him.*]

PISCHIN. What happened? Come on, tell us!

LUBOV. Is the cherry orchard sold?

LOPAKHIN. It is sold.

LUBOV. Who bought it?

[LUBOV ANDREYEVNA *is overwhelmed; she would fall if she were not standing by an armchair and a table.* VARYA *takes her keys off her belt, throws them on the floor, into the middle of the room, and goes out.*]

LOPAKHIN. I bought it! Wait, ladies and gentlemen, please, my head's going round, I can't talk. . . .[*Laugh.*] When we got to the sale, Deriganov was there already. Leonid Andreyevitch had only fifteen thousand roubles, and Deriganov offered thirty thousand on top of the mortgage to begin with. I saw how matters were, so I grabbed hold of him and bid forty. He went up to forty-five, I offered fifty-five. That means he went up by fives and I went up by tens. . . .Well, it came to an end. I bid ninety more than the mortgage; and it stayed with me. The cherry orchard is mine now, mine! [*Roars with laughter.*] My God, my God, the cherry orchard's mine! Tell me I'm drunk, or mad, or dreaming. . . . [*Stamps his feet.*] Don't laugh at me! If my father and grandfather rose from their graves and looked at the whole affair, and saw how their Ermolai, their beaten and uneducated Ermolai, who used to run barefoot in the winter, how that very Ermolai has bought an estate, which is the most beautiful thing in the world! I've bought the estate where my grandfather and my father were slaves, where they weren't even allowed into the kitchen. I'm asleep, it's only a dream, an illusion. . . . It's the fruit of imagination, wrapped in the fog of the unknown. . . . [*Picks up the keys, nicely smiling.*] She threw down the keys, she wanted to show she was no longer mistress here. . . . [*Jingles keys.*] Well, it's all one! [*Hears the band tuning up.*] Eh, musicians, play, I want to hear you! Come and look at Ermolai Lopakhin laying his ax to the cherry orchard, come and look at the trees falling! We'll build villas here, and our grandsons and great-grandsons will see a new life here. . . . Play on, music! [*The band plays.* LUBOV ANDREYEVNA *sinks into a chair and weeps bitterly.* LOPAKHIN *continues reproachfully.*] Why then, why didn't you take my advice? My poor, dear woman, you can't go back now. [*Weeps.*] Oh, if only the whole thing was done with, if only our uneven, unhappy life were changed!

PISCHIN. [*Takes his arm; in an undertone:*] She's crying. Let's go into the drawing room and leave her by herself. . .come on. . . .

[*Takes his arm and leads him out.*]

LOPAKHIN. What's that? Bandsmen, play nicely! Go on, do just as I want you to! [*ironically*] The new owner, the owner of the cherry orchard is coming! [*He accidentally knocks up against a little table and nearly upsets the candelabra.*] I can pay for everything now!

[*Exit with* PISCHIN.]

[*In the reception room and the drawing room nobody remains except* LUBOV ANDREYEVNA, *who sits huddled up and weeping bitterly. The band plays softly.* ANYA *and* TROFIMOV *come in quickly.* ANYA *goes up to her mother and goes on her knees in front of her.* TROFIMOV *stands at the drawing-room entrance.*]

ANYA. Mother! mother, are you crying? My dear, kind, good mother, my beautiful mother, I love you! Bless you! The cherry orchard is sold, we've got it no longer, it's true, true, but don't cry mother, you've still got your life before you, you've still your beautiful pure soul. . . . Come with me, come, dear, away from here, come! We'll plant a new garden, finer than this, and you'll see it, and you'll understand, and deep joy, gentle joy will sink into your soul, like the evening sun, and you'll smile, mother! Come, dear, let's go!

ACT IV

The stage is set as for Act I. There are no curtains on the windows, no pictures; only a few pieces of furniture are left; they are piled up in a corner as if for sale. The emptiness is felt. By the door that leads out of the house and at the back of the stage, portmanteaux and traveling paraphernalia are piled up. The door on the left is open; the voices of VARYA *and* ANYA *can be heard through it.* LOPAKHIN *stands and waits.* YASHA *holds a tray with little tumblers of champagne. Outside,* EPIKHODOV *is tying up a box. Voices are heard behind the stage. The peasants have come to say goodbye. The voice of* GAEV *is heard:* "Thank you, brothers, thank you."]

YASHA. The common people have come to say goodbye. I am of the opinion, Ermolai Alexeyevitch, that they're good people, but they don't understand very much.

[*The voices die away.* LUBOV ANDREYEVNA *and* GAEV *enter. She is not crying but is pale, and her face trembles; she can hardly speak.*]

GAEV. You gave them your purse, Luba. You can't go on like that, you can't!
LUBOV. I couldn't help myself, I couldn't!   [*They go out.*]
LOPAKHIN [*in the doorway, looking after them*]. Please, I ask you most humbly! Just a little glass to say goodbye. I didn't remember to bring any from town and I only found one bottle at the station. Please, do! [*Pause.*] Won't you really have any? [*Goes away from the door.*] If I only knew—I wouldn't have bought any. Well, I shan't drink any either. [YASHA *carefully puts the tray on a chair.*] You have a drink, Yasha, at any rate.
YASHA. To those departing! And good luck to those who stay behind! [*Drinks.*] I can assure you that this isn't real champagne.
LOPAKHIN. Eight roubles a bottle. [*Pause.*] It's devilish cold here.
YASHA. There are no fires today; we're going away. [*Laughs.*]
LOPAKHIN. What's the matter with you?
YASHA. I'm just pleased.
LOPAKHIN. It's October outside, but it's as sunny and as quiet as if it were summer. Good for building. [*looking at his watch and speaking through the door*] Ladies and gentlemen, please remember that it's only forty-seven minutes till the train goes! You must go off to the station in twenty minutes. Hurry up.

[TROFIMOV, *in an overcoat, comes in from the grounds.*]

TROFIMOV. I think it's time we went. The carriages are waiting. Where the devil are my goloshes? They're lost. [*through the door*] Anya, I can't find my goloshes! I can't!
LOPAKHIN. I've got to go to Kharkov. I'm going in the same train as you. I'm going to spend the whole winter in Kharkov. I've been hanging about with you people, going rusty without work. I can't live without working. I must have something to do with my hands; they hang about as if they weren't mine at all.
TROFIMOV. We'll go away now and then you'll start again on your useful labors.
LOPAKHIN. Have a glass.
TROFIMOV. I won't.
LOPAKHIN. So you're off to Moscow now?
TROFIMOV. Yes. I'll see them into town and tomorrow I'm off to Moscow.
LOPAKHIN. Yes.... I expect the professors don't lecture nowadays; they're waiting till you turn up!
TROFIMOV. That's not your business.

LOPAKHIN. How many years have you been going to the university?

TROFIMOV. Think of something fresh. This is old and flat. [*looking for his goloshes*] You know, we may not meet each other again, so just let me give you a word of advice on parting: "Don't wave your hands about! Get rid of that habit of waving them about. And then, building villas and reckoning on their residents becoming freeholders in time—that's the same thing; it's all a matter of waving your hands about.... Whether I want to or not, you know, I like you. You've thin, delicate fingers, like those of an artist, and you've a thin, delicate soul...."

LOPAKHIN. [*Embraces him.*] Goodbye, dear fellow. Thanks for all you've said. If you want any, take some money from me for the journey.

TROFIMOV. Why should I? I don't want it.

LOPAKHIN. But you've nothing!

TROFIMOV. Yes, I have, thank you; I've got some for a translation. Here it is in my pocket. [*nervously*] But I can't find my goloshes!

VARYA [*from the other room*]. Take your rubbish away!

[*Throws a pair of rubber goloshes on to the stage.*]

TROFIMOV. Why are you angry, Varya? Hm! These aren't my goloshes!

LOPAKHIN. In the spring I sowed three thousand acres of poppies, and now I've made forty thousand roubles net profit. And when my poppies were in flower, what a picture it was! So I, as I was saying, made forty thousand roubles, and I mean I'd like to lend you some, because I can afford it. Why turn up your nose at it? I'm just a simple peasant....

TROFIMOV. Your father was a peasant, mine was a chemist, and that means absolutely nothing. [LOPAKHIN *takes out his pocketbook.*] No, no.... Even if you gave me twenty thousand I should refuse. I'm a free man. And everything that all you people, rich and poor, value so highly and so dearly hasn't the least influence over me; it's like a flock of down in the wind. I can do without you, I can pass you by. I'm strong and proud. Mankind goes on to the highest truths and to the highest happiness such as is only possible on earth, and I go in the front ranks!

LOPAKHIN. Will you get there?

TROFIMOV. I will. [*Pause.*] I'll get there and show others the way.

[*Axes cutting the trees are heard in the distance.*]

LOPAKHIN. Well, goodbye, old man It's time to go. Here we stand pulling one another's noses, but life goes its own way all the time. When I work for a long time, and I don't get tired, then I think more easily, and I think I get to understand why I exist. And there are so many people in Russia, brother, who live for nothing at all. Still, work goes on without that. Leonid Andreyevitch, they say, has accepted a post in a bank; he will get sixty thousand roubles a year.... But he won't stand it; he's very lazy.

ANYA [*at the door*]. Mother asks if you will stop them cutting down the orchard until she has gone away.

TROFIMOV. Yes, really, you ought to have enough tact not to do that.

[*Exit.*]

LOPAKHIN. All right, all right...yes, he's right. [*Exit.*]

ANYA. Has Fiers been sent to the hospital?

YASHA. I gave the order this morning. I suppose they've sent him.

ANYA [*to* EPIKHODOV, *who crosses the room*]. Simeon Panteleyevitch, please make inquiries if Fiers has been sent to the hospital.

YASHA [*offended*]. I told Egor this morning. What's the use of asking ten times!

EPIKHODOV. The aged Fiers, in my conclusive opinion, isn't worth mending; his forefathers had better have him. I only envy him. [*Puts a trunk on a hat box and squashes it.*] Well, of course. I thought so!   [*Exit.*]

YASHA [*grinning*]. Two-and-twenty troubles.

VARYA [*behind the door*]. Has Fiers been taken away to the hospital?

ANYA. Yes.

VARYA. Why didn't they take the letter to the doctor?

ANYA. It'll have to be sent after him.

[*Exit.*]

VARYA [*in the next room*]. Where's Yasha? Tell him his mother's come and wants to say goodbye to him.

YASHA [*waving his hand*]. She'll make me lose all patience!

[*Dunyasha has meanwhile been bustling round the luggage; now that Yasha is left alone, she goes up to him.*]

DUNYASHA. If you only looked at me once, Yasha. You're going away, leaving me behind.

[*Weeps and hugs him round the neck.*]

YASHA. What's the use of crying? [*Drinks champagne.*] In six days I'll be again in Paris. Tomorrow we get into the express and off we go. I can hardly believe it. Vive la France! It doesn't suit me here, I can't live here...it's no good. Well, I've seen the uncivilized world; I have had enough of it. [*Drinks champagne.*] What do you want to cry for? You behave yourself properly, and then you won't cry.

DUNYASHA. Somebody's coming.

[*He bustles around the luggage, sing-ing softly. Enter* LUBOV ANDREYEVNA, GAEV, ANYA, *and* CHARLOTTA IVANOVNA.]

GAEV. We'd better be off. There's no time left. [*Looks at* YASHA.] Somebody smells of herring!

LUBOV. We needn't get into our carriages for ten minutes.... [*Looks round the room.*] Goodbye, dear house, old grandfather. The winter will go, the spring will come, and then you'll exist no more, you'll be pulled down. How much these walls have seen! [*Passionately kisses her daughter.*] My treasure, you're radiant, your eyes flash like two jewels! Are you happy? Very?

ANYA. Very! A new life is beginning, mother!

GAEV [*gaily*]. Yes, really, everything's all right now. Before the cherry orchard was sold we all were excited and we suffered, and then, when the question was solved once and for all, we all calmed down, and even became cheerful. I'm a bank official now, and a financier...red in the middle; and you, Luba, for some reason or other, look better, there's no doubt about it.

LUBOV. Yes. My nerves are better, it's true. [*She puts on her coat and hat.*] I sleep well. Take my luggage out, Yasha. It's time. [*to* ANYA] My little girl, we'll soon see each other again.... I'm off to Paris. I'll live there on the money your grandmother from Yaroslav sent along to buy the estate—bless her!—though it won't last long.

ANYA. You'll come back soon, soon, mother, won't you? I'll get ready, and pass the exam at the Higher School, and then I'll work and help you. We'll read all sorts of books to one another, won't we? [*Kisses her mother's hands.*] We'll read in the autumn evenings; we'll read many books, and a beautiful new world will open up before us.... [*thoughtfully*] You'll come, mother....

LUBOV. I'll come, my darling.

[*Embraces her.*]

[*Enter* LOPAKHIN. CHARLOTTA *is singing to herself.*]

GAEV. Charlotta is happy; she sings!

CHARLOTTA. [*Takes a bundle, looking like a wrapped-up baby.*] My little baby, bye-bye. [*The baby seems to answer,* "Oua! Oua!"] Hush, my nice little boy. ["Oua! Oua!"] I'm so sorry for you! [*Throws the bundle back.*] So please find me a new place. I can't go on like this.

LOPAKHIN. We'll find one, Charlotta Ivanovna, don't you be afraid.

GAEV. Everybody's leaving us. Varya's going away...we've suddenly become unnecessary.

CHARLOTTA. I've nowhere to live in town. I must go away. [*Hums.*] Never mind.

[*Enter* PISCHIN.]

LOPAKHIN. Nature's marvel!

PISCHIN [*puffing*]. Oh, let me get my breath back....I'm fagged out.... My most honored, give me some water....

GAEV. Come for money, what? I'm your humble servant, and I'm going out of the way of temptation.   [*Exit.*]

PISCHIN. I haven't been here for ever so long...dear madame. [*to* LOPAKHIN] You here? Glad to see you... man of immense brain...take this... take it....[*Gives* LOPAKHIN *money.*] Four hundred roubles....That leaves 840....

LOPAKHIN. [*Shrugs his shoulders in surprise.*] As if I were dreaming. Where did you get this from?

PISCHIN. Stop...it's hot....A most unexpected thing happened. Some Englishmen came along and found some white clay on my land....[*to*

LUBOV ANDREYEVNA] And here's four hundred for you...beautiful lady.... [*Gives her money.*] Give you the rest later.... [*Drinks water.*] Just now a young man in the train was saying that some great philosopher advises us all to jump off roofs. "Jump!" he says, and that's all. [*astonished*] To think of that, now! More water!

LOPAKHIN. Who were these Englishmen?

PISCHIN. I've leased off the land with the clay to them for twenty-four years....Now, excuse me, I've no time....I must run off....I must go to Znoikov and to Kardamonov...I owe them all money....[*Drinks.*] Goodbye. I'll come in on Thursday.

LUBOV. We're just off to town, and tomorrow I go abroad.

PISCHIN [*agitated*]. What? Why to town? I see furniture...trunks.... Well, never mind. [*crying*] Never mind. These Englishmen are men of immense intellect....Never mind.... Be happy....God will help you.... Never mind....Everything in this world comes to an end....[*Kisses* LUBOV ANDREYEVNA's *hand.*] And if you should happen to hear that my end has come, just remember this old ...horse and say: "There was one such and such a Simeonov-Pischin, God bless his soul...." Wonderful weather . . . yes. . . . [*Exit deeply moved, but returns at once and says in the door:*] Dashenka sent her love!

[*Exit.*]

LUBOV. Now we can go. I've two anxieties, though. The first is poor Fiers. [*Looks at her watch.*] We've still five minutes....

ANYA. Mother, Fiers has already been sent to the hospital. Yasha sent him off this morning.

LUBOV. The second is Varya. She's used to getting up early and to work, and now she's no work to do she's like a fish out of water. She's grown thin and pale, and she cries, poor thing. ...[*Pause*.] You know very well, Ermolai Alexeyevitch, that I used to hope to marry her to you, and I suppose you are going to marry somebody?

[*Whispers to* ANYA, *who nods to* CHARLOTTA, *and they both go out.*]

She loves you, she's your sort, and I don't understand, I really don't, why you seem to be keeping away from each other. I don't understand!

LOPAKHIN. To tell the truth, I don't understand it myself. It's all so strange.... If there's still time, I'll be ready at once.... Let's get it over, once and for all; I don't feel as if I could ever propose to her without you.

LUBOV. Excellent. It'll only take a minute. I'll call her.

LOPAKHIN. The champagne's very appropriate. [*looking at the tumblers*] They're empty, somebody's already drunk them. [YASHA *coughs*.] I call that licking it up....

LUBOV [*animated*]. Excellent. We'll go out. Yasha, allez. I'll call her in.... [*at the door*] Varya, leave that and come here. Come! [*Exit with* YASHA.]

LOPAKHIN. [*Looks at his watch.*] Yes. ...[*Pause*.]

[*There is a restrained laugh behind the door, a whisper, then* VARYA *comes in.*]

VARYA [*looking at the luggage in silence*]. I can't seem to find it...

LOPAKHIN. What are you looking for?

VARYA. I packed it myself and I don't remember. [*Pause*.]

LOPAKHIN. Where are you going to now, Barbara Mihailovna?

VARYA. I? To the Ragulins.... I've got an agreement to go and look after their house...as housekeeper or something.

LOPAKHIN. Is that at Yashnevo? It's about fifty miles. [*Pause*.] So life in this house is finished now....

VARYA [*looking at the luggage*]. Where is it?...perhaps I've put it away in the trunk.... Yes, there'll be no more life in this house....

LOPAKHIN. And I'm off to Kharkov at once...by this train. I've a lot of business on hand. I'm leaving Epikhodov here...I've taken him on.

VARYA. Well, well!

LOPAKHIN. Last year at this time the snow was already falling, if you remember, and now it's nice and sunny. Only it's rather cold....There's three degrees of frost.

VARYA. I didn't look. [*Pause*.] And our thermometer's broken.... [*Pause*.]

VOICE AT THE DOOR. Ermolai Alexeyevitch!

LOPAKHIN [*as if he has long been waiting to be called*]. This minute.

[*Exit quickly.*]

[VARYA. *sitting on the floor, puts her face on a bundle of clothes and weeps gently. The door opens.* LUBOV ANDREYEVNA *enters carefully.*]

LUBOV. Well? [*Pause*.] We must go.

VARYA. [*Not crying now, wipes her eyes.*] Yes, it's quite time, little mother. I'll get to the Ragulins today, if I don't miss the train....

LUBOV [*at the door*]. Anya, put on your things.

[*Enter* ANYA, *then* GAEV, CHARLOTTA IVANOVNA. GAEV *wears a warm overcoat with a cape. A servant and drivers come in.* EPIKHODOV *bustles around the luggage.*]

Now we can go away.

ANYA [*joyfully*]. Away!

GAEV. My friends, my dear friends! Can I be silent, in leaving this house for evermore?—can I restrain myself, in saying farewell, from expressing those feelings which now fill my whole being...?

ANYA [*imploringly*]. Uncle!

VARYA. Uncle, you shouldn't!

GAEV [*stupidly*]. Double the red into the middle.... I'll be quiet.

[*Enter* TROFIMOV, *then* LOPAKHIN.]

TROFIMOV. Well, it's time to be off.

LOPAKHIN. Epikhodov, my coat!

LUBOV. I'll sit here one more minute. It's as if I'd never really noticed what the walls and ceilings of this house were like, and now I look at them greedily, with such tender love....

GAEV. I remember, when I was six years old, on Trinity Sunday, I sat at this window and looked and saw my father going to church....

LUBOV. Have all the things been taken away?

LOPAKHIN. Yes, all, I think. [*to* EPIKHODOV, *putting on his coat*] You see that everything's quite straight, Epikhodov.

EPIKHODOV [*hoarsely*]. You may depend upon me, Ermolai Alexeyevitch!

LOPAKHIN. What's the matter with your voice?

EPIKHODOV. I swallowed something just now; I was having a drink of water.

YASHA [*suspiciously*]. What manners....

LUBOV. We go away, and not a soul remains behind.

LOPAKHIN. Till the spring.

VARYA. [*Drags an umbrella out of a bundle and seems to be waving it about.* LOPAKHIN *appears to be frightened.*] What are you doing?... I never thought...

TROFIMOV. Come along, let's take our seats...it's time! The train will be in directly.

VARYA. Peter, here they are, your goloshes, by that trunk. [*in tears*] And how old and dirty they are....

TROFIMOV [*putting them on*]. Come on!

GAEV [*deeply moved, nearly crying*]. The train...the station.... Cross in the middle, a white double in the corner....

LUBOV. Let's go!

LOPAKHIN. Are you all here? There's nobody else? [*Locks the sidedoor on the left.*] There's a lot of things in there. I must lock them up. Come!

ANYA. Goodbye, home! Goodbye, old life!

TROFIMOV. Welcome, new life.

[*Exit with* ANYA.]

[VARYA *looks round the room and goes out slowly.* YASHA *and* CHARLOTTA, *with her little dog, go out.*]

LOPAKHIN. Till the spring, then! Come on...till we meet again!   [*Exit.*]

[LUBOV ANDREYEVNA *and* GAEV *are left alone. They might almost have been waiting for that. They fall into each other's arms and sob restrainedly and quietly, fearing that somebody might hear them.*]

GAEV [*in despair*]. My sister, my sister....

LUBOV. My dear, my gentle, beautiful orchard! My life, my youth, my happiness, goodbye! Goodbye!

ANYA'S VOICE [*gaily*]. Mother!

TROFIMOV'S VOICE [*gaily, excited*]. Coo-ee!

LUBOV. To look at the walls and the windows for the last time.... My dead mother used to like to walk about this room....

GAEV. My sister, my sister!

ANYA'S VOICE. Mother!

TROFIMOV'S VOICE. Coo-ee!

LUBOV. We're coming! [*They go out.*]

[*The stage is empty. The sound of keys being turned in the locks is heard and then the noise of the carriages going away. It is quiet. Then the sound of an ax against the trees is heard in the silence, sadly and by itself. Steps are heard.* FIERS *comes in from the door on the right. He is dressed as usual, in a short jacket and white waistcoat, slip-*]

pers on his feet. He is ill. He goes to the door and tries the handle.]

FIERS. It's locked. They've gone away. [*Sits on a sofa.*] They've forgotten about me. . . . Never mind, I'll sit here. . . . And Leonid Andreyevitch will have gone in a light overcoat instead of putting on his fur coat. . . . [*Sighs anxiously.*] I didn't see . . . Oh, these young people! [*Mumbles something that cannot be understood.*]

Life's gone on as if I'd never lived. [*lying down*] I'll lie down . . . You've no strength left in you, nothing left at all. . . . Oh, you . . . bungler!

[*He lies without moving. The distant sound is heard, as if from the sky, of a breaking string, dying away sadly. Silence follows it, and only the sound is heard, some way away in the orchard, of the ax falling on the trees.*]

The Visit

When the burgomaster of Güllen suggests that the millionairess Claire Zacha-nassian is the only hope of the village "under God," he speaks more in the future style of the townspeople than he realizes. As they gradually substitute the capricious and trying money goddess for "those principles which form the soul of our Western culture" (as the teacher edifyingly puts it), they dedicate to her a set of rites normally reserved for the veneration of divine beings. That it is misapplied veneration goes without saying. The teacher associates her with the underworld and fate, and certainly to Schill two of her retinue qualify for furies come back to torment him. In a sense, money fills in the emptied fibers of social values as minerals replace wood in petrifying trees. The "divine" visitation does remove the curse laid on the community and create a new social covenant, but the covenant is a parody of what it should be.

In other respects the plot is a version of the sellout that finds a representative western European town wanting in humanistic values but inventive in rhetoric. Initially split into comic choruses, trios, and duets, the factions of the poverty-stricken community eventually become unified celebrants of the goddess, cleansing themselves of murder by anthems to her. Both amateurs and experts in public relations set to work doctoring reality to make it palatable to moral sensitivity. Claire captures big city types, movie stars, and scholars as securely as she does shopkeepers, factory owners, and housewives.

The production of public motives for an inexcusable act (equivalent to Claire's own substitution, in the original version of the play, of a wooden leg and an ivory hand for real limbs) is a countermovement to the intrigue against Schill. The meaning of the play emerges from both movements together, the satiric comedy of the degenerating public choruses and the undermined romance of the two old lovers, and the increasing peril and dignity of Schill as tragic victim. If we look into each of these closely, we see how skillfully Friedrich Düerrenmatt (1921—) has balanced them. Schill's masking of guilt by appeals to necessity and romantic fate is dashed aside in a retrial of his youthful betrayal. He pays for being saved from public election with costly but ennobling self-knowledge. Meanwhile, the press and the outsiders who follow Claire to Güllen commit the village to the spurious motives of western civilization and welcome it into the western economy. Thus as Schill's life is stripped of pretense and exposed to brutality, the other Gülleners are busy putting on public justification with their new clothes.

In keeping with this twofold movement, the method of the play is a combination of satiric caricature, moral parable, and mock-tragedy. It is designed not so much to imitate social manners and motives in their complexity as to expose the bare mechanism by which murder becomes an acceptable—even holy—act. The speeches are generally bare and clean like those of parables, and the characters are two-dimensional for the most part. The opening scene, for instance, employs a form of divided chorus that reveals a like-mindlessness in Güelleners One, Two, Three, Four, and So Forth. These characterless (but easily recognizable) creatures come in punctually thereafter, justifying Claire's faith in them. Given the proper stimuli, they respond like frogs to changes in the weather, fumbling clownishly in learning the ceremonies of prosperity that less out-of-the-way centers of culture have long ago perfected. At the same time the underlying seriousness of the act they perform prevents the play from becoming pure comedy. The play combines stylized caricature with fantasy and occasionally with realism. On one hand, the dignity of Schill's romantic reminiscences in the wood is undermined by various kinds of incongruity; but on the other hand, the grotesqueness of the blinded witnesses, Claire's maiming, and the softness of old age cut through the formality of the play with reminders that behind the laughable pageantry are certain unavoidable realities. The poverty of the Gülleners, after all, is a fact, and Düerren-matt's nature outside the village is scarcely an earthly paradise.

That the play manages to fuse these disparate modes from parable to satire to realism is due largely to its implicit awareness of staging as a reality in its own right. It concerns the staging of social attitudes and the substitution of many styles of appearance for truth, beginning with the planned reception of Claire (the mayor's staging of a typical burgher-play with the sideshow antics of musical comedy) and ending with ritualized murder. Each Güllener is hunting for the mask best adapted to his part in the pageantry and creditable to the public at large as it reads about the show in the papers. Schill himself, of course, has long ago paid witnesses to perjure themselves on behalf of his good name, and it is fit retribution that he be forced to play an entirely different role in the second trial and execution—while commentators quote the burgomaster's memorable words "Died of joy" for the edification of those who cannot be there personally.

But the public strangling produces no beneficial spiritual release, as the sacrifice of victims does in Greek tragedy, because the goddess-visitor represents too belittling a reality. Recognition that their curse is divine prepares the citizens of a Greek *polis* to accept their harrowing experience; but the underlying truth about Gülleners requires that they rewrite their roles in grander style. As the goddess leaves on a much improved train with their civilization in her purse, the villagers send her off in proper form, now given entirely over to their fiction. They divide in the original version into two choruses like those of Greek tragedy and chant of the catastrophes of earth (tidal waves, earthquakes, the atom bomb, poverty) and render thanks for their prosperity: the women have their clothes, the men their new sports cars, the doctors the best of equipment, and they all have Piety. They hail Claire as their benefactress, the priest says "let us pray," and the combined chorus asks for the protection henceforth of their "sacred possessions." The price they have paid for their flashy economy is an obvious debasement of religious motives and a general dullness. In effect they have substituted a seriocomic newspaper drama for tragic awareness.

The Visit

HOFBAUER *first man*
HELMESBERGER *second man*
WECHSLER *third man*
VOGEL *fourth man*
PAINTER
STATION MASTER
BURGOMASTER
TEACHER
PASTOR
ANTON SCHILL
CLAIRE ZACHANASSIAN
CONDUCTOR
PEDRO CABRAL
BOBBY
POLICEMAN
FIRST GRANDCHILD

SECOND GRANDCHILD
MIKE
MAX
FIRST BLIND MAN
SECOND BLIND MAN
ATHLETE
FRAU BURGOMASTER
FRAU SCHILL
DAUGHTER
SON
DOCTOR NÜSSLIN
FRAU BLOCK *first woman*
TRUCK DRIVER
REPORTER
TOWNSMAN

The action of the play takes place in and around the little town of Güllen, somewhere in Europe.
There are three acts.

ACT I

A railway-crossing bell starts ringing. Then is heard the distant sound of a locomotive whistle. The curtain rises.

The scene represents, in the simplest possible manner, a little town somewhere in Central Europe. The time is the present. The town is shabby and ruined, as if the plague had passed there. Its name, Güllen, is inscribed on the shabby signboard which adorns the façade of the railway station. This edifice is summarily indicated by a length of rusty iron paling, a platform parallel to the proscenium, beyond which one imagines the rails to be, and a baggage truck standing by a wall on which a torn timetable, marked "Fahrplan," is affixed by three nails. In the station wall is a door with a sign: "Eintritt Verboten."[1] This leads to the STATION MASTER'S *office.*

Left of the station is a little house of gray stucco, formerly whitewashed. It has a tile roof, badly in need of repair. Some shreds of travel posters still adhere to the windowless walls. A shingle hanging over the entrance, left, reads: "Männer."[2] On the other side the shingle reads: "Damen."[3] Along the wall of the little house there is a wooden bench, backless, on which four men are lounging cheerlessly, shabbily dressed, with cracked shoes. A fifth man is busied with paintpot and brush. He is kneeling on the ground, painting a strip of canvas with the words: "Welcome, Clara."

The warning signal rings uninterruptedly. The sound of the approaching train comes closer and closer. The STATION MASTER *issues from his office, advances to the center of the platform, and salutes.*

The train is heard thundering past in a direction parallel to the footlights and is lost in the distance. The men on the bench follow its passing with a slow movement of their heads, from left to right.

FIRST MAN. The "Emperor." Hamburg-Naples.

SECOND MAN. Then comes the "Diplo-mat."

THIRD MAN. Then the "Banker."

FOURTH MAN. And at eleven twenty-seven the "Flying Dutchman." Venice-Stockholm.

FIRST MAN. Our only pleasure—watching trains.

[The station bell rings again. The STATION MASTER *comes out of his office and salutes another train. The men follow its course, right to left.]*

FOURTH MAN. Once upon a time the "Emperor" and the "Flying Dutchman" used to stop here in Güllen. So did the "Diplomat," the "Banker," and the "Silver Comet."

SECOND MAN. Now it's only the local from Kaffigen and the twelve-forty from Kalberstadt.

THIRD MAN. The fact is, we're ruined.

FIRST MAN. What with the wagon-works shut down...

SECOND MAN. The foundry finished...

FOURTH MAN. The Golden Eagle Pencil Factory all washed up...

FIRST MAN. It's life on the dole.

SECOND MAN. Did you say life?

THIRD MAN. We're rotting.

FIRST MAN. Starving.

SECOND MAN. Crumbling.

FOURTH MAN. The whole damn town.

[The station bell rings.]

THIRD MAN. Once we were a center of industry.

PAINTER. A cradle of culture.

FOURTH MAN. One of the best little towns in the country.

FIRST MAN. In the world.

SECOND MAN. Here Goethe slept.

FOURTH MAN. Brahms composed a quartet.

THIRD MAN. Here Berthold Schwarz invented gunpowder.

PAINTER. And I once got first prize at the Dresden Exhibition of Contemporary Art. What am I doing now? Painting signs.

---

[1] No Entrance.   [2] Men.   [3] Ladies.

[*The station bell rings. The* STATION MASTER *comes out. He throws away a cigarette butt. The men scramble for it.*]

FIRST MAN. Well, anyway, Madame Zachanassian will help us.
FOURTH MAN. If she comes...
THIRD MAN. If she comes.
SECOND MAN. Last week she was in France. She gave them a hospital.
FIRST MAN. In Rome she founded a free public nursery.
THIRD MAN. In Leuthenau, a bird sanctuary.
PAINTER. They say she got Picasso to design her car.
FIRST MAN. Where does she get all that money?
SECOND MAN. An oil company, a shipping line, three banks, and five railways—
FOURTH MAN. And the biggest string of geisha houses in Japan.

[*From the direction of the town come the* BURGOMASTER, *the* PASTOR, *the* TEACHER, *and* ANTON SCHILL. *The* BURGOMASTER, *the* TEACHER, *and* SCHILL *are men in their fifties. The* PASTOR *is ten years younger. All four are dressed shabbily and are sad-looking. The* BURGOMASTER *looks official.* SCHILL *is tall and handsome, but graying and worn; nevertheless a man of considerable charm and presence. He walks directly to the little house and disappears into it.*]

PAINTER. Any news, Burgomaster? Is she coming?
ALL. Yes, is she coming?
BURGOMASTER. She's coming. The telegram has been confirmed. Our distinguished guest will arrive on the twelve-forty from Kalberstadt. Everyone must be ready.
TEACHER. The mixed choir is ready. So is the children's chorus.
BURGOMASTER. And the church bell, Pastor?
PASTOR. The church bell will ring. As soon as the new bell ropes are fitted. The man is working on them now.
BURGOMASTER. The town band will be drawn up in the market place and the Athletic Association will form a human pyramid in her honor—the top man will hold the wreath with her initials. Then lunch at the Golden Apostle. I shall say a few words.
TEACHER. Of course.
BURGOMASTER. I had thought of illuminating the town hall and the cathedral, but we can't afford the lamps.
PAINTER. Burgomaster—what do you think of this?

[*He shows the banner.*]

BURGOMASTER. [*Calls.*] Schill! Schill!
TEACHER. Schill!

[SCHILL *comes out of the little house.*]

SCHILL. Yes, right away. Right away.
BURGOMASTER. This is more in your line. What do you think of this?
SCHILL. [*Looks at the sign.*] No, no, no. That certainly won't do, Burgomaster. It's much too intimate. It shouldn't read: "Welcome, Clara." It should read: "Welcome, Madame ..."
TEACHER. Zachanassian.
BURGOMASTER. Zachanassian.
SCHILL. Zachanassian.
PAINTER. But she's Clara to us.
FIRST MAN. Clara Wäscher.
SECOND MAN. Born here.
THIRD MAN. Her father was a carpenter. He built this.

[*All turn and stare at the little house.*]

SCHILL. All the same...
PAINTER. If I...
BURGOMASTER. No, no, no. He's right. You'll have to change it.
PAINTER. Oh, well, I'll tell you what I'll do. I'll leave this and I'll put "Welcome, Madame Zachanassian"

on the other side. Then if things go well, we can always turn it around.

BURGOMASTER. Good idea. [*to* SCHILL] Yes?

SCHILL. Well, anyway, it's safer. Everything depends on the first impression.

[*The train bell is heard. Two clangs. The* PAINTER *turns the banner over and goes to work.*]

FIRST MAN. Hear that? The "Flying Dutchman" has just passed through Leuthenau.

FOURTH MAN. Eleven twenty.

BURGOMASTER. Gentlemen, you know that the millionairess is our only hope.

PASTOR. Under God.

BURGOMASTER. Under God. Naturally. Schill, we depend entirely on you.

SCHILL. Yes, I know. You keep telling me.

BURGOMASTER. After all, you're the only one who really knew her.

SCHILL. Yes, I knew her.

PASTOR. You were really quite close to one another, I hear, in those days.

SCHILL. Close? Yes, we were close, there's no denying it. We were in love. I was young—good-looking, so they said—and Clara—you know, I can still see her in the great barn coming toward me—like a light out of the darkness. And in the Konradsweil Forest she'd come running to meet me—barefooted—her beautiful red hair streaming behind her. Like a witch. I was in love with her, all right. But you know how it is when you're twenty.

PASTOR. What happened?

SCHILL. [*Shrugs.*] Life came between us.

BURGOMASTER. You must give me some points about her for my speech.

[*He takes out his notebook.*]

SCHILL. I think I can help you there.

TEACHER. Well, I've gone through the school records. And the young lady's marks were, I'm afraid to say, absolutely dreadful. Even in deportment. The only subject in which she was even remotely passable was natural history.

BURGOMASTER. Good in natural history. That's fine. Give me a pencil.

[*He makes a note.*]

SCHILL. She was an outdoor girl. Wild. Once, I remember, they arrested a tramp, and she threw stones at the policeman. She hated injustice passionately.

BURGOMASTER. Strong sense of justice. Excellent.

SCHILL. And generous...

ALL. Generous?

SCHILL. Generous to a fault. Whatever little she had, she shared—so goodhearted. I remember once she stole a bag of potatoes to give to a poor widow.

BURGOMASTER [*writing in notebook*]. Wonderful generosity—

TEACHER. Generosity.

BURGOMASTER. That, gentlemen, is something I must not fail to make a point of.

SCHILL. And such a sense of humor. I remember once when the oldest man in town fell and broke his leg, she said, "Oh, dear, now they'll have to shoot him."

BURGOMASTER. Well, I've got enough. The rest, my friend, is up to you.

[*He puts the notebook away.*]

SCHILL. Yes, I know, but it's not so easy. After all, to part a woman like that from her millions—

BURGOMASTER. Exactly. Millions. We have to think in big terms here.

TEACHER. If she's thinking of buying us off with a nursery school—

ALL. Nursery school!

PASTOR. Don't accept.

TEACHER. Hold out.

SCHILL. I'm not so sure that I can

PAINTER. But the "Flying Dutchman" never stops!

FIRST MAN. It's stopping.

SECOND MAN. In Güllen!

THIRD MAN. In the poorest—

FIRST MAN. The dreariest—

SECOND MAN. The lousiest—

FOURTH MAN. The most God-forsaken hole between Venice and Stockholm.

STATION MASTER. It cannot stop!

[*The train noises stop. There is only the panting of the engine.*]

PAINTER. It's stopped!

[*The* STATION MASTER *runs out.*]

OFFSTAGE VOICES. What's happened? Is there an accident?

[*A hubbub of offstage voices, as if the passengers on the invisible train were alighting.*]

CLAIRE [*offstage*]. Is this Güllen?

CONDUCTOR [*offstage*]. Here, here, what's going on?

CLAIRE [*offstage*]. Who the hell are you?

CONDUCTOR [*offstage*]. But you pulled the emergency cord, madame!

CLAIRE [*offstage*]. I always pull the emergency cord.

STATION MASTER [*offstage*]. I must ask you what's going on here.

CLAIRE [*offstage*]. And who the hell are you?

STATION MASTER [*offstage*]. I'm the station master, madame, and I must ask you—

CLAIRE. [*Enters.*] No!

[*From the right* CLAIRE ZACHANASSIAN *appears. She is an extraordinary woman. She is in her fifties, red-haired, remarkably dressed, with a face as impassive as that of an ancient idol, beautiful still, and with a singular grace of movement and manner. She is simple and unaffected, yet she has the haughtiness of a world power. The entire effect is striking to the point of the unbelieva-*] ble. *Behind her comes her fiancé,* PEDRO CABRAL, *tall, young, very handsome, and completely equipped for fishing, with creel and net, and with a rod case in his hand. An excited* CONDUCTOR *follows.*]

CONDUCTOR. But, madame, I must insist! You have stopped "The Flying Dutchman." I must have an explanation.

CLAIRE. Nonsense. Pedro.

PEDRO. Yes, my love?

CLAIRE. This is Güllen. Nothing has changed. I recognize it all. There's the forest of Konradsweil. There's a brook in it full of trout, where you can fish. And there's the roof of the great barn. Ha God! What a miserable blot on the map.

[*She crosses the stage and goes off with* PEDRO.]

SCHILL. My God! Clara!

TEACHER. Claire Zachanassian!

ALL. Claire Zachanassian!

BURGOMASTER. And the town band? The town band! Where is it?

TEACHER. The mixed choir! The mixed choir!

PASTOR. The church bell! The church bell!

BURGOMASTER [*to the* FIRST MAN]. Quick! My dress coat. My top hat. My grandchildren. Run! Run!

[FIRST MAN *runs off. The* BURGOMASTER *shouts after him.*]

And don't forget my wife!

[*General panic. The* THIRD MAN *and* FOURTH MAN *hold up the banner, on which only part of the name has been painted:* "Welcome Mad—". CLAIRE *and* PEDRO *re-enter, right.*]

CONDUCTOR [*mastering himself with an effort*]. Madame. The train is waiting. The entire international railway schedule has been disrupted. I await your explanation.

CLAIRE. You're a very foolish man. I

do it. You know, she may have forgotten me completely.

BURGOMASTER. [*He exchanges a look with the* TEACHER *and the* PASTOR.] Schill, for many years you have been our most popular citizen. The most respected and the best loved.

SCHILL. Why, thank you...

BURGOMASTER. And therefore I must tell you—last week I sounded out the political opposition, and they agreed. In the spring you will be elected to succeed me as burgomaster. By unanimous vote.

[*The others clap their hands in approval.*]

SCHILL. But, my dear Burgomaster—!

BURGOMASTER. It's true.

TEACHER. I'm a witness. I was at the meeting.

SCHILL. This is—naturally, I'm terribly flattered—It's a completely unexpected honor.

BURGOMASTER. You deserve it.

SCHILL. Burgomaster! Well, well—! [*briskly*] Gentlemen, to business. The first chance I get, of course, I shall discuss our miserable position with Clara.

TEACHER. But tactfully, tactfully—

SCHILL. What do you take me for? We must feel our way. Everything must be correct. Psychologically correct. For example, here at the railway station, a single blunder, one false note, could be disastrous.

BURGOMASTER. He's absolutely right. The first impression colors all the rest. Madame Zachanassian sets foot on her native soil for the first time in many years. She sees our love and she sees our misery. She remembers her youth, her friends. The tears well up into her eyes. Her childhood companions throng about her. I will naturally not present myself like this, but in my black coat with my top hat. Next to me, my wife. Before me, my two grandchildren all in

white, with roses. My God, if comes off as I see it! If only i off. [*The station bell begins ri* Oh, my God! Quick! We m dressed.

FIRST MAN. It's not her train. It the "Flying Dutchman."

PASTOR [*calmly*]. We have stil hours before she arrives.

SCHILL. For God's sake, don't let' our heads. We still have a full hours.

BURGOMASTER. Who's losing heads? [*to* FIRST *and* SECOND M When her train comes, you Helmesberger and Vogel, will hold the banner with "Welcome Mad Zachanassian." The rest will appla

THIRD MAN. Bravo! [*He applaud*

BURGOMASTER. But, please, one thing no wild cheering like last year w the government relief committee. made no impression at all and still haven't received any loan. Wh we need is a feeling of genuine si cerity. That's how we greet with fu hearts our beloved sister who ha been away from us so long. B sincerely moved, my friends, that' the secret; be sincere. Remember you're not dealing with a child. Next a few brief words from me. Then the church bell will start pealing—

PASTOR. If he can fix the ropes in time.

[*The station bell rings.*]

BURGOMASTER. —Then the mixed choir moves in. And then—

TEACHER. We'll form a line down here.

BURGOMASTER. Then the rest of us will form in two lines leading from the station—

[*He is interrupted by the thunder of the approaching train. The men crane their heads to see it pass. The* STATION MASTER *advances to the platform and salutes. There is a sudden shriek of air brakes. The train screams to a stop. The four men jump up in consternation.*]

wish to visit this town. Did you expect me to jump off a moving train?

CONDUCTOR [*stupefied*]. You stopped the "Flying Dutchman" because you wished to visit the town?

CLAIRE. Naturally.

CONDUCTOR [*inarticulate*]. Madame!

STATION MASTER. Madame, if you wished to visit the town, the twelve forty from Kalberstadt was entirely at your service. Arrival in Güllen, one seventeen.

CLAIRE. The local that stops at Loken, Beisenbach, and Leuthenau? Do you expect me to waste three-quarters of an hour chugging dismally through this wilderness?

CONDUCTOR. Madame, you shall pay for this!

CLAIRE. Bobby, give him a thousand marks.

[BOBBY, *her butler, a man in his seventies, wearing dark glasses, opens his wallet. The townspeople gasp.*]

CONDUCTOR [*taking the money in amazement*]. But, madame!

CLAIRE. And three thousand for the Railway Widows' Relief Fund.

CONDUCTOR [*with the money in his hands*]. But we have no such fund, madame.

CLAIRE. Now you have.

[*The* BURGOMASTER *pushes his way forward.*]

BURGOMASTER. [*He whispers to the* CONDUCTOR *and* TEACHER.] The lady is Madame Claire Zachanassian!

CONDUCTOR. Claire Zachanassian? Oh, my God! But that's naturally quite different. Needless to say, we would have stopped the train if we'd had the slightest idea. [*He hands the money back to* BOBBY.] Here, please. I couldn't dream of it. Four thousand. My God!

CLAIRE. Keep it. Don't fuss.

CONDUCTOR. Would you like the train to wait, madame, while you visit the town? The administration will be delighted. The cathedral porch. The town hall—

CLAIRE. You may take the train away. I don't need it any more.

STATION MASTER. All aboard!

[*He puts his whistle to his lips.* PEDRO *stops him.*]

PEDRO. But the press, my angel. They don't know anything about this. They're still in the dining car.

CLAIRE. Let them stay there. I don't want the press in Güllen at the moment. Later they will come by themselves. [*to* STATION MASTER] And now what are you waiting for?

STATION MASTER. All aboard!

[*The* STATION MASTER *blows a long blast on his whistle. The train leaves. Meanwhile, the* FIRST MAN *has brought the* BURGOMASTER'S *dress coat and top hat. The* BURGOMASTER *puts on the coat, then advances slowly and solemnly.*]

CONDUCTOR. I trust madame will not speak of this to the administration. It was a pure misunderstanding.

[*He salutes and runs for the train as it starts moving.*]

BURGOMASTER. [*Bows.*] Gracious lady, as burgomaster of the town of Güllen, I have the honor—

[*The rest of the speech is lost in the roar of the departing train. He continues speaking and gesturing, and at last bows amid applause as the train noises end.*]

CLAIRE. Thank you, Mr. Burgomaster.

[*She glances at the beaming faces and lastly at* SCHILL, *whom she does not recognize. She turns upstage.*]

SCHILL. Clara!

CLAIRE. [*Turns and stares.*] Anton?

SCHILL. Yes. It's good that you've come back.

CLAIRE. Yes. I've waited for this moment. All my life. Ever since I left Güllen.
SCHILL [*a little embarrassed*]. That is very kind of you to say, Clara.
CLAIRE. And have you thought about me?
SCHILL. Naturally. Always. You know that.
CLAIRE. Those were happy times we spent together.
SCHILL. Unforgettable.

[*He smiles reassuringly at the* BURGO-MASTER.]

CLAIRE. Call me by the name you used to call me.
SCHILL. [*Whispers.*] My kitten.
CLAIRE. What?
SCHILL [*louder*]. My kitten.
CLAIRE. And what else?
SCHILL. Little witch.
CLAIRE. I used to call you my black panther. You're gray now, and soft.
SCHILL. But you are still the same, little witch.
CLAIRE. I am the same? [*She laughs.*] Oh, no, my black panther, I am not at all the same.
SCHILL [*gallantly*]. In my eyes you are. I see no difference.
CLAIRE. Would you like to meet my fiancé? Pedro Cabral. He owns an enormous plantation in Brazil.
SCHILL. A pleasure.
CLAIRE. We're to be married soon.
SCHILL. Congratulations,
CLAIRE. He will be my eighth husband. [PEDRO *stands by himself downstage, right.*] Pedro, come here and show your face. Come along, darling— come here! Don't sulk. Say hello.
PEDRO. Hello.
CLAIRE. A man of few words! Isn't he charming? A diplomat. He's interested only in fishing. Isn't he handsome, in his Latin way? You'd swear he was a Brazilian. But he's not— he's a Greek. His father was a White Russian. We were betrothed by a

Bulgarian priest. We plan to be married in a few days here in the cathedral.
BURGOMASTER. Here in the cathedral? What an honor for us!
CLAIRE. No. It was my dream, when I was seventeen, to be married in Güllen cathedral. The dreams of youth are sacred, don't you think so, Anton?
SCHILL. Yes, of course.
CLAIRE. Yes, of course. I think so, too. Now I would like to look at the town.

[*The mixed choir arrives, breathless, wearing ordinary clothes with green sashes.*]

What's all this? Go away. [*She laughs.*] Ha! Ha! Ha!
TEACHER. Dear lady—[*He steps forward, having put on a sash also.*] Dear lady, as rector of the high school and a devotee of that noble muse, Music, I take pleasure in presenting the Güllen mixed choir.
CLAIRE. How do you do?
TEACHER. Who will sing for you an ancient folk song of the region, with specially amended words if you will deign to listen.
CLAIRE. Very well. Fire away.

[*The* TEACHER *blows a pitch pipe. The mixed choir begins to sing the ancient folk song with the amended words. Just then the station bell starts ringing. The song is drowned in the roar of the passing express. The* STATION MASTER *salutes. When the train has passed, there is applause.*]

BURGOMASTER. The church bell! The church bell! Where's the church bell?

[*The* PASTOR *shrugs helplessly.*]

CLAIRE. Thank you, Professor. They sang beautifully. The big little blond bass—no, not that one—the one with the big Adam's apple—was most impressive.

[*The* TEACHER *bows. The* POLICEMAN *pushes his way professionally through the mixed choir and comes to attention in front of* CLAIRE ZACHANASSIAN.]

Now, who are you?

POLICEMAN. [*Clicks heels.*] Police Chief Schultz. At your service.

CLAIRE. [*She looks him up and down.*] I have no need of you at the moment. But I think there will be work for you by and by. Tell me, do you know how to close an eye from time to time?

POLICEMAN. How else could I get along in my profession?

CLAIRE. You might practice closing both.

SCHILL. [*Laughs.*] What a sense of humor, eh?

BURGOMASTER. [*Puts on the top hat.*] Permit me to present my grandchildren, gracious lady. Hermine and Adolphine. There's only my wife still to come.

[*He wipes the perspiration from his brow and replaces the hat. The little girls present the roses with elaborate curtsies.*]

CLAIRE. Thank you, my dears. Congratulations, Burgomaster. Extraordinary children.

[*She plants the roses in* PEDRO'S *arms. The* BURGOMASTER *secretly passes his top hat to the* PASTOR, *who puts it on.*]

BURGOMASTER. Our pastor, madame.

[*The* PASTOR *takes off the hat and bows.*]

CLAIRE. Ah. The pastor. How do you do? Do you give consolation to the dying?

PASTOR [*a bit puzzled*]. That is part of my ministry, yes.

CLAIRE. And to those who are condemned to death?

PASTOR. Capital punishment has been abolished in this country, madame.

CLAIRE. I see. Well, it could be restored, I suppose.

[*The* PASTOR *hands back the hat. He shrugs his shoulders in confusion.*]

SCHILL. [*Laughs.*] What an original sense of humor!

[*All laugh, a little blankly.*]

CLAIRE. Well, I can't sit here all day —I should like to see the town.

[*The* BURGOMASTER *offers his arm.*]

BURGOMASTER. May I have the honor, gracious lady?

CLAIRE. Thank you, but these legs are not what they were. This one was broken in five places.

SCHILL [*full of concern*]. My kitten!

CLAIRE. When my airplane bumped into a mountain in Afghanistan. All the others were killed. Even the pilot. But as you see, I survived. I don't fly any more.

SCHILL. But you're as strong as ever now.

CLAIRE. Stronger.

BURGOMASTER. Never fear, gracious lady. The town doctor has a car.

CLAIRE. I never ride in motors.

BURGOMASTER. You never ride in motors?

CLAIRE. Not since my Ferrari crashed in Hong Kong.

SCHILL. But how do you travel, then, little witch? On a broom?

CLAIRE. Mike—Max!

[*She claps her hands. Two huge bodyguards come in, left, carrying a sedan chair. She sits in it.*]

I travel this way—a bit antiquated, of course. But perfectly safe. Ha! Ha! Aren't they magnificent? Mike and Max. I bought them in America. They were in jail, condemned to the chair. I had them pardoned. Now they're condemned to my chair. I paid fifty thousand dollars apiece for them. You couldn't get them now for twice the sum. The sedan chair comes from the Louvre. I fancied it so much that the president of France gave it to me. The French are so impulsive, don't you think so, Anton? Go!

[MIKE *and* MAX *start to carry her off.*]

BURGOMASTER. You wish to visit the cathedral? And the old town hall?

CLAIRE. No. The great barn. And the forest of Konradsweil. I wish to go with Anton and visit our old haunts once again.

PASTOR. Very touching.

CLAIRE [*to the butler*]. Will you send my luggage and the coffin to the Golden Apostle?

BURGOMASTER. The coffin?

CLAIRE. Yes. I brought one with me. Go!

TEACHER. Hip-hip—

ALL. Hurrah! Hip-hip, hurrah! Hurrah!

[*They bear off in the direction of the town. The townspeople burst into cheers. The church bell rings.*]

BURGOMASTER. Ah, thank God—the bell at last.

[*The* POLICEMAN *is about to follow the others, when the two* BLIND MEN *appear. They are not young, yet they seem childish—a strange effect. Though they are of different height and features, they are dressed exactly alike, and so create the effect of being twins. They walk slowly, feeling their way. Their voices, when they speak, are curiously high and flutelike, and they have a curious trick of repetition of phrases.*]

FIRST BLIND MAN. We're in—

BOTH BLIND MEN. Güllen.

FIRST BLIND MAN. We breathe—

SECOND BLIND MAN. We breathe—

BOTH BLIND MEN. We breathe the air, the air of Güllen.

POLICEMAN [*startled*]. Who are you?

FIRST BLIND MAN. We belong to the lady.

SECOND BLIND MAN. We belong to the lady. She calls us—

FIRST BLIND MAN. Kobby.

SECOND BLIND MAN. And Lobby.

POLICEMAN. Madame Zachanassian is staying at the Golden Apostle.

FIRST BLIND MAN. We're blind.

SECOND BLIND MAN. We're blind.

POLICEMAN. You've had a lot to do with me, then. I'll take you there.

FIRST BLIND MAN. Thank you, Mr. Policeman.

SECOND BLIND MAN. Thanks very much.

POLICEMAN. Hey! How do you know I'm a policeman, if you're blind?

BOTH BLIND MEN. By your voice. By your voice.

FIRST BLIND MAN. All policemen sound the same.

POLICEMAN. You've had a lot to do with the police, have you, little men?

FIRST BLIND MAN. Men he calls us!

BOTH BLIND MEN. Men!

POLICEMAN. What are you then?

BOTH BLIND MEN. You'll see. You'll see.

[*The* POLICEMAN *claps his hands suddenly. The* BLIND MEN *turn sharply toward the sound. The* POLICEMAN *is convinced they are blind.*]

POLICEMAN. What's your trade?

BOTH BLIND MEN. We have no trade.

SECOND BLIND MAN. We play music.

FIRST BLIND MAN. We sing.

SECOND BLIND MAN. We amuse the lady.

FIRST BLIND MAN. We look after the beast.

SECOND BLIND MAN. We feed it.

FIRST BLIND MAN. We stroke it.

SECOND BLIND MAN. We take it for walks.

POLICEMAN. What beast?

BOTH BLIND MEN. You'll see—you'll see.

SECOND BLIND MAN. We give it raw meat.

FIRST BLIND MAN. And she gives us chicken and wine.
SECOND BLIND MAN. Every day—
BOTH BLIND MEN. Every day.
POLICEMAN. Rich people have strange tastes.
BOTH BLIND MEN. Strange tastes— strange tastes.

[*The* POLICEMAN *puts on his helmet.*]

POLICEMAN. Come along, I'll take you to the lady.

[*The two* BLIND MEN *turn and walk off.*]

BOTH BLIND MEN. We know the way— we know the way.

[*The station and the little house vanish. A sign representing the Golden Apostle descends. The scene dissolves into the interior of the inn. The Golden Apostle is seen to be in the last stages of decay. The walls are cracked and moldering, and the plaster is falling from the ancient lath. A table represents the café of the inn. The* BURGOMASTER *and the* TEACHER *sit at this table, drinking a glass together. A procession of townspeople, carrying many pieces of luggage, passes. Then comes a coffin and, last, a large box covered with a canvas. They cross the stage from right to left.*]

BURGOMASTER. Trunks. Suitcases. Boxes. [*He looks up apprehensively at the ceiling.*] The floor will never bear the weight. [*As the large covered box is carried in, he peers under the canvas, then draws back.*] Good God!
TEACHER. Why, what's in it?
BURGOMASTER. A live panther. [*They laugh. The* BURGOMASTER *lifts his glass solemnly.*] Your health, Professor. Let's hope she puts the foundry back on its feet.
TEACHER. [*Lifts his glass.*] And the wagonworks.
BURGOMASTER. And the Golden Eagle Pencil Factory. Once that starts

moving, everything else will go. *Prosit.*[4]

[*They touch glasses and drink.*]

TEACHER. What does she need a panther for?
BURGOMASTER. Don't ask me. The whole thing is too much for me. The pastor had to go home and lie down.
TEACHER. [*Sets down his glass.*] If you want to know the truth, she frightens me.
BURGOMASTER. [*Nods gravely.*] She's a strange one.
TEACHER. You understand, Burgomaster, a man who for twenty-two years has been correcting the Latin compositions of the students of Güllen is not unaccustomed to surprises. I have seen things to make one's hair stand on end. But when this woman suddenly appeared on the platform, a shudder tore through me. It was as though out of the clear sky all at once a fury descended upon us, beating its black wings—

[*The* POLICEMAN *comes in. He mops his face.*]

POLICEMAN. Ah! Now the old place is livening up a bit!
BURGOMASTER. Ah, Schultz, come and join us.
POLICEMAN. Thank you. [*He calls.*] Beer!
BURGOMASTER. Well, what's the news from the front?
POLICEMAN. I'm just back from Schiller's barn. My God! What a scene! She had us all tiptoeing around in the straw as if we were in church. Nobody dared to speak above a whisper. And the way she carried on! I was so embarrassed I let them go to the forest by themselves.
BURGOMASTER. Does the fiance go with them?
POLICEMAN. With his fishing rod and

_____
4 Your health.

his landing net. In full marching order. [*He calls again.*] Beer!

BURGOMASTER. That will be her seventh husband.

TEACHER. Her eighth.

BURGOMASTER. But what does she expect to find in the Konradsweil forest?

POLICEMAN. The same thing she expected to find in the old barn, I suppose. The—the—

TEACHER. The ashes of her youthful love.

POLICEMAN. Exactly.

TEACHER. It's poetry.

POLICEMAN. Poetry.

TEACHER. Sheer poetry! It makes one think of Shakespeare, of Wagner. Of Romeo and Juliet.

[*The* SECOND MAN *comes in as a waiter. The* POLICEMAN *is served his beer.*]

BURGOMASTER. Yes, you're right. [*solemnly*] Gentlemen, I would like to propose a toast. To our great and good friend, Anton Schill, who is even now working on our behalf.

POLICEMAN. Yes! He's really working.

BURGOMASTER. Gentlemen, to the best-loved citizen of this town. My successor, Anton Schill!

[*They raise their glasses. At this point an unearthly scream is heard. It is the black panther howling offstage. The sign of the Golden Apostle rises out of sight. The lights go down. The inn vanishes. Only the wooden bench, on which the four men were lounging in the opening scene, is left on the stage, downstage right. The procession comes on upstage. The two bodyguards carry in* CLAIRE'S *sedan chair. Next to it walks* SCHILL. PEDRO *walks behind, with his fishing rod. Last come the two* BLIND MEN *and the butler.* CLAIRE *alights.*]

CLAIRE. Stop! Take my chair off somewhere else. I'm tired of looking at you.

[*The bodyguards and the sedan chair go off.*]

Pedro darling, your brook is just a little further along down that path. Listen. You can hear it from here. Bobby, take him and show him where it is.

BOTH BLIND MEN. We'll show him the way—we'll show him the way.

[*They go off, left.* PEDRO *follows.* BOBBY *walks off, right*]

CLAIRE. Look, Anton. Our tree. There's the heart you carved in the bark long ago.

SCHILL. Yes. It's still there.

CLAIRE. How it has grown! The trunk is black and wrinkled. Why, its limbs are twice what they were. Some of them have died.

SCHILL. It's aged. But it's there.

CLAIRE. Like everything else. [*She crosses examining other trees.*] Oh, how tall they are. How long it is since I walked here, barefoot over the pine needles and the damp leaves! Look, Anton. A fawn.

SCHILL. Yes, a fawn. It's the season.

CLAIRE. I thought everything would be changed. But it's all just as we left it. This is the seat we sat on years ago. Under these branches you kissed me. And over there under the hawthorn, where the moss is soft and green, we would lie in each other's arms. It is all as it used to be. Only we have changed.

SCHILL. Not so much, little witch. I remember the first night we spent together, you ran away and I chased you till I was quite breathless—

CLAIRE. Yes.

SCHILL. Then I was angry and I was going home, when suddenly I heard you call and I looked up, and there you were sitting in a tree, laughing down at me.

CLAIRE. No. It was in the great barn. I was in the hayloft.

SCHILL. Were you?

CLAIRE. Yes. What else do you remember?

SCHILL. I remember the morning we went swimming by the waterfall, and afterwards we were lying together on the big rock in the sun, when suddenly we heard footsteps and we just had time to snatch up our clothes and run behind the bushes when the old pastor appeared and scolded you for not being in school.

CLAIRE. No. It was the schoolmaster who found us. It was Sunday and I was supposed to be in church.

SCHILL. Really?

CLAIRE. Yes. Tell me more.

SCHILL. I remember the time your father beat you, and you showed me the cuts on your back, and I swore I'd kill him. And the next day I dropped a tile from a roof top and split his head open.

CLAIRE. You missed him.

SCHILL. No!

CLAIRE. You hit old Mr. Reiner.

SCHILL. Did I?

CLAIRE. Yes. I was seventeen. And you were not yet twenty. You were so handsome. You were the best-looking boy in town.

[*The two* BLIND MEN *begin playing mandolin music offstage, very softly.*]

SCHILL. And you were the prettiest girl.

CLAIRE. We were made for each other.

SCHILL. So we were.

CLAIRE. But you married Mathilde Blumhard and her store, and I married old Zachanassian and his oil wells. He found me in a whorehouse in Hamburg. It was my hair that entangled him, the old golden beetle.

SCHILL. Clara!

CLAIRE. [*She claps her hands.*] Bobby! A cigar.

[BOBBY *appears with a leather case. He selects a cigar, puts it in a holder, lights it, and presents it to* CLAIRE.]

SCHILL. My kitten smokes cigars!

CLAIRE. Yes. I adore them. Would you care for one?

SCHILL. Yes, please. I've never smoked one of those.

CLAIRE. It's a taste I acquired from old Zachanassian. Among other things. He was a real connoisseur.

SCHILL. We used to sit on this bench once, you and I, and smoke cigarettes. Do you remember?

CLAIRE. Yes. I remember.

SCHILL. The cigarettes I bought from Mathilde.

CLAIRE. No. She gave them to you for nothing.

SCHILL. Clara—don't be angry with me for marrying Mathilde.

CLAIRE. She had money.

SCHILL. But what a lucky thing for you that I did!

CLAIRE. Oh?

SCHILL. You were so young, so beautiful. You deserved a far better fate than to settle in this wretched town without any future.

CLAIRE. Yes?

SCHILL. If you had stayed in Güllen and married me, your life would have been wasted, like mine.

CLAIRE. Oh?

SCHILL. Look at me. A wretched shopkeeper in a bankrupt town!

CLAIRE. But you have your family.

SCHILL. My family! Never for a moment do they let me forget my failure, my poverty.

CLAIRE. Mathilde has not made you happy?

SCHILL. [*Shrugs.*] What does it matter?

CLAIRE. And the children?

SCHILL. [*Shakes his head.*] They're so completely materialistic. You know, they have no interest whatever in higher things.

CLAIRE. How sad for you.

[*A moment's pause, during which only the faint tinkling of the music is heard.*]

SCHILL. Yes. You know, since you went

away my life has passed by like a stupid dream. I've hardly once been out of this town. A trip to a lake years ago. It rained all the time. And once five days in Berlin. That's all.

CLAIRE. The world is much the same everywhere.

SCHILL. At least you've seen it.

CLAIRE. Yes. I've seen it.

SCHILL. You've lived in it.

CLAIRE. I've lived in it. The world and I have been on very intimate terms.

SCHILL. Now that you've come back, perhaps things will change.

CLAIRE. Naturally. I certainly won't leave my native town in this condition.

SCHILL. It will take millions to put us on our feet again.

CLAIRE. I have millions.

SCHILL. One, two, three.

CLAIRE. Why not?

SCHILL. You mean—you will help us?

CLAIRE. Yes.

[*A woodpecker is heard in the distance.*]

SCHILL. I knew it—I knew it. I told them you were generous. I told them you were good. Oh, my kitten, my kitten.

[*He takes her hand. She turns her head away and listens.*]

CLAIRE. Listen! A woodpecker.

SCHILL. It's all just the way it was in the days when we were young and full of courage. The sun high above the pines. White clouds, piling up on one another. And the cry of the cuckoo in the distance. And the wind rustling the leaves, like the sound of surf on a beach. Just as it was years ago. If only we could roll back time and be together always.

CLAIRE. Is that your wish?

SCHILL. Yes. You left me, but you never left my heart. [*He raises her hand to his lips.*] The same soft little hand.

CLAIRE. No, not quite the same. It was crushed in the plane accident. But they mended it. They mend everything nowadays.

SCHILL. Crushed? You wouldn't know it. See, another fawn.

CLAIRE. The old wood is alive with memories.

[PEDRO *appears, right, with a fish in his hand.*]

PEDRO. See what I've caught, darling. See? A pike. Over two kilos.

[*The* BLIND MEN *appear onstage.*]

BOTH BLIND MEN [*clapping their hands*]. A pike! A pike! Hurrah! Hurrah!

[*As the* BLIND MEN *clap their hands,* CLAIRE *and* SCHILL *exit, and the scene dissolves. The clapping of hands is taken up on all sides. The townspeople wheel in the walls of the café. A brass band strikes up a march tune. The door of the Golden Apostle descends. The townspeople bring in tables and set them with ragged tablecloths, cracked china, and glassware. There is a table in the center, upstage, flanked by two tables perpendicular to it, right and left. The* PASTOR *and the* BURGO-MASTER *come in.* SCHILL *enters. Other townspeople filter in, left and right. One, the* ATHLETE, *is in gymnastic costume. The applause continues.*]

BURGOMASTER. She's coming!

[CLAIRE *enters upstage, center, followed by* BOBBY.]

The applause is meant for you, gracious lady.

CLAIRE. The band deserves it more than I. They blow from the heart. And the human pyramid was beautiful. You, show me your muscles. [*The* ATHLETE *kneels before her.*] Superb.

Wonderful arms, powerful hands. Have you ever strangled a man with them?

ATHLETE. Strangled?

CLAIRE. Yes. It's perfectly simple. A little pressure in the proper place, and the rest goes by itself. As in politics.

[*The* BURGOMASTER'S *wife comes up, simpering.*]

BURGOMASTER. [*Presents her.*] Permit me to present my wife, Madame Zachanassian.

CLAIRE. Annette Dummermuth. The head of the class.

BURGOMASTER. [*He presents another sour-looking woman.*] Frau Schill.

CLAIRE. Mathilde Blumhard. I remember the way you used to follow Anton with your eyes, from behind the shop door. You've grown a little thin and dry, my poor Mathilde.

SCHILL. My daughter, Ottilie.

CLAIRE. Your daughter...

SCHILL. My son, Karl.

CLAIRE. Your son. Two of them!

[*The town* DOCTOR *comes in, right. He is a man of fifty, strong and stocky, with bristly black hair, a mustache, and a saber cut on his cheek. He is wearing an old cutaway.*]

DOCTOR. Well, well, my old Mercedes got me here in time after all!

BURGOMASTER. Dr. Nüsslin, the town physician. Madame Zachanassian.

DOCTOR. Deeply honored, madame.

[*He kisses her hand.* CLAIRE *studies him.*]

CLAIRE. It is you who signs the death certificates?

DOCTOR. Death certificates?

CLAIRE. When someone dies.

DOCTOR. Why certainly. That is one of my duties.

CLAIRE. And when the heart dies, what do you put down? Heart failure?

SCHILL. [*laughing*]. What a golden sense of humor!

DOCTOR. Bit grim, wouldn't you say?

SCHILL. [*Whispers.*] Not at all, not at all. She's promised us a million.

BURGOMASTER. [*Turns his head.*] What?

SCHILL. A million!

ALL. [*Whisper.*] A million!

[CLAIRE *turns toward them.*]

CLAIRE. Burgomaster.

BURGOMASTER. Yes?

CLAIRE. I'm hungry. [*The girls and the waiter fill glasses and bring food. There is a general stir. All take their places at the tables.*] Are you going to make a speech?

[*The* BURGOMASTER *bows.* CLAIRE *sits next to the* BURGOMASTER. *The* BURGOMASTER *rises, tapping his knife on his glass. He is radiant with good will. All applaud.*]

BURGOMASTER. Gracious lady and friends. Gracious lady, it is now many years since you first left your native town of Güllen, which was founded by the Elector Hasso and which nestles in the green slope between the forest of Konradsweil and the beautiful valley of Pückenried. Much has taken place in this time, much that is evil.

TEACHER. That's true.

BURGOMASTER. The world is not what it was; it has become harsh and bitter, and we too have had our share of harshness and bitterness. But in all this time, dear lady, we have never forgotten our little Clara. [*Applause.*] Many years ago you brightened the town with your pretty face as a child, and now once again you brighten it with your presence. [*Polite applause.*] We haven't forgotten you, and we haven't forgotten your family. Your mother, beautiful and robust even in her old age— [*He looks for his notes on the table.*]

—although unfortunately taken from us in the bloom of her youth by an infirmity of the lungs. Your respected father, Siegfried Wäscher, the builder, an example of whose work next to our railway station is often visited—[SCHILL *covers his face.*]—that is to say, admired—a lasting monument of local design and local workmanship. And you, gracious lady, whom we remember as a golden-haired—[*He looks at her.*]—little red-headed sprite romping about our peaceful streets—on your way to school—which of us does not treasure your memory? [*He pokes nervously at his notebook.*] We well remember your scholarly attainments—

TEACHER. Yes.

BURGOMASTER. Natural history...Extraordinary sense of justice...And, above all, your supreme generosity. [*Great applause.*] We shall never forget how you once spent the whole of your little savings to buy a sack of potatoes for a poor starving widow who was in need of food. Gracious lady, ladies and gentlemen, today our little Clara has become the world-famous Claire Zachanassian who has founded hospitals, soup kitchens, charitable institutes, art projects, libraries, nurseries, and schools, and now that she has at last once more returned to the town of her birth, sadly fallen as it is, I say in the name of all her loving friends who have sorely missed her: Long live our Clara!

ALL. Long live our Clara!

[*Cheers. Music. Fanfare. Applause.* CLAIRE *rises.*]

CLAIRE. Mr. Burgomaster. Fellow townsmen. I am greatly moved by the nature of your welcome and the disinterested joy which you have manifested on the occasion of my visit to my native town. I was not quite the child the burgomaster described in his gracious address...

BURGOMASTER. Too modest, madame.

CLAIRE. In school I was beaten—

TEACHER. Not by me.

CLAIRE. And the sack of potatoes which I presented to Widow Boll, I stole with the help of Anton Schill, not to save the old trull from starvation, but so that for once I might sleep with Anton in a real bed instead of under the trees of the forest. [*The townspeople look grave, embarrassed.*] Nevertheless, I shall try to deserve your good opinion. In memory of the seventeen years I spent among you, I am prepared to hand over as a gift to the town of Güllen the sum of one billion marks. Five hundred million to the town, and five hundred million to be divided per capita among the citizens.

[*There is a moment of dead silence.*]

BURGOMASTER. A billion marks?

CLAIRE. On one condition.

[*Suddenly a movement of uncontrollable joy breaks out. People jump on chairs, dance about, yell excitedly. The* ATHLETE *turns handsprings in front of the speaker's table.*]

SCHILL. Oh, Clara, you astonishing, incredible, magnificent woman! What a heart! What a gesture! Oh—my little witch! [*He kisses her hand.*]

BURGOMASTER. [*Holds up his arms for order.*] Quiet! Quiet, please! On one condition, the gracious lady said. Now, madame, may we know what that condition is?

CLAIRE. I will tell you. In exchange for my billion marks, I want justice.

[*Silence.*]

BURGOMASTER. Justice, madame?

CLAIRE. I wish to buy justice.

BURGOMASTER. But justice cannot be bought, madame.

CLAIRE. Everything can be bought.

BURGOMASTER. I don't understand at all.

CLAIRE. Bobby, step forward.

[*The butler goes to the center of the stage. He takes off his dark glasses and turns his face with a solemn air.*]

BOBBY. Does anyone here present recognize me?

FRAU SCHILL. Hofer! Hofer!

ALL. Who? What's that?

TEACHER. Not Chief Magistrate Hofer?

BOBBY. Exactly. Chief Magistrate Hofer. When Madame Zachanassian was a girl, I was presiding judge at the criminal court of Güllen. I served there until twenty-five years ago, when Madame Zachanassian offered me the opportunity of entering her service as butler. I accepted. You may consider it a strange employment for a member of the magistracy, but the salary—

[CLAIRE *bangs the mallet on the table.*]

CLAIRE. Come to the point.

BOBBY. You have heard Madame Zachanassian's offer. She will give you a billion marks—when you have undone the injustice that she suffered at your hands here in Güllen as a girl. [*All murmur.*]

BURGOMASTER. Injustice at our hands? Impossible!

BOBBY. Anton Schill...

SCHILL. Yes?

BOBBY. Kindly stand.

[SCHILL *rises. He smiles, as if puzzled. He shrugs.*]

SCHILL. Yes?

BOBBY. In those days, a bastardy case was tried before me. Madame Claire Zachanassian, at that time called Clara Wäscher, charged you with being the father of her illegitimate child. [*Silence.*] You denied the charge. And produced two witnesses in your support.

SCHILL. That's ancient history. An absurd business. We were children. Who remembers?

CLAIRE. Where are the blind men?

BOTH BLIND MEN. Here we are. Here we are.

[MIKE *and* MAX *push them forward.*]

BOBBY. You recognize these men, Anton Schill?

SCHILL. I never saw them before in my life. What are they?

BOTH BLIND MEN. We've changed. We've changed.

BOBBY. What were your names in your former life?

FIRST BLIND MAN. I was Jacob Hueblein. Jacob Hueblein.

SECOND BLIND MAN. I was Ludwig Sparr. Ludwig Sparr.

BOBBY [*to* SCHILL]. Well?

SCHILL. These names mean nothing to me.

BOBBY. Jacob Hueblein and Ludwig Sparr, do you recognize the defendant?

FIRST BLIND MAN. We're blind.

SECOND BLIND MAN. We're blind.

SCHILL. Ha-ha-ha!

BOBBY. By his voice?

BOTH BLIND MEN. By his voice. By his voice.

BOBBY. At that trial, I was the judge. And you?

BOTH BLIND MEN. We were the witnesses.

BOBBY. And what did you testify on that occasion?

FIRST BLIND MAN. That we had slept with Clara Wäscher.

SECOND BLIND MAN. Both of us. Many times.

BOBBY. And was it true?

FIRST BLIND MAN. No.

SECOND BLIND MAN. We swore falsely.

BOBBY. And why did you swear falsely?

FIRST BLIND MAN. Anton Schill bribed us.

SECOND BLIND MAN. He bribed us.

BOBBY. With what?

BOTH BLIND MEN. With a bottle of schnapps.

BOBBY. And now tell the people what happened to you. [*They hesitate and whimper.*] Speak!

FIRST BLIND MAN [*in a low voice*]. She tracked us down.

BOBBY. Madame Zachanassian tracked them down. Jacob Hueblein was found in Canada. Ludwig Sparr in Australia. And when she found you, what did she do to you?

SECOND BLIND MAN. She handed us over to Mike and Max.

BOBBY. And what did Mike and Max do to you?

FIRST BLIND MAN. They made us what you see.

[*The* BLIND MEN *cover their faces.* MIKE *and* MAX *push them off.*]

BOBBY. And there you have it. We are all present in Güllen once again. The plaintiff. The defendant. The two false witnesses. The judge. Many years have passed. Does the plaintiff have anything further to add?

CLAIRE. There is nothing to add.

BOBBY. And the defendant?

SCHILL. Why are you doing this? It was all dead and buried.

BOBBY. What happened to the child that was born?

CLAIRE [*in a low voice*]. It lived a year.

BOBBY. And what happened to you?

CLAIRE. I became a whore.

BOBBY. Why?

CLAIRE. The judgment of the court left me no alternative. No one would

trust me. No one would give me work.

BOBBY. So. And now, what is the nature of the reparation you demand?

CLAIRE. I want the life of Anton Schill.

[FRAU SCHILL *springs to* ANTON's *side. She puts her arms around him. The children rush to him. He breaks away.*]

FRAU SCHILL. Anton! No! No!

SCHILL. No— No— She's joking. That happened long ago. That's all forgotten.

CLAIRE. Nothing is forgotten. Neither the mornings in the forest, nor the nights in the great barn, nor the bedroom in the cottage, nor your treachery at the end. You said this morning that you wished that time might be rolled back. Very well—I have rolled it back. And now it is I who will buy justice. You bought it with a bottle of schnapps. I am willing to pay one billion marks.

[*The* BURGOMASTER *stands up, very pale and dignified.*]

BURGOMASTER. Madame Zachanassian, we are not in the jungle. We are in Europe. We may be poor, but we are not heathens. In the name of the town of Güllen, I decline your offer. In the name of humanity. We shall never accept.

[*All applaud wildly. The applause turns into a sinister ryhthmic beat. As* CLAIRE *rises, it dies away. She looks at the crowd, then at the* BURGOMASTER.]

CLAIRE. Thank you, Burgomaster. [*She stares at him a long moment.*] I can wait.   [*She turns and walks off.*]

ACT II

The façade of the Golden Apostle, with a balcony on which chairs and a table are set out. To the right of the inn is a sign which reads: "Anton Schill, Handlung."[1] *Under the sign the shop is represented by a broken counter.*

---

[1] "Anton Schill, Merchandise."

Behind the counter are some shelves with tobacco, cigarettes, and liquor bottles. There are two milk cans. The shop door is imaginary, but each entrance is indicated by a doorbell with a tinny sound.
It is early morning.
SCHILL *is sweeping the shop. The* SON *has a pan and brush and also sweeps. The* DAUGHTER *is dusting. They are singing "The Happy Wanderer."*

SCHILL. Karl—

[KARL *crosses with a dustpan.* SCHILL *sweeps dust into the pan. The doorbell rings. The* THIRD MAN *appears, carrying a crate of eggs.*]

THIRD MAN. 'Morning.
SCHILL. Ah, good morning, Wechsler.
THIRD MAN. Twelve dozen eggs, medium brown. Right?
SCHILL. Take them, Karl. [*The* SON *puts the crate in a corner.*] Did they deliver the milk yet?
SON. Before you came down.
THIRD MAN. Eggs are going up again, Herr Schill. First of the month.

[*He gives* SCHILL *a slip to sign.*]

SCHILL. What? Again? And who's going to buy them?
THIRD MAN. Fifty pfennig a dozen.
SCHILL. I'll have to cancel my order, that's all.
THIRD MAN. That's up to you, Herr Schill. [SCHILL *signs the slip.*]
SCHILL. There's nothing else to do. [*He hands back the slip.*] And how's the family?
THIRD MAN. Oh, scraping along. Maybe now things will get better.
SCHILL. Maybe.
THIRD MAN [*going*]. 'Morning.
SCHILL. Close the door. Don't let the flies in. [*The children resume their singing.*] Now, listen to me, children. I have a little piece of good news for you. I didn't mean to speak of it yet awhile, but well, why not?

Who do you suppose is going to be the next burgomaster? Eh? [*They look up at him.*] Yes, in spite of everything. It's settled. It's official. What an honor for the family, eh? Especially at a time like this. To say nothing of the salary and the rest of it.
SON. Burgomaster!
SCHILL. Burgomaster. [*The* SON *shakes him warmly by the hand. The* DAUGHTER *kisses him.*] You see, you don't have to be entirely ashamed of your father. [*Silence.*] Is your mother coming down to breakfast soon?
DAUGHTER. Mother's tired. She's going to stay upstairs.
SCHILL. You have a good mother, at least. There you are lucky. Oh, well, if she wants to rest, let her rest. We'll have breakfast together, the three of us. I'll fry some eggs and open a tin of the American ham. This morning we're going to breakfast like kings.
SON. I'd like to, only—I can't.
SCHILL. You've got to eat, you know.
SON. I've got to run down to the station. One of the laborers is sick. They said they could use me.
SCHILL. You want to work on the rails in all this heat? That's no work for a son of mine.
SON. Look, Father, we can use the money.
SCHILL. Well, if you feel you have to.

[*The son goes to the door. The* DAUGHTER *moves toward* SCHILL.]

DAUGHTER. I'm sorry, Father. I have to go too.
SCHILL. You too? And where is the young lady going, if I may be so bold?
DAUGHTER. There may be something for me at the employment agency.
SCHILL. Employment agency?
DAUGHTER. It's important to get there early.

SCHILL. All right. I'll have something nice for you when you get home.

SON *and* DAUGHTER. [*Salute.*] Good day, Burgomaster.

[*The* SON *and* DAUGHTER *go out. The* FIRST MAN *comes into* SCHILL'S *shop. Mandolin and guitar music are heard offstage.*]

SCHILL. Good morning, Hofbauer.

FIRST MAN. Cigarettes. [SCHILL *takes a pack from the shelf.*] Not those. I'll have the green today.

SCHILL. They cost more.

FIRST MAN. Put it in the book.

SCHILL. What?

FIRST MAN. Charge it.

SCHILL. Well, all right, I'll make an exception this time—seeing it's you, Hofbauer.

[SCHILL *writes in his cash book.*]

FIRST MAN [*opening the pack of cigarettes*]. Who's that playing out there?

SCHILL. The two blind men.

FIRST MAN. They play well.

SCHILL. To hell with them.

FIRST MAN. They make you nervous? [SCHILL *shrugs. The* FIRST MAN *lights a cigarette.*] She's getting ready for the wedding, I hear.

SCHILL. Yes. So they say.

[*Enter the* FIRST *and* SECOND WOMEN. *They cross to the counter.*]

FIRST WOMAN. Good morning, good morning.

SECOND WOMAN. Good morning.

FIRST MAN. Good morning.

SCHILL. Good morning, ladies.

FIRST WOMAN. Good morning, Herr Schill.

SECOND WOMAN. Good morning.

FIRST WOMAN. Milk please, Herr Schill.

SCHILL. Milk.

SECOND WOMAN. And milk for me too.

SCHILL. A liter of milk each. Right away.

FIRST WOMAN. Whole milk, please, Herr Schill.

SCHILL. Whole milk?

SECOND WOMAN. Yes. Whole milk, please.

SCHILL. Whole milk, I can only give you half a liter each of whole milk.

FIRST WOMAN. All right.

SCHILL. Half a liter of whole milk here, and half a liter of whole milk here. There you are.

FIRST WOMAN. And butter please, a quarter kilo.

SCHILL. Butter, I haven't any butter. I can give you some very nice lard?

FIRST WOMAN. No. Butter.

SCHILL. Goose fat? [*The* FIRST WOMAN *shakes her head.*] Chicken fat?

FIRST WOMAN. Butter.

SCHILL. Butter. Now, wait a minute, though. I have a tin of imported butter here somewhere. Ah. There you are. No, sorry, she asked first, but I can order some for you from Kalberstadt tomorrow.

SECOND WOMAN. And white bread.

SCHILL. White bread.

[*He takes a loaf and a knife.*]

SECOND WOMAN. The whole loaf.

SCHILL. But a whole loaf would cost . . .

SECOND WOMAN. Charge it.

SCHILL. Charge it?

FIRST WOMAN. And a package of milk chocolate.

SCHILL. Package of milk chocolate—right away.

SECOND WOMAN. One for me, too, Herr Schill.

SCHILL. And a package of milk chocolate for you, too.

FIRST WOMAN. We'll eat it here, if you don't mind.

SCHILL. Yes, please do.

SECOND WOMAN. It's so cool at the back of the shop.

SCHILL. Charge it?

WOMEN. Of course.

SCHILL. All for one, one for all.

[*The* SECOND MAN *enters.*]

SECOND MAN. Good morning.
THE TWO WOMEN. Good morning.
SCHILL. Good morning, Helmesberger.
SECOND MAN. It's going to be a hot day.
SCHILL. Phew!
SECOND MAN. How's business?
SCHILL. Fabulous. For a while no one came, and now all of a sudden I'm running a luxury trade.
SECOND MAN. Good!
SCHILL. Oh, I'll never forget the way you all stood by me at the Golden Apostle in spite of your need, in spite of everything That was the finest hour of my life.
FIRST MAN. We're not heathens, you know.
SECOND MAN. We're behind you, my boy; the whole town's behind you.
FIRST MAN. As firm as a rock.
FIRST WOMAN [*munching her chocolate*]. As firm as a rock, Herr Schill.
BOTH WOMEN. As firm as a rock.
SECOND MAN. There's no denying it— you're the most popular man in town.
FIRST MAN. The most important.
SECOND MAN. And in the spring, God willing, you will be our burgomaster.
FIRST MAN. Sure as a gun.
ALL. Sure as a gun.

[*Enter* PEDRO *with fishing equipment and a fish in his landing net.*]

PEDRO. Would you please weigh my fish for me?
SCHILL. [*Weighs it.*] Two kilos.
PEDRO. Is that all?
SCHILL. Two kilos exactly.
PEDRO. Two kilos!

[*He gives* SCHILL *a tip and exits.*]

SECOND WOMAN. The fiancé.
FIRST WOMAN. They're to be married this week. It will be a tremendous wedding.
SECOND WOMAN. I saw his picture in the paper.
FIRST WOMAN. [*Sighs.*] Ah, what a man!
SECOND MAN. Give me a bottle of schnapps.
SCHILL. The usual?
SECOND MAN. No, cognac.
SCHILL. Cognac? But cognac costs twenty-two marks fifty.
SECOND MAN. We all have to splurge a little now and again—
SCHILL. Here you are. Three Star.
SECOND MAN. And a package of pipe tobacco.
SCHILL. Black or blond?
SECOND MAN. English.
SCHILL. English! But that makes twenty-three marks eighty.
SECOND MAN. Chalk it up.
SCHILL. Now, look. I'll make an exception this week. Only, you will have to pay me the moment your unemployment check comes in. I don't want to be kept waiting. [*suddenly*] Helmesberger, are those new shoes you're wearing?
SECOND MAN. Yes, what about it?
SCHILL. You too, Hofbauer. Yellow shoes! Brand new!
FIRST MAN. So?
SCHILL [*to the women*]. And you. You all have new shoes! New shoes!
FIRST WOMAN. A person can't walk around forever in the same old shoes.
SECOND WOMAN. Shoes wear out.
SCHILL. And the money. Where does the money come from?
FIRST WOMAN. We got them on credit, Herr Schill.
SECOND WOMAN. On credit.
SCHILL. On credit? And where all of a sudden do you get credit?
SECOND MAN. Everybody gives credit now.
FIRST WOMAN. You gave us credit yourself.
SCHILL. And what are you going to

pay with? Eh? [*They are all silent.* SCHILL *advances upon them threateningly.*] With what? Eh? With what? With what?

[*Suddenly he understands. He takes his apron off quickly, flings it on the counter, gets his jacket, and walks off with an air of determination. Now the shop sign vanishes. The shelves are pushed off. The lights go up on the balcony of the Golden Apostle, and the balcony unit itself moves forward into the optical center.* CLAIRE *and* BOBBY *step out on the balcony.* CLAIRE *sits down.* BOBBY *serves coffee.*]

CLAIRE. A lovely autumn morning. A silver haze on the streets and a violet sky above. Count Holk would have liked this. Remember him, Bobby? My third husband?

BOBBY. Yes, madame.

CLAIRE. Horrible man!

BOBBY. Yes, madame.

CLAIRE. Where is Monsieur Pedro? Is he up yet?

BOBBY. Yes, madame. He's fishing.

CLAIRE. Already? What a singular passion!

[PEDRO *comes in with the fish.*]

PEDRO. Good morning, my love.

CLAIRE. Pedro! There you are.

PEDRO. Look, my darling. Four kilos!

CLAIRE. A jewel! I'll have it grilled for your lunch. Give it to Bobby.

PEDRO. Ah—it is so wonderful here! I like your little town.

CLAIRE. Oh, do you?

PEDRO. Yes. These people, they are all so—what is the word?

CLAIRE. Simple, honest, hard-working, decent.

PEDRO. But, my angel, you are a mind reader. That's just what I was going to say—however did you guess?

CLAIRE. I know them.

PEDRO. Yet when we arrived it was all so dirty, so—what is the word?

CLAIRE. Shabby.

PEDRO. Exactly. But now everywhere you go, you see them busy as bees, cleaning their streets—

CLAIRE. Repairing their houses, sweeping—dusting—hanging new curtains in the windows—singing as they work.

PEDRO. But you astonishing, wonderful woman! You can't see all that from here.

CLAIRE. I know them. And in their gardens—I am sure that in their gardens they are manuring the soil for the spring.

PEDRO. My angel, you know everything. This morning on my way fishing I said to myself, look at them all manuring their gardens. It is extraordinary—and it's all because of you. Your return has given them a new—what is the word?

CLAIRE. Lease on life?

PEDRO. Precisely.

CLAIRE. The town was dying, it's true. But a town doesn't have to die. I think they realize that now. People die, not towns. Bobby!

[BOBBY *appears.*]

A cigar.

[*The lights fade on the balcony, which moves back upstage. Somewhat to the right, a sign descends. It reads: "Polizei." The* POLICEMAN *pushes a desk under it. This, with the bench, becomes the police station. He places a bottle of beer and a glass on the desk and goes to hang up his coat offstage. The telephone rings.*]

POLICEMAN. Schultz speaking. Yes, we have a couple of rooms for the night. No, not for rent. This is not the hotel. This is the Güllen police station.

[*He laughs and hangs up.* SCHILL *comes in. He is evidently nervous.*]

SCHILL. Schultz.

POLICEMAN. Hello, Schill. Come in. Sit

down. Beer?

SCHILL. Please. [*He drinks thirstily.*]

POLICEMAN. What can I do for you?

SCHILL. I want you to arrest Madame Zachanassian.

POLICEMAN. Eh?

SCHILL. I said I want you to arrest Madame Zachanassian.

POLICEMAN. What the hell are you talking about?

SCHILL. I ask you to arrest this woman at once.

POLICEMAN. What offense has the lady committed?

SCHILL. You know perfectly well. She offered a billion marks—

POLICEMAN. And you want her arrested for that?

[*He pours beer into his glass.*]

SCHILL. Schultz! It's your duty.

SCHULTZ. Extraordinary! Extraordinary idea! [*He drinks his beer.*]

SCHILL. I'm speaking to you as your next burgomaster.

POLICEMAN. Schill, that's true. The lady offered us a billion marks. But that doesn't entitle us to take police action against her.

SCHILL. Why not?

POLICEMAN. In order to be arrested, a person must first commit a crime.

SCHILL. Incitement to murder.

POLICEMAN. Incitement to murder is a crime. I agree.

SCHILL. Well?

POLICEMAN. And such a proposal—if serious—constitutes an assault.

SCHILL. That's what I mean.

POLICEMAN. But her offer can't be serious.

SCHILL. Why?

POLICEMAN. The price is too high. In a case like yours, one pays a thousand marks, at the most two thousand. But not a billion! That's ridiculous. And even if she meant it, that would only prove she was out of her mind. And that's not a matter for the police.

SCHILL. Whether she's out of her mind or not, the danger to me is the same. That's obvious.

POLICEMAN. Look, Schill, you show us where anyone threatens your life in any way—say, for instance, a man points a gun at you—and we'll be there in a flash.

SCHILL. [*Gets up.*] So I'm to wait till someone points a gun at me?

POLICEMAN. Pull yourself together, Schill. We're all for you in this town.

SCHILL. I wish I could believe it.

POLICEMAN. You don't believe it?

SCHILL. No. No, I don't. All of a sudden my customers are buying white bread, whole milk, butter, imported tobacco. What does it mean?

POLICEMAN. It means business is picking up.

SCHILL. Helmesberger lives on the dole; he hasn't earned anything in five years. Today he bought French cognac.

POLICEMAN. I'll have to try your cognac one of these days.

SCHILL. And shoes. They all have new shoes.

POLICEMAN. And what have you got against new shoes? I'm wearing a new pair myself.

[*He holds out his foot.*]

SCHILL. You too?

POLICEMAN. Why not?

[*He pours out the rest of his beer.*]

SCHILL. Is that Pilsen you're drinking now?

POLICEMAN. It's the only thing.

SCHILL. You used to drink the local beer.

POLICEMAN. Hogwash.

[*Radio music is heard offstage.*]

SCHILL. Listen. You hear?

POLICEMAN. "The Merry Widow." Yes.

SCHILL. No. It's a radio.

POLICEMAN. That's Bergholzer's radio.

SCHILL. Bergholzer!

POLICEMAN. You're right. He should close his window when he plays it. I'll make a note to speak to him.

[*He makes a note in his notebook.*]

SCHILL. And how can Bergholzer pay for a radio?

POLICEMAN. That's his business.

SCHILL. And you, Schultz, with your new shoes and your imported beer —how are you going to pay for them?

POLICEMAN. That's my business. [*His telephone rings. He picks it up.*] Police Station, Güllen. What? What? Where? Where? How? Right, we'll deal with it. [*He hangs up.*]

SCHILL. [*He speaks during the* POLICE-MAN'S *telephone conversation.*] Schultz, listen. No. Schultz, please— listen to me. Don't you see they're all...Listen, please. Look, Schultz. They're all running up debts. And out of these debts comes this sudden prosperity. And out of this prosperity comes the absolute need to kill me.

POLICEMAN [*putting on his jacket*]. You're imagining things.

SCHILL. All she has to do is to sit on her balcony and wait.

POLICEMAN. Don't be a child.

SCHILL. You're all waiting.

POLICEMAN. [*Snaps a loaded clip into the magazine of a rifle.*] Look, Schill, you can relax. The police are here for your protection. They know their job. Let anyone, any time, make the slightest threat to your life, and all you have to do is let us know. We'll do the rest...Now, don't worry.

SCHILL. No, I won't.

POLICEMAN. And don't upset yourself. All right?

SCHILL. Yes. I won't. [*then suddenly, in a low tone*] You have a new gold tooth in your mouth!

POLICEMAN. What are you talking about?

SCHILL [*taking the* POLICEMAN'S *head in his hands and forcing his lips open*]. A brand new, shining gold tooth.

POLICEMAN. [*Breaks away and involuntarily levels the gun at* SCHILL.] Are you crazy? Look, I've no time to waste. Madame Zachanassian's panther's broken loose.

SCHILL. Panther?

POLICEMAN. Yes, it's at large. I've got to hunt it down.

SCHILL. You're not hunting a panther and you know it. It's me you're hunting!

[*The* POLICEMAN *clicks on the safety and lowers the gun.*]

POLICEMAN. Schill! Take my advice. Go home. Lock the door. Keep out of everyone's way. That way you'll be safe. Cheer up! Good times are just around the corner!

[*The lights dim in this area and light up on the balcony.* PEDRO *is lounging in a chair.* CLAIRE *is smoking.*]

PEDRO. Oh, this little town oppresses me.

CLAIRE. Oh, does it? So you've changed your mind?

PEDRO. It is true, I find it charming, delightful—

CLAIRE. Picturesque.

PEDRO. Yes. After all, it's the place where you were born. But it is too quiet for me. Too provincial. Too much like all small towns everywhere. These people—look at them. They fear nothing, they desire nothing, they strive for nothing. They have everything they want. They are asleep.

CLAIRE. Perhaps one day they will come to life again.

PEDRO. My God—do I have to wait for that?

CLAIRE. Yes, you do. Why don't you go back to your fishing?

PEDRO. I think I will.

[PEDRO *turns to go.*]

CLAIRE. Pedro.

PEDRO. Yes, my love?

CLAIRE. Telephone the president of Hambro's Bank.[2] Ask him to transfer a billion marks to my current account.

PEDRO. A billion? Yes, my love.

[*He goes. The lights fade on the balcony. A sign is flown in. It reads: "Rathaus."*[3] *The* THIRD MAN *crosses the stage, right to left, wheeling a new television set on a hand truck. The counter of* SCHILL'S *shop is transformed into the* BURGOMASTER'S *office. The* BURGOMASTER *comes in. He takes a revolver from his pocket, examines it, and sets it down on the desk. He sits down and starts writing.* SCHILL *knocks.*]

BURGOMASTER. Come in.

SCHILL. I must have a word with you, Burgomaster.

BURGOMASTER. Ah, Schill. Sit down, my friend.

SCHILL. Man to man. As your successor.

BURGOMASTER. But of course. Naturally.

[SCHILL *remains standing. He looks at the revolver.*]

SCHILL. Is that a gun?

BURGOMASTER. Madame Zachanassian's black panther's broken loose. It's been seen near the cathedral. It's as well to be prepared.

SCHILL. Oh, yes. Of course.

BURGOMASTER. I've sent out a call for all able-bodied men with firearms. The streets have been cleared. The children have been kept in school. We don't want any accidents.

SCHILL [*suspiciously*]. You're making quite a thing of it.

BURGOMASTER. [*Shrugs.*] Naturally. A panther is a dangerous beast. Well? What's on your mind? Speak out.

We're old friends.

SCHILL. That's a good cigar you're smoking, Burgomaster.

BURGOMASTER. Yes, Havana.

SCHILL. You used to smoke something else.

BURGOMASTER. Fortuna.

SCHILL. Cheaper.

BURGOMASTER. Too strong.

SCHILL. A new tie? Silk?

BURGOMASTER. Yes. Do you like it?

SCHILL. And have you also bought new shoes?

BURGOMASTER. [*Brings his feet out from under the desk.*] Why, yes. I ordered a new pair from Kalberstadt. Extraordinary! However did you guess?

SCHILL. That's why I'm here.

[*The* THIRD MAN *knocks.*]

BURGOMASTER. Come in.

THIRD MAN. The new typewriter, sir.

BURGOMASTER. Put it on the table. [*The* THIRD MAN *sets it down and goes.*] What's the matter with you? My dear fellow, aren't you well?

SCHILL. It's you who don't seem well, Burgomaster.

BURGOMASTER. What do you mean?

SCHILL. You look pale.

BURGOMASTER. I?

SCHILL. Your hands are trembling. [*The* BURGOMASTER *involuntarily hides his hands.*] Are you frightened?

BURGOMASTER. What have I to be afraid of?

SCHILL. Perhaps this sudden prosperity alarms you.

BURGOMASTER. Is prosperity a crime?

SCHILL. That depends on how you pay for it.

BURGOMASTER. You'll have to forgive me, Schill, but I really haven't the slightest idea what you're talking about. Am I supposed to feel like a criminal every time I order a new typewriter?

SCHILL. Do you?

BURGOMASTER. Well, I hope you haven't

---

[2] One of the principal banks of England.
[3] City Hall.

come here to talk about a new type-writer. Now, what was it you wanted?

SCHILL. I have come to claim the protection of the authorities.

BURGOMASTER. Ei! Against whom?

SCHILL. You know against whom.

BURGOMASTER. You don't trust us?

SCHILL. That woman has put a price on my head.

BURGOMASTER. If you don't feel safe, why don't you go to the police?

SCHILL. I have just come from the police.

BURGOMASTER. And?

SCHILL. The chief has a new gold tooth in his mouth.

BURGOMASTER. A new—? Oh, Schill, really! You're forgetting. This is Güllen, the town of humane traditions. Goethe slept here. Brahms composed a quartet. You must have faith in us. This is a law-abiding community.

SCHILL. Then arrest this woman who wants to have me killed.

BURGOMASTER. Look here, Schill. God knows the lady has every right to be angry with you. What you did there wasn't very pretty. You forced two decent lads to perjure themselves and had a young girl thrown out on the streets.

SCHILL. That young girl owns half the world. [*A moment's silence.*]

BURGOMASTER. Very well, then, we'll speak frankly.

SCHILL. That's why I'm here.

BURGOMASTER. Man to man, just as you said. [*He clears his throat.*] Now—after what you did, you have no moral right to say a word against this lady. And I advise you not to try. Also—I regret to have to tell you this—there is no longer any question of your being elected burgomaster.

SCHILL. Is that official?

BURGOMASTER. Official.

SCHILL. I see.

BURGOMASTER. The man who is chosen to exercise the high post of burgomaster must have, obviously, certain moral qualifications. Qualifications which, unhappily, you no longer possess. Naturally, you may count on the esteem and friendship of the town, just as before. That goes without saying. The best thing will be to spread the mantle of silence over the whole miserable business.

SCHILL. So I'm to remain silent while they arrange my murder?

[*The* BURGOMASTER *gets up.*]

BURGOMASTER [*suddenly noble*]. Now, who is arranging your murder? Give me the names and I will investigate the case at once. Unrelentingly. Well? The names?

SCHILL. You.

BURGOMASTER. I resent this. Do you think we want to kill you for money?

SCHILL. No. You don't want to kill me. But you want to have me killed.

[*The lights go down. The stage is filled with men prowling about with rifles, as if they were stalking a quarry. In the interval the* POLICEMAN'S *bench and the* BURGOMASTER'S *desk are shifted somewhat, so that they will compose the setting for the sacristy. The stage empties. The lights come up on the balcony.* CLAIRE *appears.*]

CLAIRE. Bobby, what's going on here? What are all these men doing with guns? Whom are they hunting?

BOBBY. The black panther has escaped, madame.

CLAIRE. Who let him out?

BOBBY. Kobby and Lobby, madame.

CLAIRE. How excited they are! There may be shooting?

BOBBY. It is possible, madame.

[*The lights fade on the balcony. The sacristan comes in. He arranges the set and puts the altar cloth on the altar. Then* SCHILL *comes on. He is looking for the* PASTOR. *The* PASTOR *enters, left. He is wearing his gown and carrying a rifle.*]

SCHILL. Sorry to disturb you, Pastor.

PASTOR. God's house is open to all. [*He sees that* SCHILL *is staring at the gun.*] Oh, the gun? That's because of the panther. It's best to be prepared.

SCHILL. Pastor, help me.

PASTOR. Of course. Sit down. [*He puts the rifle on the bench.*] What's the trouble?

SCHILL. [*Sits on the bench.*] I'm frightened.

PASTOR. Frightened? Of what?

SCHILL. Of everyone. They're hunting me down like a beast.

PASTOR. Have no fear of man, Schill. Fear God. Fear not the death of the body. Fear the death of the soul. Zip up my gown behind, Sacristan.

SCHILL. I'm afraid, Pastor.

PASTOR. Put your trust in heaven, my friend.

SCHILL. You see, I'm not well. I shake. I have such pains around the heart. I sweat.

PASTOR. I know. You're passing through a profound psychic experience.

SCHILL. I'm going through hell.

PASTOR. The hell you are going through exists only within yourself. Many years ago you betrayed a girl shamefully, for money. Now you think that we shall sell you just as you sold her. No, my friend, you are projecting your guilt upon others. It's quite natural. But remember, the root of our torment lies always within ourselves, in our hearts, in our sins. When you have understood this, you can conquer the fears that oppress you; you have weapons with which to destroy them.

SCHILL. Siemethofer has bought a new washing machine.

PASTOR. Don't worry about the washing machine. Worry about your immortal soul.

SCHILL. Stockers has a television set.

PASTOR. There is also great comfort in prayer. Sacristan, the bands. [SCHILL *crosses to the altar and kneels. The sacristan ties on the* PASTOR'S *bands.*] Examine your conscience, Schill. Repent. Otherwise your fears will consume you. Believe me, this is the only way. We have no other. [*The church bell begins to peal.* SCHILL *seems relieved.*] Now I must leave you. I have a baptism. You may stay as long as you like. Sacristan, the Bible, Liturgy, and Psalter. The child is beginning to cry. I can hear it from here. It is frightened. Let us make haste to give it the only security which this world affords.

SCHILL. A new bell?

PASTOR. Yes. Its tone is marvelous, don't you think? Full. Sonorous.

SCHILL. [*Steps back in horror.*] A new bell! You too, Pastor? You too?

[*The* PASTOR *clasps his hands in horror. Then he takes* SCHILL *into his arms.*]

PASTOR. Oh, God, God forgive me. We are poor, weak things, all of us. Do not tempt us further into the hell in which you are burning. Go, Schill, my friend, go my brother, go while there is time.

[*The* PASTOR *goes.* SCHILL *picks up the rifle with a gesture of desperation. He goes out with it. As the lights fade, men appear with guns. Two shots are fired in the darkness. The lights come up on the balcony, which moves forward.*]

CLAIRE. Bobby! What was that shooting? Have they caught the panther?

BOBBY. He is dead, madame.

CLAIRE. There were two shots.

BOBBY. The panther is dead, madame.

CLAIRE. I loved him. [*Waves* BOBBY *away.*] I shall miss him.

[*The* TEACHER *comes in with two little girls, singing. They stop under the balcony.*]

TEACHER. Gracious lady, be so good as to accept our heartfelt condolences. Your beautiful panther is no more. Believe me, we are deeply pained that so tragic an event should mar your visit here. But what could we do? The panther was savage, a beast. To him our human laws could not apply. There was no other way—

[SCHILL *appears with the gun. He looks dangerous. The girls run off, frightened. The* TEACHER *follows the girls.*]

Children—children—children!
CLAIRE. Anton, why are you frightening the children?

[*He works the bolt, loading the chamber, and raises the gun slowly.*]

SCHILL. Go away, Claire—I warn you. Go away.
CLAIRE. How strange it is, Anton! How clearly it comes back to me! The day we saw one another for the first time, do you remember? I was on a balcony then. It was a day like today, a day in autumn without a breath of wind, warm as it is now— only lately I am always cold. You stood down there and stared at me without moving. I was embarrassed. I didn't know what to do. I wanted to go back into the darkness of the room, where it was safe, but I couldn't. You stared up at me darkly, almost angrily, as if you wished to hurt me, but your eyes were full of passion. [SCHILL *begins to lower the rifle involuntarily.*] Then, I don't know why, I left the balcony and I came down and stood in the street beside you. You didn't greet me, you didn't say a word, but you took my hand and we walked together out of

the town into the fields, and behind us came Kobby and Lobby, like two dogs, sniveling and giggling and snarling. Suddenly you picked up a stone and hurled it at them, and they ran yelping back into the town, and we were alone. [SCHILL *has lowered the rifle completely. He moves forward toward her, as close as he can come.*] That was the beginning, and everything else had to follow. There is no escape.

[*She goes in and closes the shutters.* SCHILL *stands immobile. The* TEACHER *tiptoes in. He stares at* SCHILL, *who doesn't see him. Then he beckons to the children.*]

TEACHER. Come, children, sing. Sing.

[*They begin singing. He creeps behind* SCHILL *and snatches away the rifle.* SCHILL *turns sharply. The* PASTOR *comes in.*]

PASTOR. Go, Schill—go!

[SCHILL *goes out. The children continue singing, moving across the stage and off. The Golden Apostle vanishes. The crossing bell is heard. The scene dissolves into the railway-station setting, as in Act I. But there are certain changes. The timetable marked "Fahrplan" is now new, the frame freshly painted. There is a new travel poster on the station wall. It has a yellow sun and the words: "Reist in den Süden."[4] On the other side of the Fahrplan is another poster with the words: "Die Passionsspiele Oberammergau."[5] The sound of passing trains covers the scene change.* SCHILL *appears with an old valise in his hand, dressed in a shabby trench coat, his hat on his head. He looks about with a furtive*

---

[4] Travel in the South. [5] The Oberammergau Passion Play, portraying the suffering and death of Jesus, is performed in the south German village every ten years.

air, walking slowly to the platform. Slowly, as if by chance, the townspeople enter, from all sides. SCHILL *hesitates, stops.*]

BURGOMASTER [*from upstage, center*]. Good evening, Schill.

SCHILL. Good evening.

POLICEMAN. Good evening.

SCHILL. Good evening.

PAINTER. [*Enters.*] Good evening.

SCHILL. Good evening.

DOCTOR. Good evening.

SCHILL. Good evening.

BURGOMASTER. So you're taking a little trip?

SCHILL. Yes. A little trip.

POLICEMAN. May one ask where to?

SCHILL. I don't know.

PAINTER. Don't know?

SCHILL. To Kalberstadt.

BURGOMASTER [*with disbelief, pointing to the valise*]. Kalberstadt?

SCHILL. After that—somewhere else.

PAINTER. Ah. After that somewhere else.

[*The* FOURTH MAN *walks in.*]

SCHILL. I thought maybe Australia.

BURGOMASTER. Australia!

ALL. Australia!

SCHILL. I'll raise the money somehow.

BURGOMASTER. But why Australia?

POLICEMAN. What would you be doing in Australia?

SCHILL. One can't always live in the same town, year in, year out.

PAINTER. But Australia—

DOCTOR. It's a risky trip for a man of your age.

BURGOMASTER. One of the lady's little men ran off to Australia...

ALL. Yes.

POLICEMAN. You'll be much safer here.

PAINTER. Much!

[SCHILL *looks about him in anguish, like a beast at bay.*]

SCHILL [*low voice*]. I wrote a letter to the administration at Kaffigen.

BURGOMASTER. Yes? And?

[*They are all intent on the answer.*]

SCHILL. They didn't answer.

[*All laugh.*]

DOCTOR. Do you mean to say you don't trust old friends? That's not very flattering, you know.

BURGOMASTER. No one's going to do you any harm here.

DOCTOR. No harm here.

SCHILL. They didn't answer because our postmaster held up my letter.

PAINTER. Our postmaster? What an idea.

BURGOMASTER. The postmaster is a member of the town council.

POLICEMAN. A man of the utmost integrity.

DOCTOR. He doesn't hold up letters. What an idea!

[*The crossing bell starts ringing.*]

STATION MASTER. [*Announces.*] Local to Kalberstadt!

[*The townspeople all cross down to see the train arrive. Then they turn, with their backs to the audience, in a line across the stage.* SCHILL *cannot get through to reach the train.*]

SCHILL [*in a low voice*]. What are you all doing here? What do you want of me?

BURGOMASTER. We don't like to see you go.

DOCTOR. We've come to see you off.

[*The sound of the approaching train grows louder.*]

SCHILL. I didn't ask you to come.

POLICEMAN. But we have come.

DOCTOR. As old friends.

ALL. As old friends.

[*The* STATION MASTER *holds up his paddle. The train stops with a screech of brakes. We hear the engine panting offstage.*]

VOICE [*offstage*]. Güllen!

BURGOMASTER. A pleasant journey.
DOCTOR. And long life!
PAINTER. And good luck in Australia!
ALL. Yes, good luck in Australia.

[*They press around him jovially. He stands motionless and pale.*]

SCHILL. Why are you crowding me?
POLICEMAN. What's the matter now?

[*The* STATION MASTER *blows a long blast on his whistle.*]

SCHILL. Give me room.
DOCTOR. But you have plenty of room.

[*They all move away from him.*]

POLICEMAN. Better get aboard, Schill.
SCHILL. I see. I see. One of you is going to push me under the wheels.
POLICEMAN. Oh, nonsense. Go on, get aboard.
SCHILL. Get away from me, all of you.
BURGOMASTER. I don't know what you want. Just get on the train.
SCHILL. No. One of you will push me under.
DOCTOR. You're being ridiculous. Now, go on, get on the train.
SCHILL. Why are you all so near me?
DOCTOR. The man's gone mad.
STATION MASTER. 'Board!

[*He blows his whistle. The engine bell clangs. The train starts.*]

BURGOMASTER. Get aboard man. Quick.

[*The following speeches are spoken all together until the train noises fade away.*]

DOCTOR. The train's starting.
ALL. Get aboard, man. Get aboard.

The train's starting.
SCHILL. If I try to get aboard, one of you will hold me back.
ALL. No, no.
BURGOMASTER. Get on the train.
SCHILL. [*In terror, crouches against the wall of the* STATION MASTER'S *office.*] No—no—no. No. [*He falls on his knees. The others crowd around him. He cowers on the ground, abjectly. The train sounds fade away.*] Oh, no—no—don't push me, don't push me!
POLICEMAN. There. It's gone off without you.

[*Slowly they leave him. He raises himself up to a sitting position, still trembling. A* TRUCK DRIVER *enters with an empty can.*]

TRUCK DRIVER. Do you know where I can get some water? My truck's boiling over. [SCHILL *points to the station office.*] Thanks. [*He enters the office, gets the water, and comes out. By this time,* SCHILL *is erect.*] Missed your train?
SCHILL. Yes.
TRUCK DRIVER. To Kalberstadt?
SCHILL. Yes.
TRUCK DRIVER. Well, come with me. I'm going that way.
SCHILL. This is my town. This is my home. [*with strange new dignity*] No, thank you. I've changed my mind. I'm staying.
TRUCK DRIVER. [*Shrugs.*] All right.

[*He goes out.* SCHILL *picks up his bag, looks right and left, and slowly walks off.*]

ACT III

Music is heard. Then the curtain rises on the interior of the old barn, a dim, cavernous structure. Bars of light fall across the shadowy forms, shafts of sunlight from the holes and cracks in the walls and roof. Overhead hang old rags, decaying sacks, great cobwebs. Extreme left is a ladder leading to the loft. Near it, an old haycart. Left, CLAIRE ZACHANASSIAN *is sitting in her gilded sedan chair, motionless, in her magnificent bridal gown and veil. Near the chair stands an old keg.*

BOBBY. [*Comes in, treading carefully.*] The doctor and the teacher from the high school to see you, madame.

CLAIRE [*impassive*]. Show them in.

[BOBBY *ushers them in as if they were entering a hall of state. The two grope their way through the litter. At last they find the lady and bow. They are both well dressed in new clothes but are very dusty.*]

BOBBY. Dr. Nüsslin and Professor Müller.

DOCTOR. Madame.

CLAIRE. You look dusty, gentlemen.

DOCTOR. [*Dusts himself off vigorously.*] Oh, forgive us. We had to climb over an old carriage.

TEACHER. Our respects.

DOCTOR. A fabulous wedding.

TEACHER. Beautiful occasion.

CLAIRE. It's stifling here. But I love this old barn. The smell of hay and old straw and axle grease—it is the scent of my youth. Sit down. All this rubbish—the haycart, the old carriage, the cask, even the pitchfork —it was all here when I was a girl.

TEACHER. Remarkable place.

[*He mops his brow.*]

CLAIRE. I thought the pastor's text was very appropriate. The lesson a trifle long.

TEACHER. I Corinthians 13.[1]

CLAIRE. Your choristers sang beautifully, Professor.

TEACHER. Bach. From the "St. Matthew Passion."

DOCTOR. Güllen has never seen such magnificence! The flowers! The jewels! And the people.

TEACHER. The theatrical world, the world of finance, the world of art, the world of science...

CLAIRE. All these worlds are now back in their Cadillacs, speeding toward the capital for the wedding reception. But I'm sure you didn't come here to talk about them.

DOCTOR. Dear lady, we should not intrude on your valuable time. Your husband must be waiting impatiently.

CLAIRE. No, no, I've packed him off to Brazil.

DOCTOR. To Brazil, madame?

CLAIRE. Yes. For his honeymoon.

TEACHER *and* DOCTOR. Oh! But your wedding guests?

CLAIRE. I've planned a delightful dinner for them. They'll never miss me. Now what was it you wished to talk about?

TEACHER. About Anton Schill, madame.

CLAIRE. Is he dead?

TEACHER. Madame, we may be poor. But we have our principles.

CLAIRE. I see. Then what do you want?

TEACHER. [*He mops his brow again.*] The fact is, madame, in anticipation of your well-known munificence, that is, feeling that you would give the town some sort of gift, we have all been buying things. Necessities...

DOCTOR. With money we don't have.

[*The* TEACHER *blows his nose.*]

CLAIRE. You've run into debt?

DOCTOR. Up to here.

CLAIRE. In spite of your principles?

TEACHER. We're human, madame.

CLAIRE. I see.

TEACHER. We have been poor for a long time. A long, long time.

DOCTOR. [*He rises.*] The question is, how are we going to pay?

CLAIRE. You already know.

TEACHER [*courageously*]. I beg you, Madame Zachanassian, put yourself in our position for a moment. For twenty-two years I've been cudgeling

---

[1] See I Corinthians 13:13: "But now abideth faith, hope, love, these three; and the greatest of these is love."

my brains to plant a few seeds of knowledge in this wilderness. And all this time, my gallant colleague, Dr. Nüsslin, has been rattling around in his ancient Mercedes, from patient to patient, trying to keep these wretches alive. Why? Why have we spent our lives in this miserable hole? For money? Hardly. The pay is ridiculous.

DOCTOR. And yet, the professor here has declined an offer to head the high school in Kalberstadt.

TEACHER. And Dr. Nüsslin has refused an important post at the University of Erlangen. Madame, the simple fact is, we love our town. We were born here. It is our life.

DOCTOR. That's true.

TEACHER. What has kept us going all these years is the hope that one day the community will prosper again as it did in the days when we were young.

CLAIRE. Good.

TEACHER. Madame, there is no reason for our poverty. We suffer here from a mysterious blight. We have factories. They stand idle. There is oil in the valley of Pückenried.

DOCTOR. There is copper under the Konradsweil Forest. There is power in our streams, in our waterfalls.

TEACHER. We are not poor, madame. If we had credit, if we had confidence, the factories would open, orders and commissions would pour in. And our economy would bloom together with our cultural life. We would become once again like the towns around us, healthy and prosperous.

DOCTOR. If the wagonworks were put on its feet again—

TEACHER. The foundry.

DOCTOR. The Golden Eagle Pencil Factory.

TEACHER. Buy these plants, madame. Put them in operation once more, and I swear to you, Güllen will flourish and it will bless you. We don't need a billion marks. Ten million, properly invested, would give us back our life, and incidentally return to the investor an excellent dividend. Save us, madame. Save us, and we will not only bless you, we will make money for you.

CLAIRE. I don't need money.

DOCTOR. Madame, we are not asking for charity. This is business.

CLAIRE. It's a good idea...

DOCTOR. Dear lady! I knew you wouldn't let us down.

CLAIRE. But it's out of the question. I cannot buy the wagonworks. I already own them.

DOCTOR. The wagonworks?

TEACHER. And the foundry?

CLAIRE. And the foundry.

DOCTOR. And the Golden Eagle Pencil Factory?

CLAIRE. Everything. The valley of Pückenried with its oil, the forest of Konradsweil with its ore, the barn, the town, the streets, the houses, the shops, everything. I had my agents buy up this rubbish over the years, bit by bit, piece by piece, until I had it all. Your hopes were an illusion, your vision empty, your self-sacrifice a stupidity, your whole life completely senseless.

TEACHER. Then the mysterious blight—

CLAIRE. The mysterious blight was I.

DOCTOR. But this is monstrous!

CLAIRE. Monstrous. I was seventeen when I left this town. It was winter. I was dressed in a sailor suit and my red braids hung down my back. I was in my seventh month. As I walked down the street to the station, the boys whistled after me, and someone threw something. I sat freezing in my seat in the Hamburg Express. But before the roof of the great barn was lost behind the trees, I had made up my mind that one day I would come back...

TEACHER. But, madame—

CLAIRE. [*She smiles.*] And now I have. [*She claps her hands.*] Mike. Max. Take me back to the Golden Apostle. I've been here long enough.

[MIKE *and* MAX *start to pick up the sedan chair. The* TEACHER *pushes* MIKE *away.*]

TEACHER. Madame. One moment. Please. I see it all now. I had thought of you as an avenging fury, a Medea, a Clytemnestra—but I was wrong. You are a warm-hearted woman who has suffered a terrible injustice, and now you have returned and taught us an unforgettable lesson. You have stripped us bare. But now that we stand before you naked, I know you will set aside these thoughts of vengeance. If we made you suffer, you too have put us through the fire. Have mercy, madame.

CLAIRE. When I have had justice, Mike!

[*She signals to* MIKE *and* MAX *to pick up the sedan chair. They cross the stage. The* TEACHER *bars the way.*]

TEACHER. But, madame, one injustice cannot cure another. What good will it do to force us into crime? Horror succeeds horror, shame is piled on shame. It settles nothing.

CLAIRE. It settles everything.

[*They move upstage toward the exit. The* TEACHER *follows.*]

TEACHER. Madame, this lesson you have taught us will never be forgotten. We will hand it down from father to son. It will be a monument more lasting than any vengeance. Whatever we have been, in the future we shall be better because of you. You have pushed us to the extreme. Now forgive us. Show us the way to a better life. Have pity, madame—pity. That is the highest

justice. [*The sedan chair stops.*]

CLAIRE. The highest justice has no pity. It is bright and pure and clear. The world made me into a whore; now I make the world into a brothel. Those who wish to go down, may go down. Those who wish to dance with me, may dance with me. [*to her porters*] Go.

[*She is carried off. The lights black out. Downstage, right, appears* SCHILL's *shop. It has a new sign, a new counter. The doorbell, when it rings, has an impressive sound.* FRAU SCHILL *stands behind the counter in a new dress. The* FIRST MAN *enters, left. He is dressed as a prosperous butcher, a few bloodstains on his snowy apron, a gold watch chain across his open vest.*]

FIRST MAN. What a wedding! I'll swear the whole town was there. Cigarettes.

FRAU SCHILL. Clara is entitled to a little happiness after all. I'm happy for her. Green or white?

FIRST MAN. Turkish. The bridesmaids! Dancers and opera singers. And the dresses! Down to here.

FRAU SCHILL. It's the fashion nowadays.

FIRST MAN. Reporters! Photographers! From all over the world! [*in a low voice*] They will be here any minute.

FRAU SCHILL. What have reporters to do with us? We are simple people, Herr Hofbauer. There is nothing for them here.

FIRST MAN. They're questioning everybody. They're asking everything. [*The* FIRST MAN *lights a cigarette. He looks up at the ceiling.*] Footsteps.

FRAU SCHILL. He's pacing the room. Up and down. Day and night.

FIRST MAN. Haven't seen him all week.

FRAU SCHILL. He never goes out.

FIRST MAN. It's his conscience. That was pretty mean, the way he treated poor Madame Zachanassian.

FRAU SCHILL. That's true. I feel very badly about it myself.

FIRST MAN. To ruin a young girl like that—God doesn't forgive it. [FRAU SCHILL *nods solemnly with pursed lips. The* BUTCHER *gives her a level glance.*] Look, I hope he'll have sense enough to keep his mouth shut in front of the reporters.

FRAU SCHILL. I certainly hope so.

FIRST MAN. You know his character.

FRAU SCHILL. Only too well, Herr Hofbauer.

FIRST MAN. If he tries to throw dirt at our Clara and tell a lot of lies, how she tried to get us to kill him, which anyway she never meant—

FRAU SCHILL. Of course not.

FIRST MAN. —Then we'll really have to do something! And not because of the money—[*He spits.*] But out of ordinary human decency. God knows Madame Zachanassian has suffered enough through him already.

FRAU SCHILL. She has indeed.

[*The* TEACHER *comes in. He is not quite sober.*]

TEACHER. [*Looks about the shop.*] Has the press been here yet?

FIRST MAN. No.

TEACHER. It's not my custom, as you know, Frau Schill—but I wonder if I could have a strong alcoholic drink?

FRAU SCHILL. It's an honor to serve you, Herr Professor. I have a good Steinhäger.[2] Would you like to try a glass?

TEACHER. A very small glass.

[FRAU SCHILL *serves bottle and glass. The* TEACHER *tosses off a glass.*]

FRAU SCHILL. Your hand is shaking, Herr Professor.

TEACHER. To tell the truth, I have

_____
[2] A kind of gin.

been drinking a little already.

FRAU SCHILL. Have another glass. It will do you good.

[*He accepts another glass.*]

TEACHER. Is that he up there, walking?

FRAU SCHILL. Up and down. Up and down.

FIRST MAN. It's God punishing him.

[*The* PAINTER *comes in with the* SON *and the* DAUGHTER.]

PAINTER. Careful! A reporter just asked us the way to this shop.

FIRST MAN. I hope you didn't tell him.

PAINTER. I told him we were strangers here.

[*They all laugh. The door opens. The* SECOND MAN *darts into the shop.*]

SECOND MAN. Look out, everybody! The press! They are across the street in your shop, Hofbauer.

FIRST MAN. My boy will know how to deal with them.

SECOND MAN. Make sure Schill doesn't come down, Hofbauer.

FIRST MAN. Leave that to me.

[*They group themselves about the shop.*]

TEACHER. Listen to me, all of you. When the reporters come I'm going to speak to them. I'm going to make a statement. A statement to the world on behalf of myself as rector of Güllen High School and on behalf of you all, for all your sakes.

PAINTER. What are you going to say?

TEACHER. I shall tell the truth about Claire Zachanassian.

FRAU SCHILL. You're drunk, Herr Professor; you should be ashamed of yourself.

TEACHER. I should be ashamed? You should all be ashamed!

SON. Shut your trap. You're drunk.

DAUGHTER. Please, Professor—

TEACHER. Girl, you disappoint me. It

is your place to speak. But you are silent and you force your old teacher to raise his voice. I am going to speak the truth. It is my duty and I am not afraid. The world may not wish to listen, but no one can silence me. I'm not going to wait—I'm going over to Hofbauer's shop now.

ALL. No, you're not. Stop him. Stop him.

[*They all spring at the* TEACHER. *He defends himself. At this moment,* SCHILL *appears through the door upstage. In contrast to the others, he is dressed shabbily in an old black jacket, his best.*]

SCHILL. What's going on in my shop? [*The townsmen let go of the* TEACHER *and turn to stare at* SCHILL.] What's the trouble, Professor?

TEACHER. Schill, I am speaking out at last! I am going to tell the press everything.

SCHILL. Be quiet, Professor.

TEACHER. What did you say?

SCHILL. Be quiet.

TEACHER. You want me to be quiet?

SCHILL. Please

TEACHER. But, Schill, if I keep quiet, if you miss this opportunity—they're over in Hofbauer's shop now...

SCHILL. Please.

TEACHER. As you wish. If you too are on their side, I have no more to say.

[*The doorbell jingles. A* REPORTER *comes in.*]

REPORTER. Is Anton Schill here? [*Moves to* SCHILL.] Are you Herr Schill?

SCHILL. What?

REPORTER. Herr Schill.

SCHILL. Er—no. Herr Schill's gone to Kalberstadt for the day.

REPORTER. Oh, thank you. Good day.

[*He goes out.*]

PAINTER. [*Mops his brow.*] Whew! Close shave.

[*He follows the* REPORTER *out.*]

SECOND MAN [*walking up to* SCHILL]. That was pretty smart of you to keep your mouth shut. You know what to expect if you don't.

[*He goes.*]

FIRST MAN. Give me a Havana. [SCHILL *serves him.*] Charge it. You bastard!

[*He goes.* SCHILL *opens his account book.*]

FRAU SCHILL. Come along, children—

[FRAU SCHILL, *the* SON, *and the* DAUGHTER *go off, upstage.*]

TEACHER. They're going to kill you. I've known it all along, and you too, you must have known it. The need is too strong, the temptation too great. And now perhaps I too will join against you. I belong to them and, like them, I can feel myself hardening into something that is not human—not beautiful.

SCHILL. It can't be helped.

TEACHER. Pull yourself together, man. Speak to the reporters; you've no time to lose.

[SCHILL *looks up from his account book.*]

SCHILL. No. I'm not going to fight any more.

TEACHER. Are you so frightened that you don't dare open your mouth?

SCHILL. I made Claire what she is, I made myself what I am. What should I do? Should I pretend that I'm innocent?

TEACHER. No, you can't. You are as guilty as hell.

SCHILL. Yes.

TEACHER. You are a bastard.

SCHILL. Yes.

TEACHER. But that does not justify your murder. [SCHILL *looks at him.*] I wish I could believe that for what

they're doing—for what they're going to do—they will suffer for the rest of their lives. But it's not true. In a little while they will have justified everything and forgotten everything.

SCHILL. Of course.

TEACHER. Your name will never again be mentioned in this town. That's how it will be.

SCHILL. I don't hold it against you.

TEACHER. But I do. I will hold it against myself all my life. That's why—

[*The doorbell jingles. The* BURGOMASTER *comes in. The* TEACHER *stares at him, then goes out without another word.*]

BURGOMASTER. Good afternoon, Schill. Don't let me disturb you. I've just dropped in for a moment.

SCHILL. I'm just finishing my accounts for the week. [*A moment's pause.*]

BURGOMASTER. The town council meets tonight. At the Golden Apostle. In the auditorium.

SCHILL. I'll be there.

BURGOMASTER. The whole town will be there. Your case will be discussed and final action taken. You've put us in a pretty tight spot, you know.

SCHILL. Yes. I'm sorry.

BURGOMASTER. The lady's offer will be rejected.

SCHILL. Possibly.

BURGOMASTER. Of course, I may be wrong.

SCHILL. Of course.

BURGOMASTER. In that case—are you prepared to accept the judgment of the town? The meeting will be covered by the press, you know.

SCHILL. By the press?

BURGOMASTER. Yes, and the radio and the newsreel. It's a very ticklish situation. Not only for you—believe me, it's even worse for us. What with the wedding, and all the publicity, we've become famous. All of a sudden our ancient democratic institutions have become of interest to the world.

SCHILL. Are you going to make the lady's condition public?

BURGOMASTER. No, no, of course not. Not directly. We will have to put the matter to a vote—that is unavoidable. But only those involved will understand.

SCHILL. I see.

BURGOMASTER. As far as the press is concerned, you are simply the intermediary between us and Madame Zachanassian. I have whitewashed you completely.

SCHILL. That is very generous of you.

BURGOMASTER. Frankly, it's not for your sake, but for the sake of your family. They are honest and decent people.

SCHILL. Oh—

BURGOMASTER. So far we've all played fair. You've kept your mouth shut and so have we. Now can we continue to depend on you? Because if you have any idea of opening your mouth at tonight's meeting, there won't be any meeting.

SCHILL. I'm glad to hear an open threat at last.

BURGOMASTER. We are not threatening you. You are threatening us. If you speak, you force us to act—in advance.

SCHILL. That won't be necessary.

BURGOMASTER. So if the town decides against you?

SCHILL. I will accept their decision.

BURGOMASTER. Good. [*A moment's pause.*] I'm delighted to see there is still a spark of decency left in you. But—wouldn't it be better if we didn't have to call a meeting at all? [*He pauses. He takes a gun from his pocket and puts it on the counter.*] I've brought you this.

SCHILL. Thank you.

BURGOMASTER. It's loaded.

SCHILL. I don't need a gun.

BURGOMASTER. [*He clears his throat.*] You see? We could tell the lady that we had condemned you in secret

session and you had anticipated our decision. I've lost a lot of sleep getting to this point, believe me.

SCHILL. I believe you.

BURGOMASTER. Frankly, in your place, I myself would prefer to take the path of honor. Get it over with, once and for all. Don't you agree? For the sake of your friends! For the sake of our children, your own children—you have a daughter, a son—Schill, you know our need, our misery.

SCHILL. You've put me through hell, you and your town. You were my friends, you smiled and reassured me. But day by day I saw you change—your shoes, your ties, your suits—your hearts. If you had been honest with me then, perhaps I would feel differently toward you now. I might even use that gun you brought me. For the sake of my friends. But now I have conquered my fear. Alone. It was hard, but it's done. And now you will have to judge me. And I will accept your judgment. For me that will be justice. How it will be for you, I don't know. [*He turns away.*] You may kill me if you like. I won't complain, I won't protest, I won't defend myself. But I won't do your job for you either.

BURGOMASTER [*takes up his gun*]. There it is. You've had your chance and you won't take it. Too bad. [*He takes out a cigarette.*] I suppose it's more than we can expect of a man like you. [SCHILL *lights the* BURGOMASTER'S *cigarette.*] Good day.

SCHILL. Good day.

[*The* BURGOMASTER *goes.* FRAU SCHILL *comes in, dressed in a fur coat. The* DAUGHTER *is in a new red dress. The* SON *has a new sports jacket.*]

What a beautiful coat, Mathilde!

FRAU SCHILL. Real fur. You like it?

SCHILL. Should I? What a lovely dress, Ottilie!

DAUGHTER. *C'est très chic, n'est-ce pas?*[3]

SCHILL. What?

FRAU SCHILL. Ottilie is taking a course in French.

SCHILL. Very useful. Karl—whose automobile is that out there at the curb?

SON. Oh, it's only an Opel. They're not expensive.

SCHILL. You bought yourself a car?

SON. On credit. Easiest thing in the world.

FRAU SCHILL. Everyone's buying on credit now, Anton. These fears of yours are ridiculous. You'll see. Clara has a good heart. She only means to teach you a lesson.

DAUGHTER. She means to teach you a lesson, that's all.

SON. It's high time you got the point, Father.

SCHILL. I get the point. [*The church bells start ringing.*] Listen. The bells of Güllen. Do you hear?

SON. Yes, we have four bells now. It sounds quite good.

DAUGHTER. Just like Gray's Elegy.

SCHILL. What?

FRAU SCHILL. Ottilie is taking a course in English literature.

SCHILL. Congratulations! It's Sunday. I should very much like to take a ride in your car. Our car.

SON. You want to ride in the car?

SCHILL. Why not? I want to ride through the Konradsweil Forest. I want to see the town where I've lived all my life.

FRAU SCHILL. I don't think that will look very nice for any of us.

SCHILL. No—perhaps not. Well, I'll go for a walk by myself.

FRAU SCHILL. Then take us to Kalberstadt, Karl, and we'll go to a cinema.

SCHILL. A cinema? It's a good idea.

FRAU SCHILL. See you soon, Anton.

SCHILL. Goodbye, Ottilie. Goodbye,

---

[3] It's very smart, isn't it?

Karl. Goodbye, Mathilde.

FAMILY. Goodbye.   [*They go out.*]

SCHILL. Goodbye. [*The shop sign flies off. The lights black out. They come up at once on the forest scene.*] Autumn. Even the forest has turned to gold.

[SCHILL *wanders down to the bench in the forest. He sits.* CLAIRE'S *voice is heard.*]

CLAIRE [*offstage*]. Stop. Wait here.

[CLAIRE *comes in. She gazes slowly up at the trees, kicks at some leaves. Then she walks slowly center. She stops before a tree, glances up the trunk.*]

Bark-borers. The old tree is dying.

[*She catches sight of* SCHILL.]

SCHILL. Clara.

CLAIRE. How pleasant to see you here. I was visiting my forest. May I sit by you?

SCHILL. Oh, yes. Please do. [*She sits next to him.*] I've just been saying goodbye to my family. They've gone to the cinema. Karl has bought himself a car.

CLAIRE. How nice.

SCHILL. Ottilie is taking French lessons. And a course in English literature.

CLAIRE. You see? They're beginning to take an interest in higher things.

SCHILL. Listen. A finch. You hear?

CLAIRE. Yes. It's a finch. And a cuckoo in the distance. Would you like some music?

SCHILL. Oh, yes. That would be very nice.

CLAIRE. Anything special?

SCHILL. "Deep in the Forest."

CLAIRE. Your favorite song. They know it.

[*She raises her hand. Offstage, the mandolin and guitar play the tune softly.*]

SCHILL. We had a child?

CLAIRE. Yes.

SCHILL. Boy or girl?

CLAIRE. Girl.

SCHILL. What name did you give her?

CLAIRE. I called her Genevieve.

SCHILL. That's a very pretty name.

CLAIRE. Yes.

SCHILL. What was she like?

CLAIRE. I saw her only once. When she was born. Then they took her away from me.

SCHILL. Her eyes?

CLAIRE. They weren't open yet.

SCHILL. And her hair?

CLAIRE. Black, I think. It's usually black at first.

SCHILL. Yes, of course. Where did she die, Clara?

CLAIRE. In some family. I've forgotten their name. Meningitis, they said. The officials wrote me a letter.

SCHILL. Oh, I'm so very sorry, Clara.

CLAIRE. I've told you about our child. Now tell me about myself.

SCHILL. About yourself?

CLAIRE. Yes. How I was when I was seventeen in the days when you loved me.

SCHILL. I remember one day you waited for me in the great barn. I had to look all over the place for you. At last I found you lying in the haycart with nothing on and a long straw between your lips...

CLAIRE. Yes. I was pretty in those days.

SCHILL. You were beautiful, Clara.

CLAIRE. You were strong. The time you fought with those two railway men who were following me, I wiped the blood from your face with my red petticoat. [*The music ends.*] They've stopped.

SCHILL. Tell them to play "Thoughts of Home."

CLAIRE. They know that too.

[*The music plays.*]

SCHILL. Here we are, Clara, sitting together in our forest for the last time. The town council meets tonight.

They will condemn me to death, and one of them will kill me. I don't know who and I don't know where. Clara, I only know that in a little while a useless life will come to an end.

[*He bows his head on her bosom. She takes him in her arms.*]

CLAIRE [*tenderly*]. I shall take you in your coffin to Capri. You will have your tomb in the park of my villa, where I can see you from my bedroom window. White marble and onyx in a grove of green cypress. With a beautiful view of the Mediterranean.

SCHILL. I've always wanted to see it.

CLAIRE. Your love for me died years ago, Anton. But my love for you would not die. It turned into something strong, like the hidden roots of the forest; something evil, like white mushrooms that grow unseen in the darkness. And slowly it reached out for your life. Now I have you. You are mine. Alone. At last, and forever, a peaceful ghost in a silent house.

[*The music ends.*]

SCHILL. The song is over.

CLAIRE. Adieu, Anton.

[CLAIRE *kisses* ANTON, *a long kiss. Then she rises.*]

SCHILL. Adieu.

[*She goes.* SCHILL *remains sitting on the bench. A row of lamps descends from the flies. The townsmen come in from both sides, each bearing his chair. A table and chairs are set upstage, center. On both sides sit the townspeople. The* POLICEMAN, *in a new uniform, sits on the bench behind* SCHILL. *All the townsmen are in new Sunday clothes. Around them are technicians of all sorts, with lights, cameras, and other equipment. The townswomen are absent. They do not vote. The* BURGOMASTER *takes his place at the table,*

center. The DOCTOR *and the* PASTOR *sit at the same table, at his right, and the* TEACHER *in his academic gown, at his left.*]

BURGOMASTER. [*At a sign from the radio technician, he pounds the floor with his wand of office.*] Fellow citizens of Güllen, I call this meeting to order. The agenda: There is only one matter before us. I have the honor to announce officially that Madame Claire Zachanassian, daughter of our beloved citizen, the famous architect Siegfried Wäscher, has decided to make a gift to the town of one billion marks. Five hundred million to the town, five hundred million to be divided per capita among the citizens. After certain necessary preliminaries, a vote will be taken, and you, as citizens of Güllen, will signify your will by a show of hands. Has anyone any objection to this mode of procedure? The pastor? [*Silence.*] The police? [*Silence.*] The town health official? [*Silence.*] The rector of Güllen High School? [*Silence.*] The political opposition? [*Silence.*] I shall then proceed to the vote— [*The* TEACHER *rises. The* BURGOMASTER *turns in surprise and irritation.*] You wish to speak?

TEACHER. Yes.

BURGOMASTER. Very well.

[*He takes his seat. The* TEACHER *advances. The movie camera starts running.*]

TEACHER. Fellow townsmen. [*The photographer flashes a bulb in his face.*] Fellow townsmen. We all know that by means of this gift, Madame Claire Zachanassian intends to attain a certain object. What is this object? To enrich the town of her youth, yes. But more than that, she desires by means of this gift to re-establish justice among us. This desire expressed by our benefactress raises an all-important question. Is it true that our community harbors in its soul such a burden of guilt?

BURGOMASTER. Yes! True!

SECOND MAN. Crimes are concealed among us.

THIRD MAN. [*He jumps up.*] Sins!

FOURTH MAN. [*He jumps up also.*] Perjuries.

PAINTER. Justice!

TOWNSMEN. Justice! Justice!

TEACHER. Citizens of Güllen, this, then, is the simple fact of the case. We have participated in an injustice. I thoroughly recognize the material advantages which this gift opens to us—I do not overlook the fact that it is poverty which is the root of all this bitterness and evil. Nevertheless, there is no question here of money.

TOWNSMEN. No! No!

TEACHER. Here there is no question of our prosperity as a community, or our well-being as individuals—The question is—must be—whether or not we wish to live according to the principles of justice, those principles for which our forefathers lived and fought and for which they died, those principles which form the soul of our Western culture.

TOWNSMEN. Hear! Hear! [*Applause.*]

TEACHER [*desperately, realizing that he is fighting a losing battle, and on the verge of hysteria*]. Wealth has meaning only when benevolence comes of it, but only he who hungers for grace will receive grace. Do you feel this hunger, my fellow citizens, this hunger of the spirit, or do you feel only that other profane hunger, the hunger of the body? That is the question which I, as rector of your high school, now propound to you. Only if you can no longer tolerate the presence of evil among you, only if you can in no circumstances endure a world in which injustice exists, are

you worthy to receive Madame Zachanassian's billion and fulfill the condition bound up with this gift. If not—[*Wild applause. He gestures desperately for silence.*] If not, then God have mercy on us!

[*The townsmen crowd around him, ambiguously, in a mood somewhat between threat and congratulation. He takes his seat, utterly crushed, exhausted by his effort. The* BURGOMASTER *advances and takes charge once again. Order is restored.*]

BURGOMASTER. Anton Schill—[*The* POLICEMAN *gives* SCHILL *a shove.* SCHILL *gets up.*] Anton Schill, it is through you that this gift is offered to the town. Are you willing that this offer should be accepted?

[SCHILL *mumbles something.*]

RADIO REPORTER. [*Steps to his side.*] You'll have to speak up a little, Herr Schill.

SCHILL. Yes.

BURGOMASTER. Will you respect our decision in the matter before us?

SCHILL. I will respect your decision.

BURGOMASTER. Then I proceed to the vote. All those who are in accord with the terms on which this gift is offered will signify the same by raising their right hands. [*After a moment, the* POLICEMAN *raises his hand. Then one by one the others. Last of all, very slowly, the* TEACHER.] All against? The offer is accepted. I now solemnly call upon you, fellow townsmen, to declare in the face of all the world that you take this action, not out of love for worldly gain...

TOWNSMEN [*in chorus*]. Not out of love for worldly gain...

BURGOMASTER. But out of love for the right.

TOWNSMEN. But out of love for the right.

BURGOMASTER. [*Holds up his hand, as if taking an oath.*] We join together, now, as brothers...

TOWNSMEN. [*Hold up their hands.*] We join together, now, as brothers...

BURGOMASTER. To purify our town of guilt...

TOWNSMAN. To purify our town of guilt...

BURGOMASTER. And to reaffirm our faith...

TOWNSMEN. And to reaffirm our faith ...

BURGOMASTER. In the eternal power of justice.

TOWNSMEN. In the eternal power of justice. [*The lights go off suddenly.*]

SCHILL [*a scream*]. Oh, God!

VOICE. I'm sorry, Herr Burgomaster. We seem to have blown a fuse. [*The lights go on.*] Ah—there we are. Would you mind doing that last bit again?

BURGOMASTER. Again?

THE CAMERAMAN. [*Walks forward.*] Yes, for the newsreel.

BURGOMASTER. Oh, the newsreel. Certainly.

THE CAMERAMAN. Ready now? Right.

BURGOMASTER. And to reaffirm our faith...

TOWNSMEN. And to reaffirm our faith ...

BURGOMASTER. In the eternal power of justice.

TOWNSMEN. In the eternal power of justice.

THE CAMERAMAN [*to his assistant*]. It was better before, when he screamed "Oh, God."

[*The assistant shrugs.*]

BURGOMASTER. Fellow citizens of Güllen, I declare this meeting adjourned. The ladies and gentlemen of the press will find refreshments served downstairs, with the compliments of the town council. The exits lead directly to the restaurant.

THE CAMERAMAN. Thank you.

[*The newsmen go off with alacrity. The townsmen remain on the stage. SCHILL gets up.*]

POLICEMAN. [*Pushes SCHILL down.*] Sit down.

SCHILL. Is it to be now?

POLICEMAN. Naturally, now.

SCHILL. I thought it might be best to have it at my house.

POLICEMAN. It will be here.

BURGOMASTER. Lower the lights. [*The lights dim.*] Are they all gone?

VOICE. All gone.

BURGOMASTER. The gallery?

SECOND VOICE. Empty.

BURGOMASTER. Lock the doors.

THE VOICE. Locked here.

SECOND VOICE. Locked here.

BURGOMASTER. Form a lane. [*The men form a lane. At the end stands the ATHLETE in elegant white slacks, a red scarf around his singlet.*] Pastor. Will you be so good?

[*The PASTOR walks slowly to SCHILL.*]

PASTOR. Anton Schill, your heavy hour has come.

SCHILL. May I have a cigarette?

PASTOR. Cigarette, Burgomaster.

BURGOMASTER. Of course. With pleasure. And a good one.

[*He gives his case to the PASTOR, who offers it to SCHILL. The POLICEMAN lights the cigarette. The PASTOR returns the case.*]

PASTOR. In the words of the prophet Amos—

SCHILL. Please—[*He shakes his head.*]

PASTOR. You're no longer afraid?

SCHILL. No. I'm not afraid.

PASTOR. I will pray for you.

SCHILL. Pray for us all.

[*The PASTOR bows his head.*]

BURGOMASTER. Anton Schill, stand up!

[*SCHILL hesitates.*]

POLICEMAN. Stand up, you swine!

BURGOMASTER. Schultz, please.

POLICEMAN. I'm sorry. I was carried away. [SCHILL *gives the cigarette to the* POLICEMAN. *Then he walks slowly to the center of the stage and turns his back on the audience.*] Enter the lane.

[SCHILL *hesitates a moment. He goes slowly into the lane of silent men. The* ATHLETE *stares at him from the opposite end.* SCHILL *looks in turn at the hard faces of those who surround him and sinks slowly to his knees. The lane contracts silently into a knot as the men close in and crouch over. Complete silence. The knot of men pulls back slowly, coming downstage. Then it opens. Only the* DOCTOR *is left in the center of the stage, kneeling by the corpse, over which the* TEACHER's *gown has been spread. The* DOCTOR *rises and takes off his stethoscope.*]

PASTOR. Is it all over?

DOCTOR. Heart failure.

BURGOMASTER. Died of joy.

ALL. Died of joy.

[*The townsmen turn their backs on the corpse and at once light cigarettes. A cloud of smoke rises over them. From the left comes* CLAIRE ZACHANASSIAN, *dressed in black, followed by* BOBBY. *She sees the corpse. Then she walks slowly to center stage and looks down at the body of* SCHILL.]

CLAIRE. Uncover him. [BOBBY *uncovers* SCHILL's *face. She stares at it a long moment. She sighs.*] Cover his face.

[BOBBY *covers it.* CLAIRE *goes out, up center.* BOBBY *takes the check from his wallet, holds it out peremptorily to the* BURGOMASTER, *who walks over from the knot of silent men. He holds out his hand for the check. The lights fade. At once the warning bell is heard, and the scene dissolves into the setting of the railway station. The gradual transformation of the shabby town into a thing of elegance and beauty is now accomplished. The railway station glitters with neon lights and is surrounded with garlands, bright posters, and flags. The townsfolk, men and women, now in brand new clothes, form themselves into a group in front of the station. The sound of the approaching train grows louder. The train stops.*]

STATION MASTER. Güllen-Rome Express. All aboard, please. [*The church bells start pealing. Men appear with trunks and boxes, a procession which duplicates that of the lady's arrival, but in inverse order. Then come the* TWO BLIND MEN, *then* BOBBY, *and* MIKE *and* MAX *carrying the coffin. Lastly* CLAIRE. *She is dressed in modish black. Her head is high, her face as impassive as that of an ancient idol. The procession crosses the stage and goes off. The people bow in silence as the coffin passes. When* CLAIRE *and her retinue have boarded the train, the* STATION MASTER *blows a long blast.*] 'Bo—ard!

[*He holds up his paddle. The train starts and moves off slowly, picking up speed. The crowd turns slowly, gazing after the departing train in complete silence. The train sounds fade.*]

All That Fall

Like his visual mime *Act Without Words II* in which two men are goaded succes-sively into leaving burlap bags and going through morning routines, Samuel Beckett's radio play *All That Fall* concerns the monotony of daily and weekly cycles. These cycles put together become falling spirals: the organism gradually disintegrates—its movements slowing down, its health failing, its spirit mustering only brief flares of energy. A radio play has a special contribution to make both to the repetition of the routines and the falling pattern. It can raise echoes of former sounds and build aural structures of them, and it can annihilate a varied world of creatures, storms, trains, and voices as quickly as it can summon them. Beckett (1906—) makes it do both here with reckless abandon. Character itself is com-posed moment by moment in sound; one might almost say *of* sound: as Hugh Kenner writes, "pulsating in acoustic space, the soundscape asserts a provisional reality, at every instant richly springing forth and dying. The background of a play for voices is silence, a silence amidst which the specifically human asserts itself with a special torque." Speech, composed "into sentences, whose Ionic elegance, even as the silence claims it, cries aloud to enter an immobility in which to be savored."*

But ironically the silence threatens to become more than background. It may be a momentary vacuum or a kind of permanent nothingness into which things dis-appear, some obviously not to be heard again—disappearing with a sudden squawk in the case of the chicken that follows his instinct into the path of Mr. Slocum's car. Though we never hear their voices, the child run over by the train and the girl abandoned by "one of those new mind doctors" are further disproof of the axiom "the Lord upholdeth all that fall and raiseth up all those that be bowed down." Pilgrims in need of upholding must rely instead on the likes of Slocum, Miss Fitt, and Dan Rooney, who cannot permanently keep them from falling.

The radio's modulations of sound and illusions of distance emphasize not only the all-receiving silence but also the moment of disappearance. The nostalgia of the fading past is caught both by the lyric elegies of the play and by the retreating cow-songs, the sudden wind symphonies, and the drumming rain of the sound-effects man. Mrs. Rooney's journey is a series of wheezing echoes, dragging feet, dying murmurs, and other weakened waves from things slowly running down. The dialogue itself sometimes suggests the weariness of talk that only momentarily asserts its form against its own termination. Mrs. Rooney asks Christy:

> How is your poor wife?
> No better, Ma'am.
> Your daughter then?
> No worse, Ma'am.
>
> (*Silence.*)

* Hugh Kenner, *Samuel Beckett: A Critical Study* (Grove Press, Inc., New York, 1961), p. 171.

The sameness of the day-to-day condition leaves them speechless, hibernating in silence until a new burst of energy carries them into the next dull rite.

The texture of these downward spirals is basically the stuff of tragicomedy, which does not decline evenly but by slips and skids. In the wife and daughter of Christy or the weekly trip of Mrs. Rooney we obviously do not have falls of tragic proportion, completed dramatically at some point of reversal and disclosure. Each moment of the play tells its own story, which repeats the story of every other moment. Nor do we have a series of comic falls that add up to comic form. The play is punctuated with drops from the lyric to the farcical, and these are often rapid enough to raise laughter; but because the condition is incurable, they are never unmixed in feeling. As the daily clock prods Mrs. Rooney toward her terminal, for instance, she thinks of similar indignities still in store for her:

> Heavens, there is that up mail again, what will become of me! (*The dragging steps resume.*) Oh I am just a hysterical old hag, I know, destroyed with sorrow and pining and gentility and church-going and fat and rheumatism and childlessness. (*Pause. Brokenly.*) Minnie! Little Minnie! (*Pause.*) Love, that is all I asked, a little love, daily, twice daily, fifty years of twice daily love like a Paris horse-butcher's regular, what normal woman wants affection? A peck on the jaw at morning, near the ear, and another at evening, peck, peck, till you grow whiskers on you.

Partly because the language throughout is filled with sharp strokes against her dignity, the collapse in the last phrase does not quite cancel Mrs. Rooney's resonant manner. But obviously the end that she predicts for herself is not high, and the last deflation is blunt enough to demand an ironic view of what are very modest demands to begin with.

Despite the play's reliance on sound, it paradoxically makes us visualize almost continuously—just as for the blind, ditches and steps are the more omnipresent because they are not seen. Liberated from the stage's visual objects, delimited space, and physical movement, a radio play can conjure the nonexistent as easily as the existent. In a sense it introduces the subjunctive mood, which only language and imagination can summon, defining *aural* space by contrast to the *solid* things that inhabit the world of indicative fact. We are made briefly to imagine worlds that one might walk through with fewer complaints—cars less difficult to get in and out of (and quicker to start) than Slocum's, or an Arcadia in which, as Mrs. Rooney says poetically, the "pretty little woolly lamb" cries to suck its mother. Quite unlike this Golden Age of the imagination on the far borders of sound effects, the Rooneys have merely the horrors of home life, all the present-tense, incessant activities whose repetition makes them inescapable, "the dusting, sweeping, airing, scrubbing, waxing, waning, washing, mangling, drying, mowing, clipping, racking, rolling, scuffling, shovelling, grinding, tearing, pounding, banging and slamming." One declines and keeps on the move, yet dreams "of other roads, in other lands. Of another home."

The imagination can fill the mind with woolly lambs only momentarily, however, before the real world of smashed chickens comes hurtling through the sound waves again. Neither our ears nor our radio speakers can sustain consummate sound; the sense of hearing offers only one thing at a time or a few things in concert (though it offers these with commanding presence), and it offers nothing for more than a few moments. Whereas the players of *Act Without Words II* creep back into their enclosing sacks and remain real, vulnerable to the next prod, the voices and the footfalls of *All That Fall* vanish entirely when they pass beyond hearing. In replacing them, the tempest of wind and rain (a storm of reality) buffets the radio speaker vigorously, asserting its primacy—and then comes with finality the quiet that has been waiting its largest role.

All That Fall

MRS. ROONEY (MADDY) *a lady in her seventies*
CHRISTY *a carter*
MR. TYLER *a retired bill-broker*
MR. SLOCUM *Clerk of the Racecourse*
TOMMY *a porter*
MR. BARRELL *a station-master*

MISS FITT *a lady in her thirties*
A FEMALE VOICE
DOLLY *a small girl*
MR. ROONEY (DAN) *husband of* MRS. ROONEY, *blind*
JERRY *a small boy*

[*Rural sounds. Sheep, bird, cow, cock, severally, then together.*]

[*Silence.*]

[*Mrs. Rooney advances along country road towards railway-station. Sound of her dragging feet.*]

[*Music faint from house by way. "Death and the Maiden." The steps slow down, stop.*]

MRS. ROONEY. Poor woman. All alone in that ruinous old house.

[*Music louder. Silence but for music playing.*]

[*The steps resume. Music dies. Mrs. Rooney murmurs melody. Her murmur dies.*]

[*Sound of approaching cartwheels. The cart stops. The steps slow down, stop.*]

MRS. ROONEY. Is that you, Christy?
CHRISTY. It is, Ma'am.
MRS. ROONEY. I thought the hinny was familiar. How is your poor wife?

Samuel Beckett, "All That Fall," in Krapp's Last Tape and Other Dramatic Pieces. *Copyright* © *1957 by Samuel Beckett, 1958, 1959, 1960 by Grove Press, Inc.*

CHRISTY. No better, Ma'am.
MRS. ROONEY. Your daughter then?
CHRISTY. No worse, Ma'am.

[*Silence.*]

MRS. ROONEY. Why do you halt? [*Pause.*] But why do I halt?

[*Silence.*]

CHRISTY. Nice day for the races, Ma'am.
MRS. ROONEY. No doubt it is. [*Pause.*] But will it hold up? [*Pause. With emotion.*] Will it hold up? [*Silence.*]
CHRISTY. I suppose you wouldn't—
MRS. ROONEY. Hist! [*Pause.*] Surely to goodness that cannot be the up mail I hear already?

[*Silence. The hinny neighs. Silence.*]

CHRISTY. Damn the mail.
MRS. ROONEY. Oh thank God for that! I could have sworn I heard it, thundering up the track in the far distance. [*Pause.*] So hinnies whinny. Well, it is not surprising.
CHRISTY. I suppose you wouldn't be in need of a small load of dung?
MRS. ROONEY. Dung? What class of dung?
CHRISTY. Stydung.

with time and to spare.

MRS. ROONEY [*sobbing*]. What? What's all this now? [*Calmer.*] Can't you see I'm in trouble? [*With anger.*] Have you no respect for misery? [*Sobbing.*] Minnie! Little Minnie!

MR. TYLER. Come, Mrs. Rooney, come, the mail has not yet gone up, just take my free arm and we'll be there with time and to spare.

MRS. ROONEY [*brokenly*]. In her forties now she'd be, I don't know, fifty, girding up her lovely little loins, getting ready for the change...

MR. TYLER. Come, Mrs. Rooney, come, the mail—

MRS. ROONEY [*exploding*]. Will you get along with you, Mr. Rooney, Mr. Tyler I mean, will you get along with you now and cease molesting me? What kind of a country is this where a woman can't weep her heart out on the highways and byways without being tormented by retired bill-brokers! [*Mr. Tyler prepares to mount his bicycle.*] Heavens, you're not going to ride her flat! [*Mr. Tyler mounts.*] You'll tear your tube to ribbons! [*Mr. Tyler rides off. Receding sound of bumping bicycle. Silence. Cooing.*] Venus birds! Billing in the woods all the long summer long. [*Pause.*] Oh cursed corset! If I could let it out, without indecent exposure. Mr. Tyler! Mr. Tyler! Come back and unlace me behind the hedge! [*She laughs wildly, ceases.*] What's wrong with me, what's wrong with me, never tranquil, seething out of my dirty old pelt, out of my skull, oh to be in atoms, in atoms! [*Frenziedly.*] ATOMS! [*Silence. Cooing. Faintly.*] Jesus! [*Pause.*] Jesus!

[*Sound of car coming up behind her. It slows down and draws up beside her, engine running. It is Mr. Slocum, the Clerk of the Racecourse.*]

MR. SLOCUM. Is anything wrong, Mrs. Rooney? You are bent all double. Have you a pain in the stomach?

[*Silence. Mrs. Rooney laughs wildly. Finally.*]

MRS. ROONEY. Well, if it isn't my old admirer, the Clerk of the Course, in his limousine.

MR. SLOCUM. May I offer you a lift, Mrs. Rooney? Are you going in my direction?

MRS. ROONEY. I am, Mr. Slocum, we all are. [*Pause.*] How is your poor mother?

MR. SLOCUM. Thank you, she is fairly comfortable. We manage to keep her out of pain. That is the great thing, Mrs. Rooney, is it not?

MRS. ROONEY. Yes, indeed, Mr. Slocum, that is the great thing, I don't know how you do it. [*Pause. She slaps her cheek violently.*] Ah these wasps!

MR. SLOCUM [*coolly*]. May I then offer you a seat, Madam?

MRS. ROONEY [*with exaggerated enthusiasm*]. Oh that would be heavenly, Mr. Slocum, just simply heavenly. [*Dubiously.*] But would I ever get in, you look very high off the ground to-day, these new balloon tires, I presume. [*Sound of door opening and Mrs. Rooney trying to get in.*] Does this roof never come off? No? [*Efforts of Mrs. Rooney.*] No...I'll never do it...you'll have to get down, Mr. Slocum, and help me from the rear. [*Pause.*] What was that? [*Pause. Aggrieved.*] This is all your suggestion, Mr. Slocum, not mine. Drive on, Sir, drive on.

MR. SLOCUM [*switching off the engine*]. I'm coming, Mrs. Rooney, I'm coming, give me time, I'm as stiff as yourself.

[*Sound of Mr. Slocum extracting himself from driver's seat.*]

MRS. ROONEY. Stiff! Well I like that!

And me heaving all over back and front. [*To herself.*] The dry old reprobate!

MR. SLOCUM [*in position behind her*]. Now, Mrs. Rooney, how shall we do this?

MRS. ROONEY. As if I were a bale, Mr. Slocum, don't be afraid. [*Pause. Sounds of effort.*] That's the way! [*Effort.*] Lower! [*Effort.*] Wait! [*Pause.*] No, don't let go! [*Pause.*] Suppose I do get up, will I ever get down?

MR. SLOCUM [*breathing hard*]. You'll get down, Mrs. Rooney, you'll get down. We may not get you up, but I warrant you we'll get you down.

[*He resumes his efforts. Sound of these.*]

MRS. ROONEY. Oh!...Lower!...Don't be afraid!...We're past the age when ...There!..Now!..Get your shoulder under it...Oh!..[*Giggles.*] Oh glory!..Up! Up!..Ah!..I'm in! [*Panting of Mr. Slocum. He slams the door. In a scream.*] My frock! You've nipped my frock! [*Mr. Slocum opens the door. Mrs. Rooney frees her frock. Mr. Slocum slams the door. His violent unintelligible muttering as he walks round to the other door. Tearfully.*] My nice frock! Look what you've done to my nice frock [*Mr. Slocum gets into his seat, slams driver's door, presses starter. The engine does not start. He releases starter.*] What will Dan˙ say when he sees me?

MR. SLOCUM. Has he then recovered his sight?

MRS. ROONEY. No, I mean when he knows, what will he say when he feels the hole? [*Mr. Slocum presses starter. As before. Silence.*] What are you doing, Mr. Slocum?

MR. SLOCUM. Gazing straight before me, Mrs. Rooney, through the windscreen, into the void.

MRS. ROONEY. Start her up, I beseech you, and let us be off. This is awful!

MR. SLOCUM [*dreamily*]. All morning she went like a dream and now she is dead. That is what you get for a good deed. [*Pause. Hopefully.*] Perhaps if I were to choke her. [*He does so, presses the starter. The engine roars. Roaring to make himself heard.*] She was getting too much air!

[*He throttles down, grinds in his first gear, moves off, changes up in a grinding of gears.*]

MRS. ROONEY [*in anguish*]. Mind the hen! [*Scream of brakes. Squawk of hen.*] Oh mother, you have squashed her, drive on, drive on! [*The car accelerates. Pause.*] What a death! One minute picking happy at the dung, on the road, in the sun, with now and then a dust bath, and then —bang!—all her troubles over. [*Pause.*] All the laying and the hatching. [*Pause.*] Just one great squawk and then...peace. [*Pause.*] They would have slit her weasand in any case. [*Pause.*] Here we are, let me down. [*The car slows down, stops, engine running. Mr. Slocum blows his horn. Pause. Louder. Pause.*] What are you up to now, Mr. Slocum? We are at a standstill, all danger is past and you blow your horn. Now if instead of blowing it now you had blown it at that unfortunate—

[*Horn violently. Tommy the porter appears at top of station steps.*]

MR. SLOCUM [*calling*]. Will you come down, Tommy, and help this lady out, she's stuck. [*Tommy descends the steps.*] Open the door, Tommy, and ease her out.

[*Tommy opens the door.*]

TOMMY. Certainly, Sir. Nice day for

the races, Sir. What would you fancy for—

MRS. ROONEY. Don't mind me. Don't take any notice of me. I do not exist. The fact is well known.

MR. SLOCUM. Do as you're asked, Tommy, for the love of God.

TOMMY. Yessir. Now, Mrs. Rooney.

[*He starts pulling her out.*]

MRS. ROONEY. Wait, Tommy, wait now, don't bustle me, just let me wheel round and get my feet to the ground. [*Her efforts to achieve this.*] Now.

TOMMY [*pulling her out*]. Mind your feather, Ma'am. [*Sounds of effort.*] Easy now, easy.

MRS. ROONEY. Wait, for God's sake, you'll have me beheaded.

TOMMY. Crouch down, Mrs. Rooney, crouch down, and get your head in the open.

MRS. ROONEY. Crouch down! At my time of life! This is lunacy!

TOMMY. Press her down, Sir.

[*Sounds of combined efforts.*]

MRS. ROONEY. Merde!

TOMMY. Now! She's coming! Straighten up, Ma'am! There!

[*Mr. Slocum slams the door.*]

MRS. ROONEY. Am I out?

[*The voice of Mr. Barrell, the stationmaster, raised in anger.*]

MR. BARRELL. Tommy! Tommy! Where the hell is he?

[*Mr. Slocum grinds in his gear.*]

TOMMY. [*hurriedly*]. You wouldn't have something for the Ladies Plate, Sir, I was given Flash Harry.

MR. SLOCUM [*scornfully*]. Flash Harry! That carthorse!

MR. BARRELL [*at top of steps, roaring*]. Tommy! Blast your bleeding bloody —[*He sees Mrs. Rooney.*] Oh, Mrs. Rooney... [*Mr. Slocum drives away in a grinding of gears.*] Who's that crucifying his gear-box, Tommy?

TOMMY. Old Cissy Slocum.

MRS. ROONEY. Cissy Slocum! That's a nice way to refer to your betters. Cissy Slocum! And you an orphan!

MR. BARRELL [*angrily to Tommy*]. What are you doing stravaging down here on the public road? This is no place for you at all! Nip up there on the platform now and whip out the truck! Won't the twelve thirty be on top of us before we can turn round?

TOMMY [*bitterly*]. And that's the thanks you get for a Christian act.

MR. BARRELL [*violently*]. Get on with you now before I report you! [*Slow feet of Tommy climbing steps.*] Do you want me to come down to you with the shovel? [*The feet quicken, recede, cease.*] Ah, God forgive me, it's a hard life. [*Pause.*] Well, Mrs. Rooney, it's nice to see you up and about again. You were laid up there a long time.

MRS. ROONEY. Not long enough, Mr. Barrell. [*Pause.*] Would I were still in bed, Mr. Barrell. [*Pause.*] Would I were lying stretched out in my comfortable bed, Mr. Barrell, just wasting slowly painlessly away, keeping up my strength with arrowroot and calves-foot jelly, till in the end you wouldn't see me under the blankets any more than a board. [*Pause.*] Oh no coughing or spitting or bleeding or vomiting, just drifting gently down into the higher life, and remembering, remembering... [*the voice breaks*]...all the silly unhappiness ...as though...it had never happened...what did I do with that handkerchief? [*Sound of handkerchief loudly applied.*] How long have you been master of this station now, Mr. Barrell?

MR. BARRELL. Don't ask me, Mrs. Rooney, don't ask me.

MRS. ROONEY. You stepped into your father's shoes, I believe, when he took them off.

MR. BARRELL. Poor Pappy! [*Reverent pause.*] He didn't live long to enjoy his ease.

MRS. ROONEY. I remember him clearly. A small ferrety purple-faced widower, deaf as a doornail, very testy and snappy. [*Pause.*] I suppose you'll be retiring soon yourself, Mr. Barrell, and growing your roses. [*Pause.*] Did I understand you to say the twelve thirty would soon be upon us?

MR. BARRELL. Those were my words.

MRS. ROONEY. But according to my watch, which is more or less right— or was—by the eight o'clock news, the time is now coming up to twelve ...[*Pause as she consults her watch*] ... thirty-six. [*Pause.*] And yet upon the other hand the up mail has not yet gone through. [*Pause.*] Or has it sped by unbeknown to me? [*Pause.*] For there was a moment there, I remember now, I was so plunged in sorrow I wouldn't have heard a steam roller go over me. [*Pause. Mr. Barrell turns to go.*] Don't go, Mr. Barrell! [*Mr. Barrell goes. Loud.*] Mr. Barrell! [*Pause. Louder.*] Mr. Barrell!

[*Mr. Barrell comes back.*]

MR. BARRELL [*testily*]. What is it, Mrs. Rooney, I have my work to do.

[*Silence. Sound of wind.*]

MRS. ROONEY. The wind is getting up. [*Pause. Wind.*] The best of the day is over. [*Pause. Wind. Dreamily.*] Soon the rain will begin to fall and go on falling, all afternoon. [*Mr. Barrell goes.*] Then at evening the clouds will part, the setting sun will shine an instant, then sink, behind the hills. [*She realizes Mr. Barrell has gone.*] Mr. Barrell! Mr. Barrell! [*Silence.*] I estrange them all. They come towards me, uninvited, bygones, full of kindness, anxious to help...[*the voice breaks*]...genuinely pleased...to see me again... looking so well...[*Handkerchief.*] A few simple words...from my heart ...and I am all alone...once more ...[*Handkerchief. Vehemently.*] I should not be out at all! I should never leave the grounds! [*Pause.*] Oh there is that Fitt woman, I wonder will she bow to me. [*Sound of* MISS FITT *approaching, humming a hymn. She starts climbing the steps.*] Miss Fitt! [*Miss Fitt halts, stops humming.*] Am I then invisible, Miss Fitt? Is this cretonne so becoming to me that I merge into the masonry? [*Miss Fitt descends a step.*] That is right, Miss Fitt, look closely and you will finally distinguish a once female shape.

MISS FITT. Mrs. Rooney! I saw you, but I did not know you.

MRS. ROONEY. Last Sunday we worshipped together. We knelt side by side at the same altar. We drank from the same chalice. Have I so changed since then?

MISS FITT [*shocked*]. Oh but in church, Mrs. Rooney, in church I am alone with my Maker. Are not you? [*Pause.*] Why, even the sexton himself, you know, when he takes up the collection, knows it is useless to pause before me. I simply do not see the plate, or bag, whatever it is they use, how could I? [*Pause.*] Why even when all is over and I go out into the sweet fresh air, why even then for the first furlong or so I stumble in a kind of daze as you might say, oblivious to my coreligionists. And they are very kind, I must admit—the vast majority—very kind and understanding. They know me now and take no umbrage. There she goes, they say, there goes the dark Miss Fitt, alone with her Maker, take no notice of her. And they step down off the path to avoid my running into them. [*Pause.*] Ah yes, I am distray, very distray, even on week-days. Ask Mother, if you do not believe me. Hetty, she says, when I start eating my doily instead of the thin bread and butter, Hetty, how can you be so distray? [*Sighs.*] I suppose the truth is I am not there, Mrs. Rooney, just not really there at all. I see, hear, smell, and so on, I go through the usual motions, but my heart is not in it, Mrs. Rooney, but heart is in none of it. Left to myself, with no one to check me, I would soon be flown...home. [*Pause.*] So if you think I cut you just now, Mrs. Rooney, you do me an injustice. All I saw was a big pale blur, just another big pale blur. [*Pause.*] Is anything amiss, Mrs. Rooney, you do not look normal somehow. So bowed and bent.

MRS. ROONEY [*ruefully*]. Maddy Rooney, née Dunne, the big pale blur. [*Pause.*] You have piercing sight, Miss Fitt, if you only knew it, literally piercing. [*Pause.*]

MISS FITT. Well...is there anything I can do, now that I am here?

MRS. ROONEY. If you would help me up the face of this cliff, Miss Fitt, I have little doubt your Maker would requite you, if no one else.

MISS FITT. Now now, Mrs. Rooney, don't put your teeth in me. Requite! I make these sacrifices for nothing— or not at all. [*Pause. Sound of her descending steps.*] I take it you want to lean on me, Mrs. Rooney.

MRS. ROONEY. I asked Mr. Barrell to give me his arm, just give me his arm. [*Pause.*] He turned on his heel and strode away.

MISS FITT. Is it my arm you want then? [*Pause. Impatiently.*] Is it my arm you want, Mrs. Rooney, or what is it?

MRS. ROONEY [*exploding*]. Your arm! Any arm! A helping hand! For five seconds! Christ, what a planet!

MISS FITT. Really...Do you know what it is, Mrs. Rooney, I do not think it is wise of you to be going about at all.

MRS. ROONEY [*violently*]. Come down here, Miss Fitt, and give me your arm, before I scream down the parish!

[*Pause. Wind. Sound of Miss Fitt descending last steps.*]

MISS FITT [*resignedly*]. Well, I suppose it is the Protestant thing to do.

MRS. ROONEY. Pismires do it for one another. [*Pause.*] I have seen slugs do it. [*Miss Fitt proffers her arm.*] No, the other side, my dear, if it's all the same to you, I'm left-handed on top of everything else. [*She takes Miss Fitt's right arm.*] Heavens, child, you're just a bag of bones, you need building up. [*Sound of her toiling up steps on Miss Fitt's arm.*] This is worse than the Matterhorn, were you ever up the Matterhorn, Miss Fitt, great honeymoon resort. [*Sound of toiling.*] Why don't they have a handrail? [*Panting.*] Wait till I get some air. [*Pause.*] Don't let me go! [*Miss Fitt hums her hymn. After a moment Mrs. Rooney joins in with the words.*]...the encircling gloo-oom [*Miss Fitt stops humming*]...tum tum me on. [*Forte.*] The night is dark and I am far from ho-ome, tum tum—

MISS FITT [*hysterically*]. Stop it, Mrs. Rooney, stop it, or I'll drop you!

MRS. ROONEY. Wasn't it that they sung on the Lusitania? Or Rock of Ages? Most touching it must have been. Or was it the Titanic?

[*Attracted by the noise a group, including Mr. Tyler, Mr. Barrell and Tommy, gathers at top of steps.*]

MR. BARRELL. What the—[*Silence.*]

MR. TYLER. Lovely day for the fixture.

Loud titter from Tommy cut short by Mr. Barrell with backhanded blow in the stomach. Appropriate noise from Tommy.

FEMALE VOICE [*shrill*]. Oh look, Dolly, look!

DOLLY. What, Mamma?

FEMALE VOICE. They are stuck! [*Cackling laugh.*] They are stuck!

MRS. ROONEY. Now we are the laughing-stock of the twenty-six counties. Or is it thirty-six?

MR. TYLER. That is a nice way to treat your defenceless subordinates, Mr. Barrell, hitting them without warning in the pit of the stomach.

MISS FITT. Has anybody seen my mother?

MR. BARRELL. Who is that?

TOMMY. The dark Miss Fitt.

MR. BARRELL. Where is her face?

MRS. ROONEY. Now, deary, I am ready if you are. [*They toil up remaining steps.*] Stand back, you cads!

[*Shuffle of feet.*]

FEMALE VOICE. Mind yourself, Dolly!

MRS. ROONEY. Thank you, Miss Fitt, thank you, that will do, just prop me up against the wall like a roll of tarpaulin and that will be all, for the moment. [*Pause.*] I am sorry for all this ramdam, Miss Fitt, had I known you were looking for your mother I should not have importuned you, I know what it is.

MR. TYLER [*in marvelling aside*]. Ramdam!

FEMALE VOICE. Come, Dolly darling, let us take up our stand before the first-class smokers. Give me your hand and hold me tight, one can be sucked under.

MR. TYLER. You have lost your mother, Miss Fitt?

MISS FITT. Good-morning, Mr. Tyler.

MR. TYLER. Good-morning, Miss Fitt.

MR. BARRELL. Good-morning, Miss Fitt.

MISS FITT. Good-morning, Mr. Barrell.

MR. TYLER. You have lost your mother, Miss Fitt?

MISS FITT. She said she would be on the last train.

MRS. ROONEY. Do not imagine, because I am silent, that I am not present, and alive, to all that is going on.

MR. TYLER [*to Miss Fitt*]. When you say the last train—

MRS. ROONEY. Do not flatter yourselves for one moment, because I hold aloof, that my sufferings have ceased. No. The entire scene, the hills, the plain, the racecourse with its miles and miles of white rails and three red stands, the pretty little wayside station, even you yourselves, yes, I mean it, and over all the clouding blue, I see it all, I stand here and see it all with eyes... [*the voice breaks*]... through eyes...oh, if you had my eyes...you would understand...the things they have seen...and not looked away...this is nothing... nothing...what did I do with that handkerchief? [*Pause.*]

MR. TYLER [*to Miss Fitt*]. When you say the last train—[*Mrs. Rooney blows her nose violently and long*]— when you say the last train, Miss Fitt, I take it you mean the twelve thirty.

MISS FITT. What else could I mean, Mr. Tyler, what else could I *conceivably* mean?

MR. TYLER. Then you have no cause for anxiety, Miss Fitt, for the twelve thirty has not yet arrived. Look. [*Miss Fitt looks.*] No, up the line. [*Miss Fitt looks. Patiently.*] No, Miss Fitt, follow the direction of my index. [*Miss Fitt looks.*] There. You see now. The signal. At the bawdy hour of nine. [*In rueful afterthought.*] Or three alas! [*Mr. Barrell stifles a guffaw.*] Thank you, Mr. Barrell.

MISS FITT. But the time is now getting on for—

MR. TYLER [*patiently*]. We all know, Miss Fitt, we all know only too well what the time is now getting on for, and yet the cruel fact remains that the twelve thirty has not yet arrived.

MISS FITT. Not an accident, I trust! [*Pause.*] Do not tell me she has left the track! [*Pause.*] Oh darling mother! With the fresh sole for lunch!

[*Loud titter from Tommy, checked as before by Mr. Barrell.*]

MR. BARRELL. That's enough old guff out of you. Nip up to the box now and see has Mr. Case anything for me. [*Tommy goes.*]

MRS. ROONEY [*sadly*]. Poor Dan!

MISS FITT [*in anguish*]. What terrible thing has happened?

MR. TYLER. Now now, Miss Fitt, do not —

MRS. ROONEY [*with vehement sadness*]. Poor Dan!

MR. TYLER. Now now, Miss Fitt, do not give way...to despair, all will come right...in the end. [*Aside to Mr. Barrell.*] What *is* the situation, Mr. Barrell? Not a collision surely?

MRS. ROONEY [*enthusiastically*]. A collision! Oh that would be wonderful!

MISS FITT [*horrified*]. A collision! I knew it!

MR. TYLER. Come, Miss Fitt, let us move a little up the platform.

MRS. ROONEY. Yes, let us all do that. [*Pause.*] No? [*Pause.*] You have changed your mind? [*Pause.*] I quite agree, we are better here, in the shadow of the waiting-room.

MR. BARRELL. Excuse me a moment.

MRS. ROONEY. Before you slink away, Mr. Barrell, please, a statement of some kind, I insist. Even the slowest train on this brief line is not ten minutes and more behind its scheduled time without good cause, one imagines. [*Pause.*] We all know your station is the best kept of the entire network, but there are times when that is not enough, just not enough. [*Pause.*] Now, Mr. Barrell, leave off chewing your whiskers, we are waiting to hear from you—we the un-fortunate ticket-holders' nearest if not dearest. [*Pause.*]

MR. TYLER [*reasonably*]. I do think we are owed some kind of explanation, Mr. Barrell, if only to set our minds at rest.

MR. BARRELL. I know nothing. All I know is there has been a hitch. All traffic is retarded.

MRS. ROONEY [*derisively*]. Retarded! A hitch! Ah these celibates! Here we are eating our hearts out with anxiety for our loved ones and he calls that a hitch! Those of us like myself with heart and kidney trouble may collapse at any moment and he calls that a hitch! In our ovens the Saturday roast is burning to a shrivel and he calls that—

MR. TYLER. Here comes Tommy, running! I am glad I have been spared to see this.

TOMMY [*excitedly, in the distance*]. She's coming. [*Pause. Nearer.*] She's at the level-crossing!

[*Immediately exaggerated station sounds. Falling signals. Bells. Whistles. Crescendo of train whistle approaching. Sound of train rushing through station.*]

MRS. ROONEY [*above rush of train*]. The up mail! The up mail! [*The up mail recedes, the down train approaches, enters the station, pulls up with great hissing of steam and clashing of couplings. Noise of passengers descending, doors banging,* MR. BARRELL *shouting "Boghill! Boghill!," etc. Piercingly.*] Dan!..Are you all right?..Where is he?..Dan!..Did you see my husband?..Dan!.. [*Noise of station emptying. Guard's whistle. Train departing, receding. Silence.*] He isn't on it! The misery I have endured, to get here, and he isn't on it!..Mr. Barrell!..Was he not on it? [*Pause.*] Is anything the matter, you look as if you had seen a ghost. [*Pause.*] Tommy!..Did you see the master?

TOMMY. He'll be along, Ma'am, Jerry is minding him.

[*Mr. Rooney suddenly appears on platform, advancing on small boy Jerry's arm. He is blind, thumps the ground with his stick and pants incessantly.*]

MRS. ROONEY. Oh, Dan! There you are! [*Her dragging feet as she hastens towards him. She reaches him. They halt.*] Where in the world were you?

MR. ROONEY [*coolly*]. Maddy.

MRS. ROONEY. Where were you all this time?

MR. ROONEY. In the men's.

MRS. ROONEY. Kiss me!

MR. ROONEY. Kiss you? In public? On the platform? Before the boy? Have you taken leave of your senses?

MRS. ROONEY. Jerry wouldn't mind. Would you, Jerry?

JERRY. No, Ma'am.

MRS. ROONEY. How is your poor father?

JERRY. They took him away, Ma'am.

MRS. ROONEY. Then you are all alone?

JERRY. Yes, Ma'am.

MR. ROONEY. Why are you here? You did not notify me.

MRS. ROONEY. I wanted to give you a surprise. For your birthday.

MR. ROONEY. My birthday?

MRS. ROONEY. Don't you remember? I wished you your happy returns in the bathroom.

MR. ROONEY. I did not hear you.

MRS. ROONEY. But I gave you a tie! You have it on! [*Pause.*]

MR. ROONEY. How old am I now?

MRS. ROONEY. Now never mind about that. Come.

MR. ROONEY. Why did you not cancel the boy? Now we shall have to give him a penny.

MRS. ROONEY [*miserably*]. I forgot! I had such a time getting here! Such horrid nasty people! [*Pause. Pleading*]. Be nice to me, Dan, be nice

to me today!

MR. ROONEY. Give the boy a penny.

MRS. ROONEY. Here are two halfpennies, Jerry. Run along now and buy yourself a nice gobstopper.

JERRY. Yes, Ma'am.

MR. ROONEY. Come for me on Monday, if I am still alive.

JERRY. Yessir. [*He runs off.*]

MR. ROONEY. We could have saved sixpence. We have saved fivepence. [*Pause.*] But at what cost?

[*They move off along platform arm in arm. Dragging feet, panting, thudding stick.*]

MRS. ROONEY. Are you not well?

[*They halt, on Mr. Rooney's initiative.*]

MR. ROONEY. Once and for all, do not ask me to speak and move at the same time. I shall not say this in this life again.

[*They move off. Dragging feet, etc. They halt at top of steps.*]

MRS. ROONEY. Are you not—

MR. ROONEY. Let us get this precipice over.

MRS. ROONEY. Put your arm round me.

MR. ROONEY. Have you been drinking again? [*Pause.*] You are quivering like a blanc-mange. [*Pause.*] Are you in a condition to lead me? [*Pause.*] We shall fall into the ditch.

MRS. ROONEY. Oh, Dan! It will be like old times!

MR. ROONEY. Pull yourself together or I shall send Tommy for the cab. Then, instead of having saved sixpence, no, fivepence, we shall have lost... [*calculating mumble*]...two and three less six one and no plus one one and no plus three one and nine and one ten and three two and one... [*normal voice*] two and one, we shall be the poorer to the tune of two and one. [*Pause.*] Curse that sun, it has gone in. What is the day doing? [*Wind.*]

MRS. ROONEY. Shrouding, shrouding, the best of it is past. [*Pause.*] Soon the first great drops will fall splashing in the dust.

MR. ROONEY. And yet the glass was firm. [*Pause.*] Let us hasten home and sit before the fire. We shall draw the blinds. You will read to me. I think Effie is going to commit adultery with the Major. [*Brief drag of feet.*] Wait! [*Feet cease. Stick tapping at steps.*] I have been up and down these steps five thousand times and still I do not know how many there are. When I think there are six there are four or five or seven or eight and when I remember there are five there are three or four or six or seven and when finally I realize there are seven there are five or six or eight or nine. Sometimes I wonder if they do not change them in the night. [*Pause. Irritably.*] Well? How many do you make them to-day?

MRS. ROONEY. Do not ask me to count, Dan, not now.

MR. ROONEY. Not count! One of the few satisfactions in life?

MRS. ROONEY. Not steps, Dan, please, I always get them wrong. Then you might fall on your wound and I would have that on my manure-heap on top of everything else. No, just cling to me and all will be well.

[*Confused noise of their descent. Panting, stumbling, ejaculations, curses. Silence.*]

MR. ROONEY. Well! That is what you call well!

MRS. ROONEY. We are down. And little the worse [*Silence. A donkey brays. Silence.*] That was a true donkey. Its father and mother were donkeys.

[*Silence.*]

MR. ROONEY. Do you know what it is, I think I shall retire.

MRS. ROONEY [*appalled*]. Retire! And live at home? On your grant!

MR. ROONEY. Never tread these cursed steps again. Trudge this hellish road for the last time. Sit at home on the remnants of my bottom counting the hours—till the next meal. [*Pause.*] The very thought puts life in me! Forward, before it dies!

[*They move on. Dragging feet, panting, thudding stick.*]

MRS. ROONEY. Now mind, here is the path...Up!...Well done! Now we are in safety and a straight run home.

MR. ROONEY [*without halting, between gasps*]. A straight...run!..She calls that...a straight...run!..

MRS. ROONEY. Hush! do not speak as you go along, you know it is not good for your coronary. [*Dragging steps, etc.*] Just concentrate on putting one foot before the next or whatever the expression is. [*Dragging feet, etc.*] That is the way, now we are doing nicely. [*Dragging feet, etc. They suddenly halt, on* MRS. ROONEY's *initiative.*] Heavens! I knew there was something! With all the excitement! I forgot!

MR. ROONEY [*quietly*]. Good God.

MRS. ROONEY. But you must know, Dan, of course, you were on it. What ever happened? Tell me!

MR. ROONEY. I have never known anything to happen.

MRS. ROONEY. But you must—

MR. ROONEY [*violently*]. All this stopping and starting again is devilish, devilish! I get a little way on me and begin to be carried along when suddenly you stop dead! Two hundred pounds of unhealthy fat! What possessed you to come out at all? Let go of me!

MRS. ROONEY [*in great agitation*]. No, I must know, we won't stir from here till you tell me. Fifteen minutes late! On a thirty minute run! It's unheard of!

MR. ROONEY. I know nothing. Let go of me before I shake you off.

MRS. ROONEY. But you must know! You were on it! Was it at the terminus? Did you leave on time? Or was it on the line? [*Pause.*] Did something happen on the line? [*Pause.*] Dan! [*Brokenly.*] Why won't you tell me!

[*Silence. They move off. Dragging feet, etc.*]

[*They halt. Pause.*]

MR. ROONEY. Poor Maddy! [*Pause. Children's cries.*] What was that?

[*Pause for Mrs. Rooney to ascertain.*]

MRS. ROONEY. The Lynch twins jeering at us. [*Cries.*]
MR. ROONEY. Will they pelt us with mud to-day, do you suppose? [*Cries.*]
MRS. ROONEY. Let us turn and face them. [*Cries. They turn. Silence.*] Threaten them with your stick. [*Silence.*] They have run away.

[*Pause.*]

MR. ROONEY. Did you ever wish to kill a child? [*Pause.*] Nip some young doom in the bud. [*Pause.*] Many a time at night, in winter, on the black road home, I nearly attacked the boy. [*Pause.*] Poor Jerry! [*Pause.*] What restrained me then? [*Pause.*] Not fear of man. [*Pause.*] Shall we go on backwards now a little?
MRS. ROONEY. Backwards?
MR. ROONEY. Yes. Or you forwards and I backwards. The perfect pair. Like Dante's damned, with their faces arsy-versy. Our tears will water our bottoms.
MRS. ROONEY. What is the matter, Dan? Are you not well?
MR. ROONEY. Well! Did you ever know me to be well? The day you met me I should have been in bed. The day you proposed to me the doctors gave me up. You knew that, did you not? The night you married me they came for me with an ambulance. You have not forgotten that, I suppose?

[*Pause.*] No, I cannot be said to be well. But I am no worse. Indeed I am better than I was. The loss of my sight was a great fillip. If I could go deaf and dumb I think I might pant on to be a hundred. Or have I done so? [*Pause.*] Was I a hundred to-day? [*Pause.*] Am I a hundred, Maddy? [*Silence.*]
MRS. ROONEY. All is still. No living soul in sight. There is no one to ask. The world is feeding. The wind— [*brief wind*]—scarcely stirs the leaves and the birds—[*brief chirp*]— are tired singing. The cows—[*brief moo*]—and sheep—[*brief baa*]— ruminate in silence. The dogs— [*brief bark*]—are hushed and the hens—[*brief cackle*]—sprawl torpid in the dust. We are alone. There is no one to ask. [*Silence.*]
MR. ROONEY [*clearing his throat, narrative tone*]. We drew out on the tick of time, I can vouch for that. I was—
MRS. ROONEY. How can you vouch for it?
MR. ROONEY [*normal tone, angrily*]. I can vouch for it, I tell you! Do you want my relation or don't you? [*Pause. Narrative tone.*] On the tick of time. I had the compartment to myself, as usual. At least I hope so, for I made no attempt to restrain myself. My mind—[*Normal tone.*] But why do we not sit down somewhere? Are we afraid we should never rise again?
MRS. ROONEY. Sit down on what?
MR. ROONEY. On a bench, for example.
MRS. ROONEY. There is no bench.
MR. ROONEY. Then on a bank, let us sink down upon a bank.
MRS. ROONEY. There is no bank.
MR. ROONEY. Then we cannot. [*Pause.*] I dream of other roads, in other lands. Of another home, another— [*he hesitates*]—another home. [*Pause.*] What was I trying to say?
MRS. ROONEY. Something about your mind.

MR. ROONEY [*startled*]. My mind? Are you sure? [*Pause. Incredulous.*] My mind?.. [*Pause.*] Ah yes. [*Narrative tone.*] Alone in the compartment my mind began to work, as so often after office hours, on the way home, in the train, to the lilt of the bogeys. Your season-ticket, I said, costs you twelve pounds a year and you earn, on an average, seven and six a day, that is to say barely enough to keep you alive and twitching with the help of food, drink, tobacco and periodicals until you finally reach home and fall into bed. Add to this—or subtract from it—rent, stationery, various subscriptions, tramfares to and fro, light and heat, permits and licences, hairtrims and shaves, tips to escorts, upkeep of premises and appearances, and a thousand unspecifiable sundries, and it is clear that by lying at home in bed, day and night, winter and summer, with a change of pyjamas once a fortnight, you would add very considerably to your income. Business, I said—[*A cry. Pause. Again. Normal tone.*] Did I hear a cry?

MRS. ROONEY. Mrs. Tully, I fancy. Her poor husband is in constant pain and beats her unmercifully. [*Silence.*]

MR. ROONEY. That was a short knock. [*Pause.*] What was I trying to get at?

MRS. ROONEY. Business.

MR. ROONEY. Ah yes, business. [*Narrative tone.*] Business, old man, I said, retire from business, it has retired from you. [*Normal tone.*] One has these moments of lucidity.

MRS. ROONEY. I feel very cold and weak.

MR. ROONEY [*narrative tone*]. On the other hand, I said, there are the horrors of home life, the dusting, sweeping, airing, scrubbing, waxing, waning, washing, mangling, drying, mowing, clipping, raking, rolling, scuffling, shovelling, grinding, tearing, pounding banging and slamming. And the brats, the happy little hearty little howling neighbours' brats. Of all this and much more the week-end, the Saturday intermission and then the day of rest, have given you some idea. But what must it be like on a working-day? A Wednesday? A Friday! What must it be like on a Friday! And I fell to thinking of my silent, back-street, basement office, with its obliterated plate, rest-couch and velvet hangings, and what it means to be buried there alive, if only from ten to five, with convenient to the one hand a bottle of light pale ale and to the other a long ice-cold fillet of hake. Nothing, I said, not even fully certified death, can ever take the place of that. It was then I noticed we were at a standstill. [*Pause. Normal tone. Irritably.*] Why are you hanging out of me like that? Have you swooned away?

MRS. ROONEY. I feel very cold and faint. The wind—[*whistling wind*]— is whistling through my summer frock as if I had nothing on over my bloomers. I have had no solid food since my elevenses.

MR. ROONEY. You have ceased to care. I speak—and you listen to the wind.

MRS. ROONEY. No no, I am agog, tell me all, then we shall press on and never pause, never pause, till we come safe to haven. [*Pause.*]

MR. ROONEY. Never pause...safe to haven...Do you know, Maddy, sometimes one would think you were struggling with a dead language.

MRS. ROONEY. Yes indeed, Dan, I know full well what you mean, I often have that feeling, it is unspeakably excruciating.

MR. ROONEY. I confess I have it sometimes myself, when I happen to overhear what I am saying.

MRS. ROONEY. Well, you know, it will be dead in time, just like our own poor dear Gaelic, there is that to be said. [*Urgent baa.*]

MR. ROONEY [*startled*]. Good God!

MRS. ROONEY. Oh, the pretty little woolly lamb, crying to suck its mother! Theirs has not changed, since Arcady. [*Pause.*]

MR. ROONEY. Where was I in my composition?

MRS. ROONEY. At a standstill.

MR. ROONEY. Ah yes. [*Clears his throat. Narrative tone.*] I concluded naturally that we had entered a station and would soon be on our way again, and I sat on, without misgiving. Not a sound. Things are very dull to-day, I said, nobody getting down, nobody getting on. Then as time flew by and nothing happened I realized my error. We had not entered a station.

MRS. ROONEY. Did you not spring up and poke your head out of the window?

MR. ROONEY. What good would that have done me?

MRS. ROONEY. Why to call out to be told what was amiss.

MR. ROONEY. I did not care what was amiss. No, I just sat on, saying, If this train were never to move again I should not greatly mind. Then gradually a—how shall I say—a growing desire to—er—you know—welled up within me. Nervous probably. In fact now I am sure. You know, the feeling of being confined.

MRS. ROONEY. Yes yes, I have been through that.

MR. ROONEY. If we sit here much longer, I said, I really do not know what I shall do. I got up and paced to and fro between the seats, like a caged beast.

MRS. ROONEY. That is a help sometimes.

MR. ROONEY. After what seemed an eternity we simply moved off. And the next thing was Barrell bawling the abhorred name. I got down and Jerry led me to the men's, or Fir as they call it now, from Vir Viris I suppose, the *V* becoming *F*, in accordance with Grimm's Law. [*Pause.*] The rest you know. [*Pause.*] You say nothing? [*Pause.*] Say something, Maddy. Say you believe me.

MRS. ROONEY. I remember once attending a lecture by one of these new mind doctors, I forget what you call them. He spoke—

MR. ROONEY. A lunatic specialist?

MRS. ROONEY. No no, just the troubled mind, I was hoping he might shed a little light on my lifelong preoccupation with horses' buttocks.

MR. ROONEY. A neurologist.

MRS. ROONEY. No no, just mental distress, the name will come back to me in the night. I remember his telling us the story of a little girl, very strange and unhappy in her ways, and how he treated her unsuccessfully over a period of years and was finally obliged to give up the case. He could find nothing wrong with her, he said. The only thing wrong with her as far as he could see was that she was dying. And she did in fact die, shortly after he washed his hands of her.

MR. ROONEY. Well? What is there so wonderful about that?

MRS. ROONEY. No, it was just something he said, and the way he said it, that have haunted me ever since.

MR. ROONEY. You lie awake at night, tossing to and fro and brooding on it.

MRS. ROONEY. On it and other... wretchedness. [*Pause.*] When he had done with the little girl he stood there motionless for some time, quite two minutes I should say, looking down at his table. Then he suddenly raised his head and exclaimed, as if he had had a revelation, The trouble with her was she had never been really born! [*Pause.*] He spoke throughout without notes. [*Pause.*] I left before the end.

MR. ROONEY. Nothing about your buttocks? [*Mrs. Rooney weeps. In affectionate remonstrance.*] Maddy!

MRS. ROONEY. There is nothing to be done for those people!

MR. ROONEY. For which is there? [*Pause.*] That does not sound right somehow. [*Pause.*] What way am I facing?

MRS. ROONEY. What?

MR. ROONEY. I have forgotten what way I am facing.

MRS. ROONEY. You have turned aside and are bowed down over the ditch.

MR. ROONEY. There is a dead dog down there.

MRS. ROONEY. No no, just the rotting leaves.

MR. ROONEY. In June? Rotting leaves in June?

MRS. ROONEY. Yes dear, from last year, and from the year before last, and from the year before that again. [*Silence. Rainy wind. They move on. Dragging steps, etc.*] There is that lovely laburnum again. Poor thing, it is losing all its tassels. [*Dragging steps, etc.*] There are the first drops. [*Rain. Dragging feet, etc.*] Golden drizzle. [*Dragging steps, etc.*] Do not mind me, dear, I am just talking to myself. [*Rain heavier. Dragging steps, etc.*] Can hinnies procreate, I wonder.

[*They halt, on Mr. Rooney's initiative.*]

MR. ROONEY. Say that again.

MRS. ROONEY. Come on, dear, don't mind me, we are getting drenched.

MR. ROONEY [*forcibly*]. Can what what?

MRS. ROONEY. Hinnies procreate. [*Silence.*] You know, hinnies, or is it jinnies, aren't they barren, or sterile, or whatever it is? [*Pause.*] It wasn't an ass's colt at all, you know, I asked the Regius Professor. [*Pause.*]

MR. ROONEY. He should know.

MRS. ROONEY. Yes, it was a hinny, he rode into Jerusalem or wherever it was on a hinny. [*Pause.*] That must mean something. [*Pause.*] It's like the sparrows, than many of which we are of more value, they weren't sparrows at all.

MR. ROONEY. Than many of which... You exaggerate, Maddy.

MRS. ROONEY [*with emotion*]. They weren't sparrows at all!

MR. ROONEY. Does that put our price up?

[*Silence. They move on. Wind and rain. Dragging feet, etc. They halt.*]

MRS. ROONEY. Do you want some dung? [*Silence. They move on. Wind and rain, etc. They halt.*] Why do you stop? Do you want to say something?

MR. ROONEY. No.

MRS. ROONEY. Then why do you stop?

MR. ROONEY. It is easier.

MRS. ROONEY. Are you very wet?

MR. ROONEY. To the buff.

MRS. ROONEY. The buff?

MR. ROONEY. The buff. From buffalo.

MRS. ROONEY. We shall hang up all our things in the hot-cupboard and get into our dressing-gowns. [*Pause.*] Put your arm round me. [*Pause.*] Be nice to me! [*Pause. Gratefully.*] Ah Dan! [*They move on. Wind and rain. Dragging feet, etc. Faintly same music as before. They halt. Music clearer. Silence but for music playing. Music dies.*] All day the same old record. All alone in that great empty house. She must be a very old woman now.

MR. ROONEY [*indistinctly*]. Death and the Maiden. [*Silence.*]

MRS. ROONEY. You are crying. [*Pause.*] Are you crying?

MR. ROONEY [*violently*]. Yes! [*They move on. Wind and rain. Dragging feet, etc. They halt. They move on. Wind and rain. Dragging feet, etc. They halt.*] Who is the preacher tomorrow? The incumbent?

MRS. ROONEY. No.

MR. ROONEY. Thank God for that. Who?

MRS. ROONEY. Hardy.

MR. ROONEY. "How to be Happy though Married"?

MRS. ROONEY. No no, he died, you remember. No connexion.

MR. ROONEY. Has he announced the text?

MRS. ROONEY. "The Lord upholdeth all that fall and raiseth up all those that be bowed down." [*Silence. They join in wild laughter. They move on. Wind and rain. Dragging feet, etc.*] Hold me tighter, Dan! [*Pause.*] Oh yes! [*They halt.*]

MR. ROONEY. I hear something behind us. [*Pause.*]

MRS. ROONEY. It looks like Jerry. [*Pause.*] It is Jerry.

[*Sound of Jerry's running steps approaching. He halts beside them, panting.*]

JERRY [*panting*]. You dropped—

MRS. ROONEY. Take your time, my little man, you will burst a bloodvessel.

JERRY [*panting*]. You dropped something, Sir, Mr. Barrell told me to run after you.

MRS. ROONEY. Show. [*She takes the object.*] What is it? [*She examines it.*] What is this thing, Dan?

MR. ROONEY. Perhaps it is not mine at all.

JERRY. Mr. Barrell said it was, Sir.

MRS. ROONEY. It looks like a kind of ball. And yet it is not a ball.

MR. ROONEY. Give it to me.

MRS. ROONEY [*giving it*]. What *is* it, Dan?

MR. ROONEY. It is a thing I carry about with me.

MRS. ROONEY. Yes, but what—

MR. ROONEY [*violently*]. It is a thing I carry about with me!

[*Silence. Mrs. Rooney looks for a penny.*]

MRS. ROONEY. I have no small money. Have you?

MR. ROONEY. I have none of any kind.

MRS. ROONEY. We are out of change, Jerry. Remind Mr. Rooney on Monday and he will give you a penny for your pains.

JERRY. Yes, Ma'am.

MR. ROONEY. If I am alive.

JERRY. Yessir.

[*Jerry starts running back towards the station.*]

MRS. ROONEY. Jerry! [*Jerry halts.*] Did you hear what the hitch was? [*Pause.*] Did you hear what kept the train so late?

MR. ROONEY. How would he have heard? Come on.

MRS. ROONEY. What was it, Jerry?

JERRY. It was a—

MR. ROONEY. Leave the boy alone, he knows nothing! Come on!

MRS. ROONEY. What was it, Jerry?

JERRY. It was a little child, Ma'am.

[*Mr. Rooney groans.*]

MRS. ROONEY. What do you mean, it was a little child?

JERRY. It was a little child fell out of the carriage. On to the line, Ma'am. [*Pause.*] Under the wheels, Ma'am.

[*Silence. Jerry runs off. His steps die away. Tempest of wind and rain. It abates. They move on. Dragging steps, etc. They halt. Tempest of wind and rain.*]

APPENDIX: Biographical Notes

Anonymous   The *Second Shepherds' Pageant* is one of several plays preserved in a fifteenth-century manuscript housed in the library of Towneley Hall in Lancashire, England. The so-called Towneley plays were performed by the medieval craft-guilds of Wakefield, who helped remove English drama from the precincts of the church and replaced Latin with vernacular English, thus making available a greater range of dramatic technique and, as this play indicates, opening up comic possibilities previously unexplored. Basically, the Wakefield cycles depart from drama as ritual in favor of drama as an interaction of characters in tense situations, unfolding toward a resolution with broad strokes of melodrama. Since each dramatized topic is taken from what to the medieval audience was a connected story (ranging from the Creation to the Last Judgment), the particular episode and the biblical context reinforce each other, one enhancing the significance of the other.

Anonymous   *Everyman* belongs to a family of late-medieval morality plays that contrast on one hand with the mystery cycles and on the other with subsequent developments in realism. Unlike the mystery cycles, the moralities are not concerned with a specific episode of scriptural narrative or specific aspects of divine mystery. Instead they take for granted the directives that come from the Christian circumstances of the action and examine certain categories of the moral life that are fixed in and defined by the Christian framework. The personified virtues and vices that Everyman encounters and struggles against, for instance, are not so much aspects of imitative character as quantities deductively arrived at: given the Day of Judgment and Everyman's personal reckoning, what happens to worldly goods, knowledge, good deeds, etc. when he goes in search of assistance? What view of the major categories of morality does death, so conceived, afford? The answers are conventional, and their presentation owes as much to the nature of allegory as to the nature of drama. In contrast to later developments in dramatic realism, the play's dependence on fixed abstractions makes complexity and evolution of character undesirable. It also gives the form a definite conclusion insofar as these abstractions are fully definable by their relationship to a definite end. The clash between them and Everyman is caused by Everyman's ignorance alone. Knowledge about them roots out all motives and inclinations that might carry him into subplots or diversions and sets him on his appointed path.

Samuel Beckett   A contemporary Irish novelist, poet, and playwright, Samuel Beckett has lived most of his productive career in Paris and writes primarily in French. His dark humor and taste for the bizarre link him with modern playwrights such as Genet, Ionesco, and Brecht, but unlike these writers he usually emphasizes the isolated drama of one or two characters rather than a social panorama fantasy. Beckett's people waste and pine in a world in which politics and public affairs are remote. From his friend James Joyce, he inherits a concern for words as objects in themselves and a sense of the last extremity to which a form can be pushed before it destroys itself. His novels are virtually antinovels, as *Waiting for Godot* is, in part, a demonstration of what to do in the theater while waiting for a play. Time, isolation, physical deterioration, the comic needling of one person by another, the small rituals of daily habit, and waiting are recurrent themes.

All That Fall was first presented by the B.B.C. in 1957. In addition to this radio play, Beckett has written another, *Embers;* two mimes for two players (each); a one act, one man play, *Krapp's Last Tape;* and perhaps his best known works, *Endgame* and *Waiting for Godot.* (His main novels are *Watt, Murphy, Malloy, Malone Dies,* and *The Unnamable.*)

Anton Pavlovich Chekhov   Chekhov, like the character Lopakhin in *The Cherry Orchard,* was the descendant of peasants, the son of a shopkeeper, and like Trofimov, he complained of the meaningless, boorish provincial life of Tsarist Russia and looked forward to its betterment. He considered himself a realist in dramatic method and style and thought that traditional means of obtaining theatrical effects were false and distorting. Like his immediate predecessor Ibsen, however, he invented means of preventing the submergence of his plays in drabness and insignificance. He makes symbols of key phrases and motifs, for instance, as in *The Cherry Orchard* the nursery, music, the orchard, the train, Lopakhin's watch, and Gaev's game of billiards are brought forward from the dull material of the characters' lives. These objects and recurrent phrases give the language metaphoric density and cause the central action to emerge less as startling melodrama, standing clear of ordinary life, than as an inevitable extension of the entire fabric of the play. Whereas Ibsen's realism is often merely a restriction on the means by which a startling and critical action is presented, Chekhov's is the very substance of the play, shaped into a carefully modulated blend of comedy and seriousness.

Chekov's major plays—*The Sea Gull, Uncle Vanya, The Cherry Orchard,* and *The Three Sisters*—were written during the last years of a life devoted mainly to the practice of medicine and the writing of short stories. They were all produced by the Moscow Art Theatre under the direction of Stanislavsky, whom Chekhov accused of ruining *The Cherry Orchard* by underplaying its comedy and overemphasizing its melodrama.

Friedrich Düerrenmatt   Dürrenmatt was born in a Swiss village, grew up in a strict Protestant atmosphere, and went to the university in Zurich, where his first play, *Thus It Is Written,* was performed in 1947. His other works since that time include *Romulus the Great* (1949), *The Marriage of Mr. Mississippi* (1952), and *An Angel Comes to Babylon* (1953). Typically, his plays combine parody, satire, dark humor, allegory, fantasy, and didacticism in the expressionist manner of post-realist writers. His use of the grotesque sometimes suggests Ionesco, and his criticism of capitalism and parabolic extensions of the dramatic action suggest Brecht—as does the unexpected heroism of small people victimized by their rapacious brothers. These elements are most effectively combined in *Der Besuch der Alten Dame (The Visit),* which was published in Zurich in 1956. The translation used here, by Maurice Valency, is slightly altered from the original version.

Henrik Ibsen   Born in Skien, Norway, Ibsen began writing plays in his early twenties and wrote prolifically until over seventy. Living in several places in Norway and Europe (including Munich and Rome), he earned a certain notoriety that brought him both adulation and severe attacks. The method of his plays ranges from romantic fantasy to strict realism. Despite their appearance, however, even his realistic plays have a good deal of melodrama about them and unfold in well-marked stages of revelation and passion. These stages coincide with act divisions and are signaled by the increasing significance of certain symbols—a wild duck, ghosts from the past, or a master builder's steeple. When he wrote *The Master Builder* (1892), he was near the middle of his most productive years, which brought a play every two years almost regularly: *A Doll's House* (1879), *Ghosts* (1881), *An Enemy of the People* (1882), *The Wild Duck* (1884), *Rosmersholm* (1886), *Hedda Gabbler* (1890), *Little Eyolf* (1894), *John Gabriel Borkman* (1896), and the last play *When We Dead Awaken* (1899), to name the main ones. The translation reprinted here is William Archer's.

Jean Baptiste Poquelin (Molière)   Molière is usually regarded as the finest of French comic dramatists. The son of a prosperous upholsterer at the royal court, he studied at first to become a lawyer but in 1643 turned to the theater and adopted the stage name of Molière. After a long period touring the provinces, his company obtained the patronage of the King's brother and finally of the King himself, Louis XIV. Like Shakespeare, Molière acted in, as well as wrote, plays for a theater in which he was part owner. His early plays are highly farcical; his greatest plays, which begin to appear about 1660, are satiric comedies of manners specializing in the depiction of stock comic character types of the sort suggested by their titles—*The Misanthrope* (1666), *The Miser* (1668), *The Gentleman Burgher* (1670), *The Intellectual Ladies* (1672), and *The Hypochondriac* (1673). By ironic coincidence, it was while acting in the latter play that Molière, who had suffered several years from a lung disease, burst a blood vessel and subsequently died.

Joe Orton   Joe Orton was born in Leicester, England, and was killed in 1967. Not much is known about his life. He held a number of different jobs, moved around here and there, got in and out of jail, and wrote his first play, which was never produced, after a stint in prison. *Entertaining Mr. Sloane,* awarded a prize as the best new British play of 1964, was his second play. Some indication of what he was like may be gathered from a story he told while on a British television show of how he spent six months in jail on a charge of defacing library books. He had, it seems, an obsession about the amount of public money spent by libraries on copies of books on cookery and etiquette and other such fatuous subjects and, therefore, pasted clippings of nude females over the dust-jacket portraits of matronly British authors. Since his wrath seems to have embraced hundreds of publications of this sort, browsing through dust jackets in his local library must have been, at least before the authorities moved in, a popular pastime.

Jean Racine   The son of a lawyer, he spent his early years at the Jansenist seminary at Port-Royal, near Paris, where he received a rigorous Catholic upbringing and a solid grounding in classical studies. On moving to the Collège d'Harcourt to study philosophy, he became attracted to the theater, wrote three plays (all rejected by theatrical companies) and a few poems, and somewhat scandalized his devout relatives by this literary libertinism. They sent him off to the province of Languedoc in hopes that his uncle, the vicar-general of the diocese, might assist him into the ministry. Two years later, in 1663, he returned to Paris and resumed writing. A congratulatory "Ode on the King's Convalescence" brought him a gift of six hundred livres from Louis XIV, and not long thereafter his play *The Thebaide,* inspired by the Oedipus plays of Sophocles, was accepted by Molière and presented by his company at the Palais-Royal. The performance was badly received, as was that of his next play, *Alexander the Great,* whereupon Racine broke with Molière and went over to a rival company. During the next ten years or so, Racine set his Jansenist background vigorously behind him, enjoying the high life of Paris and the favors of various actresses and writing a series of great tragedies (including *Andromache, Berenice, Mithridates,* and *Iphigenia*) and his only comedy, *The Pleaders,* which satirized lawyers. In 1677, however, after *Phaedra* was jeered by his enemies, he quit the theater, married the wealthy Catherine de Romanet, and settled down to a life of scholarship and piety. In 1689 and 1691 he wrote two final plays, *Esther* and *Athaliah,* based on Biblical subjects.

William Shakespeare   Shakespeare was born in the rural town of Stratford-on-Avon, the eldest son of John Shakespeare, a well-to-do glover, and his wife Mary Arden, who came from a prosperous farming family. Little is known of his early life except that he probably attended the excellent Stratford grammar school and at the age of eighteen married Anne Hathaway, with whom he had three children. About ten years later, around 1590, he was in London writing poems and plays and acting in one of the two major theatrical companies of the time, the Lord Chamberlain's Company. During the next twenty years, he wrote two long narrative poems (*Venus and Adonis* and *The Rape of Lucrece*), well over a hundred sonnets, and nearly forty plays. His income as an actor, playwright, and, most of all, a shareholder in the Globe Theater enabled him to retire around 1610 to Stratford. His plays were collected after his death by his longtime friends and acting colleagues, Heminges and Condell, and published in what is called the First Folio of 1623, where they are first grouped as tragedies, comedies, and histories.

Shakespeare's literary career is usually divided into three phases, the first (from about 1590 to 1600) dominated by comedy—e.g., *Love's Labour's Lost, A Midsummer Night's Dream, Much Ado about Nothing, As You Like It, Twelfth Night;* the second (from about 1600 to 1608) dominated by tragedy—e.g., *Hamlet, Othello, King Lear, Macbeth;* and the third (from about 1608 to 1613) dominated by a form of comedy heavily indebted to romance—e.g., *A Winter's Tale* and *The Tempest.*

George Bernard Shaw   Shaw was born in Dublin of English parents. At sixteen, after an intermittent schooling, he became a clerk with a real-estate firm. After a few years he grew weary of office work, left Ireland with his mother and actress sister, and spent the years 1879–83 in London writing five novels, all of which went unpublished. Impressed by Marx, he joined the Fabian Society—a group of British intellectuals devoted to a gradual, nonrevolutionary movement toward socialism—and between 1884 and 1911 wrote numerous socialist tracts. He also wrote brilliant music criticism during the nineties for *The Star* and *The World,* as well as dramatic criticism for the *Saturday Review.* In 1898 he married an Irish heiress, Charlotte Payne-Townshend, and from this point on devoted himself almost entirely to playwriting. Of his early period as a dramatist, he later said (in the Preface to *Back to Methuselah*), "I tried slum-land-lordism, doctrinaire Free Love (pseudo-Ibsenism), prostitution, militarism, marriage, history, current politics, natural Christianity, national and individual character, paradoxes of conventional society, husband hunting, questions of conscience, professional delusions and impostures." As such a list would suggest, the range of his interests was wide, and his dramas were highly intellectual in their usually satiric dissection of current institutions, attitudes, and practices. Iconoclastic in most things, Shaw ridiculed the romantic conventions of the nineteenth century theater, substituting for its melodramatics a theater of ideas that is essentially comic in spirit and form and that frequently centers on the tension between an outmoded, mechanical system of morality and the human impulse toward a freer and more vital life. Some of his best plays are *Mrs. Warren's Profession, Candida, Man and Superman, Major Barbara, Pygmalion, Heartbreak House, Back to Methuselah,* and *Saint Joan.*

Sophocles   Sophocles was born in an Athenian suburb, Colonus, where his father Sophillus was a prosperous tradesman. Reputed to have been handsome, athletic, and well-liked, he played the leading role in his earliest plays but gave up acting because of a weak voice. He married twice and had three children, of whom one, Iophon, was also a tragic dramatist. In contrast to the good fortune that seems to have marked his private life as well as his public career as a dramatist (he was supposed to have won first or second prize at the dramatic contests in Athens twenty-four times), his own plays are distinguished by a severe and grimly ironic tragic vision. Of the more than 100 plays he is said to have written, only seven have survived entire—*Ajax, Antigone, Electra, Oedipus at Colonus, Oedipus Rex, Philoctetes,* and *Trachiniae*—and an eighth, the satyr play *Ichneutae,* has survived in large part. Sophocles' contributions to the tragic theater include the addition of a third actor (one actor and a chorus originally presented the play; then Aeschylus added a second actor and Sophocles a third, who played various roles), the expansion of the chorus from twelve to fifteen members, and the use of painted scenery.

William Butler Yeats   Yeats is best known for his lyric poetry, which is so distinguished that T. S. Eliot has called him the finest lyric poet of our time, perhaps of all time. Nevertheless, Yeats wrote more than thirty plays during his life, and in them he helped, like Eliot himself, to bring about a reconciliation between poetry and drama after their long theatrical estrangement. Most of his plays were written for the Irish Literary Theater (the Abbey Theater, as it was called), which he and Lady Gregory founded in the hope that it would become the center of the Irish literary renaissance. Though the Abbey Theater became both famous and notorious as the vehicle for the plays of Yeats and John Millington Synge, the poetic drama that Yeats longed for never got firmly established. His own plays reflect his interests in magic and the occult; his belief in a spiritual reality accessible in part through dream, reverie, and the artistic imagination; and his urge to unite the myths and legends of pagan Ireland to the technical resources and forms of the oriental theater.

Some of Yeats' early plays, based largely on Irish legends, are *The Countess Kathleen* (1889–92), *The Land of the Heart's Desire* (1894), and *On Baile's Strand* (1903). Some of his later plays based on the Noh drama (see headnote to *Purgatory*) are *At the Hawk's Well* (1916), *The Only Jealousy of Emer* (1918), and *The Dreaming of the Bones* (1918).